ONTARIO SERIES

XIII

WILLIAM ALLAN, c. 1850 Metropolitan Toronto Library T 15159

The BANK of
UPPER CANADA

PETER BASKERVILLE

Carleton Library Series No. 141

CARLETON UNIVERSITY PRESS
OTTAWA, CANADA
1987

THE

BANK OF

UPPER CANADA

A Collection of Documents

Edited with an Introduction by

Peter Baskerville

TORONTO

THE CHAMPLAIN SOCIETY
IN COOPERATION WITH
THE ONTARIO HERITAGE FOUNDATION
CARLETON UNIVERSITY PRESS
1987

ISBN 0-88629-059-7 (paperback)

Printed in Canada

Canadian Cataloguing in Publication Data

Baskerville, Peter A. (Peter Allan), 1943–
    The Bank of Upper Canada

(The Carleton library ; 141)
(The Publications of the Champlain Society. Ontario
    series ; XIII)
Co-published with: Champlain Society.
Includes index.
Bibliography: p.
ISBN 0-88629-059-7

    1. Bank of Upper Canada—History.   2. Banks and
banking—Ontario—History.   I. Champlain Society.
II. Title.   III. Series.   IV. Series: The
Publications of the Champlain Society.   Ontario
series ; XIII.

HG2708.B37B38 1987   332.1'2'09713   C87-090160-5

Distributed by: Oxford University Press Canada
                70 Wynford Drive
                DON MILLS, Ontario, Canada
                M3C 1S9
                (416) 441-2941

Major funding towards this publication was provided by the Ontario Heritage Foundation, Ontario Ministry of Citizenship and Culture

FOREWORD

THE Bank of Upper Canada was founded through political manoeuvring by which interests at tiny York defeated a group at Kingston, then the province's largest urban centre. One-quarter of its shares were initially held by the Government of Upper Canada, which also appointed four of its fifteen directors. For many years under the Union of the Canadas, the bank acted as banker to the Canadian government. Its story offers one of the first Canadian cases of government-business relationships in the development and regulation of financial institutions. More than just the study of a bank, this is an extended account of the financial politics and practices of two governments, those of Upper Canada and of the Province of Canada.

When the bank opened, Ontario was largely a forest frontier. By the time the bank failed, Ontario was a growing industrial economy, focused on Toronto by railroads in which the bank was much involved. Because it was at once one of the province's largest businesses and a major source of credit for other businesses, the bank's story tells much about how that more complex business world developed.

This volume is the latest in the Ontario Series of the Champlain Society, which is Canada's oldest publisher of historical documents. The Series began in the 1950s, sparked by the interest of then Premier Leslie Frost in developing a more informed understanding of the province's heritage. The Society publishes the Series which is largely funded by the Government of Ontario, through the Ontario Heritage Foundation. Volumes in the Series present the main documents for their particular subjects, thereby giving readers direct access to the original materials of history. The Society selects volume editors for their particular knowledge of the subject matter, and the editors select, organize, and annotate these materials and provide an extensive introduction.

The Series includes volumes of both regional and thematic character, the latter having lately predominated. The next volume, the fourteenth in the Series, will return to a regional approach, as it will be on the Upper Ottawa Valley to 1854. Volumes are also in preparation on the early history of the Niagara area and on the region at the head of Lake Ontario.

Professor Peter Baskerville, who prepared this volume, has studied and taught in Ontario, and now teaches at the University of Victoria. He is well known for his publications on the history of Upper Canada, many of which have focused on its business history; and he is currently organizing the second Canadian Business History Conference. In preparing this volume, he has had to exercise great ingenuity, for the Bank of Upper Canada's own records, as the volume sadly records, were destroyed in the 1870s. It is a tribute to the editor's achievements, and also to the political and regulatory processes which resulted in publication of a good deal of information about provincial banks, that so much of the story can nevertheless be told.

Queen's Park,   DAVID PETERSON
Toronto   *Premier of Ontario*
March 1987

PREFACE

SINCE the pioneering work of Adam Shortt at the turn of the
century, little of a scholarly nature has been written on the
Bank of Upper Canada. This is unfortunate, but easily
understandable. The Bank of Upper Canada, unlike many
nineteenth-century banks, was not taken over by any other bank
and thus has no direct corporate successor in today's world. Its
papers, instead of being preserved by a "parent" bank, were
destroyed, sold in the 1870s at $20 a ton to a paper manufacturer.
Doubtless many private and public figures breathed a sigh of
relief after the sale. But posterity has been cheated. It is now
impossible to reconstruct on a systematic and disaggregated level
a coherent picture of the bank's routine business. Thus, while we
can infer and surmise from fragmentary data and some aggregate
figures (which must be used with great caution and sensitivity)
the general nature of the bank's loan portfolio and corporate
strategy over time, a detailed depiction and analysis of everyday
lending activity is impossible.

Given that no central archive of the bank's papers exists, I have
attempted to collect materials from the other end. A list of the
bank's probable major customers by economic sector, company,
government, and individual was compiled and an attempt to
survey the relevant surviving papers carried out. This involved
searching many repositories in Ontario, Quebec, the United
States, and Great Britain. Representative selections from good
runs of information on the bank's relations with government,
other financial institutions, and financiers and major corporations
(especially railways) are reproduced in this volume. This material
is supplemented by extracts from a rich series of published
sessional papers and legislative assembly reports. Comparable
material related to "representative" individuals seems unavailable. While I have made every reasonable attempt to secure
permission to publish the documents included here, I would
appreciate being informed of any oversights in this regard.

Invariably the custodians and archivists in charge of the sources
consulted have been of great help. It was especially pleasant to
work in the congenial and professional surroundings of the Public
Archives at Ottawa and the Provincial Archives of Ontario at
Toronto. The staff of the Metropolitan Toronto Library's Baldwin

Room, of the Queen's University Archives, and of the Regional History Collection, University of Western Ontario, were equally attentive. Funds from the University of Victoria's administered Social Sciences and Humanities Research Council research grants helped defray the costs of research travel.

The late Max Magill assured me that a study of this sort could be done. I believe him now and thank him for pointing the way. Angela Redish, a member of the Economics Department at the University of British Columbia, read an early draft of the introduction. Subsequent drafts have profited from her careful review. While this study commenced under the editorship of William Ormsby, his successor, Doug McCalla, had to confront and comment on the submitted material. Doug is an exemplary editor: professional, assiduous, thought-provoking, and supportive. It has been a pleasure working with him. Diane Mew helped assure stylistic consistency and trimmed loose ends. June Belton and Eleanor Lowther shared the burden of typing a manuscript which was, in the beginning, even fatter than it is now. They made the chore appear easy. Fran did more than keep me sane and Ian, Leslie, and Danielle provided the necessary perspective. It is to my family that this book is dedicated.

CONTENTS

APPENDIXES

TABLES

THE BANK OF
UPPER CANADA

INTRODUCTION

A COLONY WITHOUT A BANK

FOR FORTY-FOUR YEARS Upper Canada had as its central financial institution the Bank of Upper Canada. In its origins, as in its subsequent operations, the bank reflected the tensions inherent in the colony's economic and, to a lesser degree, political and social development. The bank was not the central agency behind that development; on the contrary, it was often forced to respond to activities initiated by others, often from forces exterior to the colony. The Bank of Upper Canada was pre-eminently a colonial bank. It did not create the economic and political context within which it operated. It emerged from it. What gives to the study of this institution its greatest fascination, however, is the fact that the Bank of Upper Canada did not always follow rules that others set for it. Through its deviations, it did foster change within a colonial context.

Appropriately, then, the study of such an institution should begin with an overview of that environment: an examination of the economic, political, and social milieu within which the bank commenced. The Constitutional Act of 1791 provided the legislative underpinnings for this context. That act approved a division of the old province of Quebec into Upper and Lower Canada and gave to each section an appointed legislative and executive council and an elected assembly. A governor general represented the monarch in Lower Canada and a lieutenant-governor did the same in the initially less populated colony, Upper Canada.[1] All legislation was subject to the sanction of His Majesty's local representative, a sanction which could be overruled by the crown, if done within two years.

The colonies thus created were very much a part of what has been called Great Britain's formal empire. Ultimate legislative control rested with the monarch. Yet within this formal structure there was some possibility of flexibility and freedom concerning various local issues. The 1791 act granted representative assemblies the right to levy local taxes. Consistent with the self-denying ordinance of 1778, the British government remained aloof from that important function. The extent to which flexibility existed in other economic areas was less clear. A minority opinion held that

[1]The division of the two resulted from an order-in-council.

the clause which allowed the crown on the recommendation of the local legislatures "to make laws for the peace, welfare and good government" of the colonies was limited only by the stipulation that those laws could not be "repugnant to this Act." On fiscal matters the single power specifically reserved for Britain concerned external trade and navigation. Did this mean that the colonies were not subject to existing British banking legislation? Some, both outside and within the Colonial Office, answered in the affirmative: in a legal/constitutional sense it did seem possible that colonists could establish a banking system of their own choosing.[2] As we shall see, other more pragmatic realities dictated that variance from British ideals would be difficult.

Not that there existed, in the early years of the nineteenth century, a homogeneous British banking system to which the colonials could, even if they so desired, aspire. At the formative period of colonial banking, British banking consisted of several disparate elements. While there was a general consensus, the exact pattern for the future was the subject of much heated discussion. The largest and most powerful of the British banks was, of course, the Bank of England. Conceived in the late seventeenth century as a mechanism to provide money for government expenditure and to facilitate increased circulation of a limited amount of specie, the bank prospered in this role for the next century. While the bulk of its business remained with the government, it increasingly dealt directly with London merchants, and, as the official bank of issue, its note circulation gradually extended beyond London into the provinces. Because of the bank's respectability and standing – occasioned in large part by its close government connections – the public came to accept the idea of paper serving the function of specie. And, related to this, bankers came to realize that "the privilege of legal tender for notes . . . had to be gained by the public approval of a prudent administration of the bank over time."[3]

This prudence, coupled with the bank's primary focus on government finance, left the door open for the emergence of other banking institutions. Yet because the bank had been granted near monopolistic control in the early eighteenth century, alternatives were slow to develop. Within London itself there already existed

[2]Paul Knaplund, "James Stephen on Canadian Banking Laws, 1821–46," *Canadian Historical Review* [hereafter *CHR*], xxxi (1960), pp. 177–87.
    [3]B.L. Anderson and P.L. Cottrell, *Money and Banking in England, 1694–1914* (London, 1974), pp. 17–18.

private banks primarily involved with the financing of their own particular international mercantile pursuits. By the mid-eighteenth century these firms began to specialize and to finance the business of others in addition to their own. Glyn, Mills, the Baring Brothers, and the Rothschilds were pre-eminent examples.[4]

Despite the restrictions on private banking – such firms were limited to six partners, all subject to unlimited liability – such institutions began to emerge outside London after 1750. These country banks provided a variety of local services including, in many cases, the underwriting of industrial development.[5] During the two decades prior to the formation of the Bank of Upper Canada, however, dramatic failures occurred in this sector of the financial community. Partly because of this, investigations into the state of British banking parallelled the emergence of banks in the Canadas.

In one sense prospective colonial bankers had available to them models other than those provided by Great Britain. Following Adam Shortt's publications on Canadian banking in the 1890s, most writers have argued that the origin of Canadian banks lay in the United States, not in England. As Shortt painstakingly demonstrated, the actual model for both the Bank of Montreal and the Bank of Upper Canada was the charter of the first Bank of the United States drawn up by Alexander Hamilton. It is also true that both the Canadian banks solicited advice from American bankers with regard to their early operations. Finally, reflecting southward trade and financial flows, one of the first foreign agents of both banks was the New York firm of Prime Ward and Sands.[6]

What this process really led to, however, was not the complete Americanization of Canadian banking, but rather, the introduction into the Canadas via the United States of one particular variant of the British banking system. The Bank of England's charter provided the model for Alexander Hamilton's bank. Hamilton followed the British example by establishing a close relationship with the government, requiring that only an incorporated company could issue notes, and providing for periodic

---

[4]For histories of Glyn, Mills and the Baring Brothers, see respectively, Roger Fulford, *Glyn's: 1753–1953* (London, 1953); R.W. Hidy, *The House of Baring in American Trade and Finance, 1763–1861* (Cambridge, 1949).

[5]L.S. Presnell, *Country Banking in the Industrial Revolution* (Oxford, 1956), *passim*.

[6]A. Shortt, "Origin of the Canadian Banking System," *Journal of the Canadian Bankers Association* [hereafter *JCBA*] IV (1896), pp. 1–19.

revision of the bank's charter. All these factors were to be central aspects of the Bank of Upper Canada. The one important refinement to the Bank of England adopted from Hamilton by Canadian banks was the practice of branch banking. Even in this case the Bank of England had established branches, albeit not to any great extent. Equally influential in the operations of Canadian banks were the practices of the private banking sector in London. Prime Ward and Sands was, after all, the American agent for the Baring Brothers. The Baring Brothers advised the Bank of Montreal on their choice of British agents.[7] Both the Bank of Montreal and the Bank of Upper Canada followed Baring's suggestion and operated through Thomas Wilson and Company in London.

It is important to note that the only sector of early nineteenth-century British banking without influence in the Canadas was that of the country banks. And, as suggested above, the operations of these banks tended to differ from those of the London private bankers and the Bank of England. The former often provided capital for industrial or long-term, speculative (at least in the sense of new and untried) ventures. By contrast, both the latter institutions ascribed to what has been called the real bills doctrine in the transaction of their non-governmental business. This meant that they would lend money – i.e., discount bills – only to legitimate mercantile traders who were engaged in the exchange of actual goods.[8] Speculative dealings or discounting notes not backed by such goods were to be avoided. Transactions were to be short term in nature and if this policy was consistently followed, it was believed that the amount of money in actual circulation would correspond exactly to the needs of the economy.

This perception of the proper fiscal system underlay the economic policies of the Tory governments in England between 1815 and 1830. As Boyd Hilton has demonstrated, the Tories did not wish to initiate a period of unlimited growth or "progress"; rather, they desired to stabilize and balance an economy that they feared was "working too fast – building too fast."[9] Whenever these leaders considered the issue, they concluded that a fiscal system designed to achieve stable and balanced growth in the

---

[7]Merrill Denison, *Canada's First Bank* (Toronto, 1966), I, pp. 97, 125.

[8]The Bank of England would lend to country banks which in turn lent to industry, however. Boyd Hilton, *Corn, Cash and Commerce: The Economic Policies of the Tory Governments, 1815–30* (Oxford, 1977), p. 204.

[9]Ibid., 229, n. 113. The quote is from Robert Peel in 1825.

mother country was equally appropriate for the achievement of the same general ends in her colonies.

The fact that British country banking was held in disrepute in the early years of the nineteenth century, however, only partly accounts for its lack of influence on the genesis of Canadian banks. Of more importance was the primary economic role accorded to the colonies by Great Britain. That role was simply to supply natural products – staples – to the imperial centre for both consumption and refinement. It followed, then, that the financial system best suited to serve this economic structure was one which facilitated the movement of goods, not one which encouraged the growth of local industry.

These two factors – the disrepute of British country banking and Canada's staple colony role – have often been seen as sufficient causes for the emergence of Upper Canada's commercial banking system. As the writings of Joseph Schumpeter and Fritz Redlich make clear, however, commercial banking structures also emerged in non-colonial countries.[10] This broader perspective suggests that similar *local* conditions fostered similar financial responses.[11] In Canada's case, the role of the mother country and Canada's staple colonial structure may have prolonged, rather than created, this system.[12]

In fact, imperial authorities only slowly became aware of the ways in which a financial system could, if not create original wealth, at least distribute existing wealth to the mother country's advantage. To appreciate this, it is necessary to look more closely at the mechanics of colonial trade. By the last quarter of the eighteenth century, the financing of North America's trade was a matter of considerable complexity. In the first place only British coins of standard weight and fineness could be legal tender and all trade transactions had to be reckoned in terms of that currency. The specie which the Canadas possessed was of three main types: French coins introduced prior to the British conquest, British specie from England, and the Spanish dollar, obtained via trade with the American seaboard colonies. In order to equate the

---

[10]For the influence of the colonial structure on the development of Canadian banking, see Tom Naylor, "The Rise and Fall of the Third Commercial Empire of the St. Lawrence," in Gary Teeple, ed.. *Capitalism and the National Question in Canada* (Toronto, 1972), pp. 1–42. For a broader perspective, see Fritz Redlich, *The Moulding of American Banking* ɪ, (New York, 1968, reprint) and Joseph Schumpeter, *Business Cycles*, abr. ed., R. Fels, ed. (Toronto, 1964), pp. 85–97.

[11]This is explored in more detail in Section B.

[12]This is returned to in Section C.

relative value of these coins, Great Britain legislated what contemporaries referred to as "the par of exchange." After 1777 the
Spanish dollar was rated at 4s. 6d. in England and 5s. in British
North America. This meant that for a British colonist to acquire
£100 sterling he had to pay £111.11 of his local currency.

Not all coinage received the same rating. Because of this it is
quite probable that only low-quality specie circulated in the
Canadas. Good-quality coinage – i.e., that which was highly
rated – tended to be hoarded or shipped out to satisfy international
creditors. This differential rating of coinage had the effect of
allowing bad money to drive good money away and led to
continual colonial complaints concerning the scarcity and uneven
quality of local coinage.[13]

Due to the expense, dangers, and simple inconvenience of
shipping specie, trade was usually transacted via bills of
exchange. A mechanism which enabled an individual "to satisfy
an obligation in some distant place,"[14] the bill of exchange
closely resembled a modern post-dated cheque. Thus individual A
in Upper Canada might ask B in England to pay a certain sum to C
in England at a particular time – usually thirty to ninety days after
sight – that is, after the bill reached England. There are, however,
two differences between a post-dated cheque and a bill of
exchange. The latter was used for purposes of external trade and
could be made payable in any currency; it could also be bought
and sold. If individual A in Upper Canada did not have an English
contact on whom he could draw to pay C, he could purchase a bill
from D in Upper Canada who did have such a contact (E) who
could pay, at the appropriate time, the proper sum to C.

Of crucial importance, from both the imperial and colonial
points of view, was the fact that the buying and selling of these
bills did not always occur at the official rate or "par of
exchange." While many factors could cause exchange to fluctu-
ate, one of the more important of them centred on the colony's
balance of payments. In a period of heavy imports the rate of
exchange was high and the colonist had to pay a sum above par in
order to purchase a sterling bill. In a time of heavy exports, the

[13]For an extended discussion of this, see Angela Redish, "Why Was Specie Scarce
in Colonial Economies? An Analysis of the Canadian Currency, 1796–1830," *Journal
of Economic History* [hereafter *JEH*] xLIV (1984), pp. 713–28.

[14]John J. McCusker, *Money and Exchange in Europe and America, 1600–1775; A
Handbook* (Chapel Hill, 1978), p. 19; A.B. McCullough, *Money and Exchange in
Canada to 1900* (Toronto, 1984), pp. 17–23.

rate was low or below par and the colonist paid less to purchase the same bill. The exchange rate also varied according to the amount and quality of specie available in the colony. When little or poor-quality specie existed, the rate was low. If good specie was readily available, the rate usually rested at par or above.

Severe fluctuations in the exchange rate were usually looked on with disfavour by both the colonial commercial community and the imperial government. Generally speaking, both groups desired a stable financial context within which the exchange of goods and money could be conducted. The seasonal nature of Canada's trade made this difficult.[15] The importation of specie at times when the exchange rate fell was one way to maintain stability. For obvious reasons this was impossible to accomplish on a regular basis. A second way was for individuals or institutions to sell bills in the colony, not for actual goods or money, but on credit – for goods or money to be received at a later date. As Julian Gwyn has shown, this actually occurred in the 1770s and early 1780s at Quebec, Halifax, and New York. Agents for the British army contractors who were responsible for paying and supplying the British army in America were continually hampered in their work by the lack of good local specie. To augment this, they sold bills on credit, despite written instructions to the contrary from London. The precipitous calling in of these debts in 1783 led to a celebrated series of local bankruptcies at Quebec and indicated that the imperial government failed to understand the relationship between credit and a stable exchange rate in a trading economy characterized by dramatic seasonal fluctuations.[16]

Following the Revolutionary War, increased trade between Quebec and the United States further complicated the financial and trade exchange of the colonies with England. In general terms, imports from Great Britain into Quebec were more than offset by the combination of colonial exports to Great Britain plus British direct expenditure on military establishments, Loyalist claims, and pensioners. Beginning in the 1790s and most dramatically during the first decade of the 1800s, the colonies experienced a balance of payments in their favour and there was,

---

[15]Professor Douglas McCalla suggests, and he may very well be correct, that the seasonal issue only "threatened" to make matters difficult and in reality provided money-making opportunities for merchants "in smoothing the fluctuations."

[16]Julian Gwyn, "The Impact of British Military Spending on the Colonial American Money Markets, 1760–1783," Canadian Historial Association, *Historical Papers* [hereafter *HP*], pp. 77–99.

therefore, a surplus of sterling bills for sale.[17] The exchange rate was further weakened by the fact that Canada's trade with the United States was at an imbalance and this deficit had to be paid for by the existing metallic currency. The southward flow of specie made the sale of bills in the colony even more difficult. Because America ran a deficit in her trade with Great Britain, however, this specie did not remain in the United States. With bills of exchange more costly in New York and Boston, Americans sent money across the border to purchase below par bills at Montreal for use or resale in the two American cities (A 1). Through this process some balance was maintained in the colonial exchange system.[18]

Within this general context, however, available evidence suggests that much fluctuation and instability persisted in the exchange market.[19] From an imperial point of view – the British lost money when the exchange was low – some mechanism which would exert greater control over that market was required. Despite contemporary criticism (A 1), the imperial centre once again did nothing to remedy the situation.[20] In the fiscal sector, colonial policy on the eve of the War of 1812 remained, as it had been in 1783, out of touch with both colonial economic realities and its own best interest.

It remained for the colonials themselves to initiate change in this area. For several reasons the first attempts, including the first successful attempt, to establish a bank in the Canadas emerged from Lower Canada. Especially in the early nineteenth century, Upper Canada was merely an economic tributary to the lower province. As Adam Shortt has said, what the former lacked was not simply good currency, but capital.[21] Yet the actual beginning of banking in both colonies was only a little over a year apart and the Bank of Upper Canada was the first *chartered* bank to operate

[17]The suspension of specie payments by Great Britain in 1797 also affected the exchange rate. Currency that remained tied to silver or gold rose in value when compared to the irredeemable bank notes issued by Great Britain between 1797 and 1820. See McCullough, *Money and Exchange*, pp. 81, 252–53, 265.

[18]A. Shortt, "The Early History of Canadian Banking, 1791–1812," *JCBA* IV (1897), pp. 235–52; R.C. McIvor, *Canadian Monetary Banking and Fiscal Development* (Toronto, 1958), chapter 2.

[19]McIvor, *Canadian Monetary Banking*, pp. 17–18; McCullough, *Money and Exchange*, p. 262.

[20]A. Shortt, "The First Banks in Lower Canada," *JCBA* IV (1897), pp. 342–43. It is possible that colonial demand for British goods increased when the exchange rate favoured the colonies and thus in a general sense Britain did not lose money at all.

[21]A. Shortt, "The First Banks in Upper Canada," *JCBA* V (1897), pp. 1–21.

in either of the colonies. To understand how this came about it is necessary to examine with care the aims and mentalité of the local colonial leaders who participated in the imperial economic system.[22] Once again the Constitutional Act of 1791 provides a good starting point.

The act was not a measure designed to foster the interests of the mercantile element in either of the colonies. In Lower Canada, English merchants dominated the import-export sector. But these merchants were in turn but a small minority of the colony's population and had to function within what was, from their point of view, an antiquated French civil law code for the transaction of their provincial business. As events demonstrated, they had little hope of ever dominating the assembly and thus changing this situation from within.

Nor was the mercantile element in Upper Canada especially favoured. Lacking a direct outlet to the sea, Upper Canadian merchants depended on Lower Canadians to handle imports from and exports to Great Britain and in this situation the Upper Canadians were generally the junior partners. As was true of almost all frontier colonies within the British Empire, the major source of governmental revenue was customs duties. Upper Canada depended on a share of the customs revenues collected by Lower Canada. For various reasons this dependence became increasingly intolerable and, as will be seen, controversy over the distribution of customs duties contributed to the establishment of the Bank of Upper Canada at York.

If the Constitutional Act made capital accumulation in Upper Canada, whether for mercantile or other pursuits, problematic, it also accorded little social recognition to mercantile endeavour. Nor should this be surprising for, as Pierre Tousignant has made clear, that act reflected the social, economic, and political precepts of its framers. Those involved in its genesis and implementation gave primacy to the values of a landed-military elite. The future of Lower Canada was vested in the seigneurial class and Upper Canada's future rested with half-pay officers and Loyalists as landholders.[23] Yet it is often pointed out that John Graves Simcoe, Upper Canada's first lieutenant-governor, succeeded in

[22]For a review of literature on the relationship between colonial leaders and the imperial government, see R.W. Winks, "On Decolonization and Informal Empire," *American Historical Review* LXXXI (1976), pp. 540–56.

[23]Pierre Tousignant, "Problématique pour une nouvelle approche de la constitution de 1791," *Revue d'histoire de l'Amérique française* XXVII (1973), pp. 181–234.

establishing only a pale imitation of a society imbued with the values of the British squirearchy. Despite clergy and administrative land reserves, early land abundance acted as a social leveller. Servants, as Mrs. Simcoe complained, were hardly to be found. By the early nineteenth century, Americans, or, as they were called, late Loyalist land-grabbers, bulked large in Upper Canada's population. The establishment of an Anglican Church became quickly threatened by Methodist circuit-riders from the south. Nor, much to Simcoe's chagrin, did a purely landed-military elite ever emerge to dominate Upper Canadian affairs. Rather, men engaged in mercantile matters gradually assumed positions of prominence and power.

The local financial and marketing systems both gave to the merchant his power and severely limited his potential growth. In the absence of a sufficient circulating medium, Upper Canadian merchants followed a practice begun in the lower province and issued their own paper notes, known as bons, to the local settlers. They would redeem these notes at par only in October of each year: at any other date the settler had to pay a $12^1/_2$ per cent discount.[24] The merchant sold the produce he obtained to one of three outlets: the British commissariat, for local consumption; his controlling partner in Lower Canada, for consumption there, or re-export to England; or across Lake Ontario to New York State for American consumption. In the early 1790s the British commissariat probably provided the single largest market. In return for goods (including some imports), the commissariat issued sterling bills of exchange. This enabled the merchant to turn his capital over much more quickly than the average settler could and facilitated his emergence to a position of economic power in the colony.[25]

. Those merchants who did gravitate to the centre of power, however, were merchants of a certain sort. As Bruce Wilson has clearly shown in his case study of the Hamiltons at early Niagara, to succeed such men required the right bearing, the appropriate

---

[24]McIvor, *Canadian Monetary Banking*, p. 17; McCullough, *Money and Exchange*, pp. 76–77, 97, n.9.

[25]John McGill to J.G. Simcoe, 8 Jan. 1793, in E.A. Cruikshank, ed., *The Correspondence of Lieutenant-Governor John Graves Simcoe*, I (Toronto, 1923), pp. 272–75. For a challenging interpretation of this era, see Douglas McCalla, ''The 'Loyalist' Economy of Upper Canada,'' *Histoire sociale/Social History* [hereafter *HS/SH*] XVI (1983), pp. 279–304.

contacts, and the proper beliefs.[26] In this sense, the precepts underlying the Constitutional Act of 1791 blended with local circumstances to produce an elite that possessed many of the values of the British landed class – social stability, social deference, balanced and orderly growth – but applied these values to the pursuit of mercantile ends. Not surprisingly, their general views on the appropriate fiscal arrangement for the colonies accorded well with British Tory ideas on the proper financial complex for the mother country.

The initial system employed by the commissariat in the letting of contracts acted as a prism through which the appropriate economic leaders could emerge. Since no pretence was made of open bidding, several long-settled merchants tended to dominate this activity and, due to this advantage, were able both to maintain their superior position when open bidding was instituted and to extend their influence over the gradual expansion of Upper Canada's trade into the export of wheat, potash, and lumber to Quebec and New York.[27] As John S. Cartwright acknowledged in 1841:

Anyone acquainted with the trade of the Canadas . . . must be aware that prior to 1820 [Upper Canada] was but a slight degree removed from a system of barter – long credit and large profits were the order of the day. The Country Merchant received from the farmer the products of his toil, and he sent them to his correspondent in Lower Canada . . . a few only had capital, it was the [custom?] of them to meet together, affix the price at which they would receive the product of the country.[28]

He spoke on good authority: his father, Richard, was one of the pre-eminent Upper Canadian merchants in that era.

Yet it would be misleading to overemphasize the extent of the merchants' economic power in this period. Research by Douglas McCalla and Bruce Wilson has pointed to the degree of failure and uncertainty in even the highest economic ranks and suggested that competition rather than monopoly characterized the overall system.[29] As the local merchant moved from being a supplier of the commissariat to an exporter of produce, he became more

[26]Bruce Wilson, "The Struggle for Wealth and Power at Fort Niagara, 1775–1783," *Ontario History* LXVIII (1976), pp. 137–54, and *The Enterprises of Robert Hamilton: A Study of Wealth and Influence in Early Upper Canada: 1776–1812* (Toronto, 1983).

[27]On the relationship between length of settlement and economic standing, see D.A. Norris, "Household and Transiency in a Loyalist Township: The People of Adolphustown, 1784–1822," *HS/SH* XIII (1980), pp. 399–416.

[28]Kingston *Chronicle and Gazette*, 4 Sept. 1841.

[29]See the works by McCalla and Wilson cited in footnotes 25 and 26 supra.

firmly a part of an international system of long credit. He became, in a sense, doubly dependent. His controlling partner in Lower Canada handled his British business and to receive a return on goods sent to Great Britain, the Upper Canadian merchant had often to wait for two years. This, coupled with the unstable market for sterling bills, gave him little, if any, control over what his actual rate of return would be. As the colony gradually became part of this international trading system, its merchants began to press, in 1809–10, for a mechanism through which they could obtain local short-term credit and a more stable exchange market.[30]

They also, especially following the War of 1812, began to press for a more rational and widely accepted circulating medium. During the war, army bills, totalling over £1,200,000, had been issued by the Lower Canadian government under imperial guarantee. These bills quickly became the main circulating medium of both Canadas and facilitated the smooth operation of the relatively buoyant economy occasioned by the war. In fact, many contemporaries erroneously believed that the sound paper currency caused rather than aided the economic boom of those years. Following the redemption of the bills and the abrupt return of the British garrisons to England at war's end, Upper Canadian merchants found themselves overstocked and overcommitted in terms of current orders. As a temporary stop gap, they resorted to auctions.[31] As a long-term measure, they pressed again for the founding of a local banking facility to issue notes, provide credit, and manage a market for bills of exchange.

[30]Kingston *Gazette*, Dec. 1810 and Jan. 1811. Upper Canadian merchants were receiving some short-term credit from their controlling partners in Lower Canada.

[31]Provincial Archives of Ontario [hereafter PAO], Ridout Papers, T.G. Ridout to Thomas Ridout, 8 June 1816.

A. GETTING STARTED, 1817–22

THE EVENTS leading to the opening of the Bank of Upper Canada at York in July 1822 underline the difficulties of initiating economic change within an imperial-colonial framework and point to the emergence of regional conflict and a transfer of economic power within Upper Canada. They mark the gradual congruence at an economic level of imperial interests and the aims of the York elite. Against a backdrop of languishing trade, scarce specie, and a complicated circulating medium composed of local merchants' bons and depreciated American nonconvertible bank notes (A 2), Upper Canadians presented two petitions to the Assembly in 1817. One (3 March) pleaded for the establishment of a bank at Kingston, the colony's largest trading centre; the second (17 March) asked for a separate bank at York, the colony's capital. The Assembly ignored the York petition and passed, with Legislative Council approval, the Kingston bill. According to the act, the charter would be "forfeited for nonuser" if the company did not commence operations before 1 January 1819. Favourably impressed, Lieutenant-Governor Gore forwarded the bill in early May to London for the Colonial Office's consideration.[1]

In passing the Kingston rather than the York bank bill, the Assembly had acted sensibly. Kingston was probably twice York's size in 1817 and, thanks to its position at the junction of the St. Lawrence and Lake Ontario and to the existence of a large military establishment at that point, Kingston was Upper Canada's leading commercial centre.[2] That the Legislative Council, often said at this time to have been under the control of the Reverend John Strachan, the chief petitioner for the York bank and a leading member of Upper Canada's political elite, acquiesced in the Assembly's decision, accentuates Kingston's commercial superiority. In part the preponderance of Loyalists and well-established merchants amongst the incorporators of the Kingston bank helped make that institution palatable to both the

---

[1]*Journals of the Legislative Assembly of Upper Canada* [hereafter *JUC*], Mar. and Apr. 1817, *Report of the Bureau of Archives for the Province of Ontario, 1912* [hereafter *Report of Archives*].

[2]G. Stelter, "Urban Planning and Development in Upper Canada," in G. Stelter *et al.*, eds., *Urbanization in the Americas: The Background in Comparative Perspective* (Ottawa, 1980), p. 147.

lieutenant-governor and to the colony's small governing elite clustered at York. Indeed, some of the promoters had been students of Strachan himself.[3] Of more importance, however, the York group realized that without Kingston's financial assistance, they lacked the necessary capital to initiate such a venture. Nor, in 1817, could York look to the lieutenant-governor for aid.

Since the relationship between York and the lieutenant-governor was crucial in determining York's ultimate success in acquiring a bank, the situation in 1817 requires some explanation. From the imperial point of view, the lieutenant-governor saw no need for establishing a close relationship with any bank in that year. In fact Gore believed that the government's financial situation was strong enough to support additional responsibility for some civil government expenses traditionally paid from imperial sources. Since 75 to 80 per cent of Upper Canada's revenue came from its share of the customs duties levied in Lower Canada, the signing of a two-year agreement in May 1817 whereby Upper Canada would receive one-fifth of all such duties contributed to the lieutenant-governor's optimism. From 1797 to 1817 the division of these monies had been determined on a yearly basis. Although not all disputes over prior allocations had been settled, the agreement seemed a step toward both stability and the recognition by Lower Canada of the upper province's just requirements.[4] In this context, then, it is not surprising that the Kingston bank's charter contained no mention of government participation. Nor should it be surprising that York received no imperial preferment.

Several weeks after Gore had forwarded the Kingston bill to England, promoters of the Bank of Montreal published their Articles of Association in the Quebec *Gazette*. Frustrated for the past three years in their attempts to push a bill through the Lower Canadian Assembly, that bank's promoters decided to commence operations as an unchartered institution. The bank opened its doors in November and, by June 1818, had established agencies at Kingston and York, Upper Canada.[5]

Alarmed by this intrusion and unwilling to wait longer for

---

[3]Amongst the Loyalists and well-established merchants were Thomas Markland, Peter Smith, Lawrence Herkimer, John Kirby, Allan McLean, and Thomas Graham. For information on all the above, see Richard Preston, ed., *Kingston Before the War of 1812* (Toronto, 1959), *passim*.

[4]G.M. Craig, *Upper Canada: The Formative Years, 1784–1841* (Toronto, 1963), p. 100; *JUC*, 24 Nov., 22 Dec. 1821, in *Report of Archives, 1914*, pp. 18, 104, 108, 109.

[5]Denison, *Canada's First Bank*, i, chapters 5 and 6.

Colonial Office sanction, a Kingston group followed suit and published similar Articles of Association on 14 July 1818.[6] There was almost no overlap between the incorporators of the 1817 bill and the promoters of the unchartered, or what came to be known as the Pretended Bank, in 1818. Included in the 1818 promoters were Americans, relatively minor Kingston merchants, political reformers, and independent conservatives.[7] This contrast in personnel alarmed both the new lieutenant-governor, Sir Peregrine Maitland, and members of the York elite. Strachan, for example, remarked on "the want of respectability in the Members" (A 10) and Maitland pointed with distaste to the bank's American character.[8] Perhaps because of this lack of acceptance in important circles, it took the promoters until April 1819 to acquire the £10,000 paid in capital required to commence operations. By that time a branch of yet another Lower Canadian bank, the Bank of Canada, had appeared in Kingston.[9] By that time, too, competition was about to re-emerge from within Upper Canada.

The receipt in May 1819 of the royal assent to Kingston's 1817 bank bill provided the opportunity for this re-emergence. It is not clear why the Colonial Office took over two years to return the bill, thus causing forfeiture. It is doubtful that the York elite played any part in this. Review procedures concerning colonial fiscal matters were complex involving the Board of Trade, the Treasury Board, and the Colonial Office. One student of the Colonial Office has claimed that ten or eleven separate steps were taken before a final recommendation appeared. Certainly the Treasury Board was notorious for its dilatoriness in such matters. Very likely the time taken simply reflected the low priority Upper Canada possessed at the Colonial Office in the early nineteenth century.[10]

Whatever the reasons for the delay, York's elite quickly

[6]Kingston *Gazette*, 14 July 1818.

[7]Benjamin Whitney, the bank's president, was American. Peter Smythe was a representative minor merchant. Thomas Dalton was reformist in politics and C.A. Hagerman, an independent conservative, defeated the candidate who was Strachan's choice in the 1820 provincial elections.

[8]Public Archives of Canada [PAC], Colonial Office Papers, vol. 42, [hereafter CO 42], p. 362, Maitland to Goulburn, 1 May 1819.

[9]For the establishment of the branch, see Kingston *Gazette*, 20 Oct. 1818. For the bank's start-up, see ibid., 23 Apr. 1819.

[10]Paul Knaplund, *James Stephen and the British Colonial System 1813–47* (Madison, 1953), p. 209; D.B. Swinfen, *Imperial Control of Colonial Legislation, 1813–65* (Oxford, 1970), p. 13; A.S.J. Baster, *The Imperial Banks* (New York, 1929, reprint 1977), chapter 2.

attempted to take advantage of it. A scant four days after Kingston interests had submitted a petition to the Assembly to revive their bank, the York group, led by William Allan, a rising member of the local elite, reactivated their old 1817 petition. Once again – although by only three votes – the Assembly passed the Kingston bill and ignored the York petition. This time, however, the York-dominated Legislative Council requested a conference with the Assembly. The appointed delegates produced two bills both of which were immediately passed by the council. The first bill differed from the Kingston act in four ways: the names of the Kingston promoters had been replaced by York promoters, the head office was to be at the seat of government, the government was given power to own stock, and the charter was not to expire for nonuser until 1 January 1822. A second bill, to incorporate "the Bank of Kingston," was also sent down to the Assembly. Unlike the first, it was to have its head office in Kingston, it contained no provisions for government participation, and it was to expire for nonuser 1 January 1821. By such means did the York elite hope to pacify Kingston and at the same time acquire their own dominant banking institution.[11]

The Assembly passed both bills. On 12 July Lieutenant-Governor Maitland gave the royal assent to the second bill and, much to York's chagrin, reserved the first for the consideration of the Colonial Office. Maitland acted as he did for several reasons. In the first place the original 1817 bill which had received the belated royal assent provided for a bank at Kingston and did not provide for the right of government participation. In a strict constitutional sense, Maitland acted correctly in sanctioning the bill which most closely resembled the original Kingston act and reserving the York bill, with its substantially different clauses, for royal review. Although some members of the unchartered Pretended Bank were actually promoting the 1819 bill, so, too, were many of the original 1817 incorporators and in fact, the latter outnumbered the former.[12] Maitland did have confidence in the bank's promoters.

Beyond these points, however, it seems clear that Maitland did

[11]*JUC*, 8, 9, and 12 July 1819, in *Report of Archives, 1913. Journal*, Legislative Council of Upper Canada, 8, 9, 12 July 1819, in *Report of Archives, 1911*. For the York bank's charter, see 59 Geo. iii, c. 24, and Appendix 2 in this volume.

[12]Compare Kingston *Gazette*, 15 July 1817 and 23 Apr. 1819 with *JUC*, 8 July 1819 in *Report of Archives, 1913*, p. 191.

not feel any pressing need for a bank with close government connections. Once again the government's financial context helps to explain his position. The two-year agreement with Lower Canada concerning the division of customs duties had only expired on 1 July. There was every reason to expect that a new arrangement could be effected and that Upper Canada's share, reflecting its growing population, would be increased. In 1819 the lieutenant-governor remained sanguine concerning his colony's financial future. The economic needs of the lieutenant-governor and the economic aims of the York elite had yet to merge.

Making the best of an undesirable situation, John Strachan advised his former pupil and Kingston contact, John Macaulay, that once the Kingston bank commenced operations an amendment could be passed providing for government participation (A 5). In this way, presumably, he hoped to gain control of the Kingston bank's operations through the Legislative Council. For his part, William Allan went quietly back to being the Bank of Montreal's York agent and awaited further developments.[13] For their part the Kingston promoters tried valiantly to raise the £20,000 paid in capital as required by their charter in order to commence operations before forfeiture on 1 January 1821.

They failed. Funds of that magnitude were simply unavailable. Upper Canada's economy, never terribly buoyant after the war, was at the beginning of an even more dramatic downturn. Between 1819 and the end of 1822 the prices of wheat, livestock, and land fell by at least 50 per cent.[14] In part this was an inevitable consequence of an international recession involving both of Upper Canada's major trading associates, Great Britain and the United States. This impact was intensified by the operation of the British Corn Law of 1815. That act provided for the competitive entry of colonial wheat and flour into the British market only when British prices were at 67s. per quarter or above. This price range had been maintained through 1816–19. But in 1820 British farmers enjoyed a bumper crop, prices fell and colonial wheat was excluded. Thus did the situation remain until a revision of the act in 1822 allowed greater freedom of entry in 1823. By that

---

[13]He had been so appointed in June 1818. PAC, Bank of Montreal Resolve Book 1, 16 June 1818, 63.

[14]R.L. Jones, *History of Agriculture in Ontario, 1613–1880* (Toronto, 1946), pp. 39–40; T.W. Acheson, "The Nature and Structure of York Commerce in the 1820s," in J.K. Johnson, ed., *Historical Essays on Upper Canada* (Toronto, 1975), pp. 180–84.

time, too, the general economic situation in Great Britain and the
United States was on the upturn. From the point of view of the
Kingston bank promoters, however, it was a case of too little, too
late.

Capitalizing on Kingston's failure to raise the required funds,
the York group once again moved into action. This time they
enjoyed the eager support of the lieutenant-governor. Maitland,
in fact, was quite desperate and ready to seize on almost any
means to raise capital for his government. A general disruption of
Lower Canadian politics led by Louis-Joseph Papineau had been
used as a pretext by the Lower Canadians to postpone negotiating
a new settlement of customs receipts. As a result, in 1819 and
again in 1820 Upper Canada had received little money from its
major source of revenue. Nor, as 1821 progressed, did Lower
Canada seem at all in a hurry to commence negotiations.[15]
Severely pressed, Maitland sanctioned laws that authorized public borrowing to meet government obligations (A 6). And while it
is true that the Pretended Bank at Kingston continued to operate
through all this, Maitland also continued to view that bank with
considerable distrust. Although the bank enjoyed a large note
circulation, especially in eastern Upper Canada, the government
generally refused to accept its paper in payment of government
accounts.[16] This decision had a deleterious effect on the bank's
operations which, coupled with bad and perhaps dishonest management and poor economic conditions, led to its collapse in
1822. In these circumstances the notion of the government actually borrowing from the existing Kingston bank was never
entertained.

Maitland looked to a new bank for financial assistance. It is
worth emphasizing this point. His and, by extension, his government's involvement in the Bank of Upper Canada at York was not
undertaken simply to feather the nest of a private elite. He and his
predecessor had, after all, twice resisted pandering to York.
Certainly the personnel in command of the bank had to be of
appropriate background and standing in the colony. Equally
certainly, had the chartered bank at Kingston been successful
Maitland would have happily dealt with it. The unstated but very
real precepts which underlay the Constitutional Act of 1791 still

[15]*JUC*, 22 Dec. 1821, in *Report of Archives*, 1913, pp. 96–114.
[16]PAC, RG 19 B2b, Department of Finance, Receiver General of Upper Canada,
Letterbooks, vol. 1172, J.H. Dunn to C.A. Hagerman, 21 Dec. 1820; Dunn to J.
Spencer, 28 July 1821.

set the ground rules for activity within Upper Canada. Yet no matter what private advantage might accrue – and one obviously did and only certain private groups could realistically aspire to it – the lieutenant-governor viewed the bank as a means of improving a desperate financial situation. This distinction of interest persisted, much to the bank's dissatisfaction, well into the future. In 1821, however, the economic interests of both the lieutenant-governor and York's elite could best be achieved through mutual cooperation.

The ultimate result was better than even the York promoters could have legitimately anticipated. In order to forestall a move to amend the Kingston bank's charter by lowering the required paid up capital and in the process reactivating the company, they supported, but did not initiate, a bill creating a "Provincial Bank" to be called the Bank of Upper Canada. To qualify for a branch, Kingston had first to subscribe for fourteen hundred shares.[17] On 14 April 1821, the lieutenant-governor gave it his assent. It was stillborn. A scant few days later news was received that the royal assent had been given to the bill of 1819 setting up the Bank of Upper Canada at York (A 8). The York promoters proceeded under the bill. And why not? It gave them what they wanted: a bank at York, government participation, no requirement for a Kingston branch and no need for concern about any "Provincial" interest.

It remained to put it in operation. According to the charter, £50,000 (four thousand shares) had to be taken up before directors could be elected. The bank could commence operations only when £20,000 in gold or silver was actually paid in. The government could subscribe for a maximum of two thousand shares. This the government did on 16 October 1821 and by early November the bank announced that four thousand shares had been taken up (A 14). At this point, York's bank ran into the same problem that had faced the defunct chartered bank at Kingston: capital to the extent of £20,000 was simply not available for investment in Upper Canada in the early 1820s.

Like the Kingston effort, York's bank did not, therefore, commence operations before its charter became forfeit for non-user on 1 January 1822. Unlike Kingston, York successfully exercised its political power, reactivated the bank and in the

---

[17]*JUC*, 12 Apr. 1821, in *Report of Archives, 1913*, pp. 484–85. The bill resulted from a petition from Prince Edward County.

process amended the charter to allow business to commence upon the payment of £10,000.[18] Maitland gave the royal assent to the amended bill on 17 January 1822. One week later the first directorate was chosen (A 15, A 16) and on 29 January the first request for a 10 per cent payment was issued to all subscribers.[19] After the mandatory sixty-day wait a second call for 10 per cent was issued, due 10 June 1822.[20] Business commenced in July.

The fact that the bank obtained the necessary start-up money at a time of severe specie shortage and absence of ready investment capital has led to the claim, first published in 1885, that the bank obtained a shortfall in specie from the imperial military chest.[21] Writing in 1897 Adam Shortt embellished on this and, on the basis of some dubious calculations, asserted that the bank received at least £1,500 over and above the government's subscription from that source. Those in the twentieth century who have written on the bank have generally echoed Shortt.[22] The temptation to do so is understandable. The lieutenant-governor, despite imperial reluctance, had himself drawn on the military chest to meet pressing provincial needs.[23] Moreover, the alleged activity corresponds neatly with a traditional view of the York elite, or Family Compact, as grasping, unethical, and in complete control of all government activity. It provides corroboration for the future criticisms made by William Lyon Mackenzie and other reformers of the bank as a "political engine of dangerous power."[24]

What seems to have actually transpired, while somewhat less colourful than the picture painted by Shortt, is nonetheless revealing of the nature of bank–government and, to a degree, Family Compact–government relations in the early 1820s. The bank's charter stipulated that the paid-in capital had to be in specie.

[18]*JUC*, 4 Jan. 1822, in *Report of Archives, 1914*.

[19]PAC RG 19 B2a, Department of Finance, Receiver General of Upper Canada, Letters Received, vol. 1131, T.G. Ridout to J.H. Dunn, 29 Jan. 1822.

[20]*Upper Canada Gazette*, 2 Apr. 1822.

[21]See R.M. Breckenridge, "The Canadian Banking System, 1817–90," *JCBA* II (1894–95), p. 139, n. 1, for 1885 reference.

[22]Shortt, "The First Banks in Upper Canada," pp. 20–21. He claims only £10,640 was paid up at the end of 1823 and this after a third call for 5 per cent. In fact, £13,415 had been paid up on 4,293 shares. As each share was worth £12 10S, the paid-in capital was exactly 25 per cent. See *Journals of the Legislative Assembly of the Province of Canada* [hereafter *JLA*], 1841, Appendix O, Section G; Acheson, "York Commerce," pp. 186–87; Denison, *Canada's First Bank*, p. 158; C.L. Vaughan, "The Bank of Upper Canada in Politics, 1817–40," *Ontario History*, LX (1968), p. 187.

[23]PAC, CO 42, vol. 369, Dalhousie to G. Harrison, 11 Oct. 1821.

[24]*JUC*, 1829, Appendix, First Report of the Committee of Finance, 8 Mar. 1829.

Notes were not sufficient. Yet, as has been suggested, that amount of gold and silver was simply not readily available in Upper Canada. Even the government rarely received specie in the conduct of its general business and accepted Montreal bank notes instead (A 21). Out of necessity York's bank, too, accepted these notes in lieu of coin from its subscribers. Evidently it intended to collect and present them either to the Bank of Montreal for redemption in specie or exchange them in American markets for gold and silver. While the bank was willing to accept notes from private subscribers, it was less willing to do so from the government. Sympathetic to the bank's problem, but without ready specie in Upper Canada, Receiver General Dunn, the government's principal financial figure and an imperial appointee, offered to change some of the bank's holdings of paper currency into specie at Montreal (A 22). He made a special trip to Lower Canada for that purpose and by 19 June he had converted £2,500 of government-owned notes (the government's second instalment) into American half-dollars. Since this was the only coin he could obtain and since it was obviously quite bulky to transport, he refused to exchange any of the notes the bank had obtained from private subscribers (A 23).

The available evidence strongly suggests that Dunn used his contacts at the military commissariat in Montreal to effect this exchange and therein lies the origin of the story as developed by Shortt. While hardly a routine transaction – the commissariat was itself always in search of coin to pay salaries and supplies – it is none the less clear that the military chest did not provide the bank extra money. Both the timing and method of conversion employed by the bank concerning its notes from private subscribers remain, however, unknown. Very likely the bank, in violation of its charter, commenced operations with a combination of specie and Bank of Montreal notes in its vault. Since no audit, independent or otherwise, was made of the bank's holdings before it commenced operations, one will never really know.

This episode points up, yet again, the severe fiscal problems besetting Upper Canada in the early 1820s. It also suggests the extent to which the government was willing to assist the bank. In 1817 it had failed to raise a finger. In 1819 York was again by-passed. By 1821 the government, in a straitened financial condition, allowed the sudden receipt of the royal assent to York's 1819 bill to take precedence over all else. There can be no doubt but that the lieutenant-governor wanted the bank to commence operations as soon as possible. In fact on Maitland's orders, the receiver general had delayed borrowing in private quarters in the hopes that the bank could soon meet the government's needs.[25] Thus to fulfill the letter of the government's obligations, Dunn went to a great deal of trouble and some expense. In the end, however, he did no more. To place the York elite in the role of master manipulator oversimplifies a more complex series of events. Colonial Office sanctions floated in at totally unexpected moments: they could be reacted to; they could not be anticipated. The lieutenant-governor had his own agenda and his actions can only be understood in relation to it. Rather than assuming that an intimate relationship existed between the bank and government, one should be aware that a real distinction of interests persisted throughout this era. One should also remember that the government with which the bank had to deal was a complex and often discordant apparatus. Given its multi-level structure, a one-to-one relationship could rarely be effected.

[25]PAC, RG 19 B2b, vol. 1172, Dunn to Thomas Clark, 14 July 1821.

B.   PERSONNEL, PRINCIPLES AND PRACTICE: THE ALLAN ERA, 1822–35

ECONOMIC THEORY POSITS that the basic functions of financial intermediaries are to "allocate financial resources efficiently and augment the flows of savings and investments."[1] For two reasons banks are especially suited to fulfill these functions. They have an advantage over other financial institutions in that their liabilities – in this period, bank notes – circulate as money. Banks also have power to do more than simply collect money from some and distribute it to others. Because they can issue notes in excess of specie on hand, banks can also *create* money and thereby stimulate growth and development in the area they serve.

Historians have generally concluded that the Bank of Upper Canada achieved only partial success in carrying out its role as a financial intermediary in the pre-Union era. It has been charged with excessively favouring Upper Canada's political elite, locking up its funds in government debentures, and pursuing a narrow mercantile-oriented discount policy. While Upper Canada grew rapidly in this period, its economic growth was not diversified nor well-dispersed geographically. For these reasons, some economic historians have concluded that the Bank of Upper Canada and indeed the whole nineteenth-century Canadian banking system did not "fit" well with Canada's developmental needs.[2]

A close look at the bank's early years suggests, however, that much of the above interpretation stands in need of some degree of revision. This is especially true of the bank's political and government dealings. And while it is less true of the bank's discount policies, the strategies adopted by the bank in this area require clarification.

I

The men who directed the Bank of Upper Canada's affairs in the

[1]Richard Sylla, "American Banking and Growth in the Nineteenth Century: A Partial View of the Terrain," *Explorations in Economic History* IX (1971–72), p. 211.

[2]See, for example, Acheson, "York Commerce," pp. 185–91; Naylor, "The Rise and Fall of the Third Commercial Empire of the St. Lawrence," pp. 6–7; and H.C. Pentland, "The Role of Capital in Canadian Economic Development Before 1875," *Canadian Journal of Economics and Political Science* XVI (1950), pp. 472–74.

1820s were closely associated with an elite which, after three decades of internal growth and consolidation, stood poised to extend its power throughout Upper Canada.[3] The political and social aspects of that group's expansion have been well documented; its economic side has been relatively ignored. Demographic forces external to Upper Canada coupled with fortuitous geographical conditions within York's hinterland, the Home District, are seen as sufficient explanations for that area's strong population and economic growth in the 1820s and early 1830s. York's elite, the Family Compact, so active and domineering in a political and social sense, is characterized as passive and unskilled when dealing with economic affairs.[4]

When looked at from this perspective, the Bank of Upper Canada seems somewhat of an anomaly. It did enjoy immense success in this period. Especially after 1824, it dominated much of Upper Canada's financial affairs. Unlike its major competitor, the Bank of Montreal, it paid regular dividends throughout the 1820s and on five occasions between 1823 and 1835 it issued substantial bonuses as well.

This paradox of an elite without economic talent successfully operating an institution of some financial complexity is generally resolved in two ways. The root of its success, it is claimed, lay in the nature of its political connections.[5] The fact that nine of the first fifteen directors were members of the Legislative and/or Executive councils and that several others held various government appointments is often seen as conclusive proof of this point. Via these political links the bank obtained generally unspecified but, by implication, abundant financial preferment.[6] As an alleged tool in the hands of the Tory Family Compact, the bank achieved both notoriety and success.

This interpretation gains further substance from the claim that only one of the bank's early directors possessed the appropriate experience and talent to run a bank. Thus William Allan, the "only true merchant" on the board, became the bank's president

---

[3]R. Burns, "God's Chosen People: The Origins of Toronto Society, 1793–1818," *HP* (1973), pp. 213–28.

[4]For a brief review of the literature on the Family Compact as entrepreneurs, see P. Baskerville, "Entrepreneurship and the Family Compact: York-Toronto, 1822–55," *Urban History Review* ix, no. 3 (Feb. 1981), pp. 15–16.

[5]One would be hard put to find anything written on the bank which does not argue this.

[6]See, for example, A. Shortt, "Prosperity and Expansion in Upper Canada," *JCBA* viii (1900–1), p. 231.

and guided its affairs for twelve of its first thirteen years.[7] The others, or as one contemporary put it, the "Gentry Directors," contributed, by implication, little to the bank's economic and financial administration (A 16).

No attempt will be made in these pages to overturn completely this interpretation. Much can be seen by examining the bank's operations through a political lens. The existing picture, however, requires both refinement and enlargement. A closer look at the bank's directorate suggests that the possession of political power did not preclude the existence of experience in other areas.[8] William Allan was not the only director with a mercantile or business background. Thirty-five of the fifty-three directors active between 1822 and 1840 had significant business and financial experience. Twenty-one of these were merchants, making them the largest single occupational group on the directorate. In fact, aggregate statistics understate mercantile presence. Since merchants persisted as directors for an average period greater than that of any other occupational group, they numbered just over or just under half of most directorates in the years under review. Supplementing the merchants and their economic experience were eight general financiers and businessmen, four millers, and two directors who had had extensive experience working with merchants as officials in the Commissariat Department.[9]

It is true that these directors were in the main merchants and businessmen of an accepted sort. Whether they had cultivated the proper contacts and established themselves as first-generation York residents – as William Allan, John McGill, George Crookshank, Duncan Cameron, and Alexander Wood had – or inherited status as sons of first-generation parents – as the Boultons and Gambles had – or benefited from contact with John Strachan – as Peter Robinson had – most fitted easily into the dominant conservative ideology which underlay the Constitutional Act of 1791. As such they were individuals with whom the colony's ruling political groups could generally be quite comfort-

[7]Vaughan, "Bank of Upper Canada," p. 188.

[8]Many contemporary supporters of the bank, such as H.J. Boulton, emphasized government connections in order to accentuate stability and trustworthiness and to be able to claim that undue favouritism – i.e., excessive discounting to mercantile directors – would not result. It was not meant to imply that the directors lacked financial or economic experience (B 17).

[9]Of the remaining eighteen, eight were lawyers, seven army officers, and three medical doctors. See Appendix 1A and 1B, for list of directors.

able. In this sense, the directorate and the government were indeed congruent.

Yet it is the other side of the equation that requires emphasis. To a degree not properly appreciated, the Bank of Upper Canada possessed a directorate whose characteristics approximated those of other bank directorates in this period.[10] The personnel who oversaw the bank's early operations were not simply bureaucratic placemen under John Strachan's thumb. A large number had an economic life separate from government largesse. Significant financial and economic experience existed even within the group who did profit directly from government appointment. And, it should be noted, those who were most active in the bank's day-to-day operations were those who possessed the most extensive financial and business experience[11] (A 15, B 11, B 91). This suggests that the bank may well have possessed the necessary expertise to operate independent of government support.[12]

A second general point concerning the characteristics of the directors should also be mentioned. Throughout the 1820s and beyond some reform representation did exist in the bank's inner circle. Not all of York's elite were Tories. In the early years members of the Baldwin and Ridout families represented the reform interest on the bank's board. While both families were well established in York and had benefited from political patronage before 1820, they were not typical members of "God's Chosen People." In 1816 Thomas Gibbs Ridout, the bank's cashier from 1822 to 1861, referred bitterly to "the great men of

[10]This was especially the case in the sense that men with mercantile experience controlled the management. See Redlich, *The Moulding of American Banking*, p. 18, for a comment on American bank directorates. For a contrary view of the Bank of Upper Canada, a view that reflects the traditional perspective, see Pentland, "The Role of Capital," p. 472n.

[11]Certainly William Allan shouldered most of the work in this period. But others such as G. Crookshank, J.S. Baldwin, and J.H. Dunn were at various times considered as alternatives to Allan as president. And Crookshank did assume that position for one year.

[12]Allan's critical remarks on the abilities of many of his co-directors should not be accepted as the last word on this matter. Doubtless some were of little use. Yet Allan was a typical merchant in that he only reluctantly delegated authority. Throughout his life he willingly assumed much public as well as private responsibility. Many of his co-directors accepted his leading role because they agreed with his policies. Given an opportunity, many, at least in light of their backgrounds, might have performed with equal ability (B 9); M.L. Magill, "William Allan: A Pioneer Business Executive," in F.H. Armstrong *et al.*, eds., *Aspects of Nineteenth Century Ontario* (Toronto, 1974), pp. 101–13.

little York": and alluded to his own family's "independent principles" and capacity for future "vengeance."[13] Two years later John Ridout, Thomas's brother, was killed in a duel. The victor, S.P. Jarvis, went on to become an active director of the bank.

Not surprisingly, the annual elections for directors were hotly contested affairs. After gradually increasing their strength in 1823 and 1824, the Baldwin-Ridout group made a determined effort to dominate the board in 1825. Despite extensive canvassing for votes in Niagara and Kingston, they were soundly defeated and the Jarvises, Robinsons, and Boultons from York, supported by Macaulay in Kingston and Thomas McCormick (a relative of S.P. Jarvis) and others in Niagara controlled the directorate for the remainder of the period (B 10, B 11, B 12). Given the nature of the divisions, however, even after 1825 the board's deliberations continued to be characterized by political and familial as well as economic disputes[14] (B 34, B 35, B 36).

II

Some understanding of the principles upon which the bank based its operations can be gained by looking at its charter and at its seventeen-page booklet of *Rules and Regulations*, published in 1822 (A 24). As a bank of issue it was permitted to print and circulate notes above the denomination of five shillings. Other than note issue, the bank's main functions were buying and selling gold and silver and dealing in bonds, promissory notes, and bills of exchange. It was, in other words, created to standardize and institutionalize the functions hitherto performed by many individual merchants. It was for these reasons that most merchants looked forward to the bank's commencement. Only those who were financially independent could view the bank as a potential competitor in these affairs. Few mercantile houses of that stature operated in Upper Canada.

Explicit restrictions on the bank's operations were few. Market conditions governed dealings in exchange. Interest on loans and discounts could not exceed 6 per cent. No ceiling was placed on the quantity of notes which could be issued, although the bank had to redeem in gold or silver any note brought to its head office.

---

[13]PAO, Ridout Papers, T.G. Ridout to George Ridout, 1 June 1816, cited in E.G. Firth, ed., *The Town of York 1815–34* (Toronto, 1966), pp. 90–91.

[14]*Colonial Advocate*, 3 Apr. 1834.

Should it fail to do so, it had to cease operations and could only recommence when it had acquired the necessary specie. When debt, other than deposits, exceeded three times the paid-in capital stock, all directors responsible for allowing that excess became personally liable in the event of default. Since the bank's notes were put into circulation via discounts and since no specific limit existed as to the amount of notes that could be issued, the bank was free to discount as much paper as it desired.

Two particular beliefs, both current in British ruling circles, underlay much of the Bank of Upper Canada's charter. Convertibility was expected to prevent excess speculation and encourage stability. Under this system it was assumed that banks would have to maintain sufficient specie reserves to cover outstanding debts.[15] Related to this was the comforting, but misguided, notion that by financing reliable short-term mercantile transactions – that is, real bills – overspeculation was made impossible and the bank's note issue would correspond directly to the needs of the economy.[16] Consistent with this notion and this definition of a country's business, loans on the direct security of land were forbidden and loans on the security of other assets discouraged.

Because these principles underlay the bank's intended activities, the Colonial Office sanctioned its operations (A 2). And since the early practice of the Bank of Upper Canada was in part conditioned by these beliefs, some further general comments are necessary. The real bills doctrine was a product of a laissez-faire age. The economy was assumed to be self-regulating. Some modern economists have argued, however, that the real bills theory took inadequate account of the effects of price and interest levels on the supply of and demand for money and have questioned whether the monetary needs of business can be determined at any time with any precision. An even more substantial weakness in the real bills doctrine is its failure to acknowledge the fact that a "real" bill could be discounted more than once before the transaction upon which it was first issued was completed and thus the equation upon which that doctrine rested – one bill equalled one transaction – did not reflect reality.

The theory also failed to explain how a banker could be 100 per cent accurate in only discounting the bills of responsible mer-

---

[15] Hilton, *Corn, Cash and Commerce*, pp. 61–62.
[16] One did not have to be an adherent of one to espouse the other. See Lloyd W. Mints, *A History of Banking Theory in Great Britain and the United States* (Chicago, 1945), chapter 6.

chants engaged in real transactions. Discounting decisions were made on the basis of the director's interpretation of available information. That information varied in perfection as did the director's ability to interpret it. Nor did the principle of convertibility help in this regard. To the extent that convertibility inspired public confidence in the bank's notes and thus encouraged their use and reuse, the principle was effective and specie was rarely called for. Confidence itself, however, could not prevent the occurrence of periodic economic crises. When these occurred and redemption rather than reuse of notes increased, banks, along with conservative and speculative merchants, were vulnerable. Within the dictates of these prevailing doctrines, then, much potential for instability existed.[17]

In reality, too, both the bank's enabling legislation and its rules and regulations permitted some deviance from these underlying principles. Land could be accepted as collateral, or security of last resort. In this fashion a bank could acquire an unlimited amount of land and, to the extent that it did, tie up its assets in non-commercial areas. The rules and regulations of the Bank of Upper Canada permitted the lending of money on the security of its own stock even to the point of granting accommodation notes – a note the proceeds of which were to be paid to the drawer.[18] Other applicants were required to present notes with two responsible names or with one name and adequate security – presumably of a collateral sort such as land. Discounts could run for ninety days and could be renewed either upon the payment of 20 per cent or, with the directors' unanimous consent, without any payment. In effect this meant that part, at least, of the initial loan could run for fifteen months and thus the meaning of short-term became itself quite elastic.[19]

Finally, the Bank of Upper Canada, like the Bank of England and the Bank of the United States, had obligations implicit in the

[17]In addition to Mints and McIvor, *Canadian Monetary Banking*, this discussion of the real bills doctrine is drawn from A. Shortt, "Reconstruction and New Schemes," *JCBA* VIII (1900–1), pp. 1–2; Sylla, "American Banking and Growth," pp. 202–9; Schumpeter, *Business Cycles*, pp. 85–97 and comments from Professor Angela Redish, Department of Economics, University of British Columbia.

[18]This practice of discounting on the security of the bank stock was apparently discontinued sometime in the 1820s. See Feb. 1834, Appendix, *Report of the Select Committee on the Subject of Banking*, J.S. Baldwin, p. 167 [hereafter *Report on Banking*, 1834].

[19]Discounts apparently often did run for fifteen months and did put a strain on the bank's operations (B 74).

nature of its origins which were not a part of the real bills' view of the economic world. The provisions for significant government investment, for the head office to be at the seat of government and, after 1823, for government-selected representatives on the board, pointed to the final reason for the bank's existence: to assist the government, by loan if necessary, in the conduct of its financial affairs. In this the Bank of Upper Canada differed from other British North American banks. It was created, not simply to serve mercantile needs, but also, or so it appeared, to minister to affairs of state.

III

The bank's non-governmental business can be separated into two general areas: foreign exchange, and discounts and loans. Since it is often claimed that the bank's exchange transactions operated "at the expense of discounts" and "to the detriment of commercial development,"[20] this area of the bank's affairs will be considered first.

As a dealer in foreign exchange, the bank was of great potential use to merchants. It maintained deposits in London, New York, and Montreal throughout this period and could therefore sell bills on those places at any season of the year. In 1837 Ridout testified that about one-third of the bank's business had "been to enable the merchant to transact through its medium and assistance his remittances to other countries" (C 31). In return for this service the bank charged the merchant a premium on the normal rate of exchange.[21] The commercial community complained that banks, through their large capital resources, could unfairly control exchange transactions – in other words, banks could purchase bills of exchange on their foreign agents which were not directly tied to the purchase or sale of any specific commodity, and the selling price of such bills might not, so the merchants argued, reflect current market demands. The merchants feared that this would lead to excessive profit-taking on the part of the banks and in the process raise their own costs. They also argued that when a bank tied its capital up in the purchase of large bills of exchange,

---

[20]Denison, *Canada's First Bank,* I, p. 302.
[21]A. Shortt, "Criticism, Prosperity and Expansion," *JCBA* VIII (1900–1), p. 153; Gwyn, "Impact of British Military Spending," pp. 77–99.

general discounts would be curtailed and the mercantile community would suffer.[22]

The available evidence does not seem to indicate that the Bank of Upper Canada routinely speculated in exchange ''at the expense of discounts.'' Although detailed statistics on all aspects of that business are not available, the general context within which it occurred can be indicated and, for one major part, profit and loss figures can be constructed.

Commencing in the early 1820s, the cost of sterling bills increased dramatically. In fact, although it was not officially recognized until 1858, the real par of exchange jumped from £111.11 cy. to about £121.67 cy. for every £100 stg. This increase has traditionally been linked to a supposed negative balance of trade between the Canadas and both Great Britain and the United States resulting in an outflow of specie. For these reasons, as T.G. Ridout explained in 1828, the rate of exchange in Upper Canada was ''governed by the money market at New York.'' Merchants bought bills on London from the bank and sent them instead of specie to New York in payment for imports. Defending the bank against criticism of the high rates it charged for such bills, Ridout maintained that ''The constant export of specie from Canada to the United States compels the Banks to keep up the high rates in order to create funds to bring the specie back again'' (B 25).

Recent research has suggested, however, that the mechanisms governing the exchange rate were much more complicated than that. Beyond the fact that detailed statistics on Canadian balance of payments do not yet exist, factors other than trade flows and the influence of the American exchange market may have been of equal importance in setting the exchange rate. The reintroduction of specie payments in Great Britain, the decline of the market price of silver, a general deterioration in the intrinsic value of the principal colonial coins, coupled with the legal overvaluation of some of these same coins by the colony, all contributed to the overall increase in exchange costs.[23]

Within this changing environment, the bank, according to Ridout, attempted to make a profit of about 0.5 to 1 per cent for

[22]Journals of the Legislative Assembly of Lower Canada [hereafter *JLC*], 1830, Appendix cited in PAC, MG 30/D101.

[23]See McIvor, *Canadian Monetary Banking*, pp. 29–30, for the traditional view. McCullough, *Money and Exchange*, pp. 260–62 and Redish, ''Why Was Specie Scarce. . .?'' provide useful introductions to more recent interpretations.

bills on Montreal and 1.5 per cent for bills on London. In the 1830s, however, the latter rate became increasingly difficult to attain due to the "constant fluctuation" in exchange between the colony and Great Britain.[24] Between 1824 and 1830 the bank made 1.1 per cent estimated net profit from the sale of £326,913 exchange on London. In 1826 and 1827 these transactions represented about 16 per cent of the bank's overall net profit. Between 1831 and 1834 the bank eked out a bare .01 per cent return on exchange dealings which totalled £554,336[25] (see Table 4). As the Commercial Bank's cashier reflected, in early 1835, "fluctuation for some months past in the rate of premium has been so great that it has defied the most experienced in those matters."[26]

The exchange business was made even more complex by the motley state of the currency circulating in the Canadas during these years.[27] Because the colonies possessed no currency of their own, they accepted almost all coins and rated them against the nominal money of account, the pound currency. As noted earlier, a major part of that coinage, the Spanish dollar, had an official rating of 5s cy. in the colony and 4/6 d stg. in England. To conform with North American usage the Bank of Upper Canada issued its notes in dollar, not pound, denominations and adopted the Spanish dollar/pound rating system.[28]

Depending on their rating, other coins were often worth more outside than inside the colony. As a result, when it was required to redeem its notes, the bank would often do so in coinage which had the least value outside the colony and keep for its own speculative uses coinage with a greater exterior value.[29] This, of course,

[24]*JUC*, 1835, Appendix, Report of the Select Committee on the Establishment of a Provincial Bank [hereafter Provincial Bank Report, 1835], pp. 8–9, 12, 14.

[25]Computed from *JLA*, 1841, Appendix, Section G. It would, of course, be helpful to know how long these funds were tied up earning this rate of return.

[26]Provincial Bank Report, 1835, p. 14. This fluctuation is at least partly attributable to the unsteady wheat exports in this period, (B 52). See also D. McCalla, *The Upper Canada Trade, 1834–72: A Study of the Buchanans' Business* (Toronto, 1979), p. 18.

[27]A. Shortt, "Early Metallic Currency and its Regulation," *JCBA* vii (1899–1900), pp. 209–26 and "One Currency for the Empire," ibid., pp. 311–32. PAC, CO 42, vol. 438, T.G. Ridout's Observations on Currency, 29 Apr. 1837.

[28]Before 1821 in Upper Canada, however, accounts were normally kept in accordance with the New York rating of 8s. On the eve of the Bank of Upper Canada's commencement, a law was passed making it impossible for anyone to claim legal assistance in the collection of debts so valued and the 8s. rating gradually passed into disuse. See Geo. iv, c. 13, 1821.

[29]Denison, *Canada's First Bank*, p. 257; *JUC*, Feb. 1830; Appendix, Report of the Select Committee on the State of the Currency, J. Cawthra and T.G. Ridout, pp. 22, 29 [hereafter Report on Currency, 1830]; A. Shortt, "Reconstruction and New Schemes," *JCBA* viii (1900–1901), p. 8; Redish, "Why Was Specie Scarce. . .?" pp. 722–23.

made even more indispensable the bank's role as an intermediary in the transfer of funds for merchants to exterior creditors. When the opportunity offered, the bank speculated on its own behalf in the sale of this coinage to American markets. The extent to which the Bank of Upper Canada engaged in these several transactions is not known. It never submitted a profit and loss statement on this aspect of its operations.

IV

The conduct of the bank's discount and loan business divides into two periods: pre-1829 when the bank operated as the only locally chartered financial institution in the colony, and post-1829 when it had to contend with the emergence of local and non-local competition. In the carrying out of its affairs the bank adhered to some tenets of the real bills doctrine and, under the pressure of local circumstances, overlooked or modified others. As a result, and especially in the 1820s, the bank exhibited both a restrictive and an expansive visage.

The expansive quality can be best illustrated by contrasting its operations with those of its principal competitor, the Bank of Montreal. The major assets of both banks expanded significantly in this decade. Between 1825 and 1830 the Bank of Montreal's specie and discounts/loans grew at the same pace. In the Bank of Upper Canada, discounts/loans outpaced specie by 73 per cent. Compared to the Bank of Montreal, York's bank placed proportionately more of its assets in a relatively non-liquid form. By contrast the Montreal bank exhibited a more balanced growth.

As Table 1 indicates, York's bank, relative to the Bank of Montreal, was overextended in terms of its ability to redeem its notes in specie and only slightly less so in terms of its capital stock to bank note ratio. In 1828, the bank had a reserve ratio (specie to notes outstanding) of 17.3 per cent. By contrast, the Bank of Montreal's reserve ratio was generally above 47 per cent. Despite possessing at times less than one-third of the Bank of Montreal's paid-in capital, the Bank of Upper Canada's circulation fell just short of that of its rival. Nor, on average, did the Bank of Upper Canada maintain a contingency fund – for the covering of bad debts – close to the size of the Bank of Montreal's.

Historians have generally been critical of the Bank of Upper Canada's expansive tendencies in the 1820s.[30] Curiously enough

[30]See, for example, Acheson, "York Commerce," pp. 186–91.

the fact that the bank consistently realized a handsome return on its paid-in capital has been seen a further indication of unjustifiable business practices. Throughout the 1820s York's bank paid higher dividends than did the Bank of Montreal. In 1827 and in 1830 it paid dividends of 14% and it averaged about 10% per year for the decade. In 1826, 1829, and 1830, it actually realized a greater profit than did its much larger rival (see Table 3).

Looked at from the perspective of what one historian has labelled "the soundness school"[31] – an approach sympathetic to the real bills theory of banking – the Bank of Upper Canada's activities seem open to some criticism. Less profit-taking, more restrictive discounting practices, and an increased ratio of specie reserves to liabilities were required for the bank to become a member in good standing in this school. There are, however, other perspectives from which to view and understand the bank's activities in the 1820s. Rather than comparing the bank with banks in more established and developed centres such as Montreal, New York, Boston, or London, England – most of which did pay smaller dividends and did generally operate in a conservative fashion – a more constructive comparison can be gained by looking at banks in roughly similar contexts. A study of bank behaviour before 1830 in six different states has concluded that banks in less settled areas paid higher dividends and operated with lower specie reserve ratios than did banks in more developed centers.[32] In this context, the Bank of Upper Canada was not at all unusual.

Why did these frontier banks act as they did? Richard Sylla, an American banking historian, has suggested one general hypothesis. The absence of extended systems of financial intermediaries made the transfer of funds from developed to underdeveloped areas difficult. This fact, coupled with uncertain communication systems, left it up to local banks to provide credit in capital-scarce newly settled regions. By acting in a relatively expansive manner and thereby creating money and credit, these local banks responded directly to local needs.

[31]Sylla, "American Banking and Growth," p. 198. This approach is found in the works of Acheson, Shortt, Denison, and V. Ross, The History of the Canadian Bank of Commerce (Toronto, 1920).

[32]Joseph Van Fenstermaker, "Bank Profitability in the 1820s," in Fred Bateman and J.D. Forest, eds., Papers of the Fifteenth Annual Meeting of the Business History Conference (Indiana, 1968), pp. 72–85. As Peter Temin has pointed out, a low reserve ratio can be a good or a bad sign. Temin, The Jacksonian Economy (New York, 1969), pp. 73, 75.

This general outline does seem to fit the Bank of Upper Canada's situation. The bank operated in a capital-starved region which lacked any developed system of financial intermediaries.[33] Yet there is a corollary to Sylla's credit creation hypothesis which seems less applicable to the York bank's behaviour. Sylla has suggested that when banks acted in this manner they contributed in an innovative way to a country's economic growth and development. And since many of the banks that acted in this fashion seemed quite profitable, Sylla concluded that "credit creation, rather than distorting resource allocation, may well have served to improve it."[34]

Whatever the general merits of this conclusion, it does not seem to be entirely applicable to the particular case of the Bank of Upper Canada. That the bank realized a consistent profit on its operations in the 1820s does suggest that it was underwriting solid business development. It does not suggest that it was behaving at all in an innovative fashion. Nor does Sylla's conclusion address the question as to which groups most benefited from the alleged improvement in resource allocation.[35] The Bank of Upper Canada, at least, does not seem to have veered far from the central dictum of the real bills doctrine that the only acceptable bank business is that transacted with a reliable and active merchant. Although it was the official treasurer for both the Welland and Burlington Bay canal companies and although the bank and Welland directorships overlapped, the bank consistently refused to lend directly to either of these corporations. Only if, and then not always, canal company directors pledged personal security, would the bank consent to lend any money (C 15). Nor did the bank fund steamboat development in the 1820s and early 1830s.

Instead the bank pursued what Joseph Schumpeter has called the "classic case of credit creation," the financing of traditional merchant activities.[36] While detailed accounts are not available, several pieces of general evidence suggest that in this sector in the 1820s the bank exhibited a fair degree of aggressiveness. In addition to operating at a low reserve ratio level, the bank contravened another precept of commercial banking theory by

[33]See H.G.J. Aitken, "A Note on the Capital Resources of Upper Canada," *Canadian Journal of Economics and Political Science* xviii (1952), pp. 528–29.

[34]Sylla, "American Banking and Growth," p. 219.

[35]Fritz Redlich, "American Banking and Growth in the Nineteenth Century: Epistemological Reflections," *Explorations in Economic History* x (1972–73), pp. 306, 311.

[36]Schumpeter, *Business Cycles*, p. 94.

customarily granting renewals on ninety-day loans for periods up to fifteen months. By this practice at least some merchants engaged in the seasonal lumber and agricultural trades benefited. The bank's decision in the early 1820s to refuse to lock up its capital in government debentures (explored at length below pp. lxvi–lxvii) provides a further indication of that institution's commitment to the commercial sector.

At a general level, the bank responded to two pressures: one was the pressure of satiating the needs of a capital-starved region; the second was the pressure to accomplish this within the teachings of the real bills or commercial school of banking. The confluence of these pressures presented the bank with an operational dilemma. Reference has already been made to the problems the bank experienced in raising the capital necessary to commence operations. Once it was operative, the problem became one of keeping a sufficient specie reserve on hand for note redemption. Strategies had to be developed to keep its notes from being redeemed at too sudden or excessive a rate. Banks often achieved this result by establishing a large number of agencies through which they could obtain a wide circulation for their bank notes. With redemption possible only at head office, the dangers of large and sudden redemptions were minimized. In the case of the Bank of Upper Canada, however, local circumstances rendered this solution inadequate.

The first of these local circumstances concerned the nature of metropolitan ambition at York. The desire to maintain metropolitan control coupled with the necessity of maintaining scrutiny over the granting of discounts – to guard against excessive defaults – contributed to a conservative policy with regard to branch expansion in the 1820s. The bank established only two agencies: at Kingston in 1823, and, after some delay, at Niagara in 1824.[37] Neither had much autonomy. The bank stipulated that all discounts receive York approval; that note redemption could occur only at York; that transactions with New York were to be limited; and that weekly – at times twice weekly – reports be submitted[38] (B 14). The local agent could advise; rarely could he act independently. York's policy of close control over a limited number of agencies served as a conservative counterweight to its expansive note issue policy. Rather than attempting, via a large

---

[37]PAO, Macaulay Papers, Strachan to Macaulay, 12 Dec. 1822 (private and confidential); PAC, A. Shortt Papers, i, *Weekly Register*, 25 Nov. 1824.
[38]Macaulay Papers, Robinson to Macaulay, 15 Nov. 1824.

agency system, to distribute its notes as widely as possible, the bank opted for close control over its discount and loan operations and thereby minimized defaults and helped to maintain its notes in the community.

At the core of this policy lay a particular perception of the role of York and its elite within Upper Canada. As John Strachan informed his friend and soon-to-be Kingston agent for the bank, John Macaulay, it mattered not that most of the bank's shares were in York hands: "we should be left in a great measure to ourselves in the commencement for to succeed we ought to move cautiously and not be distracted by contending interests." And, he went on, any Kingston branch would remain firmly under the "control" of York directors (A 10). Under the guidance of William Allan in the 1820s the bank remained faithful to this conservative perception of metropolitan dominance.

This perception helped also to determine just which groups would benefit most directly from the bank's credit creation policy. Under this system York's interests received prime attention. Whenever discounts were suspended, as in 1825–26, they were first stopped at "outposts" and first recommenced at York[39] (B 16). It is probable, too, that the bank's renewal policy further restricted the distribution of loans. Very likely York area merchants tended to restrict the bank's discounting practice by taking advantage of the "slow re-payments" policy (B 74). This discriminatory treatment, coupled with delays in receiving credit and limits on the amount of credit that could be granted, caused increased dissatisfaction outside York. Even Niagara and Kingston chafed at these restrictions. As the 1820s drew to a close, other urban centres, lacking any formal financial institutions, began to pressure the York bank to expand its agencies.

The nature of the bank's rivalry with Lower Canadian banks further inhibited branch expansion and wide note distribution. At first the Bank of Canada, operating from its agencies at both Kingston and York, collected Bank of Upper Canada notes and presented them for immediate redemption in specie (B 3). This threat inhibited the bank's ability to expand its note issue and discounts. Nor could the York bank readily respond in kind since the Lower Canadian banks only redeemed their notes at their Montreal headquarters. The bank dealt with this matter by having an act passed in 1824 that prohibited banks from carrying on

[39]Ibid., J.B. Robinson to Macaulay, 29 March 1826; Metropolitan Toronto Library [hereafter MTL], S.P. Jarvis Papers, T. McCormick to Jarvis, 9 Sept. 1825.

business in Upper Canada without also redeeming their notes in specie in that place.[40] No Lower Canadian bank elected to do this. As a result York's bank was able to expand its note issue with more confidence.

This legislation gave to the Bank of Upper Canada strong control over the financing of the colony's domestic trade. Its credit creation policies, then, benefited those entrepreneurs, especially those close to York, most involved in that internal trade. There were, however, other layers to Upper Canadian mercantile activity. The largest Upper Canadian merchants dealt with suppliers outside Upper Canada. As payment for the excess of imports over exports, these merchants had to ship currency outside the colony. They looked to the bank for assistance in this respect. The nature of these financial transactions further refined the bank's policies and directly affected the bank's relations with Upper Canada's largest merchants.

As a service to the import-export sector of the Upper Canadian mercantile community, the Bank of Upper Canada initially redeemed its notes in specie at Montreal. In effect this saved the Upper Canadian merchant the expense of shipping specie to Montreal to pay for desired imports; he could instead ship Upper Canadian bank notes and leave to the bank the expense and trouble of providing specie for their redemption. But Lower Canada was more than a major import centre, it was also the centre for the payment of customs duties. Since these payments had to be in specie, enterprising merchants could take advantage of the York bank's redemption policy and obtain their specie from that source.[41] To an extent, then, the notes redeemed at Montreal were sent there not simply to cover import payments, but also to meet customs duties. As a result, at any one time, roughly one-quarter of all York bank notes in circulation were in the lower province[42] (B 17).

This situation affected the bank's ability to keep its notes in circulation and thus put a great deal of pressure on its credit creation policy. It also cut into the bank's profit margin. The bank had to suffer the inconvenience, expense, and fear of loss in the shipment of specie. More importantly, to protect its note issue, it had to curtail the expansion of its operations within Upper

[40]*JUC*, 19 Jan. 1824 in *Report of Archives*, 1914.
[41]A. Shortt, "Criticism, Prosperity and Expansion," *JCBA* viii (1900–1), pp. 150–51, and "Prosperity and Expansion in Upper Canada," ibid., pp. 228–29.
[42]*Upper Canada Gazette*, 19 Aug. 1826.

Canada. Business, as William Allan explained, "to all appearances as good as any . . . we *have* done" had to be declined from Brockville and further east "for fear of our notes finding their way . . . to Montl" (B 18). In this context and after much deliberation, the bank decided to cease redemption at Montreal effective 1 June 1826.[43]

This decision was in line with contemporary banking practices. After 1818 the Bank of the United States had declined to redeem its notes at other than its head office. The Bank of Montreal did not redeem its notes in Quebec City or in Upper Canada. While wealthy merchants could possibly take advantage of this situation by starting or expanding a private exchange market, the decision was not popular with most merchants in either of the colonies.[44] Short of shipping their own specie, merchants were left with two options. They could pay a 1.5 per cent discount to the Bank of Montreal for the privilege of redeeming Upper Canadian bank notes in Lower Canada (B 22). Or they could pay a commission to the Bank of Upper Canada at York and have that bank issue a draft on the Bank of Montreal and thereby rely once again on the York bank to transfer the necessary specie.

In normal circumstances the bank did an active trade in these drafts (B 20). In fact, Allan believed that by ceasing redemption the bank would now have close control over its specie reserves at Montreal and could, as a result, "advance to every person who requires what we cannot ever *count* upon as long as we do *retire*" (B 18). In 1825–26, however, a financial collapse in Great Britain precipitated the collapse of several large Montreal forwarders.[45] The bank had discounted drafts in the amount of £11,000 on Montreal houses which were now in shaky financial situations. As well, there were rumours that the bank's London agent, Thomas Wilson & Co. was "going to the Wall" (B 19, B 20). Finally, the bank was slowing its business in anticipation of a run on its vaults after it announced the stoppage of redemption at Montreal (B 18, B 20). Indeed, it was in the process of importing £25,000 in specie from New York to meet this even-

[43]Ibid., 25 May 1826.
[44]A. Shortt, "Criticism, Prosperity and Expansion," pp. 148–52. I am indebted to Doug McCalla for the comment on a private exchange market.
[45]The largest were McGillivray & Co., and Maitland, Garden & Auldjo. See Robert Sweeny, "Colony and Crisis: Montreal and the First Capitalist Crisis," unpublished paper presented at the CHA meeting, Vancouver, June 1983.

tuality.[46] In this context the bank became increasingly reluctant to transact business that would involve the transfer of specie or its equivalent to Lower Canada. As a result, the bank became "very cautious in taking any dfts. on Lower Canada" and Upper Canadian importers suffered accordingly (B 20).

It would be wrong to conclude, however, that this sector of the Upper Canadian mercantile community was systematically mistreated by the bank in the 1820s.[47] While the available evidence is scanty, it seems clear that the larger merchants suffered along with the rest. In 1825–26, the bank not only limited its drafts on Lower Canada, it also, in each year, temporarily discontinued all discounting[48] (B 16). If the various manoeuvres employed by the bank in these years at times alienated the mercantile community, they none the less served the bank's main purpose. By focusing redemption solely at York, it could now expand its Upper Canadian business and thereby achieve a wider and safer distribution of its notes. In this sense the bank was better prepared to pursue its policy of credit creation following the return of prosperity in 1827 (see Table 12A).

V

For the next eight years the bank enjoyed the fruits of economic expansion in Upper Canada. Between 1828 and 1836 the local population doubled to more than 350,000. Land under cultivation increased by a factor of twelve to roughly 1,600,000 acres. Expenditure on the Welland and Rideau canals exceeded £1,250,000. Imports rose steadily as did, up to 1832, the exports of wheat.[49]

Between 1828 and 1835 the bank nearly doubled its circulation to £243,000, did double its capital to £200,000, and more than doubled its profits to £21,500. It achieved these gains by adjusting its operating policy – adjustments which, in the minds of the bank managers, were necessitated by a sharp rise in local competition.

[46]PAC, Bank of Montreal Papers, I, 28 July 1826. *JLA*, 1841, Appendix O, Section G.

[47]As Acheson does; see "York Commerce," pp. 190–91.

[48]S.P. Jarvis Papers, T. McCormick to S.P. Jarvis, 9 Sept., 6 Oct. 1825. Macaulay Papers, Allan to Macaulay, 20 Apr. 1826.

[49]D. McCalla, "The Wheat Staple and Upper Canadian Development," *HP* (1978), pp. 37–38; H.G.J. Aitken, *The Welland Canal Company* (Cambridge, Mass., 1954), pp. 147–48; George Raudzens, *The British Ordnance Department and Canada's Canals, 1815–55* (Waterloo, Ont., 1979), p. 95.

As mentioned above, the bank's conservative policy concerning branch expansion, its tight control over its several agencies, and its discriminating treatment of non-York applicants excited much opposition throughout Upper Canada. Up to 1829 the bank had successfully used its influence in the Legislative Council to maintain a privileged position within the colony. As the bank quickly came to realize, however, there were limits to that influence. In 1824 the Legislative Council had amended the act restricting "foreign" agencies so that it would expire three years after the end of the then-current legislative session[50] (B 3). When it did, in 1829, the Bank of Montreal quickly re-established Upper Canadian operations.[51]

The Bank of Upper Canada responded by petitioning the Legislative Assembly for the re-enactment of restrictive legislation (B 29). On three separate occasions the Assembly voted no and in at least one instance it did so on the grounds that the public interest demanded open banking.[52] As Chief Justice and Family Compact stalwart John Beverley Robinson explained in a related court case:

Supposing the foreign bank solvent, and well secured and their paper good, the general advantage arising from their circulating it here might, according to circumstances, much outweigh the consideration of loss to our own bank from diminished business; and if it were otherwise, it would rest with the Legislature . . . and not with this court, to determine the question of policy and to protect the public interest.[53]

Left to his own devices, Allan responded with an aggressive three-pronged attack. He transferred the bank's agency business from the Bank of Montreal to a Montreal merchant house[54] (B 26). He undercut the Bank of Montreal's Upper Canadian agents in the purchase of treasury bills (B 30). And most importantly, he engaged in a "specie war" with his Lower Canadian competitor (B 26, B 27). This involved the accumulation of large amounts of the competitor's notes and the sudden presentation of same for immediate payment in specie. The battle was fierce: the Bank of Upper Canada imported £70,225 in specie – more than it had in the previous three years combined – and even then it had a

---

[50]*JUC*, 14 Jan. 1824 in *Report of Archives*, 1914, p. 648. For the complete bill, see Upper Canada, Unrevised Statutes, c. 13, 19 Jan. 1824.

[51]*JLC*, 9 Feb. 1829, cited in A. Shortt Papers, I.

[52]Report on Currency, 1830; *JUC*, 11 Jan. 1832 and 19 Feb. 1834; Toronto *Patriot*, 25 Feb. 1834.

[53]*Bank of Montreal* v. *D. Bethune*, *Upper Canada, Queen's Bench Reports*, O.S., IV , 1834–36, pp. 349–50.

[54]Macaulay Papers, Allan to Macaulay, 1 Jan. 1829.

reserve ratio of 16.5 per cent at one point in the year[55] (Table 1). By the end of 1829, however, the Montreal bank conceded and agreed to withdraw all but its Kingston agent from Upper Canada. In return, the York bank moved its agency back to the Bank of Montreal, ceased its specie war, and agreed to settle all balances by drafts or bills of exchange[56] (B 27, B 72, C 41).

While this victory buoyed the spirits of the York bank's managers, the withdrawal of all but one of the Bank of Montreal's agencies dismayed many others in Upper Canada (B 31). In fact the victory itself added fuel to the rising demands for separate banking establishments outside York. With Legislative Council support, the Bank of Upper Canada initially defeated these initiatives. In each case, however, the victory was costly. While the Legislative Council vetoed new charters, the Assembly refused to sanction a request to double the Bank of Upper Canada's capital. Since the amount of business which the bank could conduct without incurring director liability was tied to the size of its paid-in capital, this refusal may have hampered its operations in a period of general economic growth.[57] To the degree that this restricted credit in Upper Canada, it also adversely affected Upper Canada's economy.

What is interesting is that the bank did not capitulate under this pressure: the Legislative Council did. Recognizing that the interests of Upper Canada as a whole were being endangered, the council, over Allan's continued objections, passed a bill granting a bank to Kingston early in 1832[58] (B 45). The Assembly reciprocated and the Bank of Upper Canada received its bill authorizing an increase in capital with, however, the stipulation that no stock could be sold until six months after the act became law. Designed as it was to give the new Kingston bank an opportunity to sell its stock unhampered by York competition, this clause was reluctantly accepted by the York bank supporters.

Nor, to the shock of most Upper Canadians, did the matter rest there. In 1833 the Colonial Office overturned both bank bills on the grounds that their charters were defective. This unexpected

---

[55]*JLA*, 1841, Appendix O, Section G.

[56]B. Holmes to A. Steven, 5 Feb. 1837, cited in Ross, *Canadian Bank of Commerce*, I, pp. 189–91. When the commissariat business for Upper Canada was given to the York Bank, the Bank of Montreal withdrew from Kingston also. See below, p. lxiv.

[57]Macaulay Papers, J. Strachan to Macaulay, 10 Mar. 1830; R. Stanton to Macaulay, 20 Mar. 1831.

[58]Ibid., W. Kirby to Macaulay, 4 Dec. 1831; Montreal *Gazette*, 19 Jan. 1832.

ruling gave rise to a great outcry on the part of the colonial banking interests and only after much correspondence was a compromise effected[59] (B 66, B 75). Quite clearly the Bank of Upper Canada did not consistently control any level of colonial government.

Perhaps the most intriguing point to emerge from this discussion of bank legislation is the marked difference in perspective between the bank and the Legislative Council. At crucial times the council adopted the perspective of the greater good and voted against the immediate interests of the bank. Robert Fraser has suggested that the notion of greater good was shared by the gentry members of the council. Merchants and businessmen allegedly adopted a more narrow profit-oriented view. Men such as Strachan and Robinson, Fraser has argued, looked to the development of Upper Canada along the lines of an agricultural Eden. In policy terms this meant the funnelling of a vast sum of money into the development of transportational routes – especially into the construction of canals. To the extent that the bank would assist in the attainment of these ends, it received their support. At other times it was to be viewed, if not with suspicion, then certainly with resignation.[60]

Throughout all this legislative wrangling, the bank engaged in a very profitable and seemingly expansive business. Its outstanding capital (some £23,000) was called up in 1830.[61] Steps were taken to expand its agencies and grant greater discounting privileges to Kingston (B 39). Renewals continued to be extended for up to fifteen months. According to Allan, the negotiation of bills on New York and especially on Montreal "in aid" of the wheat, flour, and export trade averaged £500,000 per annum in these years (B 43). Operating ratios, compared to those of the Bank of Montreal, continued to reflect a frontier, capital-scarce environment.

Allan, however, believed that he was operating in a very conservative fashion. He pointed out that the bank often held government debentures as a hedge against bad debts and that it maintained large balances in New York, London, and Montreal

---

[59]PAC, CO 42, v. 415, Allan to Colborne, 29 July 1833; Report on Banking, 1834; PAC, CO 42, v. 428, J. Stephen to T. Lack, 31 July 1835.
[60]R.L. Fraser, " 'Like Eden in Her Summer Dress'; Gentry, Economy and Society, 1812–40" (Ph.D. Thesis, University of Toronto, 1979).
[61]Report on Currency, 1830, p. 24.

which could be readily converted into specie[62] (B 43). Because of this it required neither a large contingency fund (and by implication justified its large bonuses to shareholders) nor a large specie reserve. In fact, he asserted, were it not for the publication of the bank's statements and the public's ignorance concerning banking operations, he would maintain even less specie in his vaults (B 78).

Ultimately, although Allan did not admit this, the key to his operating policy in the early 1830s was the same as in the 1820s. As long as the bank did not unduly expand its agencies (indeed in the late 1820s, it had cut back its Niagara business), he could exert a tight centralized control over discounting policy. Within this context he was able to extend his note issue to what many historians have claimed to be a speculative degree.[63] Yet it was speculation within a conservative frame. And it was a strategy that sowed the seeds of its own destruction. With the commencement of competition from the Commercial Bank of the Midland District in mid-1832 and the very real possibility of more banks soon to be chartered in other centres, the bank dismantled that frame and modified the strategy of its first decade.

In an attempt to head off increased competition, the bank, by July 1832, employed agents or cashiers at eleven different Upper Canadian centres.[64] In addition, Kingston and Niagara received local boards of directors and increased discounting privileges. A gradual reduction in operating ratios parallelled this physical expansion. Throughout 1832 temporary discount stoppages were common[65] (B 52, B 61), and by year's end discussion had commenced concerning an even more fundamental policy change (B 63).

Throughout the 1820s and the early 1830s the bank's managers had prided themselves on their policy of providing relatively long-term support (fifteen months) for merchants involved in the wheat and lumber trades. ''[A]s soon as the Commercial Bank went into operation [however],'' Ridout explained, ''our notes

[62]S.P. Jarvis Papers, W. McCormick to S.P. Jarvis, 31 Aug. 1831. On the debenture claim, see pp. lxvi–lxvii.

[63]In addition to Acheson, ''York Commerce,'' see Shortt. ''Prosperity and Expansion in Upper Canada,'' pp. 240–41 and Breckenridge, ''The Canadian Banking System, 1817–90,'' p. 158.

[64]PAC, CO 42, vol. 417, p. 188, newspaper clipping of 4 July 1832 in W.L. Mackenzie to Lord Goderich, 14 Mar. 1833.

[65]Queen's University Archives [QUA], J.S. Cartwright Papers, vol. 2, W. Stennet to Cartwright, 11 June 1832.

returned upon us much quicker than before, and it was, consequently, rendered a matter of necessity to change the system.''
Commencing October 1833, the bank granted renewals only upon
the payment of one-third of the amount due, thus reducing its
loans from fifteen to nine months[66] (B 74).

How did these policy changes alter the bank's role as a financial
intermediary? In the absence of disaggregated financial data, one
can only suggest general answers to this question. It seems clear
that both the lumber and agricultural sectors suffered in the
ensuing general competition for scarce funds. The bank acknowledged this but claimed that the new competitive context plus the
limited size of its capital permitted it to supply less than ''half as
much as is required.'' The bank also attempted to discount only
for people of undoubted value. Those of more ''moderate'' means
obtained less accommodation (B 74). Offsetting these restrictions, however, was the probability that the bank's capital was, in
a geographical sense, more widely available after 1832.[67] It is
also possible that the system of shorter-term discounts facilitated
a more rapid turnover of capital. Instead of locking resources up
in renewable notes – a practice one contemporary described as
''advancing dead capital''[68] – new business (if it fit the bank's
guidelines) could be more rapidly accommodated.

The commercial community responded in various ways to
these measures. Petitions for more banks, longer discounting
policies, and stricter control over profit distribution (the bank paid
26 per cent in dividends in 1832) were common. Less easily
documented, but doubtless very pervasive, was a second
response. Reliance on accommodation notes to finance mercantile and other transactions became increasingly widespread. This
financial practice directly challenged Allan's classic credit creation policy. These notes differed from real bills in the sense that
no ''consideration had passed between the maker and endorser''
and as a result there was no obvious collateral available for
security. Rather the security rested on the ''presumed solidity'' of

---

[66]Provincial Bank Report, 1835, p. 13 (Francis Harper); Upper Canada *Courier*, 24
July 1833.

[67]The bank's continuing policy of stopping its discounts at its agencies while
maintaining them at York, however, probably curtailed this expansion. See Canadian
Imperial Bank of Commerce (CIBC), Toronto Gore Bank Letterbook, 1832–34, Aug.–
Sept. 1833.

[68]CIBC, Gore Bank Minutebook, 1836–43, 4 May 1836.

the people who signed the note.[69] Had the bank been willing to accept these notes, more than simply merchants would have had access to longer term capital. As one American financier put it, "accommodation paper could produce business in contrast to genuine trade paper that sprang from business."[70]

Under Allan's leadership, the Bank of Upper Canada rarely directly created credit "for the purpose of innovation." He maintained this stance not because of any *a priori* commitment to abstract theory. During the financial crisis of 1826 he had closely observed how the Bank of Montreal had suffered from supporting shipbuilding activities undertaken by large Montreal forwarders. To a lesser degree the Bank of Upper Canada had itself been hurt in these affairs[71] (B 18, B 19, B 20). Operating within a general North American context of rapid boom and within a local environment in which the "rage of the day is improvement . . . anything you choose to ask for – money, thousands of it . . .,"[72] Allan therefore advocated a tight money policy and in particular argued for a discounting strategy well within the real bills tradition.

While Allan did not bend under the pressure for expansion, others within the bank and especially at its agencies did. J.G. Bethune, the bank's cashier at Cobourg, for example, not only applied for and received a number of accommodation notes to finance his own transportation schemes, but also, and despite York's central control, permitted others in the Cobourg area to participate in his credit creation policy. When Allan learned that, as a consequence, some £8,000 was in arrears at Cobourg, Bethune was summarily dismissed[73] (B 69, B 70). Yet this, when added to several similar incidents that occurred at the same time, suggests that behind the bank's stipulated policy, credit creation for innovation could and did occur.[74] It should be noted, too, that

[69]J.R. McCulloch, *A Dictionary of Commerce and Commercial Navigation* (London, 1869), p. 113; *Queen's Bench Reports O.S.*, IV, 1834–36, *Bank of Montreal v. D. Bethune*, pp. 350, 355–56. As McCalla has noted, very often renewals to large merchants were granted on the strength of their reputations, rather than on any particular goods as collateral. McCalla, *The Upper Canada Trade*, p. 24.

[70]Cited in Redlich, *The Moulding of American Banking*, I, p. 11.

[71]On this shipbuilding activity, see Sweeney, "Colony and Crisis," pp. 22 ff.

[72]PAC, MG 24, I. 126, Alexander Hamilton Papers, vol. 4, Robert Hamilton to Alexander Hamilton, 10 Jan. 1833.

[73]Macaulay Papers, Allan to Macaulay, 21 Sept. 1833.

[74]For more detail on this, see P. Baskerville, "The Entrepreneur and the Metropolitan Impulse: James Grey Bethune and Cobourg, 1825–36," in J. Petryshyn, ed.,

the bank's charter permitted the granting of notes on the security of the endorsers. While the extent of this was limited by Allan's policies, the fact that it did occur suggests that banking capital may have been employed for a wider variety of uses than is generally assumed.[75]

This, then, was very much a transitional period for the bank and its management. No longer did it have the financial sector all to itself. By the end of 1835 it faced competition from two other chartered banks – the Commercial Bank at Kingston and the Gore Bank at Hamilton – and from three private or joint stock banks – the Agricultural Bank, the Farmers' Bank and the People's Bank, all at Toronto.

Increasingly strident demands were being made for a more flexible and accommodating discount policy. Upper Canadian expectations in the early 1830s knew few bounds. Within this environment the bank did more than alter its operational strategies. It also presented to the public and its political representatives a general scheme for the restructuring of Upper Canada's financial system. It was a proposal which the bank argued would better enable the financial sector to meet Upper Canada's developmental needs. Since this proposal was in part a response to financial rearrangements sponsored by the government, an examination of bank-government business relations must precede consideration of the bank's plan.

VI

Like the law-making apparatus, the administrative system in the pre-Confederation era was complex and multi-faceted. Power was not well focused. Government departments in England were only beginning to be subjected to some form of central accountability. The operating norms of one department were not necessarily shared by others. In colonial matters decentralization of control was often even more pronounced. A strong-minded imperial appointee resident in the colonies enjoyed much autonomy

---

Victorian Cobourg: A Nineteenth Century Profile (Belleville, 1976), pp. 56–70; and "Donald Bethune's Steamboat Business: A Study of Upper Canadian Commercial and Financial Practice," *Ontario History* LXVII (1975), pp. 135–49.

[75]See also McCalla's comment on the "mutability" of capital in "The Wheat Staple . . .," p. 39, n.13.

and, depending on his position, could exercise considerable personal power.[76]

The position of the receiver general, Upper Canada's most important financial administrator, is a case in point. The lieutenant-governor and the Executive Council did not control this position. Rather the British Treasury Department appointed the receiver general, held a large amount of his personal securities "for the due discharge of his duties" and oversaw his general activities. Next to the lieutenant-governor, the receiver general was the most important public administrator with whom the bank had to deal. He managed the public debt and personally administered the collection, safekeeping, and ultimate disbursement of most of the government's revenue.[77] To obtain the receiver general's account was in effect to become the government's bank of deposit.

The Bank of Upper Canada assumed that this was indeed its intended role and, in December 1822, formally applied for that position. John Henry Dunn, receiver general from 1820 to 1843, vetoed the application (B 1, B 2). Although he was required to present a financial statement twice yearly to both the local government and the Lords of the Treasury and had, when called upon, to show the daily state of the government's finances, he was not required to explain where the government's money was kept or even the terms upon which it was held. Dunn viewed the safekeeping of public money as his personal responsibility and he refused to give up this control to a public bank. Since the bulk of Upper Canada's revenue was derived from customs duties levied in Lower Canada, he, in fact, kept most of the money with his Montreal agents, the merchants, Forsyth and Richardson.[78]

The basic point seems clear. The nature of departmental administration in the pre-Union period suggests that general assumptions concerning the closeness of bank-government relations are

---

[76]Raudzens, *British Ordnance Department*, presents a good analysis of one such functionary.

[77]PAC, Governor General's Office, RG 7 G14, vol. 46, Receiver General's Memorandum, 25 Mar. 1847; RG 19 B 26 vol. 1175, Return of the Receiver General's Department for the year 1839, 30 Mar. 1840.

[78]Initially he kept his account with McGillivray and Thain, Montreal merchants. When they went bankrupt in 1824–25, he transferred to Forsyth and Richardson. PAC, MG 24 A2, Ellice Papers, C4634, S. McGillivray to E. Ellice, 6 Dec. 1825. Between 1824 and 1830 Dunn oversaw an average balance of £24,000 and in February 1830 he had £30,000 at his disposal in Lower Canada. PAC, CO 42, vol. 416, pp. 78–79, T.L. Largent to Lords of the Treasury, 1 Apr. 1833 and Report on Currency, 1830, p. 33.

not completely warranted. The two did not always act in unison. A better approach is to allow for the existence of several entities which sometimes moved in tandem and at other times operated at cross purposes. It was within this more complex context that the bank sought to capitalize on its government connections.

An excellent example of one such attempt concerns the distribution of imperial money for payment of the 1812 War Losses claims. In 1822 the British government had agreed to contribute 5s. in the pound for a total of £57,412 stg. toward payment of these claims. When this became known in the colony, a number of mercantile firms offered to handle the distribution of these funds. So, too, did the Bank of Upper Canada. Even "if the transaction should afford them a trifling benefit," J.B. Robinson informed the colonial secretary, "it might yet be an object to them in the infancy of their institution."[79]

The transaction was far from trifling. If the money sent was specie, then the bank could pay the claimants in its own notes and sell the specie at a profit in New York. If the money was transferred in bills of exchange on London, then the bank could again pay in its own notes and have a considerable amount of exchange to sell at a profit. In either case, however, Dunn would be by-passed: the bank would be acting as both a government depository and as a dispenser of government funds. Dunn considered these tasks to be his private preserve. As a result, he asked the Commissariat Department at Montreal – to which the imperial government had transferred the £57,412 – to transfer the specie to his agents, Forsyth and Richardson. This, he believed, would keep the monies in his hands and out of the direct hands of any bank. He could then pay the various Upper Canadian claimants via drafts on his Montreal agents.

Nor, he argued, would this be to the Bank of Upper Canada's disadvantage. The drafts received by the colonial claimants would likely be discounted at the Bank of Upper Canada and then the bank could sell the government drafts at a premium in Montreal (B 7). As a further sweetener he promised to ship to the bank – presumably at public expense – £10,000 of this money, in specie, from Montreal "upon the opening of navigation" in 1824.[80] By such means Dunn maintained control over what he considered to be his proper business. At the same time both the

---

[79]PAC, CO 42, vol. 371, J.B. Robinson to W. Horton, 2, 28 Jan. 1823.
[80]Ibid., vol. 66, Dunn to Hillier, 4 Mar. 1824.

Bank of Upper Canada and Forsyth and Richardson profited from the arrangement.

Although the bank did not control the receiver general's deposits, it did play a role in the distribution of government accounts in Upper Canada. While this was advantageous to the bank in the sense that it facilitated the expansion of its note issue, it was, in two other respects, disadvantageous. Because the bank disbursed government funds, the general public assumed that it had on hand large "Deposits of the Public money" from which it derived a great interest (B 91). For much of the period under review, however, this was not the case. Rather, the system worked in the following manner. When the receiver general required cash, he would draw on his Montreal agents at twenty days sight. The bank credited his account when the draft was purchased and at that time Dunn drew it out to meet payments in Upper Canada. For its part the bank had to wait at least twenty days before it received the funds from Montreal and for an unspecified time period it had also to pay 2 per cent to the Bank of Montreal for the issuance of the draft. Not only was the bank prevented from gaining interest on public money, but this system forced the institution to lend the government money, interest free. Thus in 1835 Allan could bitterly complain to a fellow director that:

we have been in advance sometimes as much as £12 to £13,000 and last winter when we made our Return to the Legislature out of £180,000 of Deposits the Bank held there was only £817 – deposited by the Receiver General. We lost by our transaction with him for many years, nearly £200 a year (B 91, C 27).

Throughout this period, then, the bank was denied the receiver general's deposit. There were, however, other sources of "government" monies in the colony. The Crown Lands department had kept some of its money with the bank.[81] Of more importance were the funds under control of the British military. In 1831 the imperial commissariat decided to transfer the disbursement of its funds in the Canadas to local banks (B 43). Initially the Bank of Montreal was granted major control (B 63). In 1833 Allan, using a contact at the Colonial Office, obtained control of all Upper Canadian payments. These totalled between £40,000 and £50,000 per year and each month's requirements were deposited one month in advance (B 64, C 27). The deposits were either sterling drafts or specie against which the bank would issue its

---

[81]*JUC*, 1839–40, Appendix, Report on Public Departments, p. 161.

THOMAS GIBBS RIDOUT, c. 1860 *Metropolitan Toronto Library T 32035*

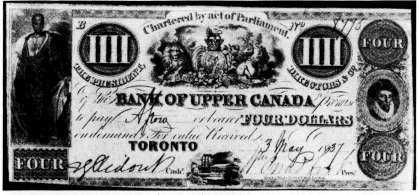

BANK OF UPPER CANADA $1 AND $4 NOTES, 1831, 1837 *Currency Museum, Bank of Canada (photographer Zagon, Ottawa)*

own notes and then sell the exchange (drafts or specie) at a profit. In fact the bank's competitors often complained that the control of the commissariat's account gave to the bank control of the general price of all exchange on Britain![82] (C 50).

The nature of the government deposit reflected the nature of the government structure. There was no centralized account and of the two major deposits, the bank obtained full use of only one. Although it was a very lucrative arrangement, it was obtained only near the end of the period under review and from that time until the Rebellion the commissariat deposit never exceeded 10 to 12 per cent of the total deposits in the bank.[83] While the use of government monies contributed to the bank's profitability, it was hardly the major determinant of that profitability.

The significant growth of bank deposits in the 1830s (from £33,621 in January 1831 to £180,735 in January 1835) had more to do with the influx of immigrants than to the government account. Some 150,000 immigrants arrived at Quebec in those years. Probably two-thirds of them proceeded to Upper Canada. The bank was prepared for their arrival. It had already made arrangements with several British, Scottish, and Irish banks to receive deposits from prospective emigrants and to issue letters of credit on the York bank for same.[84] According to a past president of the Bank of Montreal, emigrants deposited £60,000 and brought "Scrip for deposits made in England for £65,000 more" to the York bank between May 1831 and January 1832.[85] Although in 1834 both the Agricultural and the Commercial banks granted interest on deposits, the Bank of Upper Canada, probably because of its head start, did not feel it necessary to do so. Francis Harper, the Commercial Bank's cashier, commented ruefully that these "large sums deposited . . . without interest . . . add considerably to their profits. . . ."[86] While this was

.

[82]PAC, RG 5 A1, Upper Canada Sundries, Petition of merchants and others of the town of Kingston in the Province of Upper Canada, to The Right Honourable the Lords Commissioners of His Majesty's Treasury, 6 Oct. 1832.

[83]*JUC*, 1837, Appendix, Report of the Select Committee on the Monetary System of the Province [hereafter Report on the Monetary System, 1837], pp. 31, 37.

[84]CIBC, Gore Letterbrook, 1835–36, A. Steven to Reid Irving and Company, 16 Mar. 1836; ibid., 1837–40, A. Steven to Reid Irving & Co., 6 Dec. 1839; "It is in small County Towns that many individuals deposit their means for credit in Canada as I see a great many credits from the Agents of the British Linen Corp. addressed to the Bank of Montreal and the Bank of Upper Canada."

[85]PAC, Ellice Papers, C 4635, S. Gerrard to Ellice, 9 Feb. 1832.

[86]Provincial Bank report, 1835, p. 14.

undoubtedly true, the Bank of Upper Canada, in common with other banks in this era, did not employ deposits as effectively as they would when cheques began to become common in the later 1850s.[87]

The second general area of government-bank financial contact – the system of government borrowing – also stands in need of reappraisal. It was over this issue that two opposing development strategies for Upper Canada emerged. The resolution of this debate and the consequent restructuring of the financing system helped to lay the framework within which Canada's banks evolved throughout the remainder of the century.

After 1821 the government could not operate without recourse to public borrowing (B 4). There were two reasons for this. For the short term, Upper Canada was squeezed by Lower Canada's failure to share customs duties. The passage of the Canada Trade Act late in 1822, which gave to Upper Canada one-fifth of all the customs duties levied in the lower colony – a figure that was to be revised every three years – solved part of this problem. Before its passage, however, £25,000 had had to be borrowed to meet militia payments. In 1824 a further £16,000 was required to meet the general costs of the public service. The year 1824 also saw the commencement of a second and long-term program: public financing of transportation routes, in this case an £8,000 debenture issue in favour of the Burlington Bay Canal Company. Between 1824 and April 1834, the government issued £368,640 in debentures payable in Upper Canada.[88] Seventy-seven per cent of the money raised was spent on various transportation schemes.

Initially the government looked to the bank for a substantial amount of these funds. It quickly became obvious, however, that there was no way for the bank to meet the increasingly heavy demands of government and at the same time provide for the growing needs of the mercantile community. Although the bank supplied less than one-quarter of the £40,000 borrowed by the government between 1822 and 1824, government debt represented 37 per cent of all debt owed the bank in 1823. As a result, mercantile discounts were curtailed and, rather than lend more money to the government in 1824, the bank sold 20 per cent of the debentures it had on hand to private individuals.

With this transaction the bank commenced an important and

---

[87]C.D.W. Goodwin, "John Rae: Undiscovered Exponent of Canadian Banking," *The Canadian Banker* LXVI (1959), pp. 113–14.

[88]For a listing of government debentures, 1822–41, see *JLA*, 1841, Appendix B.

not well understood financial role in Upper Canada. It decided
that it could not be a long-term holder of government debentures
and meet the needs of the general business community. Instead it
elected to exercise the role of broker. Between 1826 and 1834 it
purchased or repurchased at least £180,327 of government debentures. It sold at least £169,878 of them. This freed up the bank's
capital for general mercantile pursuits: between 1824 and 1834
the amount owed the bank by the government roughly fluctuated
between 6 and 14 per cent of all debt owed the bank (Table 5).
And while it is important to note that the bank was not a slave to
the capital needs of the government, the bank's role has signifi-
cance in other respects. By purchasing from those who desired
cash and wished to sell and selling to those who had cash and
wished to invest, the bank stimulated a market for public debentures and in so doing helped the government realize necessary
funds. As T.G. Ridout explained in 1834, the bank kept the
public debt ''in motion as so much cash, convertible at any time
into money or bills of exchange'' (B 24, B 68, B 74).

It is probably true, as Ridout went on to claim, that this system
''brought much foreign capital into this country'' (B 74). Certainly few other than the bank purchased debentures directly from
the government. Even after the receiver general instituted a
system of public tenders in the hopes of lowering the interest rate
and issued debentures in the £25 to £100 range in the hopes of
attracting a large number of small investors, the bank and several
wealthy merchants continued to control the direct buying.[89]
Because the bank received a commission on each resale, it
undoubtedly wished to dominate this aspect of the system. Probably to simplify its own bookkeeping, the government capitulated
to the bank on this matter and whenever the bank bid for the total
issue, it received it, regardless of whether there were other
bidders at the same interest rate.[90] Nevertheless, small purchasers
rarely directly approached the government. Even the merchants
who competed with the bank often acted as agents for others. This
fact, plus scattered fragments of evidence which suggest that
William Allan and T.G. Ridout operated as general investment
agents for a number of wealthy British financiers, lends credence
to Ridout's claim[91] (B 85). In this way the bank acted as a conduit

[89]PAC, RG 1 E1, Executive Council of Canada, Minute Books, Upper Canada,
C-98, Dunn to Hillier, 12 Mar. 1827.
[90]PAC, RG 19 B2a, vol. 1131, Hillier to Dunn, 17 May 1827.
[91]Ellice Papers, IX, Ridout to Ellice, 31 May 1833.

through which a limited amount of foreign funds flowed into Upper Canada in the years before 1834.

By the late 1820s, however, many in the government were concluding that available capital was both insufficient and too costly.[92] In an attempt to benefit from lower interest payments, a favourable exchange rate and a greater capital pool, the government attempted to borrow £90,000 stg. at 4 per cent directly in England.[93] It failed in 1830, but in 1834, working through Thomas Wilson and Co., a London banking house and agent of the Bank of Upper Canada, the government raised £200,000 stg. at 5 per cent interest payable in London. The government intended to use this money to redeem the debentures already issued in Upper Canada. In 1835 it contracted for a further £400,000 stg. through Thomas Wilson and Co. and the Baring Brothers[94] (B 68).

This new arrangement for selling government debentures in London threatened to end the bank's lucrative middleman role. Not surprisingly, led by Allan and Ridout, the bank strenuously objected. It was to no avail. Once again the bank and government went in separate directions. The funding arrangements instituted in 1834 persisted throughout the rest of the century.

The debate that took place over the transfer of the government loan suggests that at the levels of both self-interest and principle, the government's financial leaders and the bank's financial managers were irreconcilably opposed. Self-interest was common to both sides: Dunn, the prime mover of the new arrangements, wished to save the government money; Allan wished to preserve the bank's profits. Perhaps because Dunn owed his appointment to the imperial government, he saw nothing dangerous about transferring the loan to London (B 79). Partly because of his local banking position, Allan saw the move as an erosion of colonial power.

Yet each side possessed a larger view. The roots of the disagreement stemmed from differing perceptions of the proper way to stimulate Upper Canada's development. Dunn argued that

[92]*JUC*, Jan.–Mar. 1828, Appendix, Report of the Select Committee appointed to examine and report on the public accounts; PAC, RG 5 Al, vol. 94, J. Dunn to Sir J. Colborne, 27 June 1829.

[93]PAC RG 19 B2a, vol. 1133, An act to borrow a sum of money in England at a reduced rate of interest to cancel the public debt of this province, 12 Mar. 1830; ibid., Baring Bros. to Dunn, 5 June 1830.

[94]Ibid., B2b, vol. 1173, Dunn to Thomas Wilson and Co., 6 Feb. 1834; M.L. Magill, "John H. Dunn and the Bankers," *Ontario History* LXII (1970), pp. 83–100.

the new arrangements would benefit the colony by more than the savings in interest and the presumed profit from exchange. By funding government projects from the large British capital pool, Dunn hoped to encourage local investors "to look to private investment and assist private enterprise" (B 76). "Money is abundant," he explained in October 1835,

and Securities are scarce, a very short time I trust will prove to the Public, the benefit of compelling Capitalists in Upper Canada, to look to other than Public Securities and Private persons will be able to avail themselves of their Real Estate in the way of Mortgage. When this object is accomplished I shall be satisfied. (C 9).

In effect, by redeeming debentures issued in Upper Canada and transporting the government loan from the colony, Dunn's policy was designed to create forced savings at the local level. He then hoped that this idle local capital would be invested in non-governmental pursuits.

Because the chartered banks were prohibited from lending money on the direct security of land, Dunn wished to complement, if not undercut, these institutions by privately encouraging the establishment of British joint stock banks. If managed "cautiously," he felt that these private partnerships would, by lending on land, assist "the various operations of the farmer, the merchant and improvements generally." He even considered initiating such a venture himself.[95]

These ideas appealed to those Upper Canadians who desired a more speculative environment. The promise of capital for increased canal construction, greater land sales and, in more ambiguous terms, increased private enterprise, commanded the support of both the gentry and the more independent entrepreneurs such as the merchant and canal promoter, William Hamilton Merritt. This coalition proved powerful enough to outvote the bank's supporters in both the Assembly and the Legislative Council.

Because of the tendency to subsume the bank within the state, Canadian historians have generally ignored the alternative program for financing Upper Canadian development put forward by Allan and Ridout. As Allan pointed out, this program was not simply grounded in the fear of losing profits: under the new arrangement the bank would benefit nicely from the government's exchange business. For Allan, the key advantage of the old system was the fact that by making the loans locally "persons

[95]PAC, MG 24 E1, W.H. Merritt Papers, vol. 9, J.H. Dunn to Merritt, 7 Nov. 1834.

would have . . . inducements to bring money and invest it, *Where the Interest would be Spent & the Principal retained"* (C 10, C 26). Under the new system, an Upper Canadian who wished to invest in his government's development plans would have to send his money to London and collect both interest and principal at that place. By paying in the colony, Allan felt, local fund concentration would increase because the investor, be he local or foreign, would be more apt to reinvest at that spot.

Secondly, Allan argued that a wide range of local investment opportunities were required to attract wealthy immigrants and to keep capital in the country. Investing in mortgages, as he put it, "does not suit everybody." Allan believed that Dunn's policy made it especially difficult for the new immigrant, who was ignorant of local land values and only able to afford short-term investments. Under the new system the opportunity for a convenient, safe, and quickly redeemable investment no longer existed. Thus, while Allan agreed that Dunn's policy would create forced savings, he predicted that the capital would either lie dormant in the bank or would leave the country (B 85).

Implicit in the government's financial rearrangements was the assumption that Upper Canada's chartered banks were not doing enough to promote the colony's development. In the 1830s, as we have seen, complaints arose about the bank's reluctance to finance canals, to provide long-term accommodation for the lumber business, and, on occasion, to provide adequate financing for the agricultural trade[96] (C 14). The Bank of Upper Canada recognized these complaints but claimed that the problems did not arise from narrow interests or the lack of effort to serve Upper Canadian needs. Rather, the problem was inherent in the structure of the Canadian banking system. There were, the bank's directors asserted, too many banks and those that existed were underfunded. Within this context, the bank did all it could to promote Upper Canadian development. To do more, its president claimed, would be fiscally irresponsible. The bank's directors responded to these restrictions, to the debt transfer scheme, and to the demands for larger and longer running discounts, by supporting the general idea of chartering a provincial bank with a capital between £500,000 and £1,000,000[97] (B 45, B 73, B 74).

---

[96]PAC, RG 5 A1, Bytown Lumber Merchants Petition, 28 Nov. 1836; Montreal *Gazette*, 8 Oct. 1833.

[97]A. Shortt Papers, vol. 3, Lord Glenelg to Head, 27 Nov. 1837 (copy).

Despite the obvious self-interest of the proposal – the bank hoped that it would become the new provincial institution – there was a developmental side to the idea. The bank's directors contended that a larger bank could handle the government's growing financial needs, meet the requirements of the general commercial community, and facilitate continued local control of the colony's investments in a manner that a larger number of less capitalized banks could not.[98]

How credible was the bank's position? Generally its support of a provincial institution has been interpreted as yet another attempt to establish a narrow monopolistic position in the colony. It was this widespread fear of creating a huge "political engine" that led to the repeated defeat of the proposal both within Upper Canada and within the Colonial Office.[99] Yet if the bank *was* correct – if it was hampered by the financial structure in meeting Upper Canadian needs – then its proposal to change that structure ought to command serious attention. H.C. Pentland has pointed out that nineteenth-century banking "failed to fit into the developing Canadian economy in a wholly satisfactory manner." The question at issue here is why was this so? Pentland and others point to the mercantile character of nineteenth-century banking: the propensity to finance the movement rather than the production of goods and the tendency to lend on a short-term rather than a long-term basis.[100] If the Bank of Upper Canada's arguments can be believed, however, the problem was as much due to limited size and excessive competition. Certainly, as we have seen, the bank, on being faced with the new competitive context following 1832, did adopt a shorter discount policy.

Viewed from a larger perspective, the degree to which the bank would have operated differently had it expanded becomes less important. In a more measurable way, the bank's failure to increase its size, restrict competition, and maintain local control of Upper Canada's debt marked a turning point in the evolution of the Upper Canadian financial system. It gave to the Bank of Montreal an opportunity to dominate colonial banking. Lower

[98]See *JUC*, 18 Dec. 1833, Appendix, Report of Select Committee on Petition of the President and Directors of the Bank of Upper Canada; Provincial Bank Report, 1835, pp. 9–10 (Ridout), pp. 18–20 (B. Thorne).

[99]A. Shortt, "Experiment and Inflation," *JCBA*, viii(1900–1), 319–20; Shortt Papers, vol. 3, Lord Glenelg to F.B. Head, 27 Nov. 1837 (copy).

[100]Pentland, "Canadian Economic Development," 471–74; Naylor develops this in "The Rise and Fall of the Third Commercial Empire of the St. Lawrence," and in *The History of Canadian Business, 1867–1914*, i (Toronto, 1975).

Canada did not have a J.H. Dunn to influence local banking development. The Montreal bank controlled Lower Canada's government funds and enjoyed much closer financial relations with that government than the Bank of Upper Canada did with its government. Relatively unhindered by local competition, the Bank of Montreal, even before the Union, began to move into Upper Canada. After the mid-1830s no Upper Canadian bank could successfully resist such expansion.

The carving up of the Upper Canadian banking system in the 1830s encouraged the perpetuation of that system's general mercantile orientation. Competition rendered it more difficult to grant long-term accommodation to local enterprise. Reliance for such capital increasingly fell on outside sources. In fact, following the debt refunding, those Canadians who wished to invest in long-term local projects had to do so via Great Britain. The refunding inaugurated the practice of sending money out of the Canadas in order to invest in the Canadas. In this case, the money was rechannelled through London.[101] In the modern era Canadian funds are often reinvested via New York.[102]

VII

Between 1822 and 1835, the Bank of Upper Canada exerted a narrow, if important, influence on Upper Canadian development. It provided a secure medium of exchange and contributed toward the growth of a stable money supply. By the provision of short-term capital, it underwrote the routine business of the more substantial members of the commercial community. While it was far from being a "government" bank in this era, its activities did complement the government's developmental policies. In addition to financing commercial growth, the bank, as a broker, facilitated the sale of government securities. In this sense it seems to have acted efficiently as a distributor of available financial resources.

In the end, it failed to move from its policy of classic credit creation. The possibility of such a transformation was present in the mid-1830s. Under pressure to expand, the bank presented a series of general proposals that, it claimed, would enable it to loosen and expand its business. A tradition of large profit-taking

---

[101]It is entirely possible, of course, that this structure discouraged rather than encouraged local investment in large capital projects.
[102]Kari Levitt, *Silent Surrender* (Toronto, 1970).

and a general perception of close government collusion had, however, led to widespread public distrust of the bank's credibility.[103] Its desire to increase its capital and re-emerge as the colony's dominant financial institution was, therefore, seen by the public as a purely self-interested policy. The government's most powerful financial administrator, John Henry Dunn, shared the public's general perceptions, and in this context the developmental side of the bank's program was given little consideration.

---

[103]Allan realized that his position required him "to please the Public and do Justice to the Stockholders." While he succeeded in the latter, he failed in the former (B 71).

C.   SEARCH FOR A FOCUS: 1835–48

As PRESIDENT, WILLIAM ALLAN had resisted constant pressure for expansion of discounts and agencies. He had balanced, however roughly, government and general commercial business. Although he did not enjoy it, he had reluctantly accepted the necessity of attempting to please the "Public" as well as the "Stockholders" (B 71). In June 1835, tired of it all, he resigned to become the governor of the British America Fire and Life Assurance Company (B 91).

John Macaulay, the bank's Kingston agent, once complimented Allan on his "prudence in always having a *horse in the stable*" (B 52). Not all of his associates, however, shared this perception. For those who did not, Allan's resignation provided an opportunity to kick the door asunder and ride unfettered in the public's pasture. By the time the bank's new president, the York merchant William Proudfoot – assisted by the ever-present and increasingly powerful cashier, Thomas Ridout – realized the dangers that could accompany such new-found freedom, the damage had been done.

The initial policies pursued by the new managers permitted the Commercial Bank's emergence as a powerful local competitor, increasingly angered other banks and the wider business community, and on the eve of the union of Upper and Lower Canada, left the bank ill-prepared to confront the profound political, economic and financial changes of the 1840s.

I

A scant year after his resignation, Allan confided to a correspondent that his successors "have deviated from my System & my Management very much, and I am inclined to think they [reap?] in the folly & effects of it and are not over flush" (C 13). Aggregate figures and scattered literary evidence suggest that the bank's new managers had embarked on an aggressive course of credit creation and that they did so within a speculative rather than a conservative frame. The £479,321 of discounts outstanding in February 1836 was not to be exceeded until 1845 and represented a 27 per cent increase over the January 1835 figure. Deposits at New York and London had plummeted to a new recorded low and overdue debts as a percentage of all debts reached a new recorded high in November. Most of the doubtful discounts, Ridout later explained, had been granted by the bank's agencies and thus after March 1838 no new discounts – excepting drafts on Lower Canada – were granted outside of Toronto.[1]

This suggests that the problem Allan had pinpointed in Cobourg continued to bedevil the bank's business. Head office maintained insufficient control over the discounting practices of its outlying areas and as a result had to allocate more of its capital to renewals and salvage operations at the expense of new loans. Some contemporaries charged that the bank had begun to invest in long-term loans, thus defying accepted principles of commercial banking by withdrawing capital from general mercantile usage. Critics also questioned the extent of capital the bank had tied up in unsaleable real estate. While disaggregated figures are not available, it is doubtless true that excessive discounting at both the agencies and head office, an increased proportion of long-term loans, and increased accumulation of real estate – as collateral for overdue debts – did occur in 1836 and the first half of 1837.[2]

The bank's managers saw little reason for concern. Profits reached a record high at the end of 1836. Even more encouraging, government business seemed increasingly lucrative. If Ridout and Proudfoot "deviated" from Allan's general business operations, they initially followed his strategy vis-à-vis government relations. Even while the bank opposed the government's fiscal arrangements and pressed unsuccessfully for changes in the colony's financial structure, its managers took steps to benefit from the existing state of affairs. These steps marked the beginning of a significant change in the bank's general business orientation. As the decade progressed, the bank looked increasingly to the government as the major source of its profits. To the extent that it did, the general mercantile community and the public at large suffered.

The government's loan operations of 1834–36 were designed to realize two ends: to refund and transfer the existing debt and to raise new capital for continued canal construction, especially on the St. Lawrence River. The government earmarked most of the

---

[1]*JUC*, 1839, Appendix, Third Report of the Committee on Banking, [hereafter Third Report on Banking, 1839] pp. 765 and 782 (Ridout's testimony).

[2]For indications of this see QUA, J.S. Cartwright Papers, vol. 2, Archibald McLean to Cartwright, 15 Jan. 1839; Third Report on Banking, 1839, Hincks's testimony; PAC RG 19 CI, vol. 1181, Prime Ward and King to Ridout, 11 Oct. 1839.

£200,000 raised in 1834 for debenture redemption and the transfer of Upper Canada's debt to London, England. Dunn strongly supported this procedure, it will be recalled, in part because he believed that the government could profit from the public sale of bills of exchange on the London funds. He had confidence in this plan because the adverse balance of trade that North America had with Britain in this era generally created a demand both within the colony and at New York for good bills with which to pay British suppliers.[3]

While opposed to this plan in principle, the Bank of Upper Canada attempted to profit from its implementation. It wished to purchase government exchange at a low rate and sell at a high rate to the general commercial community. Strong competition from other financial institutions, however, often blocked the bank from acquiring government exchange. When this occurred the bank fell back on what might diplomatically be termed aggressive business tactics to attain its end. The York bank frequently possessed the debentures slated for redemption. In the cases where a competitor purchased the requisite exchange, the Bank of Upper Canada refused to accept payments in the notes of rival institutions and demanded instead full payment in specie. This stipulation prevented the bank's competitors from increasing their note circulation and neutralized their anticipated exchange transactions.

The bank first successfully carried out this manoeuvre under Allan's presidency in November 1834, and, in the words of the receiver general, "produced a good deal of difficulty to me and not a little to the Commercial Bank." The Bank of Upper Canada's rivals promptly informed the government that they would not tender for exchange without a guarantee that their paper would be received in payment (B 81). In order to prevent the Bank of Upper Canada from monopolizing the exchange business, Dunn agreed and promised such in all future advertisements (C 2). This made it incumbent on the government to provide specie should a similar situation arise in the future.

In June 1835, that situation arose. The Bank of Montreal offered 9¼ per cent premium for some £25,000 of government exchange; the Bank of Upper Canada offered 8 per cent. The latter held most of the debentures to be redeemed and when questioned by the receiver general's office stated that it would only accept specie as payment. The government gave in and sold

---

[3]*JUC*, 1835, Appendix, First Report of the Committee on Public Accounts, 27 Mar. and Second Report, 4 Apr.

the exchange to the Bank of Upper Canada even though it had presented the lowest of four bids.[4]

The government capitulated because Dunn had left for England on 1 June in order to raise a second large loan.[5] Any dispute within the colony over the redemption of current debentures would have ruined his chances and would probably have forced Upper Canada's debentures to a serious discount on the London market.[6] From Ridout's perspective the time was right for turning the screw. It is also noteworthy that the government could not afford to pay £25,000 in specie at that particular time. At year's end the receiver general had overspent his provincial revenue by some £6,400.[7] To Ridout, the message must have seemed clear: not only could the bank profit from the government's financial weakness, but, in the course of so doing, it could deny its major competitors lucrative business. That the general public suffered indirectly from the loss of profit to the government concerned Ridout and the bank's directorate not at all.

The proceeds of some of the £200,000 loan negotiated in 1834 and most of the £400,000 loan negotiated in 1835–36 were earmarked for canal construction. When the government sold exchange for this purpose, rather than for redeeming debentures, it might be expected that the Bank of Upper Canada would lose its market advantage. To a degree this was true. Without debentures in hand the bank could no longer pressure the government in order to get its way. In two other respects, however, the bank continued to enjoy an advantage over its rivals. The Executive Council, not the receiver general, controlled the final disposition of all exchange contracts. Whenever possible the council favoured the Bank of Upper Canada[8] (C 8). Yet it would be wrong to exaggerate the council's power in this regard. Even with this support, between 1834 and 1836 the bank acquired only 29 per cent of the receiver general's bills drawn on the London loans. While this made it the largest single purchaser, the bank hardly dominated the market.[9]

[4]PAC, RG 19 B2a, vol. 1173, Minute in Council (copy), 2 July 1835; Turquand to Rowan, 30 June 1835.

[5]*JUC*, 1836, Appendix 1, no. 7, Dunn to Bond Head, 18 June 1836.

[6]QUA, Magill Papers, Long Sheets, p. 128.

[7]*JUC*, 1837, Appendix 2, Public Accounts.

[8]PAC, RG 19 B2a, vol. 1137, Harper to Turquand, 26 Aug. 1835; ibid., RG 19 B2b, vol. 1173, Turquand to Harper, 1 Sept. 1835.

[9]Computed from *JLA*, 1841, Appendix B, General Statement of the Receiver General's Bills of Exchange drawn on London, on account of Debentures negotiated in England [hereafter General Debentures Statement].

A second level of influence partially compensated for the bank's failure to purchase a greater percentage of the canal exchange. When a bank purchased these bills, it expected that the government would pay the contractors, suppliers and labourers in the buyer's bank notes. The possibility of putting notes in circulation in such a safe way – they would be well dispersed and take a long time returning to the bank – provided a major stimulus for bidding in the first place.[10] The receiver general recognized this and stated that the bank buying the exchange would be given "every advantage" in circulating its paper.[11]

Jonas Jones, the chairman of the commission superintending the construction of the St. Lawrence Canal, had other ideas. A conservative member of Brockville's elite, closely allied with Toronto's Family Compact and a past, if not current, debtor to the Bank of Upper Canada, he disbursed all money spent on the canal (B 40). Whenever possible he did so in Bank of Upper Canada notes, whether that institution had bought the exchange or not.[12] Put simply, this meant that Jones would often exchange the buyer's paper for Bank of Upper Canada notes at the latter's Brockville agency. The bank's agent would then send these notes to the purchaser's head office for immediate redemption in specie or its equivalent. This provided the Bank of Upper Canada added benefit from increased circulation; the demand for redemption provided its competitor only unanticipated trouble and expense[13] (C 4, C 5, C 6).

While profiting from the government's financial practices, the Bank of Upper Canada continued to petition for an increase in both its capital and its status to that of a provincial bank. In 1837 the local legislature acceded to the bank's wishes and, in addition, passed other bills which, had they received royal assent, would have increased the colony's banking capital by nine times to £4,500,000 cy.[14] Even as the lieutenant-governor referred these bills to London, however, rumours of impending financial disaster crossed the ocean. The decade which had commenced with such economic promise threatened to close amidst financial uncertainty and economic distress. British speculation in railroads and canals, American speculation in canals and banks, and

[10]PAC, RG 19 B2a, 1137, C. Castle to Turquand, 25 Aug. 1835.
[11]Ibid., RG 19 B2b, 1173, Dunn to Castle, 23 Feb. 1836.
[12]PAC, A. Shortt Papers, vol. 9, J. Jones to R.B. Sullivan, 7 July 1837 (copy).
[13]PAC, RG 19 B2a, vol. 1137, Jones to Turquand, 27 July 1835, Castle to Turquand, 25 Aug. 1835; ibid., RG 19 B2b, vol. 1173, Dunn to Castle, 23 Feb. 1836.
[14]Shortt Papers, vol. 3, Glenelg to Bond Head, 27 Nov. 1837 (copy).

widespread American crop failures caused Anglo-American trade to grind to a halt. In May 1837 New York banks suspended specie payments. In June, Thomas Wilson and Co., the bank's and Upper Canada's principal London financial agent, suspended all operations. It had in its hands £83,000 stg. of the government's money and some £10,000 to £15,000 stg. of the bank's funds.[15] Government expenditures outran revenues and new London agents, Glyn, Mills and Company, had to assist the Baring Brothers in advancing money for interest payments on the government's large and in some cases overdue debt. Glyn also guaranteed payment of the bank's British obligations, thus commencing a long relationship with the colony and its major financial institution.

Despite rising wheat prices – due mainly to the needs of the American market – Upper Canadian crop failures stymied growth and contributed to a general sense of economic instability.[16] Against this troubled backdrop, William Lyon Mackenzie staged his abortive uprising late in 1837. The consequent infusion of British capital to pay for the men and munitions necessary to put down both Mackenzie's fiasco and the much more serious revolt in Lower Canada, and to protect against a series of imagined uprisings in 1838, facilitated a gradual return to financial normalcy in the decade's closing year.

This financial crisis had an immediate impact on the Bank of Upper Canada's desire and ability to maintain normal operations. The general suspension of specie payments by New York banks led to a shortage of specie and a demand arose in New York for redeemable Upper Canadian bank notes. Proudfoot feared that as much as one-half of the bank's £200,000 note issue would be "bought up by speculators and brought here for redemption."[17] Nor, in the initial stages of the crisis, did this projection seem totally unreasonable. Fuelled by Mackenzie's strident rhetoric, by the desperate need of private banks for specie, and by foreign demand, a noteholder run commenced and on the very day Proudfoot made his estimate, the bank had had to pay out £10,000 in specie.[18]

Proudfoot and Ridout could respond in one of two ways to this

[15]PAC, RG 19 B2b, vol. 1175, Dunn to Macaulay, 8 July 1838; PAC, Glyn, Mills Papers, MG 24 D36, A541, Proudfoot to Glyn, Mills, 13 Sept. 1841.
[16]R.L. Jones, *History of Agriculture,* p. 124.
[17]PAC, RG 5 A1, Proudfoot to Bond Head, 16 May 1837.
[18]See Table 6.

problem. They could continue to pay out specie until the bank's reserves were depleted and then close the institution pending the acquisition of new funds to meet outstanding notes. Or they could follow the lead of American and Lower Canadian banks and suspend specie payments but continue discounting. While the latter course required special legislation (the bank's charter prohibited the conduct of business while specie payments were suspended), it would enable the bank to support mercantile activity and thus help to stimulate and buttress the general economy in a troubled period. Upper Canada's merchants firmly supported this option. If the former course were pursued, discounting would cease, old loans would be recalled, and mercantile credit would dry up.

Despite a serious split within the directorate,[19] the bank refused to suspend payments and thereby exemplified what Sir Francis Bond Head, the lieutenant-governor, called "the commercial integrity of the British Empire."[20] It is important to note that more than Bond Head's celebrated anti-Americanism lay behind this stance. His views on the necessity of "faithfully liquidating"[21] echoed the social and moralistic pronouncements of the British bullionists in the 1820s and 1830s. Underlying their program was the desire to protect a traditional landed aristocracy against the presumed ravages of an overly speculative commercial and industrial order. Just as the bullionists assumed that convertibility and tight credit would kill off "improvident and unreasonable speculation," so Bond Head argued that only those "who had been in the habit of receiving from the Banks what is termed Accommodation" would suffer.[22] Like the bullionists, Bond Head believed convertibility would cleanse the economy and thereby protect the status quo. Small wonder that he could declare that redemption would "tend most materially to assist in crushing the enemy of Civilization – democracy."[23]

That the views of the British bullionists had no relevance to social and economic conditions in Upper Canada – or indeed, little relevance to economic affairs in Great Britain – worried

[19]Report on Monetary System, 1837, p. 2; PAC, Upper Canada Sundries, Macaulay to Hagerman, May 1837.
[20]PAC, CO 42, vol. 438, Bond Head to Proudfoot, 17 May 1837.
[21]Ibid.
[22]For the British bullionists, see B. Hilton, *Corn, Cash and Commerce*, pp. 58–64. PAC, CO 42, 438, Bond Head to Glenelg, 12 July 1837.
[23]Ibid., Bond Head to Proudfoot, 17 May 1837.

neither Bond Head nor the Bank of Upper Canada. In fact Proudfoot and Ridout were not motivated by any ideological or class concerns when they turned their back on Upper Canada's mercantile community. The Bank of Upper Canada allied itself with Bond Head out of simple self-interest. The bank's managers believed that they could profit more from government preferment than from the continuance of general commercial business. In this sense the bank's behaviour during the economic recession marked the culmination of a trend first clearly visible late in 1834.

The lieutenant-governor promised to use his influence and obtain for the bank £50,000 in treasury bills from the Commissariat Department. Disappointed in this attempt and prodded by the Bank of Upper Canada, he convinced the receiver general to deposit all his monies, in specie if possible, with the bank (C 34). Finally, under severe pressure from the mercantile community, Bond Head acceded to a law which permitted suspension at the discretion of the lieutenant-governor and Executive Council. He made it clear, however, that only the notes of specie-paying banks would be accepted for government business. In order to prevent a bank from suspending and employing large specie reserves for speculation on the exchange markets, he further decreed that the amount of specie in the vault at the time of suspension could not exceed the total of one dollar notes in circulation (C 33).

In the meantime the Bank of Upper Canada endeavoured to protect its specie reserves by importing £40,000 in silver from New York between 3 May and 27 June and by borrowing $50,000 in notes from the Bank of Montreal.[24] The bank used these non-redeemable notes, rather than its own redeemable paper, to maintain a certain level of activity in the area of Lower Canadian trade. By August the bank's affairs had stabilized. Its specie reserves began to increase and its note issue continued to contract. Aided by the receiver general's deposit (the bank transported from Lower Canada £24,000 in specie in early August),[25] the reserves reached £139,000 in January 1838. During the last half of 1837 Ridout and Proudfoot discounted only £40,000 to £50,000 of new paper while calling in roughly £200,000 of old

[24]Report on Monetary System, 1837, Statement "A" and p. 859; PAC, Bank of Montreal, Resolve Books, vol. 3, p. 116, 30 May 1837. By so doing the Bank of Montreal significantly increased its circulation.
[25]*JUC*, 1837–38, Appendix, Public Accounts, p 28; PAC, RG 19 B2a, Vol. 1138, Proudfoot to Turquand, 24 July 1837.

discounts and reducing notes in circulation by 60 per cent to £80,000.[26]

Despite the drastic curtailment of its normal business operations, the bank suffered only a minimal 25 per cent decrease in profits from the record year of 1836. Ninety per cent of these profits came from the sale of exchange on London (Table 4). Between April 1834 and April 1837 the bank obtained 30 per cent of all the exchange issued by the government on its London loans. From May to December 1837, the bank purchased over 90 per cent of the government's exchange on its London loans and this represented over 40 per cent of all the exchange on London purchased by the bank in this period.[27] The bank's share of this business increased because Bond Head refused to sell bills "to any person or Institution for the Notes of a Bank which has suspended specie payments."[28] Even though the government had consistently obtained a higher price for its exchange in Lower Canada, this decree effectively ended competition from that quarter and enabled the Bank of Upper Canada to realize a 10 per cent return on the sale of £165,074 of London exchange in 1837[29] (Table 4).

The Commercial Bank adopted a course different from that of its Upper Canadian competitor. Never as successful as its rival in garnering government business, whether in terms of exchange or deposits, the Commercial Bank decided to concentrate on meeting the needs of its mercantile customers and suspended specie payments in September 1837.[30] This was a further boon to the Bank of Upper Canada as individuals dealing with the government had to use Bank of Upper Canada notes.[31] By late 1837,

---

[26]For figures for new discounts see *JUC*, 1837–38, Appendix, Third Report of the Select Committee on Finance [hereafter Third Report on Finance, 1837–38], p. 95 (Ridout). For a contradictory figure, see *JUC*, 1838, Appendix, Report of the Select Committee on the Subject of Banking [hereafter Report on Banking, 1838], p. 215. Other figures computed from Table 6. While Table B3, Appendix O, 1841, *JLA*, Bank of Upper Canada Monthly Discounts, 1836–41, cannot be trusted (it understates the amounts), it does support the trend suggested here.

[27]Computed from data in General Debentures Statement, and *JLA*, 1841, Appendix O, Monthly Statement on Exchange on London Purchased and Sold by the Bank of Upper Canada, 1836–41.

[28]PAC, RG 19 B2b, vol. 1173, Turquand to Forsyth & Richardson, 14 July 1837.

[29]Third Report on Finance, 1837–38, p. 101 (Turquand); the normal rate of return anticipated by bankers was 1½ per cent; see above, Section B.

[30]PAC, CO 42, vol. 439, Bond Head to Glenelg, 29 Sept. 1837.

[31]It had the immediate effect of swelling the bank's deposits by £37,000. The Commercial Bank had to pay this amount over to the government as the price of suspension. PAC, RG 19 B2b, vol. 1175, Dunn to Macaulay, 3 Nov. 1838.

then, virtually all local government departments accepted payments only in Bank of Upper Canada paper, deposited their funds with that bank and paid their expenses via drafts on that bank.

As a suspended bank, the Commercial could no longer directly obtain exchange or specie from the government. Instead, the Kingston bank began to "procure" from private individuals receiver general and Commissariat cheques on the Bank of Upper Canada and present the same to that bank for payment in specie (C 39). Arguing that this took unfair advantage of specie-paying institutions, Ridout paid the cheques in Commercial Bank notes. Since the Commercial Bank desired specie for exchange purposes, it was put in the anomalous position of refusing to accept its own notes and demanding specie instead. Despite the Commercial's plea that it deserved consideration for having suspended to relieve "the commercial community," the government's Banking Committee supported the Bank of Upper Canada on this issue.[32]

In yet another way the bank altered past policies to strengthen its monopoly position. In 1836, acting on the request of the Gore Bank, Ridout and Proudfoot had set the York bank up as a clearing house for the notes of all Upper Canadian financial institutions. Differences in account between the various banks were to be paid by drafts on Montreal, New York or London[33] (C 17). This practice minimized specie raids and imparted greater stability to the general banking system. Following the economic downturn of 1837, however, the Bank of Upper Canada dismantled that structure. The bank's competitors hoped to use the note exchange system as a means to collect exchange on London and thus break Ridout and Proudfoot's control. Despite both the attempts of the Commercial and Gore banks to reinstitute the practice and the positive recommendations of an 1839 Banking Committee, the Bank of Upper Canada refused to accommodate its Upper Canadian rivals.[34]

The Mackenzie uprising in December allowed the bank to strengthen further its hold on general government business. Until the outbreak, the Commissariat Department had been reluctant to

---

[32]Report on Banking, 1838.

[33]CIBC, Gore Letterbook, 1835–36, Steven to Harper, Ridout, Dupuy, Truscott and Green, Leslie, and Ross, 25 June 1836 [all bankers]; Steven to Truscott, Green and Co., 27 July 1836.

[34]A. Shortt, "Crisis and Resumption," *JCBA* ix (1901–2), p. 115–16; Third Report on Banking, 1839, pp. 761–62.

deposit much of its funds with any Canadian bank and had maintained the greater part of its capital under its own control.[35] Rebellion in Upper and Lower Canada changed this. The department required immediate and large outlays to finance the military's response. As a result it accepted a short-term £50,000 loan from the Bank of Upper Canada and appointed that bank as its agent in the upper province.[36] The bank received, according to an angry John Cartwright, president of the Commercial Bank, some £150,000 of sterling bills from the commissary general by mid-February (C 39). In return, of course, the Upper Canada bank issued, whenever possible, its own notes and hoped to profit, as it had in 1837, by the sale of this exchange in the New York market.

On this latter point, the bank severely miscalculated. The high exchange rate in 1837, coupled with the general downturn in economic activity in the United States, contributed to low imports from Great Britain in 1838. Primarily for this reason the overall trade balance generally favoured the United States throughout that year.[37] This meant that bills of exchange on London remained around par in this period.[38] And that meant that the Bank of Upper Canada could no longer enjoy substantial profits from the sale of government bills in New York. As a result the bank's London deposits increased from a deficit in early January to more than £200,000 by March (C 44). Its note circulation – occasioned by Commissariat payments – doubled and its specie reserves – due to other banks collecting Bank of Upper Canada notes and demanding specie in redemption – declined by 55 per cent. In these circumstances the bank refused to import specie from Great Britain, claimed that border troubles prevented the shipment of coinage from New York, threatened to cease purchasing government debentures and petitioned for suspension of specie payments in order to continue its program of supporting government activity (C 47).

That Lower Canadian and most American banks were preparing to resume payments at this time, did not trouble the bank's managers. Nor did it trouble the people's representatives. On the

[35]PAC, RG 7 G1, vol. 35, A.J. Spearman to I. Routh, 6 July 1837.

[36]Shortt, "Crisis and Resumption," p. 111.

[37]Peter Temin, The Jacksonian Economy, pp. 149–52; D.C. North, "The United States Balance of Payments, 1790–1860," in National Bureau of Economic Research, vol. 24, Trends in the American Economy in the Nineteenth Century (Princeton, 1960), p. 605.

[38]PAC, CO 42, vol. 445, Bond Head to Glenelg, 20 Mar. 1838.

final day of the legislative sitting the conservative-dominated Assembly and the friendly Council acceded to the bank's wishes and, with Bond Head's support, not only permitted suspension but allowed the Bank of Upper Canada's notes to continue to be accepted by the government. Although the Commercial Bank, when it suspended, had had its note issue restricted to its paid-up capital, the Bank of Upper Canada was permitted to issue double that figure. At no time in its history had the Toronto bank enjoyed a cosier relationship with the Upper Canadian government.[39]

Over the time of the bank's suspension (March 1838 to November 1839) Ridout's justification changed to suit the moment. Border disturbances and the imminent threat of civil unrest headed the list. A second favourite related to the habit of Lower Canadian banks paying specie in depreciated and non-current (in Upper Canada) French half crowns. To prevent Upper Canada from being inundated with such coinage after resumption, Ridout repeatedly requested an act that would establish a standard coinage system throughout the colonies[40] (C 44). While relations with Lower Canadian banks were at a low point in this period and the existence of different currencies did interfere with colonial trade, it seems clear that in this case, as in the claims of civil unrest and border troubles, Ridout greatly exaggerated the extent of the problems[41] (C 41, C 43, C 56, C 60).

The bank's business practices between March 1838 and November 1839 provide a truer measure of the reasons for suspension. Ridout and Proudfoot continued to focus on government business and to grant only secondary attention to the general commercial community. The expanding note issue – it reached a recorded high of £341,163 in February 1839, a figure not exceeded until 1853 – resulted from Commissariat and general government disbursements, not from increased discounts.[42] Government debentures represented close to one-third of the bank's debts due in 1838 (Table 5). Important mercantile customers began to desert the bank, finding they could obtain cheaper bills of exchange from other institutions[43] (C 22, C 25, C 42). From

[39]Shortt, "Crisis and Resumption," p. 112. Other suspended banks were accorded a similar privilege at this time.

[40]PAC, Colborne Papers, MG 24 A40, vol. 16, Ridout to Colborne, 28 Feb. 1839.

[41]PAC, Bank of Montreal Resolve Book, vol. 3, 6 Dec. 1839. Shortt, "Crisis and Resumption," pp. 113–14.

[42]*JLA*, 1841, Appendix O, D2; the discount trend can be seen in ibid., Appendix O, B3, but see footnote 26 above.

[43]Third Report on Banking, 1839, pp. 772, 776, 777.

the date of suspension until well into 1839 the bank ceased discounting entirely at all its branches and curtailed discounts at its head office.[44] Merchants doing business with the Commissariat Department received preference; others looked elsewhere (C 48).

Ultimately this strategy backfired. Not only did the bank lose credibility in the minds of the merchants and public at large, but it also suffered where it really hurt – on the profit and loss statement. In 1837 the bank had enjoyed a 10 per cent profit on the sale of bills on London. In 1838 this profit margin decreased to a still respectable 2 per cent. By the end of that year, however, the bank had £300,000 of exchange on deposit in London, unsold. Eighteen thirty-nine proved to be the year of reckoning. The legislation permitting suspension was extended from May to November 1839 and even Ridout realized that the chances of obtaining a further extension were impossible. As the year progressed and the Commissariat began to curtail its expenditures, the bank began, while under suspension, to reduce its note issue and, in order to build up its local specie reserve, sell its large London exchange holdings[45] (Table 6). Due to unstable economic conditions in the United States,[46] these holdings were disposed of at a net loss of 2 per cent or £12,702. The loss decreased the bank's overall profits by half and forced Ridout to take over £4,000 from the contingency fund to meet normal dividend payments (tables 4 and 12 B).

The bank's policies also led to strained relations between it and the Bank of Montreal in the later 1830s. Probably desiring to cover balances owed the Montreal bank via the payment of inflated British silver (it was rated at a higher level in Upper than in Lower Canada) and thus contravening the long-standing 1830 agreement, the bank only reluctantly backed down in April 1838[47] (C 41). Even then peace was fleeting. In order, as the bank explained, "to protect our notes," it opened a Montreal agency in September and proceeded to redeem its notes at a slight discount.[48] Angered, the Bank of Montreal cancelled the 1830

[44]Third Report on Banking, 1839, *passim*.

[45]*JLA*, 1841, Appendix O, D2, and B3. For a different perspective on this period, see A. Redish, "Why Was Specie Scarce?" especially pp. 208–9. Both the interpretation offered here and that of Redish revise Shortt, "Crisis and Resumption."

[46]Temin, *Jacksonian Economy*, pp. 152 ff.

[47]CIBC, Gore Letterbook, 1837–40, Steven to Castle, 30 Apr. 1838; A. Shortt, "Metallic Currency before the Union," *JCBA* ix (1901–1902), p. 283.

[48]Shortt Papers, vol. 4, Goldsmith to Murdock, 18 May 1840 (copy).

arrangement and entered into a short-lived alliance with the Commercial Bank. When this, too, broke down, the Montreal bank purchased the People's Bank at Toronto and commenced a fateful course of expansion throughout Upper Canada.[49] Faced with this competitive onslaught, the Bank of Upper Canada re-established a working agreement with the Lower Canadian institution (C 60). It was, however, a case of too little, too late: the Bank of Montreal was in Upper Canada to stay.

The Bank of Upper Canada's strategy led to a further and ironical result. The bank's desire to monopolize government business led to a clearly demarcated division of affairs between it and its major local rival, the Commercial Bank. Denied govern-ment preferment, the Commercial focused on general mercantile business. The irony is that by so doing it enjoyed its highest profits to that date. In 1837 and 1838 those profits approximated the Bank of Upper Canada returns; in 1839, the Kingston bank's profits surpassed those of its older rival (Table 3). Large gains were to be had from playing the exchange market, but, as the experience of 1833–34 ought to have suggested, substantial losses could also occur. That the Commercial Bank realized substantial profits at a time of apparent recession suggests that the Upper Canadian economy might have been in better shape than most economic historians have assumed. Since the Commercial engaged in a strong business selling bills of exchange on New York in this period, Upper Canadian-American trade might not have been as hard hit as Upper Canadian-British trade.[50] At any rate, it is clear that Ridout and Proudfoot's quest for short-term gain opened the door to its newly established rival and allowed the Commercial Bank to attain a position of respect and credibility with the business public. Measured by paid-in capital, circula-tion, discounts and specie, the Commercial Bank was every bit the equal of the Bank of Upper Canada. Only in size of deposits did the York bank exhibit a clear superiority.

II

The Bank of Upper Canada had not succeeded in wresting all it desired from the legislature in the 1830s. Competition had emer-ged. Repeated attempts to transform itself into an official provin-

---

[49]Denison, *Canada's First Bank*, I, pp. 360–64.
[50]*JLA*, 1841, Appendix O, B4.

cial bank had failed. Yet it was at the centre of much of the legislative wrangling and certainly between 1837 and 1839, it enjoyed a cosier and more privileged relationship with the government than at any time in its past.

That position and perspective the bank would not enjoy again for some time. The first portent of change came in 1840. Desperate to meet its interest payments on loans provided by Barings and Glyns, the government sold its Bank of Upper Canada stock and thereby severed its formal link with that institution. In May 1841, the Commissariat Department withdrew its profitable account[51] (C 57). The political union of Upper and Lower Canada, in June 1841, occasioned an even more dramatic change in Bank of Upper Canada–government affairs. With the commencement of the Union, the "Old Lady" of the upper province became only one of ten banks operating in the united colony. At the commencement of the 1830s the Bank of Upper Canada monopolized the colony's banking business; in July 1841 it controlled only 9 per cent of the Union's banking capital, 12 per cent of its discounts, 14 per cent of its specie, 15 per cent of its circulation and 18 per cent of its deposits.[52]

The bank also had to face an aggressive imperial attempt to restructure the existing colonial financial system. Although Upper Canadians had taken their banking seriously (no fewer than ten committees produced lengthy reports on the current state and future direction of local banking in the 1830s), several fundamental banking and currency problems had still to be solved. These problems included the continuing debate over a provincial bank, the merits of a fluctuating note issue, and the imperial govern-

---

[51]PAC, RG 19 B2b, vol. 1175, Dunn to S.B. Harrison, 25 Feb. 1840; Dunn to Macaulay, 2 June 1840; M.L. Smith, ed., *Young Mr. Smith in Upper Canada* (Toronto, 1980), p. 61.

[52]This comparison is in one sense unfair: the colony of 1841 was much larger than Upper Canada in the 1830s. After the Act of Union, however, the Bank of Upper Canada was faced with much more dramatic competition, for both its domestic and obviously for its government business, from Lower Canada (Canada East) than had been the case in the pre-Union era.

An alternative measurement using data only from banks with head offices in Upper Canada yields the following rounded percentages:

Capital: 34%
Discounts: 37%
Specie: 32%
Circulation: 32%
Deposits: 55%

Computed from information in *JLA*, 1841, Appendix O, F; and R.M. Breckenridge, *The History of Banking in Canada* (Washington, 1910), pp. 43, 85.

ment's role in colonial financial affairs. The Union's first governor general, Charles Poulett Thomson (Lord Sydenham), came
equipped with what he considered to be satisfactory solutions for
all these problems.

As a past president of the Board of Trade in England, Sydenham had overseen much colonial banking and currency legislation. He had not been favourably impressed. Only under duress
had he assented to "those bad Banking Acts" from Upper Canada
in the mid 1830s.[53] An advocate of the Currency School of
Banking, he believed that guaranteed convertibility of notes into
coin was the *sine qua non* of an effective financial system. Too
many independent banks would result in over-issues and a speculative environment. To forestall this, he wished to create a
provincial bank with sole control of note issues. The government
would benefit from an additional revenue of £35,000 per year; the
colony would benefit from a stable banking structure; and
England would benefit from this advanced experiment in banking
systems.[54]

Many in the colony sympathized with Sydenham's ends. The
most recent committee on banking had, in fact, focused on the
matter of excessive note issues.[55] Francis Hincks, a local banker
and reform politician, for one, believed that most Upper Canadian
banks were ill-managed and speculatively inclined. Fewer,
however, sympathized with the governor general's means. Certainly the local bankers had other ideas. Arguing that the loss of
note-issuing privileges would lead to total ruin, J.S. Cartwright,
president of the Commercial Bank, and Benjamin Holmes and
Peter McGill, respectively cashier and president of the Bank of
Montreal, led the fight against Sydenham. In a private letter to the
governor general, McGill put the bankers' position in an uncom-
promising fashion:

Your Lordship's threatened hostility to the banks, if they refuse to come into views, as
respects the Bank of Issue, will not be carried into effect – The war would not be with
the Banks – *but with the debtors of the Banks*, a very large and influential class.[56]

[53]Lucy F. Brown, *The Board of Trade and the Free Trade Movement, 1830–42*
(Oxford, 1958), *passim*. Quote from Shortt Papers, vol. 3, C.P. Thomson to Glenelg, 8
Jan. 1836 (private, copy).
    [54]P. Knaplund, ed., *Letters from Lord Sydenham to Lord John Russell* (London,
1931), pp. 149–51; G. Poulett Scrope, *Life of Lord Sydenham* (London, 1843),
pp. 248–49, 385–91.
    [55]Third Report on Banking, 1839, pp. 760–62.
    [56]Shortt Papers, vol. 4, 2 Aug. 1841 (copy); for Cartwright's position, see E. Nish,
ed., *Debates of the Legislative Assembly of Canada*, ɪ (Montreal, 1970), 31 Aug. 1841.

Fearing restricted credit from the banks, the mercantile community fell in line against Sydenham and the Assembly soundly
defeated the bank-of-issue scheme.[57]

The Bank of Upper Canada's role in these matters is somewhat
obscure. No member of the bank played a prominent part in the
defeat of Sydenham's plan. Nor was this the first indication that
the bank's managers preferred not to confront directly imperial
authority. In 1840 when, in common with other Upper Canadian
banks, the Toronto institution applied for an increase in capital, it
acceded to new imperial regulations that the others refused to
accept (C 59). Proudfoot and Ridout hoped to curry government
favour by, whenever possible, bowing to imperial desires and,
when not possible, allowing others to take the forefront in
attacking them. By such tactics they hoped to maintain their
privileges.

Such hopes soon proved forlorn. During discussion of the
bank's charter in the Assembly, its competitors had the conces-
sions "struck out" (C 59). As a result the imperial government
refused to assent to any of the revised charters. Sydenham, failing
to realize the main prop of his banking plan, fell back on
secondary and, from the banking community's point of view, far
from palatable alternatives. The exaction of a 1 per cent tax on
note issues headed these measures. In addition to raising capital
for the government, the tax penalized banks for using their note-
issuing privileges "as a means of creating capital."[58] Despite
prolonged objections from the banks, the government had collected over £95,000 by the end of 1849. Even the Bank of Upper
Canada argued that the tax was unfair and excessive. Proudfoot
claimed that this impost cost some banks one-twelfth of their
annual profits and, in fact, his bank did pay £12,800 to the
province, a figure in excess of one-twelfth of its profits for the
decade[59] (C 83).

Itemized in the Fourth Report of the 1841 banking committee,
the remaining measures followed closely many of the suggestions
recently forwarded from the Imperial Board of the Treasury.[60]
Double liability for shareholders, the restriction of issues to the
extent of paid-up capital, and the strict confinement of discounts
to commercial transactions were the more important of these. To

[57]A. Shortt, "Lord Sydenham's Measure," *JCBA* x (1902–3), pp. 26–33.
[58]Hincks's phrase; see Nish, ed., *Debates*, p. 748.
[59]Figures calculated from *JLA*, 1849, Appendix Z, and 1850, Appendix 7.
[60]Shortt Papers, vol. 4, J. Russell to C.P. Thomson, 4 May 1840 (copy).

obtain an increase in capital the Bank of Upper Canada and many of its competitors agreed to the above terms. After 1842 the only significant differences between imperial government desires and local practice – excepting a central bank of issue – concerned the issuance of notes below one pound.[61] Imperial authorities wished to outlaw these issues; local bankers, pleading an absence of specie for small change, argued for their retention. In the end, the local banks compromised to the extent of limiting such issues to 20 per cent of the total.

Taken together, these measures accentuated a process begun in the mid-1830s – the institutionalization of a specifically focused financial system.[62] The banking legislation supported an economic structure already in existence. It made it more difficult, but, as will be demonstrated, not impossible, for banks to change from simply servicing a commercial-mercantile clientele, to underwriting an emerging industrial economy. Whenever banks like the Bank of Upper Canada even inadvertently transgressed imperially defined limits, they were open to judicial penalties and substantial loss. The full implications of this legislation did not hit the bank until the end of the decade.

Throughout the 1840s the fluctuating state of government finances dictated the nature of provincial government-bank business relations. In this context one of the most important measures proposed by Sydenham was an imperial guarantee of the interest payable on a £1,500,000 stg. loan to be raised in England at 4 per cent. Accepted in principle by the imperial authorities, the loan transaction reached completion late in 1842 under Sydenham's successor, Governor General Bagot. To carry on public works during negotiations, the provincial government borrowed from local banks. Along with other institutions, the Bank of Upper Canada eagerly obliged.[63] Between June 1840 and December

---

[61]*JLA*, 1847, Appendix W.

[62]The disallowance by the imperial government of Upper Canadian legislation incorporating a Trust and Loan Company in 1837 and again in 1844 underlines this process. As John Denis Haeger has demonstrated, similar companies in the United States were formed to underwrite long-term investments and thus take the pressure off commercially oriented banks. By contrast, the imperial government did not want any colonial financial institution to undertake that role. See Haeger, "Eastern Financiers and Institutional Change: The Origins of the New York Life Insurance and Trust Company and the Ohio Life Insurance and Trust Company," *JEH* xxxix (1979), pp. 259–73.

[63]See PAC, RG 19 B2b, vol. 1174, May–July 1842, for reaction of the banking community.

1842, Ridout and Proudfoot advanced at least £66,000 to the government at 6 per cent interest.[64]

The imperial loan provided banks a second avenue for profit. As with the loans of 1834–36, the government transferred the funds from England to the colony via the sale of exchange. As in the 1830s, banks competed for this business. From the Bank of Upper Canada's perspective, however, circumstances had dramatically altered. No longer could it bring special leverage to bear on the provincial government. While Ridout and Proudfoot acquired a reasonable proportion of the amount issued (around 20 per cent), they did so at competitive rates and at average profit levels.[65]

Nor, as they had in the late 1830s, could Ridout and Proudfoot control the disbursement of funds on the various public works projects. Two factors accounted for this change. Before 1841, local commissioners of public works, such as Jones in Brockville, oversaw construction and distributed funds in their areas. Sydenham replaced this decentralized structure with a central Board of Works.[66] The Bank of Upper Canada lacked direct links to the directors of this new apparatus. Of crucial importance, the mode of payments was even further centralized. Acting under the advice of the imperial government, Francis Hincks, the inspector general, arranged a system whereby payments from the government to the contractors came under the ultimate control of the receiver general's office.[67] While much of this system broke down in practice, one element remained constant: the financial agency that controlled the receiver general's account received the lion's share of the public works business.

Dunn, the receiver general, continued to keep as much of the government's funds out of the direct hands of banks as he could. As part of a general restructuring of the government's financial apparatus, Hincks ended this practice and distributed the account to several banks throughout the Union[68] (C 79). The system

[64]Ibid., Receiver General's Office to R. Rawson, 26 Aug. 1842; Dunn to S.B. Harrison, 12 Dec. 1842.

[65]*JLA*, 1844–45, Appendix 5. The bigger institutions did, however, have an advantage over the smaller (C 80).

[66]D. Owram, " 'Management by Enthusiasm': The First Board of Works of the Province of Canada, 1841–46," *Ontario History* LXX (1978), p. 171.

[67]R.S. Longley, "Francis Hincks and Canadian Public Finance," CHA, *Annual Report* (1934), p. 35.

[68]Ibid.; PAC, RG 19 B2, vol. 1174, Dunn to Forsyth Richardson and Co., 10 Oct. 1843.

against which the Bank of Upper Canada had fought since 1822 had finally ended, but not, as it turned out, in a wholly satisfactory manner. Under the new arrangements the larger Bank of Montreal received the major portion of government funds and, accordingly, enjoyed the major share of public works business.[69]

A final unpleasant alteration of the bank's relationship with the government occurred in the mid-1840s. Taking advantage of the fact that the imperial loan provided the province with large current balances, the new receiver general, William Morris, in September 1844 demanded that all banks pay interest on public accounts. Perhaps because the Bank of Upper Canada received only one-sixth the amount of funds deposited in the Bank of Montreal, it initially refused to comply. Unsympathetic, the receiver general cancelled his deposit on September 30. Ten days later Morris accepted Ridout's offer of $3^{1}/_{2}$ per cent on all daily balances![70] (C 81).

Clearly, the bank's relations with the colonial government had undergone marked change since the later 1830s. In this context, the decision to rely on the government for a major portion of the bank's business had proved extremely short-sighted. The 1840s demanded an alternative strategy.

The dramatic increase in local competition, however, made significant operating adjustments difficult. By 1844 both the Commercial Bank and the Bank of Montreal operated more "Out Stations" in Upper Canada than did the Bank of Upper Canada.[71] Peter McGill emphasized that the "prosperity of Montreal and Quebec depend principally on the commerce of the fertile regions of the West . . ." and the bank's directors congratulated themselves on the fact that "the business of the Bank has been increased considerably by the establishment in the Western Sec-

[69]PAC, RG 7 G14, vols. 46 and 48 contain information on distribution of the receiver general's account in 1844 and 1847. See also RG 19 B2b, vol. 1174, Turquand to Steven, 19 Feb. 1844. To ensure good relations, Holmes, cashier of the Bank of Montreal, acted as a surety for Turquand, the deputy receiver general. PAC, Bank of Montreal, Resolve Book 4, p. 90, 9 Jan. 1844.

[70]PAC, RG 19 B2b, vol. 1174, Morris to J. Cury, 31 Sept. 1844; Morris to Ridout, 9 Oct. 1844.

[71]See returns filed by the various banks in PAC, RG 19 B2a, vol. 1143; quote from ibid., Harper to Turquand, 11 Mar. 1844. Bank of Montreal, Resolve Book 4, pp. 58–59, 232, 450–51.

tion of the Province, of several Branches and Agencies. . . ."[72]
To underwrite this expansion, in 1845, the Bank of Montreal
raised £250,000 more paid-up capital, making its total £750,000.
By 1848, 58 per cent of the bank's full-time employees and eight
of its nine part-time agents worked in the western district.[73] The
smaller Gore Bank attempted, within the limits of its capital, to
stake claim to the area west of Hamilton, and the much larger
Bank of British North America operated at least two and probably
more outlets in the upper colony.

With some reluctance, Ridout and Proudfoot responded by
increasing from eight to twelve agencies in 1845 and adding an
additional outlet in 1846.[74] They also, in common with the
Commercial Bank, attempted to increase their capital from
£200,000 to £500,000. Unlike the Bank of Montreal, both Upper
Canadian banks experienced great difficulty in attracting new
investors. Despite receiving legislative permission to open offices
and sell stock directly in London, the Bank of Upper Canada
obtained only £71,000 by December 1845. At decade's end, the
bank fell £120,000 short of its goal (Table 12 C).

The degree to which the Bank of Upper Canada attempted to
shift its focus from government business to that of general trade
and commerce is difficult to ascertain. Sources which provide
information on the internal operations of the bank in the 1840s are
very scarce. On the basis of some financial data and scattered
literary evidence, however, some conclusions can be offered.

The bank's note issue conformed closely to the seasonal swings
of Upper Canada's wheat and lumber economy. As Figure 1
indicates, on average the note issue of the Bank of Upper Canada
and of its major competitors peaked in the February to April and
September to October periods. It bottomed out in the summer
months. This fluctuation in circulation suggests that the bank
provided capital in September-October to facilitate the purchase
of that season's harvest and in the winter and early spring to allow

---

[72]C.J. Cuneo, "Surplus Labour in Staple Commodities: Merchant and Early
Industrial Capitalism," *Studies in Political Economy* VII (1982), p. 68; Bank of
Montreal, Resolve Book 4, p. 95, 26 Jan. 1844.

[73]Ibid., pp. 232, 450–51.

[74]PAC, RG 19 B2a, vol. 1143, Ridout to Turquand, 12 Mar. 1844; vol. 1146,
Ridout to Morris, 17 Dec. 1845, 12 June 1846.

lumberers and produce merchants to bring to market the results of the previous season's efforts.[75]

Figure 1 also suggests that the Bank of Upper Canada's peaks and troughs were somewhat less dramatic than those of most of its competitors. In particular, the bank's note issue exhibited only a shallow decline in the summer months. One explanation for this summer stability is that the Bank of Upper Canada financed more public works projects and could, therefore, circulate more of its notes in the peak summer construction period.

As Table 7 indicates, during the middle years of the 1840s, when canal construction was at its peak, the Bank of Upper Canada issued more of its bank notes in the summer than did any of its resident Upper Canadian competitors. The fact that the Bank of Montreal also experienced a relatively marginal summer decline and that that bank was heavily involved in public works projects provides further support for this conclusion.[76] The pattern of the Bank of Upper Canada's note issue, then, suggests that Ridout and Proudfoot did not significantly alter their general operating strategy. While not ignoring general commercial affairs, they continued to rely as much as possible on government preferment.

The average behaviour depicted in Figure 1 masks the economic and financial drama of the 1840s. In some ways it was a decade of spectacular growth. Population doubled. The government expended £1,500,000 stg. on canal construction. In the ten years following 1837 over $2,500,000 was invested in agricultural land. Between 1842 and 1851 wheat production increased by nearly 300 per cent. While precise figures for Upper Canadian wheat exports are not available, one estimate suggests that exports per farm expanded from forty-five bushels in 1845 to eighty bushels in 1850.[77]

Interestingly, bank profits did not show a corresponding increase. Profit as a percentage of paid-in capital averaged 7 per cent over the decade for the Bank of Upper Canada and the Bank

[75]This analysis is consistent with the comments of A. Shortt, "Lord Sydenham's Measures," *JCBA* x (1902–3), pp. 28–29; R.C. McIvor, *Canadian Monetary Banking*, p. 47 and T.G. Ridout in Report on Currency, 1830, 29.

[76]The more dramatic rise in the note issue of the Montreal bank is due to the payment of customs duties in Montreal and Quebec.

[77]John McCallum, *Unequal Beginnings: Agriculture and Economic Development in Quebec and Ontario Until 1870* (Toronto, 1980), p. 15; Cuneo, "Surplus Labour in Staple Commodities," p. 66; Pentland, "The Role of Capital in Canadian Economic Development Before 1875," pp. 461–63.

of Montreal. Both figures fell far below the respective averages for the 1830s and the early 1850s. While comparable profit figures cannot be determined for the Commercial Bank in this decade, it is clear from dividend payments, contingency fund additions and stock prices that the Kingston bank enjoyed more stable profits than its major competitors.

Why, then, did the Bank of Upper Canada not realize greater profits in this period of significant economic growth? In the first place development was uneven. In 1840 and 1841 crops were good, markets strong, exports high and expectations of future expansion via the large imperial loan pervasive. In these two years all banks realized substantial profits. Due to a slumping economy in Great Britain and the United States, however, a severe downturn occurred in the spring of 1842 and continued until the autumn of 1843.[78] In part, bank behaviour reflected this economic malaise. Instead of an increasing note issue following the 1842 harvest, the Bank of Upper Canada's circulation fell 24 per cent by the end of November. The Gore and Commercial banks experienced similar declines.[79] Banks tightened discounts and the merchant community found itself without access to ready capital.

The behaviour of the Upper Canadian banks in curtailing discounts and restricting note issues was not simply a response to the general economic downturn. Two further factors account for the banking community's reluctance to assist merchants during this troubled economic period. Impending changes in the colony's currency laws – which, by adjusting coinage values, would have the effect of almost equalizing exchange rates between Upper and Lower Canada – put the banks, according to one merchant, "into a perfect panic . . . and they will do nothing until they see what effect its operation will have upon their circulation"[80] (C 71). In addition to cutting circulation, banks attempted to unload on the public and their competitors all the specie they believed would be devalued by the new law. Astute noteholders, unsure which coin would be devalued, waited until the law came into force at the end of April 1842, and then presented their notes for payment. The ensuing run on the banks

---

[78]McCalla, *The Upper Canada Trade*, chapter 4.
[79]Calculated from figures in *JLA*, 1849, Appendix Z.
[80]A. Shortt, "Currency and Exchange as Influenced by the Union," *JCBA* x (1902–3), pp. 25–40.

BANK OF UPPER CANADA $2 AND $5 NOTES, 1852, 1861 *Currency Museum,*
Bank of Canada (photographer Zagon, Ottawa)

BANK OF UPPER CANADA BUILDING, ADELAIDE AND GEORGE
STREETS, TORONTO, c. 1859 *Metropolitan Toronto Library T 30675*

BANK OF UPPER CANADA, ONE PENNY TOKEN *Currency Museum, Bank of
Canada (photographer Zagon, Ottawa)*

caused further curtailment of discounts and note issues and thus contributed to the general commercial deterioration.

The second factor relates to the provincial government's reliance on the banking community for funds throughout 1842. As mentioned above, all banks willingly accommodated the government. This resulted in the commercial community complaining "of a want of accommodation" and "great inconvenience." Even the receiver general admitted that "it is not advisable for Government to employ Banking capital which more or less deprives the commercial community of that accommodation" (C 73).

It is interesting to note, too, that while the Bank of Upper Canada curtailed discounts and note issues, it, in common with the Commercial Bank, did not curtail profit-taking. In the process of raising new capital, the two major Upper Canadian banks in 1843 issued substantial bonuses to old stockholders. Despite realizing the lowest rate of profits since its first year of operation,[81] the Bank of Upper Canada paid out £32,617 in dividends, reducing its contingency fund from £26,600 to £4,900. The Commercial paid out £36,000, reducing its fund from £31,291 to £7,992. As a result neither bank could well handle a sustained economic downturn.

It seems clear that factors other than the general economic situation affected banking behaviour in this period. Banks operated in ways which (they conceived) would best suit their interests. In the long term, their profits were obviously tied to the economic fortunes of the wider community. In the short term, opportunities for profit maximization and for profit-taking – dumping suspect coin, large dividend payouts – existed which operated against the economic interest of the wider commercial community. The Bank of Upper Canada was not alone in availing itself of these opportunities.

Fortunately for the bank, the rapid infusion of capital for canal construction, economic upswings in England and the United States, continued good harvests in Upper Canada and the passage of the Canada Corn Act in 1843 all contributed to a buoyant economy in the middle years of the 1840s. The Canada Corn Act applied only a nominal duty of one shilling per quarter on all Canadian wheat entering Great Britain. In addition, it defined as

---

[81]Measured as a percentage of paid-in capital.

Canadian any flour milled in Canada and shipped out of the St. Lawrence. Despite the existence of a small tariff designed to protect Upper Canadian farmers, American producers took full advantage of this imperial legislation and exports out of the St. Lawrence boomed between 1844 and 1847.[82] American legislation in 1845 and 1846 further stimulated the export of Upper Canadian produce. Called the Drawback Acts, these measures allowed all Canadian flour destined for Great Britain to be shipped, free of tariff charges, across the border, down the Erie Canal and out of the port of New York.

In this context, banks operating in Upper Canada had several courses open to them. They could, like the Bank of Montreal, concentrate on government business and on facilitating the shipment of produce down the Great Lakes and out the ports of Montreal and Quebec. In this way the Bank of Montreal tied itself firmly to the traditional British-colonial economic relationship.[83] After 1846, when the major portion of the imperial loan had been expended, that bank became almost totally reliant on the traditional trading relationships – a preferred position in the British marketplace – for its major profits.

The Bank of Upper Canada also sought as much government business as it could. Probably to a degree greater than the Bank of Montreal, and like the Commercial Bank, it financed Upper Canadian-American as well as Upper Canadian–British trade.[84] Despite this relative diversification, the Bank of Upper Canada, in certain important ways, relied on the continuation of the traditional imperial economic connection. Following the Canada Corn Act of 1843, Ridout and Proudfoot seem to have underwritten expansion within the Canadian milling industry. That expansion was in part dependent on the imperial definition of Canadian flour and on the continuance of a preferred British market. Change in either of these conditions would cause American producers to ship via the cheaper New York route and thus cause contraction within the milling sector in Canada.

The bank's operating strategy depended on British lawmakers in a second way. The British Navigation Acts provided a priv-

---

[82]*JLA*, 1849, Appendix Z.
[83]See Cuneo, "Surplus Labour in Staple Commodities," and Denison, *Canada's First Bank: A History of the Bank of Montreal*, II (Toronto, 1967).
[84]That the two banks did so is probably less a reflection of conscious strategy on their part than a consequence of the fact that most Upper Canadian merchants participated in both trade avenues.

ileged position to shippers of British or colonial registry. Some of these privileges related to the shipping trade on inland waters, in particular on the Great Lakes.[85] This protection, coupled with the increased export of flour and grain from Upper Canada and the increased immigration into Upper Canada in the 1840s, stimulated the development of a local shipbuilding industry. Not only did the bank provide funds for this sector, it also underwrote the activities of several of the major shippers in this period. The protection afforded the local shippers by the Navigation Acts was one important factor in the success of both shipbuilding and shipping enterprises.

These tendencies can be more clearly determined by an examination of banking affairs following the general economic crisis in the western world's economy and the Repeal of the Corn Laws in 1846. As in the early 1840s, economic downturns in Great Britain and the United States adversely affected Canadian commerce. This unsettling trend was, for some, further exacerbated by new imperial legislation providing for complete free trade in wheat by 1849. The abolition of colonial preference and, in 1849, the repeal of the Navigation Acts resulted in the dismantlement of the traditional imperial-colonial economic relationship. Of the three banks considered here, the one most closely tied to British markets suffered the most. In the two years following repeal, the Bank of Montreal's contingency fund fell from £82,865 to £15,250. In 1847–48 the bank suffered an estimated operating loss of 1 per cent on its paid-in capital. "All the great interests of the country," McGill explained to disgruntled shareholders in 1848, "have suffered severely"[86] (Table 3).

In point of fact, few financial institutions suffered to the extent of his bank. While all three banks relied on short-term financing from their respective British agents, the Montreal bank's situation was so severe that its normal agreement "was virtually abrogated"[87] (C 94, C 95). The Commercial Bank realized a profit of between 7 and 8 per cent on paid-in capital in 1848. It increased its contingency fund by some £4,000 over 1846. The price of its stock remained strong throughout the 1847–49 period (C 93). That the Commercial Bank continued to conduct a relatively

---

[85]MTL, Broadside Collection, 21 Dec., Mr. Bethune's Speech.
[86]Cuneo, "Surplus Labour in Staple Commodities,"pp. 76–77.
[87]PAC, Glyn, Mills Papers, A545, P. McGill to Glyn, Mills & Co., 27 May 1848; PAC, Buchanan Papers, MG 24 D16, vol. 67, P. Buchanan to James Law, 15 Sept. 1848.

stable business at a time when the Bank of Montreal experienced heavy losses can be explained by differences in their operating strategies. Following 1846, Upper Canadian wheat exports continued strong, finding markets through Montreal in Quebec and the Maritimes, via the Erie Canal to Great Britain, and, after 1847, across the Great Lakes for local American consumption.[88] Not as tied to the traditional British export trade, the Commercial Bank could operate relatively insulated from changes in that sector. In this sense the Commercial Bank reflected the economic strength of Upper Canada; the Bank of Montreal reflected the problems associated with the imperial connection.

This appraisal of the conditions of two of the Bank of Upper Canada's major competitors provides a useful context from which to examine that bank's situation in the later 1840s. Following the repeal of the Corn Laws and during the general commercial crisis of the late 1840s, the bank's profits fell to a low of 2 per cent on paid-in capital in 1848, rising in 1849 to about 4 per cent. Its contingency fund declined from £13,000 in 1846 to £5,600 in 1848. Put simply, the Bank of Upper Canada stood at a rough mid-point between the Commercial and Montreal banks and this position also reflected its relative dependence on the imperial market.

Its most visible losses occurred in those areas most vulnerable to British legislation. The Niagara Harbour and Dock Company, a major shipbuilding enterprise located at Niagara, suffered a severe downturn in the later 1840s. In 1848 the company owed the bank at least £12,000 in overdue debts. Many of the boats constructed by the company had been purchased by Donald Bethune, a Lake Ontario shipper. To help finance his business the bank had advanced £30,000 by 1845. Bethune declared bankruptcy in 1848.[89] Finally the bank lost an undetermined amount of money on the milling enterprises of, among others, the Gamble family.

A close look at the lending practices of the bank in this era is revealing. "I do not think the [Bank of Upper Canada] has lost

---

[88]McCallum, *Unequal Beginnings*, chapter 2 and p. 124. The differences between the operations of the Commercial Bank and the other banks might, of course, be only apparent. They could be a result of different accounting procedures although, in the Commercial's case, there were no large public defaults or rumours of same (C 93).

[89]For information and sources on these businesses, see Peter Baskerville, "Donald Bethune's Steamboat Business," pp. 135–49 and Bruce A. Parker, "The Niagara Harbour and Dock Company," *Ontario History* LXXII (1980), pp. 93–121.

much,'' Larratt Smith, an informed Toronto lawyer wrote in June 1848,

but its funds are very much tied up awaiting the wills of two or three estates being wound up and reaping the fruit of that most foolish policy of locking up their funds with two or three large houses, the failure of any of which entails a severe loss, instead of doing a more general business, and getting over a hundred securities all over the countries instead of one . . . .

Smith was referring in particular to the fortunes of three large enterprises: Ross, Mitchell and Company, a Toronto wholesale drygoods business which failed in 1847 and again, for good, in 1857; Thomas Clarkson and Company, a Toronto grain dealer; and Thorne and Parsons, millers and wholesalers in Thornhill (C 93). His comments on the restricted or narrow approach followed by the bank in its lending policies are also borne out both by the bank's past behaviour in 1838–39 and by its relationship with the Niagara Harbour and Dock Company, the Bethune steamboat business and the Gamble enterprises.

The principals of all these businesses either overlapped with or were closely connected to the bank's directorate. When the Niagara Dock Company first borrowed money, its president, William Cayley, sat on the bank's directorate. In 1843 Cayley refused to run for the bank's presidency because, he admitted, Proudfoot "has supported me on very many occasions and I am not disposed to forget it."[90] In June 1843 the company secured its liabilities by granting to Clarke Gamble, the bank's solicitor, ownership of all its assets. Although Gamble later testified that the bank knew nothing of this transfer, it is undoubtedly the case that the bank used its solicitor to hold this property, since the bank's new charter did not allow banks to accept mortgages on boats or to own and operate manufacturing enterprises.[91]

In the 1830s Donald Bethune had been a lawyer for the bank at Kingston. He had also been a substantial borrower. In the 1840s he traded on this past relationship, on the fact that his brother Angus sat on the board, and on the fact that he owed the Niagara Dock Company considerable money, which if unpaid would jeopardize the bank's loans, to obtain large advances from the Bank of Upper Canada. When Bethune's businesses appeared to be sinking in 1847, the bank accepted a note for £16,000 endorsed

[90]MTL, S.P. Jarvis Papers, Misc., W. Cayley to S.P. Jarvis, 11 Mar. 1843.
[91]Upper Canada Court of Queen's Bench, *Reports* VIII (1850–51), *Cayley* v. *McDonell et al.*, Assignees of Bethune, pp. 463–64.

by J.D. Smith, the uncle of Bethune's wife and the father of the
bank's longtime agent at Port Hope. When Smith failed to meet
the note in 1848, Ridout and Proudfoot, increasingly
"uneasy,"[92] obtained direct operating control of a number of
Bethune's boats. This contravened their 1842 charter and left the
bank open to protracted litigation and substantial losses.[93]

More than the pressure of a collapsing economy in 1848 caused
the bank to forego the use of an agent to manage Bethune's
business. Clarke Gamble, the lawyer overseeing the Niagara
Harbour and Dock Company, was himself personally indebted to
the bank. He and his legal partner, William Boulton, owed well
over £16,000, obtained, an insider wrote, via "discount(s) over
the counter" advanced by "old Tom and Proudfoot, I believe
. . ." (C 86, C 94). apparently part of these funds were used to
support the milling enterprises of Gamble's brothers, William and
John.[94] The point to note here is that on account of the irregularity
of Gamble's debt and his position as owner of the Niagara Dock
Company – which was itself in an "unsaleable"state[95] – the bank
could not afford to sue for the loans' retrieval. By the end of the
1840s the company, the steamboat operation and the Gamble
affairs were so interconnected that if one fell, all might fall. In this
situation the bank assumed ownership of the boats in a last
attempt to prop up an unstable house of cards.

The Niagara Dock Company continued to rest in Gamble's
hands and after several attempts to lease and sell it, the bank
finally took direct control in 1857. In 1870 the company still owed
the bank's trustees $31,000.[96] Bethune's business was buffeted
about in various courts, with a final and somewhat obscure
settlement not taking place until the late 1850s. Gamble and
Boulton, shrouded, according to one contemporary, "in a great
mystery," avoided legal proceedings and continued as the bank's
prime solicitors. The bank foreclosed on William Gamble's
mortgages in 1862 but Clarke Gamble became the lawyer for the
bank's trustees in 1866 and in the process became the man

---

[92]Baskerville, "Donald Bethune's Steamboat Business," p. 145.

[93]It had already contravened its charter by lending money on the security of ships.
See ibid. and Upper Canada Court of Queen's Bench, *Reports* vii (1849–52), *McDonell
v. Bank of Upper Canada* for details on the litigation and losses.

[94]University of Toronto Library, Thomas Fisher Rare Book Library [hereafter UTL-
TF], Elmsley Papers, Elmsley to E. Hale, 25 May 1848.

[95]*Cayley v. McDonell*, p. 464.

[96]Parker, "Niagara Harbour and Dock Company"; PAC, RG 19 C1, Department of
Finance, Bank of Upper Canada, vol. 1195, Real Estate Trust Account, p. 451.

primarily responsible for winding up the Bank of Upper Canada's bankrupt affairs.[97]

It is worth noting that there does not appear to be a simple political bias inherent in the bank's lending policies. Certainly old Family Compact families such as the Jarvises, Gambles and Boultons continued to borrow freely. But John D. Smith and his son, the bank's Port Hope agent, were "zealous discreet and firm reformer(s)" and Thomas Clarkson, despite Toronto Tory policy, chaired the Toronto Annexation Association in 1849[98] (C 74). In fact both tories and reformers sat on the bank's directorate in the 1840s, and in 1848 several of the more impecunious of the former were unceremoniously removed from the board and in their place William Cawthra and J.G. Goodhue, both merchants and reformers, appeared.

From one perspective the bank's lending policies in the decade had an adventuresome quality about them. The only other bank to finance the Niagara Harbour and Dock Company had been the American-based Niagara Suspension Bridge Bank. Upon its collapse in the early 1840s, the Bank of Upper Canada took over. This, and the bank's involvement with the Bethune business and several milling enterprises, suggests a willingness, surprising in view of the restrictive imperial legislation, to underwrite new and not simply mercantile enterprises. From a developmental point of view this evidence of diversification warrants note.

It would be wrong to make too much of this. In the final analysis, it seems clear that if the bank had any preference it was to underwrite, whenever possible, government activity. A second tendency, as suggested by its relative stability in 1848, was its willingness to finance Upper Canadian-American as well as Upper Canadian-British trade. Other than this, there does not appear to be a conscious policy on Ridout and Proudfoot's part to support any particular sector of either the commercial community or the fledgling industrial area. Millers, shipbuilders and merchants received credit, it seems, on the strength of their relationship to or connection with the bank's directorate and managers. Since the board was not a closed political preserve, its lending policies favoured neither party. The necessity for a personal connection, however, probably underlay Smith's depiction of the

---

[97]Elmsley Papers, Elmsley to E. Hale, 25 May 1848; Norah Storey, "William Gamble," *Dictionary of Canadian Biography* [hereafter *DCB*] xi (Toronto, 1982), p. 332.

[98]F.H. Armstrong, "Thomas Clarkson," *DCB* x (Toronto, 1972), pp. 173–74.

bank's lending to the few and ignoring the many. In an era when the value of a note was largely determined by the worth of the endorser, this policy of lending to those one knew well could make sense. Unfortunately, in the Bank of Upper Canada's case, personal connections seemed to blind the bank's managers to the real personal worth of the "friends" to whom they advanced the bank's funds. It also led them, inadvertently, towards a somewhat diversified loan policy. Decisions made in 1848 indicate that Proudfoot and Ridout had little understanding of the problems and pitfalls involved in such a course. Whether they could learn and successfully adjust remained to be seen.

D. UNDERWRITING STRUCTURAL CHANGE: THE BANK AND THE UNION, 1849–57

MOST MAJOR INDICES suggest that the decade of the 1850s was one of the most buoyant periods of economic development for Canada in the nineteenth century. The rate of growth of the Gross National Product exceeded that of any other decade. Capital imports reached $100 million, nearly tripling those of the 1840s. By 1861 some $75 million had been spent on the construction of 1,360 miles of railway in Upper Canada alone. Measured both by number and size, iron foundries, tanneries, carding, fulling, grist and saw mills all expanded. H.C. Pentland has argued that a concentration on surface exploitation – fur and timber – diminished and in their stead the production of agricultural products and home manufacturing increased.[1]

Prior to 1850 it is clear that the Bank of Upper Canada, both because of the general financial and economic structure within which it operated and because of the nature of its managers, did not systematically encourage the development of fixed capital enterprise. The question to be considered here, then, is what role did the Bank of Upper Canada play in facilitating the dramatic economic growth and the significant structural transformation which occurred in the decade and a half prior to Confederation? This section and the one following will demonstrate that the bank participated in these changes in both a direct and an indirect fashion; that the role played by the bank complemented the role played by the London investors; and that the nature of its past evolution, the particular characteristics of the ongoing structural changes and the personal capacities of its managers conditioned the quality of that participation.

I

No private financial institution was more closely involved in the economic developments of the 1850s than the Bank of Upper Canada. In part this involvement resulted from a decision taken by the bank's managers in January 1850 to apply for the position

---

[1] W.L. Marr and D.G. Paterson, *Canada: An Economic History* (Toronto, 1980), p. 19; H.C. Pentland, *Labour and Capital in Canada, 1650–1860* (Toronto, 1981), chapter 5; McCallum, *Unequal Beginnings*, p. 77. Parts of this section follow closely P. Baskerville, "The Pet Bank, the Local State and the Imperial Centre, 1850–1864," *Journal of Canadian Studies* xx, no. 3, (1985).

of the government's bank. Given Ridout and Proudfoot's past desires, the decision itself was hardly surprising. That the government selected their bank over the much larger Bank of British North America and Bank of Montreal does, however, require explanation.

During the closing years of the 1840s, the government found itself in dire financial straits. Although the imperial loan had been exhausted in 1846, public works continued and were increasingly paid for out of current revenue. With the downturn in trade in 1847–48, the major source of this revenue, customs duties, declined dramatically and expenditure outpaced revenue by 20 per cent.[2] In this situation the government looked to the Bank of British North America and the Bank of Montreal, joint government bankers, for interim assistance. Perhaps, as Receiver General Viger ruefully admitted, because of "the knowledge the Banks possess of the state of our Chest," the government met with unfavourable responses[3] (D 1). This "timidity" plus Ridout's offer to advance £50,000 at any one time (his competitors offered only £20,000) led to the Bank of Upper Canada becoming for the first time the government's official bank – a position which it held until January 1864 (D 2, D 3).

At the time the bank assumed its new role, the government continued in a pressured financial state. For the short term it borrowed from Ridout and also issued one, two and five dollar debentures for the payment of local expenses. This freed up cash to meet interest payments due in London. For the longer term it depended on the successful negotiation in London by Francis Hincks, the inspector general, of a £500,000 bond issue at a rate of 6 per cent payable in twenty-five years. At the end of October, Hincks successfully completed the sale and the government account became a prize worth possessing[4] (D 31).

And so it seemed to remain for the following six years. Between 1851 and 1856 imports doubled, exports increased by two and one half times and revenue increased by one and one half. The government's direct net liabilities decreased by slightly over £750,000 by the end of 1855. Between August 1852 and October

---

[2]M.J. Piva, "The Canadian Public Debt, 1848–56," unpublished paper presented to the CHA, Montreal, June 1980, p. 3.

[3]PAC, RG 19 B2b, vol. 1160, Viger to Hincks, 29 June 1849.

[4]PAC, RG 19 E1A, Department of Finance, Departmental Correspondence, vol. 3368, Reiffenstein to A. Galt, 25 Jan. 1859; Piva, "Canadian Public Debt," pp. 4–8.

1854, government cash on hand in the colony and in England increased from £672,839 to £1,012,933.[5]

The Bank of Upper Canada profited nicely from both the general economic upswing and from its position as government banker. Profits increased from 6 per cent return on paid-in capital in 1850 to an incredible 19 per cent return in 1854 (Table 3). Between 1850 and 1856 the bank received a slightly higher average return on capital than did its much larger rival, the Bank of Montreal. Such success was not without cost. Competitors' criticisms were echoed by the general public. Known as the Pet Bank, the Bank of Upper Canada became a favourite target for frustrated entrepreneurs and ascerbic editorial writers (D 12).

Ridout resented these attacks. He argued that the bank was often in advance to the government rather than the reverse. The receiver general's office stood by Ridout. Deputy Receiver General C.E. Anderson commented publicly on the bank's generosity (especially when compared to its predecessors) and underlined, from an administrative and economic point of view, the desirability of having one rather than several government banks (D 13).

The management of the government account did appear to be a simple and lucrative affair. Certainly the contract Ridout signed in January 1850 seemed disarmingly straightforward. The bank would collect all government monies and pay out all government cheques. It would provide exchange on London at the lowest current bank rates and provide £50,000 credit should the province require it (D 3).

The London loan and the economic upswing meant that the province only officially borrowed £20,000 from the bank and then for just three months in 1850. The provision of exchange did not seem onerous. When required to meet the twice-yearly interest payments on the government's borrowings, the bank's predecessors had required compensation "at least one month previous" to the due date and thus were never out of pocket (D 31). Although the bank did not charge for collecting and paying out government money, the indirect profits from these transactions were significant. Government payments were grist to the bank's mill. Made in Bank of Upper Canada notes, the payments were

---

[5]All calculations based on evidence in following sources: *JLA*, 1861, Appendix 3; ibid., 1863, Appendix 6; ibid., 1852, Appendix DD; PAC, RG 19 E1A, vol. 3368, Jan. 1859, Memo of Public Debt of Canada; ibid., B2b, vol. 1161, 1 Oct. 1854.

many, often small and well dispersed. The bank could count on its paper receiving a much wider and longer circulation than would have been the case in normal mercantile transactions.

As the collector and chief depository of government monies, the Bank benefited in several ways. Increased deposits provided a larger base from which to extend discounts. Ridout admitted that, on average, he relied on £75,000 of the government deposit in this way (D 31). The nature of the government revenue also operated to the advantage of the bank and to the disadvantage of its competitors. As had been in the case in the 1820s, so in the 1850s customs duties comprised the bulk of the province's income. These seasonally concentrated payments had to be paid into the Bank of Upper Canada. Since not all payees had an account at that institution other banks had to increase their discounts to meet the demand for customs money. They did this knowing that the Bank of Upper Canada would be immediately receiving their paper and would be calling on them for redemption in specie or exchange. This caused these institutions to alter their normal discounting practices and often to draw on their London agents for exchange to meet the Bank of Upper Canada's demands. Lower Canadian banks also complained that this practice resulted in a capital drain from the Lower to the Upper province and thus constituted an unfair sectional bias (D 12, D 14, D 15, D 16).

Both criticisms were to some degree valid. It should be noted, however, that competitors like the Commercial Bank also had sizeable government deposits (at interest) and could extend their discounts accordingly. And the balances against the Bank of Upper Canada at Toronto and in favour of the Lower Canadian banks far outweighed the seasonal advantage enjoyed by the Bank of Upper Canada in Lower Canada (D 31). But these are minor qualifications. Had the government account operated in the manner sketched above, the Bank of Upper Canada would have had no cause for any cavil.

Much of the criticism of the Bank's privileged role was based on the periodic publication of government accounts. These indicated that government deposits in the Bank of Upper Canada between 1851 and 1856 often approached one-half of all government funds in local banks (Table 8). In two significant ways, however, the published accounts tended to be deceptive. The floating deposits stated to be at call, especially in the Bank of Upper Canada, tended to be overstated and the government's general debt picture to be understated. The combination of these two factors ultimately put the bank into a very tight situation. To understand the beginnings of this squeeze, each of these factors must be examined.

In May 1851 Ridout, at the government's behest, altered the arrangement for paying the province's London debts. In return for a ½ per cent commission above the going rate of exchange at New York, the bank agreed to forward the semi-annual interest payments to London and wait for repayment by warrant after production of receipts[6] (D 10). The government believed that this system would "ensure without risk and on most favourable terms, the punctual payment of the interest. . . ." For its part the bank had to wait at least one month and often longer before being reimbursed. This new system was quickly extended to all government exchange requirements, with the result that the bank at times found itself upwards of £250,000 stg. out of pocket with no interest compensation, and no recognition recorded in the public accounts until receipts had been presented.[7]

The above arrangement accounts for some of the differences between the published and actual deposits. The structure of the government's financial administration accounts for the rest. Despite Hincks's reforms in 1842, central accountability for the revenue and expenditure of the provincial government had yet to be effected. In theory the inspector general and receiver general oversaw the government's finances. In practice each department continued to operate with a great deal of autonomy. As a result the receiver general, or the province's "cashier," often had no knowledge of what monies had been spent and his own private and published accounts were accordingly "so much waste paper" (D 32, D 46, D 47, D 48, E 4).

Within this financial system (or lack thereof), the Bank of Upper Canada came to play the pivotal and ultimately very risky role of facilitator. By acting as a go-between, with the receiver general as custodian of the public revenue on one side and the various government departments on the other, the bank helped to prolong a decentralized and increasingly outmoded financial apparatus. Paradoxically, while operating within this context, the bank began to underwrite the structural transformation which

[6]PAC, RG 1 E7, Executive Council, Canada, Submission to Council, 36, Taché to His Excellency, 16 May 1851.
[7]PAC, RG 19 E2a, vol. 2745, Ridout to Taché, 26 Oct. 1854; QUA, Magill Papers, p. 222.

rendered that apparatus obsolete. Unfortunately, the habits it acquired in this period proved to be so deeply ingrained that it became a casualty of the very processes it helped initiate.

Public works expenditures provide a good example of that system at work. Acting simply on the signature of the commissioner, secretary or resident engineer of that department, Ridout advanced money to contractors. He then sent the certificates to the receiver general who, via an order-in-council, issued a warrant for repayment. While this proved to be an ideal way to issue the bank's notes, the bank was again out-of-pocket for sums not recorded in the receiver general's books for upwards of a month[8] (D 32, D 46, D 47, D 48, E 4). Because of the lack of central accountability, the bank ran the risk of various departments overspending their alloted money or, in the case of the Public Works Department, of various contractors exceeding their expenses and thus of the receiver general refusing to reimburse the bank for what were, from his point of view, unsanctioned advances[9] (E 6, E 111). The Bank of Montreal had temporarily quit as the government bank over just such a situation in 1845.[10]

Obviously, as Ridout's letters in February 1855 to Begley, secretary to the Department of Public Works, indicate, the bank considered these risks well worth taking[11] (D 35, D 36). It could be, as John Langton, the auditor general, suggested, that Ridout discounted these advances to the contractors; if so, the business probably equalled any other that the bank could obtain[12] (D 48). In this rather casual and somewhat protected fashion, Ridout fell into the routine of advancing money for fixed capital development. Like most habits, it fed on itself. Once commenced, it was difficult to accept reasons to stop. Even more insidious, as time progressed, the degree of government protection became increasingly difficult to define.

The bank, then, profited in various ways from the public account even though the money at its disposal was rarely of the

[8]*JLA*, 1854, Appendix JJ, Second Report of Standing Committee on Public Accounts, Ridout testimony, pp. 94–105.

[9]PAC, RG 58 B2b, Auditor General's Records, vol. 1, Langton to Cayley, 4 Feb. 1857; ibid., RG 19 E1A, vol. 3367, Woodside to Rose, 28 Apr. 1858; ibid., RG 11, Department of Public Works Records, vol. 636, pp. 19953–55.

[10]PAC, RG 11, vol. 6, B. Holmes to H. Killaly, 22 Sept. 1845; ibid., vol. 119, H. Killaly to D. Daly, 25 Nov. 1845; PAC, RG 19 B2A, vol. 1145, P. McGill to A. Morris, 24 Nov. 1845.

[11]PAC, RG 11 A1, 22, Ridout to Begley, 13 Feb. 1855.

[12]Magill Papers, p. 241A.

magnitude the public imagined and rarely even of the size the receiver general believed. At a time of dramatic economic growth the ultimate pitfalls inherent in this loose financial system could be ignored. Before extending this analysis into the era of economic recession following 1856, however, the second deceptive characteristic of the government accounts – the understatement of its debt – requires comment.

In the aftermath of the dismantlement of the British mercantile system a spirit of economic nationalism emerged in the Canadas.[13] In policy terms this took the form of a gradual increase in tariff protection for "home manufacturers" and a dramatic increase in state support for railroad construction. The Guarantee Act of 1849 provided the government's guarantee for interest on loans up to 6 per cent for all railroads of seventy-five miles or longer. The guarantee would apply once half of the construction had been completed.

British capitalists were not impressed. Glyn and Baring, the government's London agents, advised that Canada should extend the guarantee to principal as well as interest. Acting on the advice of Francis Hincks, the Canadian government went one step further and in 1851 passed legislation which not only provided the government guarantee on principal as well as interest for certain designated "trunk" railroads, but also allowed those roads to raise capital via the issuance of provincial bonds.[14] Under this system the government had guaranteed £4.4 million stg. in loans to railroad companies by the end of 1855 (Table 9).

Few believed that the government would have to take responsibility for these debts; as a result their increasing size received only passing mention in the period under review.[15] Looking back from the vantage point of 1863, John Langton commented:

The Railway debt was only nominally a burden upon the country, as the interest upon it was not paid by the Province, while the expenditure of such a large sum, with much more from other sources, gave an immense stimulus to trade, and increased our revenues beyond the ordinary requirements of those years. The consequence was, that, although we continued to expend largely upon other public improvements, and although the increased expense of living and the abundance of funds caused a heavy addition to almost every branch of the ordinary expenditure of the country, yet during those four

---

[13]See A.A. Den Otter, "Alexander Galt, the 1859 Tariff and Canadian Economic Nationalism," *CHR* LXIII (1982), pp. 151–78.

[14]Provincial debentures commanded a higher premium than railroad bonds, even if the latter were guaranteed by the province; see Piva, "Canadian Public Debt," pp. 10–12.

[15]See Galt's budget speech in *JLA*, 1861, Appendix 3.

years our net liabilities (excluding the Railway debt) had been diminished to the extent of $3,000,000.[16]

The prevailing optimism seemed, then, warranted. It would have been surprising had the Bank of Upper Canada been able to stand apart from the buoyant development ethos of that period. The bank's special connections with government and its particular involvement in the mechanics of administering the blossoming indirect debt rendered such a stance, even had the bank's managers wished it, impossible.

The railway-government-bank link existed at several levels. The government designated the bank as the payor for all interest due on provincial bonds granted to railroads. Similar to the system for the payment of the interest due on the government's direct debt, the bank arranged for the semi-annual interest payments on behalf of the St. Lawrence and Atlantic, the Great Western; and the Ontario, Simcoe and Huron Union railway companies[17] (D 26). One important difference did exist: "the Interest [so paid] will have to be collected from those Companies on which account they [the guaranteed bonds] are issued"[18] (D 26). From the government's point of view this system lessened the chance of any abrupt default. If a railroad failed to meet its interest payments, the bank, not the British bondholder or the government, would have to absorb the first shock. The government's guarantee and credit rating would be protected and time would be available for emergency adjustments. While the bank made some profit on the exchange transactions involved, it was out of pocket a substantial and growing sum for upwards of a month several times a year. In 1851, for example, the government expected the bank to advance £115,400 stg. By January 1854, this outlay had increased to £199,690.[19] Of this sum, £53,024 represented interest on railroad debt and, as Table 9 indicates, the amounts advanced to railroads had yet to take off.

Interaction between the bank, railways and government also existed at a more informal but equally significant level. In 1851 the Bank of Upper Canada advanced money to the Great Western

[16]*JLA*, 1863, Appendix 6.
[17]PAC, RG 19 B2b, 1161, Taché to Ridout, 15 Apr., 28 July 1854.
[18]Ibid., Taché to Ridout, 12 Nov. 1853 (enclosure); 28 July 1854.
[19]Figures for 1854 calculated from ibid., Tabular Statement showing the periods which the dividends on Canadian bonds in the English market fall due in 1854, 12 Nov. 1853.

Railway[20] (D 9). The context within which these early advances occurred became the norm for future bank-government-railway relations. In the first instance the Great Western received £50,000 on the security of municipal debentures. At this period these securities lacked any semblance of a provincial guarantee and thus were unsaleable in the British market.[21] The Bank of Montreal had categorically refused to lend to the railroad on a similar security.[22] The key to Ridout's action rests with the informal pressure of Francis Hincks (D 9). Sensitive to government desires – they had just received the government account – Ridout and Proudfoot acceded to this pressure and, albeit with some reluctance, met the Great Western's wishes.

When the Great Western reappeared at the bank's door later in the year, the context had somewhat altered. The railroad requested £60,000 additional credit to be repaid by provincial debentures issued under the recently passed Main-Line Railway Act. The advances would, as the railroad's president put it, enable "the Company to *anticipate* the proceeds of those Debentures."[23] On the surface this seemed to promise the bank firmer security for its loans. In fact, much ambiguity continued to characterize the bank-government-railway relationship.

Ridout agreed to this second set of loans under the expectation that the government would provide the wherewithal for repayment. Yet no contract bound the government to protect the bank in any of these advances. Nor had the government, at the time the loans took place, agreed to give the Great Western provincial debentures at any time in the future. In fact, early in 1852 strong evidence existed which suggested the contrary. Francis Hincks, increasingly involved in the promotion of what was to become the Great Western's main rival, the Grand Trunk Railway, began to adopt a hard line toward the former road. He decreed that the Grand Trunk's gauge (5′6″) would be the national standard and any road desiring provincial aid would have to conform to that regulation. Having just entered into an agreement with American financiers for a 4′8½″ gauge, the Great Western found itself in an

---

[20]PAC, John Young Letterbook, MG 24 D80, vol. 4, R.W. Harris to Ridout, 26 Nov., 23 Dec. 1850; Harris to Proudfoot, 3 Nov. 1851.

[21]A private member's bill had enabled municipalities to aid the Great Western only. Province of Canada Statutes, 14 Vic. c. 79.

[22]PAC, Bank of Montreal, Resolve Book 5, 15 Oct. 1850.

[23]John Young Letterbook, vol. 4, Harris to Proudfoot, 3 Nov. 1851; Young to Forbes, 7 Nov. 1851.

awkward position. After protracted negotiations, the Americans compromised, the Great Western adopted the wider gauge and the government issued £200,000 of debentures in November 1852.[24] From the bank's perspective, these first series of loans can be viewed as a trial balloon. Had disaster occurred, the bank would have been wounded, but not fatally. The fact that the loans turned out to be successful – from the Great Western's, the government's and the bank's point of view – cemented an ambiguous relationship and provided a precedent for similar activity in the future.

The bank became increasingly caught up in the development mania of the era. Almost immediately Ridout and Proudfoot extended this system of interim financing (or in some cases variations of it) to other railways. Before October 1854 they advanced £155,000 to the Ontario, Simcoe and Huron Railway, £72,000 to the Buffalo, Brantford and Goderich, and an unknown amount to the St. Lawrence and Atlantic (D 18, D 31). In addition, and completely on its own initiative, the bank discounted notes of railroad contractors and issued contractors advances secured only by shares of the road under construction (D 45). In these later transactions the government did not have even an ambiguous presence.

The personal activity of Thomas G. Ridout, the bank's chief manager, parallelled these initiatives. The Great Western appointed his son as an assistant engineer. Ridout himself became an active promoter of the Great Western and its subsidiary lines, the Hamilton and Toronto, and London and Sarnia. He also became the treasurer of the Grand Trunk Railway (and soon a director) and convinced both the Great Western and the Grand Trunk to erect stations on property he owned, thus raising the value of his adjoining holdings[25] (D 20, D 21, D 22, D 42). Both the bank and its personnel became increasingly intertwined with the fortunes of Upper Canada's railways.

The Bank of Upper Canada was not the only bank to assist railway companies and contractors in this period. The Bank of Montreal provided limited short-term financing to the St. Lawrence and Atlantic and the Grand Trunk as well as discounting the

---

[24]P. Baskerville, "Americans in Britain's Backyard: The Railway Era in Upper Canada, 1850–80," *Business History Review* LV (1981), pp. 315–24.

[25]PAC, John Young Papers, vol. 1, Ridout to Young, 27 Jan., 3 Feb., 1852; PAC, RG 30, Canadian National Railway Papers, vol. 1000, 19 Oct. 1853; 14 Jan. 1856, Resolution 14.

notes of the Grand Trunk's principal contractors, Peto, Brassey and Company. As Merrill Denison has outlined, that bank also became rather heavily involved in financing two lines in northern New York and New England (D 25). The Commercial Bank, too, provided short-term money to the Grand Trunk.[26] The extent, rather than the fact, of involvement separated the Bank of Upper Canada's activities from the behaviour of its two major competitors. The nature of the government account explains the different degrees of participation.

Railways accounted for the largest proportion of the government's indirect debt. The second-largest percentage was that borrowed by municipalities, often to aid in the construction of various local lines. In November 1852 legislation was passed enabling municipalities to raise money for local works via bond issues. While the act creating the Consolidated Municipal Loan Fund did not explicitly designate the government as guarantor for these loans, the debentures so issued were labelled government debentures. As well, before 1855 government spokesmen often publicly assumed the posture of guarantor.[27] In the midst of this ambiguity, the Bank of Upper Canada once again played a significant role as facilitator.

Officially the receiver general's office effected all sales of municipal debentures. A record would be made of each municipality's borrowings and an official repayment schedule set up.[28] In practice the Bank of Upper Canada acted as broker or middleman in the sale of these securities. By the end of 1854 the bank and its agents had marketed 62 per cent of the £1,172,916 issued.[29] It purchased the securities outright with no guarantee from the government should it then be unable to dispose of them. On this matter the receiver general, Etienne Taché, was adamant (D 33). In this context, then, the bank saved the government a significant and possibly risky short-term outlay. And it did so without any charge to the government for the service.

[26]PAC, Glyn, Mills Papers, A 545, A. Simpson to Glyn, Mills, 4 July 1853 (private and confidential); Denison, *Canada's First Bank,* II, chapter 3.

[27]Province of Canada Statutes, 16 Vic. c. 22, "An Act to Establish a Consolidated Municipal Loan Fund for Upper Canada"; *JLA,* 1854, Appendix JJ, Second Report of Standing Committee on Public Accounts; Dickinson testimony, question 137.

[28]Ibid., Dickinson testimony, questions 122–25.

[29]Calculated from information in: *JLA,* 1861, Sessional Paper, vol. 3; PAC, RG 19 B2b, vol. 1162, Memo of Bonds received by Bank of Upper Canada, Feb. 1855; Magill Papers, p. 216. Of the £722,316 placed by the bank £154,416 were taken up by the government's special funds.

The province also relied on the bank to keep the market for these securities at par or better. As the letter from the deputy receiver general, C.E. Anderson, to John A. Macdonald in August 1855 suggests, whenever a large block of debentures threatened to come on the market at a discount, the bank purchased and held the same until either it or the government could dispose of them at a satisfactory price. In this particular instance it is worth noting that the bank held the £25,000 for eight months longer than had been pledged (D 41). The bank, of course, routinely received 6 per cent on these bonds and on its general advances to railroad companies. It was to that extent hardly out of pocket. The ultimate problem with this system related more to the bank's overall liquidity and in particular to its ability to serve simultaneously the government and the wider commercial community. To evaluate the bank's ability to serve both sectors in this period, a close look at its general business activity is required.

Similar to most other economic areas, the financial sector expanded rapidly in the early 1850s. Six new banks appeared. Almost all the existing banks received capital increases. Between 1852 and 1856 paid-up capital grew by 62 per cent. Expansion occurred at such a pace that, as Ridout's letter to Anderson in August 1856 suggests, the established institutions had no time to evaluate the worth of the new entries[30] (D 54).

Ridout and Proudfoot responded aggressively to this competition. Although they experienced difficulty placing shares in England, the bank's paid-up capital increased by 20 per cent more than the average gain for all banks between 1850 and 1856 (D 50). Not only did they keep pace with branch expansion in Upper Canada, but they also increased their presence in Lower Canada by adding, to their branch in Montreal, one in Quebec City and an agency in Three Rivers. The Quebec branch, opened to handle the government account when the capital was at that city, proved to be very profitable, netting £50,000 during its first eight years of operation.[31]

---

[30]PAC, RG 19 B2b, vol. 1162, Provincial Banks, 15 Dec. 1855. The Free Banking Act of 1850, while designed to increase banking facilities by permitting any person or corporation to engage in banking after depositing certain securities with the government, failed in this regard largely because much of the bank's assets would be tied up in those relatively low yield securities. See A. Shortt, "Free Banking and Currency Amendments," *JCBA* x (1902–1903), pp. 12–29.

[31]PAO, Mackenzie-Lindsey Papers, *Journal of Banking, Commerce and Finance*, 1859; *Cases in the Privy Council*, I (1867), *Bank of Upper Canada* v. *J.L. Bradshaw*, p. 480.

To meet general business demand and competitive pressure, Ridout and Proudfoot engaged in capital creation to a degree greater than at any time in their past. While the circulation of all banks increased by 194 per cent between 1850 and 1854, the Bank of Upper Canada's increased by 284 per cent. Its reserve ratio declined from 25.6 per cent in 1850 to 10.2 per cent in 1855–56 (Table 2). Of the eight largest chartered banks, the Bank of Upper Canada had the lowest reserve ratio between 1854 and 1856.[32] This ratio, of course, could mean many things. In the 1820s and 1830s the bank had also engaged in capital creation. Under the aegis of William Allan, it had done so within a conservative frame and had progressed satisfactorily.

What steps did Ridout and Proudfoot take to protect their large circulation? They issued a good percentage of their notes as payments to government employees and as wages for labourers on public works and railway construction. This circulation was considered to be safe. The notes were widely dispersed and rarely came back upon the bank as quickly as notes issued in connection with mercantile affairs. In a larger sense, bankers regarded the Canadas in the early 1850s as a banking paradise. "[T]he people of Canada," one banker commented, "were foolish enough and rich enough to hold bank notes to an amount relatively only second to Ireland, the best circulating country in the world for the Banks, but a fact that tells against their thrift and knowledge of the value of money." In common with most of its competitors, the Bank of Upper Canada took full advantage of this tendency of the rural population to hoard their notes "in old chests, 'holes in the wall' and other outlandish natural Banks of deposit," and profited accordingly (D 63).

Discounts also rose dramatically. In 1854 they were 2.7 times greater than in 1850 and this increase exceeded that of the banking sector as a whole by 0.5 times. That almost one-third of the bank's discount increase (28 per cent) occurred between July 1850 and June 1851 can be attributed to the acquisition of the government account and to a general increase in commercial activity (tables 11 and 12 B). Railway borrowing accounted for less than 15 per cent of that year's growth. By contrast, during 1853 and 1854, when the largest spurt in discounts occurred, (46 per cent of the total gain) railway financing probably accounted

---

[32]Calculated from figures in Province of Canada, *Journals of the Legislative Council* [hereafter *JOLC*], 1856, Appendix 2.

for close to half of the increase.[33] These aggregate figures suggest that as the mid-decade approached, Ridout and Proudfoot allotted an ever larger percentage of their new business to fixed capital enterprises. It also suggests that railroad financing did not dominate the bank's overall business; it continued to expand in other areas as well.

Legislation passed in 1850 underlay this general expansion. Prior to that date banks were in a very ambiguous legal position concerning their right to acquire property. "An Act to confer certain rights upon the Chartered Banks," quietly passed in 1850, made it legal for banks to purchase at sheriffs' sales any land mortgaged to them "by way of additional security for debts." The legislation placed no limit upon the amount of land so acquired. Nor did it place any limit on the length of time a bank could own such land. In 1856 this latitude was extended to mortgages on ships and "other personal property in this province" taken by way of collateral security.[34]

The Bank of Upper Canada took full advantage of this legislation. Land values, which had been increasing since the Union, experienced their greatest spurt in the 1852–56 period. In common with many others, Ridout and Proudfoot personally speculated heavily in the real estate market[35] (E 5). So too, in terms of its discounts, did the institution they managed. As early as June 1852, 12.4 per cent of all debts owed were in the form of mortgages. Interestingly, after this date the bank usually hid this figure within its general discounts, although the law required a finer breakdown. This suggests that the amount of mortgage debt increased rapidly as the decade progressed. And, as the investigation of the bank's position subsequent to 1857 will reveal, such was indeed the case.

In addition to expanding discounts on the basis of land as collateral security, the bank relied on the backing of its growing deposits. Between 1850 and 1854 deposits almost doubled. Throughout the period they exceeded the value of notes in circulation. Before a parliamentary committee in 1854 Ridout,

[33]Calculated from various sources, the most important being PAC, RG 30, 5 and *JLA*, 1854, Appendix EE.

[34]Province of Canada Statutes, 14 Vic. c. 22, "An Act to confer certain rights upon the chartered banks of this province and to declare the rights already possessed by them in certain cases"; ibid., 18 Vic. c. 71, "An Act to Amend and Consolidate the Acts forming the Charter of the Bank of Upper Canada." See Appendix 2 for 1856 act.

[35]For Proudfoot see Glyn, Mills Papers, A 542, Proudfoot to Glyn, Mills, 2 Aug. 1858.

the picture of prudence, assured a hostile MP, Luther Holton, that the bank relied on only £75,000 of its large government deposit and 50 per cent of its private deposits for the purpose of discounting. In fact, however, figures provided by Ridout to that committee and to the Legislative Council tell a different story.

Bank of Upper Canada Average Principal Assets and Liabilities, 1853–54

Specie – £98,430 cy.	Capital – £498,000
Discounts – £1,657,590	Notes in
	circulation – £641,590
	Deposits: 1) Private – £536,000
	2) Gov't. – £311,000

A brief glance at this simplified balance sheet suggests that Ridout severely understated his use of deposits for discounts (D 31). To have working capital (capital, minus 10 per cent lodged in public securities with the government, plus notes, plus deposits) equal to discounts, he would have had to rely on closer to 92 per cent of average private deposits. Not only was this ratio far in excess of what Ridout claimed to rely on, but it also far exceeded the 66 per cent figure the manager of the Bank of British North America declared to be the maximum permissible.[36] Obviously the Bank of Upper Canada operated extremely close to the edge and had little liquid margin available to it at a time of crisis.

Suggestions of a major problem surfaced in the summer of 1854. In power since 1851, the Hincks-Morin ministry began to fall apart under the strong attack of both more reform and more conservative-minded opponents.[37] Given its relationship with the government, the bank became the centre of many of these criticisms. Rumours that it had misused the government deposit, over-extended itself, and diverted resources from the mercantile community prompted demands for a public inquiry into the nature of the government account. Amidst this political censure, pressure on the bank's financial resources took two forms. In May the Great Western upped its borrowings to £218,000 (Table 10) and at that time had no specific guarantee from the government concerning the issuance of more government debentures. Increasingly worried, Ridout urged the railway's directors to

---

[36]*JOLC*, 1856, Appendix 2. For an analogous use of working capital, see A. Shortt, "The Crisis of 1857–58," *JCBA* xi (1903–1904), pp. 206–207. Ridout may well have relied more heavily on the government deposit, but the risks here were of an even higher magnitude, given that deposit's relative volatility.

[37]See J.M.S. Careless, *The Union of the Canadas* (Toronto, 1967), pp. 189–92.

press for immediate government assistance. After much lobbying, the railway succeeded in freeing up £300,000 stg. in June.
An inactive British market, however, prevented the sale of these
bonds until late September. In the interim the bank extended its
advances to £317,108, a figure equal to approximately 17 per cent
of its debts due and 75 per cent of its paid-in capital[38] (D 27,
D 28, D 29, D 30).

In part because a high percentage of railway loans took the
form of notes rather than exchange, the bank's circulation
increased by 78 per cent between June 1853 and October 1854
(Table 12 B). The bank attempted to protect its increasingly
extended position by curtailing circulation in August 1854 and by
importing four times as much specie between March 1853 and
March 1855 as it had in the two previous years.[39]

Even while Ridout and Proudfoot undertook these protective
measures, a further and ominous pressure on the bank's resources
began to be felt. Between October 1853 and October 1854,
private deposits dropped by 40 per cent.[40] Commencing in July
1854, the government also began to exert heavy pressure on its
deposits. The establishment of an imprest account allowed the
receiver general to withdraw large sums on no notice to meet
special needs. Such withdrawals often went unrecorded in the
public accounts and the bank did not receive interest on any
overdrafts. And according to the bank's figures, in October 1854
the government had overdrawn its current account by some
£28,000.[41]

Due to the collapse of the Hincks-Morin government in late
June and an election in July and August, an inquiry into the bank's
affairs did not take place until October. By that time it had
received money from the sale of the Great Western debentures in
England. Thus Ridout could truthfully testify that most major
railway advances had been repaid and that the government
account was not the unmixed blessing that many assumed it to be
(D 31). While this testimony tended to quiet many of the bank's
critics, it did not solve all of the bank's problems.

Lower revenues, the coming due of large bond repayments and

---

[38]Albany Institute of Art and History [hereafter AI], Corning Papers, W. Longsdon
to E. Corning, 31 July 1854; PAC, RG 30, 2, 9 June 1854.
[39]*JOLC*, 1856, Appendix 2.
[40]Calculated from figures in *JLA*, 1854, Appendix EE, no. 1, Weekly Statement, 1
Jan. 1853–23 Oct. 1854.
[41]Ibid., no. 2, Weekly Balances . . . 1 Jan. 1853–23 Oct. 1854.

inept investments of government money by Taché and Hincks contributed to the continuing decline of the government account throughout 1855. In February, for example, Taché admitted that his current balances at the Bank of Upper Canada were "completely exhausted" (D 33). Faced with increased government penury, Ridout attempted to restrict his business and, as his correspondence with the receiver general in September 1855 suggests, look for every means to increase the bank's liquid capital[42] (D 44).

Despite his avowed intentions, advances to the Great Western topped £120,000 in January, payments to Glyn, Mills and Company, his London agents, fell temporarily in arrears in July, the Grand Trunk received a £75,000 advance in August and, not surprisingly, the bank's circulation continued to expand throughout 1855 and into the first quarter of 1856. Perhaps reflecting this evidence of Ridout's failure to curtail business, the bank's stock began to sell at a discount for the first time in several years[43] (D 40).

Financial affairs worsened throughout 1856. For the first time the real nature of the government's debt situation became clear. In January the Ontario, Simcoe and Huron Railway defaulted on interest payments due on its government-guaranteed loan. In April the Grand Trunk admitted that it could not meet the interest on its bonds and approached the inspector general "for advice." In May the bank, already overdrawn at its London agents, learned that it would have to meet the Grand Trunk payments as well as the government's normal half-yearly interest payments in London on July 1[44] (D 49). The government had to borrow £100,000 from Barings and Glyn to meet the July payments. Pressed by the government, the bank did advance £42,900 to the Grand Trunk to enable it to meet interest payments due in the United States and £12,166 to the Ontario, Simcoe and Huron Railway so it could pay general working expenses. In addition Ridout, seemingly oblivious to the accumulating signs of impending crisis, granted the Grand Trunk a further £29,000 stg. loan, without any govern-

---

[42]PAC, RG 1 E7, vol. 42, J. Bradshaw to C.E. Anderson, 27 Sept. 1855.
[43]Ibid., RG 30, vol. 1002, 16 Aug. 1855; *JOLC*, 1856, Appendix 2; Mackenzie-Lindsey Papers, 721D, Stock Table, 1853–56.
[44]PAC, RG 30, vol. 1000, 9 Apr. 1856.

ment guarantee, so that the railway could meet its everyday working expenses[45] (D 51, D 52, D 53).

To provide for the Grand Trunk's needs, in the summer of 1856, the government passed a Relief Act which allowed the line to issue £2 million in preference bonds to rank ahead of provincially guaranteed and ordinary bonds. Although the railway could use the money for general purposes, it had also to provide assistance from it to various financially troubled feeder lines in Upper and Lower Canada.[46] This latter provision had the effect of drawing the bank even more deeply into the tangled world of government-railway financing. Initially on the government's recommendation and ultimately via negotiations directly with the Grand Trunk, the bank advanced these subsidiary lines the needed capital. Repayment would occur after the sale of the new bonds and after the feeder lines provided the Grand Trunk with suitable security. Late in July Ridout commenced a long series of such advances by issuing £13,000 to the Ottawa and Prescott Railway.[47]

Glyn, Mills and Company, heavy investors in the Grand Trunk and London agents of both the government and the bank, grew worried. In order to better protect their interests, the London bankers had T.G. Ridout appointed to the Grand Trunk's Canadian board. Suitably impressed, Ridout promised that, "as far as my abilities will allow," the interests of the British shareholders would be looked after. By the end of 1856 Ridout was the resident banker of a heavily pressed provincial government, of a near bankrupt Grand Trunk, and of that railway's chief competitor, the increasingly straitened Great Western. With the world money market already in a "rigid state," Ridout in November assured Glyn, Mills that he was "preparing for it accordingly, by reducing our daily discounts" (D 57). It was to become an all-too-familiar refrain.

Between 1850 and 1856 exports of Upper Canadian wheat doubled in volume and tripled in value. For the first five of those years crop yields fluctuated between average and excellent, and markets – especially between 1854 and 1856 when the

---

[45]PAC, RG 1 E8, Executive Council of Canada, State Records, Taché to His Excellency, 30 May 1856; Ibid., RG 19 B2b, vol. 1162, Memo of Advances to Grand Trunk since 1 April 1856, 23 Oct. 1856.

[46]A.W. Currie, *The Grand Trunk Railway of Canada* (Toronto, 1957), pp. 45, 92.

[47]*JLA*, 1858, Appendix 4, Standing Committee on Public Accounts, questions 294–344.

Reciprocity Treaty and Crimean War created new demands –
remained buoyant. Riding the wave of prosperity, importers
made record orders in 1856. That year, however, saw the end of
the Crimean War and a softening of wheat markets. This coin-
cided with the beginning of a series of poor harvests in Upper
Canada. Importers had trouble selling their wares in 1857. Downturns in the British and American economies exacerbated these
local conditions.[48] By October 1857 major American banks had
suspended specie payments.[49] Foreign capital flows into the
Canadas dried up, local land values plummeted and railroad
construction ground to a virtual halt as traffic returns on existing
lines failed to meet working expenses. The government, faced
with declining revenue (expenditure exceeded income for the first
time since 1848) and increased debt burden (in January 1857 the
Great Western joined the list of railway defaulters), searched
desperately for short- and long-term solutions to the developing
economic crisis.

In this changed context, the Bank of Upper Canada found it
increasingly difficult to exercise successfully its multi-faceted
role as facilitator. At the same time the government required that
assistance more than at any time in its past. Mutual need led to
adjustments. In January the bank paid ''Interest on a portion of
the Public Debt'' in London (£205,000) and was reimbursed by
the sale of £150,000 stg. 6 per cent provincial debentures credited
to its London account. Not paid, but listed as ''transmitted'' in the
public accounts for the year ending December 1856, however,
was the £60,000 stg. required for the sinking fund set up to retire
the imperial loan of 1842. Because the bank was ''not in funds,''
it did not send over any money on that account in 1856. Nor did it
meet a similar payment required for 1857, although the public
accounts for that year were as ambivalent as they had been a year
previous.

This did not mean that the bank received and used for its own
purposes £60,000 stg. from the government. Rather the receiver
general held warrants ready for issuance upon receipt of proof of
payment. Since neither the bank nor the government was out of
pocket, neither desired to press the other and so it went until the

---

[48]See McCallum, *Unequal Beginnings*, chapter 4; McCalla, *Upper Canada Trade*,
chapter 7.

[49]PAO, Merritt Papers, vol. 34, W.H. Merritt, Jr. to W.H. Merritt, Sr., 14 Oct.
1857.

close questioning of the Committee on Public Accounts for 1858 brought the episode to light and the government then hastily sent over the delinquent sums.[50]

Unfortunately for the bank, the government expected other, more onerous kinds of accommodation. The receiver general's account remained overdrawn an average of £78,400 between November 1856 and May 1857.[51] Advances issued to various railway companies on account of the government in 1856 remained unpaid and increased in 1857. As the Grand Trunk sought more and more relief, the general public (incited especially by George Brown) became increasingly disillusioned and angry and consequently the government dared not approach Parliament for open grants. Instead the receiver general, J.C. Morrison, and the inspector general, William Cayley, leant heavily on the bank to provide covert relief in the form of advances to the Grand Trunk to be repaid by the province sometime in the future. By July 30 advances of this type to various railroads amounted to £180,000 (D 61).

For reasons of a more personal nature, the receiver general also took pains to assist a rival of the Bank of Upper Canada, the Zimmerman Bank, operating out of Niagara Falls. Samuel Zimmerman, almost the sole shareholder, and a major Upper Canadian railroad contractor, used this bank to underwrite many of his far-flung operations. A close friend of Zimmerman, J.C. Morrison had profited from the contractor's assistance in past elections. To repay these past kindnesses, Morrison, on his own initiative, deposited some £62,000 of government money in Zimmerman's bank. While excessive, given the bank's relatively low paid-in capital, this transaction was not illegal since the receiver general had the right to place government funds in any Canadian chartered bank. Upon Zimmerman's sudden death in May 1857, however, it turned out that the vault was empty. To prevent scandal, Morrison quickly made a paper transfer of £61,990 from Zimmerman's bank to the credit of the Bank of Upper Canada. He also relied on the latter to redeem outstanding Zimmerman Bank notes. All told, this increased the Bank of Upper Canada's obligation by some £150,000. Not only could this obligation not be publicly acknowledged, but £61,990 of it

---

[50]*JLA*, 1858, Appendix 4, questions 486–99, 659–76 and 829–43.
[51]PAC, RG 19 B2a, vol. 1149, Statement of Balances due by government to Bank of Upper Canada, 8 Nov. 1856–30 Apr. 1857, T.G. Ridout, 8 June 1857.

was listed as part of the provincial deposit at the Bank of Upper Canada from that time forward. For this particular assistance, the bank received security in the form of land from the Zimmerman estate. Over-valued, the land could not be sold and simply added to the large unsaleable securities already in the bank's possession[52] (D 59, E 27).

By July 30, and after reimbursing the bank £307,265 stg. for its half-yearly interest payments, the government admitted owing the Bank £396,227. Of this, £73,000 represented the unpaid sinking fund account and should be subtracted. On the other hand, the government did not include the Zimmerman debt, nor did it include a £24,000 payment due on account of advances to François Baby, a contractor, who had worked under government contract in the mid 1850s. Leaving aside the Zimmerman debt (securities had, after all, been provided for its ultimate repayment), the government owed £347,000 a sum representing roughly 20 per cent of all the bank's debts due and close to half the Bank's paid-in capital (D 60, D 61).

The worsening financial situation affected the bank in yet another area of its indirect government business. Prior to 1856 it had acted very efficiently in selling and maintaining a buoyant market for Municipal Loan Fund debentures. By March 1857, however, a local market could not be found and Ridout had on hand at least £150,000 of unsold debentures. Since this seriously affected the bank's liquidity, he requested the government to convert £100,000 of these to sterling bonds for sale in London[53] (D 68). Ridout hoped, in the short term, to profit from the exchange arising from this transaction, and in the medium to long term, to profit by the sale of the debentures in the larger British market. Suspicious of the ambivalent guarantee afforded these bonds by the provincial government, British investors refused to buy and the securities remained a drag on the bank's limited working capital.[54] (E 8).

---

[52]On Zimmerman's general operations and relations with Morrison, see P. Baskerville, "Americans in Britain's Backyard," pp. 324–28; P. Baskerville, "The Boardroom and Beyond: Aspects of the Upper Canadian Railroad Community," (Ph.D. thesis, Queen's University, 1973); and J.K. Johnson, "'One Bold Operator': Samuel Zimmerman, Niagara Entrepreneur, 1843–57," *Ontario History* LXXIV (1982), pp. 26–44. For specific events related here, see PAC, RG 19 B2b, vol. 1162, C.E. Anderson on Zimmerman Bank, May 1857; Canada, Financial and Departmental Commission, *First Report*, May 1863, pp. 45–46 and Evidence, pp. 156–57, 164–65 and 174–75.

[53]PAC, RG 19 B2b, vol. 1163, John Ross to Ridout, 15 May 1858.

[54]Glyn, Mills Papers, A 542, Ridout to Glyn, Mills, 24, 29 May, 27 Sept. 1858.

Throughout 1857 it is clear that the Bank of Upper Canada provided a significant degree of direct and indirect assistance to a financially strapped provincial government. The amount it had advanced, according to the government's own figures, exceeded the bank's 1850 contractual obligations by nearly seven times (D 61). This accommodation put dangerous pressure on the bank's general operations. The deepening of the financial crisis in October found it with discounts 6 per cent higher than the previous year and a circulation in excess of ten times specie in hand (Table 11). Not surprisingly, Ridout eagerly engaged in discussion with several other Upper Canadian banks in an attempt to settle monthly balances via exchange rather than specie. Since Lower Canadian banks refused to participate, the resultant agreement was largely ineffectual.[55]

Even before October, Proudfoot and Ridout, desperate for working capital, had attempted to call in the debts of some of their larger borrowers. Railways ranked high in this category. By July the Great Western owed £70,000, the Grand Trunk £60,000 (separate from government-sponsored advances) and the Zimmerman estate, £75,000 (on account of Zimmerman's railway interests). The Zimmerman estate, of course, consisted of unsaleable land. The Grand Trunk had government backing and thus required support. The Great Western became the target. Pushed by his board, Ridout reluctantly threatened to sue if prompt payment was not forthcoming. Indignant, the Great Western immediately transferred its account to the Commercial Bank and ultimately paid off its loan in October 1857[56] (D 56, D 58, D 62).

Both the government and the bank began to build up large overdrafts at their London bankers, Glyn, Mills and, in the province's case, the Baring Brothers. In mid-September Glyn wrote two letters warning Ridout to avoid advancing more funds to the Grand Trunk and to stop "depend[ing] in your operations upon such large advances from us." By mid-November the government owed its London bankers £302,000. In these circumstances and in a depressed market, Glyn and Baring sold £500,000 of provincial debentures for the lowest premium ever received. While this transaction excited a great deal of controversy during the public accounts investigation of 1858, the

---

[55]Shortt, "The Crisis of 1857–58," p. 212.
[56]The deterioration in GWR/BUC relations can also be traced in PAC, Buchanan Papers, vol. 52, Ridout to Radcliffe, 2, 29 Sept. 1856.

proceeds did pay off the overdraft and provide the government with some working capital throughout the year[57] (D 65).

The Bank of Upper Canada had no such recourse. Between 1850 and 1856 it had become an essential component of a system that provided needed short-term financing for large capital-intensive development projects. Although under heavy stress, it had continued to perform that role in 1857. The demands of that position, coupled with the results of an overly expansive general discount policy prior to 1857, were soon to take their toll.

[57]*JLA*, 1858, Appendix 4.

E.   A CASUALTY OF CHANGE: 1858–66

FOR MANY, THE ATTRACTIVENESS of the internal system that had evolved throughout the 1850s to help finance capital construction in the Canadas lay in the absence of rigid rules. The government, sundry railways, and, up to 1857, the Bank of Upper Canada had all benefited from flexible standards and informal relationships. When, under accumulated pressures, the bank began to decline after 1857, Alexander Tilloch Galt, the new inspector general, G.C. Glyn, Grand Trunk managers and Grand Trunk contractors began to push for the infusion of new, more systematic and rigid managerial standards at the bank. At the same time, failing to construct an alternative system suitable for their immediate and pressing financial needs, Galt and the Grand Trunk continued to press the faltering bank in the traditional ways. Increasingly fierce competition within the financial sector added to this pressure. Between 1855 and 1857 twelve new banks had been chartered (although not all became operative) and several new savings and loan and fire and life insurance companies commenced business.[1] In this context the Bank of Upper Canada performed its last acts as facilitator and upon completion was cut adrift to die a slow and, significantly, little-lamented death.

Aggregate statistics provide one indication of the bank's failure to cope after 1856. Measured as a percentage of total bank notes in circulation in the Canadas, the Bank of Upper Canada's share reached a record high in October 1856. It exceeded that record in the four following years. Examination of the bank's share of total discounts in the Canadas reveals a similar trend (Table 11).

In certain circumstances both indices might point to unparallelled prosperity. Reference to the bank's reserve ratio, its discounts to paid-in capital and to the behaviour of the bank's two major competitors, the Bank of Montreal and the Commercial Bank, however, underlines the fact that the Toronto bank was running out of control. In 1856 the Bank of Upper Canada ranked second in discounts and in circulation outstanding. Its discounts fell £1 million short and its circulation about £175,000 short of those of its larger rival, the Bank of Montreal. Over the next three years the gap closed and in July 1859, the Bank of Upper

---

[1] H.A. Innis and A.R.M. Lower, *Select Documents in Canadian Economic History, 1783–1885* (Toronto 1937), p. 660.

Canada's circulation exceeded that of the Montreal bank by £10,000 and its discounts fell only £250,000 short. In 1860, despite the fact that the Bank of Montreal possessed just about twice the paid-in capital, the Toronto bank attained the dubious distinction of ranking first in discounts and circulation outstanding. Although, following 1857, the Commercial Bank's paid-in capital exceeded the Bank of Upper Canada's by roughly a third, the Kingston bank fell £750,000 short in discounts and £250,000 short in circulation in 1860.[2]

In retrospect it seems clear that by late 1860 the Bank of Upper Canada was virtually in a moribund state. Evidence presented at its annual meeting that year indicated that a disproportionate amount of its discounts were locked up in overdue debt and secured by unsaleable real estate. Its stock languished some seventeen points below par while other banks were selling at 112 and 113.[3] Led by its president, William Proudfoot, some of the bank's informed shareholders (present and/or past directors) began to unload their shares between 1857 and 1860.[4] Both Glyn, Mills and the government threatened to foreclose loans and sever connections. The fact that neither did saved the bank for six more years. The following analysis explains how and why Glyn, Mills and the government continued their support. In the process it sheds further light on both the mechanics and structure of Canadian public finance on the eve of Confederation.

I

Managerial reform emerged as one answer to the bank's problems. When Galt became finance minister, the new term for inspector general, the government's financial administration was in the midst of a major renovation. Commenced by John Langton, the auditor general, attempts were being made to centralize

[2]Calculations made from sources used for Table 11. As this section makes clear, however, accounting principles were quite loose and such comparisons on the basis of published data are problematic.

[3]By December 1861 the bank's stock had dropped to 47 while all other major bank issues remained above 100. A. Shortt, "The Passing of the Upper Canadian and Commercial Banks," *JCBA*, 1904–1905, xii, pp. 204 and 208.

[4]Proudfoot dropped from 305 shares in 1857 to 11 shares in 1860. Thirty-two present or past directors held 5,683 shares in 1857. The same people held 4,562 shares for an overall decline of 20 per cent in 1860. It should be noted that nine of the thirty-two actually increased their holdings and a further nine maintained the same number in these years.

financial control, provide consolidated statements of all revenue and expenditure, and allocate responsibility and accountability with more clarity. The Bank of Upper Canada had always expressed itself in favour of this modernization[5] (D 46, D 55, E 3). The advancement of monies only after the receipt of warrants seemed to preclude the repetition of payment delays similar to the Macdonald and Baby affairs (D 61, E 6). It offered the opportunity to set the bank-government relationship on a much firmer and less ambiguous footing.

Three factors, however, made successful adjustment by the bank's managers extremely improbable. In the first place Ridout and Proudfoot were incapable of significant change. As one shrewd observer put it, they were two "old men" surrounded by assorted "cantankerous noodles" (the directors). Conditioned by years of loose and casual business dealings, they lacked the expertise and desire to systematize and rationalize the bank's *modus operandi*[6] (E 54).

Not that they differed significantly in this respect from the behaviour exhibited by the managers of their two oldest Upper Canadian rivals, the Commercial and Gore banks. Both were managed by men who had been active since the 1830s and both were burdened with overdue debts. In the case of the Commercial, the parallel was even closer: at this very time it was in the process of casually funnelling $1,600,000 into the Great Western Railway's American subsidiary, the Detroit and Milwaukee Railroad.[7] Only a small percentage of this was repaid. Not surprisingly, the Commercial closed its doors a scant year after the Bank of Upper Canada and soon after the smallest of the three oldest Upper Canadian chartered banks, the Gore, avoided bankruptcy by being absorbed into the new Canadian Bank of Commerce.

Clearly, the Upper Canadian banking system suffered from a crisis in management. Old habits and attitudes were unsuited to this era of structural change from a commercial to an emerging industrial economy. Yet equally clearly the ultimate key to a turnaround in the fortune of the Bank of Upper Canada and its rivals lay outside their management. As a newly appointed

---

[5]PAC, RG 58 E1, vol. 1, Memo, John Langton, 10 Mar. 1856; Langton to Cayley, 9 Jan. 1856 [*sic*].
[6]PAC, RG 58 B2b, vol. 1, Langton to Galt, 12 Nov. 1859.
[7]P. Baskerville, "The Boardroom and Beyond . . .," p. 280.

assistant superintendent for the Bank of Upper Canada explained in June and August, 1859, "a rather careless system of discounting" in the days of heady speculation plus the severe downturn of the previous two years led to a decline in government deposits (relative to the pre-1856 period) and the "locking up" of the bank's capital (E 27, E 37). It mattered little that Ridout was now avowedly reducing discounts to their smallest possible figure;[8] only an economic upswing that would put funds into the pockets of the bank's clients and/or raise the value of assets held as collateral could free capital already committed. The prospects for such a happening were slim.

In addition to the problems of managerial talent and economic malaise, there loomed a more subtle and in some respects a more difficult obstacle. The government and the major railroads expected the bank to reform itself even when it became clear that they were falling far short of success in reforming their own operations. Ambiguity rather than clarity continued to characterize bank-government-railway business relations and lack of central accountability continued to pervade general government administration.[9] This climate rendered reform of a systematic sort difficult indeed.

Through increased borrowing in London and increased customs duties the government's current financial condition marginally improved throughout 1858 and 1859. By May 1858 the province had begun to reimburse the bank and, after allowing for a debt of £155,000, it had a balance in its current account of £240,000. Early in January 1859 the receiver general paid £78,227 as a further reduction of all "direct and indirect" debts. For a brief period in January, the account ran at a deficit, but from that point it ran at a credit balance of over £200,000[10] (E 12).

Despite the improvement in the government account, the Bank of Upper Canada's financial position continued to decline. The Municipal Loan Fund debentures that Ridout had for sale in London (increased by a further transfer in March 1858) remained unsaleable. Economic conditions in the Canadas continued poor. While general banking discounts declined between October 1857

---

[8]PAC, Glyn, Mills Papers, A 452, Ridout to Glyn, Mills, 8 Aug. 1859.
[9]See Canada, Financial and Departmental Commission, *First Report*, May 1863, *passim*.
[10]PAC, RG 19 E1A, vol. 3367, Cayley to Galt, 10 Aug. 1858 and enclosure, 17 May 1858; Financial and Departmental Commission, May 1863, *Evidence*, p. 182.

and March 1858 by 7 per cent, the Toronto bank's declined by
only 2 per cent, suggesting collection problems (Table 11).

In addition to depending on Glyn, Mills for the provision of
working capital, Ridout began to rely on the provincial government. The bank required assistance to meet the interest payments
in July 1858. In December, Galt purchased £18,000 stg. Municipal Loan Fund debentures from the bank even though it was
clearly in the province's interests to have the bonds run to
maturity. The purchase, of course, represented a clear reversal of
traditional bank-government functions[11] (E 17).

The first of a series of crises seems to have been reached by
mid-1859. Not only did Ridout fail to provide any of the bank's
money for the government's July interest payments, "but," Galt
explained to Thomas Baring in a private note, "I find the removal
by the Bank as I directed of so large an amount of *our* Balances to
London would be exceedingly inconvenient for them," and
therefore he asked the London agents to advance the required
sum. That same month Galt and Sherwood, the receiver general,
encountered severe criticisms from their cabinet colleagues for
giving the Bank of Upper Canada £100,000 of exchange without
prior cabinet approval (E 31). As a final accommodation Galt
agreed to purchase £150,000 stg. more municipal debentures in
order to prevent the bank from making a forced sale and depressing the market in London[12] (E 27).

Even this extent of government assistance proved to be insufficient. Ridout had already used the debentures as collateral for
advances from Glyn, Mills. As a result, their sale brought only
£15,000 cash into the bank's vaults. To put the London account
on a firmer footing and to provide a satisfactory amount of
working capital for future operations, Glyns granted a £200,000
stg. line of credit secured by land from the Zimmerman estate. By
September, however, Ridout had run the bank's borrowings to
well over double that sum. Frustrated by these problems, Galt
wrote to Baring in August that "it [the Bank] is a source of

[11]Glyn, Mills Papers, A 542, Ridout to Glyn, Mills, 19 Apr. 1858; QUA, Magill
Papers, p. 271.

[12]PAC, Baring Papers, MG 24 D21, A 834, Galt to T. Baring, 6 June 1859 (private);
Galt to Baring & Glyn, 14 July 1859; PAC, RG 19 E1A, vol. 3376, Galt to Baring &
Glyn, 6 June 1859. In early June, the bank had £261,356 of the government's total bank
deposits amounting to £336,050 and according to Ridout, this had run down to £70,000
by 4 July.

weakness to us at present . . ." and could not be used as Baring would have liked[13] (E 27, E 36, E 37). As a large investor in the Grand Trunk, Baring, of course, wished for the continuance of the traditional system whereby the bank would provide short-term capital for the railway and obtain repayment when traffic returns increased, bond sales climbed, or a political climate favourable for the provision of government aid emerged. In fact, throughout 1858 Ridout and Proudfoot had continued to advance money directly to the Grand Trunk, to various subsidiary lines and to Gzowski and Company, the railway's major local contractors. Unfortunately for the bank, none of the prerequisites necessary for repayment appeared and by November, despite soothing from the Grand Trunk's administrators, Ridout had become increasingly uneasy[14] (E 1, E 2, E 7, E 11).

So, too, had the Grand Trunk's local managers. Aware of the bank's difficult financial position, Thomas Blackwell, the general manager, John Ross, the president, and Casimir Gzowski, the chief contractor, explored the possibility of dumping the Bank of Upper Canada and chartering their own institution (E 9, E 10, E 14). Unsuccessful in this, they continued to pressure the government to press the bank to aid the railroad[15] (D 67, E 18). Ridout and Proudfoot succumbed, and, without consulting with or reporting to the bank's board, continued to support the Grand Trunk (E 21, E 23).

By late April 1859 the railroad owed the bank, $560,000. To finance these outlays, the bank had itself to borrow from Glyn, Mills[16] (E 19, E 22, E 25, E 26). (The Grand Trunk's credit was too low to enable it to do so directly.) Other than as a means of expanding its note circulation, these advances, while of benefit to the Grand Trunk, were of no profit to the bank. The Grand

---

[13]PAC, Galt Papers, MG 27 D8, vol. 1, T. Baring to Galt, 22 July 1859; by 3 September, the debt was in excess of $2,600,000. Glyn, Mills Papers, A 542, General Statement of Bank of Upper Canada, 3 Sept. 1859, enclosed in Ridout to Glyn, Mills, 19 Sept. 1859.

[14]Ibid., Ridout to Glyn Mills, 12 Apr., 18 Oct., 27 Dec. 1858; Baring Papers, A 835, Blackwell to T. Baring, 4 Dec. 1858.

[15]Glyn, Mills Papers, A 542, Ridout to Glyn, Mills, 11 Jan. 1858; Baring Papers, A 835, Blackwell to Baring, 29 Jan. 1859.

[16]Glyn, Mills Papers, A 542, Ridout to Glyn, Mills, 24 Jan. 1859. The Canadian Government changed from sterling to the decimal system effective 1 Jan. 1858. Throughout 1858 usage gradually adjusted to the new system. Generally, for 1859 and after, this chapter will report funds in dollars, where necessary, at conversion rate of £1 cy = $4.00; £1 stg = $5.00.

Trunk's voracious appetite, coupled with the large amount of the bank's capital already locked up in overdue debt and unsaleable securities, precipitated the crisis of July 1859.

Galt's attempts to deal with the threatened disintegration of the government-bank-railway association bolstered the informal and ambiguous administrative context within which that relationship had evolved. His measures underline the difficulty, if not the impossibility, of the bank's undergoing any substantial reform of a systematic nature. Galt's response was twofold.

In January 1859 Ridout believed that the government promised to maintain a balance of $600,000 to $700,000 in his institution[17] (E 13, E 16, E 17). Undoubtedly the finance minister hoped that this sum would assist the bank to assist the railroad. The promise, however, was made in a typically informal way. No order-in-council accompanied it and throughout the year the bank complained that Galt failed to adhere to it (E 38, E 39). Early in 1860 Sherwood denied all knowledge of such a commitment (E 46) and before a committee of investigation in 1863 Galt admitted that at one time he had intended to effect such a program but, after consultation with his colleagues, had changed his mind.[18] The extent to which the bank's managers understood this change of heart is not clear. It is possible that Cayley, for example, continually referred to the alleged promise in his correspondence with Glyn in order to pacify the London agent. For his part, Ridout felt that the government was at least "morally bound to keep us covered" because of the Zimmerman affair (E 26). Galt, while sympathetic, probably declined to put any such agreement in writing for fear of future political consequences.

The intangible nature of such an arrangement led to frustrated expectations on both sides. Increasingly Galt came to believe that his general financial measures were being undermined by having to come to the aid of the faltering bank. To a degree this feeling was justified. Yet, in fairness to the bank, Galt really did not know the full extent of the bank's loans to the Grand Trunk. Thus he thought that the provision of $400,000 in exchange would more than pay off the Grand Trunk's indebtedness to the bank in July 1859 (E 32). In fact the debt exceeded that by $200,000 and

---

[17]PAC, RG 19 E1A, vol. 3369, Galt to Ridout, 22 Jan. 1859 (private).
[18]Financial and Departmental Commission, May 1863, *Report*, p. 46, and *Evidence*, question 1142.

by the time the bank actually received the money in question, the debt had climbed to $800,000.[19] Perhaps not surprisingly, a relationship characterized by unofficial arrangements was weakened by insufficient communication.

In June, Galt attempted to update the bank's administration by the appointment of William Cayley as assistant superintendent and by the election (through the use of Proudfoot's proxies) of David Lewis Macpherson and John Ross as directors. The background of the new personnel accentuated the ambiguity inherent in the bank-government-railway connection. Despite Galt's avowed intent to encourage reform in the bank, the men he introduced were far from disinterested and objective managers. Cayley, a past director of the bank and recently inspector general, was currently a director of the Grand Trunk. Macpherson, a rich Toronto businessman, was a partner with Gzowski, the major local contractor for the Grand Trunk and a firm to which the bank was currently granting large advances. John Ross, president of the Executive Council and minister of agriculture, was also the president of the Grand Trunk. Given the nature of these new appointments, the Grand Trunk could rest easy in its attempts to charter a new bank; it had virtually acquired an old one.

Two severe jolts to the bank's position in 1860 led to the final overhaul of its operations: the appointment of a new cashier, the election of a new president, and the introduction of a revamped capital structure. Precipitated by the revelations of a recently fired employee, the first problem surfaced in early summer (E 53, E 60). By themselves the accusations of J.H. Hopkins, published by William Lyon Mackenzie, should have caused only a minor upset.[20] When coupled with longstanding rumours about the bank's weakened position plus the equally longstanding determination of the Bank of Montreal to take advantage of that weakness, they resulted in a serious crisis.[21] In early May the Bank of Montreal demanded daily settlements of balances payable in gold, in place of the existing system of weekly and monthly settlements payable in exchange (E 54). This necessitated large drafts on Glyn, Mills for the purpose of procuring the specie. To preserve the bank's New York credit, Ridout had to pay off some $400,000 in loans from the Bank of the Interior at

[19]Glyn, Mills Papers, A 542, Bank of Upper Canada Statement, 3 Sept. 1859, in Ridout to Glyn, Mills, 19 Sept. 1859.
[20]Ibid., Memo re Mr. Hopkins, 4 Apr. 1860.
[21]Ibid., Ridout to Glyn, Mills, 8 Apr. 8, Aug. 1859.

Albany (E 57, E 58). Despairing of the bank's future, Glyn seriously considered selling all his shares (E 59). Galt, equally seriously, considered withdrawing the government account "unless [the Bank] strengthens itself instantly and places itself beyond immediate risk."[22]

Problems in communication and ineffective management continued to hamper adjustments and underline the hazards of operating within the Union's public financial system. Cayley complained that the government failed to keep enough funds in its account to permit the bank to advance the July interest payments (E 58). Galt complained that despite large current accounts in the bank, he could not withdraw the interest money or the bank might collapse.[23] Despite Ridout's assurances of curtailing discounts, the bank had in late winter issued a large accommodation to grain and lumber dealers of four to six months' duration "to enable [them] to get their products to market." And finally, underlying the crisis, the amount due the Bank from the Grand Trunk exceeded $500,000 in April and May (E 62).[24]

Before advancing any funds to the bank, Glyn demanded good security. The bank's response indicates the severity of its financial situation. Ridout sent over $260,000 of municipal debentures. These bonds, however, were a portion of those which the government required all banks to hold (up to one-tenth of their paid-in capital) as security for their Canadian operations. In effect Ridout had forwarded, in the guise of first-rate security, collateral already on deposit as guarantee for the bank's general operations. It is possible that Ridout had successfully employed this manoeuvre in the past. This time Glyn, having no knowledge of the real nature of the security proferred, desired cash quickly and had the government redeem the bonds, leaving the bank without sufficient debentures on hand to meet local legislative requirements. Unperturbed, Ridout petitioned the cabinet in August to purchase a like amount of debentures to replace those "which had been lodged in the hands of Glyn, Mills and by them through misapprehension handed over to the government and redeemed. . . ." The bank did this, Cayley explained to Glyn, in order to prevent problems with the monthly publication of the bank's statement. He was enabled to do this, it would seem, because the

---

[22]Ibid., Galt to Glyn, 18 May 1860.
[23]Baring Papers, A 834, Galt to Baring, 20 May 1860 (private).
[24]Glyn, Mills Papers, A 542, Ridout to Glyn, 26 Apr. 1860.

government had exerted pressure on the Grand Trunk to reduce, with the aid of Glyn and Baring, its large bank loans (E 69).[25]

All this suggests that the bank was fast taking on the characteristics of a revolving door. Money taken in from one point quickly exited to meet debts due at a second point. Little remained at the bank. Not surprisingly, no sooner had this crisis been papered over than another, unmatched for severity, commenced.

In September 1860, Glyn and Baring, worried about advances in excess of $4 million which they had made to the Grand Trunk, took steps to protect their position. These included the exercising of a lien on Grand Trunk rolling stock – collateral on which the Bank of Upper Canada had also made large advances (by November the railroad's debt to the bank had soared to $905,320) (E 71, E 72, E 82). When Glyn's actions became publicly known, Ridout's New York agents refused to accept any more drafts on Glyn, Mills without firm guarantee from London that they would be honoured. The bank could not procure specie without access to a New York agent, and without specie it could easily be closed by its Canadian rivals. In this situation Galt provided temporary exchange on London and pressured Canadian bankers to effect a more permanent solution. The other major banks ultimately agreed to endorse Ridout's bills on London in return for special deposits of the Bank of Upper Canada's commercial bills (up to $400,000) as security[26] (E 74, E 75, E 77, E 78).

Under instructions from Galt and Glyn, Ridout curtailed discounts. Depositors, accustomed to temporary advances, now used their savings and both deposits and circulation declined drastically, causing a severe weakening of the bank's capital resources[27] (E 84, E 85, E 86). The situation became so serious that Glyn, Mills was reduced to holding overdue bills from the Grand Trunk as security for the Bank of Upper Canada's overdrawn account[28] (E 91). In this context Glyn and Baring permitted the bank to rank with them as claimants both on the railway's

---

[25]Ibid., A 540, Glyn to Cayley, 5 June 1860; PAC, RG 1E8, vol. 73, 3 Aug. 1860 (quote from here).

[26]Glyn, Mills Papers, A 542, Cayley to Glyn, Mills, 12 Nov. 1860; ibid., A 545, Galt to Glyn, Mills, 25 Oct., 5 Nov. 1860; PAC, RG 19 E1A, vol. 3376, Galt to Proudfoot, 23 Oct. 1860.

[27]Glyn, Mills Papers, A 542, Cayley to Glyn, Mills, 15 Nov. 1860.

[28]Ibid., Ridout to Glyn, Mills, 18 Oct. 1860; PAC, Galt Papers, vol. 2, Glyn to Galt, 15 Mar. 1861.

rolling stock and ultimately on other securities as well[29] (E 73, E 99).

The government and the London agents came to the bank's aid for one primary reason: in prolonging the bank's existence they saw a last opportunity to save the Grand Trunk and protect their immense investments. Indirect aid through the bank no longer sufficed for the Grand Trunk: its capital requirements necessitated parliamentary intervention in the form of a further large relief measure. The Grand Trunk, however, was hardly a popular corporation in the Canadas at this time. By comparison, the Bank of Upper Canada had strong support, especially in the rural areas of the upper province. Of equal importance, it possessed direct financial ties to a large number of voters and legislators in the form of shareholders, borrowers and depositors. The Grand Trunk's major borrowings took place outside the country and thus it lacked a similar political following. Initially this situation led Ross, Galt and Cayley to conclude that unless the Bank of Upper Canada received support Canadians would blame the Grand Trunk for its collapse and the chances of the railroad ever receiving parliamentary assistance would be slim. It was this argument which convinced Glyn and Baring to provide support to the Grand Trunk so that railway could repay the bank in June 1860[30] (E 63, E 72).

During and following the September crisis, Galt and others (including his political opponent, Luther Holton) began to push the political logic inherent in this situation a bit further. Direct relief to the Grand Trunk could be made politically palatable by being marketed as indirect relief for the Bank of Upper Canada. In this sense it became important to keep the bank slowly sinking, but not capsized; or, as Galt put it in March 1861, the "Bank is now in great difficulty, but I cannot attempt its relief, until our GT policy is settled – my best argument would be lost in this case"[31] (E 73, E 77, E 79, E 80, E 81, E 94, E 95).

Nor did Galt miss the final logic of this policy. Once the Grand Trunk received relief the bank could be left more and more to its own devices. Whether looked at from a political point of view – i.e., the railroad would be safe from any political fallout follow-

---

[29]Glyn, Mills Papers, A 540, Glyn to Ross, 11 Oct. 1860; Glyn to Cayley, 25 Oct. 1860; ibid., A 545, T. Ward to Glyn, 8 Nov. 1860.
[30]Baring Papers, A 835, Galt to Baring, 13 Oct. 1859 (confidential).
[31]Glyn, Mills Papers, A 542, A.T. Galt to Glyn, 5 Nov. 1860; Baring Papers, A 834, Galt to Baring, 8, 21 Mar. 1861.

ing the bank's collapse – or a financial point of view – i.e., if the railroad paid off its loans, the bank ought not to collapse – it would be less and less necessary for the government to come to its aid. With this in mind, Galt warned Glyn, Mills in March 1861, "that the government would so far as lay in their power, sustain the Bank until the Grand Trunk affair was settled" (E 95).

Not that he intended to cut the bank immediately adrift. Rather, after a long search, he had finally secured "them the services as *absolute manager* of a really able man." Galt hoped that this addition to the management coupled with the ultimate payment of the Grand Trunk's debts would "resuscitate" the Bank and facilitate its re-emergence as a support to and not a drag on the government (E 95).

The man Galt had attracted, Robert Cassels, a banker of thirty years experience with the Bank of British North America and widely respected throughout the Canadas, had undertaken a formidable task.[32] The bank had yet to reacquire a New York agency; Glyn, owed in excess of $2 million, threatened to discontinue all business; the Grand Trunk debt equalled one-sixth of all debts due; close to 12 per cent of the remaining debts were under collection; and approximately one-fifth of the bank's resources were tied up in real estate. Conditional on receiving an optimistic report, Galt privately promised to maintain an amount of $600,000 and provide a guarantee of $400,000 to Glyn for all new debt transacted. After criticizing past management and stipulating that the Grand Trunk debt had to be repaid, Cassels submitted the required report. Glyn, Mills once again came to the bank's aid and agreed to the separation of old and new debts, taking the Zimmerman lands as part security for the old loans[33] (E 98, E 100).

All these transactions remained in the realm of private business. Not only did the public not learn about the government support, but, following a practice probably initiated by Cayley in 1859, Cassels included the large sum owed Glyn, Mills in the bank's 1861 financial statements under the entry "Cash deposits bearing interest."[34] On several counts, this latter manoeuvre was a shrewd piece of subterfuge. While both were indeed liabilities,

---

[32]See Peter Baskerville, "Robert Cassels," *DCB* xi (Toronto, 1982), pp. 156–57.
[33]Glyn, Mills Papers, A 543, Cassels to Glyn, 11 May, 14 June, 30 Sept., 11 Nov. 1861; ibid., A 540, Glyn to Cassels, 16 Oct. 1861.
[34]Ibid., A 542, Bank of Upper Canada Statement, 3 Sept. 1859, in Ridout to Glyn, 19 Sept. 1859; ibid., A 543, Cassels to Glyn, 7 Nov. 1861.

a significant distinction existed between amounts owed other bankers (the category under which the Glyn debt belonged) and deposits at interest. Banks, of course, commonly loaned money on the basis of their deposits and especially on deposits at interest, since these sums were often left in for a fixed term and thus banks had firm control over them. Not only did this falsify the bank's lending position, but the inflated deposits at interest also gave the impression that many wealthy Canadians continued to believe so strongly in the bank's future that they willingly committed their money for a fixed period of time to that institution.

Again following precedents, Cassels doctored the statements in a second, albeit less dramatic, way. The amount owed by the Zimmerman estate, which Cassels publicly put at $596,000 was not included under the general heading of debts due. Rather it was put in with balances due from other banks, a much more secure category of debt than general debts due.[35] Technically this designation was correct: at least part of the debt had been derived from Zimmerman's banking business. In the absence of information to the contrary, however, the unwary observer would naturally assume that the banks and agencies in this category were operative and not bankrupt.

The manoeuvres worked. In the public's eye, the bank seemed far more secure than it in fact was. At the June 1861 meeting the shareholders vented their spleen on the old management (Cayley, Proudfoot and Ridout were not elected or appointed to any position in the bank) and under Cassels's advice, accepted a 40 per cent reduction in capital from $50 to $30 a share. This freed up $1,274,440 to cover estimated bad debts amounting to $1,250,507 (E 101, E 102).

Cassels supplemented his public activities with a major overhaul of the bank's operations. He closed weak branches and arranged with competitors to handle government business in the areas affected (E 103). General loans and discounts were, yet again, tightened and more effective mechanisms for collecting old debts and selling real estate were instituted.[36] He took small creditors to court and where feasible forced large debtors such as the Kingston Brewery and Distillery owned by James Morton (owing $210,000), the Lyn Tannery near Brockville ($124,000)

---

[35]Ibid. The stability of the figures in balance due from the banks from 1859 on suggests that the practice commenced that year.
[36]Magill Papers, vol. 316A.

and the Chippawa Distillery and Tannery at St. Catharines ($128,000) into trusteeship to be managed on behalf of the bank. Although Cassels acted as trustee or co-trustee of the three firms, the bank failed to realize very much on any of these debts.[37] By contrast, as a trustee Cassels received commissions and, along with his brother Richard, a manager of one of the bank's branches, he purchased the Lyn Tannery at far below book price in the late 1860s and continued to operate it until 1879.[38]

By February 1862, however, the continued weakness of the bank's position had become all too apparent. In private letters to Galt, Cassels asked for more forbearance and pressed gently for ''the Grand Trunk money.'' In late March he travelled to Quebec to lobby for an effective relief measure (E 104, E 105, E 106, E 108). Grand Trunk supporters remained unsympathetic (E 107, E 109). The measure through which the bank hoped to be reimbursed was merely a part of a larger bill designed to amalgamate all major Upper Canadian railroads. The spectre of excessive monopoly proved sufficient to hold up proceedings. The government itself remained curiously passive concerning the question and John Sandfield Macdonald, without having mastered the issue, introduced it as a private member's bill. Thomas Galt, A.T. Galt's brother, later claimed that the whole matter had been mishandled from beginning to end.[39]

Frustrated, Cassels, in addition to employing the by now standard argument that the railroad would not receive Upper Canadian support without assurances that the bank's claim would be paid, laid bare the essence of the railway-bank-government linkage. The bank ''advanced their money on the faith of a promise by one of their own Directors who was President of the Co. [G.T.], and also a member of the [government]. . . .'' For that reason the bank deserved immediate and preferential consideration. The argument failed to convince Grand Trunk spokesmen. All that may be true, John Rose informed Thomas Baring, but ''*you* [also advanced money] on the pledge of securities which a member of the [government] represented he had power to use for that purpose. . . .''[40] (E 109).

---

[37]See PAC, RG 19, C1, vol. 1195, *passim*.
[38]For adverse public reaction to Cassels's management of one of these trusts see E 142.
[39]See Toronto *Globe*, 26, 29 Mar., 24, 28 Apr., 7, 13, 16 May 1862; Glyn, Mills Papers, A 545, T. Galt to Glyn, 21 June 1862.
[40]*Globe*, 2 June 1862.

The fragility of the bank's position could not have been clearer. Beyond the obvious problems of relying on informal promises from government members, Cassels and the bank were faced with even greater difficulties. By mid-May, John Ross, the promise-maker, was no longer a bank director, a railroad president or a government member. His replacement as Grand Trunk president, Edward Watkin, a British appointee, refused to admit that the bank should be given rights prior to those of its London creditors. In this he was supported by Thomas Baring, who, unlike Glyn, had no stake in the Bank of Upper Canada.[41]

Ross's resignation as a member of the government was part of the general resignation of the Conservative ministry over the defeat of their Militia Bill in mid-May. In place of Ross, Galt and Cayley, Cassels and the bank had now to work with a reform-oriented government headed by J.S. Macdonald and Louis-Victor Sicotte.[42] In the short term this new relationship worked to Cassels's advantage. The new administration possessed only the slimmest of majorities. In this context the fact that it immediately reintroduced, albeit in revised form, contentious legislation to aid the Grand Trunk (and indirectly the Bank of Upper Canada) is noteworthy. The fact that the bill passed, in a further revised form, due to a majority of Upper Canadian members voting in its favour, and that, on the day of its passage, the bank and the railroad had entered into the beginnings of a final arrangement of their financial problems, are likely more than simple coincidence.[43] This series of events suggests that neither the new government nor ultimately the Grand Trunk could ignore Cassels's claims of strong Upper Canadian support for the bank: to capitalize on sympathy for the bank, the government took a chance on pushing the railroad measure; to secure its passage, the Grand Trunk agreed to enter into formal negotiations with the bank.

Watkin dragged out the negotiations as long as he could. A final settlement of all claims was only reached in late November 1863. By that time, from the bank's point of view, it was too

---

[41]Glyn wanted the Grand Trunk to pay the bank. Galt Papers, vol. 2, Glyn to Galt, 25 Feb. 1862 (private). Although Glyn owned five hundred shares, worth $25,000 in 1860 and $15,000 in 1863 and 1865, their fate was hardly his major concern.

[42]*Globe*, 21 May 1862. For an analysis of this ministry, see P. Baskerville, "Imperial Agendas and 'Disloyal' Collaborators: Decolonization and the John Sandfield Macdonald Ministries, 1862–64," forthcoming.

[43]*Globe*, 2, 3, 6, 7, 11 June 1862; PAC, RG 30, Deposit 55, 6 June 1862; Magill Papers, p. 361.

little, too late. In the first place the bank did not receive cash; rather, the Grand Trunk assigned to it postal and equipment bonds plus sundry mortgages valued at $1,105,000 and obtained a release from all debts. The bank could not fully realize on these securities "until [the] Grand Trunk *may be in funds*"[44] (E 138, E 139).

Secondly, by late 1863, the bank had fallen behind on its payments to Glyn, Mills. As a result Glyn demanded and received first rights to all the Grand Trunk securities in return for which the bank subtracted $890,000 from its Glyn debt. While this, as the bank's solicitor later claimed, might have been a "most favourable" arrangement for the bank – in unloading questionable Grand Trunk security on Glyn – the transaction underlines yet again the bank's position as a revolving door (E 138). Even after the Grand Trunk paid its debt, the bank's working capital remained nil.

Finally, and most importantly, a final resolution of bank-government affairs occurred. It was an ending the bank neither sought nor welcomed. Following the passage of the Grand Trunk Arrangements Act, relations between the bank and government had swiftly deteriorated. Denying the existence of any written agreement to keep a minimal balance at the bank, the new receiver general reluctantly acceded to Cassels's requests for aid, but granted only temporary support.[45] Luther Holton's appointment as the new finance minister in 1863 proved to be the death blow to Cassels's hopes for continued sufferance. When the bank failed to provide sufficient funds to meet the July interest payments, Cassels only barely staved off the transfer of the government account to the Bank of Montreal.[46]

Holton had little patience with the bank's problems. One of his main goals as finance minister was to lessen Canada's financial dependence on Glyn and Baring. If the Bank of Upper Canada could not help him in this, he was quite prepared to employ another local institution. In fact he was eager to do so. He had long viewed the bank as the essential and corrupt link between the

---

[44]PAC, RG 30, Deposit 55, vol. 9630, 10 July, 10 Aug., 18 Nov. 1863; Magill Papers, pp. 371, 379; PAC, RG 19 C1, vol. 1192, 26; Baring Papers, A 835, Hickson to Grant, 5 July 1867.
[45]PAC, RG 19 B2b, vol. 1165, J. Morris to Cassels, 11 June, 26 July 1862. Financial and Departmental Commission, May 1863, *Evidence*, p. 154.
[46]Glyn, Mills Papers, A 543, Cassels to Glyn, 29 June 1863 (private); Bank of Montreal, Resolve Book 6, 26 May 1863.

Conservative government, the Grand Trunk and the London financiers. He believed that cutting the bank adrift would be a nice counterpoint to the thorough public investigation he had initiated into the financial administration of past Conservative governments. "I believe," he wrote a doubting George Brown, "[that] the severance of the Connection between the government and this instrument of manifold Corruption [the Bank] would be the most striking endeavour that could be given that we have entered upon a New era" (E 116, E 118).

Political logic had dictated that the Conservatives prop up an ailing institution. From Holton's perspective that same logic dictated the removal of all such props. It was no longer desirable to sustain the bank to assist the Grand Trunk; rather, it was now necessary to terminate the bank to undermine the railroad. His "plan would," he fervently hoped, "be a staggering blow to the Grand Trunk influence both in this Country and in England"[47] (E 116, E 117, E 118).

Both financial and political considerations, then, led Holton to override Cassels's "bullying, coaxing and whining," and to transfer the government account to the Bank of Montreal, effective January 1864. Negotiations between Cassels and Holton (throughout November and December) resulted in the government leaving substantial deposits in the form of loans in the bank to be repaid at low interest over a series of years[48] (E 119, E 120, E 121, E 122). By August 1864 the bank fell behind in its repayments. Fortunately for Cassels, Galt, once again finance minister, permitted a renegotiation of the repayment schedule.[49] In February 1865, Galt also forestalled an attempt by the Grand Trunk to remove its account from the faltering institution (E 126).

But these were temporary reprieves. It is significant that Galt made no known attempt to transfer the government account back to the bank of Upper Canada. The reform interlude had saved him the nasty necessity of effecting the transfer himself. Quite clearly the bank had not revived and remained too dependent on government sufferance. Lacking such aid, it could no longer support any large business undertaking. Accordingly, in December 1864 the Great Western transferred its account to the Bank of Montreal (E 125). When the Grand Trunk followed suit in October 1865

---

[47]Financial and Departmental Commission, May 1863.
[48]PAC, RG 1 E7, vol. 62, 25 Nov. 1863; ibid., E8, vol. 81, 8 Dec. 1863.
[49]Ibid., 6 Aug. 1864.

(E 127), this did not signal the end of the financial system which had evolved in the 1850s.[50] Rather, the traditional bank-government-railway connections had re-emerged with but one change in the cast: the Bank of Montreal had replaced the Bank of Upper Canada.

Perhaps fittingly, eight months later the Bank of Montreal supplied the ultimate *coup de grâce* by demanding immediate payment in gold for its Bank of Upper Canada notes. When the government (perhaps under pressure from the Bank of Montreal) reneged on a loan of £100,000, the Bank of Upper Canada suspended specie payments and, on 18 September, 1866, closed its doors forever.[51]

The bank's administration attempted to keep firm control over the wind-up of its affairs. Clarke Gamble, the long-time solicitor, drew up the deed of assignment. The bank's directors appointed three of themselves, Cassels and one government representative, as trustees to carry out the final distribution of assets (E 132). According to a statement prepared by Cassels and presented to a "very stormy" group of shareholders in November, assets exceeded liabilities by $1,488,862. Even allowing for bad debts, he believed that "a considerable surplus will ultimately remain for division amongst [them]. . . ." In defence of his own management he pointed out that liabilities had been reduced significantly since he took control (E 132). Between May 1861 and November 1866 liabilities were reduced by $5.4 million – viz., Glyn's debt declined by $1.6 million, circulation by $1.3 million, and deposits by $2.5 million (the latter decline, of course, being an indication of lack of public confidence in the bank, especially since the decline occurred against a backdrop of a general rise in banking deposits). What Cassels did not point to was the even more dramatic decline in assets of just over $7 million.[52] Nor did he have to remind the shareholders that they had already lost $1.3 million by a capital reduction to cover bad debts. Nor did he, other than in the vaguest of terms, allude to the fact that of the largest asset category, discounts, 36 per cent were already past

[50]Baring Papers, A 835, Hickson's Report, 8 Apr. 1864 (private and confidential), p. 4, Rose to Baring, 20 Oct. 1865 (private); Watkin to Baring, 23 Oct. 1865; Bank of Montreal, Resolve Book 6, 25 Nov. 1864.

[51]*Globe*, 19 Sept. 1866; PAC, RG 1 E8, vol. 89, 1 Sept. 1866; ibid., E7, vol. 67, file 568; ibid., vol. 86, file 29.

[52]MTL, Larratt Smith Diary, 13 Nov. 1866. The May 1861 figures were published; Cassels used unpublished April figures for his calculation.

due.[53] He also failed to mention that, under his management, one Edward Berry, a ship-owner operating out of Kingston and Quebec had, on no security other than his own name, received $327,736 in discounts. This roughly equalled 15 per cent of all discounts outstanding in November 1866. The bank lost all but $12,000 of this money.[54] And finally, he passed over the fact that he had speculated unsuccessfully with bank money in stock purchases and that this, plus activities as a trustee operating the Lyn, Chippawa and Kingston properties, left him open to a claim from the bank of $35,763[55] (E 133).

Other members of the bank's recent administration also figured in the debtor category. Thomas Ridout, the late cashier, owed $11,130. William Proudfoot, past president, owed $5,220. George Allan, the retiring president, owed $25,000. The first two debts were written off and only $12,500 was realized on the last.[56]

When Cassels's personal transactions came to light he resigned (10 July 1867) and by year's end the remaining in-house appointees also retired. The government, anxious to wrap up the bank's affairs as quickly and as quietly as possible, appointed two trustees to represent the creditors and the shareholders appointed one to protect their interests.

John A. Macdonald, the prime minister, had both public and private reasons for desiring a swift and peaceful, conclusion to the wind-up. He did not want the shareholders to be forced to meet their double liability requirements. Such an exaction could prove to be embarrassing on several counts. Seventy to 80 per cent of the stockholders resided in Canada and they could excite considerable anti-Conservative feeling if the government, the largest creditor, demanded such a payment. The shareholders would also require a full, searching and public investigation into the bank's affairs in order to satisfy themselves that all debts had been collected and securities realized before they would pay. Not only would such an investigation uncover Macdonald's private debt of $17,195 (written off as a loss on 30 July 1870),[57] but it might also uncover, in a more general sense, "food for those opposed to the government" (E 134).

[53]PAC, RG 19 C1, vol. 1195, p. 40.

[54]Ibid., vol. 1184, Schedule C, Bills and Notes, Nov. 1866; ibid., vol. 1195, p. 644.

[55]Ibid., vol. 1212, 1, 22 May, 18, 21 Sept. 1867, 16 Dec. 1868.

[56]Ibid., vol. 1210, Aug. 1868; ibid., vol. 1195, p. 657. Ridout also owed money to the Gore Bank. CIBC Letter Book, 1863–69, 3 Aug. 1863.

[57]PAC, RG 19 C1, vol. 1195, p. 660.

For reasons such as these, the government took a further step to centralize and expedite settlement by formally assuming control of the wind-up in August 1870 and appointing none other than Clarke Gamble to oversee the remaining details.[58] Gamble and Francis Hincks, the new finance minister, agreed to sell to a "paper maker" up to ten tons of the bank's books in November 1870 at $20 a ton. According to Gamble, after the destruction of these books, there remained only one person alive who had any intimate knowledge of the bank's financial operations: and that man, Robert Cassels, left no memoirs (E 138, E 139, E 143).

It is difficult to calculate with any precision the amount of money lost by the bank's creditors. Many depositors were also borrowers and in such cases the trustees accepted a bookkeeping transfer as legitimate payment. Similarly, many borrowers had Bank of Upper Canada notes on hand or could purchase them at 70 to 75 per cent of face value and receive 100 per cent value for them in repayment of their debts.[59] After December 1868 bank liabilities were redeemed at 75 cents on the dollar. Very likely, losses to noteholders and depositors exceeded $290,000. Glyn, Mills, the largest private creditor, received its final payment in September 1872 – although just when the firm realized on the Grand Trunk securities is unclear[60] (E 141). It is clear that shareholders lost $3,170,000 and that the government received only about 10 cents on the dollar, losing around $1 million.[61]

While these losses were, in the aggregate, quite severe (amounting to about 15 per cent of the province's existing banking capital), contemporary sources point almost unanimously to the minimal impact on the general financial community of the bank's closure.[62] The reasons for this are clear. The capital had been severely reduced four years prior to the suspension of activities. The continuance of the government deposit gave to the bank the illusion of stability, if not prosperity. Between 1861 and 1866, the bank's general business had declined

---

[58]PAC, RG 55 A3, Treasury Board Records, 14 Sept. 1870.

[59]University of Western Ontario [hereafter UWO], Becher Papers, F.J. Joseph to H.C.R. Becher, 29 Sept. 1866.

[60]PAC, RG 55 A1, vol. 2001, 18 Sept. 1872.

[61]PAC, RG 19 C1, vol. 1187, Memo re Bank of Upper Canada, 27 Mar. 1882; ibid., vol. 1188, Memo re Bank of Upper Canada, 5 Feb. 1885; ibid., vol. 1184, Memo re Bank of Upper Canada, 27 Mar. 1888.

[62]See, for example, Baring Papers, vol. 4, Rose to Baring, 5 Oct. 1866 (confidential).

to such an extent that few other than the shareholders, Glyn, Mills and the government had made significant financial commitments to it. As Adam Shortt has written, the picture of a bank dying a slow death is rather unusual.[63] But then, given the political context within which the lingering end took place, it could hardly have been otherwise.

[63]Shortt, "The Passing of the Upper Canada and Commercial Banks."

CONCLUSION

A COLONIAL BANK:
THE UPPER CANADIAN FINANCIAL SYSTEM AND THE
IMPERIAL CENTRE

THE PARTICULAR CHARACTERISTICS of its local managers shed much light on the nature of the bank's evolution. The persistence of its key personnel is remarkable. For the first forty years of its existence only three people played major roles in its operation and of these only William Allan dominated affairs. His leadership exhibited a consistent policy orientation and a thoroughness in implementation lacking during the tenure of his successors. Under the guidance of Ridout and Proudfoot, the bank at times appeared rudderless: policies were more a response to the moment and less a result of reasoned strategy. Infirmities of age exacerbated these tendencies and by the time new management appeared, the bank could not be resuscitated.

While there is no doubt that this contrast in personnel is real, it would be wrong to make too much of it. In the first place, Ridout and Proudfoot managed in a much more complex era. Allan's resignation, in fact, reflected an unwillingness to confront such emerging problems as the new government funding scheme, increased competition, and pressure for diversification and expansion of discounting. Whether he could have adjusted successfully to the changing context is largely unanswerable.

Secondly, it is clear that Ridout and Proudfoot did make bad managerial decisions: relying on government to the exclusion of general commercial business in the late 1830s, thus allowing the Commercial Bank to emerge as a strong competitor; failing to control the borrowing of personal favourites in the 1840s; advancing money to public works' contractors on improper authority causing delays in repayment and at times refusals to repay (the Bank of Montreal, in 1845, had refused to permit this); overextending general discounts and in effect speculating on real estate in the early 1850s; and continuing, despite their close knowledge of the Grand Trunk's bankrupt state, to advance large sums to the railway in the late 1850s. But it would be insufficient to focus on the merits or demerits of sundry managers. After all, the managers of the Commercial and Gore Banks fared little better. The context within which these decisions took place is of primary importance. In this sense the bank's history sheds light on more than the character of the personnel who managed it. The Bank of Upper Canada emerged as a direct response to a particular set of local economic problems and throughout its forty-four-year history, its operations mirrored, however indirectly, the successes and failures of Upper Canada's economic development. Capital-creation policies implemented by William Allan addressed the colony's perennial problem – capital scarcity – and thereby facilitated commercial growth. The bank helped to underwrite the most pervasive economic activity of the period, the general trade in agriculture and lumber products. Its active foreign exchange operations permitted greater specialization in trade. Expansion of branch banking contributed to an efficient movement of internal exchange. Yet, and perhaps surprisingly in view of the general literature on the period, it did more than contribute to commercial expansion. If William Allan could resist making direct advances to fixed capital enterprises – canals and steamboats – many of his employees could not. Throughout the 1840s the Bank of Upper Canada, although somewhat unsystematically, underwrote mills, steamboats and, via the Department of Public Works, canal construction. It continued such activity throughout the 1850s and 1860s.[1] In those decades the bank also, of course, became involved in the foremost economic activity of the era – railroad construction. That it ultimately became a casualty of that involvement,[2] should not obscure the benefits which railroads and, presumably through them, the general Canadian public derived from such participation.

The fact that the three major Upper Canadian banks passed from the scene in the 1860s suggests that, despite different operational emphases, certain underlying influences affected all Upper Canadian institutions in a similar way. Following an initial period of monopoly, the Bank of Upper Canada bowed to the pressures of regional and metropolitan rivalries in the mid-1830s. Dunn's financial system in part recognized the legitimacy of these rivalries and as a result Upper Canada's financial business became carved up amongst several local institutions. This development

[1]See various account books of the bank, PAC, RG 19 C1, vols. 1188, 1194, 1195, *passim.*

[2]In addition to the involvement already outlined, the bank had advanced $462,000 to John Fowler and Henry Covert, two general railway contractors, all of which was past due in July 1865. PAC, RG 19 C1, vol. 1194, p. 68.

provided the much larger Bank of Montreal with a grand opportunity to capitalize on that city's traditional economic dominance
by expanding and severely challenging the upper colony's more
fragmented banking structure following the Union.

During the expansive years of the early 1850s, all local Upper
Canadian institutions speculated, in retrospect unwisely, on continued growth. The stability of the resident Upper Canadian
banks, however, depended on a continual turnover of short-term
loans. By the mid-fifties too much of their capital had become tied
up in real estate. When the Bank of Upper Canada and the
Commercial Bank attempted to underwrite fixed capital investment according to the same principles, they suffered even more
severely in the economic downturn of 1857–58. That the Bank of
Montreal was better able to withstand the financial shocks of the
later fifties (evidence suggests that it, too, had over-speculated in
the early years), reflects the continuing economic and financial
dominance exerted by Montreal over much of the upper colony.
The pressures of operating within what was still a frontier economic environment during a period of fundamental change
proved too strong for the Upper Canadian financial community to
handle. Their collective failure, it should be emphasized, did not
result from undue passivity; rather, their at times overly enthusi-
astic support of commercial growth and structural change demonstrated both the complexity and the limits of commercial banking
in a frontier environment.

The Bank of Upper Canada's history also provides insights into
a favourite theme of Canada's business historians – government-
business interaction. Following William Lyon Mackenzie, most
commentators assume that the bank had government under its
firm control. There was indeed an important connection. It is true
that only certain individuals deemed acceptable by government
leaders – in terms of birth, ideology and economic standing –
could hope to succeed as bankers in the pre-Union period. Yet a
close look at the history of one bank highlights the complex and
reciprocal nature of government-business interaction. In the pre-
and to a degree the post-Union eras, government was a multi-
levelled and often discordant apparatus. The bank and parts of
that government intersected at various times, but rarely ever
completely merged. A distinction of interest formed the basis of
most interaction.

Equally misleading is the tendency among Canadian historians
to rest content with concluding that the government acted as the

prime agent of nineteenth-century economic development. While in the aggregate this may well be correct, the conclusion runs the risk of obscuring the dynamics of such development. Throughout its history, the bank played a significant role in the implementation of the government's financial policies. It brought some foreign capital to the colony via its brokerage of government debentures prior to 1835 and performed a similar function through the mediation of Municipal Loan Fund debentures in the 1850s. It was at the centre of the debate which surrounded the significant changes in government financial policy implemented by Dunn in the mid-1830s. A study of the bank's unsuccessful proposals adds clarity to the options available at that time. The bank's function, in underwriting, both directly and indirectly, fixed capital development in the 1850s reveals a more complex picture of government and foreign financing of railroad expansion than that found in most standard accounts. The bank's history suggests that micro-studies of business institutions can be the means of charting the fluid interaction evident between the private and public sectors in nineteenth-century Canada.

Its history can also be approached from a broader perspective. The Canadian banking system was the most advanced and independent of all such systems operating in the British colonies during the first half of the nineteenth century.[3] In part, this occurred because of the proximity of the United States and the example of its banking system. More importantly, British administrators feared that by denying Canadians a local banking structure, they might push them firmly into the American orbit and thus strengthen a major trading competitor. Yet it remains true that the Bank of Upper Canada was a colonial bank. As such it had particular roles to play within the colonial-imperial relationship. From this perspective the bank's major economic rationale was to underwrite the export of natural products to England and to facilitate the import of finished products from the mother country. The constant resistance by imperial overseers to colonial banks investing in fixed capital enterprises reflected the primary economic goal of that empire.

When the goals of empire began to change, most visibly in the 1840s and 1850s, from direct to indirect economic control, the Bank of Upper Canada's role also shifted. London investor-bankers desired local institutions capable of supporting their

[3]See A.S.J. Baster, *The Imperial Banks* (New York, 1929).

personal colonial investment programs. The local government assumed a primary role in this context. Because of the Bank of Upper Canada's contractual links with that government, it too became an important element in this investment process.

The imperial investors expected the bank to tide over or prop up large capital-intensive projects during periods of drought in the London financial market. By so doing, it could protect existing British investment as well as facilitate further development. When the bank, because of the accumulated pressures outlined in Section E, could no longer serve adequately in this role, the first to be exasperated were men such as Thomas Baring, a heavy investor in Canadian railways. As long as new issues of government debentures remained saleable, Glyn and Baring rarely minded advancing money to pay interest on old issues. They did so under the expectation that new money raised, or a good part of it, would be used to support their Canadian interests. When the Bank of Upper Canada began to act as a drain on, instead of a contributor to, their investment flow, from the imperial perspective the time was right for a change.

Yet there was danger in too radical an alteration. When the Bank of Montreal became the government's new banker in 1864, the concerns of men such as Baring shifted from how to handle a weak institution, to how to keep a strong one from competing directly with them in terms of raising money in the London market.[4] From the imperial perspective a proper balance had to be maintained. The Bank of Upper Canada, through its infirmities, tipped the balance unacceptably in one direction. The Bank of Montreal, through its strength, threatened to tip it in the other. The proper sense of proportion, after all, dictated that a colonial bank remain in the colony.

[4]PAC, Baring Papers, vol. 4, Rose to Baring, 29 July 1867 (private).

DOCUMENTS

A. GETTING STARTED, 1817–1822

A 1   HUGH GRAY TO [?]
Quebec, December 1807

[*Hugh Gray*, Letters from Canada, Written During a Residence There in the Years, 1806, 1807, & 1808 (*London, 1809*), *pp. 182–86*]

. . . Amount of exports from Canada	66,586	8	2
Amount of ditto from			
United States	175,546	11	6
Balance against Canada	£108,960	3	4 [1806]

This balance the Americans carry out of Canada in cash. There are a great variety of coins in circulation in Canada:– we have the Spanish, French, American, and British, gold and silver coins. The Spanish dollar is in most general use, and these the Americans prefer, because they generally bear a premium in New York and Boston, to the amount sometimes of 2 per cent. The Americans want them for their China trade. . . .

In the present case, if the Americans by carrying cash out of Canada create a scarcity, both the government and the merchants will find a difficulty in procuring it. The government want large sums for paying the troops, and the expences of the civil department – the merchants want money to pay for the *produce* they purchase for exportation. They draw bills on England, which they sell to the holders of cash. Now, when the holders of cash find that money is much wanted, they will give it to those who for 100£. bill on England will take the smallest amount of cash from them. Payments are made in the currency of the country. Sterling is 11 1/9th per cent. more valuable – this is the *par of exchange*. When there are many *drawers*, the number of bills for sale, lowers their value; and the demand for cash raises its value; so that the holders of cash can get sterling bills under par, that is, they get a bill for 100£. sterling for less currency than 111 1/9£.– Suppose five per cent under par – five pounds are deducted from one hundred pounds, and currency *at par* is given corresponding to 95£. sterling, by which there is evidently a gain to the holder of cash, and a loss to the drawer of bills – 95£. sterling being equal to 105£.11s. 1 3/9d. currency, which he gets instead of 111£.2s. 2 6/9d. the par. It follows that the holders of cash wish to lower the exchange, and the drawers to raise it. If I want a bill on England, to remit, the less currency I give for it the better for me; and if I wish to dispose of a bill, the more currency I get for it the better for me.

The Americans by taking cash out of the country, increase the value of what remains, and the exchange falls. It has sometimes fallen so low, that sterling has been given for currency, whereby drawers of bills suffered a loss of 11 1/9 per cent.

In New York and Boston, the exchange on Britain is in general high, that is to say, bills on London bear a premium, sometimes as much as eight per cent. For a 100£. bill, you get currency corresponding to 108£. Cash is more plentiful than bills.– In Canada it is quite the reverse; and when the exchange is, in consequence, low, it becomes extremely advantageous for the holders of cash, in Boston and New York, to send it to Canada for the purchasing of bills (which they get at a discount), rather than purchase bills at home, which are sold at a premium. Thus the cash carried out of Canada by one set of men, is brought back again by another set. In consequence of which, the exchange in Canada approaches *par*, and the circulating medium regains its level.

Government, as well as individuals, who have occasion to draw bills in Canada, suffer very heavy losses by the discount on bills. I cannot help thinking that it would be a very easy matter for government to prevent any great loss by exchange. All they have to do is to keep themselves advised of the state of exchange in New-York, and draw at three or four per cent. more favourable for the holders of cash than the course at New-York offers. There can be no doubt that the cash would immediately come into Canada. Instead of government bills in Canada being at a discount of seven or eight per cent. they would rarely be below par; for in New-York bills in general bear a premium sufficiently high to induce the holders of cash to carry it to Canada for government bills, at par, or very little below it. The expence of bringing in cash from New-York, to Quebec or Montreal, is not above three to three and a half per cent. insurance included. The risks to be insured against are, thieves, and the danger of loss in crossing lakes and rivers. . . .

A 2   LT. GOVERNOR FRANCIS GORE[1] TO EARL BATHURST[2]
York, 8 May 1817
[*PAC, CO 42, v. 359, p. 149*]

Captain MacGregor, who leaves this place for England, has obligingly offered to be the bearer of the several Acts passed in the last Session of the Provincial Legislature, or reserved for the signification of His Majesty's pleasure; which I now have the honor to transmit by that Gentleman, with a short notice of the considerations which induced me to give, or with hold His Majesty's Assent to them respectively. – They are Ten in number. . . .

[1]Francis Gore (1769–1852) was lieutenant-governor of Upper Canada, 1806–17, on leave in England, 1811–15.
[2]Henry, Third Earl Bathurst (1762–1834) was colonial secretary, 1812–27.

The Tenth, to Incorporate a Bank,[3] is Reserved, for the signification of His Majesty's pleasure.

It does not appear that any of the British Statutes Militate with such an Establishment in the Colonies, the great scarcity of Specie having occasioned an Inundation of paper from the United States, to supply the place of Army Bills, and it appears to me to be reasonable, to give the preference to such of His Majesty's Provinces as may wish to lend their Aid to remove the Evil. I do not doubt but some such Establishment, either common to both provinces, or the issue of Army Bills sanctioned by His Majesty's Government, would conduce much to the Interest of Agriculture, and commerce in this Province.

A 3   JOHN STRACHAN[4] TO JOHN MACAULAY[5]
York, 8 February 1819
[PAO, Macaulay Papers]

. . . I should have been sorry for the loss of the Bank Bill passed two years ago had it not contained one clause foisted on by its enemies which in my opinion destroyed its advantage. The clause was that a full statement [books?] & all should be made annually to the Legislature instead of a General Abstract signed by the Directors. This would have exposed all the Secrets of the Company if any person would have given them a scent under such circumstances. . . .

A 4   JOHN BEVERLEY ROBINSON,[6] ATTORNEY GENERAL, TO
LT. GOVERNOR P. MAITLAND[7]
York, 10 July 1819
[PAC, RG 5 A1, v. 48]

I have examined the following Bills which have passed the Honorable the Legislative Council, and House of Assembly during this session – namely – . . .

---

[3]This refers to the attempt to charter a bank at Kingston.

[4]John Strachan (1778–1867), born in Aberdeen, Scotland, came to Upper Canada in 1799. In 1803 he was ordained a priest in the Church of England and in 1823 was appointed general superintendent of education for Upper Canada. He sat on the Legislative Council, 1820–41, and on the Executive Council, 1817–36. A member of the Bank of Upper Canada's directorate in 1822, he held shares in the bank in the 1830s, but not in the 1850s and 1860s.

[5]John Macaulay (1792–1857) was born in Kingston and educated by Strachan at Cornwall. He became surveyor general in 1836 and between 1838 and 1842 held the post of inspector general. At Kingston he was variously a postmaster, a magistrate and from 1823 to 1836 agent for the Bank of Upper Canada. In 1837 and 1838 he sat as a government appointee on the Bank of Upper Canada's directorate. A director of the British America Fire & Life Assurance Company, he was also for a time in the 1840s president of the Commercial Bank of the Midland District.

[6]John Beverley Robinson (1791–1863), born in Quebec, was also educated by Strachan at Kingston and Cornwall. He represented York in the Legislative Assembly from 1820 to 1829 and was recognized as the government leader for much of that time.

On these Bills for the incorporation of two several Banking Companies, the one to be called the Bank of Upper Canada, and the other the Bank of Kingston, I have to remark to Your Excellency that, as their paper is not made a legal tender, I see no objection to their receiving the Royal Assent – The preambles involved an inconsistency, for they are the same in both bills, – Each declaring the expediency of establishing a Bank in the Province of Upper Canada, whereas without assigning any necessity in either, they have in fact established two –

I imagine if they become laws, some of their Clauses will be found to require alteration and explanation, and indeed in bills of this nature it is scarcely possible it should be otherwise –

As one instance of this kind – (and as it strikes me at present it is rather a material error,) – there is a general Clause providing that all their bills shall be negotiable and binding upon the Corporation *in the same manner as bills issued by private persons are by law negotiable and binding*; and the same legal remedies are given to enforce the payment of them – Now by the Laws of England, which we have adopted, bills issued by any person under twenty shillings (and the bank bills here are appointed to be as small as five shillings) are *neither negotiable, nor binding*, and so far from there being any remedy to recover their amount it is made penal to issue them –

A 5   JOHN STRACHAN TO JOHN MACAULAY
YORK, 26 JULY 1819
[*PAO, Macaulay Papers*]

. . . You must be alert with your Bank try to make it as much Provincial as you can and should Gov't wish to hold shares a short bill to that effect & containing any other modifications as might appear beneficial to all parties might be introduced next Session. The great object now is to get it in operation.

A 6   JOHN McGILL[8] TO GEORGE CROOKSHANK[9]
York, 14 April 1821
[*PAO, Crookshank-Lambert Papers*]

After a long session our Legislature was prorogued at 6 O'clock this

He became chief justice in 1829 and sat on the Executive Council, 1829–31, and the Legislative Council, 1830–41. He was a director of the Bank of Upper Canada from 1824 to 1826.

[7]Sir Peregrine Maitland (1777–1854) was lieutenant-governor of Upper Canada, 1818–28.

[8]John McGill (1752–1834) arrived in Upper Canada in 1792 after fighting with the Queen's Rangers in the American Revolution. He became commissary of stores and provisions (1792), inspector general (1801–13) and receiver general (1814–19). He sat on the Executive Council, 1796–1818, and on the Legislative Council, 1797–1834. He was a director of the Bank of Upper Canada in 1822, 1823 and 1825.

[9]George Crookshank (1773–1859) was born in New York and moved to Saint John,

afternoon, upwards of thirty Bills received the Royal Assent, amongst which is one authorising the Lt. Governor or rather the Receiver General to borrow £25,000 to pay the arrears of Militia Pensions. One to establish a Bank at York, to be called the Upper Canada Bank, Capital to be £80,000 – each share 50 dollars, when £10,000 specie is deposited then to go into operation – Books of subscription to be opened immediately. . . .

A 7   WILLIAM ALLAN,[10] D. BOULTON, JR.[11] AND W. B. ROBINSON[12]
TO MAJOR HILLIER[13]
York, 5 May 1821
[*PAC, Executive Council Minutes, Upper Canada, 14 May, 1821*]

Being appointed a Committee of Management, by the Petitioners named in an Act to incorporate Sundry Persons, under the Stile and Title, of the President, Directors, and Company, of the Bank of Upper Canada, for the purpose of carrying the provisions of the said Act into effect, We take the liberty of apprizing you, that Books will be opened for receiving subscriptions on the 21 day of May Instant, And we should be happy to receive an early signification of His Excellency's pleasure, as to the Amount of stock to be taken by the Government, as it may have an important effect upon the success of the Subscription throughout the Province –

New Brunswick, after the Revolution. On coming to York in 1796 he worked with his brother-in-law, John McGill, in the Commissary Department. He was acting receiver general, 1819–20, and a member of the Legislative Council, 1821–41. He possessed extensive business contacts in New York City, was a director of the Bank of Upper Canada between 1822 and 1826, and acted as its president, in William Allan's absence, in 1825. In 1857 he owned four hundred shares in the Bank of Upper Canada. His estate owned ten in 1860.

[10]William Allan (1770–1853), born in Scotland, came to Montreal in 1787 and moved to York about 1796. He sat on the Legislative Council, 1825–41, and the Executive Council, 1836–41. Up to 1822 his primary occupation was that of a merchant. With the exception of 1825, he was president of the Bank of Upper Canada from 1822 to 1835. During this period he was at times, collector of customs, inspector of stills and taverns, postmaster of York, treasurer of the Home District, commissioner of the Canada Company, first president of the Toronto Board of Trade, president of the Toronto & Lake Huron Railway Company and, after resigning from the bank, governor of the British America Fire & Life Assurance Company.

[11]D'Arcy Boulton Jr. (1785–1846), eldest son of Judge D'Arcy Boulton, was called to the bar in 1807 and between 1810 and 1825 operated as a merchant in partnership with Peter Robinson and later with William Proudfoot. He was a director of the Bank of Upper Canada in 1824–26, 1828 and 1831–33. Later he became a director of the British America Fire & Life Assurance Company.

[12]William Benjamin Robinson (1797–1873), third son of Christopher Robinson and brother of John Beverley Robinson, represented Simcoe in the Legislative Assembly in 1830–40, and again in 1845–57.

[13]Major George Hillier (d. 1841) was Lieutenant-Governor Maitland's aide-de-camp, military, and later civil secretary.

A 8   LT. GOVERNOR P. MAITLAND TO EARL BATHURST
York, 12 May 1821
[*PAC, CO 42, v. 366, p. 131*]

The Bill for the establishment of a provincial Bank originated in a Report of a Committee of the House of Assembly, upon petitions from different parts of the province complaining of the great want of a circulating medium and the depressed and embarrassed state of Trade in consequence – Loan Offices were prayed for which the Legislature could not sanction and which I could not have assented to, but it was thought that the Establishment of a Bank by Legislative provisions, and under proper restrictions would go every length it would be prudent or practicable to go in removing the Evil. To ensure its going into operation the amount of Capital necessary and of course of paper to be circulated was comparatively small, and it was framed in all respects upon the bill authorizing a bank at Kingston, to which His Majesty had assented but which had become ineffectual from the failure in subscribing the stock within the time prescribed. I assented to it from a conviction of the general and immediate necessity of such an Establishment, and from the hope of its enabling the Government to obtain within the province, and in the most convenient way the loan which we were compelled to resort to to [*sic*] pay the public Creditors the arrears which have accrued during the suspension of our receipts from Lower Canada. Almost immediately after the termination of the Session, the bill passed in 1819 for establishing a provincial bank, which it was apprehended would not be returned within the limited period, now nearly expired, came out with a signification of His Majesty's Gracious Assent which has been accordingly proclaimed – Altho' the time which remains for carrying its provisions into effect is short, I trust its object may succeed, and at all events as the purpose of both is similar, and the bill now sent would certainly not have been passed had there been any assurance that the other would have been returned in time, and may be considered as superseded and rendered unnecessary by it. Your Lordship will, I doubt not, feel it necessary to suggest that it be disallowed by His Majesty.

A 9   W.D. POWELL,[14] TO MAJOR HILLIER
York, 14 May 1821
[*PAC, Executive Council Minutes, Upper Canada*]

The Committee of the Executive Council, considering Your Excellency's reference of this date, of the Letter from the Bank Committee, of Management, as requiring its opinion and advice, respectfully submit, that Your Excellency should engage the Public, to the Extent

---

[14]William Dummer Powell (1755–1834) born in Boston, came to Canada in 1799. Between 1816 and 1825 he was chief justice.

authorised by Law, And that if Your Excellency's determination be such, it should be made known to the subscribers, which the Committee apprehend, would afford equal encouragement as the Actual subscription for Two thousand shares, and Yet, leave it open to Individuals to furnish all the shares if so inclined.

A 10　JOHN STRACHAN TO JOHN MACAULAY
York, 5 July 1821
[PAO, Macaulay Papers]

I have abstained hitherto from saying a word to you concerning our bank but I think the period is arrived when I ought to speak. 1st I think that there is no doubt of our being able to put it in operation. 2 If well managed it appears to me to posess advantages which cannot fail of rendering it in time lucrative. In regard to subscriptions from Kingston or indeed out of York I was never sanguine for I declared at the first meeting that I did not expect four hundred Shares to be taken up out of the District – This excited division but I believe I shall be found correct.

Now I am not sorry that we should be left in a great measure to ourselves at the commencement for to succeed we ought to move cautiously and not to be distracted by contending interests. But it will soon be for our advantage to have an agent at Kingston and at no distant period an office of deposit with all the powers of a branch but carried on at less expense and more under our control. I looked forward to you as the Proper person for this Agency and ultimately Cashier of the deposit and I have no doubt but that it would afford a handsome remuneration in a very short time – to pave the way for this if you think it likely to be an object it will be necessary for you if your circumstances will permit to subscribe at least 20 Shares to qualify yourself for being a Director. Before doing this however you may write a confidential letter to the Attorney General telling him your view in subscribing and that you will depend upon his assistance in procuring you the Agency etc. when the proper time arrives but that if he be engaged in the favor of any other person your present circumstances compel you to decline. This will be agreeable to him and anticipate any other application and I think we shall have no difficulty in managing the matter. I wish you to revolve this thing seriously before you decide. You need not fear the present Kingston Bank it is not likely that we shall have any thing to do with it. I shall be decidly against it for many reasons 1st the want of respectability in the Members 2 The assumption of their debts. 3 The Expence of a Branch not completely under our control 4. The little aid they could afford us in respect to Capital. I take it that our answer will be if they propose an union, "Our books are open you may subscribe." I write confidentially, nor need any body know that I have addressed you on the subject.

A 11 JOHN MCGILL TO GEORGE CROOKSHANK
York, 22 July 1821
[*PAO, Crookshank-Lambert Papers*]

. . . It is not as yet ascertained whether there are sufficient subscribers to the Upper Canada Bank to commence operations. My own opinion is that it will be a losing business, tho' I have been dragged into subscribe for more than was perhaps prudent. I really cannot see what good business a Bank can do here – The Lower Canada Bank, I am told, has not been able to pay a dividend for the last year, owing to bad debts.

A 12 JOHN SPENCER[15] TO JOHN H. DUNN[16]
26 July 1821
[*PAC, RG 19 B2A, v. 1130*]

. . . I take the liberty to suggest the great inconvenience experienced by Lessees – and others in my Bailiwick – in consequence of the refusal of Bills of the Upper Canada Bank[17] on account of the public – which is almost the only circulating medium with us.

A 13 MAJOR HILLIER TO JOHN H. DUNN
8 October 1821
[*PAC, RG 19 B2A, v. 1130*]

I am commanded by His Excellency the Lieutenant Governor to request that you will be pleased to attend the meeting of the Subscribers to the Bank of Upper Canada which is to be held tomorrow (the 9th) & subscribe the Books on behalf of the Government for exactly the number of shares (& no more) that will, with the subscription of private individuals enable the Bank to go into operation.

I have further to request you will be pleased to acquaint me for His Excellency's information with the amount which you shall have subscribed for on behalf of the Government. . . .

A 14 JOHN H. DUNN TO MAJOR HILLIER
York, 16 October 1821
[*PAC, RG 5 A1, v. 54*]

I have the honor to acquaint you for the information of His Excellency the Lieutenant Governor that pursuant to his directions I attended the

[15]John Spencer was sheriff, District of Newcastle, 1810–1827.

[16]John Henry Dunn (1794–1854), born in St. Helena, came to Upper Canada in 1820 as receiver general after a stint in the East India Service in London. He was receiver general until 1843 when he returned to England. He sat on the Executive Council in 1836 and on the Legislative Council, 1822–41. He was at times president of the Welland Canal Company, director of the British America Fire & Life Assurance Company, director of the Home District Savings Bank and Trustee of the Home District. He sat on the directorate of the Bank of Upper Canada in 1822–23, 1826–36, 1841, 1843–45.

meeting of the members of the proposed Bank, which took place to day, and the state of subscription is agreeable to the enclosed copy of a Document handed to me by Mr. William Allan, one of the Chosen Committee; by which you will perceive that without the full number of shares which I have subscribed for the Government vizt 2000 the operation of the Bank could not be affected. I remained till the close of the Proceedings, and discovering no disposition by Individuals to make any further Subscription I had no alternative left but to do as above stated, which I hope His Excellency will be pleased to approve.

[Enclosure]

Statement of a Return of Subscription to the Proposed Bank of Upper Canada, on the 16th October 1821 –

Hawksbury Shares	10	
Kingston	46	
Cobourgh	36	
Hope	136	
Queenstown	50	
Vittoria	20	
Sandwich	80	
Amherstburgh	40	
York	1452	
Dundas	40	
Total number	1910	of Shares subscribed
Government A/C	2000	Upper Canada
	3910	
Remaining to complete	90	the number prescribed by the
Act vizt –	4000	Shares to go into Operation

10/ per Centum on 4,000 Shares at £12.10 currency per share £5,000 Governments Proportion of the above £2,500 –

A 15   JOHN McGILL TO DAVID LAMBERT[18]
York, 23 January 1822
[PAO, Crookshank-Lambert Papers]

. . . The President for the Bank of Upper Canada is to be chosen tomorrow, had Mr. Crookshank been in the Province, he would have been elected, as that, in consequence of his absence cannot be done, I except that Mr. Allan will be President. . . .

A 16   W.B. ROBINSON TO S.P. JARVIS[19]
York, 28 January 1822
[PAO, Jarvis-Powell Papers]

. . . Mr. Allan was elected President unanimously last week. Thos.

[17]This refers to the so-called Pretended Bank of Upper Canada at Kingston – pretended because it operated without a charter.
[18]David Lambert (d. 1825), was the brother-in-law of George Crookshank and partner in Lambert & Company, New York.
[19]Samuel Peters Jarvis (1792–1857), born in Upper Canada and called to the bar in

Ridout,[20] Cashier (£200 a year), & the following Gentry Directors – Widmer,[21] McGill, Dunn, H.J. Boulton,[22] Dr. Strachan – Thos. Dickson[23] – Surveyor General[24] – [?], W.B.R. [William Benjamin Robinson], Col. Wells[25] – Baby[26] – George Munroe[27] & George Ridout.[28] The first instalment will be called for almost immediately to enable the Cashier to proceed to Philadelphia for plates & paper. . . .

A 17   GEORGE RIDOUT TO JOHN MACAULAY
York, 31 January 1822
[PAO, Macaulay Papers]

. . . The Pres. & Cashier were elected without a dissenting voice. This is pleasant enough. The Boultons secretly having canvassed for Mr Dunn but finding that it would not take made a virtue of necessity: & [?] fell in with the majority.

A 18   EXTRACTS FROM DIARY OF THOMAS GIBBS RIDOUT
[PAO, Ridout Diaries]

[Montreal, 15 April 1822]
. . . waited upon Mr Griffen[29] Cashier of the Montreal Bank & handed him Mr Allans letter of Introduction – also presented his draft in my favor for Two Thousand pounds on acct. [account] of the Bank of Upper Canada to be left as a Deposit – was received with much politeness by Mr Gerrard[30] the President and permitted to take a list of their Bank Books – and obtain all the information which the Gentlemen of the bank could give –
    called in Co. [company] with W. R. [William Radenhurst][31] at the Canada Bank and left a parcel of Gold for them handed to me at

---

1815, was from 1814 to 1839 employed in the provincial secretary's office. He married a daughter of W.D. Powell. He was a director of the Bank of Upper Canada, 1825–44 and 1846–47.

[20]Thomas Gibbs Ridout (1792–1861) was born in Canada, moved to York from Niagara in 1797, and was educated by John Strachan at Cornwall. During the War of 1812, he was deputy assistant commissary general for Upper Canada and remained with the Commissary Office until 1820. By his first marriage he became the brother-in-law of R.B. Sullivan and Robert Baldwin. From 1822 until 1861 he was cashier of the Bank of Upper Canada.

[21]Christopher Widmer (1780–1858), born in England, came to Upper Canada as an army surgeon during the War of 1812 and became one of York's most acclaimed medical men. He sat on the Legislative Council, 1843–58. He was a director of the Bank of Upper Canada, 1822–24, 1827–56, and vice president, 1843–48.

[22]Henry John Boulton (1790–1870) was born in England, second son of D'Arcy Boulton. He was appointed solicitor general for Upper Canada in 1818 and attorney general, 1829–33. He was a member of the Legislative Assembly, 1830–34, 1841–44 and 1846–56. He was a director of the Bank of Upper Canada, 1822–28 and, until 1833, when he became chief justice of Newfoundland, the bank's lawyer at York. He owned 320 shares of the Bank of Upper Canada in 1857, 242 in 1860. By 1863 he owned no shares.

Kingston by George Markland[32] and also two parcels of Paper money given to me at Kingston by Mr Ferguson[33] of the U.C. Bank – . . .

[New York, 28 April 1822]
. . . dined at 2 with Mr Morris Robinson Cashier of the United States Bank – . . . he recommended us to issue as many small notes as possible – not to discount upon accommodation notes or suffer any to be renewed without paying 20 per cent on the principal promises to give me every information on my return – . . . I must buy a few bottles of Ink soaked in oil for filling up Bank Post Notes and for signatures as it cannot be extracted from the paper –

[Hartford, 6 May 1822]
. . . After dinner went to the Phoenix Bank and remained there until 5 o'clock copied some forms. . . .
great care must be taken to have the notes well pressed as they wear longer and are not so apt to soil – water mark no security –

[23]Thomas Dickson, member of a wealthy Niagara family, was collector of customs at Queenston and represented Lincoln in the Legislative Assembly, 1812–16. Robinson was probably incorrect in referring to him as a bank director. His name does not appear in any other source.

[24]Thomas Ridout (1754–1829) was the father of T.G. Ridout. He was surveyor general from 1810–29, and a director of the Bank of Upper Canada, 1822–23.

[25]Joseph Wells (1773?–1853) a half-pay officer from England, came to Canada in 1815. He sat on the Legislative Council, 1820–41, and the Executive Council, 1830–36. From 1827 to 1839 he was bursar of King's College and a director of the Bank of Upper Canada, 1822–26 and 1828–38.

[26]James Baby (1763–1833) was born at Detroit. He sat on the Executive and Legislative councils, 1792–1833, and was inspector general, 1815–33. He was prominent in the Catholic Church at York and a director of the Bank of Upper Canada, 1822–32.

[27]George Monroe (1801–78) was born in Scotland and came to York in 1802. An Anglican and a merchant, he was a director of the Bank of Upper Canada, 1822–24 and 1829–31. In 1865 he owned ninety-one shares of the bank.

[28]George Ridout (1791–1871) brother of T.G. Ridout, was called to the bar in 1813. He was a director of the Bank of Upper Canada in 1822 and 1824.

[29]Robert Griffen, cashier of the Bank of Montreal, 1817–27, and brother of the Bank of Montreal's first notary, Henry Griffen, became a celebrated land speculator underwriting an area known as Griffentown in Montreal.

[30]Samuel Gerrard (1767–1857), a merchant, came to Canada from Ireland in 1787. He was active in the North West Fur Trading Company. He resigned from his mercantile business in 1821 and was president of the Bank of Montreal, 1820–26.

[31]William Radenhurst was a discount clerk and teller for the Bank of Montreal in the 1820s.

[32]George Herchmer Markland (ca. 1790–1862), son of a Kingston merchant and loyalist, educated at Strachan's Cornwall school, was a member of the Legislative Council, 1820–40, and the Executive Council, 1822–36, treasurer of the Midland District, 1821–37, and inspector general of Upper Canada, 1833–38. In 1818 he was the Kingston agent for the Bank of Montreal. He sat on the Bank of Upper Canada directorate as a government appointee in 1833.

[33]John Ferguson, judge of the Midland District Court, 1802–26, was a director of the Pretended Bank of Upper Canada at Kingston.

They ought to be filled up with a good free running hand – good ink & figures well made – this being the greatest difficulty counterfeiters meet with as they cannot obtain good writers – their figures are generally bad –

[Hartford, 7 May 1822]
. . . obtained from Mr Hudson a Book of Statutes contg. [containing] the Charters of several Banks of this State X – called at the Graphic office to see how our plates were getting on. . . .

[New York, 10 May 1822]
. . . employed till 12 o clock in copying the rules of the United States Bank. . . .

[New York, 11 May 1822]
. . . The advantage which a Canadian Bank derives from redeeming their notes in New York arises from the currency they obtain in the back part of the States – as all the trade centers in New York. They are remitted as cash here and the agent purchases them at 1 or $1^1/_2$ p^r discount beyond which it would not be prudent to go – New York also regulates the exchange of the continent & Sterling bills remitted here find ready sales at the highest rates. then the agent disposes of at $^1/_4$ p. c. [per cent] the proceeds of which keeps him in funds to meet the notes.

A 19   JOHN H. DUNN TO MAJOR HILLIER
York, 4 June 1822
[*PAC, RG 5 A1, v. 56*]

. . . The enclosed is a letter I got from Mr. Allan which is on the subject of the instalment due by the Government to be paid on or before the 10TH Instant. Mr. Allan feels himself under the absolute necessity of requiring this sum to be paid in Specie and I really am at a loss to know how far I may be able to accomplish this matter. [?] you will be good enough to speak to the Commissary for his assistance, who has some right to accommodate me, as I have done so for him on a former occasion. If you were to draw on the Military Chest at Quebec I should go down myself or send in order that I may get it in hand [?] the $^1/_2$ per Cent allowed, would assist to cover the expense. It is I presume a matter of little importance as the money you may draw if not expended will be liable to be returned at no charge and it will be as carefully lodged in my custody as the Commissarys – *This is between us* –

A 20   DIARY OF THOMAS GIBBS RIDOUT
[*MTL, T.G. Ridout, Diary*]

[New York, 7 June 1822]
. . . in speaking to Mr. Catlin[34] about agency here he offered to become

---

[34]Lynde Catlin had been cashier of the New York branch of the Second Bank of the United States and was, in 1822, president of the Merchants' Bank at New York.

our agent on the same terms that he acts for the Bank of Canada which is 1/4 per cent for negotiating the sale of Bills of Exchange – on all monies deposited in his hands subject to drawing he allows 5 per cent during the time it remains undrawn. should he be overdrawn he allowed at the rate of 7 per cent – a settlement takes place every 3 or 6 months according to the magnitude of the transactions.

A 21   JOHN H. DUNN TO MAJOR HILLIER
York, 7 June 1822
[*PAC, RG 19 B2b, v. 1172*]

I have received your letter of this days date and In reply I beg to inform you that I am perfectly prepaired to meet the Warrant you allude to, for the sum of £2500 provided that the President of the Bank will receive that sum from Me in Notes of the Montreal or any other Bank in Canada or a Draft on my Agents at Montreal As to Specie it is impossible. I am under the absolute necessity of accepting Paper currency from the great scarcity of Specie and the most of the Persons from whom the Provincial Revenue is derived have no other means of transmitting money to me but in paper through the channel of the Post office in the Province – with regard to the money received by my Agents in the Lower Province I am under the necessity of drawing to this place by Draft, for which I receive paper, when ever it happens, that I receive Specie, it is always paid out towards the demands against the Public.

A 22   JOHN H. DUNN TO WILLIAM ALLAN
York, 10 June 1822
[*PAC, RG 19 B2b, v. 1172*]

As I feel much interested, both on account of the Concern which the Government have in the Bank, as well as for its general success, induces me to offer you any assistance I can render, in the transaction of the change of the Paper Currency which I am aware you have been necessitated to receive from the Subscribers, into Specie, as it is my intention to proceed to Montreal by the next Steam Boat, which will offer a conveying on Wednesday and shall return as speedy as possible, I beg to request you will be pleased to enter the Instalment due by the Government as paid and as soon as I am able it shall be deposited in your possession agreeable to the terms of the act (viz in specie)

A 23   JOHN H. DUNN TO MAJOR HILLIER
Montreal, 19 June 1822
[*PAC, RG 5 A1, v. 56*]

I arrived here on Monday and I have so far settled my Business that I have got the Sum of £2500 in Specie, but I am sorry to say all in 1/2 Dollars, Gold is not to be got under any other circumstances than a High Premium. I am rather at a loss to decide in what manner these 1/2 Dollars are to be conveyed to York. They are so bulky that unless I am able to procure some safe mode I should not like to take the Risk on myself. I however will apply for a Military Guard of a confidential Adjutant, and if I succeed I shall leave this on Saturday next or Monday. As I shall be under the necessity of proceeding by Water my absence from York will be longer than I anticipated, at all events I shall make all possible speed .... I cannot help wishing myself safe back again to York with this Money and if you see Allan have the goodness to tell him that I cannot think of burthening myself with any larger sum, and that I have not seen Mr. Ridout, and am not aware if he has returned from the States.

A 24 RULES AND REGULATIONS FOR CONDUCTING THE BUSINESS OF THE CHARTERED BANK OF UPPER CANADA
York 1822
[*MTL*]

III.

. . . The Stock of every member of this Corporation shall be considered to be pledged to the Company for any and all monies, which such member may at any time owe the bank, and actually due; and the Board of Directors may, if they see cause, refuse to make any transfer, or pay any Dividend upon such stock, until such debt is fully discharged.

IV.

The bank may take charge of the Cash of all such persons as shall choose to place it there free of expense, and shall keep it subject to the order of the depositor, payable at sight . . . .

VI.

A majority of votes shall determine all questions, except in cases of Discount, when two of the Board voting in the negative, shall be sufficient to check the passing of a note, and all decisions shall be by ballot.

VII.

All Bills and notes offered for discount, shall be delivered in the Bank on Tuesday in each week, and laid before the Board of Directors, by the Cashier, on the succeeding Wednesday, at ten o'clock, together with a statement of the Funds and situation of the Bank, on which days the discount shall be settled, and such as are admitted shall be paid, or placed to the credit of the applicants, on the day on which they are discounted, and may be drawn for at any time after one o'clock, and the notes or bills not discounted, shall be returned at any time after one o'clock on the same day.

VIII.

Discounts shall not be made for a longer time than ninety days, with the usual grace, unless by an unanimous vote of the Directors present at a meeting of the Board, and no discount shall be made without two responsible names, but if such property as shall be approved by the Board, be deposited and pledged, to an amount sufficient to secure the payment, with all damages, then one responsible name may be taken; but no accommodation note, (i.e. a note, the proceeds of which are to be placed to the credit of the drawer,) shall be discounted, unless its payment be secured by a deposit of the Stock of this Bank, or such other property as shall be approved by the Board, together with an express authority to the Bank, to sell the deposit in case of non-payment, at any time after the note shall become due. And no notes, bills, or acceptances, shall be discounted for a less time than ten days, nor for a less sum than twenty-five pounds.

IX.

No renewal of a note shall be made unless twenty per cent of the amount be paid, except by the unanimous consent of the Directors present . . . .

XII.

No credit shall be given, on any pretence whatever, to any person who may be at the time a defaulter at the Bank, whether the defalcation be on paper discounted or left for collection, as maker, drawer, acceptor or endorser; and in order that the Board may be enabled to carry this regulation into exact operation, it shall be the duty of the Cashier, to lay before the Board at each meeting for discount, the names of all defaulters, designating those on discount, and those on notes left for collection.

XIII.

Discounts may be made on notes payable to the President and Directors of the Bank, on such personal pledges, and other securities as the Board of Directors may deem expedient . . . .

XVII.

No individual or co-partnership responsibility as drawer, maker, acceptor, or endorser, shall be received to an amount exceeding One Thousand Pounds, unless by the unanimous consent of the Board.

XVIII.

No Director, without special authority from the Board, shall be permitted to inspect the cash account of any person with this Bank.

XIX.

It shall be the duty of the President to sign the Bills and Post Notes of the Bank, and to deliver them when signed to the Cashier, who shall give duplicate receipts, to be taken in a book especially to be kept by the President for that purpose. The other receipt to be lodged with the Accountant for the time being, who on his leaving his office in the Bank, shall deliver the said receipts to his successor, unless otherwise ordered by the Board of Directors . . . .

XXI.

The Board of Directors shall be divided into weekly committees of one each who shall be styled Director for the week; and who shall have power with the President, in the recess of the Board, to manage such concerns of the Bank, as do not require the advice and interference of the full Board. The weekly committee shall have no authority to revise or change any decision made by the Board on any note . . . .

XXIII.

Every officer of the Bank shall be engaged on the express condition that their duties may be increased or altered at the pleasure of the Directors. And it is the intention of the Directors, and they reserve the right and power to themselves, to vary the duties of the several officers, and to call on one to assist in the performance of the duties of another, and for such alteration or increase of services, no officer shall be entitled to any increase of salary . . . .

XXX.

1st. – It shall be the duty of the Cashier to countersign at the Bank, all Bills or notes to be signed by the President, or by order of the Board; to take charge of all Bills, notes, obligations, money deposits, and pledges, and at the close of the business of each day, shall have the whole thereof in his possession, and see that the same are safely deposited in the vaults of the Bank; and daily examine the settlement of the cash accounts, and whenever the actual amount disagrees with the balance of the cash account, report the same to the President and Directors without delay; to attend all meetings of the board, keep a fair and regular account of its proceedings, and promptly furnish a copy of all resolutions of the Board to any of the Directors who may apply therefore; give such information to the Board as may be required – consult with committees when requested, on subjects referred by the Board – and also, to perform such other services as may be required of him. Carefully to observe the conduct of all persons employed under him, and report to the board such instances of neglect, incapacity, or bad conduct, as he may discover in any of them. It shall also be the duty of the Cashier, to cause the officers, clerks, and servants of the Bank, to attend to and execute their respective duties, in conformity to such rules and regulations as may be prescribed by the Board of Directors, and to take a general superintendence of the concerns of the Bank. To see that the books and accounts are kept in an orderly and methodical manner, and never suffer them to be behind the duties of the day, to the end that whenever a clear and perfect exhibit of the state of the Bank shall be required, it may be speedily produced. The Cashier shall also on every discount day, make out and lay before the Board of Directors, a distinct abstract of the state of their Funds, which abstract shall ascertain, the amount of the debts and credits of the Bank, amount of notes issued, and then in circulation, the amount of cash on hand, and shall likewise distinguish in the account of cash on hand, how much thereof is in specie, and how much in the several kinds of Bank notes, designating those of this Bank and the notes of other Banks. He shall also at all times have a list of all the discounts made, and arranged in a perspicuous manner, subject to the inspection of every Director when called for.

2nd. – The Cashier shall also perform the duty of Teller; make all payments from the Bank, including all Notes or Bills discounted, and to receive payment of such Notes or Bills due; all Checks on this Bank received by him, shall be delivered on the day of their receipt to the Bookkeeper to be entered by him; and if he shall pay any Check drawn on this Bank, the person drawing the same, not having the amount thereof to his credit in the Bank, he shall be charged with the amount overdrawn, provided the same was done without application to the Bookkeeper, but if the Bookkeeper shall have declared the Check to be good, he shall be responsible for the amount overdrawn. He shall also receive all Money Bills or Checks brought to the Bank to be deposited, and enter the same to the credit of the persons depositing the same, or to the credit of such person as the depositor shall direct; he giving a list of such deposits, also he shall receive payment of all Notes, Bills, and Demands left for collection, and when the proprietor thereof shall desire it, he shall pass to their credit the amount of Bills and Notes discounted. He shall also keep a Debit and Credit Journal of all Monies passing through his hands; from which, the Bookkeeper posts to the several accounts in the business Ledger.

3rd. – The Cashier shall also take a register of the Notes of this Bank, in the usual manner, and a Vault Book, shewing the daily amount of Cash in the Vault, designating the amount in Specie and Notes separately. The Cashier shall also keep the Stock Journal and Transfer Book, and Stock Ledger; and do and perform such other services as may be required of him . . . .

B. PERSONNEL, PRINCIPLES AND PRACTICE: THE ALLAN
ERA, 1822–35

B 1   Copy of a Resolution Adopted by the Board of
Directors of the Bank of Upper Canada
York, 31 December 1822
[*PAC, RG 19 B2A, v. 1131*]

Whereas the Government holds a considerable share of the Stock of this
Bank and would equally participate with Individuals in all the advantages and benefits arising from its prosperity, and whereas upon the
establishment of the Institution, it was generally understood and supposed that the Public monies of this Province would be deposited
therein, the Board unanimously agreed to and adopted the following
resolution.

Resolved that the President, Directors and company of the Bank of
Upper Canada are ready to bring up all the Revenue and balances of
Revenue which now are or may hereafter become due by the Province
of Lower Canada to this Province and that they will pay the drafts of the
Receiver General at sight to the amount thereof either in specie or their
own notes as may be required.

B 2   John H. Dunn to William Allan
York, 3 January 1823
[*PAC, RG 19 B2b, v. 1172*]

I have received your note and the accompanying Resolutions of the
Bank of Upper Canada, upon which I beg to remark that I have no wish
to place the Public Funds under my Charge, in possession of the Bank,
and I think I intimated to the Reverend Doctor Strachan one of your
Directors, who agitated this subject in my presence on a former
occasion, that he must obtain an order for doing so from the Lords
Commissioners of His Majesty's Treasury in England until then I
should pursue the same line of conduct as I have hitherto done.

With regard to the Public Money, now in the Course of payment at
Quebec and the offer you have made of bringing it up to this Place I can
have no objection provided that I have a satisfactory security for its safe
deliverence to me in specie but at this moment I am not aware that my
Agents at Montreal have been able to acquit the Warrant, to receive the
Public money now due, from the Lower Province, at the same time I
have to say, that in future, that according to the demand I have for
money, your Bank shall have my Drafts on Montreal; as all Individuals
receiving Public Money from me under the Proper Authority, shall have
the power of receiving your Bank Notes, or those of the Montreal Bank,
which I have deemed proper to receive from my subaccountants, under

the impression of its respectability, and the Confidence I have placed in that Institution.

B 3   BANK OF UPPER CANADA PETITION TO
LT.-GOVERNOR P. MAITLAND
York, 3 July 1823
[PAC, RG 5 A1, v. 61, pp. 32175–7]

. . . The President Directors and Company of the Bank of Upper Canada Beg leave respectfully to represent.

That this Institution established by an act of the Legislature of this Province for the general prosperity of the colony, has advanced with a success and benefit to the Public beyond what could have been anticipated from so recent a commencement.

This Board however regret to have occasion to complain to your Excellency that the Bank of Upper Canada as well the Province at large suffer great injustice by means of a pretended Bank, which has for some time past carried on business as such at Kingston, under the title and pretence of being a Branch of the Bank of Canada, which is by an act of the Lower Province, established at Montreal: an injustice which your Excellency will be pleased to observe requires an early remedy.

That the Bank of Upper Canada notwithstanding the public disadvantages of this illegal establishment at Kingston, has nevertheless been guided by the most liberal views towards that Bank, and did accordingly about the time of their commencing business at Kingston direct its agent there (in answer to an application made by the persons conducting that pretended Branch Bank at Kingston) to express a readiness on the part of the Bank of Upper Canada to establish with that Bank a mutual accommodation by exchanging the respective notes of both Institutions as they might occasionally accumulate with each, in the course of regular business, and also made a similar communication to the person acting for that Bank at York, offering at every exchange of notes, to pay the difference in specie at the Bank or by Bills of Exchange on Montreal at par, as might suit their convenience.

That in disregard of this liberal offer the Branch Bank of Canada has declined any such exchange either at Kingston or this place and continues to carry on their business at Kingston, thereby putting in circulation large sums of money in Bank notes made at Montreal, and there alone payable, and by such means collecting very considerable Sums in the notes of the Bank of Upper Canada.

That at three several times large amounts of the notes of the Bank of Upper Canada thus collected by the aforesaid Branch Bank at Kingston have been presented for payment at the Bank of York and payment in specie insisted on, and at the same time an absolute and total refusal given by them to accept or take in exchange their own notes, then in considerable accumulation in the Bank of Upper Canada and offered at the same time that the notes of the Bank of Upper Canada were so presented for payment.

That this conduct on the part of the Bank of Canada, so contrary to that liberal spirit which the Bank of Upper Canada, would willingly cultivate with them, and other similar Institutions, proves not only a private injury to this authorized Institution but also a public grievance in as much as it draws the specie from this Province and yields to their Stockholders in the Lower Province, an interest on their capital, derived from the people of this Province, and subjects the Bank of Upper Canada to serious disadvantages by obliging them at considerable expense and risque to send for the necessary supplies of specie from Montreal to make good the specie so drained from this Bank, by the aforesaid illegal Branch Bank at Kingston to which may be added the very great inconvenience sustained by the Public of the Upper Province from such an in-undation of Bank paper which is only redeemable in Lower Canada.

That the Bank of Upper Canada has taken all fair and honorable means to induce the Bank of Canada at Montreal and the persons acting for them in this Province to abandon a course so hostile to this Institution established by the Law of this Province, a protection of little avail if illegal undertakings, like this pretended Branch Bank at Kingston be permitted to carry on their evil designs.

That the Bank of Upper Canada authorized their President to address the President of the Bank of Canada on the subject, subsequently to which their solicitor under the direction of the Board, addressed another letter to the person assuming the office or duty of President of the said pretended Branch Bank at Kingston, both which communications have been so disregarded that the Board not unmindful of the Interest which the Government has in the protection of this Bank, deem it their duty to communicate these matters to your Excellency and respectfully request your Excellency will please to direct the Crown Officers to examine into the facts and to institute such legal proceedings against the aforesaid pretended Branch Bank as may effectually check so great a Public evil.

B 4   JOHN H. DUNN TO MAJOR HILLIER
York, 15 September 1823
[*PAC, RG 19 B2b, v. 1172*]

I beg leave to acquaint you for the information of His Excellency the Lieutenant Governor that the 2nd installment on £20,000 currency borrowed from Messrs Clark and Street[1] amounting to the sum of

[1]Thomas Clark (1770?–1837) was a merchant, grist and saw miller and forwarder of goods at Queenston, Chippawa and Fort Erie, in partnership with Samuel Street (1775–1844), a United Empire Loyalist, who took over all the business when Clark died in 1837. Street and Clark were major competitors with the Bank of Upper Canada for government debentures in the 1820s and early 1830s. Street was a director of the Bank of Upper Canada in 1840 and 1844.

£6666.13.4 is due this day agreeable to the Debentures issued by me under an act of the Provincial Assembly, and also the 1st installment of £6666.13.4 amounting to £2222.4.5/4/3 Cy. Borrowed from the Chartered Bank of Upper Canada is due on the 16th of this month, under the authority of the same act– I have therefore to request you will be pleased to inform me if it is the pleasure of His Excellency that the same should be Renewed, as I have no funds, under the disposal of the Provincial Government in my possession and have advanced near £5000 to carry on the Public Service. The Parties concerned are willing to accept Renewals.

B 5　JOHN STRACHAN TO JOHN MACAULAY (PRIVATE)
York, 29 October 1823
[PAO, Macaulay Papers]

. . . I happened to meet Mr. Allan this evening at the Old Chiefs and was sorry to find that some little misunderstanding has been excited between you and the Bank here. Now my Good Sir I can with much confidence say that it is impossible for a man to be more respected than you are by all the Directors (this I know tho' not now among their number) and the Cashier had no right to write you as He did. But the truth is he has so little tact or feeling that he is not aware of writing offensively when he is doing it. You must not therefore mind his loose expressions and accept of the very ample amends [?] which I am told goes by this Post. I am told that it is in contemplation to establish an office of deposit at Kingston if so it will be doubtless offered to you and I would advise you to accept of it on as reasonable terms as possible. it will not give you more trouble than you now have as Agent so that you will require no more assistance and you must keep in mind that it will if successful soon become an office of discount and so be a permanent establishment the direction of which would naturally fall into your hands and yield with little trouble an honourable & in time a very handsome remuneration.

B 6　WILLIAM ALLAN TO JOHN MACAULAY
York, 6 November 1823
[PAO, Macaulay Papers]

. . . I shall make known to the Board that you have withdrawn your offer of resignation and that all things are fully cleared up – on the Subject of Establishing an Office of Deposit – among other things that occurred to me, was that if upon a fair trial it was found not to answer it was that kind of Establishment that could soon be withdrawn　But I did also think that for some time it would not require much more labour or attendance than you have heretofore bestowed I should certainly require to have the office open constantly for a given time each day for the sake of receiving as well as Paying and to transact any other bussiness as to a clerk for Copying letters it did not appear to me there would be much more to do in that way than you have had till the bussiness increased and if it is found to increase in that case I can have no doubt but the Board let them be composed of whom they may would always make what further additional assistance was necessary. It can only be considered as an Experiment just now. It would of course be necessary to have the office kept separate from all other transactions   It would also be /but fair/ and Perhaps necessary, no person should have a knowledge the state of any person Account who might make a Deposit, or keep his money in any way – and I think the Entrance, and every thing apertaining to it ought to be separate – from the description you gave me some time ago of your new Building – I think that could be managed – as you say a good Iron chest in a Substantial Building where there is constantly some person in it . . . and the Books, of course every day should be put away in a safe place . . . .

B 7   John H. Dunn to Major Hillier
York, 11 February 1824
[*PAC, RG5 A1, v. 64, pp. 34403–4*]

It was my intention some time since to write to you, or to call on His Excellency on the subject of the payment of the Losses during the late War[2] but I have been prevented in consequence of indisposition, and to offer the services of my department in doing so. I have been informed it is the intention of the Commissary General to send the amount up to this Place in Specie. I have only to say, that in my humble opinion it will be doing no possible good, and the service will incur a very considerable expense. I wrote to my Agents at Montreal to know if they would in the event of my paying the Losses, receive the amount at Montreal from the Commissary Genl free of all charges, which they have handsomely agreed to do. So should His Excellency accept my services, the whole of this Matter as far as regards the Payment will be done without a fraction expense to the Public, & the mode should be adopted precisely similar to that which was done on a former occasion and approved of in England. the Bank here shall have every advantage, even as much so, as they could desire if they paid the amount in itself – . . . .

B 8   John H. Dunn to Major Hillier
York, 20 February 1824
. [*PAC, RG 5 A1, v. 65*]

. . . After Clark had been here, I received the enclosed private note from Mr. Allan. I did not contemplate that the Bank would have been willing to take any of the Debentures, as they refused to do so in September last when the second of Clark's old Debentures became due.

[2]This refers to claims for indemnity due to losses incurred by citizens during the War of 1812.

At any rate the amount they can loan will not answer the purpose. I am already upwards of £3000 in advance in the Provincial fund, and against the Provincial Fund there are some large demands for School Money and for the Board of Claims etc. And from my last letter by the Wednesday post my agents say there is not the smallest chance of getting any money from Quebec till some arrangement is made regarding the Defalcation with the Lords of the Treasury in England[3] . . . .

B 9   WILLIAM ALLAN TO JOHN MACAULAY
York, 22 April 1824
[PAO, Macaulay Papers]

. . . We have had a meeting on the subject of a further Instalment according to Law and have urged upon calling in 7 1/2 pct more. We have had for some time & have now more banking to do than our funds would allow and is a Pitty to loose it for the want of Money.

Just *Entre nous* I really don't know what we will do for *Directors* There are few or no persons *here* in business or even men of any knowledge of business in that way that are qualified enough to have for Directors and so many of those who are not interested and know nothing of mercantile transactions and concerns ought not to be there there idea of things are often [daft?] for my own part (altho I would not wish you to mention it) But I mean to decline being elected as President (and Perhaps may decline being a Director – if there appears likely a tolerable Board) not from any displeasure or any cause whatever, because I feel very sensable the Board have at all times Paid every [attention?] to what ever I Proposed or recommend, when ever I took anything upon myself (But it is very Probable I will be absent from home. Perhaps for some considerable time – and altho if they thought proper to elect me again and the Board could go on by having another Chairman or President chosen in my absence. As I mean to sign and leave a good supply of Notes still I would feel just as much Interest in case any thing went wrong as if I was Present.) for that reason I mean to decline should there be any certainty of my being able to leave *Home* this Summer of which I will be able to ascertain by the time the new Election takes place,– Don't imagine from what I say that I rate my Presence or assistance beyond that of the most inept Member of the Board . . . . I note what you say about Mr. Simpson[4] and his friend, saying the Montl Bank [are going?] to fix an Establishment at Kingston.

B 10   JOHN DALY[5] TO S.P. JARVIS
Niagara, 15 May 1825
[MTL, S.P. Jarvis Papers]

I understand you act as agent for several whom has stock in the Bank of

---

[3]The receiver general of Lower Canada was accused of using public funds for his own private interests.

U.C. as you have several Proxeys to vote upon at the ensuing election of Directors, for the Bank the R_____t, [Ridout] Party are using every means to get complete sway this year, I hope [?] you will be on the alert and pick up all the proxeys you can lay your hands upon, for you and I will be on the same side of the question and if you will exert yourself as much as I have we will play the card well. I have now the representation of 200 votes and I expect 50 more, therefore I shall be in York on the 1st of June to attend, their is a great number of votes about Smith [?] and York etc. etc. Your whole attention to this ought to be directed for you are more interested than I am, the R_____'s party are trying to get Proxeys, over here, know You ought to put in Motion every wheel in order to put them down and not let them have the controul of the Bank – try to apprize the Boultons they will be put out by the R_____d's party for they are using every Stratagem to control the Board of Directors You   furnish me with a list of Directors you would like to support, If you try hard you can get 100 votes their is your Brother stock also A Hamiltons,[6] your Mothers, Your own please do let Me know how many votes you have also Mr. McCormicks[7] dont neglect you had better if you are acquainted with the Soliciter Gen. tell him of the plan the R_____'s are going upon, as he is better liked than them.

B 11   JOHN STRACHAN TO JOHN MACAULAY
York, 30 May 1825
[*PAO, Macaulay Papers*]

. . . From what Mr. Dunn has told me great efforts are in making to get such Directors as shall insure the election of Mr. Baldwin[8] as *President* of the bank. The plan I never knew till Saturday that Mr Dunn Told me I believe they thought him a Friend and let the secret out   it is the power of Attorney which the Cashier & his Friends hold that make them so bold – I am sorry that you feel delicate in representing your power but I hope the same delicacy does not extend to others in Kingston if it do the matter is up. At Niagara they have acted differently as I am just given to understand and a person I believe comes over to vote in the name of all the Subscribers or at least the greater number . . . .

---

[4]Alexander Simpson was cashier of the Quebec branch of the Bank of Montreal.

[5]John Daly was a merchant and investor in the Niagara area.

[6]Alexander Hamilton lived in Queenston and was a son of Robert Hamilton, an influential merchant.

[7]Thomas McCormick was a longtime agent for the Bank of Upper Canada at Niagara (1824–65?). He felt himself to be an appropriate agent because he was not engaged in any mercantile activity and thus was free of any conflict of interest.

[8]John Spread Baldwin (1787–1843) younger brother of W.W. Baldwin, came to Canada from Ireland in 1799 and eventually entered into a partnership with Quetton St. George, a merchant at York. In 1814 Jules Quesnel of Montreal became a partner and Baldwin and Quesnel remained in business until 1832.

B 12 THOMAS MCCORMICK TO S.P. JARVIS
Niagara, 10 June 1825
[*MTL, S.P. Jarvis Papers*]

I have yours of yesterday. The Cashier had previously sent me a list of Directors for publication. If I am not mistaken there will be more unanimity in this Board than the last – with respect to the alteration proposed for the conducting the office here – I have had some conversation with Tannabill[9] on the subject, and shall see him again before he goes over. I believe he will generally agree with me on the subject and will be better able explain in person what is required, than I could by writing – I must however say that I am not averse to the power of Discounting being limitted for I suggested to Mr. Bolton[10] the necessity of its being so – I think £500 too large a sum to be discounted here for any one person without a reference to the Bank. I should think it would be for the Interest of the institution that I should have a voice in discounting, for I consider myself from my situation (that is, unconnected with commercial pursuits) as the most likely person to be disinterested – I should think it would be well, when there is but one Voice against the passing of a Note that it should be referred to the Bank.

Respecting the authority to the Cashier of this office, to Draw on Montl. and New York I know there are objections, but, I do not consider them insurmountable – and as it is much wished for here, perhaps it would be better to bear with a little inconvenience – what might perhaps make it less objectionable would be, for Mr. Ridout to transmit me as usual Drafts on both places and a small sum at each place left at my disposal to enable me to make up such sums as might be required – any Drafts in that case would not at any time exceed Twenty pounds Ea. – and every week I would send a detailed statement of Bills Drawn – . . .

B 13 T.G. RIDOUT TO MAJOR HILLIER
York, 2 July 1825
[*PAC, RG 5 A1, v. 73*]

In compliance with your request of the 30th ultimo, I beg to submit the underwritten Statement as the probable amount of the circulating medium of this Province, and also the average rate of Exchange on London at 30 dys. for the years 1823, 1824, & first Six Months of 1825, viz.

[9]John Tannabill, of York, was a director of the Bank of Upper Canada in 1825 and owned shares in the bank in 1830.
[10]This probably refers to Henry John Boulton, the bank's solicitor at York.

	Exchange	Bank Notes	Specie		Total
1823	– 5¹/₂ premᵐ	. . . 75,000	 25,000	=	100,000
1824	– 8 Dᵒ	. . . 87,000	 30,000	=	117,000
1825	– 7¹/₂ Dᵒ	. . 105,000	 30,000	=	135,000

The above rates of exchange are the average at which the Bank has purchased private Bills within the last three years, and the amount of Bank notes includes those of this Bank and of the Lower Canada Banks: as near as I can ascertain from the business done in this country the average of each being as per Statement on the other side – the principal issue of Montreal paper is from the Receiver General – the great increase of the General Total for the last two years, I think arises from the Montreal Capital employed in the Lumber, Potash and Flour Trade, and also the fictitious capital set afloat by the discounts of this Bank.

The supply of specie is chiefly derived from the issues of the Commissariat, and what is brought out from Europe by Emigrants – Spanish dollars are very scarce being bought up for exportation to the United States, and even French crowns are sought for – English gold bears here a premium of 1¹/₂ or 2 per Cent and is scarce –

Average amount of Bank Notes in circulation, within U.C.

		1823		1824	1825
Upper Canada	–	29,000	–	45,000	63,500
Montreal	–	30,000		35,000	35,000
Canada	–	16,000	–	7,000	6,500
		£75,000		£87,000	£105,000

B 14   THOMAS MCCORMICK TO S.P. JARVIS
Niagara, 16 July 1825
[*MTL, S.P. Jarvis Papers*]

. . . I enclose a Memorandum showing what the profits of the Bank office was to me from its first establishment to the 1st Inst. – to explain why I employed an asst. before the office was opened – by referring to the Bank you will find it was Resolved the Office should be opened when a certain quantity of stock was subscribed, when that was done it was again resolved it should be postponed untill the amount was all paid in – why it was delayed after the Stock was paid for I cannot explain – however during this time I was paying Clerk's wages, office Rent etc for the Year Commencing the 1st Inst. the expense will exceed much what I have here stated, as for the change in the mode of conducting the office I shall be under the necessity of attending solely to it –

In consequence of limiting the Credit of the office in New York – I have lost the sale of upwards of £400 – which is upwards of £8 to the Bank – as I could not draw for the sum required, untill Prime & Coy[11]

[11]Prime Ward King & Company was the successor to Prime Ward & Sands, a private banking house in New York and the American correspondent for the Baring Brothers in London, England. They were the Bank of Upper Canada's New York agents.

were authorized to place a further sum at my disposal – if there is no serious objection – it would be well if this restriction was removed – you are aware that I have to make a return to the Bank twice a week of the several sums I draw for either on Montl Bank or Prime & Coy

B 15   JAMES MACAULAY[12] TO S.P. JARVIS
18 July 1825
[*MTL, S.P. Jarvis Papers*]

Dickson said if I declined indorsing the enclosed note to ask You to do it – to fill it up with Your own name & paying into the Bank the bills in part liquidation of a note already there signed by him & the Atty Genl Now as the Bank here refused to lend a fellow *five Pounds because* I had *indorsed his note* it would not (as the Yankies say) be consistent for me to obtrude my name upon the Humble: board of Directors a second time with a view to solicit favors either for myself or friends.

B 16   THOMAS MCCORMICK TO S.P. JARVIS
Niagara, 3 December 1825
[*MTL, S.P. Jarvis Papers*]

. . . With regard to the Note mentioned in Your last Letter, I should hesitate much in recommending it for Discount unless Endorsed by the person applying to have it discounted – indeed by order of the Board at York it is one of the Rules for this office (and I should think of the Bk also) that all paper offered for Discount should be Endorsed by the person applying – I think the Bank ought not to Discount any paper from this quarter unless recommended by the Board here – it appears to me that it is full time that the instructions respecting Drafts should be removed. There is a great deal of dissatisfaction expressed at the continuance particularly since it is known that the Bank has been discounting – some time ago I wrote to the Cashier to let me know (if he could with propriety) When it was probable one would be allowed to Discount – but he did not [seem?] to take any Notion of that part of my letter. I made the application at the request of the Board but did not state so – I most sincerely wish you had some other Cashier for it is out of the question making a suggestion to him or asking advice on matters relating to the Bank – I am told he thinks that I should wish to get his place – which is perhaps the Cause of his being the [?] – however he is very much mistaken it would not be a trifling consideration that would induce me to take it . . . .
Burn this when you have read it.

---

[12]James Buchanan Macaulay (1793–1859) was born at Niagara, served in the War of 1812, was called to the bar in 1822 and became a judge of the Court of King's Bench in 1829.

B 17   H.J. BOULTON TO R.W. HORTON[13]
Downing Street, 15 December 1825
[*PAC, CO 42, v. 376, pp. 163–64*]

. . . In 1819 the Bank of U. Canada the only Institution of the kind in that Province was first Chartered by Act of the ProvL Parlt with a joint Stock Capital of £200,000 which being found larger than the state of the Colony required was by a subsequent Statute reduced one half.–

I assisted in drawing the Charter and suggested the propriety of enabling the ProvL GovR to take Stock on behalf of the Colony to the extent of one quarter of the present Capital. This I considered would give the Bank additional confidence with the public, and the nomination by the Governor of 4 Directors annually out of the 15 which constitute the Direction effectually secures the Institution from any unwarrantable speculations & gives a character to the Bank which it could not otherwise possess. Among the Directors are several Members of the Council, the Crown Officers and other Gentlemen connected with the Government with a few men in Commercial Business.

Thus constituted no private views can insinuate themselves to obstruct the proper and liberal application of the Funds of the Corporation which in most other Banks in America where the Directors are all Merchants I am afraid is not always the case.

The Bank by its Charter is required to redeem all its Bills in Gold or Silver, is prohibited from dealing in any kind of goods or Merchandize, or holding more Land than is necessary for its immediate accommodation in transacting its Business – Besides these salutory restrictions, the President & Cashier are bound to lay before Parlt at the request of either House annually a return on Oath of the Funds of the Institution. – the amount of Stock paid in, – the amount of debts and Credits – the Notes or Bills emitted & in circulation and the Specie in the Vaults at the Date of the Return – And the Directors are prohibited from incurring Debts beyond 3 times the amount of the Capital Stock paid in upon pain of their personal responsibility.

With this Constitution the Bank began Business in 1821 & have continued ever since in a state of successful operation netting after the first year from 8 to 12 per Ct profit upon the Capital paid.

The Confidence of the Public is unbounded and the notes of U.C. Bank are current along the whole line of the American frontier bordering on Canada and are only at a small discount in New York and this owing to the Commercial relations of the two Countries & not to any distrust in the soundness of the Institution.

The Business of the Bank consists chiefly in discounting promissory Notes Generally at 90 Days at the rate of 6 per Ct negotiating Bills of Exchange and buying & selling Bullion.

[13]Robert John Wilmot Horton (1784–1841) was under-secretary of state for war and the colonies, 1821–28.

From these Sources without entering into any Speculations (which Banks should never be permitted to do) they derive this Profit, which has acquired a degree of stability which probably exceeds that of most Banking Institutions in America.

The Circulation is now upwards of £70,000, and its capital paid in about half that amount; probably £50,000 of this is afloat in U. Canada and the residue abroad, in the U. States & Lower Canada. Almost the only Specie that finds its way into U. Canada is that which is issued by the Commissariat to the Troops . . . .

Banking as compared with other Branches of Commerce may I think be properly termed "non-productive" and therefore should not be permitted to be enterprised in situation when the Commercial transactions of the neighbourhood did not require the Facilities which such Institutions afford. The public convenience should be the sole object in the Law authorising the Establishment of a Bank – The only question should be does the Business of the Country require this New Bank.

A Bank is a tremendous Engine in the hands of persons entrusted with its Direction and if they are actuated by personal considerations of selfish Interest they can acquire the most entire Controul or monopoly of the Merchantile transactions of the Town in which it is placed. They may by a liberal conduct at first induce people to get large Discounts under an expectation of their being continued and then by a sudden refusal to accommodate the same persons any farther, which they can always find plausible reasons for doing, and by requiring prompt payment of all paper outstanding, may throw the whole Business of a flourishing Town into disorder, of which every one will more or less feel the Inconvenience excepting those who have caused it & who will take care to be provided with plenty of Capital against the appointed time, to take advantage of the dismay they have created.

Thereupon such a Machine should not be entrusted in the hands of private Individuals who are amenable to no one for their Conduct but it should be placed under such restrictions as will effectually prevent speculation and afford the public an opportunity of ascertaining periodically the Solvency of an Institution in which they must all be more or less interested.

B 18   William Allan to John Macaulay
York, 30 March 1826
[*PAO, Macaulay Papers*]

. . . If we could get the Specie early in May it would be very desirable for several reasons –

In course there will be a Run of our Notes I presume at Montl. to this Bank after we have made it known we are to discontinue which we will do sometime before It is actually to take place, but we will be pretty well provided and will try & provide further against that

It is the great risk [?] so many of our Notes coming up that I think most of/I have a great many applications from Montreal to purchase stock in our Bank. The Stockholders generally are not at *ease* or well pleased with the State of Montreal Bank and its affairs – *very many heavy losses*. They hold of Mr. Gillivary & Co.[14] Bills under Protest £18,000 Stg/all this to yourself/ They Consider the Expense of there institution much to great and grumble a good deal about, In course you can discount Mr. Chisholm[15] Dft on Amt on Auldjo & Co.[16] for £75 with merely the persons own endorsation. A Sum of that small amt need not be much of an object –

The fact is it is quite impossible for us to go on and allways keep to the same rule, we no doubt make resolutions that are soon altered or suspended by others, But our coming to that determination is as [?] to, too many letters of Credit from the drws. and endorsers whom we know very little about I look upon it that after we give up retiring our notes at Montreal that we will always have funds there without any interruptions – to enable us to advance to every person who requires what we cannot ever *count* upon as long as we do *retire*. Another thing we have had many applications for, what to all appearances is as good as any business we *have* done from Brockville in particular and other places below that for fear of our Notes finding their way down to Montl we have declined.

It would then be our Interest to Send our Notes in circulation as far Eastward as we can . . . .

B 19   WILLIAM ALLAN TO JOHN MACAULAY (CONFIDENTIAL)
York, 14 April 1826
[*PAO, Macaulay Papers*]

The occasion of my writing you now is to say that I have received a Communication there is some Risk of our Agents TW & Co. [Thomas Wilson][17] of London going to the Wall.

They have some considerable amount of monies of ours in their

---

[14]This refers to McGillivray, Thain & Company, a mercantile house in Montreal. Simon McGillivray and his father William had been very active in the North West Company. By 1825 the mercantile firm was in desperate financial straits. Simon was elected to the board of the Bank of Montreal in 1825.

[15]William Chisholm (1788–1842) came to Upper Canada from Nova Scotia in 1804. In the 1820s he founded the town of Oakville, and represented Halton in the Legislative Assembly, 1820–24, 1830–34 and 1836–41. He did a great deal of business with Maitland, Garden & Auldjo.

[16]This refers to Maitland, Garden & Auldjo, a leading commercial house in Montreal which did extensive business in Upper Canada. Its failure in 1826 precipitated an economic crisis in the colony. George Auldjo was a director of the Bank of Montreal in 1822.

[17]Thomas Wilson & Company was a private banking house in London, England. It operated as London agent for the Bank of Montreal and the Bank of Upper Canada before going bankrupt in 1837.

hands a large proportion of which we have drawn for through New York, but which have not reached them at the last date. I have submitted this and other circumstances to some of the Directors in confidence – and we have come to the determination of discontinuing to discount, for the present which I think will be our Intent to adhere to for some time for several reasons – So that any notes you may send on Saturday will be presented at the Board in [?] – But most likely returned, to you & after that you can say to all or any person who send in these Notes that we have discontinued – doing anything but renewals for a short time Be very carefull & very cautious in taking Dft on Lower Canada or indeed elsewhere just now get Endorsers if you can, you will use your discretion respecting of all or any person who applys for accommodation – Indeed it may be well to let it be gradually known, before applications are made.

B 20 WILLIAM ALLAN TO JOHN MACAULAY
York, 17 April 1826
[PAO, Macaulay Papers]

Your letter of the 12th Inst. is before me to which I scarcely Know what to say, you would be in possession of my private & confidential communication of Thursday last writen on a hurry on Saturday and I feel most happy to say I am relieved from a very great load of anxiety since that, by a communication from London of 6 March giving me the following Pleasing information "We learn that is doubtfull if the report respecting Messrs. Thos. Wilson & Co. had any foundation and we are morever assured they were considered as entirely safe" – So that I think we have nothing to apprehend on the other side of the water, and in course there is nothing to be apprehended of our friends at New York I trust not – In that case we should keep our heads above water with confidence notwithstanding we shall be very considerable Sufferers by the House of Maitland Garden & Auldjo – whose acceptances, for Dfts. discounted by us upon there letters of Credit entirely to the Amt £7,794 – and R. Wood & Co.[18] £3250 – that you see is upwards of Ten Thousand Pounds all those drawn upon them by Mr. Chisholm who can get Security from him. He offered frequently to give us Security on all his property. He I believe owes nobody anything of consequence as to Mr. [Barnhart?][19] I fear it is very [different?] – and I have not the best opinnion of him, I am going to try what I can do with him to day But the misfortune is we have no legal hold of them but these diff. Dfts. become due for they are all accepted at Montl. I am affraid we will still be worse of with the Dfts. on R. Wood & Coy [God?] knows who are the drawers

[18]Robert Wood & Co. were shipbuilders in Quebec City. In 1826 they were under contract with Maitland, Garden & Auldjo to build boats for them.
[19]John Barnhart was a merchant in Kingston who did a great deal of business with Maitland, Garden & Auldjo.

of them I suppose men of Straw – [McK   ?] Bethune & Comy.[20] owe us £100 – but I dread to hear by the next Post of other House, as we have discounted for Dfts. on Montreal & Quebec for a considerable amt. I wrote you we had determined to stop all discounts & that you now not send up any more Notes – only confine yourself to renewals – and be very cautious in taking any Dfts on Lower Canada without Good Endorsers. I mean all except Government Bills – you will turn what British Silver you have into Bills on the Treasury & send them up. I would not send above £1,500 – The remainder of your Specie you will send up in charge of some person coming in the Steam Boat altho we shall before along time Perhaps before we get paid these Dfts which will be coming back and we may also in the End loose some considerable, still as yet it will not effect us, as soon as we get our Specie from New York – we shall have £25,000 in our Vaults & Perhaps – we will be in Cash at New York & London besides & we hold the Government debentures – so that if there was any Run upon us I have every reason to think we can easily withstand the worst I think our Notes are so scattered about there is no danger of any large Amts. being collected. But between ourselves I think there is much more reason for to apprehend the Montl Bank going to the wall than us – They have discounted for Messrs Maitland & Co of Montl £22,000 Stg. or £27,000 cy., which will all come back besides considerable more and £18,000 they hold of McGillivary & Co In fact I know they have not less than from £60 to £70,000 in that state. If there is any persons in your part of the Country whose dfts you discounted on either of those Houses now said to have stopt or any other you hear of hereafter, you should try and get Security from those Persons as far as you can. I know you will do everything in your Power in that way – don't wait for any directions send all the Specie you have or can collect by the 1st of Month except £1,500 of bills which I wish you to send as soon as you can – as I have promised them . . . .

you had better send up all the Notes you have or can spare as you will be getting a supply from Montl constantly – and will not have occassion for money now there is no discounts. We want here all the Notes we can to prevent our issuing more, which we will not do for some time – . . . .

B 21   BANK OF MONTREAL/BANK OF UPPER CANADA RELATIONS
23 June 1826
[PAC, Bank of Montreal Resolve Book, v. 1, p. 392]

The Upper Canada Bank having ordered the sum of £4000 to be placed to the credit of this Bank with Prime Ward King & Co. at New York – as advised by Mr Ridout, the Cashier's letter dated 14 Inst.

Resolved that 1 per cent Prem. be allowed it being understood that Interest shall be charged in making up the account with the said Bank.

[20]MacKenzie, Bethune & Co. were merchants and shipbuilders operating out of Montreal.

With respect to the UC notes now receiving by this Bank at a Discount of 1^1/$_2$ P cent.

Resolved that it be proposed to the said Bank to take their Dfts on New York for the par amount of the Notes at 1% Prem.

B 22 BANK OF UPPER CANADA
[*Montreal* Gazette, *6 July 1826*]

The sudden determination of the Directors of the BANK OF UPPER CANADA not to retire their Notes at Montreal as usual, has inflicted great loss and inconvenience upon the people of this city and province, which nothing can compensate or stop but an immediate recall on the part of the Upper Canada Bank, and the appointment of a person to receive and exchange its notes within a given time. We cannot help adding that the determination in question was most improper and unjustifiable after having permitted about £100,000 worth of the Bank of the sister province to have been circulated in good faith in Lower Canada. It is true that the Montreal Bank and others take these notes at a discount of one & a half *per centum*; but does not the public lose this one and a half *per cent.* and does not the whole transaction look very much like a job. We do not say it is actually a job; but we do and must say that the whole transaction merits the investigation of the legislatures of both provinces, which is the only means of saving the public from similar impositions on the part of the Upper Canada Bank, or any other public institution claiming and obtaining the confidence of the country.

B 23 BANK OF MONTREAL/BANK OF UPPER CANADA RELATIONS
28 July 1826
[*PAC, Bank of Montreal, Resolve Book, v. 1, p. 404*]

Moved and seconded
Resolved: that the Upper Canada Bank notes be sent to York, in charge of Mr. Radenhurst as speedily as the same can be prepared & registered & that Mr. Radenhurst be instructed to receive payment for the same by check on this Bank at par or in Specie as best may suit the convenience of the Bank at Upper Canada.

B 24 T.G. RIDOUT TO JOHN H. DUNN
York, 16 January 1828
[*PAC, RG 19 B2a, v. 1132*]

. . . [re your letter] notifying that Government Debentures Nos 4 to 8 – inclusive amounting in all to 9,444.8:10^1/$_2$ Currency are in course of redemption – which I shall communicate to the several persons to whom the above debentures have been transferred by this Institution & will follow their instructions for presenting the same on or before July 13 when interest thereon ceases according to the Act of Provincial Parliament, under which the loan was effected.

B 25   T.G. RIDOUT TO MAJOR HILLIER
York, 12 September 1828
[PAC, RG 5 A1, v. 90]

In obedience to your request I beg leave to furnish the undermentioned statement of the Exchange and currency of this Province for the year 1827 – viz.

Monthly course of Exchange for Bills on London, at 60 dys, sold by this Bank during the above period –

January	11½	premium on £100. –
February	11½	dᵒ
March	10	dᵒ
April	10	dᵒ
May	10 1/4	dᵒ
June	9 3/4	dᵒ
July	10	dᵒ
August	10	dᵒ
September	10	dᵒ
October	11	dᵒ
November	11	dᵒ
December	11	dᵒ

The rate of exchange in this Province is governed by the money market at New York. – Bills on London being bought up by merchants & others as remittances to New York in lieu of specie – and besides the constant export of specie from Canada to the United States compels the Banks to keep up the high rates in order to create funds to bring the specie back again.

The average amount of specie in Upper Canada for the year 1827 – did not, I think, exceed thirty thousand pounds besides about Twenty five thousand pounds generally in the Bank vault – that, in circulation consisting chiefly of Spanish dollars, American half dollars and French Crowns – the two former in demand, for export to purchase salt & other commodities from the Americans –

The British silver coins issued by the commissariat do not pass current in the country, as they are bought up at a premium of about 8 per cent on their sterling value, for the purpose of exchange with the Commissariat for Treasury bills on London – Sovereigns and guineas, are at a like prem., for sale at New York – the principal supply is brought here, by emigrants –

An English copper coinage is very much wanted, the present copper money being issued by private individuals, and is quite worthless – The coins in most demand, are Spanish dollars, & quarters, and American half dollars.

B 26   WILLIAM ALLAN TO JOHN MACAULAY
York, 1 September 1829
[PAO, Macaulay Papers]

I duly received your last favour of the Ult. and the Post before brought us your Report, of your expedition down to Bytown, which is full and satisfactory. I do not think we need be disirous of appointing any agent down there about admitting there was any fit Person who would undertake it; as there is little doubt but Mr. A. Jones,[21] will be able to get at a Proportion of it as much so as if we had an Agent.

You have perhaps heard that our *War* of withdrawing Specie from the Montl. Bank & they from us is likely to cease now. Indeed it has ceased they have given directions to there Agents here Mr Harper[22] to take Dfts from us for all & any monies sent in there is now a negotiation [pending?] that if we determined *after* communicating with our Agent Messrs T.W. & Coy if it would not be disagreeable for to have our Agency again changed to the Montl. Bank I think they are very willing to relinquish We have [?] directed the Cashier to write to the Cashier of Montl Bank now & Submit to their Board that if they will withdraw *all* there agents from U C & leave us the entire banking of the Province, we will again give them our agency & make reciprocal arrangements whereby we shall be on a much better footing than we ever was before that is our Propositions to them will put us so – and I have every reason to think they will willingly come into *all* Indeed I am informed they have no hesitation about anything, but how to provide for A M Dupie[23] at your Place who succeeded Mr Harper as for H. they say they will Pay him his year Sallary & he has no more claim on them they [?] don't mind all his Expense here & his having had a House for three years – this they *loose* & much *more* if our arrangement takes place you shall know the Particulars (and I think will be a little surprised after all they or there agent have *vaunted* and said –

Withall their boasting & conceit of their superior means I believe they soon found out we was in Earnest & perhaps not so easy Broken as they or some of them thought When they found Mr. Ridout went down to arrange about a Regular *System* of getting a Supply of Specie from them every week – and by way of a specimen of what we could do brought with him £23,000 – they began to look about them and endeavored all they could to know if he was not authorized to Propose any terms He was not on the contrary he was told to avoid entering into any bussiness but that he was sent upon. He was as he thought urged by Mr. Molson[24] to say something and he at once Proposed they should

[21]Alpheus Jones (1794–1863), collector of customs and postmaster at Prescott, was the fourth son of Ephraim Jones, the first representative for the Johnstown District in the Legislative Assembly. In 1830 he was a large stockholder in the Bank of Upper Canada.

[22]Francis Harper, married to a cousin of John A. Macdonald, was the Bank of Montreal's agent at York in 1829. He became the first cashier of the Commercial Bank of the Midland District and manager of the Upper Canada Trust & Loan Company at Kingston in 1851.

[23]Henry Dupuy was the Bank of Montreal's first accountant and became their Kingston agent in 1829.

[24]John Molson Sr., the brewer, became president of the Bank of Montreal following the economic crisis of 1826.

withdraw all there agents from this Province that altho it staggered them did not seem to meet with much *objection*

That is the ground of our now *modest* Propositions to them. I am quite satisfied had we carried on to draw Specie from each other for Six Mths. Knowing our *means* & *Resources* besides – we would have seriously affected the Montl *Bank* added to all we have accomodated our Agents with a considerable discount, which the Montl Directors refused them – So much for all this which grew out of nothing – (all this Entre nous for the present). . . .

B 27   H. Dupuy to [?]

Kingston, 4 June 1868
[PAC, MG 24 D52-55]

. . . In the year 1829 I was appointed Manager of the Kingston Branch after having been nailed to the books for 12 years. Shortly after this a Specie war took place between the Bank of Montreal & the B. of Upper Canada thus, Kegs & Boxes of Specie would go up to Toronto, B.U.C. in payment of balances sometimes pretty large, then if the balance happened to be on the other side, the same Boxes and Kegs would make their appearances again, & this war continued for some months. At last peace was restored and both Banks agreed to settle their balances by Bills of Exch. or Drafts . . . .

B 28   Thomas McCormick to S.P. Jarvis
Niagara, 28 December 1829
[MTL, S.P. Jarvis Papers]

. . . I have a notification from the Cash. to charge 1/4 per CT. on all Drfts negotiated on Lower Canada and in addn the Discount to the time they will be paid – which includes the time it takes to go by mail [even?] or Bills at Sight – it appears to me this is rather Close Work – particularly as the Bank must be desirous of obtaining that description of paper to keep up the funds in Lower Canada and to Counter Balance the paper sent up for Collection by the Montreal Bank – however there may be many reasons for this arrangement that I am not aware of – . . .

B 29   William Allan to Lt.-Governor Colborne[25]
York, 16 January 1830
[PAC, RG 5 B23]

. . . That by their [Bank of Upper Canada] charter of Incorporation several provisions are inserted for the protection of the Public, which your petitioners conceive are equally if not more necessary to be observed by Foreign Banks and other monied Institutions carrying on

[25]Sir John Colborne (1778–1863) was lieutenant-governor of Upper Canada, 1828–36.

business in this Province by means of Agents, who are not at present responsible to any person besides their employers – . . .

. . . That altho' they have no wish to avoid competition, should the Legislature in their Wisdom deem it expedient to incorporate other Banks within the Province under the same salutary restraints that are imposed upon themselves, yet they feel that they would not do justice either to themselves or the Public if they did not state to Parliament the inconvenience which results from Foreign Banks being allowed to carry on their operations here without being subject to any restriction whatever, and more especially without being compelled to retire their Notes at their Banking House in this Province –

As the Law now stands it has been argued by some, that Foreign Banks may issue Notes and Bills to any amount they please without being responsible at all to the Courts of this Province should they fail, and without being compellable in any way to redeem their Bills at the place from whence they are issued –

Wherefore your Petitioners humbly pray that your Excellency will be pleased to pass a Bill restraining all Bodies Politic or Corporate, and all persons whatever from carrying on any kind of Banking Business except under the same restrictions limitations and conditions that affect the Bank of Upper Canada –

B 30   SELECT COMMITTEE ON THE STATE OF THE CURRENCY
6 February 1830
[JUC, *1830, Appendix, pp. 30-31*]

. . . Mr. Mackenzie[26] was called to the Chair. The Honourable William Allan . . . examined . . . .

112. Would you suggest to this Committee such provisions as in your opinion would be advisable for the better securing the public? – . . . I think the precautions that were taken with respect to the Bank of Upper Canada, when chartered, have hitherto been found, in practice, quite sufficient. It appears to me, that the leading object, in framing a constitution for monied bodies, should be, to establish and sustain them in public credit. This is promoted by extending to them the support and patronage of the Government. By the Government possessing stock and participating in the affairs and management of such an institution, gives it the complexion of an establishment partially (though not exclusively) Provincial. Over trading should be restrained; and the issue of notes, &tc. depend not only on the means of redemption, but the resources, prospects and fair demands of the business population of the country. Periodical statements of the funds, when they shew a fair and prosperous course of business, tend to confirm public confidence. – Banking

[26]William Lyon Mackenzie (1795–1861) mayor of York, 1834–35, was a reformer who led the abortive rebellion in Upper Canada in 1837. He was a long-time critic of the Bank of Upper Canada.

establishments should depend upon the field afforded for safe and useful operation. My experience does not warrant me in suggesting any new charter in this province at present. Were an increase deemed expedient in any other part of this country, measures should be taken to prevent excessive issues, and to restrain large credits if possible, and if provision could be made to discourage attempts to embarrass each other, which rival institutions of this kind are frequently from trivial causes disposed to do. As the Government could not be interested in any other Stock Companies if created, between which an emulation, at least in their trade, must always prevail. I feel quite confident it would be for the interests of the country, in preference to creating other independent Banks, to cause such amendments of the charter already granted to the Bank of Upper Canada, as might enable that corporation to have its capital enlarged; to extend its business by Branch Banks acting in co-operation with the principal establishment, would, I think, but tend to insure solvency, and secure the rights of creditors and stockholders, without abridging the public at large, of any the advantages attending such institutions . . . . With respect to the details of regulating such branches, they are at present reposed in the Directors, with whom the principal arrangements and control ought always to rest. The appointment of sub-directors to manage those Branches might be vested in the Shareholders; although by such a mode, much responsibility would be removed from the principal Board. I do not wish to be understood as intending more than to suggest the idea.

113. Were you enquiring into the circumstances of an individual, with a view to ascertain his solvency, would you consider a similar statement to that given annually by the Bank to Parliament, as containing sufficient information for you to proceed upon? – I decline answering that question.

114. Can you furnish this committee with a list of the Stockholders of the Bank of Upper Canada, with the shares held by each? – I cannot.

115. What objections can you have in refusing this list? – I decline answering that question.

116. Are there instances within your knowledge, where the Bank has refused to discount good paper? – Not to my knowledge has any piece of paper been refused by the Bank when considered good, except when cases have happened that the Bank had already gone to the extent that they thought themselves justifiable in going.

117. Can you produce to this committee, a list of the salaries paid the officers of the Bank and its branches? – I decline giving the committee any information on that subject.

118. Can you give to this committee an account of the contingent expenses of the Bank for any one year? – I decline giving any information on that subject.

119. Can you produce to this committee the last triennial account of losses and profits? – I decline giving that information.

120. What proportion of the Bank discounts or loans are awarded to its directors and officers? – Are they restricted to the same sums as private individuals, or does their paper in any way receive a preference? – It receives no preference whatever.

121. What is the nature of the exclusive privileges which you desire by the prayer of your Petition? – We wish every other institution to be obliged to redeem their paper at some place within the province.

122. Does any restriction, such as you desire, exist in the Lower Province? – Not that I know of.

123. Was not the Montreal Branch Bank established here lately, an advantage to the public? – I think quite the reverse.

124. Before the Montreal Bank withdrew its agency from Brockville, did not your agent at Prescott pay one half per cent premium upon large bills on the commissariat of Lower Canada? – In a few instances, I believe, he was authorised so to do, in order to obtain bills on the Treasury.

125. Is your agent at Prescott now authorised to pay this premium on such bills? – No.

126. Would you advise the selling out the Provincial Bank stock for any purpose whatever? – I would not.

127. What is your opinion of a Bank founded entirely on the resources of the Provincial Government. – I do not think a Bank in such a way, would be more responsible than the Provincial Bank as now constituted.

128. Why do you now call in the remainder of the Bank stock? – With the idea of applying to the Legislature for an increase of Capital Stock at a future period; which could not be properly done until the present stock was called in.

129. Is it not usual to leave uncalled in, a certain proportion, say twenty-five or thirty per cent. of the stock subscribed, to meet any unforeseen difficulties? – I believe not.

130. Would it not be advantageous to the country, were a law passed, enacting that every simple contract debt, of whatsoever nature or kind, should bear interest? – In England, the allowance of interest upon simple contract debts has been regulated by experience, and the commercial habits and customs of the country; but I am not by any means prepared to express an opinion favourable to any material changes in the law we already have here in that respect. – It is always optional with individuals to exact or forego interest, as their transactions may seem to themselves to justify, but I believe the general course of dealing upon credit in this country has not varied materially from the general rule in England – I mean, that interest is not usually exacted from the period of credit, but after the lapse of 6 or 12 months. I see no injustice in the allowance of interest upon all bills, notes, etc. from maturity; upon loans, from the time of advances; also, upon liquidated accounts, and accounts rendered, if yearly or half-yearly, in the ordinary course of

business. – It would be just too, I think that all other debts should bear interest at the end of six months; for example, all Merchants' or Tradesmen's accounts, not regularly adjusted or rendered, according to the custom of mercantile people. – A general and immediate liability to interest, in all cases, I do not conceive advisable – such a rule would not accord with the mercantile usage; which usage may be fairly adopted in relation to other transactions of accounts.

131. What average premium has the stock of the Bank of Upper Canada borne for the last few years, as near as you can remember? – Most sales are private transactions between the buyer and the seller. . . . I believe sales have been generally from 8 to 9 premium.

132. Did you ever know an instance where a Member of the House of Assembly was nominated by the Government to represent the Provincial stock in the Bank? – I have only known one instance.

133. Can you afford this Committee any further information of importance relative to the state of the Currency, or offer any other suggestions as to alterations of the present laws by which it is regulated, or as to new improvements? – . . . As respects the various denominations of coins made current by law, I believe the table established in relation to gold sufficiently protects the public interest. It is, I believe, very well known that the silver coins called French Crowns, Half-Crowns, and Pistareens, are made a legal tender here, at a sum exceeding the actual value, and their current value in the United States. They, of course form an object of speculation between the two countries, to the prejudice of Upper Canada. They should be rendered not current, (or their value be reduced:) – But the present holders, unless the Government is authorised to call them in at their present value, sustaining the loss upon a re-issue, or unless some other plan can be devised for effecting the change, without imposing individual loss. I am not now prepared to suggest any.

B 31   COMMERCIAL BANK OF UPPER CANADA: REPORT
[*Kingston* Chronicle, *6 February 1830*]

. . . 6th . . . . if the Town of Kingston can afford to support an office of the Bank of Upper Canada, and an agency of the Montreal Bank, the officers of which Banks receive liberal salaries, and are enabled to remit to the parent Institutions considerable profits, it must be evident to all, that a Bank, the profits of which would remain in the place, instead of enriching the people of York and of Montreal, would have every chance of success . . . . These circumstances combined with the flattering prospect of an increase in our trade on the completion of the Welland and Rideau Canals, convince your Committee that the proposed Bank only requires to be set in operation to prove at once its utility and success.

7th. The utility and even necessity of a Bank in Kingston is further forced on the consideration of your Committee from the manner in which the Banking business is at present conducted by the offices here. At the office of Upper Canada Bank, a discount even for the smallest sum cannot be had, without at least a delay of ten days from the time of application – the notes for discount having first to be sent to York, and there to undergo the inspection of the Directors of the Bank, persons, who, however respectable, may often have separate and rival interests from those who in Kingston apply for discounts.

The Montreal Bank Agency, although application for discounts are not attended with the same delay in it, as in the former, is upon other grounds, liable to still greater objections. It is the office of a foreign Bank the profits of which are just so much loss to this Province, the sum for discount is very limited, and is besides under the guidance of one person instead of being governed by a board of Directors. – Add to this, that the Merchants of Lower Canada, Directors in the Parent Institution, have it in their power to see at all times, the names sent in upon notes for discount at the Agency office – the two offices are not obliged to redeem the paper they issue, and in consequence of this, (as it is well known that Canada Notes are at a discount in the u.s.), if a payment has to be made on the other side of the Lake, one must either pay a premium here for current money, or at an expense, trouble and delay obtain it from York or Montreal.

8th. That besides the profit arising from the circulation of Bank paper, a very considerable sum must be raised from the premiums charged by the Agencies mentioned, both in remitting to, and drawing from, the Lower Province, which together with the Discounts, may as well be kept at home as sent to York and Montreal.

9th. Your Committee would further point out the uncertainty of these Agencies remaining here. The recent withdrawal of the Agency of the Montreal Bank from York, is sufficient to induce a belief, that no circumstances whatever, short of personal advantage to the Merchants composing the Bank of Montreal, will lead them to allow any agency of that Bank to remain here, and that as soon as that ruling principle will come to operate, neither good faith, nor Upper Canada interest will weigh a feather in the scale. Your Committee feel warranted in thus expressing themselves, from seeing the people of York so recently and so suddenly abandoned, after the hopes held out to them.

10th. That the attempt now making by the York Bank, to procure an act of the Legislature to compel all Bank Agencies to redeem the paper of their respective Banks, leads your committee to apprehend that a dangerous monopoly will be the consequence of the success of the present application, if that evil be not averted by the establishment of a Bank in Kingston . . . .

B 32   WILLIAM ALLAN TO JOHN MACAULAY
York, 8 February 1830
[*PAO, Macaulay Papers*]

I have received your two last favours of the 3d & 4th Inst. together with
the Upper Canada Herald, which contains a Copy of the proceedings &
resolutions at the meeting that was held at Kingston on the Subject of
the Bank project – which as you say is assuming form and consistence.
The subscribed I consider but small as yet considering there are several
persons who have Capital, that are promoting it. – However it is far
short of the Sum req'd, say £40,000 to be Subscribed or of the £10,000
– to be pd in I suppose Specie. I perceived some among the Committee,
who have been long very liberally accomodated by this Bank, as to
there being £25,000 taken up by People at the Head of the Lake I don't
think it Possible (with the exception of Mr J. Ross.[27] – no Persons there
have any money – nor do I think if they have they are much inclined to
Promote a Bank at Kingston – Particularly when they know this
Institution affords them every accomodation they could reasonably
expect and we have established an agent & office there Indeed I am
almost Positive they won't get £5,000 subscribed or anything like it – if
so it will only be People looking for [extreme?] accomodation. I cannot
imagine who they have at York likely to take *Stock* it is Possible there
may be, and at Brockville I have no doubt, but if any of the monied
People there have any idea of gettting up a Bank in that part of the
Country – they would not be likely to support this – as to lots of Shares
being taken up at Montreal that I much doubt also, I have had
conversation w. some of the Mont'l Gent'n. up there and they are
decidely against any other Bank – being established. However time will
tell – and we will see what it will come to. I am much inclined to think
they can have no hopes of geting a Bank Charter this Session, and a
Bank at Kingston I would think would require time to induce any person
to have much confidence in it after the Pretty specimen and the now
winding up concern of the last undertaking there.[28] If they can raise
Stock out of the ashes of the old concern I would not like to possess
much of their paper – The Mont'l Agent Mr. D ＿＿＿ [Dupuy] need not
be under any great apprehension I don't think our *liberals* here will
Comply with our Petition except by enacting other things to alter our
Charter etc which unless it is to be improved they will not [readily?] get
done; the Passing any Act will not be much pressed, and in all
Probability it may be allowed to go to Sleep for this Session. I will not
urge it on And as you observe we may continue to get the Montl Bank to
join us and make a Common cause against this new *Project* being
carryed into effect. But if it should so happen if they commence with or

[27]J. Ross was possibly a merchant situated in the Hamilton-Dundas region.
[28]This refers to the Pretended Bank of Upper Canada at Kingston. Its affairs were
still in the process of being settled.

without a charter – In course we will decline our Renewals or discounts to any Person concerned in it. Let all of them Pay up their Notes as fast as they become due or have them sent up & put in suits immediately – Dr. Sampson[29] Name has lately been on a good deal of Paper as well as some of the other folks. It is not true with respect to the York Merchants – having advantages over those of Kingston, more accomodation has been given to the Merchs of Kingston even to Double the Amt. that is asked for or given to those here – Take the year round
. . . .

In course our Profit will be generally curtailed at Kingston particularly if a Rival Institution gets into opperation we need not expect to show a Profit of £400 – in Our Montl transactions but I cannot think – it will have any other effect than that. In course if all the People in business there – wish to keep their Acct with this new Proposed institution it would be much against, but the Capital Proposed would not be long equal to the bussiness – However we should continue to keep up the rate of Ex. [exchange] & every thing that would produce us remittance at a Rate they could not afford. In fact we have a considerable Surplus fund I would sink a part of that in opposing them and we can be as great a thorn in their side as they can be in ours – We could not apply to have our Capital Increased till all the Stock was called in that is now done, and I believe it is instead of [?] making application at the next Session, for an increase of Capital. The Premium on Stock is high certainly – . . . I will sell if it is any accomodation to get Stock holders who take an Interest with us. I will sell to the Extent of Perhaps £400 or more if you will let me know immediately – but at 8 1/2 pct Premium the Current Rate and what I paid for some part of this – and I will try & get more if you think it is advised . . . .

B 33   JOHN STRACHAN TO JOHN MACAULAY
York, 26 February 1830
[*PAO, Macaulay Papers*]

. . . The Kingston bank bill has it is said passed the Lower House & will be sent up tomorrow. We have so many people among us Bank Directors or connected with the institution that it is difficult to know how to act. Had the Bank here at the time they determined to call in their Stock petitioned the Legislature to repeal the act limiting their Stock and [raising?] it to £200,000 & accompanying their request with a proposal to have a full office of discount at Kingston immediately & at Niagara and the head of the Lake as your own discretion approved and that the books should be open for subscriptions two Months in different parts of the Province & that none of the old Stock holders should be

---

[29]Dr. James Sampson, an army doctor in London, England, during the Napoleonic Wars, came to Kingston, Upper Canada, with the British military and stayed to practise medicine in that city.

allowed till the expiration of that period to take any of the additional Stock the present attempts from Kingston would never have been made. The only grain of opposition is that the affairs of the old Bank of Kingston still remain unsettled –

B 34   WILLIAM ALLAN TO JOHN MACAULAY
York, 12 April 1830
[*PAO, Macaulay Papers*]

. . . I note long ago your having in a supply of £18,000 from Montl. by a Special Messenger they sent up. You will or have sent the Cashier the Amt of Disbursement for [?] going down which will be placed to your Cr. The Navigation is now fairly open & we shall not again be at any loss about our having a Supply or being able to keep our agents in Supply of Notes. etc. I am pleased to find that the Lower Canada currency bill only extend to Pistareens: Crowns & Half Crowns are still current there we expect the Montl Bank will take back all those we have and give us Dollars or 1/2 Dollars for them and as Pistareens Still pass there at 10d we presume they will also take what we have at that value & give us other Silver that will pass here, – *if they* do we shall lose about £200 – but that is no consideration to be rid of all these *Coins;*[30] – We have not heard from Montl Bank with any Promisse of their complying – but I think there is little Doubt but they will – *In that* case altho we have now a large Amt of Cash. w. them & daily *now* larger sums accruing in Lower Canada we shall not have occassion to trouble them I think at any time this Season for other Specie – We are getting in a Supply by Mr McCormick who goes out to N. York. on his own bussiness. We will have about £45 to £50,000 in Specie in our Vaults which I think will be sufficient to meet all demands that can come against us from Ogdensburgh, Utica, Rochester, or any other place, and we have abundant of funds in London, Lower Canada & N. York – In short the state of the Bank affairs generally were never more flourishing than now. I am convinced it would be for the Interest of the Province that it was Confined to this Institution & Extend the Capital but I dont much anticipate that being the case. Indeed one objection to that of applying – is they would be for making such alterations in our charter as would not be pleasant indeed it would just give them the opp'ty they now want, for my own part I would sooner go on for two or three years as it is – But there is no saying what change may take place, before next Session. I am given to understand – that we are going to have a compleat change in our Direction. Indeed it is evident means has been taken to bring it about if they follow it up – Mr. Baldwin has within three months enabled about Eight or Ten of his Friends to be voters &

---

[30]Allan is referring to French crowns and half crowns.

even Directors by Distributing a quantity of *Stock* he held among them –
and they tell me he & his connections along with Mr George Ridout are
using every means they can to get Power of Attorney etc. for the
purpose of keeping out a Number of those that are now in the Direction
– Those Gentn who feel most anxious about it – Tell me, by way of
inducing me, to take an active part along with them, that it is the
intention of those Gentm *to put me out also* or at all events to prevent me
from being elected as *President* again However, I have never from the
Commencement interested myself either directly or indirectly for the
purpose of being either ellected a Director or that of being President and
I shall not now do so. If there is any desire on the part of any Stock
holder to prevent my being either the one or the other, I will give them
full means of doing it – It would relieve me from a good deal of Anxiety
at times – However if I was to be ellected a *Director* & not President
again, I would not continue in course. They could not if they *intend* it,
have fixt on a more favourable time, as to the State of the Bank affairs
generally than now to displace me, but how long that will continue
remains to be seen –

I am quite indifferent as to the matter altho the Board have voted me a
fair allowance for my trouble for this two or three years, it would not be
the loss of that, that would induce me to try & take any means to retain it
– If it is not the case otherwise I will not give myself any concern about
the matter, I have spoke with Several of the Members on the Subject of
allowing you another Clerk, of late on the Subject of making an
alteration in your office by extending the bussiness & if it was Possible
to have two or three Genlm eligible to be *Directors* there to have a
Board I had all this matter ready to carry before the Board some time
ago, with a Promise from several they would agree to it – But I have
since been Spoke to and they rather wish to put any change of till after
the election. They say if the Board are composed of New Members or
many new *ones* let them make what alterations They Please – and if not,
if the Board continues the same or nearly, they will then at once
determine on extending the agency & having an Establishment at
Brockville –

I think the Board will declare a *Bonus* at the time of their declaring
the dividend next month – They would not do otherwise then if there
should happen to be a very great change – It would enable the next
Board to make it or a larger dividend, than they otherwise might have
means.

Next winter I shall be an advocate if I have anything to say on it – for
giving the Legislature all the information they can by any Possibility or
with any kind of *Modesty* ask for . . . .

B 35   WILLIAM ALLAN TO JOHN MACAULAY
York, 17 May 1830
[*PAO, Macaulay Papers*]

. . . It appears that the Spanish Quarter Dollar – are not considered the full value in the States – in our Supply lately rec'd from N York, we got a quantity of them – which they charge to us at the full value of 1/3 Cy which we have complain about in consequence of the cashier of the Ogdensburgh Bank having come up here with £5,000 in our Notes. We offered him Quarter Dollars of that description, but he declined taking them & prefered retaining & taking back our Notes – which he did – I suppose he will go to the [Rideau?] & exchange our Notes there. He wanted us to come into terms about giving them Dfts on N. York for a triffling Premium. We told him we would do nothing of the kind he might put up as many of our Notes as he could, and when presented we would be prepared to give him Specie – or we would Act by them as we have agreed hereby the *Utica Bank*, supposing them to collect many of our Bills in the way of *bussiness* when ever they had accumulated in any Amt. upon being sent us we would give them Dfts on N. York, at 1/4 p.c less than we in general draw for. but if we found they made a bussiness of collecting our Notes – to put there own in circulation – we would not Promise any thing of the kind – He admitted they had made some exertions in collecting this £5,000 and in putting there own Notes in Circulation and that these Notes would be coming upon them – We have some suspicion *here* that some of the Prescot People & those about there we have accomodated with Pretty large Discount have been taking it to [?] the Ogdensburgh Bank. There is as many Gamblers in the way of tricks on our side as there is on theirs. *Enter nous* I would like to be Satisfied that our agent has no concern in the success of that Institution – We found that Messrs Prime Ward & Co. are the agent of that Bank & support it, you need not be surprised if We determine to change these Gentn as our agents. If I continue as I am I think it likely I shall recomend it for reasons [?] I will let you know hereafter One Question is who could we get to be our Agent equally good & Safe – are you personally acquainted with any *House* you could Answer for – all this to yourself M Elmsley[31] is the right kind as to *Politics*. a Good Staunch fellow in every way – unless he should [ever?] change – I hope Mr Reilly[32] will send Cameron[33] a Power of Atty – but has he owned Stock

[31]John Elmsley (1801–63) was the son of John Elmsley, chief justice of Upper Canada. In 1833 he converted from the Church of England to the Roman Catholic faith. He sat on the Legislative Council, 1831–41, and the Executive Council, 1830–33, 1836–39. He was director of the Bank of Upper Canada in 1828–30, 1832 and 1834 and a substantial stockholder in the bank in the early 1830s. He became president of the Farmer's Joint Stock Banking Company in 1835.

[32]Reilly might have been a stockholder, although his name does not appear on any lists for this period.

[33]Cameron might also have been a stockholder; his name is absent from any list for this period.

long enough to vote upon say 3 Mths before the Election I am told Mr George Ridout is trying every method & means of geting votes & Powers of Attorney it is well known that the 20 Shares that was transferred to him by *Baldwin* was only to give him a vote or make him eligible that the Stock now in his Name as well as that of Morrisson[34] & Ketchum[35] & several others all actually belong to *Baldwin* this I am told they brag of – . . .

I only Note the Contents of the late Package on the Subject of Banks in the States – if we were to be circumscribed to the issue of Bills above five Dollars – what would the Country do –

B 36 WILLIAM ALLAN TO JOHN MACAULAY
York, 19 June 1830
[*PAO, Macaulay Papers*]

. . . I do not much like making any promise of an agency to Brockville; or indeed of any other change but what has been proposed namely a Board at Kingston to discount. Indeed there is not telling what is best. I prefer keeping *within bounds* and on the Secure Side instead of Extending the bussiness of the Bank to much and afterwards to have to contract it or withdraw some of those Agencies; I note what you say of the probability of Mr Harpers errand to N. York – they understand the value of money there as well as he does – Mr Jones at Prescott or yourself – will not hereafter be at a loss for a supply of Notes now, they will come up pretty fast The Montl Bank I understand Retires about £1000 a day –

I am glad to see Mr Peter McGill[36] [win?] President – . . . Mr. Geo. Ridout – who does not know what to do or say to get himself in as a Director & get Mr. Jarvis & some of his out – He will never succeed – (I am told our *Cashier* is at the bottom of all or the prime mover of all that was attempted I am sorry for it, but I fear it is to true He is very ungratefull – but that is nothing new – He has an ungovernable temper – Him & his Brother Frank[37] in the Bank have been quarreling for the last Six Mos & complaining to me . . . .

---

[34]Dr. Thomas David Morrison (1796?–1856) was born in Quebec, arrived at York about 1816 and became a licensed doctor in 1824. A reformer in politics, he was mayor of Toronto in 1836 and after the rebellion of 1837 was acquitted on a charge of high treason. He owned twenty shares in the Bank of Upper Canada in 1830.

[35]Jesse Ketchum (1782–1867) was a tanner, a reformer in politics, and a philanthropist. He arrived in Upper Canada from New York in 1796. He owned twenty shares in the Bank of Upper Canada in 1830 and fifty-three in 1860. He was a director of the bank, 1840–44.

[36]Peter McGill (1780–1860), arrived at Montreal from his native Scotland in 1809. He assumed the name of McGill in 1821 at the request of his uncle, the Hon. John McGill and he inherited the latter's rich estate in 1835. A director of the Bank of Montreal from 1819, he was its president, 1834–60.

[37]Frank Ridout (1808–31?), the brother of Thomas Gibbs Ridout, was a discount clerk in the Bank of Upper Canada. Caught embezzling funds from the bank in 1830, he died soon after.

B 37   WILLIAM ALLAN TO JOHN MACAULAY
24 June 1830
[PAO, Macaulay Papers]

I have had Mr Jones[38] with me battling about our Establishing an office at Brockville – which as far as depends upon myself I am not in favour of at *Present* and I am Pretty certain if it was Proposed to the Board they would be against it; – or many of them would. He said what would be a great facility in affording them the accomodation they reqd from time to time – if we authorised you to discount at once without waiting for a reference to the Board here, or indeed with the formality of going before a Board at Kingston – if we could manage to Establish one there – This we may just as well [and ?] fairly do If You would be willing to undertake it. In course with no more responsibility on your part than there now is – namely you discounting such Notes as are offered with Good Endorsers according to the best of your information knowledge & belief – The same as those you recommend now to the Board as far as you know – In that case you might have the discretionary Power of discounting any Note to a certain Amount all applications beyond that Sum to be refered to the Bank. Do you think that would Answer both the People of Kingston & Brockvile they could have no excuse for delay   It would be better to all there you to discount all Notes (you thought good) not exceeding a certain Sum each that would do better than saying you might discount to a Certain Amt without limiting the respective Notes   What do you think of that   Please let me know and I will Prepare it to commence at once.

B 38   J. BABY, JOS. WELLS, JOHN H. DUNN AND JAS. WINNIETT[39]
TO Z. MUDGE[40]
York, 18 August 1830
[PAC, RG 5 B23, v. 2]

Having been appointed Directors of the Bank of Upper Canada on behalf of the Interest of the Government by His Excellency the Lieut-Governor, we feel it our duty to apprise you for His Excellency's information that a few days ago a deficiency was discovered in that Institution by the delinquency of Mr. Francis Ridout the Discount Clerk

---

[38]This may refer to Alpheus but it is probably Jonas Jones. Jonas (1791–1848) was a lawyer at Brockville and represented Grenville in the House of Assembly, 1816–28, and Leeds, 1836–37. He was a commissioner overseeing the construction of the St. Lawrence Canal and became judge of the Court of Queen's Bench in 1837.

[39]James Winniett was a lieutenant in the 68th Regiment in 1795 and retired about 1829. He became superintendent of Indian affairs on the Grand River in 1832. He was a director of the Bank of Upper Canada, 1829–32, and a large stockholder in the bank in 1830.

[40]Zachariah Mudge was civil and private secretary to the lieutenant-governor, 1828–31.

in having abstracted Discount Notes the amount of which is supposed to be about £1600. – The Board of Directors have appointed Committees of its Members to examine into the transactions with the intention of ascertaining the defalcation and calling upon the Securities of Mr. Ridout for the same. The Securities are the Honble & Venble Archdeacon of York, The Honble George Crookshank, Messrs Vilmer[41] and Samuel Ridout[42]

B 39 WILLIAM ALLAN TO JOHN MACAULAY
York, 16 December 1830
[PAO, Macaulay Papers]

. . . I attend to what you say about being perplexed as to the balloting for Notes, where the application from those of below & your own Town exceed £1250 – that may be pretty much obviated by averaging them in the manner you speak – provided you do not exceed £5,000 Per Month, I have had a conversation with the Cashier on this Subject and all the other matters (contained in your respective letters) and I have instructed him to write you fully in reference to them according to the Memo I gave him – as altho I write you myself in my hasty correspondence on many of the Bank transactions, Still as my letters are not copied for indeed they could not fore nobody could read them not even *myself* – but they are not considered to be official . . . . However I do not conceive that such a transaction as that is to be considered as any part of your limit of £40,000 – . . .

with respect to the limit of £500 to a man Credit which you say you do not like, and that a little more latitude should be given your Board when all discretion is exercised – I agree wh you and no doubt in due time you will be allowed to exercise a further discretion but your Instructions was necessary [2 words?], when your Board commenced – and in giving these Instructions it was better they should be such as could be extended after a while – than to have to curtail them, on this subject I told him to write you also, (*but the fact is* till we [receive word?] of our Capital being extended even to £20,000 its original but up to £25,000 or £200,000 so much the better, we must not be too ready in extending your discretionary Power – or exceeding in our own – you may be assured we will go all the length we can safely do in meeting the Suggestions of your *Board* or those of yourself . . . . I should like very well if you could buy of Harper in any way by Providing for him as an

[41]This may refer to Christopher Widmer.
[42]Samuel Ridout (1778–1855), the older brother of Thomas Gibbs Ridout, was sheriff of the Home District from 1815-27 and registrar of deeds. He operated a general store in partnership with Andrew Mercer. He sat on the board of the British America Fire & Life Assurance Company and in 1824, 1827, 1829, 1834 and 1838 was a director of the Bank of Upper Canada. In the 1830s he seems to have owned just enough shares in the bank to qualify for a directorship.

agent but we must take care & not hold out anything that may be committing ourselves. I have a rd. a letter from Mr Cartwright[43] with a Copy of the proposed Petition to the Legislature I Presume as you say there is no risque of any *Union* between the Brockvile folks & those of Kingston – I think [that] will serve to prevent either from succeeding –

It certainly was the meaning of our *Board* in the Instructions sent you that when a man had got to the Amt of £500 – he should not exceed even to £25 – but there maybe many exceptions – It is well you would accomodate Mr. Harper wh. the 200 and those folks opposed to us – for the present that they should not have it in their power either to say or *think* we refuse them on that Amt. or that we cannot accomodate them . . . .

. . . If you could pursuade Mr. Cartwright to write to Hagerman[44] I don't like since that Hagerman is a Member to Speak to him *myself* but Mr. Cartwright might – most of the Members to the [one word?] will support an increase of our *Capital* I know many have proposed it without saying anything to them on the subject.

> B 40   WILLIAM ALLAN TO JOHN MACAULAY
> York, 20 January 1831
> [*PAO, Macaulay Papers*]

. . . I note what you Say of having seven applications for about £2500 – of Notes before you, and that £1000 less since last discount day – There is no help we must weather through as well as you can till we see what is to be the issue of the Kingston Petition – If you I mean the Board exceed a little your limits in any particular case or for any particular Person, that is proven to be quite Safe – I will answer for your taking any authority necessary hereafter to confirm – But I should most thoroughly recomend to you and the Board to be very Watchful for everybody is Speculating now – all expect to make fortunes – none to *loose* any but look at Lower Canada & many of the Speculators there, they no doubt made as [sure?] of their Success as all our Upper Canada folks do *Jonas Jones*, notwithstanding his already accomodation – wants a further credit of no less than £5,000 entre nous he is going to Mortgage his establishment at Brockville to the Bank as Security (entre nous) he comes up here, about 27th Inst – to urge the Kingston Bank Bill or their own application, but it I have heard nothing of as yet . . . .

---

[43]John Solomon Cartwright (1804–45), the son of Richard Cartwright, was the first president of the Commercial Bank of the Midland District. He represented Lennox and Addington in the Legislative Assembly from 1836.

[44]Christopher Alexander Hagerman (1792–1847), born at Adolphustown, represented Kingston in the Legislative Assembly in the 1820s. In 1829 he became solicitor general, in 1837 attorney general and in 1840 a judge of the Court of Queen's Bench.

B 41   WILLIAM ALLAN TO JOHN MACAULAY
York, 12 February 1831
[*PAO, Macaulay Papers*]

I should have written to you two days ago, but I had nothing particular
to say – except about the Progress of the Commercial Bank Bill, which
was brought down to our House about a Week ago – When it should
have gone into Committee there was a thin House   I moved it should
be deferred to a future day and there there should be a call of all our
Members in Town as it was a Subject upon which there might be a good
deal of discussion – it was put of till last Thursday – we had a Pretty full
House   There was few to advocate it at all & Mr. Markland after
several remarks that was made by *one* or *two Members* that were against
it, which he conceived were intended to apply to him at length got up &
[spoke?]   He had not had time to examine the Bill and was not
prepared to advocate it or otherwise and He Said He admitted some
change had taken place that perhaps made it not so necessary now as last
Year   In *fact* he did not appear to be a very warm supporter of it   Mr.
Peter Robinson[45] was in favor of it as Mr. Elsmly & Capt. Baldwin   These were the only apparent *advocates*   It was put up till
Tuesday-next when it will again be in Committee – and I have no doubt
with anything like a full *House*   It will soon be disposed of under the
Table. No one now except Hagerman seems very anxious about it –
rather the Reverse – But he is much annoyed & I think he must be
pressed by his friends down with you – our application for extending
our *Charter* is in Progress but by no means in the way We proposed it –
[one word?] I fear altho it will pass – It will be *close* in several ways I
am certain Hagerman will do what he can to make it not *Palatable* to the
Stock holders and Directors – such is the way of the speculators – if they
dont get things they wish themselves they endeavor to prevent others
from getting what is fair & right – *Pray entre nous* (what do you know
of Jonas Jones affairs – I have heard not very favourable accts. &
several particulars I don't like – I am particularly anxious from having
gone out of the Common course to accomodate him at the Bank
whenever any thing was said about him at our Board, He and W.
Jones[46] were [sized?] up by some friends as being so wealthy. The
former is said to be worth £20,000 – but I understand he is considerably

---

[45]Peter Robinson (1785–1838), eldest son of Christopher Robinson and brother of
J.B. Robinson, represented Durham, Simcoe and the East Riding of York in the
Legislative Assembly from 1816–20 and York and Simcoe from 1820–24. He superin-
tended the Irish settlement at Peterborough in 1824–25, was commissioner of crown
lands, 1827–36, member of the Executive Council, 1823–36, and the Legislative
Council, 1829–38. He operated as a merchant in York in the 1820s and sat as a director
of the Bank of Upper Canada in 1823, 1825, 1827–28 and 1835. His brother considered
Peter to be the businessman of the family.

[46]W. Jones was a member of the large Jones family at Brockville.

in debt in Montl to one House in Particular who Hold a Mortgage on his Property –
Pray do all you can to get me some *private* information as I feel rather anxious – What do you think of Mr. Jones he is about giving a Mortgage to the Bank on his Property at Brockville –
this all Private
could you in any way find out by the Register of Johnston District – If Jonas Jones Esq has not given a Mortgage to Peter McGill & Co for a Pretty large Sum.

B 42   JOHN STRACHAN TO JOHN MACAULAY (PRIVATE)
York, 3 May 1831
[*PAO, Macaulay Papers*]

. . . I should have been rather inclined to have voted for the Kingston Bank Bill with a different name had the one for increasing the stock of the Bank of Upper Canada been sent up at the same time but I will not trust the House of Assembly by passing the one without the other.

I perceive certain very intemperate resolutions entered into at Kingston which would change my opinion were it grounded on personal considerations. Nothing can be more insolent or absurd than some of them are & the best method would be to give them the trouble and expense of coming up and appearing at the bar next Session. Such a lesson would have a salutary effect and teach them a little common sense but having heard this manifestation of folly it appears to me that we cannot withold without exciting more wrath than the matter is worth, a Second Bank for any long time. And what is not to be concealed the Directors of the Bank here are altogether to blame. 1. They have excited the cupidity of the whole Province by their high Dividends & bonuses – instead of keeping a large reserve of Profits as a refuge in case of loss   2 Their greed was such for I can call it nothing less that they would not apply for an increase of Capital till the whole amount of former Stock was paid in   3 The anxiety prevailed among them lest the New Stock holders should in any way partake directly or indirectly in any portion of the profits of the Old Stock   4 Their slowness in establishing a full branch at Kingston which might have destroyed all opposition or desire for a bank had it been done two or three years ago as it ought to have been   5 To proceed to the Arcana of the Bank – there are three or four Directors who for narrowness & illiberality are enough to destroy any institution what would you think of a trifling note black balled with our Friend *John McGill* endorser. – 6 There Law Agent has in many cases & without check or reprimand proceeded most improperly   7 In regard to management consider that the youngest officer [Frank Ridout] continued as they say to pillage them of large sums for five years without detection.

I certainly hold with you that the Capital of Banks should consist of profits or money not otherwise employed but as the present institution with all its defects has done much good I am inclined to increase its stock because it can then render any other bank unnecessary by establishing Branch Banks where they are required. Had this been done as I said two years ago a separate Bank would not have been called for at Kingston but as matters now stand one more Bank is perhaps expedient to stiffle the cry of Monopoly & to secure you against bad debts and in this way it may be useful to the old Bank. It is also to be observed that the wealth of the Province has trebled during the last ten years so that in this point of view two Banks may be admitted. Accustomed to the Scotch Banks in which country there are 83 I do not apprehend much danger from over issue provided the public be well secured . . . .

B 43   REPORT OF THE PRESIDENT OF THE BANK OF UPPER CANADA ON THE TREASURY DEPOSITS, SUBMITTED TO LT.-GOVERNOR COLBORNE
York, 6 June 1831
[*PAC, CO 42, v. 393, pp. 273ff*]

. . . The Dividends of the Bank are made half yearly and have been at the uniform rate of eight per cent per annum since the year 1823, – besides a Bonus twice of six per cent each.

Several Public Institutions hold Stock in this Bank.

Regulations

The Bank notes issued by the Institution consist of one, two, four, five, ten and fifty dollar bills – they are redeemable only at the Bank – and are at par with silver, throughout the province, and at Montreal in Lower Canada, they have likewise a good circulation on the frontier of the United States.

The denomination of coin chiefly paid out by the Bank is the american half dollar and the spanish dollar – The quantity of Specie in the vault is generally from £20,000 to £40,000-Cy in those coins.

The British Silver Money paid out to the Troops goes very little into circulation, it is bought up at a premium according to the rate of Exchange on London, for the purpose of purchasing Commissariat Bills on the Lords of the Treasury. Sovereigns are also purchased, and are sent to New York for exportation.

The Bank has offices at the Towns of Kingston and Niagara, and Agencies in various parts of the Province to meet the Agricultural and Commercial demands of the Country.

The foreign Agencies are as follows,

At Montreal   –   The Montreal Bank
" New York   –   Messrs Prime Ward King & Co
" London   –   Messrs Thomas Wilson & Co

The usual discounts are on promissory notes at 90 days, with one or more endorsers also on the negociation of Bills on Lower Canada, and the United States, but principally the former Country at 90 days, to aid in the purchases of Wheat, Flour and Lumber, the chief exports of the Province – Bills of this description amount to about £500,000 per annum. The Bank also purchases Treasury bills, Half pay bills, and other Exchange on England, and sells its own drafts on London, Montreal and New York from the latter place it derives its supplies of Specie . . . .

Resources

The Bank of Upper Canada has never been put to any inconvenience for want of resources, and has had as yet, no financial difficulties to contend with – having always possessed ample funds to meet every demand Besides the specie in the vault, it holds permanently large funds in Montreal, New York and London, arising from the operation of its Foreign business – and which are convertible into specie whenever required. It holds likewise Government Debentures to a large amount at times, which are transfered as occasion offers for foreign funds.

The Average deposits from Individuals and Public Institutions, amount to about thirty thousand pounds throughout the year, for which no interest whatever is allowed.

The discounts of the Bank are founded on Landed property or on commercial speculations on the staple articles of export before mentioned, viz. persons who transact business with the Bank, either are known to possess valuable landed or other property or else hold produce to meet their bills when due.

The Bank regulates its issues of notes according to the season of the year, and the state of its Foreign Funds, the largest issue is during the winter when the wheat purchases are making in the Country.

The expenditure of the Civil Government of the Province is for the most part paid by the Bank on the Receiver General's checks.

Should the Government see fit to transfer to the custody of the Bank of Upper Canada, the funds usually deposited in the Military Chests of this Province – and require security for such deposits – the Bank is not legally authorized to offer any guarantee of that nature – but an application might be made to the Legislature, authorizing a certain proportion of each share of Bank Stock to be pledged to the government – or else to set apart a certain amount of the assets of the Bank at all times as a permanent security. – the same to be held inviolate for that purpose.

With respect to what accommodations or benefit superior to those granted to private depositors the Bank might be disposed to offer to the Public, in consideration of the larger amount of Funds, that might be expected to be entrusted to them on the behalf of the Government. It would be necessary in the first place to know the nature of the business required to be transacted by the Bank, in what manner and where the payments are to be made the probable amount of the deposits – and how such deposits are effected, Whether, by specie paid in, or by bills on England before the Bank can arrive at any correct conclusion on the subject.

That it would be made from time to time by the Commissary Generals Bills at 30d/s on the Treasury, which the Bank would negociate on the most advantageous terms, and would render the Commissary General an account sales for the proceeds thereof, retaining (about 1/4) of one per cent for its commission or else the Bills would be purchased by the Bank at a rate to be agreed upon, – In such case the Bank may be induced to offer an interest of   per cent per annum for the average permanent deposit.

It would pay the Commissariat checks at the Bank, and at its offices and agencies, either in current Silver Coins or in Bank notes, at the option of the parties presenting the checks, and would render an account of the same, monthly to the proper authority – it being understood that the Bank would provide funds for these payments at all the Military Stations in the Province.

In case the Government should adopt the course proposed, or in contemplation, there can be no doubt that the measure would prove advantageous to the public. . . . As there will not be any occasion to hold over on deposit a sum of Money beyond the estimated Monthly expenditure for the Troops, or other Military purposes.

It is the opinion of the Bank that the British Silver Coinage will never become the circulating medium of Canada unless the Currency shall be changed into Sterling. – and the exchange on England be stationary at par, neither occurrence is very probable. under these circumstances, it does not appear necessary to issue such coins to the Army in this Province.

B 44   JOHN MACAULAY TO WILLIAM ALLAN
Kingston, 26 December 1831
[*MTL, Allan Papers*]

. . . I fear the Banking business will not go on as it ought in the Legislature and that the new Charter will pass without any addition being made to our capital. This I suppose cannot be helped, and yet it is very absurd to give our Bank Petitioners what they have made so great an outcry against, when we had it viz. a *monopoly*. They are now to be the only sellers of Bank stock in the market. If they are so anxious to nurse the new Institution, and are afraid it will be too ricketty an infant to survive free competition in the stock market, let them say that our new stock shall not be offered in the market until – months after the passing of the act – but it is very absurd, surely to cramp the operation of a useful institution, & compell it to remain stationary, while the country & everything in it is thriving. And in the course of improvement, of course, no new agencies or offices of discount are to be established, unless we get an increase of capital. What then are the people of the Head of the Lake and Brockville about? Probably when they find a charter granted for Kingston, they will set up for themselves – I do not think that in either quarter they should expect our Bank to put itself out of the way hereafter in order that they may be accommodated. The whole opposition I am convinced originates in a miserable jealousy of our Institution. Prosperity generally excites envy. This is the nature of man.

I do not like the appearance of things in Europe especially in England where there are signs of convulsion and revolution. . . . For this reason I would suggest the prudence of keeping our account with Wilson and Co, very low because no one at this distance can tell when a sudden panic or civil commotion may upset the firmest Commercial Establishments, and spread ruin among the Capitalists and Bankers. And as a further measure of precaution, I would always keep up a respectable contingent fund – vested in Government Debentures and thus bearing interest, in order to meet the bills that might return in case of any disastrous crisis at London . . .

B 45   WILLIAM ALLAN TO W.H. MERRITT[47]
York, 28 December 1831
[*PAO, Merritt Papers, v. 34*]

. . . I conceive a Paper Currency – of a proper value with Gold & Silver, which it profess to represent; – Is the cheapest, & best, circulating medium a country can have; and I conceive that is fully the case with all the Notes Legalay in circulation now; – Therefore my idea is there ought to be but this *one Bank* in the Province with a Capital sufficient to afford all the accomodation every part of the Country requires – When that is the case if it could then be shown that the One Institution did not do so; – Then it would be reasonable to ask to have other Institutions; –

I know I am generally represented as being against any other Bank, besides the Bank of U. Canada from *Interested* motives Now the fact is I have no Interest in the World in being against it; – I never in my life borrowed or had a shilling from this Bank, nor any other; and I hope & trust I shall never have occasion to have; as to what I have been allowed for some years as President of this Bank; I did that duty without any

[47]William Hamilton Merritt (1793–1862) was born in New York and came with his family to St. Catharines in 1796. Primarily known for his promotion of the Welland Canal, he was also active in politics representing Haldimand from 1832 and Lincoln from 1841 in the Legislative Assembly. He promoted and incorporated the Niagara District Bank in 1841.

remuneration for the first two or three years; – and I would have no objections (if I continue and the Profits of the Bank would not afford to Pay that or any remuneration – I would be as willing to do the duty without as with it; and admitting there was another Institution in opperation I am well satisfied there is *bussiness* for *two* or even *more* but I conceive it much for the interest of the Country there should be only One; with a capital sufficient for all purposes; – another Bank in full opperation would not prevent this Bank if *properly* managed from dividing the same as heretofore; –

I oppose the Kingston Bank for another reason, that if it passed into a Law; it opens the door, which cannot again in Common Justice be afterwards Shut. If that passes (which I have no doubt it will) I will most certainly support your application for a Bank at St Catherines or any other that is hereafter made – altho I differ with *your idea*, that the more Banks the better; – There is a wide difer' [difference] betweeꞯ this Province and any part of the United States; – If a Bank or Banks can be carryed on and do there bussiness without *Capital*, – They may succeed, but if I *know any thing* of the *Trade & Situation of this Country* – a Second Bank will hamper the Public generaly and many individuals particularly and a little time will tell – I really am indifferent about it. I have less reason to care, being in no line of bussiness – and if they once determine upon one more Bank; – all future applications that appear *reasonable* will have my support . . . .

B 46   JOHN MACAULAY TO WILLIAM ALLAN
Kingston, 7 January 1831 [*sic*; 1832]
[*MTL, Allan Papers*]

. . . I am in due receipt of your favour of 3rd Instant, informing me of the passing of the charter for the Bank at this place by the Legislative Council which I fancy was not to be avoided as the people here were resolved to persevere until the measure was carried, and their perseverance was sure sooner or later to wear out the opposition to it in the Upper House. They are now I find going round with their subscription Book and have already got £13,000 down on paper An appeal is made to the feeling of individuals, as inhabitants of the town, and they are easily and certainly very naturally led to believe that a Bank is all that Kingston wants to make it flourish. They say, ''Look at York – how it flourishes! All is owing to their having a Bank'' – and the people readily swallow all that is repeated to them in this way – not for a moment supposing that our Bank already does the business of two such Banks as the late pretended BUC – and that another discount office nor half a score of them can make Kingston keep pace with York in improvement. I am sure the fine back Country does infinitely more for the advancement of York than the Bank can do. I do not know what the exact effect of this new institution may be on our business. This is not easy to predict but I am inclined to think it must interfere with it very materially because so many will be interested in the new Concern as Stockholders that they will be disposed to do their business there, & there certainly is not room here at present for double our business. Perhaps the natural growth of the Country, which is rapidly improving may do much to find profitable business for both. One thing that I am convinced of is that the new Concern will be sadly puzzled to keep its account good below even though they should enter into a league with the City Bank that is talked of and another thing equally certain is that they will not for years be able to discount steadily. Some good folks therefore who are now allowed such credit may find themselves a little straitened bye & bye instead of having double their present large accounts. I wonder at the conduct of some individuals. But appeal to their feelings as inhabitants of Kingston, cannot, it seems, be resisted. If individuals abroad take shares, the sum required, will doubtless be raised, but if people in other districts are shy, there will be some difficulty to get together £10,000. They want Mr. Kirby[48] to be their President – and asked me to take stock – to which I replied I would begin to think about it when I found they made good dividends. There is a talk of getting Henry Smith's[49] brother to be Cashier instead of Harper, who is generally disliked so that I can foresee a good deal of squabbling about offices.

I am glad to learn that we are likely to get our additional capital & if we do, I suppose the Bank will at once extend its discount offices as the only effectual means of putting down petitions for new Banks, and limiting the support of the Commercial . . . .

B 47   JOHN S. BALDWIN TO J. QUESNEL[50]
York, 28 January 1832
[*Archives Nationales du Québec – Québec, Quesnel Papers*]

. . . The principal thing I have to say to you now is to answer your query about the Bank. I should have spoken to you about it before but was waiting for the matter to be settled which was only concluded a day or two ago – the fact is that all the Eastern members are very jealous of the various improvements in York and particularly at the Bank. I believe many of them would see its destruction with pleasure as also that of the town if they could but the Kingston Bank bill passed both Houses in a very handsome way with a capital of £200,000 this being done they could not refuse giving the York Bank the like capital as it now has but £100,000 but the Assembly cloged it with so many provisions that the

---

[48]John Kirby, a successful Kingston merchant and conservative in politics, was John Macaulay's uncle.

[49]The Smiths were a prominent Kingston family. Henry Smith was the first warden of the Kingston Penitentiary.

[50]Jules Maurice Quesnel (1786–1842), born in Montreal, became a partner with J.S. Baldwin in a mercantile firm.

Council rejected it with disdain. They made several amendments striking out those obnoxious points & sent it back, at last they had a compromise on it, and it passed in this way. This £100,000 Stock is not to be open for subscription till six months after the final passing of the bill. (this is to prevent its interfering with the Kingston stock which is now open for subscription) A book is to be opened in every district and no one person allowed to take more than 80 shares of £1000 for a certain time If to much is subscribed for each town is to [doc?] off in proportion till it is reduced to the proper number.

([This?] is a blow at the people of York, to prevent their engrossing to much of it, or rather to give them as *little* as *possible*) So that the day, after the six months is expired, I suspect it will be the early bird to get the first worm whoever has the luck to get a few shares in this way will come in at par. and the money to be paid by instalments as the Bank may require it I think 10 per cent at a time. This being the case the present directory will divide the present surplus fund, which is now large, to prevent the new comers benefiting by it, – this will give you some idea of the matter. I should like myself to get 80 shares & I can assure you I cannot receive them before the six months. you can let me know what you would wish . . . .

B 48   THOMAS MCCORMICK TO S.P. JARVIS
Niagara, 2 March 1832
[*MTL, S.P. Jarvis Papers*]

. . . There is no doubt, that the Bank now about to be Established at Kingston – will take advantage of every opening for Establishing Offices in different parts of the Province – I Would therefore think – that the BUC should not loose any time in placing the Several Offices on that footing – that will leave no room for Complaint – and therefore no room for them Establishing other Offices – the Commercial Bank has had a list here for the purpose of getting Stock Subscriptions and enducements held out privately which might have Succeeded – as several of the Most respectable in business think that a Board of Directors ought to be formed here as they find it very inconvenient, the Delay in transacting their business – I have stated to them my Opinion (without pledging myself as an Agent) that I thought the Bank – would not Object to the re-establishing the Board at this place provided a Sufficient Number would make themselves Eligible to act as Directors in Consequence – I believe they have all foreborn to Subscribe for any Stock in the Commercial Bank and there 4 or 5 – would take sufficient Stock in this Bank to make themselves eligible to be Directors . . . .

It appears to me that the Bank might have Managed to have had the controul of the Comc. Bk. and not allowed the [Directory?] of the Montl Bank to have it – you will find that institution a Source of Annoyance before long – or I am Mistaken (I mean the Coml. Bk).

B 49   JOHN MACAULAY TO WILLIAM ALLAN
Kingston, 26 March 1832
[*MTL, Allan Papers*]

. . . The President of the Commercial came to me today for £125 in Specie to pay in his first instalment of stock, and I gave him that amount in English shillings & sixpences. I thought it as well to accommodate him in this way & shew that we did not care or feel sore about his desertion. I hope you will think I have done what is right in the matter. He asked Mr. Ranken[51] if he could get our bye-laws to found upon them a code for the Commercial. This however is what I shall not grant – but if he speaks about it to me I shall say that I will readily let him have them if he obtains authority from you to that effect.

I have not heard what measures you have in contemplation about the Brockville office. Last winter Jonas Jones, Sherwood[52] and others said they wished Mr. Ranken to be the Cashier if I could spare him. I said that though I should like well to retain him here that should never be in the way of his advancement, & I expected that the application for his appointment would proceed from Brockville. To my great surprise, however, it has been lately hinted to me that Henry Sherwood is a candidate for the Cashier-ship himself. In fact these good folks seem to wish to engross all the offices. I hope however the Bank will not forget in its appointments, its own subordinate officers – the young men trained up in its own business. They certainly have claims for advancement, when appointments are made, & it is clearly the interest of the Bank to act on this principle. I know not what may be the views of the officers in the Bank at York nor what the Board may intend doing – but if someone there is not appointed to Brockville, I hope Mr. Ranken's claims will not be overlooked. He has been now connected with the Bank nearly ten years, understands Banking business well, is remarkably correct in accounts, and possesses great prudence, judgment and discretion. He is indeed in every aspect uncommonly well qualified for a Cashier-ship. I think he is precisely the person required for Brockville to which place some one quite a stranger and unconnected with the rival families and parties should be sent, in order to secure the best business & to prevent our establishment from being a one-sided Concern.

---

[51]Ranken was an assistant to John Macaulay, the Bank of Upper Canada's Kingston agent.
[52]Henry Sherwood (1807–55), born in Leeds County, operated as a lawyer at Prescott and York. In 1842–44 he was mayor of Toronto and he represented Toronto in the Legislative Assembly, 1843–54.

B 50   JOHN MACAULAY TO WILLIAM ALLAN
Kingston, 13 April 1832
[*MTL, Allan Papers*]

. . . I should think neither he [John Watkins][53] nor any other of the
Commercial *directors* should expect *equal accommodation* from us
from henceforth to that formerly most liberally granted. For instance
when they are obliged to suspend (as they occasionally must) their
discounts they should not be allowed to *make a convenience* of our
office. They do not deserve from us so much consideration & if they feel
the effects of this course of policy so much the better. Mr. Watkins is
one of the last men in town who should have joined an opposition to us.
However, I suppose it will be advisable not to alter our present system,
until we see how they proceed with their business. It appears to me
impossible for them to discount largely or with any regularity for a long
time to come. Cartwright has assumed a task of no ordinary delicacy
and responsibility. My present impression is that he is too straightforward a person to suit the views of most of the Stockholders and
Directors, and that when the concern is fairly afloat, they will choose
another President. He *deserves* such a retribution for his inconsistent
conduct as respects us. It appears to me your view of the subject as to
exchange of notes is perfectly correct . . . .
I find that Mr. Dupuy is paying 6% for British Half crowns, i.e.
giving 2/11 instead of 2/10¹/₂ the legal value and that they are purchased
for exportation Would it not do to ship British silver at that rate from
New York as well as from Montreal. Dupuy says the Montreal Bank
consider it a better speculation than the purchase of Exchange . . . .

B 51   WILLIAM ALLAN TO W.H. MERRITT
York, 14 April 1832
[*PAC, W.H. Merritt Papers, v. 7*]

. . . It is only 10 pct that is or can be called for; as the first Instalement
on what ever Stock is Subscribed, for on 1st Augt – and each Successive
call is 10 pct after giving due notice of 90 days I believe. However you
will no doubt see a Copy of the Act long before the period the Books are
to be opened for Subscription you better be prepared you or any of your
Friends – to take up whatever you intend as soon as the time arrives – as
I understand there is a certainty of all the Shares being taken up as fast as
the Act, will authorise it –
There are several persons, as I am told connected in this Country that
intend taking Stock (I mean persons in England/No person can exceed
in the first Instance more than 80 Shares In fact the manner of

---

[53]John Watkins operated an ironmongery shop in Kingston from 1818 and in 1829
opened a branch in York run by T.D. Harris.

Subscribing & calling in the Instalements – is exactly according to the Conditions & clauses in the Original Act. We would have had no objections to have opened Books for Sale at your place if we could but the Act did not authorise it. And we found it could not be done to promise to make any Establishment of An Agency – there & continue the One we have at Niagara. However there is no Saying what another Season may produce, I dare say all those persons about St. Catherines who have any right or Tittle to expect it will receive as much accomodation as are fair and reasonable.

If you will at a future period If I still continue as Pr. give me any *private* information as to the Situation & circumstances of all or any of the persons in business most likely to require much Credit (It will be useful and Shall be entirely *private* – . . .

B 52   JOHN MACAULAY TO WILLIAM ALLAN
Kingston, 9 May 1832
[*MTL, Allan Papers*]

. . . I am very much obliged to you for informing me of your reasons for restricting the discounts. I was well aware when I received the Cashier's letter that there must have been good cause for adopting this course, but I was curious to learn exactly what it was. I was satisfied from the amount I had recently received myself from Mr. Dupuy and forwarded, that the Montreal Bank was picking up our notes at a great rate. The slackness in trade, and the little field now offered for speculation will prevent our notes from remaining in circulation long to the same extent as they did last year. I admire your prudence in always having *a horse in the stable*. I am convinced that great caution is necessary in directing the concerns of a Bank especially in a Country like ours, where business is so conducted that debtors always calculate on the certainty of being allowed to renew, & where absolute ruin would be caused by an attempt to collect notes at the end of the first 90 days. A Horse in the stable is therefore most important where a Bank cannot possibly collect its debts in less than a year. We had on Saturday about £3000 before us & it was a sad damper to the parties when they found there was a check on the issue of our paper. They begin to complain of the Scarcity of money, forgetting that the £5 or £6000 of the *loose cash* of the town is locked up inactive in the vaults of the Commercial. How plentiful it may become when the Commercial notes take wing I cannot say. I suppose our stop will hasten the measures of the Bankers here. They have got in about 1500 and Mr. Cartwright, I am told, signed 800 on Saturday, but here they are stopped, as the Engravers are so much engaged with other Banks as not to be able to supply them in proper season – This is unfortunate. They propose issuing their paper about the middle of June. They are in treaty with me for a lot in rear of my house and offer me £250 in stock and £250 in cash payable in a twelve month . . . .

B 53 WILLIAM ALLAN TO W.H. MERRITT
York, 5 June 1832
[*PAC, W.H. Merritt Papers, v. 7*]

. . . Mr. Wenham[54] in the absence of the Cashier will reply to your application which I hope will meet your wishes – but I would advise you to avoid, as much as you can, – Having your name on other Paper, in the Bank I mean, if you have any idea of requiring any considerable Amt. for your self & Mr. P. [Phelps] –[55]
Because even now or, if I should be absent, the Board are often governed in discounting of Notes by the Amt. of Credit before given either to the Promissor or the Endorser – Now if you appear, as either Promissor or just Endorser – on other Notes besides those you may present for Mr. Phelps & yourself. It may endanger them w. Some of the Board – all this entre nous & for your Sake I mention it . . . .

B 54 T.G. RIDOUT TO JAMES HAMILTON[56]
York, 6 June 1832
[*UWO, Hamilton and Warren Papers*]

Your letters . . . [have] been duly laid before the Board of Directors; by whom I am instructed to inform you that they would have been very happy to have complied with the wishes and probably the necessities of the People in business in your part of the Country – but the great difficulty is the want of means, as the limited Capital of the Bank, altho' lately increased, barely enables the Board to afford the necessary discounts here, and at other places where offices and agencies are already formed – so that it entirely precludes the Directors from promising to establish either a Branch, or an agency at St. Thomas until a further augmentation of the Capital Stock . . . .

B 55 JOHN MACAULAY TO WILLIAM ALLAN
Kingston, 5 July 1832
[*MTL, Allan Papers*]

. . . I beg to say that I always endeavour to guard against the negotiation of accommodation paper. I am aware that Mr. MacDonell[57] does sometimes resort to this expedient – & when it is possible I refuse his drafts – sometimes he brings me drafts with 2 or 3 endorsers & then I do

---

[54]Joseph Wenham, born in England, became the Bank of Upper Canada's book-keeper in 1822. He became the bank's agent in Brockville in 1832, its agent in Montreal in the late 1830s and the Bank of Montreal's agent at Toronto in the early 1840s.

[55]Phelps may have been a merchant operating in the St. Catharines area.

[56]James Hamilton, the son of Robert Hamilton of Queenston, operated a general mercantile, milling, and shipping business with John Warren at Port Stanley. He was later sheriff of the London District.

[57]Angus Roy Mcdonell (MacDonell) was a merchant operating out of Cornwall and Kingston.

not feel that I ought to refuse – unless perfectly certain of the object – In the two cases you mention the 1st draft for £120 was to my knowledge a regular transaction. The second for £250 was negociated on a letter of credit from Mr. J.G. Bethune[58] which I did not feel that I could refuse.

I always looked on the dfts. passing between MacDonell & Stennett[59] as Kites[60] & have never received any except for collection. It is a pretty difficult thing to keep down this practice – I wish it was practicable to stop it altogether & compel people when they want money to come and apply for it in a regular way.

I cannot get an insight into the affairs of the Commercial, to ascertain how much stock they have taken up. I understand however that they do not intend to commence business until the cholera has subsided – I shall have a right to know the state of things and bye and bye as I have been tempted to become a stockholder I am half inclined to think I may repent my bargain. I intend selling out as soon as I can . . . .

B 56   JOHN MACAULAY TO WILLIAM ALLAN
Kingston, 20 July 1832
[*MTL, Allan Papers*]

. . . I am glad to hear that our discounts may now be extended when that can be done with safety. Mr. Wenham will I suppose soon commence at Brockville and that will take off 1/3 of my discount business. I wish we could secure the collecting business of the Montreal Bank. Poor Dupuy stands in the way of that – for the percentage on bills collected now does more than pay him, & the Montreal Bank would not probably know what to do with him if he were removed from this. My apprehension on this question is that the Commercial may manoeuvre bye and bye so as to secure this branch of business to themselves especially as several of the Montrealers hold their stock. That collection is a matter of importance & would greatly affect the state of the weekly exchange of notes. I am told they have a quantity of our paper in hand which of course is to be expected but they have not yet said a word to me about Exchange – I shall leave it to them to broach the subject. They have upwards of £3000 of our notes. I have not quite £1000 of theirs. Dupuy has in hand about

---

[58]James Grey Bethune (1793–1841) was a general businessman and promoter at Cobourg. He was the Bank of Upper Canada's agent at Cobourg in the early 1830s.

[59]A. Stennet was a partner with A. McDonell in merchant business.

[60]Kites were promissory notes forwarded from a merchant in one city to an account controlled by a partner in a second city. Because it took some time for the note to clear the banking system, on the strength of the first note, the merchant's partner would issue a second note, often to a third party. The same result could be achieved through the use of bills of exchange. A drew on B in another place at 60 days sight and sold the exchange to his bank. Then at 57 days or so B drew a similar bill on A which he used to pay the first bill when it came due. The common factor was, of course, the fact that the accounts drawn on could not meet the various drafts.

£1300 and must continue in collecting dfts to pick up a great deal. They discount twice a week & I am told go as low as 12.10–. They are proceeding cautiously & many who looked for discounts are disappointed. I think they are in the way of committing a great mistake by appointment [of] a numerous list of agents. There is risk in this, especially when men in trade are the agents and their standing not thoroughly known. I doubt not there is a body of *malcontents* at York ready to support an agency of the Commercial as soon as it can be set up. For my part I expect soon to see two or three more Banks agoing among us. The uncertain position of things in England will send out many capitalists to Canada, who will want employment for their money, & our Province is sure to prosper, and triple its population and its exports in a very few years. Nothing can now arrest its course but the folly of our own people. I therefore as one lament that our capital had not originally been set up at half a million. We shall see that the Province could soon find employment for it all – I am inclined to think that our new Stock will be all subscribed for the first day. I know of several thousand that will be subscribed here. Your plan of calling in the stock is a good one & I hope it will be adopted. It will serve the real capitalists and disappoint the mere speculator . . . .

B 57   JOHN MACAULAY TO WILLIAM ALLAN
Kingston, 28 July 1832
[*MTL, Allan Papers*]

. . . Though I am somewhat hurried today, I must find time to write you a few lines respecting our Exchange with the Commercial. Mr. Ridout will probably communicate the contents of my private letter to him.

I am, *entre nous*, apprehensive he lost his temper on the presentment of my draft in the manner stated and at all events, he used a very offensive expression if it be true that he accused the Commercialists of a *trick*, which is unfortunate, as it tends to make bad blood and the more so as there was no real foundation for such a charge. The President of the Commercial also used coarse language today when I told him of my recent instructions not to exchange, which I supposed originate in Mr. Harper's not instructing Ross to exchange at York. He undertook to question Mr. Ridout's veracity & said he had told untruths. I said I did not believe it – He replied he has told untruths and on more than one occasion *particularly with respect to the Montreal Bank*. I was losing my temper at this gross attack on Mr. Ridout, but managed to avoid saying anything more than that I did not believe it, that I knew Mr. Ridout's word could be relied on – & that he would not condescend to tell any untruths. I said it was a pity any misunderstanding should arise. He then said he would write to you, and has since shewn me a copy of his letter – which I hope will lead to peace. Now what could be meant by the allusion to the Montreal Bank made unguardedly by Mr. C?

[Cartwright] *Something* it is clear must be alluded to that has been stated in correspondence relative to the Commercial Bank. I mention this in confidence. It would unnecessarily annoy Mr. Ridout to mention it to him.

B 58   JAMES STEWART[61] TO LORD HOWICK[62] (COPY)
London, England, 1 August 1832
[*PAC, A. Shortt Papers, v. 2*]

. . . I am also to observe to your Lordship that my Lords perceive from some of the Papers transmitted to them relative to the several Banking Establishments in Canada, that a practice exists in the Bank at York, of making advances upon Landed security, which is in their opinion at variance with sound principle, and which, if persevered in, & carried to a greater extent, particularly in a Country where there is so much spirit of speculation in land, may be productive of the greatest difficulty, and expose the Bank to the risk of being unable under particular circumstances, to meet the Demand upon it in specie. My Lords therefore deem it their duty, as it appears that the Government of Upper Canada hold a considerable portion of the stock in the Bank, & have complete control over its operations, and as there appears an intention of applying to the Legislature for Powers to double its present Capital to call the special attention of Viscount Goderich[63] to this important point, and to request that he will consider the expediency of giving Instructions to the Lieut Governor to abstain from giving the Royal Sanction to any act for extending the Capital of that Bank, unless Provisions be made in such Act, to restrain this practice, in like manner as was done in the Act for the incorporation of the Montreal Bank.

B 59   JOHN MACAULAY TO WILLIAM ALLAN
Kingston, 4 August 1832
[*MTL, Allan Papers*]

. . . I am glad to find that Mr. Ridout was not provoked by the Commercial's agent to say anything that he could be sorry for. It is curious how such a story could have been set afloat, without there being any foundation for it. People seem to have a wonderful talent at invention in such cases.

On reference to Mr. Cartwright's letter it is clear he did not understand the arrangement I proposed to him for an Exchange of Notes. I do

---

[61]James Stewart was secretary to the commissioners of His Majesty's Treasury.

[62]Lord Henry George Howick, Third Earl Grey, was undersecretary for the colonies (1830–33) and a spokesman for the reform group in the Whig party. He became colonial secretary in 1846.

[63]Frederick John Robinson, Viscount Goderich (1782–1859), was colonial secretary, 1830–33. He was created Earl of Ripon in 1833.

not know how he could conceive that "all the Commercial paper would be transmitted from the Bank of Upper Canada to the office at Kingston to be exchanged" – Where could be the equality unless all the Bank of UC paper were also sent to York to be exchanged at the Bank? The fact is that I clearly explained to him that we would exchange notes here & if the balance were against me, I would give them a draft in the Bank & that their agent would also exchange at York with the Bank & get payment if the difference were against us as I supposed by a Bill on Montreal, not however pledging myself to that or to specie, but considering that the Bank would prefer giving the former. This is the arrangement I repeatedly mentioned to him and entered into in conformity to your own views of the matter. Whether he forgot it, or whether Harper wishes a different arrangement I know not but I think all the blame lies with the latter, who will be troublesome as soon as he has it in his power. I dislike having any transactions with him. When I gave the draft, I took it for granted that Harper would instruct the agent to receive their own notes in payment for the whole amount, if we had as many in the Bank vault. The trouble however is now, I trust, over. I shall endeavour to prevent a recurrence, by having a fair *written* understanding in all future matters with the *President*. I hope you will not mention to anyone a syllable about the expressions he uttered in a moment of irritation respecting Mr. Ridout. I thought it right *you* should know that occurrence, but no one else – I suppose there has been some little tattle in this case also.

Some of the Commercials are not a little annoyed I understand at the eagerness exhibited to obtain our new stock, but they console themselves with the hope that when ours is all taken up theirs will come into market – which is all very likely to be the case. There are many sage speculations afloat among them, which are reported to me. One scheme is to *compel* us to keep our books open two months whether we will or not because, say they, the law authorises it, & then there may be room to speculate. Another scheme is to *break our charter*, if we call in the stock, without an interval of 60 days between each instalment . . . .

B 60   WILLIAM ALLAN TO W.H. MERRITT
York, 7 September 1832
[*PAC, W.H. Merritt Papers, v. 7*]

. . . You will by this time be able to See by the News Paper, what Quantity of Stock you are to have; –

Had the Legislature thought proper to have increased the Stock to such An Amt, as the wants of the Country (now or Soon will require,) say to £3 to £400,000 – It would have enabled every One to get what ever Amt he might desire; – As it is not one fourth of those who wanted Stock could get it – during the few days the Books were Kept open, there was Considerable *more than three times* what the law authorised *Subscribed* so that has to be Cut down, –

Had the Books been Kept open for two Mos. which *some* people fancy the Act *required*; there would have to a certainty, been more stock Subscribed for than would have given *One* share to each; – I have no doubt after the first Instalment is pd up which is not till January, – There will be Stock enough to purchase as I am aware a very great many took Stock on Speculation which could not be prevented, And if you want to [purchase?] any Particular Sum in Bank Stock my *advice* is for you to have your money ready at New York/or Some other Tangible place Where no doubt you have *some* Interest for it; – And if you or any person who are desirous of obtaining a given quantity of Bank [stock] had to Pay One pCent or even more I should prefer *that* myself – as One can buy to Suit themSelves & Know what you can depend upon, in place of scrambling for it *now*, – . . .

B 61   JOHN MACAULAY TO WILLIAM ALLAN
Kingston, 25 September 1832
[*MTL, Allan Papers*]

. . . I am aware that it is important to prevent the establishment of precedents that may tend to introduce lavish expenses – but after all Mr Ranken's salary is but small. We of the *outposts* are not paid like the good folks of Head Quarters . . . .

The Cashier has stopped my drawing in New York, to the great inconvenience of our neighbours in Jefferson County . . . .

B 62   JOHN MACAULAY TO WILLIAM ALLAN
Kingston, 8 October 1832
[*MTL, Allan Papers*]

. . . You have not said anything to me about the arrangement with the Commissariat but I am led to suspect the business for this place has been grasped most unfairly and greedily by the Montreal Bank. If so, it cannot be helped but I see no reason for my part why such an arrangement should be tamely submitted to. The Commercial folks have, I hear, sent off a remonstrance to Head Quarters today on the subject. They are seeking for it and, I should not wonder if they succeeded – for it is unreasonable that a foreign bank should have the public business here. To be sure Treasury bills to the tune of £40 to £50,000 sterling a year is worth trying to keep, but I should think that will not be allowed long – and if our Bank does not interfere the Commercial will in the end secure it. The Montreal Bank should never have been allowed to retain its footing here. I think our Bank had once an opportunity of getting them off which will not soon return. Only consider what a business they will have – paying the troops etc   about £50000 sterling, and collecting nearly double that sum. . . .

B 63   JOHN MACAULAY TO WILLIAM ALLAN
Kingston, 10 October 1832
[*MTL, Allan Papers*]

. . . With respect to the plan had in view by the Bank, and intended soon to be acted on, of making people pay up without renewals, I suppose that the Board of Directors are the best judges, having more extensive knowledge of the circumstances of the Country than any other persons – I must however confess I cannot subscribe to the propriety of the measure at the present period, even though due notice be given that it will go into effect with regard to future discounts at a certain day – It is my opinion that the Country is not yet ripe for any such change in the mode of conducting its cash transactions & I therefore think the Bank will run great risk of failing in the attempt to force such a change upon it. The result will be a clamour for *more* Banks & the certain establishment of four or five new ones within 3 years. This at least is my *prophecy*. We shall see how far I am a good prophet. At any rate such a measure on our part is the very thing that will help on the Commercial, whose stock will in a twelve month be at a premium.

With respect to the payment of the Military etc I see you confirm my suspicion that the Montrealers have evinced the old spirit of greediness. I was afraid something of this sort might happen & long ago wrote to Mr. Ridout to attend closely to this matter. All that is left to our Bank is to pay a few men at York, & all the paltry outposts above – Here where the payments are about £4000 a month, the Montrealers pounce upon it. They ought not to be allowed to retain it. If we cannot get it I would rather see it in the hands of the Commercial Bank, than of a *foreign* institution. The Montreal Bank deserves to have its rapacity punished by a law prohibiting the circulation in this Province of any notes under *five* dollars. They could not complain of this as it is but an *equal* measure of retaliation.

B 64   WILLIAM ALLAN TO EDWARD ELLICE[64]
York, 27 October 1832
[*PAC, Ellice Papers, v. 7*]

. . . I am this moment induced to take the liberty of troubling you upon a subject in which you have an interest, not as a private individual but in a public capacity as Secretary of the Treasury; I mean the contemplated arrangement by which the Military disbursements of the Canadas are intended to be hereafter made through the Montreal Bank and the Bank of Up. Canada. Although no official communication has yet been received by the latter, I have nevertheless had intimation of the extent to

[64]Edward Ellice (1783–1863) was a British businessman involved in the North American fur trade who owned extensive land in New York State and the Canadas. He was secretary of the treasury, 1830–32 and secretary-at-war, 1832–34.

which it is proposed our Institution should participate in the intended mode of distribution. And I feel constrained to remark that whether from inadvertency, missapprehension, or deliberate intention the patronage does not seem to me to have been equalised between the Banks. It is said that of Montreal is not only to furnish the calls of Lower Canada but to enjoy the same privilege in this Province as far up as Kingston inclusive, restricting our Provincial Bank to York and the Western Posts . . . .

I am not aware of any good reason for a weak institution like the Montreal Bank having its origin and residence in a separate Province monopolizing any (Especially the most [lucrative?] portion of the fiscal business of the Military Department of Upper Canada but I perceive [reasons?] why each Bank should be restricted to the Local limits of its Charter. They both exist under Provincial Charters. The one emanating from the Legislature of Lower – and the other – from that of Upper Canada and of course have strictly speaking a local habitation and a name in each respective province and not elsewhere: The Legislature of one Colony could not impart to any such Institution a power to establish a branch or agency within the boundary of the other although it has not been [one word?]. The business of banking requires of course foreign Agencies through which much of its dealings in Bills &tc are conducted, and although the Montreal Bank has an individual Agent at Kingston to extend the circulation of its paper in that vicinity – still they do not retire their notes at that place nor do they keep any Specie funds for that purpose except below and however long this practice may be as at present tolerated is not for me to say. But without enlarging on the impropriety of an undue preference to the Montreal Bank to the prejudice of another equally solvent Establishment, and the indirect encouragement of a species of rivalry not contemplated in its Charter, and deemed incompatable with the interest and security of the Upper Canada Public; I will suggest some reasons which strike me as conclusive in favor of the Bank of which I have the honor to be President.

The Bank of Upper Canada in circulating Bills in any part of this Province does not exceed its constitutional limits and within which it is bound to ask redemptions. It is a Chartered Institution in which the Government has a large interest though not an absolute control/as I believe has been erroneously assumed or supposed. It enjoys unimpeached credit and of such reputation/which combined with lucrative dividends to Stock-holders as evince prudence and a knowledge and practice of correct principles of banking, and can be urged with confidence in its favor. In addition to which it has not only established local Agencies at considerable expense in many parts of the Province to afford facilities to the Public at large, but it has had from its commencement eleven years ago a regularly established Branch or office of discount and deposit at Kingston through which the Public service could be accommodated with the utmost readiness and facility. did the

Montreal Bank present greater facilities at that post or any other point that ours could furnish, the preference could be more easily accounted for – but such not being the case it is felt due to Upper Canada, and to the Bank operating under her Charter – that the latter should receive from the King's Government the same measure of confidence and patronage within this Province which may be justly claimed by, and granted to, a similar Institution seated and acting under a like local power in the other. When I add that the admission of the Montreal Bank to the advantage spoken of in Upper Canada will make a difference of £40.000 or £50.000 per Annum in Treasury Bills to the domestic Bank of this Province you will not be surprised that I should somewhat strenuously advocate our interest in the arrangement. as the Government Bills will only be received in proportion to advances made. and for sums actually paid, the Home Government can incur little danger of inconvenience and no risk of loss in the event of a failure in either Bank, but as on a representation that our business is not conducted on sound Banking principles endangering our stability may have influenced the course adopted at the Treasury – I think it proper to notice the subject.

I have reasons to apprehend that my Lords have in some way been led to believe that we made a practice of advancing loans upon landed securities. Such however is not the fact. It is not improbable that upon our receiving Official notice of the views of His Majesty's Government the Board of Directors will feel it incumbent upon them to [point out?] all unfavourable or erroneous impressions with which the Lords of the Treasury may have become possessed. In the meantime I will only further state that the Bank has been in operation upwards of eleven Years and now only owns 1999 9/10 Acres in all the Province taken in cases where debts have been incurred and no other visible means remaining for our recovery.

I, of course, have no objections to your making any use of this letter as Secretary to the Treasury which You may think proper –

B 65   REPORT OF THE SELECT COMMITTEE
appointed to inquire into the manner in which the new stock of the Bank of Upper Canada has been disposed of by the Directors of that Institution, December 6, 1832
[JUC, *1832–33, Appendix, pp 75–79*]

William Morris[65] – Chairman.
Committee — Hamnett Pinhey,[66]
William Buell[67]

. . . One thing is plain and obvious, from the evidence appended to this

[65]William Morris (1786–1858), born in Scotland, arrived in Canada in 1801. He was a merchant at Perth and represented Lanark in the Legislative Assembly, 1820–36.
[66]Hamnett Pinhey came to Bytown in 1819 from England. He was warden for

report, (even if the language of the Act is admitted to be ambiguous) namely, that the highest Law Officer in the country intended, as the House of Assembly certainly did intend, that five hundred shares of the Stock should be secured to the inhabitants of each District, provided they should be found to have subscribed that quantity. It must therefore become a matter of surprise and disappointment that the intention of the Legislature should be so far frustrated as to give to the subscribers of the Towns of York and Niagara five-eights of the whole new Stock, when those of some other District Towns has been reduced to less than one-half of the number of shares intended to be secured to the inhabitants of each District . . . .

Your Committee viewing the injury which has been inflicted on the subscribers of Stock in all the District Towns but those resident in York, Niagara and Amherstburgh, recommended the immediate passage of a bill, explanatory of the Act of last Session, and securing to the subscribers of the several Districts an amount not less than five hundred shares, according to the intent and meaning of the Act referred to . . . .

B.

Number of Shares subscribed in the several Districts of the Province, on the New Stock of the Bank of Upper Canada, in August 1832.

			£	s.	d.
York, ...	No.	10,039	125,487	10	0
Niagara, ...	No.	6,291	78,637	10	0
Brockville, ...	No.	2,824	35,300	0	0
Kingston, ...	No.	2,136	26,700	0	0
Hamilton, ...	No.	1,279	15,987	10	0
London, ...	No.	1,020	12,750	0	0
Cobourg, ...	No.	633	7,912	10	0
Cornwall, ...	No.	560	7,000	0	0
Perth, ...	No.	806	10,075	0	0
Amherstburg, ...	No.	91	1,137	10	0
Shares, ...	25,679 equal to		£320,987	10	0

Carleton County and from 1830–32 represented Carleton in the Legislative Assembly. He was a member of the Legislative Council, 1847–57.

[67]William Buell Jr. (1792–1862) was the son of William Buell, the founder of Brockville. He was editor of the *Brockville Recorder* and a reform politician.

C.

Statement of the distribution of the 8,000 Shares of the New Stock of the Bank of Upper Canada in the several Districts of the Province, in proportion to the amounts subscribed, as directed by the Act, viz:

		Shares
York, ...	Home District	No. 2817
Niagara, ...	District of Niagara	No. 2111
Kingston, ...	Midland District	No. 650
Hamilton, ...	District of Gore	No. 454
London, ...	District of London	No. 342
Cobourg, ...	District of Newcastle	No. 255
Cornwall, ...	Eastern District	No. 212
Perth, ...	Bathurst District	No. 248
Amherstburgh, ...	Western District	No. 91
Brockville, ...	Johnstown district	No. 820
Total		8,000

The Foreign Subscriptions included in the above are as follows, viz:

	Shares
At York	406
Niagara	20
Kingston	89
London	10
Brockville	31
In all	556

THOMAS G. RIDOUT,
Cashier.

Bank of Upper Canada,
York, 6th December, 1832.

B 66   THOMAS LACK[68] TO R.W. HAY[69]
Whitehall, 9 May 1833
[*PAC, CO 42, v. 416, pp. 18ff*]

. . . their Lordships have considered the provisions of the Acts passed by the Legislature of Upper Canada for altering and extending the Bank

---

[68]Thomas Lack was joint secretary of the Board of Trade, England. He retired in 1836.

[69]Robert William Hay, was permanent under-secretary for the colonies, 1825–36.

previously established in that Province, and for incorporating another Banking Company, under the Title of the Commercial Bank of the Midland District of Upper Canada, And that they beg to offer the following observations.

Their Lordships would in the first Instance refer Mr Stanley[70] to the enclosed Copy of a Minute of the Committee of Privy Council for Trade, of the 16th July 1830, and observe that many of the precautionary principles recommended by that Minute are omitted in those Acts, as well as other Provisions which appear of almost equal importance for the protection of the public Interests in all Acts for the Extension of the Capital of the existing Banks, or the Establishment of New Banks, in the Canadas; precautions rendered more necessary by an experience of the prejudicial effects which have in former periods resulted from the extension of the Banking System in the neighbouring States, without the restrictions they impose.

The adoption of these regulations appears to their Lordships indispensable; but beyond these conditions there are several others which they are of opinion ought to be insisted on, with a view to the security of the public, both as regards the certainty of convertability of the Paper issued, into Specie on demand; as well as the prevention of a series of fluctuations in the Amount and value of the paper money which are attended with consequences yet more disastrous to the community. These I am desired to recapitulate –

1st   A provision for the forfeiture of the Charter of Incorporation on any suspension of Cash Payments which may continue for the space of sixty days –

2nd   For the conversion into Specie, on demand, of Paper issued by the Branch Banks, at the Place of Issue, as well as at the principal Establishments of the Bank.

3rd   For the payment of one half at least of the subscribed Capital, prior to the Bank being opened for business; and of the whole, within a period not exceeding twelve Months from the date of such opening –

4th   For the restriction of the Amount of Paper discounted, on which the names of Directors or Officers of the Bank appear as Drawers, Acceptors, or Indorsers, to an amount not exceeding one third part of the whole Discounts of the Bank.

5th   For prohibiting the Bank, in it's corporated capacity, from purchasing or holding its own stock.

6th   For extending the provisions contained in the 2d Article of the Minute of Privy Council for Trade above referred to, and rendering it imperative on the Banks to publish half yearly, in some public Newspaper, the State of their affairs as therein specified.

In recommending the adoption of these provisions for the regulation

---

[70]Edward G. Stanley, Lord Stanley (1799–1869) was colonial secretary, 1833–34 and 1841–45. He became the Earl of Derby in 1851.

of the Banks of Upper Canada, as well as of all other Banks of Issue which may be established in our North American Colonies, The Lords of this committee would beg to state, that even these provisions do not go so far as what experience has shown, in the Neighbouring Country, the United States, to be advisable – There, especially in the State of New York, where lamentable experience of the Mischiefs arising from a bad System of Paper Issue has shown the necessity of restriction, several yet more stringent provisions have been adopted: Still There Lordships consider that those which they have suggested will be found sufficiently binding, to prevent the mischievous consequences which must in their opinion inevitably result from such a system as that proposed to be followed in the Acts submitted to them . . . .

B 67 MINUTE OF THE COMMITTEE OF THE PRIVY COUNCIL FOR
TRADE (COPY)
Whitehall, 16 July 1830
[enclosed in PAC, CO 42, v. 416, p. 18ff]

. . . the Establishment of Banking Companies . . . would tend to promote the Commerce and general prosperity . . . H.M. Colonies in which individual capitalists might be willing to undertake such Establishments; and that it would therefore be advisable to give encouragement to such undertakings by the Grant of Charters under certain conditions, of which the following should be the principal.

1st   That the Sum to which the personal responsibility of the respective Shareholders may be limited, should not be less then twice the amount of the Shares held by each.

2nd   That such Bank should make up and publish for the information of the Proprietors general half yearly Accounts, shewing the whole amount of its Debts & Assets at the close of each half year: – shewing also the amount of it's notes payable on demand, which had been in circulation in each week of such half year; – together with the Amount of the Specie & other Assets immediately available in each such week for the discharge of such notes. And that copies of such half yearly Accounts should be laid before the Government of the Colony.

3rd   That such Bank should be at all times liable to furnish to the Governor of the Colony, on his requisition, similar Accounts.

4th   That the Funds of the Bank should not be employed in Loans or advances upon Land, or other property not readily convertible into money, nor in the purchase of any such property; but be confined to what are understood to be the legitimate operations of Banking, viz. Advances upon Commercial Paper or Government Securities, and general Dealings in Money and Bills of Exchange . . . .

B 68   John H. Dunn to Col. W. Rowan[71]
York, 1 August 1833
[*PAC, RG 19 B2b, v. 1173*]

. . . I have used every exertion both in Canada and the United States of America to borrow money on the securities of the Province, by Debentures for the various objects of public improvement under the Acts of the Legislature, passed the last session and lament to inform you that I have been unsuccessful. It has produced great disappointment and I fear embarrasment to many of the Commissioners for improving the public Roads and Bridges, who have proceeded in Contracts in the full expectation that the money would be got. The failure has not been so much from the rate of Interest limited by the Legislature as from the great scarcity of money. The Bank of Upper Canada has hitherto been the principal purchasers of Government debentures, not as an investment but for the purpose of selling again, to realise money in London, New York and Montreal If the loans had been at 6 per Cent there is no doubt but the Bank would have taken to a certain extent but I still think there would have been a difficulty in realizing all the money required as there appears a more general desire with Capitalists at this time to invest in speculations holding out greater inducements than the Common Interest at 6 per Cent.

The Legislature will no doubt desire to grant from year to year larger sums of money than its own resources, for its improvement at all events it is very desirable that the debt of Upper Canada, now bearing an Interest of 6 per Cent may be if possible paid off by a new loan at a less rate.

From the best consideration I have been able to give to the subject I think that some other system must be adopted, than relying on raising money on this side of the Atlantic. There can be no better security than this Province is able to give, and there can be no doubt, if the subject is brought before Capitalists in England that money may be got for this Government on more favourable terms than could be obtained in either this Province or the United States. With this view of the matter I beg leave to acquaint you that with the permission of His Excellency I propose to proceed to London to make a personal application and at the same time to endeavour to establish a system which will enable the Legislature with a certainty to look to all the future means they may please to require upon a lower rate of Interest, and upon more favourable terms than they can ever expect to negotiate loans here . . . .

[71]Sir William Rowan (1789–1879) was civil and military secretary to Sir John Colborne, 1832–39. In 1849 he was commander-in-chief of British North America and in 1853–54 administrator of Canada.

B 69   WILLIAM ALLAN TO JOHN MACAULAY
York, 31 August 1833
[*PAO, Macaulay Papers*]

. . . it was what I have long suspected, not of those Partys in particular, but of them & others I have been for this two years past annoyed beyond anything to see the transactions between Coburgh & Montreal and that very Gentn. at your place Mr. McDonell I have had my eye upon for a much longer period I saw evidently that he & others I may say *wantonly* made use of the funds of the Bank and as I thought Imposed too much on the Good nature of those he had to do wt. [with] I assure you now & I have often told Mr Ridout to write to *you* as well as Mr Bethune[72] to say that I thought you run too much risk in the many Dfts that were discounted in the way folks were doing – as it was evident they had not one penney of money at Command but what they raised that way; And the Number of Dfts negotiated on Mr A. [Angus] Bethune[73] might have struck any one long ago This Mr McDonell carried on the same kind of Kite flying between him & Mr Stennet *here* for nearly two years Mr Stennet used to draw on him at 90 days for £5 or £600 – within a few days of that becoming due up comes McDonell Dft on Mr Stennet for the same Amt. Till at last I saw from occasionaly noticing it, That it was a shameful traffic made use of with the funds of the bank; – I at last was obliged to take Mr. Ridout to *task* for allowing such a traffic to be carryed on in that way; – The Consequence was Mr Stennet would have cut of my head if he could – for totally prohibiting this – He then went to the Montl. Bank agency & to the Commercial Bank where they commenced and I wish them joy of him as I doubt his soundness. Mr Bethune has been out of all bounds in taking Dfts [say?] Bills of Exchange he took among many others last Spring to the Amt. of £2 to £400 – from Persons who came literally on [3 words?]; It is well asscertained that there was no such person in existance as those who they were said to be upon. They were [conveyed?] all round the Town of *Dumfries* now The Drawer has gone from that part of the Country & God knows where to be found – and if found Perhaps he is not worth halfpenny –

We have seen served so in several instances within a year There was a Captn [Sticks?] who came & *flourished* here for about a year & drew bills which Mr Bethune took for £600. There have and is now several about of this Description Indeed I conceive Mr. B. [Bethune] has *too many Irons in the fire and* that the Bank Agency is not attended to besides the Young man that is employed [entirely?] in that department is neither attentive, or Correct – I am Pretty well convinced the Bank

[72]This refers to James Grey Bethune.
[73]Angus Bethune (1783–1858) was born in Upper Canada, in 1814 became a partner in the North West Company. He was a director of the Bank of Upper Canada, 1843–54.

Books are all in confusion so much so that I am going to send Mr Ridout or Mr [name not written] down to Examine them & take an account of every thing there belonging to that Agency; – You know Mr. Bethune assertained on the Investigation when we sent Mr. [?] down that he had lost £3,000 and odd or rather he appeared to have been defficient that. He assumed all the deficiency that belonged to the Bank – & when he was up here about two months ago He made an application in writing wishing to know what time would be given him for the repayment of this three thousand & upwards – when he did that I was obliged to tell the Board that not above half of that Amt belonged to the Bank because at the time of the *Robery* we knew exactly what money belonged to the Bank,[74] There was not near Two Thosand, However the Board agreed to give him three years on Paying [?] p.cent. with Interest on the Gross Amt. He & his Brother D. [Donald] Bethune[75] are on the defaulters list *here now* for upwards of £1400 – and I know Gillespie & Co.[76] House in Montl. have a very considerable claim on him, – Mr. N [Norman] Bethune[77] told Mr Moffat[78] at Montl. he had refused to allow there Dft to be protected in order to bring his friends or correspondents to settlement, – a Pretty excuse, if he had refused to accept those Dft in the first place and given that as a reason there might be some truth in it; [McDonell?] shows Property to the Amt. of £13,000 to pay debts to the Amt. of £12,200. I suppose he will pay about 5P or 6P in the Pound; – You say there will be an application for time – I dont hesitate to say that if it depended on me; – I would give no longer time than the Law will allow as I look upon these transactions in a very different light, to those of [a] person carrying on & keeping to his *regular course* of bussiness and been unfortunate – There I think every indulgence should be given, here I think *none* should be *given*; – There are others that I have often said would go to the *Wall* in the same way, you will see by & by, –

I am convinced that One Half of the Dfts that have been negotiated by those People for years & by many others have been Redrawn for at Montl. & sent up here for Collection again Indeed I must own I have no *patience* with those speculators – and have been induced to write too much already, – (all entre nous) How Mr. D. Bethune can pretend to ask

[74]The bank at Cobourg had been robbed and half of the stolen money was found apparently thrown on J.G. Bethune's front yard.

[75]Donald Bethune (1802–69), born in Upper Canada and the brother of Angus Bethune, was a lawyer and represented Kingston in the Legislative Assembly, 1828–30. In the early 1830s he was a local director and solicitor of the Bank of Upper Canada at Kingston. He operated a shipping and forwarding business on Lake Ontario from the mid-1830s to the early 1850s.

[76]Gillespie Moffatt & Company was a major mercantile house headquartered in Montreal with branches in York and England.

[77]Norman Bethune was a brother of Donald Bethune and operated a mercantile business in Montreal.

[78]George Moffatt (1787–1865) was the principal Montreal partner of Gillespie Moffatt & Company.

for *time* & indulgence to Pay so large Debts contracted in Bussiness as much out of the way of what he ought to be concerned in I cannot imagine; – I find he has in hand upwards of £15 to £1600 of Notes in Suit what state are they in or what had he done is there no money collected. You know my oppinnion long ago was that we was giving *too much Credit* to a *great many* — It is often said at our Board when Notes are objected to that such & such persons is worth Thousand of Pounds; – It is very true many have large property they value at that rate, but notwithstanding they cannot command £100 unless by having recourse to the Bank I am perfectly *sick* of seeing & hearing of the many traffics & speculations entered into as long as they can draw Dft or get Notes discounted at the Bank . . . .

I think I have understood that Mr. [J?] B owes Gillespie & Co House about £7000 . . . . Pray what professional man would you advise our employing at Kingston for I would recommend his being employed against Bethune & all his Endorsers as well as against McD. [McDonell?] & even Mr. N.B. [Norman Bethune] at Montreal . . . .

B 70   WILLIAM ALLAN TO JOHN MACAULAY
York, 2 September 1833
[*PAO, Macaulay Papers*]

. . . Should it be necessary to oblige any of the *Partys* who may refuse or object to make themselves answerable for such transactions as they are Party to as Endorsers etc you are authorised to employ a proper person to take measures against them immediately if you conceive it necessary –

This is all I can say – I hope great care & caution will be used in the way of discounting or taking up Dfts on Lower Canada or now else where; Mr Jas B. [Bethune] I think has been perfectly *wild* in taking those things – These speculators in Lower Canada that *pretend* to sell produce etc on Commission & get those who may consign any to them to be giving Dft on them is very precarious & mainly speculative. I understand that Mr. N [Norman] Bethune who has had the appearance of having transacted many Thousand Pounds worth in that way; – is not worth *Credit* now . . . .

I believe the Cashier wrote to you long ago giving a Resolution of the Board that no person was to exceed either as Drawer or Endorsers more than £2000 under any circumstances . . . .

B 71   WILLIAM ALLAN TO JOHN MACAULAY
York, 26 September 1833
[*PAO, Macaulay Papers*]

. . . I note what you say as to the dissatisfaction of your Board at not being consulted about the appointment of Mr. Bidwell[79] etc.

[79]Marshall Spring Bidwell (1799–1872) was born in Massachusetts and arrived in

Now I don't think it fair they should be so, The Board here have a hard duty to perform in trying to do everything for the Interest of the Stockholders and the Public – and they detest Mr. Bidwell *politics* one and all as much as any of you can do – but at the time that matter was first before them, It was with the understanding that our Bank bussiness at the moment req'd the assistance & advice of some professional man., immediately, particularly in matters that Mr. Bethune was even a party to himself. The whole list of Lawyers *were* gone through and there did not appear, according to the Information we then had, There was any choice except a Mr. Casady[80] & Mr. Bidwell. The latter Gentl. was said to be as punctual & correct as any man could be particularly in Collecting & Paying over money. Therefore they decided it was there duty to appoint him – under these circumstances whatever may be thought, or what now may be said I cannot see it in the light some of those Good folks in your place . . . if the Board is obliged to consult the feelings & inclinations of everybody upon any immergency – They may as well have no Power at all to exercise their own discretion. For my own part I've so much difficulty and dissatisfaction in not Pleasing everybody that I have fully determined & nothing will induce me to continue after next June if I am [one word?] till then, I consider it very unfortunate you had occassion to be absent. Why did not your Board, meet and communicate wt. us on these matters, I am sure we have always shown ourselves ready to rec. any information or advice from them. For my own part I can safely say that everybody would have given their consent to Mr. Kirkpatrick[81] being appointed in preference to all the rest for my own part. I was desirous of his being appointed in preference to Mr. Bethune – but it was carried in favour of the latter.[82] But we understood Mr. K. was on the eve of going of for Ireland if not gone . . . the minutes of your Board which was read yesterday was considered as putting the matter at rest and Mr. Bidwell was to be considered the man of bussiness (if he chooses) to accept it – So that they may rant & Rail against us as much as they *like*. *I have lived long enough in the World* & seen enough that I know that One Half of them is more or less influenced by interested motives in some way. How much did the new President of the Commercial Bank advocate ours & oppose the promoting of it – . . .

Upper Canada in 1812. He was a leader of the moderate reformers in Upper Canada. Under pressure from Sir Francis Bond Head, he left Upper Canada in 1837 for New York and lived there the rest of his life.

[80]Casady, it is assumed, was a lawyer operating in the Kingston area.

[81]Thomas Kirkpatrick (1805–70), lawyer and politician, came to Canada in 1823 from his native Ireland. He was the solicitor for the Bank of Upper Canada at Kingston from about 1837 until its collapse. He was a director of the Bank in 1846, 1848–49 and 1851–53.

[82]This refers to the appointment of Donald Bethune as the bank's first Kingston solicitor in 1832.

I suppose I hope I shall be able to work through till next year, When I shall most certainly release myself from any charge or responsibility – in a Situation Where I have [been] req'd to Please the Public & do Justice to the Stockholders.

B 72   PETER McGILL TO WILLIAM ALLAN
Montreal, 18 November 1833
[*MTL, Allan Papers*]

. . . Our Bank duly appreciate I assure You, the good feeling of your Bank towards ours, – and while I have a Seat there a reciprocity of feeling and of accomodation shall if possible be maintained – The Transfer in N. York – will of course be made When required. –

When War existed between us as You recollect – I was Mainly instrumental in restoring peace – by proposing and carrying the Measure of the withdrawal of our Agencies from all parts of U:C – with the exception of Kingston – and the other day I proposed the abolition of the Agency there also. – I wish it had been done years ago. – The Mischief done by McDonell's failure would in such case have been less extensive.

B 73   PETITION OF BANK OF UPPER CANADA, 6 DECEMBER 1833
[*PAC, RG 5 B23, v. 2*]

. . . That the Commercial and Agricultural business of the Province has increased within the last two years to such an extent, that your Petitioners find their present Capital of £200,000, is too limited to enable them at all times to furnish the necessary funds for carrying on, with advantage to the Public, the very great home and foreign trade of this rising Colony.

That this disadvantage most particularly presses upon those who are engaged in the purchase of produce during the winter season, as the proceeds of that trade are not realized, until on the opening of the Navigation in the ensuing Spring, the products are exported to a Foreign Market, and the Bank cannot afford to grant the long credits necessarily required for these operations.

. . . that altho the Bank of Upper Canada has established Offices in several parts of the Province for the more immediate accommodation of the inhabitants, yet there are many other places to which Branches would be extended, did not the limited means of the Institution render such a measure impracticable.

. . . the readiness with which Capital, both Foreign and Domestic, has been invested in this Institution, – the magnitude of business done with its present limited Stock – the extent of the deposites confided to its charge, both in this Country and in England, are sufficient to demonstrate to your Excellency, that the increase of Capital now prayed for, would be the means of offering secure and profitable opportunities of investing money – an inducement to Foreign Capitalists to emigrate to this Province – and at the same time give facilities and security to trade, and accommodation to the Merchants of the Country, extremely desirable, and almost necessary to its Commercial prosperity.

. . . Your Excellency will be pleased to pass an Act encreasing their Capital Stock to at least Five Hundred thousand Pounds . . . .

B 74   EVIDENCE OF T.G. RIDOUT BEFORE THE SELECT COMMITTEE ON THE SUBJECT OF BANKING AND FINANCE, FEBRUARY 1834 [JUC, *1833–34, Appendix, pp. 169–70*]

1.   When were the Books of subscription for Stock opened?

The books were opened at York, Kingston, Niagara, Brockville, Perth, Cornwall, Cobourg, Hamilton, London, Sandwich and Amherstburgh on the 1st day of August, 1832.

2.   At what time were they closed?

They were closed at York, on the 2nd of August, 1832, and circular letters were sent by post on that day, to the several places above mentioned, directing the books to be immediately shut – and they were closed accordingly as the letters reached their destination.

3.   Into how many Shares were the Stock divided?

Into 8,000 shares of fifty dollars each.

4.   How many Shares were subscribed?

The number of shares subscribed was 25,679.

5.   What effect had the rumours of His Majesty's intention to disallow the Acts of 1832 upon the Public and upon the Bank itself?

When the news reached this country, it created great anxiety for a few days, and the premium on Bank stock fell; but public confidence soon rallied, as the people on more mature reflection, were satisfied that the Home Government would not carry their threat into execution, as it was not only a novel interference with their money affairs, but an arbitrary stretch of power, to endeavour to enforce conditions that were impracticable, and could only exist as an annoyance, and would render Bank stock untransferable. It was, however, not believed that the measure would be carried into effect, and so the anxiety on the subject passed away. It had therefore no prejudicial effect upon the Bank of Upper Canada, although the Board by way of precaution, confined itself to moderate discounts, and to bills of short date; which, in some measure, affected the commercial interests, by a want of means to make foreign purchases; but as the produce of the country had at that time been all bought up, and on its way to market, the agricultural interest did not suffer.

6.   Did the Bank alter its mode of transacting business with the Public in consequence of the intelligence received?

The Bank formerly discounted promissory notes at 90 days, with leave to retire by payments of one-fifth every three months. This practice was found very inconvenient for the Institution as the slow repayments pressed heavily upon its foreign funds, and a total stoppage of new discounts was often times necessary; – besides, it was found not to be the practice of any Bank in the United States, or in Lower Canada; and as soon as the Commercial Bank went into operation, our notes returned upon us much quicker than before, and it was, consequently, rendered a matter of necessity to change the system. The Board, therefore, in July last gave public notice, that "after 1st October ensuing, no instalment, less than one-third of the original note, would be received." This alteration brings the money back in nine months which is, of itself, a long credit for a Bank to give. The old regulation afforded 15 months and made people very careless; – besides the trouble it gave in the accounts and books of the Bank was incalculable.

7.   What effect had the alteration?

The effect has been, that persons of moderate circumstances borrow less money, at least, no more than they can conveniently pay within the time; that our notes come back to pay these instalments, and are ready for new issues; and that they bring along with them the notes of *other* Banks, which seem to create new funds, and strengthens the Institution.

8.   Should His Majesty now annul or disallow the Acts passed in 1832, what would be the result?

The consequences of such disallowance will, no doubt, be very disastrous to the whole country; and the existence of the Bank must depend upon the forbearance of the new stockholders, in giving the Bank time to repay them their money so unfortunately invested, and by consenting to receive it back in two monthly instalments of about 10 per cent each thereby allowing time to curtail the discounts to the extent, perhaps, of £150,000. This operation will bring down ruin upon many, and derange the whole capital of the Province – reduce the price of land – lessen the imports, and diminish the value of the entire exports of the country; as all ranks of persons, whether in trade, in agriculture, or in other pursuits, will feel the pressure of this unlooked for operation; the public confidence, as to the stability of the old capital, will be very much shaken. All these ruinous consequences must ensue, for I am confident that none of the new Stockholders will hold stock on the conditions which the Home Government wish to impose; – besides it is unjust that they should be liable to laws and penalties they knew nothing of, and to a greater loss than their co-partners, who only hold old stock, and have equal benefits.

9.   Do the public require greater Banking facilities than could be afforded by the original Charter of the Bank of Upper Canada?

The interests of this Province require at least one Bank, with a capital much larger than any now in existence, in order to carry into full effect the following necessary operations, viz: – To be enabled to advance money at five and six months credit, during winter, for the purchase of produce, and for the lumber trade, and wait for the re-payment out of the sales of such produce in a foreign market. A Bank with a small capital cannot afford such an outlay: and the Bank of Upper Canada can only do so to a small extent, – not half as much as is required, and consequently the winter trade is always embarrassed, and limited to less than the actual quantity in the market at that season.

2nd. A Bank with a large capital would have it in its power to regulate the foreign exchanges, and keep the Province supplied with specie, by means of its foreign funds, and could take advantage of the proper time for so doing, without sensibly curtailing its discounts. Its notes would be current throughout the country. It would regulate the transactions of smaller Banks, and keep them within bounds; or, in case of need, it would support them in emergencies, and sustain their credit. By means of its offices and agencies, it could afford the Government, and the public, facilities in making payments wherever required in any part of the Canadas. It would encourage the investment of foreign capital, and sustain the public credit for buying and selling Government Debentures, thereby relieving those who wish to sell, and selling to those who wish to invest – so that the public debt would be kept in motion as so much cash, convertible at any time into money or bills of exchange. This system, which the Bank has adopted as far as it was able, has brought much foreign capital into this country, and it ought to be continued.

10.   Have you ever heard it asserted, that the Bank of Upper Canada is "a dangerous engine of political power in the hands of the Government?

I have read in the newspapers, charges to this effect, but I have never heard it asserted. The Government has never yet attempted to influence the Bank in any one operation. As far as the Government was concerned, it has been a free agent.

11.   Have you any reason to think the transactions of the Bank have ever afforded any foundation for such a charge against either the Bank or the Executive Government?

No partiality or prejudice has ever been shewn in the business of the institution, growing out of political opinion: such matters are never discussed at the board. The responsibility of parties, and not their political feelings, have always appeared to me to govern the decisions of the Directors in all their transactions. I am satisfied in this respect.

12.   Would not the public possess more security in the establishment of a Bank with so large a capital as to enable the Institution to leave in the hands of the Stockholders, one half the amount of Stock authorised by the Charter, to be called in upon any emergency?

Such a reserved stock, liable to be called in at any moment, would prevent both foreign and domestic investment, and it would not be readily transferable. Capitalists, Trustees, Corporate Bodies, Widows and Executors, would not venture to invest their money on such uncertain terms: it would not be a solid capital, nor would it be marketable. It would, probably, be principally held by a class of persons who, if called upon, could not pay up the remainder especially if the Bank was in any jeopardy: and as that would be the only, and the very time it would be wanted, no dependence could be placed on such a resource; besides, it must be called for, to make good the losses of the public, in consequence of the failure of the Bank, and not their own losses, as Stockholders. They would therefore rather lose the half they had already paid in, than risk any more; and many, for want of property, could not be compelled to pay, even if the law allowed actions to be brought against them.

B 75   LT.-GOVERNOR COLBORNE TO WILLIAM HAY (PRIVATE)
Toronto, 7 March 1834
[*PAC, CO 42, v. 418, pp. 135ff*]

. . . The Parliament was prorogued yesterday. I take the earliest opportunity of forwarding to you a copy of the Address to the King on the subject of the amendments to the Acts respecting the Upper Canada and Commercial Banks. This very objectionable Address was carried by 30 in a House of 31 members.[83]

Many of the Members, I understand, regreted exceedingly that such an Address should have been proposed; but in any discussion on subjects relating to the private affairs of so many persons of influence, in every part of the Province, and suffering perhaps from the refusal of the Banks to extend their discounts, under present circumstances; it is impossible to calculate on the terms that may be introduced in Addresses.

Notwithstanding the character of this Address, You may be *assured* that the good feeling of *this* Province will prevail, that the next Assembly will be well composed, and that the *respectable Colonists* which have been planted in several districts during the last three years will soon possess great influence. If I am not too sanguine as to the result of the approaching Elections, the Assemblies after the expiration of the next Parliament will be composed of an intelligent group of persons, strongly attatched to the Interests of the Mother Country. From time to time, however, many bad subjects from the United Kingdom will take up their residence in the Provinces, capable of giving all [strengthens?] with the Demagogues already now amongst us . . . .

B 76   JOHN H. DUNN TO THOMAS WILSON AND CO.
Toronto, 29 March 1834
[*PAC, RG 19 B2A, v. 1136*]

. . . I consider this transaction the commencement of a large business, in which you may rest assured that our conduct will not fail to merit

---

[83]This address was highly critical of the Colonial Office's actions and regulations concerning banking in Canada.

your esteem and confidence. I have appointed your House as our agents and which has been stated to the Government. I have acted in the absence of advices from you just as if your contract existed seeing that little, or no variation has taken place in your Money Market. The only circumstance which I lament is the very low state of Exchange. I must govern my drafts on you, as I require the money, and also with reference to the premium on Exchange. This £30,000 will enable me to supply all the most urgent necessities until I hear from you, and I will then forward a further Supply of Debentures and at the same time call in the Debt which is due, the holders of this Debt are entitled to Six Months Notice – I can assure you that it is not at all the desire of the individuals who hold the Public Debentures to surrender them, with our monied people the transfer of our Debt to London has not been carried without considerable opposition, and on my part difficult to effect. I look upon this New Capital brought into the Province as one of the most important advantages, it will of necessity oblige persons to look to private investment, and assist private enterprise . . . .

B 77   ELECTION OF DIRECTORS TO THE BANK OF UPPER CANADA
[*Toronto, Colonial Advocate, 3 April 1834*]

We are glad that Messrs. Allan and S.P. Jarvis voted against the Messrs. Cawthra[84] for directors of that institution last Saturday, and that Messrs. Billings[85] and Crookshank the late deputy and assistant commissaries up at the garrison were their choice. It is now well understood that Messrs. Allan, Jarvis and their proxies, assisted by Cashier Ridout's tact, have entirely controlled the late elections,[86] and proved Messrs. Baldwin and Dalton's[87] assertion that the Bank is a political machine. Messrs. Cawthra have twenty times as much interest in the stability of the Bank as Messrs. Billings and Crookshank; Messrs. Cawthra are honorable and wealthy merchants who never asked or wanted a shilling of bank accommodation in their lives, but are willing to employ a vast sum of *real* capital in stock in the Bank to be loaned to traders and dealers, and also, we presume, in the habit of depositing

[84]Joseph Cawthra (1759–1842) was born in Scotland and operated a general store in York. He supported the reform party. He was a director of the Bank of Upper Canada in 1835–37 and 1839. His son, William Cawthra (1801–1880), was a merchant and Bank of Upper Canada director in 1848–50, 1852–53, 1855–56 and 1858.

[85]Francis Thomas Billings (d. 1875?) was deputy assistant commissary general at York from 1814 until his appointment in 1829 as treasurer of the Home District. He was a director of the Bank of Upper Canada in 1827 and 1831.

[86]Despite the *Advocate*'s assertions, none of the men mentioned were directors in 1834. Perhaps the election referred to was an interim measure to fill vacancies prior to the normal election at the June annual meeting.

[87]Thomas Dalton (1792–1840), born in England, came to Canada in 1812. He operated a brewing business in Kingston and was associated with the Pretended Bank of Upper Canada. In 1828 he edited the *Patriot*, moving it to York in 1832. Throughout the 1830s, he commented in depth on banking affairs.

thousands of pounds with the institution the better to enable it to extend its discounts to the public. Whether are such men as these, or men who have little or no interest in the welfare of the institution or of the public the most fit for directors? Allan and Jarvis say to this – ''Ah! but the Messrs. Cawthra are liberals, they are reformers of long standing, and we dare not trust them with scheming and jobbing, and planning, and working of a tory political bank, when just on the eve of a general election.'' They are deeply interested, it is true, but they are at the same time too fond of the right and liberties of the people to be trusted as members of a discount board, at which has sat S.P. Jarvis, W. Proudfoot,[88] Archdeacon Strachan and George Monro. This is neither the time nor the place to advert at length to the Bank monopoly – but we are preparing to do our duty – England, Ireland, and Scotland has its lords and dukes, its privileged classes; here, and of a meaner and more grovelling character we have a host of bank directors, privileged to make money and all it would purchase scarce or plentiful at their pleasure.

B 78   WILLIAM ALLAN TO LT.-GOVERNOR COLBORNE
Toronto, 2 May 1834
[PAC, CO 42, v. 419, pp. 91ff]

With reference to the inquiries made by your Excellency, relative to the proportion of Specie kept by the Bank of Upper Canada (as compared with that of their notes in circulation, I beg to inform you that we have never found occasion to be *governed by any particular rule in that respect for this reason*, as we have always kept a good supply of Funds with our different Foreign Agents at Montreal, New York and London; at the two former places our notes are redeemed and particularly at Montreal where the far greater proportion of our issues find their way there in the course of business and are taken up and redeemed the same as at our own Counter: for instance, in the course of last year nearly £600,000 was taken up there.

Was it not that there is now another Chartered Bank which, in the course of business, collect our Notes in this Province so as to cause a call upon us for Specie from time to time, it would scarcely be necessary for us to keep half as much as we generally do, which is about 1/5 of what notes we have in circulation; and if we required a supply at *any* time we can always obtain it in the course of two or three weeks.

There are never any calls upon us for Specie except occasionally, by people who have collected our Notes that may be in circulation in the

[88]William Proudfoot (d. 1866?) came to York about 1816, probably from Scotland. He became a partner in a store with D'Arcy Boulton Jr. from 1816 to 1825 and operated alone until the mid-1830s. In 1834–36 he was governor of the British America Fire & Life Assurance Company. From 1835 to 1861 he was president of the Bank of Upper Canada, having already sat as a director in 1822, 1826 and 1828–34. In 1857 he owned 305 shares in the bank. In 1860 he owned eleven.

United States, and now and then in small sums by the people of the Country.

As all the Mercantile transactions in the Province are carried on by Bills of Exchange drawn by us on these our Foreign Agents, and was it not that we are called upon for a statement of the affairs of *the Bank which are made public*, whereby if it appeared we had only that small proportion of Specie, which, in reality was more than we required, it might cause apprehension by those who are ignorant of our affairs, and the mode in which our extensive business is carried on; but the moment more Banks are instituted and get into operation, the less Foreign funds they can have, and consequently all must keep a larger supply of Specie than we ever had occasion for, as the consequence will be, each Bank if multiplied will be more or less dependent on the other, and the security and circulation of Bank Notes will be a greater hazard.

The Specie kept in the Banks of the State of New York and many other of the United States Banks, are only about 1/20 of their Notes in circulation and few or any of them have any Foreign Funds, consequently they ought to have a much greater amount than we ever required, but they have less –

B 79   JOHN H. DUNN TO WILLIAM ALLAN
Toronto, 21 September 1834
[*MTL, Allan Papers*]

. . . I consider it more advantageous to the Public, and the interest of the Province, to look to London for all our Supplies, when we shall be able to get money at all times with certainty and upon more reasonable terms than the Legal Interest of Upper Canada. I am obliged for the opinion expressed in your letter as to the unwise and impolitic measure of negotiating the Provincial loans in England. I can assure you that I entertain a high respect for your knowledge acquired by long experience in this Province, and which has been fully established by the satisfactory management of the first monied Institution in the Province. It is therefore with great defference and regret, that my opinion on this subject should be so much at variance with your own. I really cannot anticipate any of those evils which you appear to apprehend and do expect to realize very beneficial effects to the Interest of this Province Generally.

B 80   PETER MCGILL TO WILLIAM ALLAN
Montreal, 24 September 1834
[*MTL, Allan Papers*]

. . . I am perfectly Satisfied with the explanation given respecting the refusal of our Bank Notes in certain cases – It could not be expected that you would do otherwise, and our Board feels quite confident that the Bank of Up: Canada will never come to a determination – which can in

any way be construed to militate against the interests of the Ml. Bank, except for the protection of its own interests against the Schemes of Such Jobbers as are alluded to –
We discountenance, every thing like trick or spite – and have frequently refused to give Your Notes at our Counter in exchange for our own preferring to give the Specie, because we well knew for what purpose, the Exchange was asked – I mean to pursue a fair, honorable straight forward course, and I wish sincerely that two other Monied Institutions, which shall be nameless would do the same . . . .

B 81   JOHN H. DUNN TO JONAS JONES
Toronto, 6 November 1834
[*PAC, RG 19 B2b, v. 1173*]

I beg to acknowledge the receipt of yr letter of the 1st Inst and to explain the nature of the transaction between the Cashier of the Bank of Upper Canada and myself on the subject of your warrant for £10,000 on account of the work on the St. Lawrence Canal. The money to be furnished you is all to be drawn from England which can be done on much better terms for the public than issuing debentures here at 6 p cent. My bills of exchange are open to competition., The last Tenders averaged 8 1/16 p cent, the Bank of Upper Canada proposing at 7.1/2 p cent. The Commercial Bank purchased £15,000 stg and Truscott Green and Co.[89] £5000 – I therefore only negociated £20,000 stg being sufficient to redeem the amount of public debt called in by me. This debt was due to the Bank of Upper Canada for they held the Debentures. The cashier demanded from the Commercial Bank for my draft the whole amount in specie which produced a good deal of difficulty to me and not a little to the Commercial Bank I was informed by the Cashier of the branch of the Commercial Bank at Toronto that that institution must decline offering for Exchanges if the proceeds are to be handed over to another Bank stating at the same time that the Bank would give at least 8 per Cent for the Exchange provided their paper was used in circulation whilst the other Bank would only give 7 1/2 p cent. Finding therefore there was likely to arise a monopoly prejudicial to the public Interest I addressed you a note on the subject and you stated that in a few days you would be here. In the mean time Mr. Ridout called with the Warrant for £10,000 and I told him all the circumstances and the subject of my letter to you and wished him to delay the Warrant a day or two as I expected you here which he seemed to agree to. About a week ago Mr. Horne[90] presented the Warrant again and I stated the same to him, that you would be here and I wished to see you before I paid it – He returned the

[89]Truscott Green & Company was a private banking firm operating in York.
[90]Dr. Robert Charles Horne (d. 1845) was born in England and came to York in *ca.* 1815. After a period as editor of the *Upper Canada Gazette*, he became chief teller of the Bank of Upper Canada at York.

Warrant to the Government Office & I explained my reasons to the Lt. Governor who wished the matter settled and I accordingly did so that day by giving a check for £10,000 – You will ere this be notified by the Bank accordingly – If the commissioners will receive my drafts on anyone of the public Banks it will ensure a fair competition for my Exchanges. There can be no difficulty or inconvenience as I understand that the Commercial and other Banks have Agents at Brockville where they will keep a proper supply of paper – I think Messrs. Morris and Co.[91] and one of your commissioners Mr. Norton, act as Agents to the Commercial Bank – I need not, I am sure, state that all the Interest I can afford the Bank of Upper Canada, I feel bound to do, both because the public have stock and because I hold a personal interest in it – My only object is to do the right thing for the Interest of the public confided in me.

B. 82   C. GAMBLE[92] TO EXECUTIVE COUNCIL
4 December 1834
[*PAC, A. Shortt Papers, v. 2*]

. . . Forgeries upon the Paper Currency of this Province are at this time being carried on to an alarming extent . . . a regular organised band of Counterfeiters are now spreading over the Country circulating forged Notes upon the Bank of Upper Canada.

B 83   T.G. RIDOUT TO W.H. MERRITT (COPY)
[JUC, *1836 Appendix No 90, Minutes of Evidence of the Welland Canal Investigation, 12 December 1834*]

Finding that your last check for 1000£. of the Welland Canal money was negotiated through the Agricultural Bank,[93] which enables them to substitute their own notes, and to call upon us for specie – I am desired to request you will inform me or Mr. M'Cormick at Niagara when you intend to draw out the remainder of the Welland Canal funds lodged in this Bank – and if it is your intention to negotiate it when so drawn in the same way; as it is necessary for this Bank to be prepared to meet such unexpected demands. Perhaps, however, when you gave the above check you were not aware that it would be immediately converted into specie – although it had no doubt the effect of preventing the circulation of our notes.

[91]James Morris (1798–1865) was a politician, merchant and banker who was born in Scotland and settled in Upper Canada in 1808. A younger brother of William Morris, he represented Leeds in the Legislative Assembly, 1837–44 and was a member of the several reform ministries in the 1850s. He acted as agent and cashier for the Commercial Bank at Brockville from 1836 until 1850.

[92]Joseph Clarke Gamble (1808–1902) was a lawyer for the Bank of Upper Canada from sometime in the 1830s until the bank's collapse in 1866. He then became the main overseer of the bank's wind-up, a process that lasted into the 1890s.

[93]Truscott Green & Company conducted their banking business under the title of the Agricultural Bank. It opened for business in York in May 1834.

B 84   T.G. RIDOUT TO JOHN H. DUNN
Toronto, 24 December 1834
[*PAC, RG 19 B2A, v. 1136*]

With reference to my previous offer for the purchase of your exchange on London, I am directed now to inform you, that this Bank will if you please buy your bills at 30d/s on Messrs. Thomas Wilson & Co to the extent of Ten Thousand, or Fifteen Thousand pounds Sterling, at an advance of six per cent for premium thereon and should you accept this offer be pleased to furnish them of the following description, viz:

5 of £1000 each	£5,000
15 of £500 each	£7,500
2 £400 ea	£800
6 £200	£1200
5 £100	£500
33 Setts making	£15,000

I should have written to you yesterday on this subject but waited for advices from New York, which I received last evening – stating that exchange on London might hold on for three or four weeks in the neighbourhood of six per cent, but after that they expected it would decline as their backward Cotton crop would then be coming in, and bills would be plentiful and would fall in value.

Under all these circumstances it is hoped that you will keep here as large a balance as you can conveniently do at this season but this is entirely as you please. We are now buying bills on London freely at 4.1/2 to 5 P. Cent Prem.

B 85   WILLIAM ALLAN TO EDWARD ELLICE
Toronto, 26 December 1834
[*PAC, Ellice Papers, v. 9*]

I wrote to you, some time ago, and owned the receipt of your letter of July last, relative to the transfer of what Government Debentures were held here in your name, by the Bank of Upper Canada (then made over by your desire to your Son Mr. Edw. Ellice Jr. and I believe I also Enclosed you the list of them with a Certificate from our *Cashier* to that effect, and I then, and I believe, before, made you *aware* that by An Arrangement our Receiver Genl. had made in the Autumn of 1833. with Mssrs. Thomas Wilson & Co. of London, that, he would negotiate & transfer what was due & outstanding of These Debentures from this Country to London, this arrangement was acquiesced in, and authorised by our *Legislature* last Winter; who Knew nothing about the matter, and did not think it worthy of refering to those who could have told them, of the *great & injurious effect* it would have, namely transfering a Debt of £200,000 from this Country to England (not only a debt but I must say the Actual money, together with the Interest that will have to be paid at home every Six Months for 20 years to come or as long as the Debt, is outstanding. It is not only this £200,000 that he negotiated for to Pay of Debentures due, in this Country, to those who held these Debentures & who never asked for their money on the Contrary *did* not require or wish to have it, as long as they recd. their Interest It is not only this £200,000 that have been called *in* & paid of in that way, but they authorised him to negotiate for Two or Three Hundred Thousand Pounds more, – (as to the former I cannot see what advantage or what inducement there was to borrow money at *One* place to *Pay* of *money* at another (when that money if left as it was or if the Debentures had been renewed to People here, it would have Kept the money in the Country and would have been an enducement for many Persons (*which has been the case*) to bring out their money to this Country and invist it in a Security that they could dispose of & get redeem'd any day in the year; –

The Consiquence is that there is now or Soon will be *no* means of *Investing* money by any *one* who has it (In a Secure & Satisfactory way that they could realise it when wanted and all this for no other reason, I Know of, than that a Sum of money will be gained by the Premium on the Bills he draws, But that gain is only to be ascertained, at the Expiration and when those Debentures are paid off. As One proof of the effect of this foolish arrangement, there is now Deposits in the Bank of U Canada *alone* to the Am*t*. of *£100,000* @ *£125,000* which the owners of have no means of Investing in any way they can *realise* Interest for it (unless by *loaning* it on Mortgages etc., – which is Good Security for Principal & Interest (but that does not Suit every body) particularly *Strangers* and persons lately come to the Country – because they cannot realize their money when they want it – I urged thus offering, the new Debentures that were authorized & issued to Redeem the £200,000 *to be given to the Holders of the old Ones* – in this Country – but that was not done, – Therefore the effect of all this is Shewing itself every day –

I fear you will not afford time to peruse this long Story – even if I have made it out to be understood, But the *sum* and *Substance* of it is to Say that among those now to be redeem'd & paid off there is about £9000 – or Perhaps more of what was held in your name & transfered to your Son; The money remains in the Bank, till he give directions how it is to be disposed of without yielding any interest whatever; – Therefore the Sooner he gives directions to the Cashier about it the better; was there or Should there, be any means of Investing *all* or any part this Winter I would take upon me to have it done, till we hear from Mr. Ellice; –

If any Debentures are to be had, that are redeemable some years hence, I will direct the Cashier to try & obtain them for him – if there is no Secure & Satisfactory way of Investing it in this Country he will have to have it remitted to him . . . .

P.S. Mr. Ridout, the Cashier of the Bank will write upon the Subject

also, but in the meantime your Son is loosing the Interest of his money –
WA

B 86   WILLIAM ALLAN TO ROBERT BALDWIN[94]
Toronto, 5 February 1835
[*MTL, R. Baldwin Papers, A32–A37*]

. . . relative to what your Uncle,[95] had intimated to you, – that of there
having been some objections made at the Board last Week, to discounting your paper – for certain reasons – That certainly was the case, These
reasons were given by some of the Directors (and the same was
mentioned at the Bank to me more than two mths [months] ago; – that
about the time you had a note of Baldwins & Sulivan[96] discounted for
£1200 – (I think, about 12th Nov. That a Check from your office was
brought to the Bank for £1500 – as I understood & paid to one of your
clerks Mr. Powell I believe which sum or a large Proportion of it was
handed over to the Agricultural Bank and brought back upon us
immediately to be paid in Specie; How that came is best known to you
or Mr. Sulivan, but the facts when I was told of them, seemed to be so
distinctly known, that I made no very particular enquiry; –
   I did consider *if it* was so, that it was not fair of M. Sulivan
particularly who had frequently been employed professionally on the
Part of our Bank; – This was the cause of the objection at the Board, the
other day, – If these facts were true; it was to be expected they would
hesitate to discount more *large* notes for the same Partys without
knowing how the proceeds were to be disposed of   And the application
I understood Mr. Sulivan had since made on behalf of the Agricultural
Bank relative to our receiving from them the Notes of the Kingston
Bank in Payt. of our own, certainly impress'd me with a belief that more
than common [Interest?] had been taken in their behalf which makes it
necessary for us to be – watchful; –
   However I am quite satisfied as what you State, and shall make
Known the Contents of your letter to other Members of the Board, who I
am sure will be equally so; – as we are most desirous that nothing but
good feeling should prevail and we wish to give every reasonable
accomodation, that could be required of us, – more particularly with
respect to you & Your Family;–
   You must naturally suppose the Directors would be *alive even* to any

[94]Robert Baldwin (1804–58), a prominent reform politician, was the eldest son of
Dr. W.W. Baldwin.
   [95]This refers to Augustus Baldwin (1776–1866), a naval officer and brother of W.W.
Baldwin. He arrived from Ireland at York in 1817. He sat on the Legislative Council,
1831–41, and the Executive Council, 1836–41. He was a director of the Bank of Upper
Canada, 1832–37, 1839, 1841, 1843–44 and 1847–56.
   [96]R.B. Sullivan (1802–53) was a lawyer who was a director of the Bank of Upper
Canada 1835–40.

supposed transaction which might tend to opperate against the Interest of the Institution –

B 87   TRUSCOTT GREEN & COMPANY TO LT.-GOVERNOR COLBORNE
(COPY)
23 February 1835
[*PAC, A. Shortt Papers, v. 3*]

Understanding that the Bank of Upper Canada as a palliation for their improper and unwarrantable conduct towards the Agricultural, makes it a plea, that we have identified ourselves with a certain political party in this City, by advancing Cash to assist the late City Council; we deem it proper to state to Your Excellency (with a view to counteract the effect such representations may make on your mind) that we have not, since our arrival here, identified ourselves with any party, and that we have not rendered pecuniary aid to any body, or individual, on account of his or their political attachments. – We deem it proper to make this unqualified statement to your Excellency, as well in defence of our Character, as from the connection of the Local Government with the Bank, against which we have too much reason to complain. – We regret that an Institution established, ostensibly, for the public welfare, and supported by the Stock of the Government, and receiving its Deposits, should so interfere with the provincial Welfare, as to employ its funds in the unjust and unworthy purchase of our paper, with a view to suppress an Institution which has already been of such essential Service to the Country, and then screen its conduct in groundless Subterfuge – Your Excellency is not perhaps aware that this Bank have employed Agents in various parts of the Country to collect in the paper of our Establishment; But such is the fact, and we feel ourselves compelled to enquire if such conduct is countenanced by the Local Government. –

B 88   T.G. RIDOUT TO JOHN H. DUNN
Toronto, 23 April 1835
[*PAC, RG 19 B2A, v. 1137*]

Your respective letters . . . were submitted to the Board yesterday and they decided upon the Bank only engaging for the present debentures to the extent of £30,000 . . . . I was therefore directed to inform you that we would take that amount provided we were not called upon for more than £15,000 in one month these to be at six percent per annum payable half yearly with the express condition that they are not to be redeemed in a less period than three years whether in the possession of the Bank or any person to whom we may have occasion to transfer them.

I beg leave to remark that what I alluded to in my letter of the 20th inst. with respect to Debentures being called in and redeemed before the period that they appeared on the face to become redeemable were those from Nos. 106-192 inclusive making a sum of £25,000 which the Bank

took up and had disposed of to different persons with the understanding (as we had not seen the act) that they were not to be called in until the years 1837, 1839 and 1841 which appeared by these debentures to be the time they would be payable being £8333.6.8 in each of those years. However they are all advertized to be paid off on the 30th of June next. To the great disappointment of many of the holders . . . .
P.S. The Bank may in the course of a couple of months find themselves enabled to take up a further amount if to be had.

B 89   JOHN H. DUNN TO COL. W. ROWAN
Toronto, 25 April 1835
[*PAC, RG 19 B2b, v. 1173*]

By an Act recently passed the Legislature, the Receiver General is authorized to borrow the sum of £400,000 in London for the purposes of prosecuting public works in progress and cancelling all the public debt now due; and until the Receiver General is able to contract for this Loan, he is enabled by the Act to borrow £100,000 in this province, at the rate of 6 per cent per annum redeemable in 5 years or at any previous time by giving 6 months notice –

As the expenditure of the St. Lawrence will very soon require from 20 to 30 thousand pounds per month and in order that the Commissioners may not be embarrassed for want of funds, I have made application to the Bank of Upper Canada, and it appears, that Institution can only advance £30,000 with the stipulation that the debentures shall not be redeemed in a shorter period than 3 years – I have very little expectation that any greater sum can be got in Upper Canada. At any rate, there is a doubt – and no doubt on such an important point should be allowed to exist where thousands of persons will be depending on contractors and contractors on the Government and it is not in my power to assure the Bank that the terms required can be complied with – I received by the last packet from Messrs. Wilson and Co. an offer to take a further sum not exceeding £200,000 at par – 'Till I can have recourse to competition in the London Market and carry into effect the intentions of the Legislature, I do not at present see how I can do better for the Province than accept the offer of Thos. Wilson and Co. of £100,000 only, and in the meantime to adopt the best mode of selling the other £300,000 by competition in London. By doing so, all anticipation of embarrassment will be removed: perhaps were I present in London I could do no better than obtain the loan on the same terms now offered by Messrs. Wilson and Co. – It was considered in London that their offer on a former occasion was liberal and I have no reason to think they would be influenced by any other motives. They are more intimately acquainted with the transactions of this Province than any other House in London being the Agents of all the Banks in Upper, and I believe in Lower Canada also – I am privately informed that the Upper Canada

Debentures have been sold in that Market for about 6 per cent premium, but on the 14th of March last it was quoted at 3 and a fraction, and not in demand.

It is clearly a great gain to the Province to borrow money in England at 5 per Cent compared to the 6 per Cent here as exhibited by the Report of the Finance Committee[97] which committee recommends strongly that all future Loans should be borrowed in London.

If there should be a premium on the £100,000 in favour of Messrs. T. Wilson and Co., The Province would lose nothing; but there will be a positive loss of more than one per Cent per annum if the £100,000 is borrowed here at 6 per Cent, besides the loss of the use of the profits of Exchange which may be estimated at about £500 per annum in addition – In the present situation of the great scarcity of money in the Province, it seems another inducement to resort to Foreign Capital, and not deprive the Banks of any means which may operate to the prejudice of individual and private accommodation.

If the value of Debentures is only about 3 per cent premium, I can scarcely expect to obtain the loan much above par, as this would be considered only a fair remuneration for a respectable money Broker in London for the trouble and expense of paying the Interest on this Loan for twenty years.

If my application for the sale of the remainder of the loan of £300,000 (A reply to which cannot be expected till the month of September) should not meet with success, I shall endeavour to make arrangements to proceed to London. My absence at this particular period when my active exertions are required in the discharge of my public duties would be attended with great inconvenience.

B 90   WILLIAM HEPBURN[98] TO W.H. MERRITT
11 May 1835
[PAO, W.H. Merritt Papers, v. 18]

. . . I have by His Excellency's direction had an interview with the President of the Bank of Upper Canada with a view of negotiating a loan sufficient to meet the present emergency – but he told me that the Bank would not (at least he should advise the Bank) not to lend money upon the security of the Indian funds without the Trustees giving at the same time *their own personal security*. This I for one will not do. However I shall tomorrow write officially to the Bank & after having ascertained definitely their determination will write to you again.

---

[97]First Report on Public Accounts, *JUC*, Appendix, 1833–34, p. 22.
[98]William Hepburn was registrar of the Court of Chancery and a trustee of the Six Nations Indian Reserve.

B 91   WILLIAM ALLAN TO JOHN MACAULAY
Toronto, 9 June 1835
[*PAO, Macaulay Papers*]

. . . I fear you give me Credit for much more than I am entitled to respecting the past management of our Bank concerns, all the *merrit* I claim or can allow I had any right to was that I paid all the attention to it I could and at all times carryed in my recolection the cheif and material things that was of consiquence to be looked after. It was a point with me never to Defer or put of anything to a future day – and I *must own* I Took upon *myself* in many instances to decide & act upon & do several things, That I conceived right & safe & for the Interest of the Institution to do – in place of refering or submitting them to the Board which often caused more prompt & a better mode of settling matters that would have been cabel'd & disputed about without any satisfactory determination – This I often found the case. Therefore the Great advantage I had in this respect was experience which my present sucessor; nor indeed any could well have except acquired in the same way, – and I have always held it as a rule that you should endeavor to understand fully – and look after what you undertake, in any Public duty – If that is done there is [2 words?] of reasonable success; –

There was a Great deal of Quareling & contention about the appointment of my sucessor, – The Governor & the Govt Party wanted to appoint Mr *Dunn* and if they had acted *fairly* & openly – The Majority would have been in his favour, but it was understood they had an underhand understanding several of them & thought they would carry it without consulting some of the others – which made them oppose him – Mr P [Proudfoot] was not ellected from the idea of his being by any means either equal to it or the best they could get He was the only [one] who was a Candidate for it, His Party I believe feared Mr. John Baldwin who if he had been a Director would perhaps have been prefered – Therefore He had but few Votes – But I believe He would not have undertaken it (at least He told me so, However he felt very *sore* at not being in the Direction; and I must say He has always prooved a Good one. However there is yet a good deal of that feeling against that *Family* & conection The *Captn* who was the candidate last year, when I proposed giving it up – declined this year, I believe the difficulty & dispute I had to encounter last Summer w. [with] The Receiver Gen'l & the Commercial Bank about the Bills of Ex and subsequently our controversy w. [with] Messrs. Truscott & Green Frightened him, But as to Mr Dunn my own opinnion is he is neither fit for to be in that Situation – nor is it right He should, – In fact any feeling that has been against the Bank of U.C. has been more on acct of the Government Having some Interest & concern in it. last Winter [we?] brought the matter before the Board to advise the Gov't to sell out their Stock, but the Governor and all the Gov. Directors were against it and got some others to join – We have the name of having large Deposits of the Public money in the Bank for which we were deriving the Interest when in fact; In place of our allmost [n]ever having any *Public* money deposited we were oftener in advance for the Receiv Genl.

In short to show you How we stood that way I Enclose you a *memo.* which I beg you will *return* to me after looking at it, That will show, we have been in advance sometimes as much as £12 to £13,000 and last winter when we made our Return to the Legislature out of £180,000 of Deposits the Bank held there was only £817 – deposited by the Reciv Genl We lost by our transaction with him for many years, nearly £200 a year. By means of his drawing on His Agent at Montl at 20 days sight always & He often got the money or drew checks for it, Before we could send of his Dft not only that but for years The Montl Bank charged a Com. of 1/4 pc for issuing Payt of his Dft – the same as all others, which was a total loss – I had a Great difficulty and a long correspondence before I could overcome that, but they eventually gave it up   His Dft on his Agent at Montl [provides?] help to our funds there much and that was the only advantage we had to continue taking them; – However what He would do if he becomes President I dont know; – Many of the members (or rather some) urged as a reason why they wanted to make him President that he was *Popular* with many Members of House of Assembly – and thus could most likely be the means of getting our Capital Increased;

His Popularity will increase with them if He lets them get what they want (He is rather a curious person, and one whose modes & manner of bussiness I *dont* admire   But I must tell you him & me are not very gratious, because I have freely given my opinnion to the Governor [own words?] – respecting the negotiations of the Loans & the removal of all the Debentures from this Province   As long as I am at hand I told the *Cashier* & Mr. *Proudfoot* also I would assit them wt. my advice at all times & contribute as much as I can but I find there is a Good deal of feeling among the present Board whether time will get the better of that or not; But it does not auger well – and Proudfoot has not stamina or [Words?] – I had many good causes for resigning I found too much was thrown on me, all the *odium* of refusals, the blame was put on me, scarcely one Half of the Directors knew anything of the affairs of the Bank, They came on a discount day and took up a NewsPaper & some scarcely knew what pass'd from the time they came in till they went away unless their attention was particularly called upon on some matter   If they got their dividend of 4 p.c. every Six Mts & a Bonus now and then that was all they cared about the Bank, – They did not as I thought Enter into the [feeling?] of Interest they should and I began to think it was needless for me to take all responsibility and trouble without a more certain compensation than the chance of some *Members* voting my Sallary Half yearly, – £250 – I thought indeed I had been in that situation long enough to entitle me to look for something more, but this did not seem to *Strike* any of them; The Canada Company in whose office I have been for six years or so Increased my Sallary without any intimation or anything being asked to £200 Sterling more, –

I thank you for the Information & communication respecting the Commercial Institution – I must own I am not impressed with the idea they & there agents act all together in that straight forw'd way I should wish to do – and the more mean & Pitiful transaction of the *famous* Private Bank; has added to the conduct of many persons who allowed themselves to be made tools of in Exchange of their Notes etc. etc

In fact I have been a good deal disgusted and our Recv Genl is as fond of Courting Popularity as any body I know, I hate & dispise all such methods, I have lived so long in the world without having recourse to any measures of that kind & I hope to continue I would not *compromise myself* nor allow any of the transactions of the Bank to be *compromised* – and I think you will quite agree with me –

. . . It is very clear the tide of emigration is a Good deal changed from the Port of Quebec – to Ports in United States   I think our progress & Improvement or even Wealth is not likely this year to increase very much   I fear the Steam Boats will not be so good a Speculation – and altho you are one of the Commissionaires for Spending so large sum of money for the Improvement of the Navigation of the St. Lawrence. I am not nor never was of opinnion that it was Good policy to expend so much just now. I prefered that a proportion of this money should have been appropriated to Improvement of *Inland* waters such as the Trent & many others – It will be long before the St. Lawrence repays the Interest of the money and not only that, but till Lower Canada Improves their Water Communication Where is the Good of this immense outlay – you are I dare say against me in this opinnion, – I am sure if you have Patience and can wade through all I have written – I should wonder but it is not every day I sit down to trouble with these long Yarns . . . .

You must consider all this private You better destroy it when you can read it all – But return me the Memo . . . .

C.   SEARCH FOR A FOCUS, 1835–48

C 1   T.G. RIDOUT TO B. TURQUAND[1]
Toronto, 11 June 1835
[*PAC, RG 19 B2A, v. 1137*]

In reply to your letter of yesterdays date, in which you desire to know if a draft at Montreal would be acceptable to this Bank on the 30th instant, in redemption of the government Debentures then due, I am directed to inform you, that I cannot enter into any pledge to that effect as it is quite uncertain at this moment, to determine, what would be the most convenient mode of payment – unless specie were offered – and then there would be no choice.

C 2   B. TURQUAND TO T.G. RIDOUT
Toronto, 11 June 1835
[*PAC, RG 19 B2A, v. 1137*]

We were much in hopes of receiving your reply to mine of yesterday's date. – Our advertizements particularly mentioning that Current Bank paper will be taken in payment for Exchange, makes it imperative on us to communicate with the other Banks, or to take measures to obviate any embarrassments that might arise from the Bank of Upper Canada requiring Specie, and as time will even now scarcely admit of our informing the Banks etc at Montreal, you will at once perceive that it is not without reason we press you for an answer.

C 3   T.G. RIDOUT TO JOHN H. DUNN
Toronto, 30 June 1835
[*PAC, RG 19 B2A, v. 1137*]

. . . N.B.

The Lower Canada Banks can afford to give a higher rate [for government exchange on London] because they redeem their notes in a depreciated coin namely French half crowns which are not a legal tender in this Province.

C 4   F. HARPER TO B. TURQUAND
Kingston, 14 July 1835
[*PAC, RG 19 B2A, v. 1137*]

I address you in the absence of Mr. Dunn to state that the amount of the

---

[1]Bernard Turquand was deputy receiver general. He had been working in that department since 1829.

check which you sent Mr. Jonas Jones on me for £5000 has been paid, and the money lodged by that gentleman in the office of the Bank of U. Canada in Brockville from whence it came up this day and this Bank has to redeem the same at once.

The terms of Mr. Dunns advertisement and your letter to the President of this Institution led this board to believe that in tendering for the Exchange that our notes would be distributed in a fair manner to the contractors on the St. Lawrence Canal and under this impression they were induced to offer a higher rate of prem. [premium] that they would otherwise have done – This course of proceeding on the part of the Acting Commission, if persisted in, will prevent this Institution from offering in future that rate of prem. which the Exchange of the Receiver General of this Province ought to command.

The Board have desired me to submit this statement to you & to ask if any instructions were given by you to Commis. of the St. Law. [Lawrence] Canal how the money so checked was to be appropriated or whether it was left to Mr. Jones to act with it as he thought proper.

C 5   B. TURQUAND TO JONAS JONES
Toronto, 22 July 1835
[PAC, RG 19 B2b, v. 1173]

. . . I avail myself of this occasion to acquaint you that the Commercial Bank M.D. have complained of the £5000 withdrawn from it by the check sent you on the branch of that institution at Brockville, being deposited in that of the B.U.C. and by it transm't. [transmitted] to Kingston; which it appears they have to redeem at once, and the Board of Directors having been led from the Rec. Gen's advertisement etc. to believe that, in tendering for the Exchange, their notes would be distributed in a fair manner to the contractors on the St. Lawrence Canal, and under that impression were induced to offer a higher rate of prem. than they would otherwise have done, adding that the course of proceeding if persisted in will prevent that institution from offering in future that rate of premium which the Exchange of the Rec. General of this Province ought to command, have requested in consequence an explanation from this office in respect thereto in reply to which, extracts of the Official Correspondence from the Rec. General's department to you as President of the Board of Commissioners for the improvement of the St. Lawrence have been transm't. to it. I beg to refer you to Mr. Dunn's letter of the 28th April last and to request you will have the goodness to give this office at least three wks. or a months notice of the amt. required from time to time, in future for the work in question.

C 6   C. CASTLE[2] TO B. TURQUAND (PRIVATE)
Montreal, 19 August 1835
[*PAC, RG 19 B2A, v. 1137*]

A few days since I made you a tender for £10,000 of Mr. Dunn's Exchange – today, I intend doing so for £20,000 additional – In doing so, however, it is necessary I should mention circumstances which must of course influence us in our office & which redound to the disadvantage of Mr. Dunn – I allude to the circulation our bills might probably obtain, when the proceeds of Exch. are to be expended on Public Works.

Mr. Holmes of the M. [Montreal] Bank – (who advises me that he will make no tender in consequence) informed me that the proceeds of the £5,000 Stg. given to the Comml. Bank in June was forwarded to Mr. Jones at Brockville in a sealed packet, – *by him sent into Mr. Wenham* – & that the packet was returned to the Comm. Bank within the week untouched! Comment is unnecessary.

Should Mr. Dunn be unable to control these circumstances I need not add that it will be useless for Banks in the Lower Province to tender hereafter, as they can subsequently purchase the same Exch. from the U.C. Bank *at a lower rate* than what they would under the benefit of circulation, offer Mr. Dunn in the first place and leave the U.C. Bank a profit beside.

Our Agent in Prescot, Mr. Patton will be glad to honor Mr. Jones' cheques to the different contractors should you deem it expedient to advise him thereof, in the event of our obtaining any portion of this Exchange.

C 7   C. CASTLE TO B. TURQUAND
Montreal, 20 August 1835
[*PAC, RG 19 B2A, v. 1137*]

I have to acknowledge receipt of your letter of 19th inst. accompanying 20 sets of Exchange of £500 each. I beg also to mention that your dft. on me through the Bank of U. Canada has been presented, & in the present instance, honored: but with reference to my tender for other £10,000 Stg. bearing date 19th inst. I have to intimate that if the same be accepted & the proceeds as in this case, are to be drawn for through the Bank of U. Canada instead of being applied in our notes for payment of works on the Canal, *on which presumption alone, both my tenders were made*, you must not be surprised to have the Exchange returned & your draft dishonored – as it is not to be supposed this Institution can afford to tender from half to one P. Cent higher than other Banks without a view to benefit by circulation.

---

[2]C.H. Castle was cashier of the City Bank in Montreal. He resigned from this position following the economic downturn in 1847.

C 8   F. HARPER TO B. TURQUAND
Kingston, 29 August 1835
[*PAC, RG 19 B2A, v. 1137*]

Having understood that the Tender for the Exchange which the President of this Institution sent to you a few days ago was at the same rate as the Bank of U Canada & that that institution has nevertheless obtained the whole of it – I am desirous to enquire of you, if this is the state of the case, & if so whether it is to be understood that in all cases when the tenders are equal with the Bank of U.C. that the said institution is to have the preference.

C 9   JOHN H. DUNN TO W.H. MERRITT
Toronto, 20 October 1835
[*PAC, W.H. Merritt Papers, v. 10*]

. . . Mr. Ridout is the best person to Sell your Stock, because persons who have Money for Investment, have their funds lodged in the Upper Canada Bank; for the purpose of taking advantage of buying Bank Stock as no Debentures are now for Sale. Money is abundant, and Securities are scarce, a very short time I trust will prove to the Public, the benefit of compelling Capitalists in Upper Canada, to look to other than Public Securities and Private persons will be able to avail themselves of their Real Estate in the way of Mortgage. When this object is accomplished I shall be satisfied . . . .

C 10   WILLIAM ALLAN TO W.H. MERRITT
Toronto, 5 November 1835
[*PAC, W.H. Merritt Papers, v. 10*]

. . . The opportunity I have every *day* of *seeing & knowing* the effects of the Policy of removing all our Prov'l. [Provincial] Loan to England is quite convincing to me, that there is nothing that could have been done that has & will prove *worse* for us in point of money concerns – But you & others *call* it bringing money into the Country (not So according to my idea/It has & will as long as it continues enable The Dift. [different] Banks to purchase His Majesty Recr. Genl. Bills – but that mode & method, will not have half the effect of bringing money to this Province the same as if these loans had been made here & persons would have had inducements to bring money and invest it, *Where the Interest would be Spent & the Principal retained – A little time will tell –* . . .

C 11   EXTRACT OF REPORT ON OFFICE AND AGENCIES OF THE BANK OF UPPER CANADA, AUGUST 1835, SENT BY THE DIRECTORS, BANK OF UPPER CANADA TO SIR JOHN COLBORNE, 30 DECEMBER 1835
[*PAC, CO 42, v. 427, pp. 469ff*]

"On the Lumber Trade"

During our stay at Quebec we took occasion to enquire into the Lumber trade – & the transactions of the principal houses engaged therein, as well as their connection with the Lumber Men of the interior, and the foreign Market. The result was that there appeared to us a general want of capital for such an extensive trade, embracing as it does the chief export of the Canadas – & from what came under our own observation, it was very apparent that a strong disposition existed in the mercantile community to take every advantage of the necessities of the Lumber Men of the interior, who are with few exceptions entirely in the power of the Quebec Merchants; so that little reliance can be placed on the former drawers of bills.

We visited the coves and were surprized at the immense quantities of timber and staves, which extended two or three miles on each side of the River – & we could not but regret that a trade so valuable, especially to Upper Canada, should be so much embarrassed for want of Banking facilities not only at this sea port – but up the Country, where the first outlay is required and tends very much to enable two or three leading Houses to monopolize the best part of the business and to govern the market.

On enquiry we learnt that the export from the Ottawa River alone, amounted to about £800,000 per annum requiring an expenditure during the Winter & Spring of about £100,000 to get the rafts as far as Bytown – of this sum one half is probably furnished in cash by drafts on Quebec negociated by this Bank and by the Bank of Montreal, & the remainder on Goods, with which the Lumbermen are supplied by their correspondents at most exorbitant prices – the costs then of taking the rafts down to Quebec, and the numberless charges and exactions when there – as well as the partial system of culling reduces the Lumberman frequently to the necessity of pledging his raft for trifling advances, and thus he is thrown more and more into the power of the export merchant, and often returns home a Bankrupt . . . .

C 12   A. STEVEN[3] TO REID IRVING & CO.[4]
Hamilton, 16 March 1836
[*CIBC, Gore Bank Letterbook, 1835–36*]

. . . [Steven wanted Reid Irving & Co. to take the Gore Bank account on the same terms as Thomas Wilson & Co. took the Bank of Upper Canada account, that is:]

Interest on every item on both sides of account but over drawn for any considerable amount 5 PCT on the sum over drawn. The Charges for Agency is 1/2 pct on one side of their account and amount of postages besides extra charges for Expenses on Bills not made payable in

---

[3] Andrew Steven (1789–1861) was cashier of the Gore Bank at Hamilton. He held this position until 1856, when he became president.

[4] Reid Irving & Company, private bankers in London, England, acted as the British agents for the Gore Bank. The company went bankrupt in 1847.

London. They receive deposits for the Bank and Issue their letters of Credit accordingly and render their account half yearly . . . .

[Steven also wanted an arrangement with the Bank of Scotland to receive deposits from prospective immigrants and issue letters of credit on the same basis as the British Linen Company Bank[5] did for the Bank of Upper Canada,]

. . . that is no allowance is made them for Agency or postage, they receive deposits on their own account and issue Letters of Credit on the Bank here against these when paid in this country the Bank of U.S. draws for on Mssrs Smith Payne & Smith[6] London @ 3 d/s and the Bills are sent to Mssrs. Thomas Wilson & Coy. London for collection on account. When these bills are drawn the British Linen Company are advised of the particular Credits that have been presented paid and Valued for – by that arrangement you will perceive that the Bank in Scotland has the use of the Deposits until drawn for on their agents in London . . . .

C 13   WILLIAM ALLAN TO W.H. MERRITT
Toronto, 3 May 1836
[*PAC, W.H. Merritt Papers, v. 11*]

. . . To tell the truth I believe the Bank of U. Canada present means won't enable them to be liberal or afford aid they have deviated from my System & my Management very much, and I am inclined to think they [reap?] in the folly & effects of it and are not over flush – . . .

C 14   WILLIAM ALLAN TO JOHN JOSEPH[7] (COPY)
3 May 1836
[*PAC, A. Shortt Papers, v. 3*]

I received your Note of yesterday Enclosing Mr. Merrit letter to you, on the subject of obtaining money from the Bank of U. Canada for the Welland Canal . . . .

. . . With respect to the Bank of U.C. I have spoke to several of the Directors (I am not one I have nothing to say) – but I fear he is not likely to be very sucessful – and the fact is *I believe* their means are not so good just now, as they have been, or as they might be if they had managed their business properly –

But I fear they have deviated a good deal from my Management for the last *Thirteen Years* – And by that means they have it not so much in

---

[5]British Linen Company Bank also acted as agent for the Bank of Montreal.

[6]Smith Payne & Smith, a private banking company in London, acted as the Bank of Montreal's general London agent (1837–41), and ultimately became agents for the Bank of British Columbia.

[7]John Joseph was civil secretary to the lieutenant-governor in Upper Canada, 1836–38.

their power to loan a few Thousand Pounds; – which I most sincerely regret, – for I can see the Canal will go to destruction – I fear the Government Directors (altho there should be *four* there they dont generally attend.) I really dont know what can be done.

It might be well if His Excellency would authorise you to write a letter to the Government Directors requesting them to make an application to the Board to give the Welland Canal Compy a Credit for £4000 – upon their offering such security as they can command that this loan would be repaid in One year – If they could do so, it might relieve them – there is nothing else I can suggest . . . .

C 15   JOHN H. DUNN TO JOHN JOSEPH (COPY)
Toronto, 6 May 1836
[*PAC, A. Shortt Papers, v. 3*]

. . . I have had, on former occasions, similar applications to the Bank of Upper Canada, but the Board never would grant Loans to the Welland Canal Co without my personal engagement and have had myself involved to very considerable Amounts, causing me much anxiety and I am unwilling to incur the like responsibility again; but as far as advocating the measure in my place as a Member of the Board, I will do all that lays in my power.

C 16   T. STAYNER[8] TO JOHN MACAULAY
Quebec, 14 May 1836
[*PAO, Macaulay Papers*]

. . . "Irresponsible" Banking as you very properly designate *private* Banking in this Country, should be put down. We already begin in Lower Canada to feel the mischevous effects of those institutions – their Notes are sent into circulation throughout the Country by Agents employed for the purpose, and the business of the chartered Banks is sadly injured thereby. I was so pestered by this paper, that I was compelled to say as I have done in my late Department Order – that I would not receive any more of it! – British Silver is not to be had in any quantity at Quebec – all I can muster is about fourteen pounds worth which I shall [consign?] to you together with some Upper Canada Notes both of the chartered and unchartered Banks – My reason for sending you the former is that Freer[9] has just notified me that Mr. Harper has written "Castle" of the City Bank that he will cash his Notes at Montreal *only when he happens to have funds there* – this will not answer my purpose, and I shall with your permission – until I can make

---

[8]Thomas Allen Stayner (1788–1868), born in Halifax, was postmaster at Quebec, 1823–27 and postmaster general of Upper and Lower Canada, 1827–51. He was director of the Bank of Upper Canada, 1854–60. In 1860 he owned 963 shares in the bank. In 1863 he owned thirty-three.

[9]Noah Freer was cashier of the Quebec Bank from the early 1820s until at least 1852.

some other arrangement, send my Upper Canada Bank Notes to you as a deposit – to be placed at my Credit by your Mother Bank – I shall probably send you some to day.

C 17 A. STEVEN TO T.G. RIDOUT
Hamilton, 8 August 1836
[*CIBC, Gore Bank Letterbook, 1835–36*]

. . . Will you be kind enough to take from the different Banks in Toronto what of our notes they may offer you in Exchange for their own sent to you from this Bank and perhaps you will soon have a chance to send them to me as well as those you have on hand when they will appear at your credit in A/C we have about £3000 of yours at present – I have written to Mssrs Truscott Green & Coy. to say that I have sent you their notes and have stated that ours will be taken by you in Exchange and if any difference in our favour I will take a dft. either on Montreal or New York @ 3 D/S at a rate of Exchange will halve the profit between the buying and selling price.

Mr. Ross[10] writes to me that you stated to him that no official correspondence had taken place between your Institution and this relative to an Exchange of notes. I fancy Mr Ross must have presented some of ours to you for payment when you had not received from me the Commercial Bank notes collected by this Bank.

It is my intention during the navigation to send down some day in each week all the notes of the Toronto Banks by the Brittania . . . .

Mr Dupuy need not have taken any of the precious metals from your vaults under the pretext of paying this Bank as he has never been asked for payment in that way nor do I intend to do so. The dft. on him enclosed herein is for the notes I left with you for him a month ago.

C 18 MEETING OF THE OTTAWA LUMBER ASSOCIATION, NOVEMBER
1836
[*Bytown* Gazette, *17 November 1836 (editorial)*]

. . . The second object for which the meeting is called, namely, to pray the Legislature to grant the wished for augmentation to the capitals of the Banks, is well deserving the attention of the merchant & agriculturist in this quarter – That there is a want of accomodation from the Banks, sufficient to supply the exigencies of the business, cannot be denied, & that this want has been severely experienced in this quarter is no less true. Let it be also borne in mind that Bytown is the main force of the Lumber Trade, the chief article of our exportation, & that the amount of fluctuating capital required for the supply of this trade is very

---

[10]Charles S. Ross was agent for the Commercial Bank at Toronto. In 1843 he opened that bank's Hamilton branch. In 1847 he was cashier for the Commercial Bank at Montreal and in the early 1860s he became, for a brief period, the bank's president.

great. There are also peculiarities regarding this trade which makes those engaged in it more dependant on Bank accomodations than perhaps any other line of business; the maker of lumber, is the merchant who furnishes him, being always under the security of keeping a supply of cash on hand to make his purchases from the farmer, as with him little credit can be expected, his trade only giving him returns once a year. The excuse the Banks make for not being able to afford the necessary accomodation is the want of capital, & in their view it is but fair that their application to the Legislature should be supported, But as regards Bytown & this section of the country, there is a further want to be supplied in order to render these establishments able to meet the wants of our commerce here. It appears the two Agents here are not authorized to discount without previously transmitting the paper to the Board of Directors at Kingston & Toronto. This ceremony is a mere farce of formality, vexatious to those applying for accomodation without adding in the least to the security. None is so able to judge of the stability of those applicants as the Bank Agent residing among them; & if he be a gentleman of such character as to be deemed trust worthy of acting as agent, why not the Banks, as in other countries, place a specific amount at his disposal for discounts in the section of the country where he resides? . . .

C 19   JOHN MACAULAY TO HIS MOTHER
2 February 1837
[*PAO, Macaulay Papers*]

. . . The Legislature is proceeding to pass so many bank Charters that I think the business will be quite overdone & Bank Stock sink to par. The Council has completely bowed to the force of public desire. Indeed it was no longer desirable to withstand the demands of the people for more Banks. The last radical Parliament passed Charters which [being] refused by the Council are now reenacted by a Tory Assembly. The people will have Banking of some sort or other & it is vain to hope we can resist the mania. Nothing will cure it but a failure or two. I much fear the following will pass both Houses: Brockville, Coburg, Niagara, Prince Edward, St Catharines, London, Sandwich; Increases of Gore capital & North American besides two Loan Companies. It will be a pretty mess if the [Royal?] Sanction should be given to the whole . . . .

C 20   R.W. HARRIS[11] TO ISAAC BUCHANAN[12]
Toronto, 6 February 1837
[*PAC, Buchanan Papers, v. 30, p. 24881*]

. . . I did not call on Mr. Carter[13] and consequently have no communi-

---

[11]Robert William Harris (1805–61), born in Ireland, came to Montreal in 1830, moving to York in 1832 and Hamilton in 1844. He operated, with Peter and Isaac

cation on the subject of the Banks, It is yet uncertain if the Bank of UC will get an addition to their capital, this uncertainty arises from the New district Banks going into operation and the jealousy of Members interested in their welfare not wishing to put the BUC stock in competition with their own Banks.

C 21   COURT TO COMMISSIONERS
London, 6 February 1837
[*PAO, Canada Company Papers, A-6-2, v. 3*]

. . . The Court should be glad to find that owing to any new competition the Bank of Upper Canada may be induced to transact their business on more favorable terms by allowing interest on deposits and affording better Rates of Exchange and extending their branches into the Company's territory.

C 22   R.W. HARRIS TO PETER BUCHANAN[14]
Toronto, 24 March 1837
[*PAC, Buchanan Papers, v. 30, p. 24887*]

I wrote you a few hurried lines yesterday when I was very warm on the shabby conduct of the Bank of UC. tho. very much annoyed I have not allowed anything to occur which places IB & Co [Isaac Buchanan & Company] on a different footing from what it was the day before. I merely told Mr. Ridout that I considered IB & Co entitled to the exchange at the rate on the 15th the day on which they were to get it and if the Bank would not give it at that rate, they might, (meantime,) write back the discounts which I suppose they have done . . . .

. . . The Office of the Bank of British North America will open here early in May and from which institution I anticipate some benefits for our business. Their Manager Mr. Smith is now here, who by the way was the bearer of two introductory letters from Montreal to me by which means I have been enabled to get some information that I should otherwise been deprived of.

Buchanan, one of the largest wholesale mercantile companies in Upper Canada. He was president of the Great Western Railway, 1849–56.

[12]Isaac Buchanan (1810–83), born in Scotland, arrived in Montreal in 1830, moved to York in 1831 and set up operations in Hamilton in 1840, moving there in 1844. In addition to his large mercantile operation, he was an active promoter of various railroads, sat in the Assembly at various times during the Union and vociferously argued on behalf of a protective tariff and irredeemable paper currency.

[13]Robert C. Carter was a London-based financier and banker who became the first agent for the Bank of British North America in Upper and Lower Canada.

[14]Peter Buchanan (1805–60), a leading merchant, was a partner with Isaac Buchanan and Robert Harris in one of Upper Canada's largest wholesale companies. He was active in railway promotion in the 1850s.

C 23   PRIME WARD & KING TO BARING BROTHERS[15]
New York, 25 March 1837
[PAC, Baring Papers, v. 80]

. . . cf. the Bills of the Bank of Upper Canada . . . they are safe – no sounder institution exists – and so far as our commitments by endorsements go – we have almost always *$100,000* of theirs, in hand – . . .

C 24   SIR F.B. HEAD[16] TO LORD GLENELG[17]
Toronto, 4 April 1837
[PAC, CO 42, v. 437, pp. 337ff]

. . . 5th. The last Bill I have to remark upon is that which is intended to create a respectable Provincial Bank, with a large Capital under strict Legislative Control, and on terms that will place it within the effectual supervision of the Government. I consider this Bill to be the most important of those I have remarked upon, and I have no doubt that it is so looked upon by the most intelligent Members of the Legislature, and of the Community in general.

When the Upper Canada Bank was established in 1822, the Government were authorized to subscribe stock in it to a Considerable amount which was not disapproved of by His Majesty's Government, and the effect has been in all respects beneficial. It has given a character to the Institution and the Government, or rather the Province, has received constantly a dividend of 8 per Cent annually on the Capital invested, besides occasional additions which have made it average about ten per cent. Your Lordship will not fail to see that under this Bill the Government would become Proprietors to a much larger extent, and you may, not impossibly, be startled at the magnitude of the project: but I trust a careful consideration of the subject will result in the determination to let the wish of the Legislature have affect. Those persons in whose judgement much confidence is placed here look with anxiety to this measure as affording the best security against injury from the possible imprudence of private Banks. It will serve, they think, as a safeguard and a reserve in difficulty and will gradually acquire the salutary power of controlling the emission and circulation of Paper Currency. Besides this it will introduce a great additional Capital into the Colony, which may be safely borrowed in England upon the Credits of the Province, since it will be employed as fast as it is borrowed, in a

---

[15]The Baring Brothers was a large banking house located in London, England. Prime Ward & King were their American correspondents. The Baring Brothers became agents for the Upper Canadian and eventually the Union government. The banking house also became heavy investors in Canadian railway enterprises in the 1850s.

[16]Sir Francis Bond Head (1793–1875) was the lieutenant-governor of Upper Canada, 1835–38.

[17]Charles Grant, (Baron Glenelg) was colonial secretary, 1835–39.

manner that will more than produce the interest for which the Government will be liable . . . .

. . . I foresee no danger from monopoly – for there will be all varieties of Banks, and unless Your Lordship perceives some decisive objection which does not present itself to me, I trust that this measure will receive the Royal assent . . . .

C 25   R.W. HARRIS TO ISAAC BUCHANAN
Toronto, 23 April 1837
[PAC, Buchanan Papers, v. 30, pp. 24895-6]

. . . I saw Mr. Ridout on Saturday and delivered your message and asked what they were drawing for, when he said 12 1/2% p cent, I told him we were getting Exchange for 10% prem and of course could not do any business with the BUC when other Banks were inclined to do our business on so much better terms – . . .

C 26   WILLIAM ALLAN TO W.H. MERRITT
Toronto, 26 April 1837
[PAC, W.H. Merritt Papers, v. 12]

. . . the fact is there will be little to do for to require any person to Succeed Mr. J. Jones in Superintending the St. Lawrence or any other Public Work – *There is no money borrowed or likely to be this year –* The money market seems to be in Such a deplorable way at home, and abroad, no Saying what will be the effect, – But I dont hesitate to Say that this Province is now in the Situation I *anticipated* when the Recr. Genl. & the House of Assembly was so determined to remove what *Debts the Province then owed*, by Redeeming all the Debentures due from the Holders and getting authority to have them transfered from the Country, – I said then, and I spoke to *you* as *well as many* others, that I considered it was *indirectly removing* £200,000 from U Canada & having a large Debt in England, your answer *to me I will recolect was that the more we were in Debt at home the more consiquence the Country would be considered and better Known*; –

Now I never thought so, I consider that if your Debt had been confined to our own Country & money'd people as they came out found a ready way of Investing their money, in the Province, It would have come here by *Degrees* as much as we ought to have required, Whereas now nobody will bring money out beyond what their business, or transactions may require; – We were told the Province would gain £20,000 by borrowing the money in England; –

But if it should so happen that the Recr Genl. Bills come back, any of them, the Province will more likely *loose* £20,000 in less than Two Years after the business was transacted; However things must take their chance, – . . .

C 27   WILLIAM PROUDFOOT TO SIR F.B. HEAD
Toronto, 18 May 1837
[*PAC, CO 42, v. 438, pp. 117ff*]

. . . By the Return accompanying this paper, it will be seen that the Bank has now £40,000 in specie against a Circulation of £200,000 – it's notes spread over this Country and the neighbouring states – as well as in Lower Canada, besides £134,000 in Deposites, of which about £70,000 belongs to the Government – to meet these demands besides the specie on hand the Bank has £25,000 in cash at New York, £15,000 in London, and about £85,000 accruing at the Montreal Bank – and £320,000 in discounted notes, Government Debentures and other public securities of this Province – the discounted notes are the Bills of a vast proportion of the Merchants Mechanics and farmers of the country, comprising many thousands of the most respectable classes and men of substantial means, and whose paper falling due daily as it does has hitherto been met by them in general with fair and punctual payments in accordance to the regulations.

It must be confessed that at this sudden call for large sums of specie the Bank has been taken by surprize – for it was not prepared to learn that a general bankruptcy had befallen the Banks of the American States – and it has been owing to the no doubt embarrassed State of our agents in London, Thomas Willson & Co. that we are now £30,000 – or £40,000 below our usual supply of cash for in 1836 we directed them to send out £35,000 in British silver by the month of October. They only shipped £5,000 sterling – that no more could be obtained – but promised to procure it early in this Spring, so as to be landed at New York in April, and upon this promise we relied until we heard of their difficulties in London. Our agents in New York were then advised that we should send out for a supply of dollars the latter end of this Month – at the same time we forwarded them £15,000 of Exchange on London, desiring them to instruct their agents the Messrs. Barings to make immediate returns in British silver coins.

Having at this moment a considerable balance at New York a messenger was dispatched hence on Tuesday night to bring in £25,000 – his return may be expected in about a Week – this will relieve immediate difficulties and afford time for further measures.

Owing to the embarrassments of our London agents our means of raising specie at New York by selling our Exchange on them has been completely cut off, and foreseeing this several applications have been lately made to the Commissary General for his Bills on the Treasury in order that we might sell them at New York – where they always command the precious metals, he has however declined, stating that he would prefer to keep up his account here by making transfers from the Montreal Bank, where he had a large balance, altho in his last letter he has promised on the next occasion to endeavour to give us his Bills.

The monthly payments made by this Bank for account of the Commissariat is from £6,000 to £8,000, and these we are obliged to make, if required, in American or Spanish Silver. This we cannot do unless the Commissary General will give us his Treasury Drafts – we have however no right to demand any during this month, as he has now about £11,000 at his credit and the agreement is that we should have an average balance on hand of at least Six weeks expenditure.

As it is clear that no other means can be devised to avert the threatened crisis, the Board have ordered the Cashier to proceed to Quebec with such letters as Your Excellency may be pleased to address to the Earl of Gosford,[18] Sir John Colborne and the Commissary General, to inform them of the great jeopardy in which all the public monies of this Province are placed – the ruin that will inevitably overtake the public Service, both in the civil and Military Departments, and the actual loss that will ensue, should the works on the St. Lawrence canal be suspended, if the Bank of Upper Canada does not obtain an immediate supply of Treasury Bills. It is considered that £50,000 will be sufficient – with these the Cashier will hasten to New York – then sell them for specie, which he will immediately forward to the Bank, and thereby avert the threatened calamity.

There can be no difficulty in carrying on the works of the St. Lawrence, and there need be no suspension of contracts – provided the Receiver General will furnish the Bank with the precise and real funds which are at his disposal. It seems that he is allowed to draw on the Messrs. Baring Brothers & Co. for the proceeds of the debentures sold to them for this particular service, and that the expenditure is about £10,000 per month. Now if he will issue to the Bank at this time £20,000 of his Bills – and continue to issue £10,000 monthly hereafter, thereby keeping the Bank One Month supplied in advance (as the Commissary General does) the Board will engage that there shall be no stoppage for want of money – for their Bills will be sold in New York for Specie, and the whole proceeds Exchange and all shall be placed at the Receiver General's credit with the Bank.

In these unprecedented times it would perhaps be necessary that Your Excellency would permit these Bills to be accompanied with an official document from the Government Office, stating that in case of need, they will be protected by the Treasury – and as Mr. Draper[19] is in London, he will make every provision for such a contingency, if advised – as per list of the Bills, furnished at the same time, either out of the proceeds of unsold Debentures remaining in London or from other

---

[18] Archibald Acheson, Second Earl of Gosford (1776–1849) was governor general of Lower Canada, 1835–37.

[19] William Henry Draper (1801–77) was born in London, England, and came to Canada in 1820. He was a lawyer, judge and leading Conservative politician. He was a director of the Bank of Upper Canada, 1833–34 and 1838–39.

sources – and should the Commissary General deem £50,000 too large a sum to be drawn for at once for Commissariat purposes – the whole or part may be refunded to the Treasury by Mr. Draper in the like manner or out of the Clergy and Indian funds which will in all probability be returned to this Province, and this Bank will then make itself account-able to Government for the amount by taking up the equivalent in 6 per Cent Debentures. It has been generally understood that the portion of revenue derived by this Province from Lower Canada has always been paid over to Messrs. Forsyth, Richardson & Co. who are the Receiver General's agents in specie – now if this is the case, and that there remains any present balance due – there can be no difficulty in procuring from the Receiver General a draft on his agents for that amount payable in specie, as they receive it – and it would be well in future to continue the practice.

Hitherto the Receiver General has generally drawn upon his agents at 20 dys which makes on an average 30 days before the Bills are paid. This has proved on many occasions extremely inconvenient to the Bank – as he has frequently checked for the whole sum – before he has drawn the Bill, sent his check to the Commissioners of the St. Lawrence Canal, who have received the money from our Office at Brockville – and the Bank Notes have been expended by the time we had received this 20d/s Dft – The Bank has frequently remonstrated against such a course of proceedings – but not wishing to lose the Government account the irregularity has been at times permitted to pass over.

It will no doubt be satisfactory to Your Excellency to learn, that in the event of Messrs. Thomas Wilson & Co., our agents in London, stopping payment on the arrival of the 10th May Packet in England, which cannot be before the first week in June, the Bills of this Bank on them will have by that time been nearly paid off, probably – £15,000 will remain outstanding but under the most disastrous circumstances, the Board have been assured that all its drafts will be protected by other Houses who have stepped forward and offered their services in case of need.

C 28   WILLIAM PROUDFOOT TO JOHN ELMSLEY (COPY)
Toronto, 22 May 1837
[PAC, A. Shortt Papers, v. 3]

The Board of Directors having been informed by their President that you expressed dissatisfaction at their having instructed the Teller, to take the Applicants for specie at their Counter in rotation, claiming preference for your runners as belonging to a Banking institution, and that you have threatened to make the Directors repent their conduct, have instructed me to convey to you their reasons for abiding by that decision.

It has long been suspected by the Board, that you had imported little or no specie for the use of your Bank and that in the event of a demand for silver you trusted solely for support to the amount of Upper Canada Bank notes collected from your friends in exchange for the notes of your Bank, which Upper Canada Bank notes you were carefully hoarding for the purpose of acting against that institution at a time when the demand for Cash, would necessarily make it both more difficult and more expensive, for the Bank to replenish its Coffers; The Board could not with these impressions regard your Bank as a friendly institution and did not therefore make any distinction in its favour.

The Board are informed that you stated on Saturday afternoon, that you had from £10,000 to £12,000 of U.C. Bank notes in your possession, *collected in the usual way of business* and locked up in your vaults as a *dernier resort*. That you should have been driven so long ago as last friday to this last resource, plainly indicates that you could have but little cash in your Vaults and so far the Directors are borne out in the suspicion before adverted to.

That you should have resorted to the means, you are known to have adopted, in order to procure U.C. Bank notes as a deposit in lieu of specie, the Board regret; for they will recollect, with what eloquent indignation, you, while a member of their Board, condemned the conduct of Messrs Truscott Green & Co. who drew their deposites out in specie. You, Sir, have the high merit of refining upon the practice, for in the first place you induced some of your friends to supply you with U.C. Bank notes in exchange for those of the Farmers' Bank, under the pretence of enabling you to exchange paper with that institution, and in the second you have waited to realize on those notes, until you could do the greatest amount of injury to the Bank, rather than adopt the more honorable Course of claiming the Balance in your favor weekly or daily as is usual among Bankers. You know, that some of those from whom you drew your supplies under the pretence before mentioned, would withdraw their aid, if they found that you were acting on the Coffers of the Bank, and that if you had honestly divulged your intentions, you would be constrained to supply yourself with specie from England, New York or Montreal as the Bank of U.C. has invariably done. This would have been a more expensive mode of operation, than deceiving your friends and through their aid procuring your resources from the U. Canada Bank, though it would undoubtedly have been far more creditable it would further have spared you the very high gratification of doing all the ill *will* in your power to the institution on whose honor and stability it appears now, that you relied for the means of fulfilling your own engagements, – a gratification which ought to be of no common class, since in the opinion of the Board, you have not hesitated to stake against it, the loss of a fair reputation.

The Board do not think upon this review of your proceedings, that they have been such as to entitle you to any favour at their hands; although your runners did receive a preference on Saturday afternoon, still less do they perceive any just cause for your threatening them with your high displeasure.

Your position as a member of the Legislative Council and as one of the Executive Government, would, beyond question, afford you the means of working ill to the U.C. Bank, provided always, the foregoing statement of facts, when published be not of sufficient weight to induce the Public to pause before they condemn an Institution whose affairs we believe to have been invariably conducted in a spirit of candour and honesty, both as regards other Banks and the public in general.

C 29   SIR F.B. HEAD ON BANKS
22 May 1837
[PAC, CO 42, v. 437, pp. 125ff]

. . . The Lieutenant Governor having reason to believe that the Chartered Banks in Upper Canada are desirous to understand explicitly what assistance, if any, the Executive Government is determined to adopt in consequence of the present unexampled foreign demand for specie, I am commanded to inform you that His Excellency most highly approves of the course which the Banks of Upper Canada are at present pursuing in honourably fulfilling, regardless of all consequences, the engagements they have solemnly entered into with the public.

The Lieutenant Governor is of opinion that a suspension by Banks of their cash payments with specie in their Vaults, is equally in America, as it is elsewhere, inconsistent with Commercial integrity, which in plain terms means a Bank honestly liquidating, so long as it has power to do so whatever it has "promised to pay in demand."

The Lieutenant Governor feels confident that within the Province of Upper Canada all well disposed people will be desirous to support the Banks in the creditable duty they are performing, but as suction from without may possibly have the affect of draining the specie from their Vaults – the Lieutenant Governor desires me to inform you that on his receiving from the President of any Chartered Bank in Upper Canada, the accompanying declaration, signed by the President, Cashier, and by the major part of the Directors, the Lieutenant Governor in Council will be prepared to assume the serious responsibility of enabling the said Banks, until thirty days after the next meeting of the Legislature, and under certain restrictions to continue their business without the necessity of redeeming their notes in specie.

The Lieutenant Governor having thus frankly stated the responsibility he has determined to assume in case the apprehensions entertained respecting the drain of Specie should be realized, wishes it to be understood that he confidently expects of the Banks and of the friends of Provincial Credit that their utmost exertions will be used to avert a stoppage of payment in specie, which under any circumstances must be considered as a great public calamity . . . .

The first impulse of this Province was to follow, by a general suspension of cash payments, the example of the adjoining Republic, but I have conversed with no man who has individually been able to maintain this recommendation against the plain homely arguments that oppose it..

If the foreign demand for specie continues, the exhaustion of the Banks is, I admit, inevitable. The only question, therefore is, shall payment be suspended with their coffers full or empty? or in other words, is specie or character of most value to this Province? In reply, I have no hesitation in affirming that Upper Canada would prefer to lose its specie rather than its character – the former may be termed its Commercial Blood, but the latter is its *life*, and it is but common policy to shed the one in defence of the other.

My Lord if the Banks of America can be permitted in rude health to agree together to suspend their payments whenever it may be deemed convenient for them to do so, the British Creditor who has trusted to their solvency, from having previously calculated their assets, is liable at any time to the application of a sponge which is destructive of all confidence or credit.

Against this levelling, anti-commercial, republican system Upper Canada is now proudly contending, and I feel confident that by maintaining its character, and consequently its connection with the Mother Country, the Province will be amply repaid for the temporary inconvenience it now labours under . . . .

C 30   BANK OF MONTREAL/BANK OF UPPER CANADA RELATIONS
23 May 1837
[*PAC, Bank of Montreal, Resolve Book, v. 3, p. 112*]

Thomas G. Ridout Esq. Cashier of the Bank of Upper Canada was introduced to the Board, when an application for £20,000 in specie to enable the Bank of Upper Canada to continue its payments in coin was discussed – whereupon the Board determined that the Bank having suspended specie payments with a view to prevent the exportation of coin, no proposal can be entertained having for its object the abstraction of Specie from the vaults of the Bank.

C 31   T.G. RIDOUT BEFORE THE SELECT COMMITTEE ON THE
MONETARY SYSTEM OF THE PROVINCE, JUNE 1837
[JUC, *1837, Appendix, pp. 2–3, 35–7*]

[T.G. Ridout, testimony]
. . . Q. – Do you consider that the suspension of payment in Specie, under the circumstances, compromises the character and credit of the Province, or will it injure, to any serious extent, the character and standing of the Banks or the Province?

A. – The character and standing of the Banks in this Province, as

elsewhere, depend upon meeting engagements entered into unconditionally, without regard to circumstances; or if they cannot do this,
upon the exertions they make to meet these engagements. I cannot
contemplate the failure of the Banks in fulfilling their engagements,
even from necessity, in any other light than as a forfeiture, to a certain
extent, of the high character which they have always maintained for
solvency; and if they should follow the example of the Banks of the
United States and Lower Canada, which have refused Specie payments,
at the same time pretending that it was from choice and not from
necessity, I cannot but see that in future the Creditor of the Banks has
two risks to run instead of one, namely, the ability of the Banks, on one
hand, and on the other, their inclination. If it should be found that Acts
of Parliament are no security, and that *ex post facto* laws can relieve
against debts incurred in good faith, and on the reliance upon former
Acts of Parliament, I cannot conceive that the character and standing of
the Banks of the Province, and of the Province itself, will not be
seriously injured, notwithstanding the example which is mentioned in
the question to which this is respectfully intended as an answer. The
suspension of Specie payments by the Banks, in my humble opinion,
compromises the character of the Province; and if such suspension is to
affect the transactions of Government, it amounts to neither more nor
less than Provincial Bankruptcy . . . .

Q. – To what extent would it be necessary to curtail the circulation of
the Notes of your Bank, with its present Capital, before it would be
possible or prudent to resume fresh Discounts?

A. – The resuming of fresh Discounts would depend upon the
resources of the Bank, founded on the foregoing case, the degree of
credit attached to its Notes in circulation, and upon the amount of its
Foreign Funds, and whether the Discount would be required in Bank
Notes or in a Foreign Bill; the latter would serve the purposes of a
Merchant best, as he seldom requires Bank Notes, and never as a
remittance to his Foreign Creditor; probably one-third of the business of
a regular Bank has heretofore been to enable the Merchant to transact
through its medium and assistance his remittances to other Countries.

Q. – Have the demands lately made for Specie, upon your Bank,
been for the use of the Country, as a circulating medium therein, or for
exportation from the Country – Or by whom, and for what purpose, has
the principal demand been made – as far as you have ascertained, or can
form an opinion?

A. – The principal drain for Specie upon the Bank of Upper Canada,
since the beginning of May last, has been made by the three Private
Banks of this City – about £21,000 or £22,000 between them; the
demand from the United States has been about £4,000 within the same
time, as nearly as we can conjecture, and the remainder has been drawn
out for the use of the Country; the latter is gradually coming back in
small sums. Before this crisis arrived, we estimated that the Private

Banks of this City took from our vaults full nine-tenths of the Specie we issued; the greater part of which it is supposed they sold in the United States, at a small advance of one or two per cent. This was an advantageous transaction, as the Money was quickly turned, and came back upon us for more supplies; indeed it appeared to form especially the chief business of the Agricultural Bank within this Province, and it was enabled to carry on with great profit, by industriously exchanging its own notes, in all parts of the Country, for those of the Bank of Upper Canada thereby compelling the Bank to import much larger quantities of Specie than the fair demand of the Country required, which was done at a considerable expense, and was a continual drain to its Foreign Funds, and impaired its means of public accommodation to a considerable degree.

Q. – Do you believe that individuals who have been transacting business with your Bank, and receiving accommodation therefrom, have been doing generally a safe, prudent, and sound business?

A. – As far as the Bank of Upper Canada can at present judge, its transactions hitherto have been with persons who were considered as doing a good, prudent, and sound business; a difference in that opinion is now, however, gaining ground; – at all events, the most of them are not prepared for these times.

Q. – It is generally believed that the Banks of this Province have been in the habit of discounting very largely to Americans, and it is alleged as a reason for so doing, that by that means funds are created in New York. To what extent has this kind of business been done by your Bank? Has it been done on account of any extraordinary gain to the Bank in the way of premium, or for the purpose of enabling the Bank to afford any particular facilities to the Mercantile Body of this Country? What amount or proportion of Bills discounted by your Bank and payable in the United States, have been dishonoured when due; and do you believe that such Bills have been generally founded upon real *bonâ fide* business transactions, or that they have been negotiated in this Country merely for the purpose of raising money? How far have transactions in foreign Exchange, and accommodation to Foreigners, affected your means of accommodation to the Public of this Province, and did you in consequence of such transactions in Exchange and with Foreigners lessen your discounts?

A. – The Bank of Upper Canada, within the last year, has discounted for American Houses between £50,000 and £60,000, which has enabled them to make large purchases of Produce in this Province; their Bills were payable in New York, and produced available Funds for the Bank, yielding a fair profit at a time when Bills on London sold there at 3 or 4 per cent. below the rate in Canada; and, consequently, Funds created from such a source could only have been done at a considerable loss – we, however, attained our object to a certain degree by discounting American Paper, and it enabled the Bank last month to supply its vaults out of those returns: – about £3,500 of those Bills are overdue, but are well secured. The above transaction did not affect the means of the Bank to afford accommodation to the Public of this Province; it rather tended to enable the Bank to assist our Merchants in making their Foreign remittances . . . .

C 32   B. TURQUAND TO WILLIAM PROUDFOOT
Toronto, 15 July 1837
[*PAC, RG 19 B2b, v. 1173*]

Having been given to understand that it would be inconvenient for the Bank of Upper Canada to accept the Receiver General's Drafts on Mssrs Forsyth Richardson & Co. his Agents at Montreal at 20 day's sight as usual, but that there would be no objection to one for £5000 at *10* days – I sent a Draft for that sum as agreed upon to your Bank on Friday but which I exceedingly regret was refused.

I now beg leave to enquire on behalf of His Majesty's Receiver General on what terms the Bank will take his Drafts on Montreal and to remark that unless some arrangement can be made for withdrawing the public monies that may be now, or that may hereafter come into the hands of the Agents at Montreal (hitherto effected through the medium of the Bank of Upper Canada) without the risk of a similar occurrence very serious inconvenience & embarrassment may be sustained by the Government.

Your early reply to this communication is respectfully requested.

C 33   SIR F.B. HEAD TO BANKS OF UPPER CANADA
Toronto, 19 July 1837
[*PAC, RG 19 B2A, v. 1150*]

The Lieut:Governor wishes the Banks of Upper Canada to understand that if any Bank shall desire to avail itself of the Provisions of the Act to authorize the Chartered Banks in this Province to suspend the redemption of their Notes in specie, it will be necessary.

1st That the said Bank shall submit to the Lieut:Governor in Council a full statement of its affairs, shewing the solvency of the Institution.

2nd That the amount of specie retained or to be retained in the said Bank at the time of its suspension shall not be more than sufficient to redeem on demand its one dollar notes, which are in circulation.

3rd That the notes of a suspended Bank cannot be used in Government transactions.

C 34   E. McMahon[20] to B. Turquand
Toronto, 22 July 1837
[*PAC, RG 19 B2A, v. 1150*]

. . . His Excellency . . . desires that in future you will not in the Receiver General's Department use the notes of any Banks in this Province or elsewhere, unless such Banks are or shall be at the time redeeming their notes in specie.

His Excellency also commands me to state to you, in reference to any Public monies, which may be in the hands of the agents of the Receiver General in Lower Canada (with the exception of the payment about to be made for duties payable from that Province to this, which His Excellency has directed you to authorize the Bank of Upper Canada to bring into the Province in specie) that he expects them to be available in this Province as required and in such a shape as to prevent any variance from the rule respecting the currency to be used by the Government. His Excellency considers the public monies at the credit of the Province with the Receiver General, as in his hands here, and not in Lower Canada. His Excellency thinks it necessary that this statement should be made to you, in consequence of your mentioning in a letter to Mr. Secretary Joseph, as a reason for your anxiety, that there should be no delay in procuring the amount of duties about to be brought in, the difficulty you had with the Bank of Upper Canada in negociating drafts on the Receiver General's agents.

His Excellency regrets that any such difficulty should have arisen, and he desires me to remark, that it could not have occurred, had these monies been in the hands of the Receiver General, or in some place of Deposit within the Province.

C 35   Prime Ward & King to Baring Brothers
New York, 1 September 1837
[*PAC, Baring Brothers Papers, v. 80*]

. . . We now find that with regard to the £10,000, as with the previous £5000 stg., no British silver is to be expected from you – and as we cannot supply it here, we are left to arrange with the Bank of Upper Canada, to whom the disappointment, at this moment, is particularly inconvenient, from the peculiar fitness of that coin, for their circulation. The course persued by you might in some quarters have proved detrimental to us – but with our friends of the Bank of Upper Canada, a long & confidential intercourse, renders explanations less difficult although far from pleasant – the more so as the handsome interference

---

[20]E.W. McMahon was chief clerk, 1812–41, and assistant to the civil secretary, John Joseph, 1836–38.

of Mssrs. Glyns[21] – in their behalf seems to have furnished the means for the protection of our signature, in an unlooked for emergency . . . .

C 36   JOHN MACAULAY TO KIRBY
Toronto, 16 September 1837
[PAO, Macaulay Papers]

. . . It seems that the Commercial Bank has actually decided on a suspension of specie payments. I wonder it was not long since done. However they can yet render essential accomodation to the trade & agriculture of the Country. Our Bank has no intention of suspending – Our stock of specie is £75,000 our notes in circulation is reduced to £97000. The Gore Bank has £27000 in circulation & about £37,000 in specie on hand – an excess of £10,000 so that until both these banks have released themselves from considerable quantity of metal by means of liberal discounts with their own paper, they cannot lawfully suspend . . . .

C 37   JOHN MACAULAY TO KIRBY
Kingston, 21 November 1837
[PAO, Macaulay Papers]

. . . Our vaults are overflowing with specie containing at this time £138,000. It speaks well for the Country that the liabilities to the Bank have been reduced to £200,000 since the suspension of cash payments in the United States.

C 38   T.G. RIDOUT TO GEORGE S. BOULTON[22]
Toronto, 15 February 1838
[JUC, 1838, Appendix, Report on Banking]

. . . I am directed by the Board to inform you, that on the 13th instant the Commercial Bank presented here for payment, some Commissariat Checks for which they refused their own Notes, and insisted upon being paid in the Notes of this Bank. A similar circumstance took place at Kingston a few days ago; where the Cashier of the Commercial Bank refused to take his own acceptance for about £1300 in payment of a Commissariat Check upon this Bank, and on speaking to Mr. Cartwright, their President, on the subject, he excused himself to the President of this Bank by saying, that their own Notes were of no value

---

[21]Glyn Hallifax & Company or Glyn, Mills & Company was a large banking house operating from London, England. Along with the Baring Brothers they became agents for the Upper Canadian and Union governments. Glyns also represented the Bank of Upper Canada following the bankruptcy of Thomas Wilson & Company. In the 1850s Glyns became heavy investors in various Canadian railways.

[22]George Strange Boulton (1797–1869), a lawyer, represented Durham in the Legislative Assembly, 1830–41.

to them, and that they were not obliged to receive them unless they pleased.

The Board therefore beg that your Honorable Committee will be pleased to take the above circumstances into consideration, and should the Suspension Act, under which the Commercial Bank shelters itself, warrant such proceedings on their part – they beg leave to suggest that some remedy may be afforded, as it is quite impossible for this Bank, or any other specie paying Bank, to maintain the credit of the country by a sound circulation, if the suspended Banks are permitted to take undue advantages of their own disabilities.

C 39   JOHN S. CARTWRIGHT TO GEORGE S. BOULTON
Toronto, 16 February 1838
[JUC, *1838, Appendix, Report on Banking*]

. . . I beg to make the following remarks: –

When the Act authorising the Suspension, (under which the Commercial Bank is now pending,) was passed, it was done for the purpose of relieving the commercial community, and not to promote the schemes of any Banking Institution, and it was generally understood that in consequence of the suspension in the United States and Lower Canada, the Banks in this Province must in self-defence avail themselves of the law, if they intended to do any business whatever. It is necessary for me to allude to the almost universal dissatisfaction which existed when it was understood that the Chartered Banks would not be allowed to avail themselves of the Act by the Executive, except on terms which were, to say the least, unexpected, and in consequence no Bank would or could accommodate the public; and had it not been for the accommodation afforded by the Montreal Bank it is impossible to foresee the consequences.

Among the conditions annexed by the Executive was the following: – That the Notes of a Suspended Bank should not be used in 'Government transactions,' and in consequence when the Commercial Bank suspended (at the earnest and repeated solicitation of business men,) their paper was not only refused at the Government Offices, and in tender for exchange, but they were compelled to pay in specie, the sum of £37,000, being the amount of the Receiver General's credit for Debentures. In all subsequent tenders for Exchange our paper was refused as inadmissible, and the tender of the Bank of Upper Canada received at a rate far below that at which we had offered to the manifest loss of the Province, though it is understood that the Bank of Upper Canada had discharged their obligations, growing out of the Exchange transactions, in paper of suspended Banks. Being thus excluded from all competition in the purchase of Exchange, to which we alone could look as a source to supply us with Specie, we naturally endeavored to procure as many checks of the Receiver General's and Commissariat as we could, and it was not to be expected that after having been compelled to pay the Receiver General a large amount in Specie, that we were to be dictated to by the Bank of Upper Canada as to the mode of payment, or to take our own paper in exchange on their own terms.

Regarding the immediate cause which seems to have given rise to the complaint of the Bank of Upper Canada, (the refusal of this Bank to receive payment in their own Notes for Commissariat Checks,) I would only remark that the Bank of Upper Canada are understood to have received from the Commisary General, Sterling Bills to the extent of £150,000, a portion of which, £40,000, was paid in Specie, and the remainder placed to the credit of the Commissariat, against which that Department are now drawing. And if the Bank of Upper Canada had given us exchange at the rate at which they received it from the Commissary General, it would have been accepted by this Bank, who are only compelled to demand Specie on Upper Canada paper, in consequence of being totally excluded from competition for exchange, and prevented from accommodating their customers who have payments to make to Government; I think all difficulty would be obviated if the restrictions now imposed on us were removed, and for which there can no longer exist any necessity, as it is a notorious fact that our paper is equal in value to that of a Specie paying Bank, and is paid out as such by the Bank of Upper Canada.

My remark to the President of the Bank of Upper Canada was, that our paper was of no use to us for the purpose of Exchange for the reasons before mentioned.

How far the Bank of Upper Canada or the Commercial Bank have been most instrumental in maintaining the credit of the country, I will not determine, but leave it to the judgment of those who are interested in neither, and can therefore form an impartial opinion.

C 40   R.W. Harris to Isaac Buchanan
Toronto, 15 March 1838
[*PAC, Buchanan Papers, v. 30, p. 24911*]

. . . on Saturday. morning last I went to Mr. Ridout about Exchange and had arranged to get £3000 on Monday, but when Monday came he said he would require to wait for board day (this day) and to day at half past one he has had no board. The plain English of all this amounts to, Mr R's expectation that exchange will be higher. the New York paper arrived on Monday morning showing an advance of 1% from the previous days advices & I have sent in some notes (which remained in the office) to the Commercial Bank for which I expect to get 1000£ or so for tomorrow's mail @ 12% (tho BUC's rate is 12¹/₂%) and I hope to send 500£ or so of sundry bills . . . . I hear the BUC does not intend discounting but I am still sanguine of getting in our outstandings during spring very well and I hope we will then be more independent of the

"Old Lady"[23] to show you more clearly the little ground the BUC has for this delay, I now enclose a list of bills now in that institution for collection and I.B. and Co. has reduced their liabilities £3000 since you left Toronto . . . .

C 41   BANK OF MONTREAL/BANK OF UPPER CANADA RELATIONS
12 April 1838
[PAC, Bank of Montreal, Resolve Book 3, p. 189]

A letter from the Cashier of the Bank of Upper Canada dated at Toronto the 4th Instant in reply to an application from the Cashier dated the 9th requiring Mr. Ridout to cover the account overdrawn to the extent of £16,952 was submitted to the Board.

Mr. Ridout declining to cover the said balance except upon terms which are considered in contravention of the agreement entered into between the two Banks in the year 1829 render it expedient in the opinion of the Board that Mr. Holmes[24] do proceed forthwith to Toronto for the purpose of coming to a clear understanding as respects the continuance of the arrangement hitherto existing or of making such other as may be consistent with the interests of this Institution & which may enable it to continue to facilitate the trade of the Country.

It was further resolved unanimously on motion of Mr. Anderson[25] seconded by Mr. Jamieson,[26] that the Notes of the Bank of Upper Canada be no longer received in payment or Deposit it being inexpedient to increase the Balance now due to this Institution.

C 42   R.W. HARRIS TO ISAAC BUCHANAN
Toronto, 1 May 1838
[PAC, Buchanan Papers, v. 30, p. 24928]

. . . that I am doing IB and Co. banking with the Commercl I am not allowing any thing to occur that would prevent me at any time offering the BUC a transaction if they were drawing at the same rates as the other Banks the BUC is again drawing @ 12$^{1/2}$% prem and I expect to get the [reissue?] for to day @ 10% . . . .

---

[23]"Old Lady" refers to the Bank of Upper Canada. The term became current in the mid-1830s. It is possible that it was first used by W.L. Mackenzie as a derogatory term. Eventually it came to denote respect and sympathy.

[24]Benjamin Holmes (1794–1865) was promoted from second teller to cashier of the Bank of Montreal in 1827, a position he held until 1846. He was a vice president of the Grand Trunk Railway and a director of the Bank of Montreal in the 1850s. He sat in the Legislative Assembly several times in the 1840s.

[25]T.B. Anderson was a director of the Bank of Montreal and became its president from 1860 to 1869.

[26]John Jamieson was a director of the Bank of Montreal.

C 43   BANK OF MONTREAL/BANK OF UPPER CANADA RELATIONS
10 August 1838
[*PAC, Bank of Montreal, Resolve Book 3, p. 212*]

. . . After the ordinary course of Discounting the President called the attention of the Board to Mr. Ridout's letter of the 3rd August, relative to the establishment of an Agency in Montreal & the Cashier submitted a private letter from Mr. Harper dated the 1st Inst. on the subject of renewing the agreement with the Commercial Bank.

The Board considered it inconsistent with the interest of this Bank, to continue as Agents, Bankers who cannot render any reciprocity, or who in fact stand in the position of a rival Institution in this City, & under this conviction direct Mr. Holmes to proceed on Monday next to Upper Canada, then & there to make such arrangements for the settlement of the account with the Bank of Upper Canada & entering into an arrangement with the Commercial Bank as may be considered advantageous.

C 44   T.G. RIDOUT TO JOHN MACAULAY
16 August 1838
[*PAC, Colborne Papers, v. 16*]

Statement of the causes, which led to the suspension of specie payments, on the part of the Bank of Upper Canada. And the reasons that may be assigned for continuing that suspension at the present time.

When the general suspension of specie payments throughout the United States and Lower Canada took place in May 1837 this Bank had £204,000 of notes in circulation [Feeling?] confident of their ability to redeem their paper, The Board determined to do so – and not to suspend and at the same time they granted to the Public every indulgence in the way of renewals And so well was the Bank prepared for the emergency, that when the insurrection broke out last December, it had £140,000 in its vaults and only £80,000 of notes in circulation.

In the above state of affairs, the [exigencies?] of Public Service suddenly required a large outlay of money which the Commissary General was quite unable to meet, and altho' he had some months before withdrawn his account, and the Bank did not contemplate its renewal, yet it at once came forward and advanced him in bulk £50,000 in dollars, leaving £40,000 of specie in its vaults, and offered besides to furnish money for the military disbursements in all parts of the Province where Posts were established, which proposals were accepted and consequently those payments amounted in January to £34,417, in February to £96,618, and in March to £88,892 by which means the issue of Bank notes were increased to £154,000 – and its specie in the vault reduced to £60,000 – and finding every probability of a continuance of those payments and it being notorious from the disturbed state of the American frontier that it would be impracticable to import

Specie from New York to replenish our coffers which were rapidly being drained by the joint attacks of the Commercial and other suspended Banks of this Province who taking advantage of the great issue made for Government by the Bank of Upper Canada, collected its notes in large sums and demanded their redemption in specie at the same time refusing to take any part of their own notes in exchange so that feeling the contest to be unequal and unfair, the Board of Directors finally determined on the sixth of March last to petition the Lieutenant Governor for leave to suspend and it was immediately granted and which we have every reason to think was concurred in by the Commissary General as it assured him the means of carrying on the service until he could receive his supplies of specie from abroad on the opening of the navigation, being well satisfied that the notes of this Bank in the mean time would afford a sound currency by its well established reputation, and he was also aware that the late extraordinary issues were based upon his Treasury Bills sold to the Bank and which it had remitted to London to the amount of more than £200,000 Sterling being in actual gold deposits more than equal to the entire circulation of its notes and that the suspension of the Bank was not under inability to pay its debts but was entirely owing, to political events of a most extraordinary nature, also, that there was a physical impossibility both on his part and on the part of the Bank to supply the Country with specie.

The Bank of Upper Canada consequently suspended specie payments with £60,000 in gold and in silver coins in its vaults and upwards of £200,000 Sterling in London against a circulation of £154,000 of its notes in this Province, not withstanding which and not from a desire to hoard up its specie, but to afford every facility to the Public Service, it was communicated to the Commissary General that the Bank would still continue to pay the Troops, Staff, and Departments in dollars, and would pay the same to his contractors if required. This the Bank has faithfully performed not only here, but at the various posts in Upper Canada and at a considerable cost for transport.

The affairs of the Bank of Upper Canada having been brought down to the present time, it remains to discuss the expediency of resuming specie payments, or the disadvantage that would be the result of such a measure at this juncture –

His Excellency the Lieutenant Governor having lately ordered the three chartered Banks to take the matter into their earliest consideration. To the foregoing [requisition?] the Commercial Bank has quietly answered, that they were ready at any moment that the Upper Canada and Gore Banks first showed the example. Such an indefinite reply needs no comment, and if the other two Bank's had answered in like manner, only reversing the order of names it would be impossible ever to arrive at a conclusion. The Board of Directors of this Bank have not however thus endeavoured to evade the question, but have maturely considered it and have requested a meeting of the three Banks by a delegation of their Presidents to take the matter into the fullest consideration. To this request the President of the Commercial Bank has replied to the effect, that as that Bank would be ready to resume specie payments as soon as the Upper Canada Bank would set the example, it was quite useless for him to attend the meeting, which he therefore declined – it remains therefore with the Upper Canada Bank and the Gore Bank to state their own opinion and to be guided thereby . . . .

That an immediate resumption of specie payments in the present distressed state of this country, owing to the late Political events, and the general want of confidence in Trade would compel the Banks to stop all further discounts and to call in their debts as fast as possible and should recourse be had to Suits at Law, which in most cases would be necessary, it is a well known fact, that no money can be realized at Sheriffs Sales, without bringing ruin on the debtors for neither goods or chattels, lands or houses will now bring one third of former prices, and so well are the Public aware of this, that there does not appear to be any general wish to enforce Specie payments. In stopping discounts, the advantages likely to arise from the rich crop of wheat now coming into market would be in a great measure paralized. For in Consequence of the scarcity of money prices would of course fall to ruinous rates or else there would be no sales for a Foreign market. At the same time the Country would be drained of its Specie by those who are daily selling off their farms and removing to the United States. It is therefore suggested as an act of prudence on the part of the Government and of consideration for the state of the country not to call upon the Banks to resume specie payments until the present crop shall have been brought to market, and that a new impulse shall have been given to the prosperity of the Province by the removal of our usual immigration from Europe and the additional capital derived from that [cause?].

Besides the foregoing, this Province labours under many other disadvantages, which might justly be brought under His Excellency's notice particularly as Mr Secretary Macaulay, in his letter, intimates that the state of the currency in all parts of the Empire is a matter in which Her Majesty's Government takes a peculiar interest. Such being the case it may be fairly urged that the currency of Upper and Lower Canada should be placed upon an equal footing, which it never can be until the circulation of the French Half Crown shall be totally abolished in the latter Province as it is in this . . . and that it shall no longer be a legal tender at 2/9 when in fact it is an old worn out smooth coin, and it is not recognized as a coin in any other Country excepting Lower Canada. And its intrinsic value as bullion in the United States is only about [10% on £1?] equal to 38 or 40 cents.

2ndly   That the base copper coinage now existing be entirely prohibited from circulation and that it be replaced by a Provincial coinage of good copper.

3rdly   It may likewise be suggested that there shall be established by an Imperial Act a certain silver coinage for the use of the British Colonies on this continent consisting of Dollars and its parts of equal weight and fineness to the United States dollar. As such a measure would put an end at once to the Banks of the Province deriving their supplies of specie from the Mint of the United States at Philadelphia, it being, a profit to the Bankers of 1 or 1½ per cent to melt down the Mexican dollar and have it reissued into American halves.

4thly   A silver coinage for the colonies will be the more acceptable, for besides abolishing the French half crown it will also abolish the circulation of the British silver coins in this Province against which the Lower Canadians' complain and which has already been brought under the notice of Lord of the Treasury by Mr. Commissary General Routh[27] as having been fixed by our Legislature at too high a rate. The act however will expire in about another year.

It is unquestionable that at the present moment the Banks of this Province are quite able to resume specie payments. The effect of which would be the withdrawal of the greater part of their notes from circulation and to deprive the country of a circulating medium of its own as silver and gold in the present political state of men's minds, would either be hoarded up or be carried out of the Province. The Bank notes of Lower Canada which are redeemable in French half crowns would then take the place of our notes and all the real inconveniences of a bad and inconvertible currency would be immediately felt. Altho' it is as yet little known as our Banks are in the daily course of redeeming their notes by Bills on London and New York within one per cent of the Montreal rates and that to any amount they may be offered.

It is not only from the depressed state of trade and the great difficulty of collecting debts that the Upper Canada Bank suffers inconvenience and would be unable to afford the Country any new discounts on a resumption of cash payments but the well known embarassed state of the Provincial Finances tends very materially to press upon Public credit and has become hindersome to this Bank. As the holders of Government debentures having for several months past been alarmed for the safety of their property in those investments have insisted upon the Bank to redeem them at par under a claim that as they bought them from the Bank so ought they to be repurchased by the Institution; this feeling has proved to be very extensive. And within the last six months the Bank of Upper Canada, in order to uphold and maintain the credit of Government has actually repurchased £40,700 of the Provincial Debts which are now unsaleable and consequently remain a dead weight in its hands. To this may be added the further sum of £39,500 Sterling of Government debentures, unsold & unsaleable in the hands of its agents in London, our last advices being that capitalists will have nothing to do with Canada bonds during the unsettled state of that Country.

[27]R.I. Routh was commissary general for the Canadas.

The Board therefore respectfully submit whether under all these circumstances hereinbefore stated, and whilst the Bank is encumbered with £80,000 of unsaleable Government debentures, many thousand pounds of which are now due but which the Receiver General is unable to pay, it can be considered prudent or proper at the present time to resume specie payments in this Province.

C 45   JOHN H. DUNN TO JOHN MACAULAY
Toronto, 5 September 1838
[*PAC, RG 19 B2b, v. 1175*]

I have the honor to enclose to you for the information of His Excellency the Lieut-Governor a letter dated the 20th July last from Mrssrs. Glynn Hallifax and Co. which I received a short time since and to state that I should have transmitted it earlier, but have waited in the hopes of being able to procure Exchange here to remit according to the desire of these Gentlemen, at the same rate, or nearly, as the quotations at New York but as long as the Banks continue suspension of Specie payments, the Exchange will be higher by 4 or 5 p cent – at New York the premium is about from 8 to 9 – here from 12 to 13 – A further delay in furnishing means to pay the dividends on £200,000 Debentures due in December next might produce embarrassment and injury to the credit of Upper Canada. I therefore beg most respectfully to submit to His Excellency whether it would not be better to purchase Exchange at the present rate, than run the risk of delay with the hopes of procuring it on more favourable terms. It will take perhaps a month to reach London and the usual sight of Bills, 60 days, will bring it nearly to the period when the dividends are payable.

C 46   T.G. RIDOUT TO MATILDA[28]
Toronto, 12 November 1838
[*PAC, Ridout Papers*]

. . . I think that we shall pass a quiet night – at all events we cannot be surprised & in case anything – should happen my guard will be increased to 50 or 60 men which will be enough to defend the Bank for several hours. We intend to have the barricades put up again so that we could hold out against anything – but artillery – I wish that we had a less quantity of gold & silver in the vault – it gives us so much anxiety & is such an Inducement to the rebels I must try & get it removed to the Garrison as soon as the vault is ready . . . .

C 47   T.G. RIDOUT TO JOHN JOSEPH
Toronto, 8 December 1838
[*PAC, RG 5 A1, v. 211*]

As it seems that various complaints are making to Govt against this

[28]Matilda Ridout (née Matilda Ann Bramley) was T.G. Ridout's second wife.

Bank – and more particularly that nothing can be obtained in exchange for our notes I beg to offer you the following explanations in reply to the charges proferred –

In the first place since our suspension of specie payments on the 6 March last this Bank has drawn upon London and New York in redemption of its notes to the amount of £320,828 cy – and has imported from England and the United States £140,000 in gold and silver coins – which are freely paid out for change for the accommodation of the Public.

In the early part of last month we found that the demand for bills on New York and London rapidly increased and that the applications were chiefly made by Americans and their friends in this country including the People's Bank[29] and as we were then on the eve as we supposed of an invasion from the United States we imagined that all this money for use of the Brigand armies and that it materially assisted in their outfit – We therefore refused to issue any more bills unless in small sums for those we knew and could depend upon – besides we were desirous of preserving our funds in London for any emergency that might happen. This restriction lasted about a fortnight – for since the Prescott affair[30] the rapid enrollment of our Militia and the augmentation of our regular Military force – we have felt more secure and it has been deemed expedient and right again to draw freely both upon London and New York. I mean for merchants – for commissariat supplies and for all ordinary purposes – and we have made it a rule to do this at one per cent below the prices of other Banks –

We refuse now even to sell our bills to the Banks of this Province and Lower Canada having discovered that they had taken shameful advantage of our fair and candid dealings – for finding that we drew bills at one per Cent below their rates – they industriously collected our notes and bought our drafts – refusing at the same time to exchange on equitable terms – as for instance we held at Kingston in the latter part of October £9000 of Commercial Bank Notes. Then Mr. Harper refused to exchange saying that he held none of our paper – when at the very same time he sent down £7000 to the Montreal Bank in our notes – which were taken in the Brougham   We were then compelled to run the later risque, and they were forwarded to this place, where by degrees we got them exchanged by Mr. Cameron. Since then we have refused the Commercial Bank notes unless in payment of debts – as we will not subject ourselves to the trouble and risque of sending them from one place to the other at their whim or caprice – We have told them that if they have a superabundance of our notes they should pay them out and we would do the same with theirs – as the notes of the chartered Banks

---

[29]The People's Bank was a private bank which commenced operations at Toronto in the mid-1830s. It was formally taken over by the Bank of Montreal in 1840.
[30]This refers to the Patriot uprising at Prescott on 11 November 1838.

were all of equal value at present and that they should redeem their own by Bills – and we should do the same with our paper

The Commercial Bank has all along refused to tell us what amount of our notes they held on hand – all their proceedings with respect to this Bank are carried on in mystery and apparently with vindictive malevolence – all our advances for a friendly intercourse have been met by treachery and bad faith.

We understand that they now hold £30,000 – of our notes – this no doubt is the sum of their joint collections with the Montreal Bank – the greater part of which has no doubt been collected at Montreal at 3 per discount – that being the rate at which the Montreal Bank receives them – for this large sum they have not yet made any demand in foreign exchange – but perhaps they intend to do so – when I think they will be most certainly refused –

We pay out the Gore notes indiscriminately with our own – and so we would the Commercial if they would do the same by us, and that is the proper course for all our Banks whilst they act under the suspension law, and would prevent all petty jealousies – and that mean and contemptible system of collecting each others paper –

As for the Public they are better served by the Bank of Upper Canada than by any other Institution· in the Province – we discount freely all good paper founded on the trade of the Country – more especially bills on Lower Canada – and if we stopt all accommodation for 2 or 3 weeks last month – it is not to be wondered at – as the threatened invasion was a sufficient excuse

If I knew of any other charges against us I would answer them at once and I trust to your satisfaction and I only conclude by saying that the officers and directors of the Commercial Bank make it their chief business to excite a sympathizing feeling against this Bank, and by long perseverance they have pretty well succeeded.

C 48   THE BANK OF UPPER CANADA'S DISCOUNT SYSTEM
[*Toronto* Examiner, *12 December 1838*]

The Bank of Upper Canada has commenced drawing on New York, at 5 per cent, *for Commissariat checks only.* This is a scandalous imposition on the public. It however establishes two facts, 1st, That this Bank is either unable or unwilling to meet all its engagements. 2nd, That it has determined to give a preference to one creditor over all others. Waiving for the present all discussion as to the propriety of such a course, and assuming that it is right and proper that as the Bank has lately received £100,000 in Sterling Bills from the Government, it should *give a preference* to its claim, we shall endeavour to shew that *even this object is not attained* by the present system. We have always considered that as long as the Banks give drafts on London or New-York for their bills, at a reasonable rate, little complaint of their suspension could fairly be made. If A. owes B. £50, and that a pressure in business takes place, it is obviously much better for B. to get an order on New York to get his £50 in silver, than to be told he must wait A's convenience. Just so it is with the Banks. We shall now give an illustration of the working of the Bank's new system. Two merchants enter into a contract with the Commissariat for £500 of clothing each. A. is an importing merchant, B. not. – Both deliver their goods and both are paid by checks on the Bank of Upper Canada. A takes his check and gets a Bill on New York for the amount, which he can easily convert into any funds he pleases, either gold, silver, or Exchange on London. B takes his check to the Bank and is paid in bills, not wanting a draft. He then pays to the importing merchants from whom he purchases, to C. £100, D. £200, and E. £200. These parties then take their bills to the Bank to get a draft, but are told *they can get nothing* at present, and must *wait the pleasure* of the Bank. Is this conduct either equitable or honourable? We are told that the principle of monarchy is Honour. The principle of the Bank of Upper Canada is to – the reader can fill up the blank.

C 49   T.G. RIDOUT TO MATILDA
18 December 1838
[*PAC, Ridout Papers*]

. . . I am now sending Coutts & Co.[31] fifty thousand pounds in bills on the [?] & to Glyn & Coy. one hundred thousand pounds of the same drawn by Commissary General Routh. We shall have £25000 more next week to forward making in all £330,000 since the 27 October last. The expenses of Government are so enormous that we expect to receive as much more before the 1st of March next.

I should like to know your opinion of the Glyns we have here a very good one of them & trust them with a great deal of money – as they have now £230,000 of our funds in cash in their hands – we shall however draw heavily upon them this winter & will probably import from London next spring 150,000 sovereigns . . . .

C 50   A. STEVEN TO C. CASTLE
Hamilton, 10 January 1839
[*CIBC, Gore Bank Letterbook, 1837–40*]

. . . I observe that Mr. Wenham and Mr. Holmes are at issue respecting Upper Canada Bank Notes and that they are now redeemed at one per cent discount.

. . . we would deduct two per cent on all collections made for you here on account of the difference of Exchange at your City and the selling rate at the Bank of Upper Canada, that Institution as things now are rules this Province in Exchange matters as the Commissary General

---

[31]Coutts and Company were merchant bankers in London, England.

gives all his dfts. to that Bank. Our Board now confirms what I wrote to you on that subject so you must charge accordingly – in the end it must all be paid by Upper Canada . . . .

C 51   A. Steven to T.G. Ridout
Hamilton, 16 January 1839
[CIBC, Gore Bank Letterbook, 1837–40]

. . . and [I] regret to learn that you have now reduced your Exchange on New York to 4½ per cent so that we will now lose by your dft. on that City for £5000 which was credited to you at 5 per cent advance. I am also informed that the Banks in Toronto are selling drafts in London at the rate you charge us so that we will only have our trouble for our pains which is not a very profitable transaction . . . .

C 52   T.G. Ridout to John Macaulay
Toronto, 9 March 1839
[PAC, RG 5 A1, v. 218, pp. 119891–2]

You will be quite correct in stating that the greater part of the British silver imported by the Banks under the act fixing its value in this Province at 6/ the crown and 1/3 the shilling has been collected by the merchants and returned to England, being the best remittance that they could make, and out of £150000 imported within the last 3 years, I really do not think that there are £5000 remaining in the country. We have not actually £50 on hand.

The merchants made a handsome profit by remitting the British half crown . . . .

PS. I have advised the finance Committee to adopt by one act the whole of the American gold and silver tariff, which includes all the coins in the world excepting the *French half crown*. This would be a good preparatory measure for the introduction of a colonial coinage.

C 53   Third Report of the Committee on Banking
March/April 1839
[JUC, 1839, Appendix, pp. 764–5, 770–72]

[T.G. Ridout examined]
Is it expedient, in your opinion, to allow the Act authorizing the Chartered Banks to suspend specie payments to expire at the end of the present session of Parliament?

In my opinion it would not be expedient, in the unsettled state of the foreign affairs of this Province, to allow that Act to expire at the end of the present session of the Legislature, as the interests of the Government, as well as the interests of the Country, require its renewal – the advantages derived from its operations by the banks are, in a great measure, imaginary; as the depression of trade and the check given to all enterprize and improvement has caused a great falling off of bank business – and as there is no probability of any extensive emigration this year – the effect of returning to cash payments would be to drain the banks of specie and totally to prevent all discounts whatever.

. . . It has been stated that the Bank of Upper Canada has withdrawn its accomodation from the public at their different offices in the outer Districts – Has that been the case, and to what extent?

It ought very little to be wondered at that the Bank of Upper Canada does not, at present, extend through its offices and agencies the same liberal accommodation to the public that it did formerly; for on reference to the large list of bills over due it will be found that a great portion of them originated at the offices, and the attention of the Bank is now more directed in securing those debts, by granting renewals and other indulgencies to the parties concerned, than in increasing their liabilities by new discounts; however, those persons of undoubted credit, character, and responsibility, who at times require advances, find no difficulty in having their notes discounted by transmitting them direct to the Bank; besides, the offices are not in any way restricted in discounting bills upon Lower Canada, founded upon the usual letters of credit . . . .

[Francis Hincks[32] examined]

Is it expedient, in your opinion, to allow the Act authorizing the Chartered Banks to suspend specie payments to expire at the end of the present session of Parliament?

Most decidedly. – The effect of a suspension of specie payments in this Province is to enable the banks to defraud the public by charging an exorbitant premium on foreign exchange. It does *not* enable them to extend their accommodation. There is, in my opinion, a very prevalent error in this subject. If a bank has to redeem its liabilities with foreign exchange, it may just as well do so with specie, except that it is enabled to charge its own price for exchange in consequence of its creditors having no alternative. It would be ruinous to the Country for the banks to suspend payment altogether, as the Bank of England formerly did, because, even assuming that public confidence would be unbounded, there are no Capitalists to hoard the notes, and thus keep them at nearly par value. For a short time the Bank of Upper Canada refused to give anything for its bills, and the inconvenience caused by this conduct was very great. The Commercial Bank Agency at Toronto has assumed a right to redeem its notes for such parties as it pleases – viz., its own customers. This is, of course, better than not paying at all, but is still very unjust. Under the present Act, the Chartered Banks are enabled to suspend payment virtually, and from the conduct of the Bank of Upper Canada, it is to be apprehended that they might do so; if they did the

---

[32]Francis Hincks (1807–85), was a banker, reform politician, journalist and colonial administrator. He arrived at York from his native Ireland in 1832. In the later 1830s he was cashier of the People's Bank at Toronto.

credit of the Province would be destroyed – specie and exchanges would be 20 or 30 per cent. premium, and every thing else in proportion. I can see no excuse for a continued suspension. I am not aware that the Government has borrowed money from any of the Chartered Banks, and I think it ought not, because all the banking capital in the Province is required to sustain the commercial interests. I feel convinced the sole object of suspension is to enable the banks to charge an exhorbitant premium on exchange, and that this will be its effect.

. . . It has been stated that the Bank of Upper Canada has withdrawn its accommodation from the public at their different offices in the outer Districts – Has than been the case, and to what extent?

I know nothing of the outer Districts, I believe there is hardly a Merchant in this City who banks with that Institution, and I have heard that its Cashier has stated that they did not want Merchants accounts – a most extraordinary assertion, if true, for the manager of a Bank. My own opinion, founded, I wish it to be understood, entirely on hearsay, is, that the Capital of the Bank of Upper Canada is so locked up in debentures, mortgages, long loans, and other unavailable securities, that it is compelled to extort exorbitant premiums on exchanges, in order to realize its usual profits. Hence the desire for continued suspension.

C 54   T.G. Ridout to B. Turquand
Toronto, 18 July 1839
[*PAC, RG 19 B2A, v. 1140*]

As this Bank is already in advance about £7700 – on your account it may perhaps be considered by you but reasonable that upon two offers at the same rate [for government Exchange] we shd. have the preference as in the Commissariat a good contractor always has. We should therefore be unwilling to give up any thing to another for which we have a shadow of claim, altho we have no right to dictate to you.

Why dont you draw for £20,000 at once?

C 55   John H. Dunn to John Macaulay
Toronto, February 1840
[*PAC, RG 19 B2b, v. 1175*]

. . . I keep balances in Montreal. When there the public have the advantage of a market for the purchase of Exchange – and the Exchange in Lower Canada is always lower than at Toronto. The Banks here charge a premium for exchange on Lower Canada but in either case there is always 1% more to send funds to Lower Canada. This province is largely indebted to Lower Canada and it must be obvious that the money in Lower Canada is better than in the Banks at Toronto. Wherever they are, I am responsibile . . . .

. . . The Amount of the public balances in my hands of any kind and description and the disposition of the same is as follows . . . .

. . . In the agents hands in Montreal	£11530. 0. 5
Bank of Upper Canada	5801.16.11
Commercial Bank Toronto	4771. 6.10
Transmitted to Glynn Halifax, Mills & Co. 8365.10.7. sterling together with prem. in exchange equal to currency	10560. 0. 0
In the chest	1361.13. 3
	£34,024.17. 5 stg

C 56   J. Bell Forsyth[33] to John S. Cartwright
Quebec, 29 February 1840
[QUA, Cartwright Papers, v. 2]

. . . I see there is a great war between the Montreal Banks and the Upper Canada institutions which I regret to see but which I am not surprised at, as the Montreal Bank will attempt to crush any individual or Rival Establishment that will not quietly do as they *command* . . . .

C 57   T.G. Ridout to John H. Dunn
Toronto, 7 April 1840
[PAC, RG 19 B2A, v. 1139]

I have the honor to acknowledge the receipt of your letter of the 3ᵈ inst. on the subject of the Bank shares ordered to be sold by Government and desiring to be informed if it would be convenient for this Bank to issue its exchanges on London for £20000 stg. under security of that stock, to which I am directed to reply, by stating that the Board would decline to make any advance upon the Government stock in this Bank, as the unsettled state of the times may prevent those ready sales which were anticipated a few weeks ago.

I was authorized last month to purchase about £7000 of Bank Stock under the expectation of your sales – since when several of the parties have bought from other persons, some at par, and others at the addition of interest from the date of the last dividend, and there remains now about £3000 only to be invested – for this however I am not empowered to make any tender for a distant day – but if offered to me I would buy at par.

I should imagine that the best mode of disposing of the Government stock would be for you to grant a letter of attorney to some person in the Bank to sell the whole 2000 shares at market price, provided that it is not below par, or the power of attorney may be in the usual form

---

[33]J. Bell Forsyth was a member of an important mercantile family situated in Montreal.

unconditional but accompanied by a letter of instructions – at the same time the Government might advertize that the said stock is for sale at the Bank, where the Public may apply.

Since the 1 January last there have been sold 724 shares equal to £9050 all at par excepting the last 80 which were sold last week with the addition of 3 months interest and I am authorized to buy 80 more shares at the same rate.

C 58   Sale of Bank of Upper Canada Stock, 22 may 1840
[PAC, RG 19 B2b, v. 1175]

Circular

To the Several parties tendering for Government Stock sold in the Bank of Upper Canada – all accepted at 1 p. Cent premium viz:

Tender No.

1	Henry Moyle[34]		£2,000	accepted	1% PRM
2	Hon Wm. Morris	80	shares at par rescinded and given to Mrs. Heath at		1% PRM
3	Ed Malloch[35]	80	shares		1% PRM
4	W.H. Boulton[36]	100	shares		1% PRM
5	Hon A. Baldwin	80	shares		1% PRM
6	J.S. Baldwin	100	shares		1% PRM
7	J.S. Macaulay	80	shares		1% PRM
8	Dr. Widmer	80	shares		1% PRM
9	Thomas Helliwell[37]	100	shares		1% PRM
10	Jn. Macaulay	100	shares		1% PRM
11	Clark Gamble	360	shares for sundry persons		1% PRM
12	Thos. G. Ridout	505	shares for ditto		1% PRM
13	J.G. Chewitt[38]	80	shares		1% PRM
14	R.R. Hunter[39]	64	shares		1% PRM
		1809	Shares		

& Mr Moyles equal to (+ a
                    fraction)   158
                    Total   1967 Shares

[34]Henry Moyle was a resident of Brantford, Upper Canada.

[35]Edward Malloch was a resident of Richmond, England.

[36]William Henry Boulton (1812–74), grandson of Chief Justice D'Arcy Boulton, was a lawyer and politician.

[37]Thomas Helliwell (1795–1862) was a brewer and merchant in York. He was a director of the Bank of Upper Canada in 1829–30, 1834–35, 1837–38, 1840–43, 1846–47, 1849–52 and 1854–58.

[38]James Grant Chewett (1793–1862), born in Cornwall, worked in the surveyor general's office. An active financier, he was a director of the Bank of Upper Canada in 1828, 1839, 1842–44 and 1846–56. In 1857 he owned 217 shares in the Bank. In 1860 he did not own any.

[39]Roger Rollo Hunter lived in Zorra, Upper Canada, and invested in many banks.

C 59   C. POULETT THOMSON[40] TO LORD JOHN RUSSELL[41] (COPY)
Montreal, 27 May 1840
[*PAC, Shortt Papers, v. 4*]

. . . These are all acts relating to banking companies – The three first are for encreasing the Capital of the three principal banks in Upper Canada . . . . I stated to the parties that they could not hope for the assent of the Crown inasmuch as they had not complied with the conditions set forth in the Board of Trade Regulations. – Inasmuch as the object sought was not the establishment of the fresh bank but the encrease of Capital, I should have been willing to overlook one or two of the provisions required, not considering them indispensable under these circumstances, but I am of opinion that the condition respecting the amount below which notes are not to be issued is of the greatest importance, and the parties having refused to conform to it, have in my opinion interposed an insuperable obstacle to the confirmation of their bills. It is fair to say that the Bank of Upper Canada was willing to assent to this condition, but it was struck out by the influence of parties interested in the other bills – . . .

C 60   BANK OF MONTREAL/BANK OF UPPER CANADA RELATIONS,
24 JUNE 1840
[*PAC, Bank of Montreal, Resolve Book 3, pp. 347–8*]

. . . Mr. Wenham stated that prior to his departure from Toronto he had a conversation with Mr. Ridout who intimated the readiness of the Bank of Upper Canada to come to a friendly understanding with the Bank of Montreal on which subject he had received communication from Mr. Holmes, which he admitted to be a liberal proposal but at the same time said it was considered by the Bank of Upper Canada that some mutually more beneficial arrangement could be proposed & the following was the substance of a conversation understood to be the basis on which a second intercourse would take place – That the Montreal Bank should make collections, & pay drafts drawn upon them without any charge for agency, the Bank of Upper Canada agreeing to keep a balance of £5000 at the credit of their account as in compensation, the Montreal Bank to redeem the Notes of the Bank of U.C. on this account at one per Cent discount, charging a ¼ per cent on the amount redeemed, & in order to continue the redemption at that rate without interruption, it was agreed that when the Bank of U.C. were not in funds, the Montreal Bank should take them on their own account, charging them to the Bank of U.C. and in receiving in payment of balances thus accruing, Bills upon London, or Drafts upon New York at ½ per cent above the rate of which

---

[40]Charles Poulett Thomson, Lord Sydenham (1799–1841) was the first governor general of the United Province, 1840–41.
[41]Lord John Russell was colonial secretary, 1839–41.

the Bank of Montreal were at the time [drawing?]. The transmission of the Notes being at the risk of the Bank of Upper Canada.

Which proposition the Directors assented to & authorized the Cashier to conclude, with the understanding – that all the Notes of the Bank of U.C. redeemed in the City be held at the risk of that Bank & subject to their order.

C 61   T.G. RIDOUT TO JOHN H. DUNN (COPY)
Toronto, 24 June 1840
[*PAC, A. Shortt Papers, v. 4*]

. . . this Bank will undertake the remainder of the Government Loan applied for – and will therefore hold itself in readiness to advance, in addition to the Twenty thousand pounds already engaged – the further sum of Ten thousand pounds in September – and Ten thousand pounds in October next on the terms which you have specified – making in all the full amount required Forty thousand pounds – Cy

C 62   ISAAC BUCHANAN TO PETER BUCHANAN
December 1840
[*PAC, Buchanan Papers, v. 9*]

. . . I mentioned to Tom Ridout the Cashier of the Bank of Upper Canada that you would be up and he expressed himself delighted at the prospect of seeing you and is quite up at the prospect of getting Bill's of Exchange on England instead of Montreal letters of credit for the purchase of the Produce of Upper Canada . . . .

C 63   JOHN H. DUNN TO S.B. HARRISON[42]
Toronto, 7 April 1840
[*PAC, RG 19 B2b, v. 1175*]

The money borrowed by authority from the Bank of Upper Canada and the Gore Bank in July and September last making together the Sum of Two thousand Six hundred pounds has been due some time – The monies granted to the Legislature for the public works for which these loans were negotiated were to be raised by Debentures and although some of these Debentures have been sold there still remain more to issue under the respective Act.

It occurs to me that the Banks would be willing to receive Debentures at par dated back on the days the monies were borrowed, which will, I think, be the best mode of discharging the debt – provided the arrangement can be made.

The list of Debentures are about to be prepared for the meeting of the

---

[42]Samuel Bealey Harrison (1802–67) was a miller, lawyer and politician. From 1841 to 1844 he was government leader in the Legislative Assembly of the Province of Canada. He was an important ally of Governor General Sydenham.

Legislature and if *these* debentures are to be issued, it will now be the best time to do so It will save the necessity of His Excellency's applying to the Legislature to reimburse these outlays which might produce discussion and perhaps some trouble.

C 64   T.G. RIDOUT TO JOHN H. DUNN
Toronto, 16 August 1841
[*PAC, RG 19 B2A, v. 1141*]

I have the honor to transmit herewith a list of 617 Government Debentures held by this Bank making in all, the sum of £193,745.15.5 Cy The interest on which is payable half yearly at your office in this City but in consequence of the removal of the Government to Kingston, no such office now exists here. I beg therefore to be informed, if you have given any directions for the payment of the said interest in this place according to the tenor of the Bonds, as it falls due monthly and where – the Board of Directors having declined to take upon themselves the responsibility of transmitting documents of so much value to your office at Kingston.

C 65   T.G. RIDOUT TO SAMUEL STREET
Toronto, 9 September 1841
[*PAO, Samuel Street Papers, v. 3*]

. . . You will perceive that the last six months interest due to Mr. Robert Gillespie[43] £250 has been carried to the credit of your account under date of the 13 July; and with respect to the accruing debenture interest due to yourself since the 1st of that month, I beg to inform you that nothing has yet been paid, as we have been for sometime past in communication with the Receiver General to cause the interest to be paid here, according to the engagement on the face of each debenture, the Board being unwilling to incur the risque of transmitting to Kingston half yearly £193,500 of those securities belonging to various persons without their express orders.

The amount due to you for the quarter ending the 30th inst. is £495 for which you may value as if it was at your credit but as we have not yet received it from Government we cannot regularly make the distribution in our books.

C 66   A. MACDONALD[44] TO JOHN S. CARTWRIGHT
Kingston, 11 October 1841
[*QUA, J.S. Cartwright Papers, v. 3*]

I communicated the contents of your favor from Prescott, to the Board

---

[43]Robert Gillespie (1785–1863), merchant and businessman, was a partner in a large mercantile house centred in Montreal.

[44]A. Macdonald was probably assistant cashier for the Commercial Bank at Kingston.

this morning, which there was a tolerably full meeting, most fortunately, as the Montreal Bank, has come down upon us in the most determined manner; Mr. Gunn[45] from Montreal is here & has presented between Thirty eight & Thirty-nine Thousand pounds of our paper, for which he demands, Specie, Exchange on London @ 9% or a Dft on Montreal at par, payable in Dollars & Halves – of course we decided upon giving him Specie & are Keeping him amused counting 1/. & 6 of British Silver, until we can obtain a supply from some where as we have here only *£38000* in the Vault. The Hon. John Hamilton[46] has Kindly anticipated his Journey to Montreal, & goes down tomorrow in hopes to meet Mr. Harper there, who will most probably return home without delay, and bring with him some means from Montreal Agency – should he not effect any Kind of settlement with Mr. Holmes, which I have advised him to try, through the medium of a third party. Mr. J.A. Macdonald[47] had gone up to Toronto to see if Mr. Cameron[48] can procure a loan from the Bank of U.C. – in the mean time, Mr. Edie[49] has received & counted *£2000* of the paper, and managed to count out *£625* of Specie in return, in conjunction with his current Duties, as we are now so weak handed, that I could not Spare anyone from the Desks to assist him. – He thinks he will manage to make them up the remainder of the £2000 tomorrow – Mr. Gunn politely offered to procure persons to assist us in counting the Specie, which I as politely declined, as it is my desire to Keep him amused until Mr. Harpers' return or until I hear from him –. Mr. Patton[50] has been here with Mr. Gunn, & threatened all sorts of things, which I calmly told them I must submit to, and when a formal demand was made today at 3 o'Clock for the full amount of paper exhibited in bulk, I quickly replied that the specie should be paid to them as fast as the Teller could count it, That during the Cashiers absence, I could not allow a particle of Specie to go out of the Vault (which was temporarily my charge) without its being faithfully counted

. . . .

---

[45]William Gunn was a senior employee with the Bank of Montreal.

[46]John Hamilton (1802–82) born at Queenston, Upper Canada, was active in a shipping and forwarding business on the Great Lakes and St. Lawrence canal system. He became president of the Commercial Bank in 1847.

[47]John A. Macdonald (1815–91) at this stage in his career was a lawyer and businessman in Kingston. He worked for the Commercial Bank and other Kingston concerns.

[48]John Cameron (d. 1867) was cashier for the Commercial Bank at Toronto from 1833 to 1855 when he resigned to set up business as a private banker.

[49]Mr. Edie was an employee of the Commercial Bank at Kingston.

[50]John Patton, was, in 1841, agent for the Bank of Montreal at Kingston.

C 67   C.C. FERRIE[51] TO JOHN H. DUNN
Hamilton, 12 November 1841
[*PAC, RG 19 B2A, v. 1141*]

I would feel obliged if you would inform me whether it is likely that anything will be done this winter or when, in the way of Public improvements. Should the Government wish to negotiate with the Chartered Banks for the necessary funds, the Directors of the Gore Bank (of which I am President) are disposed to supply money for the Improvements in this District (and probably in other Districts west of this), to a reasonable extent, and on terms not inconsistent with the interest of the Bank – say for the Burlington Canal, the Macadamized roads, and the Plank road to Port Dover. If we knew when the works would be likely to commence and what would likely be required, we might regulate the business of the Bank with a view to meeting the wishes of the Government as far as possible . . . .

Should nothing be done immediately I hope at all events that the Gore Bank will not be overlooked when Govt may be negociating with the other *larger* Institutions. The Gore Bank has Agencies in different places to the west by means of which operations might be facilitated.

C 68   W.H. MERRITT TO WILLIAM PROUDFOOT
St. Catharines, 12 November 1841
[*PAO, Samuel Street Papers, v. 3*]

I have the honor to acknowledge the receipt of the letter addressed to me by the president of the Bank of Upper Canada on the 4 Inst. apprising me that the institution would decline pledging itself to the negotiation of any stated amount of the loan required by the Welland Canal Company to carry on their operation . . . .

From the length of time this Company has confined their Business to your Bank I regret the Directors consider its continuance of so little value. Any Institution would gladly make this loan for the Company Account – large sums are collected monthly & paid out. The exchange of paper alone is no inconsiderable Sum I hope the Directors will take the proposal of the company again into consideration before compelling us to make an application in another quarter. I wish your answer before summoning a Board to make the above proposition.

The Contractors are this moment erecting Shanties and the Government are determined the work should proceed; therefore I hope your Board on reconsideration will feel it their interest to aid us in the indispensable improvement.

---

[51]Colin Campbell Ferrie (1808–56), an important Hamilton merchant, was mayor of Hamilton in 1846 and president of the Gore bank in 1847.

C 69   T.G. Ridout to H. Sherwood
Toronto, 12 March 1842
[*TCA, Toronto City Council Papers*]

. . . the loan required by you . . . for the Public service of this City, and the securities offered, having been taken into mature consideration it was unanimously resolved "That the expiration of the Bank charter in the year 1848 and the present unsettled state of the Currency of the Country, are insuperable objections to any further credits from this institution in favour of the City Corporation or for entertaining the proposition made by the mayor on the 8 inst." I beg leave therefore to communicate the same for your information and regret that it was not deemed advisable to comply with your proposal for a new City Loan.

C 70   John S. Cartwright to Sir Charles Bagot[52]
Kingston, 16 April 1842
[*PAC, A. Shortt Papers, v. 10*]

. . . I must trouble Your Excellency with a few remarks to shew why the present period is unfavourable for changing the existing order of monetary matters, until the Spring business is over –

The Geographical portion of Western Canada (excluded as they are from the ocean) is such that Montreal and Quebec are its Ports, and its business centers in those emporiums, the nature of that business requires, that the Banks in Upper Canada should during the winter give extended credits. The Capitalists of Montreal or Quebec grant letters of Credit to individuals in Upper Canada engaged in the purchase of produce, which credits are drawn for thro' the Banks, chiefly in the Months of December and January, it being generally stipulated that the produce purchased by these means shall be in the Market where the drafts mature, and from the length of the winter and nonarrival of the Spring fleet at Quebec the produce does not reach the market before the middle of June. – As this business enables the agriculturist to obtain a remunerating price, and promotes a wholesome and active business, it has uniformly been the practice of the Banks to encourage it, as in addition to the impetus given to the legitimate trade of the Country, it enables them to procure Exchange on England and thus supply the importers of Western Canada who would otherwise be unable to carry on their business, but would be compelled to buy at second hand from importers at Quebec and Montreal. – The produce in reaching market is usually sold at a credit of three months, and by this pap&r (which is discounted by the Banks of Eastern Canada) the acceptances from Upper Canada are paid but if this accommodation is withheld serious results must follow. – It has been communicated to the writer, that in

[52]Sir Charles Bagot (1781–1843) was governor general of the United Province, 1841-43.

consequence of information received by the Bank of Montreal, that the Currency Bill had been sanctioned by Her Majesty's Government, that Institution had or was about to withhold their usual accommodation, and as it has a Capital more than double any other Bank, and necessarily exercises a proportionate influence other institutions will be compelled to adopt a similar course. –

I am induced to suggest to Your Excellency the propriety of delaying the Proclamation (should the Bill arrive sooner) until about the 1st of July when the Spring business will be over.

1st Because the moment the Bill is sanctioned and promulgated all Banks must withhold accommodation as a run must follow from holders of Bank Notes, particularly in the United States, who will realise a profit of no inconsiderable amount by the change. –

2nd Because by withholding discounts, the Merchants would be paralized and the spring trade interrupted, – the sale of Produce from Western Canada now in transitu almost prevented. –

3rd Because should the Banks in Lower Canada at this particular period withhold the usual accommodation, whereby the holders of produce will be unable to realise, numerous Bankruptcies must follow. –

4 Because the uncertainty of the Bill's being sanctioned, the operations of the Trade being based on the existing Law – it being impossible to carry on business so as to meet with the existing and contemplated act. –

5 Because the Banks will not be able to loan the necessary sums required by Government, to enable them to carry on the Public Improvements. –

C 71   PETER BUCHANAN TO ISAAC BUCHANAN
New York, 25 April 1842
[*PAC, Buchanan Papers, v. 13, p. 11562*]

. . . The Banks have got into a perfect panic about this new Currency Bill and they will do nothing until they see what effect its opperation will have upon their circulation. T.G. Ridout told me that he was satisfied Three Hundred Thousand [us?] at least would be taken out of circulation or rather that that amt. of Notes wld be taken out of circulation and replaced by gold or silver and which will either find its way to the States or be hoarded fast by the farmers. If this opinion of his is borne out to one half the extent it will make a great difference in the Amount of our results and will opperate most unfavorably upon the general Trade of the Country . . . .

C 72   CURRENCY LAW AND THE BANKS
[*Montreal* Transcript, *5 May 1842 (copy), in PAC, A. Shortt Papers,
v. 10*]

We are now in a state of transition from a system which permitted an almost unrestricted issue of bank paper – to one which will force the banking institutions to watch, with a guarded vigilance, the extent of their liabilities.

They cannot, as in former days, arrange their balances by a transfer of French Crowns; neither can they defeat the intentions of the merchant desirous of placing funds in New York or England, by tendering to him that coin.

They will seek, as their customers, those whose wants do not compel them to resort to such resources; and the line of discount must be influenced by a constant reference to the state of the vault.

Cash has been scarce during the past month; but this contraction in the money market arises from the anxiety of the Banks to call in their issues, and thus place themselves upon a secure footing to meet the demands of those who hold their notes . . . .

C 73   John H. Dunn to R.W. Rawson[53]
RGO, 5 October 1842
[*PAC, RG 19 B2b, v. 1174*]

In reply to your letter of the 4th inst. on the subject of the amount of Bills drawn upon Her Majesty's Government in anticipation of the Loan guaranteed by the Imperial Parliament for the uses of this Colony I have the Honour to state – I understood that the measure was adopted to repay to the Bank advances made by them to the local Government and that they were exceedingly anxious to be repaid; it was also a matter of great consideration to do so, in consequence of the distress felt by the Commercial community complaining of a want of accommodation from the Banks and that the Government having borrowed so much of the Banking Capital produced much of this great inconvenience.

. . . and immediate additional funds will be required to enable the Government to carry on the public works, further Drafts in England will be necessary or recurrence again on the Banks for a Temporary Loan a species of accommodation that I cannot omit to state is advisable should be avoided as much as possible – When accommodation is afforded by the Bank, they insist on certain restrictions as to circulation and payment of their Paper which is found to be exceedingly inconvenient and it is not advisable for Government to employ Banking capital which more or less deprives the commercial community of that accommodation.

C 74   T.G. Ridout to Robert Baldwin
Toronto, 4 January 1843
[*MTL, Robert Baldwin Papers*]

The good of the Public Service as well as my wish to promote the

[53]R.W. Rawson was the civil secretary.

interests of an old friend and reformer induces me to recommend to your patronage Elias P. Smith[54] of Port Hope for the office of Crown Lands Agent for the Newcastle District. He is a zealous discreet and firm reformer – so is his Father John D. Smith,[55] the principal proprietor at Port Hope.

Mr. E.P. Smith has been agent for this Bank since 1832 and has given great satisfaction. He is not engaged in trade and is in good circumstances. I am sure that he will make a valuable servant to the Government . . . .

C 75   JAMES E. SMALL[56] TO ROBERT BALDWIN
17 February 1843
[MTL, Robert Baldwin Papers]

. . . The Cashier of the U.C. Bank is anxious to know whether Elias G. Smith has been appointed Crown Land agent for the Newcastle District & why it is that *he himself* is not considered worthy of a School Commissionership or Comm' of Lunatic Asylum he says he thinks *he* is entitled to some *place of honour*, under the present Government he does not want *emolument* . . . .

C 76   T.G. RIDOUT TO G. SHERWOOD[57]
Toronto, 23 March 1843
[TCA, Toronto City Council Papers]

I have the honour to acknowledge the receipt of your letter dated 15 instant stating that the Common Council of this City is desirous to obtain a loan of £50,000 sterling, in order to pay off their outstanding liabilities and to enable them to proceed with further City improvements, also stating that in the meantime & until such object can be effected they will require an advance of £2000 or £3000 to commence their intended works early this spring; – and having laid the same before the Board yesterday, I am instructed to inform you, that this Bank will decline any further advances or engagements with the corporation of this City – until an act of the Legislature shall be passed to authorize the loan now required; and that it shall also be enacted, that no further debt shall be contracted until the former shall be paid off; and likewise to prohibit the issue of corporation notes for the future[58] – it is also

---

[54]Elias P. Smith was a merchant and distiller in Port Hope and son of John D. Smith.

[55]John D. Smith, a merchant and trader, was born in New York and in 1792 founded the settlement of Port Hope. He represented Durham in the 1820s in the Legislative Assembly.

[56]James Edward Small (d. 1869) was a reformer and in 1849 county judge of Middlesex.

[57]This likely refers to Henry Sherwood who was mayor at the time.

[58]During the suspension of specie payments by the banks in the late 1830s, Toronto and other municipalities began to print their own notes for local circulation.

required, that the act shall define the property to be given in security for the said loan, and the period of time for which the new debt may be contracted – and that out of the first proceeds thereof the old Debt shall be liquidated. All which being satisfactorily accomplished this Bank will then be ready and willing to lend its aid in obtaining the said Loan, either in this Province or in England, on the most advantageous terms that can be procured for the benefit and care of the City of Toronto.

C 77   B.W. Smith[59] to Robert Baldwin
Barrie, 25 May 1843
[MTL, Robert Baldwin Papers]

. . . [I am involved in a dispute over the raising of money] and as the case is in the hands of Gamble and Boulton,[60] who have taken the pains to acquaint the Bank of U.C. I do not get the usual accommodation there, and I fear some of the Directors as well as the Bank Solicitor and Partner would be but too happy if they could oust the new Shff. [Sheriff] and therefore I do not expect any lenity at their hands . . . . Will you be writing to Mr. Ridout, BUC, if so, tell him to do what my dealings with the Bank for 12 years would justify him in doing . . . .

C 78   T.G. Ridout to H. Sherwood
Toronto, 18 September 1843
[TCA, Toronto City Council Papers]

I have the honor to acknowledge the receipt of your letter of the 31 ult. in which you request to know if it would be convenient for this Bank to negotiate a loan with the City Corporation for Twenty thousand pounds, on debentures for ten years, secured by Mortgage on the Market Block and a certain number of water lots the property of the corporation, and having laid the same before the Board – I am directed to inform you that it would have afforded the Board much gratification to have met your wishes on this subject as it would have enabled the corporation to have paid off the previous mortgage of £12240 on their property now due, which is held by this Bank; but that understanding that William Cawthra Esq. was lately in treaty with you for this very loan, the Board declined to interfere as they have no doubt that a beneficial arrangement for the City can yet be made with Mr. Cawthra for the whole sum required which I am told is £30,000 Cy.

---

[59]B.W. Smith (d. 1875), born in Upper Canada, was a merchant in Barrie and from 1842–75 sheriff of the Simcoe District.

[60]This refers to the firm of Clarke Gamble and William Henry Boulton, solicitors for the Bank of Upper Canada.

C 79   CIRCULAR, EXECUTIVE COUNCIL OFFICE
Kingston, 29 December 1843
[*PAC, RG 19 B2A, v. 1143*]

Notice is hereby given, that all persons who have to pay Monies to the Receiver General of this Province, on any Public Account whatsoever, are required henceforth to deposit the same in that part of this Province formerly Upper Canada, in the Bank of Upper Canada, in the City of Toronto, or in the Commercial Bank of the Midland District, in the Town of Kingston, or in the Gore Bank, in the Town of Hamilton; and if in that part of this Province formerly Lower Canada, then in the Bank of Montreal, in the City of Montreal, or in the Bank of Quebec, in the City of Quebec, to the Credit of the *Receiver General's Department*. Such Persons are also required to obtain from the Bank with whom any such deposits shall be made, duplicate receipts or acknowledgements thereof, signed by the Cashier or Teller of such Bank; one of which must be transmitted forthwith to the Receiver General of this Province, on receipt whereof a proper discharge countersigned by the Inspector General of Accounts will be transmitted to the person making such deposit.

C 80   A. STEVEN TO B. TURQUAND
Hamilton, 11 May 1844
[*PAC, RG 19 B2A, v. 1144*]

I was duly favoured with your letter of May 20 ultimo in reply to mine on the Subject of Exchange in England, and, I assure you this reply was any thing but satisfactory to the President and Directors, as they cannot understand why this Bank's offer for £10,000 Stg. at one per cent prem was refused, and the Bank of U. Canada and the Commercial Banks Each got £50 000 Stg. at same rate, and that enabled the Commercial Bank who has an office here to sell your dfts at much less than others, and to supply these Merchants who formerly got their Bills from us which is I assure you a serious loss and has a tendency to induce the public to think that there is some good reason why the Gore Bank was not treated as well as the other Banks of this Province.

I trust that you will bear this in mind when the Government notify the Banks of their intention to sell Exchange on England again.

C 81   W. MORRIS TO D. DALY[61]
Montreal, 11 September 1844
[*PAC, RG 19 B2b, v. 1174*]

The Public Moneys now deposited in the several Banks are in some instances permitted to remain for considerable periods to the great advantage of those Banks and I am given to understand that were the

[61]Dominick Daly was provincial secretary.

sums remaining transferred to certain of these Institutions that the Managers thereof would be willing to allow to the Province a rate of interest upon the principle of a Daily Cash Account.

If this Plan were adopted no change as to the number of Banks now authorized to receive Deposits from the various officers employed to collect the revenue need be made, but this Department would require to transfer the funds from those Banks to that with which the arrangement is made for the Payment of Interest on deposits.

Should this measure be approved of, I would not recommend that any bank with a small capital be selected for the keeping of such an Account with the public . . . .

C 82   T.G. RIDOUT TO JOHN S. CARTWRIGHT
Toronto, 19 September 1844
[PAO, J.S. Cartwright Papers]

I have received your letter of the 14th inst. and am much grieved to learn that your health has become so much impaired as you describe it to be but I hope that Providence will be merciful to you and grant you yet many happy years and prolong your days for the sake of your dear Family. The admirable state of your mind on this occasion command the respect of all your friends and I feel myself bound by those sentiments and by our old acquaintances to do everything that I am able or that I can think of to contribute towards fulfilling your wishes in the settlement of your affairs.

The Board has consented to accept the lands you offer in payment of the £1250 debt but there remains that bill of Burnetts for £600 – still unpaid for which we await your offer.

Your letter of the 17th inst. arrived yesterday after the Board adjourned but I do not think that it made any difference, as they seemed well satisfied with your first offer, indeed I hope that if there remains any surplus after making sales thereof within three years from this date, it will be paid over to you or your family, the directors are liberally disposed that way – and they will endeavour to make sales to the best advantage with that object in view.

You can have your Deed made out and executed as soon as you please – so as to have the first matter settled, and let us hear from you on the Burnet affair.

The losses that you have met with are enough to try the health and temper of any man.

C 83   WILLIAM PROUDFOOT TO LT.-GENERAL CATHCART[62] (COPY)
28 March 1846
[PAC, Executive Council Papers, 1846, in PAC, Shortt Papers, v. 5]

. . . the Tax of one per Cent per annum imposed in the year 1841, upon

[62]Charles Murray, Second Earl Cathcart was governor general of the United Canadas, 1846–47.

the circulating paper of the Banks of this Province, has been found most oppressive to the stockholders, most injurious to them in depreciating the value of their property and in reducing the amount of their profits, and it has also had a material effect in preventing the further investment of money in Banking Capital.

That this Tax has amounted to the enormous proportion of one twelfth of the whole realized profits of some of the Banks, and will have the effect of reducing their dividends even in times of commercial ease and prosperity to the common interest of money, consequently money holders will not make investments in Banking Capital, subject to the risques, losses, and fluctuations of Commerce if they are only to realize common interest.

That it is by means of the creation of a surplus fund in prosperous times, that moneyed corporations are enabled to sustain reverses in trade, without danger or injury to credit, and without loss of Capital Stock, and that therefore a tax which absorbs the profits from which a surplus fund might be created, is not only permanently injurious to the Banks but subversive of the confidence which stockholders should always be enabled to entertain, in the safety under any circumstances of the whole money invested in Capital Stock.

That while no other Income Tax is levied in the country, any tax upon the Income of Bank Stockholders, is contrary to every principle of justice, and unless the existence of Banks, can be proved to be a public evil, such a Tax is contrary to every sound maxim of expediency.

That the Tax as it at present exists, amounting to about one twelfth of the profits of the Banks, is moreover excessive, and even if the necessities of the Government required a general income Tax, Your Petitioners are convinced that it would never be placed at such an extravagant and ruinous rate.

Your Petitioners therefore humbly pray that your Excellency will be graciously pleased to concur in a bill to repeal this unequal and oppressive tax or if such a measure should not be found at present practicable, to reduce the amount of taxation within more reasonable limits . . . .

C 84   Larratt Smith[63] to his Father[64] (copy)
Toronto, 11 January 1848
[*MTL, Larratt Smith Papers*]

. . . The Banks are all right and I think will not be affected, although any attempt on their part to enforce payments, would cause a crisis, and a general smash throughout the Province – They seem to be following a

---

[63]Larratt William Violett Smith (1820–1905) arrived with his parents at Toronto from his native England in 1833. He became a lawyer and general financier. He was director of the Bank of Upper Canada, 1864–65.

[64]Captain Larratt Hillary Smith (1782–1860), was a half-pay British army officer.

prudent course, and are sustaining their customers, . . . in all cases (although not discounting) where the parties are undoubted – If I could only have got hold of your £500, I could have made a good thing out of it for you – I can buy B.U.C. Stock, less the Dividend, for I dare say, 5 or 6 Discount *at least* . . . .

C 85   S.P. Jarvis to S.P. Jarvis, Jr.
Toronto, 11 April 1848
[*PAO, Jarvis-Powell Papers*]

. . . Since you left us the firm of Gamble and Boulton have met with great reverses. Their Bookkeeper, "Mr. Williamson" almost a month ago, absconded, leaving behind him a large default. Mr. Gamble pursued him into the U.S. and altho' he overtook a part of his family he could obtain no tiding of the culprit himself, and so he returned. Mr Gamble being the Solr. to the B. of U.C. an investigation of course immediately took place to ascertain if any of the money collected for the Bank had been abstracted when it was discovered that a considerable sum was deficient, and that the books had been thrown into confusion by false entries to make them balance.

This led to an investigation of the liabilities of Gamble and Boulton and of William Boulton and Clark Gamble – individually inconnected with the firm when it was found that their indebtedness, in the several Banks, amounted to about forty or fifty thousand pounds. The consequences have been that they have made an assignment of all their property to trustees for the benefit of their creditors. Whether this property, which at a fair valuation appears to be Sufficient, to cover the amount of their indebtedness can be converted into money is very doubtful, and if a forced sale of it takes place they will not pay 10 shillings in the pound. It is a disastrous piece of business not only for themselves, but for many others' – respectable tradesmen and Mechanic's whose names are on their paper, and who in the present depressed state of the Monetary affairs of the Province, cannot pay and will be thrown into Bankruptcy. Storm[65] the builder has already gone into bankruptcy, and Ritchey[66] will have great difficulty keeping his head above water . . . .

C 86   Larratt Smith to his Father (copy)
Toronto, 22 April 1848
[*MTL, Larratt Smith Papers*]

. . . I think that our Banks are unquestionably safe, & that no better investments are held out than the purchase of Stock. I shall invest about

[65]William George Storm (1826–92) became a partner with F.C. Cumberland in an architectural firm from 1850 to 1866.
[66]John Ritchey had been a carpenter and builder in Toronto since at least 1830.

£250 in U.C. Bank Stock from 3 to 4 discount . . . And what do you
think of the failure of Gamble & Boulton, they are completely smashed
having liabilities to £50,000 & upwards, Wm Boulton owing the Bank
of U.C. on his own paper £16000, this had been going on for years past
but on a most . . . footing being in fact not on their legitimate business,
but upon business which the Bank Directors most culpably allowed
them, They got only over this largely, but have . . . several parties in
"town" & seriously injured many others, & poor Spragge[67] amongst
others is liable upon their paper for accommodation only £1600!
Ridley[68] the builder for £3000 – James McDonell[69] about £2000 –
Wadsworth[70] & Wilson[71] together £7000 – Cayley[72] & a host of others
for sums more or less, they attribute this indisposition to their Bookkeeper Williamson clearing out, a defaulter to £3000, but this is all
fudge – The lawyers in this place are without exception, the most
greedy set of men in it, & all more or less involved . . . John Gamble[73]
is ruined & . . . – he was concerned with Gamble & Boulton – all these
large firms here have either failed or been the next thing to it – Ross
Mitchell & Co,[74] Thos Clarkson & Co.,[75] & Thorne & Parsons[76] among
the principal. . . . Poor old Col Loring[77] is dead & buried, his illness
was sudden & soon terminated in his decease. He had £12000 of Fine
Stock alone, so Proudfoot told me, the bulk of his stock being in the
Bank of Upper Canada . . . .

C 87   LARRATT SMITH TO HIS FATHER (COPY)
Toronto, 5 May 1848
[*MTL, Larratt Smith Papers*]

. . . There is a good deal of Bank Stock in the market just now,
especially of the U.C. Bank, I know of £1500 – The fact of Gamble &

---

[67]Joseph Spragge (1775–1848) was a schoolteacher and general financier.
[68]This probably refers to John Ritchey.
[69]James McDonell was a merchant in Toronto.
[70]William Rein Wadsworth (1803–90) was a miller in the Weston area near Toronto.
[71]This may refer to Adam Wilson (1814–91), a prominent Toronto lawyer.
[72]William Cayley (1807–90) arrived in Upper Canada from England around 1838.
He was a lawyer, politician and general businessman. He was a director of the Bank of
Upper Canada in 1839–43 and 1845–47. In 1859 he was appointed assistant manager
and for several months in 1861 was acting president. In 1857 he owned eighty shares in
the Bank of Upper Canada. In 1860 he owned fifteen.
[73]John William Gamble (1799–1873) was a politician and manufacturer. He operated a grist and flour mill, sawmill, distillery and cloth factory in Vaughan Township
outside Toronto. He was Clarke Gamble's brother.
[74]Ross Mitchell & Company was a wholesale drygoods business operating in
Toronto. It failed in 1857.
[75]Thomas Clarkson & Company was a Toronto grain company which failed in 1857.
[76]Thorne and Parsons were millers and wholesalers in Thornhill.
[77]Robert Roberts Loring (1790?–1848) was a half-pay officer at Toronto. He was a
director of the Bank of Upper Canada from 1845–47.

Boulton's large liability to the Bank, & the great mismanagement attributable to the Directors is the main cause depression of the Stock, added of course to losses on a/c of Thorne & Co – . . . The advertisement you allude to about the Bank of B.N.A. is a very old one, & only continued because the party has not withdrawn it – This Bank is the first institution in this country, & governs all the other Banks, at the same time being the most liberal by far to it's investors . . . . It just occurs to me what arrangement you could make to get your funds home at a great saving, & this is what Cassels[78] has done with the Banks. Dispose of your stock, at the best price you can, then come upon the banks for specie, & as the amounts are very large, they will gladly give you exchange upon New York at 1 or 1$^{1}/_{2}$ at farthest to get rid of you, where you can buy at a very reduced rate – In Cassels case, he works the other banks in this way – Their circulation is tremendous, the Yankees pick up their paper & demand specie & they, to get rid of this, give them Bills on New York almost at par which they sell to Cassels for 2 per cent & he retails again to his customers at 3$^{1}/_{2}$ per cent which is the present rate – It has been as high as 5 this summer, which accounts for the disproportion in the rate between this place & New York for Bills on England – However Cassels can manage it for you, if you only come out, & will save you your expenses in the bargain, which if left to me & I have to buy Bills here must all be sunk. If you cannot manage by exchange, then get specie & take it with you – The banks will make you take American silver, as they do not keep gold & never pay large sums in gold . . . .

C 88   W. HEYDEN[79] TO ROBERT BALDWIN
Toronto, 17 May 1848
[MTL, Robert Baldwin Papers]

. . . It appears that it was humbug about the Chief Justice, Macaulay etc. giving security for the amt. due by Gamble & Boulton to the Bank as Bank Solicitors. Security has not been given neither has it been offered. When will the people here cease to be pulled by this party or compact . . . .

C 89   W. HEYDEN TO ROBERT BALDWIN
Toronto, 22 May 1848
[MTL, Robert Baldwin Papers]

I have just been at the Bank. Ridout gave me the enclosed for you to sign. It appears that an effort is being made to make *William Cayley* President & I believe to turn out Ridout himself. There is a regular civil war in the Bank. The Boultons & Cayleys are trying to [die game?] at all events. Cayley it is said is entirely insolvent . . . .

[78]Walter Cassels was the manager for the Bank of British North America at Toronto. He was a brother of Robert, the cashier of the Bank of Upper Canada in the 1860s.

[79]W. Heyden was a local businessman and friend of the Baldwin family.

C 90   W. HEYDEN TO ROBERT BALDWIN
Toronto, 27 May 1848
[*MTL, Robert Baldwin Papers*]

. . . When you draw do so through the Agency of the Bank of UC. I have the powers of Atty. for Proudfoot received this morning. I don't take as much interest in that matter as I did a few days ago. . . . Gamble has been appointed or rather confirmed in the solicitorship & without any security – for the past defalcation as solicitor it is monstrous, a fraud has been committed on the public by the report emanating from the Bank that good security had been given. I wish your Stock was disposed of at present it is out of question. No purchasers – I do not believe that there was any serious intention of changing the president and cashier. It was a threat . . . .

C 91   W. MACAULAY[80] TO JOHN MACAULAY
Picton, 31 May 1848
[*QUA, J. Macaulay Papers*]

. . . How is it that the BUC stock is at such a discount I suppose that there can be no doubt that there is "something rotten etc" there – for all have been going upon stilts there 20 or 30 years – the bubble must burst one day. I dare say however that this is nothing more than the merchants who are obliged to raise money to meet their payments, selling off at a sacrifice. At present nothing is secure – if you wish money to bring serviceable interest – it must undergo the risque – and if you put it in safe places, as you think – you will not receive anything with regularity. . . .

C 92   WILLIAM PROUDFOOT TO S.P. JARVIS (PRIVATE)
4 June 1848
[*MTL, S.P. Jarvis Papers*]

After Seeing you yesterday there was a meeting at the Bank, to agree about the appointment of new directors to serve at which I urged that you should be put on the list as one but as the others were all opposed to me the meeting broke up without coming to any understanding at which I regret Exceedingly but upon the further Consideration of this matter I am of opinion that it would not be wise in me to go in direct opposition to their views – as the agitation on this matter has already excited too much the attention of the Public. And I think it but fair to advise you that I Shall not be able to put you on my list as a director this year. And having again to Express my regret after having acted together for so many years – but the interests of the Bank are paramount to any other Consideration with me . . . .

[80]Rev. William Macaulay (1794–1874) was an Anglican minister and John Macaulay's brother.

C 93 LARRATT SMITH TO HIS FATHER (COPY)
Toronto, 29 June 1848
[*MTL, Larratt Smith Papers*]

. . . You asked me if I had consulted Cameron or Ridout on the point. They are the last people I should consult, as you may be sure they do not dream to lose you as a Stockholder, & would throw every impediment in the way – I mentioned the matter to Cameron who thinks with myself that it is a bad move to sell out at all – The banks have all with the exception of the Commercial Bank, lost a good deal, by failures – [the] Montreal, losing £120,000 alone, which has brought their stock down from 13 p c to par. The Commercial Bank is considered the best stock in the market just now, they have just declared the usual dividend at $3^{1}/_{2}$, whilst the Montreal gave 3, & the U.C. Bank as you will see in the paper divides only 2 – upon the last half year – I do not think the last Bank has lost much, but it's funds are very much tied up awaiting the wills of two or three estates being wound up & reaping the fruit of that most foolish policy of locking up their funds with two or three large houses, the failure of any of which entails a severe loss, instead of doing a more general business, & getting over a hundred securities all over the country instead of one – Since I last wrote you I have purchased Twenty five more shares in the U.C. Bank Stock @ *5 p c* discount, this with the former purchase investing your £500 in £525 of stock, this will atone for the reduction of the dividend in some measure as you will have 2 p c to receive upon £525 this time in addition to the usual dividend – and I thought moreover that if you were determined to sell out, the best plan would be to make as much as possible, in the first instance to cut off against loss, as the stock will not be lower – There has been a regular turn out in the direction, & only in time to save the Bank I believe from ruin, for if the clique headed by Sam Jarvis had succeeded in getting Sir Allan McNab[81] President & Cayley, Cashier, turning out Proudfoot and ''old Tom'', as they worked hard to do, ruin, utter ruin must have been the result – I worked hard for Proudfoot, & gave him your notes, & many others – You will see by the papers that Sam Jarvis applied to the Court for a mandamus to set the direction vide, which they very properly refused. . . . I can assure you I had a good deal of apprehension for the Bank, from it's unenviable popularity, it's just . . . in allowing Gamble & Boulton £*15000* of discount over the counter, a most shameful transaction, for which the directors ought to be made responsible, or the guilty parties (old Tom & Proudfoot I believe) as the bank will be kept out of it for some time to come if they don't lose it altogether or a great part of it – & this further blow to it's audit, by the disclosure of the fact, that a clique of worthless bankrupts were under . . . to turn out the only responsible parties in the Bank, & help

[81]Allan Napier MacNab (1798–1862) was a politician and general business promoter.

themselves to a further extent, when Cayley cannot now give the Bank security for the £5000 he owes, & Sam Jarvis the £6000 or £7000. . . . As it is all has settled down quietly again, & although the reduction in the usual dividend, has not improved it's stock it has not depreciated it, & certainly commands a better price than hereto fore – The Dividend is payable on the 24th of July – So much for Banking – . . .

C 94   GLYN, MILLS TO T.G. RIDOUT
London, 15 September 1848
[PAC, Glyn, Mills Papers, A540]

. . . we avail ourselves of the present mail to call your attention to the position of the account, which has assumed rather a new feature by remaining so long overdrawn. Refering to your letter of the 30th June, we find you alluding then to the probability of your making early remittances to cover the drafts which you had freely issued by that packet. We think on the whole the prospects of a favorable harvest excepting the potatoe crop, have been well realized and that the demand and trade in the manufacturing districts is increasing. There is no spirit of speculation and though money continue, very abundant yet the price of securities and stocks does not improve.

p.s. 4 o clock . . . the letters per Cambria have just delivered and we are in receipt of yours of the 19th August, but its' contents do not supercede the occasion of the note on the other side.

C 95   GLYN, MILLS TO T.G. RIDOUT
London, 27 October 1848
[PAC, Glyn, Mills Papers, A540]

Allow us to accompany the acknowledgement of the receipt of your note of 7th Inst with the assurance of our entire satisfaction with the general arrangement of the account. The remarks in ours of the 15th ultimo referred to an expression in a former letter from you, coupled with the prolonged use of the credit which did not appear to coincide. We have no wish to alter the mode in which the account has been generally kept or to withdraw the credit. The latter was established as an occassional convenience in the understanding that in banking business it was the exception to the general rule and that the advance which it might involve should be covered by remittances before the maturity of the drafts and as far as possible should not lead to a cash advance . . . .

D. UNDERWRITING STRUCTURAL CHANGE: THE BANK AND THE UNION, 1849–57

D 1 L.M. VIGER[1] TO FRANCIS HINCKS
2 June 1849
[*PAC, RG 19 B2b, v. 1160*]

. . . I regret to say that I have been disappointed as to my obtaining £20,000 stg in England, as referred to in my last –, from the Bank of British North America – and on my application to the Bank of Montreal the reply was "that they were not drawing" – From some cause best known to themselves the Banks seem to look forward to some great change that might affect the Government meeting their engagements, such are my conclusions from Mr. Davidson's[2] remarks and apparent timidity. And I am fully of the opinion that until satisfactory intelligence is received from the Home Government we cannot depend on any further accomodation from the Banking Institutions here: and this may also in some degree be attributed to the knowledge the Banks possess of the state of our Chest.

D 2 T.G. RIDOUT TO FRANCIS HINCKS
Toronto, 8 January 1850
[JLA, *1852, Appendix DD*]

I have the honor to acknowledge the receipt of your letter of the 8th ult., on the subject of the Government Deposit Account, and the several matters therein mentioned have been maturely considered, I am authorized to state in reply as follows: That this Bank is willing to receive without charge the Public Deposits, at all its Agencies throughout Canada, and to replace them to the credit of Government in this City.

That it will pay the Government cheques, at the several Agencies in the same manner as has heretofore been done.

That when Exchange on London shall be required, it will be willing to furnish the same at the lowest Bank rates charged at any of its Offices.

And that should it be required, the Bank will engage to afford the Government an accommodation not exceeding at any time the sum of fifty thousand pounds currency, at the usual rate of interest of six per cent per annum.

---

[1]Louis-Michel Viger (1785–1855) was president of the Banque du Peuple and became receiver general in 1848.

[2]Thomas David Davidson was cashier of the Montreal branch of the Bank of British North America. From 1855–63 he was cashier of the Bank of Montreal.

D 3 PROCEEDINGS IN COUNCIL, 8 JANUARY 1850
[*PAC, RG 1 E8, v. 34*]

The I.G. [Inspector General] has the honour to submit that in consequence of the removal of the Seat of Government to Toronto changes in
the existing arrangements with the Banks which have for some time
back kept the Government account has become necessary and as the
present arrangements were entered into after application had been made
to those banks which were supposed from the amount of their capital
and the number of their branches to be able to work the account
satisfactorily the Inspector General deemed it right to bring the subject
again under the notice of the same Banks to which he had formerly
applied and to invite proposals from each. The Commercial Bank M.D.
have declined making any proposition whatever on the subject. The
Bank of Montreal and Bank of British North America have made a
proposal which is herewith submitted in which with certain modifications they agree to take the account giving the Government a credit to
the extent of £20,000. The Bank of U.C. has also made a proposal
which is in every way most satisfactory & that Bank further proposes to
give the Government credit to the extent of £50,000 when required. The
Inspector General has the honour to recommend that the proposal of the
Bank of U.C. being much the most advantageous to the Government be
agreed to.

D 4 C.E. ANDERSON[3] TO T.G. RIDOUT
Toronto, 19 March 1850
[*PAC, RG 19 B2b, v. 1160*]

I have to acknowledge your respective favours of 15 & 17th Inst.
relative to your Mr. Hinds[4] at Kingston declining to receive some £865
of matured Provincial Debentures –
– In reply I am authorised to state that your explanation is perfectly
satisfactory, in fact your instructions to your Agents are more liberal
than was possibly expected or looked for.
When I brought the matter in question under your notice I did not
understand that it was the Bank of Montreal who had presented the
Debentures in question for payment but some private party; Had I
understood otherwise I should at once have informed Mr. Wilson[5] that
our arrangement with the Bank of Montreal was, that such Debentures
as were redeemed by that Institution were to be Cancelled and forwarded by Mail direct to this Department, where a Check would be
returned in payment thereof such is the course followed by the Parent

[3]C.E. Anderson was deputy receiver general.
[4]Hinds worked in the Bank of Upper Canada at Kingston.
[5]William Wilson was in general charge of the Bank of Montreal's Upper Canadian
business.

Bank and it is to be presumed that the Agencies have Similar instructions. The Same understanding exists and is carried out by the Bank of British North America. It would be exceedingly unfair to allow the Bank of Montreal to call on your Mr Wenham for specie or to be credited with say £5000 or £10,000 of our Debentures, when at the very time perhaps we might have a larger sum at Credit with the Bank of Montreal, or if presented here might be paid by checks on various Institutions. To day for example the Crown Lands are transferring us some £20,000 the larger amount of which are in other Banks than the Bank of U.C. and will of course be first checked out –

– I am therefore authorised both by the Receiver & Inspector General to state that it is entirely at your own option to redeem Debentures when presented by other Banks, or not just as it may suit your convenience . . . .

D 5   JAMES MORRIS[6] TO F. HARPER (COPY)
Toronto, 30 May 1850
[PAO, Letter of Morris to Stockholders of the Commercial Bank, 1850, p. 10]

. . . This morning I again alluded to our getting a share of the Government account, but Mr. Hincks silenced me by saying: "I was most anxious that your friends should have had one-half of the business, but as they declined it I cannot now give that which belongs to another." And I must say that he is right in keeping faith with Ridout. . . .

D 6   JOHN ROSS[7] TO ROBERT BALDWIN
Belleville, 22 July 1850
[MTL, Robert Baldwin Papers]

I have just been told that the British Bank propose to establish a Bank agency here and if so it would be well to forestall them in some way. I do not know better how to do this than by getting the Bank of Upper Canada to carry out their original intention of opening an office in Belleville. The amt. of public money accruing here seems to be rapidly increasing in all the departments more specifically the customs and as the Coml. has been lately endeavouring to *undermine* the U.C. Bank in the matter of their Gov't a/c it has occurred to me that this step might render it a matter of necessity for the latter bank to establish an office. At all events if we can now get the Bank of Upper Canada to open an

---

[6]James Morris worked for the Commercial Bank in Brockville.

[7]John Ross (1818–71) was a Belleville lawyer, politician and businessman. He held public office from 1851–62 and was a director of the Bank of Upper Canada in 1859–60. He owned 102 shares in the Bank in 1860 and fifty shares in 1863. He was president of the Grand Trunk Railway throughout most of the 1850s.

office I think it would prevent the British Bank doing so. No matter which Bank opens an office we shall suffer somewhat unless proper agents be appointed. If you could get Mr. William Hutton appointed the selection would be a most judicious one for the Bank of Upper Canada. W. Hutton was several years warden of the District – has been for two or three years past Supt. of Schools and knows every man in the Dst. [District].

Besides Mr. Hutton would conduct the office without reference to politics and that is what the Bank should desire. If you could further the arrangement which I have suggested it would be a very great thing now and would materially serve the interests of the Bank . . . .

D 7   H.C. BECHER[8] TO COL. THOMAS TALBOT[9]
London, 30 October 1850
[*UWO, Talbot Papers*]

. . . on the 12 Sept. I bought thro. Mr. Ridout 50 shares Bank U.C. Stock for you amounting to £625 at 20 per cent discount – for which therefore I paid £500. On the 27 Sept. I bought 8 shares more at the same price £100 Stock for £80. . . . Mr. Ridout writes me that he has engaged for the purchase of £400 more. . . . I hope by this time twelvemonth to have a large return from Bank Stocks & other Investments for you . . . .

D 8   H.C. BECHER TO G. MACBETH[10]
London, 19 November 1850
[*UWO, Talbot Papers*]

. . . I went to see Mr Ridout while in Toronto but he was at Cobourg. He'll be back when I go down at the end of the week however & I shall then try & invest nearly all of the Colonel's [Talbot] available funds with his [Ridout's] assistance – Bank Stock is rising sadly (for us) & none to be had while I was in Toronto of any amt. B.U.C. last sales 9 per cent discount – Commercial par . . . .

D 9   R.W. HARRIS TO T.C. STREET[11]
Hamilton, 24 December 1850
[*PAC, John Young Letterbook, v. 4*]

Understanding that the application of the Great Western Railway Coy,

[8]Henry Corry Rowley Becher (1817–85) was a lawyer in the London area. He also acted as a general investment agent or broker.

[9]Thomas Talbot (1771–1853) was a financier and large landowner in the London, Upper Canada, area.

[10]George Macbeth (1825–70) was a landowner, general merchant and politician in London, Upper Canada.

[11]Thomas Clark Street (1814–72), son of Samuel Street, was a wealthy lawyer, businessman and politician. Between 1862 and 1868 he was president of the Gore Bank. In 1845, 1847–51, 1853–63 and 1865 he was a director of the Bank of Upper

for an account with the Bank of U. Canada has been laid over for further consideration, waiting your presence at the Board of Directors. I think it well to inform you . . . [re] the nature of the account asked for . . . .

In September last the G.W. Coy [Great Western Railway] applied to the Bank of Montreal for an advance on the Debentures of Municipalities taking stock in the Rail Road Coy and the Dirĕctors of that institution offered to advance £20,000 cy., but which sum was considered insufficient for the wants of the Company and at the time this offer was received Mr. Hincks represented to the Directors of the Great Western that the Bank of Upper Canada could advance the amount required, on better terms than any other Bank in the Province, that their opportunities for working off debentures was better than any other institution and that under existing circumstances the account would be of importance to the Bank. An application was, therefore, made asking the Bank to advance say to the extent of 80% on said debentures being at same time empowered to sell 90% or over as opportunities afford – that the advances at any time should not exceed £50,000 cy. that the entire account should be kept with the Bank & its agencies and no interest on deposit expected so long as the Bank remains in advance, that if under unforeseen circumstances the account was not active enough for the Bank and that advances had remained uncovered for a particular time to be agreed upon (say a year) the Bank to be authorized to realize the amount of their advances out of the debentures on hand at such prices as they would bring . . . .

D 10   T.G. Ridout to E.P. Taché[12]
Toronto, 15 May 1851
[*PAC, RG 1 E7, v. 36*]

I have the honor to acknowledge the receipt of your letter of yesterday's date in which you are pleased to enquire on what terms this Bank will engage to pay the Dividends on the Canada Bonds falling due in London at various periods of the year, at the Bank of England, and at the offices of Messrs Baring Brothers & Co. and of Messrs. Glyn Mills & Co. all which having been taken into respectful consideration – I am directed to inform you in reply, that this Bank will undertake to make those payments to the above parties – at such times, and for Sums, as you may direct, taking their receipt for the Same, and that on producing those Vouchers to your Satisfaction you will cause a Warrant to be issued in favor of this Bank, for the full amount thereof at a rate of Exchange one half of one per cent above the current rate at New York, at the period, that the advices of payments are received here.

Canada. He owned 800 shares in the Bank of Upper Canada in 1857 and 1,175 shares in 1865.

[12]Sir Étienne-Paschal Taché (1795–1865) was receiver general from 1849 to 1856.

I have further to State, that in order to meet your wishes at the present time, I have this day instructed Messrs. Glyn & Co. to pay over on the 30th day of June next, the undermentioned Sums of money, to meet the Dividends due on Canada Bonds in London, on the 1st day of July ensuing.

Viz.

To the Bank of England	£20.000–
To Baring Brothers & Co.	11.858..13..3
To Glyn Mills & Co.	15.242..5..11
In all	£47.200..19..2 Sterling

To Same to be accounted for, according to the foregoing Arrangement proposed.

D 11   JOHN YOUNG[13] TO WILLIAM PROUDFOOT
Hamilton, 3 November 1851
[*PAC, John Young Letterbook, v. 4*]

. . . I would premise that the simple understanding between you & Mr Ridout on the part of the Bank, and Mr Harris the President on the part of the Company, was that the Bank agreed to advance to the Company £60,000 at a rate not exceeding £10,000 per month and that the money so advanced would be repaid to the Bank within [a few?] months out of the first Government Debentures to which the Company would be entitled under the Guarantee Act – the loan in fact enabling the Company to *anticipate* the proceeds of those Debentures, and to push forward the Works in such a manner as would entitle [them to it from?] Government and earlier than would otherwise be the Case . . . .

D 12   BANKS, THE COMMERCIAL COMMUNITY AND THE
GOVERNMENT
[*Montreal* Transcript, *23 December 1851, cited in PAC, A. Shortt Papers, v. 3*]

. . . We buy without the means of purchasing. – The importing merchant goes to the banks with the bills in his favour of country customers, expecting discounts, to be employed in purchasing exchange to remit to his correspondents at home or abroad. The banks here usually employ their whole capital and deposits in discounts, with the needful and prudent reserves. If they are to grant any more, it must be against funds realised from the sale of produce, of the bills drawn against which they are the purchasers or negociators. More than this they cannot do. Neither private individual, nor bank, can grant

---

[13]John Young (1808–73) was a merchant, business promoter and manufacturer at Hamilton, Upper Canada. He was active for a time in the Buchanan, Harris business and was a prominent promoter of the Great Western Railway.

exchange worth buying, without having funds to draw against. If they discount more than their capital, their notes come in upon them, and they must contract their issues some other way, to say nothing of their means being contracted by an enforced withdrawal of deposits by parties who find them worth more than bank interest. A bank ordinarily calculates on keeping a certain amount of paper out, in proportion to its credit and capital; but, if there is a great demand for exchange, and a diminution, either in amount and price of produce, not merely cannot it enlarge that issue, but it is compelled to diminish it, because it is eagerly sought for for purposes of remittance, and returned as fast as it is issued. There is no truth more certain than that a bank can only lend what it has; and it has nothing but its capital, circulation, deposits, and bills drawn against exports which it puts to the credit of its customers. If the last falls off, the second and third do also. And, in times of pressure, the ability of the banks to discount, is further curtailed by the necessity of increasing their reserves; for they never know in what quarter there may be a large and sudden demand for assistance, which might be dangerous to refuse. We often hear of the heavy losses of banks in sustaining their large customers; much more seldom of what they escape by doing so.

In considering the ability of a bank to make loans, there are two questions totally distinct, but often confounded, – the amount of the funds at its disposal to loan, and the parties to whom it loans them. The former is definite, and quite beyond the power of the bank to extend or to contract. The latter is discretional; and, though it matters little to the public who gets the money, it is life and death to individuals. In times of pressure there are always accusations of favouritism, which may be well founded or not; but banks have often prudential reasons for making large loans in particular quarters which they cannot make public. Their primary business is to support public credit, on which their own stability and profits depend; and, where there is not some obviously sordid motive, it is but fair to presume that they do so to the best of their judgment.

At present, there is no panic, but there is severe pressure. No more, however, than was foreseen, and as much as possible provided against; and if the exporting British houses had known as much of the probable value of Canadian exports here as the Banks, there probably would have been no pressure here in the autumn, and no cry of prosperity in the spring.

The mischief, whatever it is, the Government has done its best to aggravate. By a return moved for by Mr. Mackenzie, commented on some time ago in the *Gazette*, it appears that the Government had, on the 5th June last, just as most of the duties on the spring importations had been paid, deposits, not bearing interest:

| In the Quebec Bank | 1,927 12 9 |
| Bank of Montreal | 1,011 18 11 |

Banque du Peuple	9,944	10	4
Commercial Bank	3,557	2	0
Gore Bank	1,392	9	0
Bank of U. Canada	199,643	1	8
	217,776	14	8

At 3 per cent interest: –

With the Bank of Montreal	£19,666	13	4
With the Peoples Bank	39,083	6	8
With the Commercial Bank	85,166	13	4
With the Bank of Upper Canada	123,333	6	8
	£267,260	0	0[14]

From this it will be seen that the City Bank and the Bank of British North America were totally excluded from the business of the government, while the Bank of Upper Canada has the enormous sum of £323, 276 lent it, a large portion for a long and definite period, the understanding being that when interest is allowed by a bank, it is not pressed hastily for payment. Subsequently, the *Gazette* tells us, the whole of the balance was withdrawn from the Bank of Montreal, which is undeniably the largest institution of the kind in the province.

To understand the full enormity of this transaction, it must be understood, that these sums of money were the result of the payment of duties in checks in the different Banks of Montreal and Quebec, and their agencies, but principally in those two cities. The natural and proper course would have been to have left them in deposit in the Banks on which they were drawn, and again drawn them out in fair proportions as the exigencies of the public service required. Instead of this, almost the whole available surplus is transferred, with the least possible delay, to the Bank of Upper Canada. The effect in deranging the Commercial transactions of the country is obvious. The leading Banks of Lower Canada are, by so much, crippled in their resources, their ordinary discounts diminished to the extent of these extraordinary drafts. The Bank of Upper Canada receives the loan of a very large sum of money, to which it has no pretensions, and, also, benefits largely by the payments of its notes, in exchange for Government drafts. But in addition to this receiving such an extraordinary accession to its funds, it will, of course, employ them; and that it can only do, by extending its discounts, and to this, no doubt, is largely attributable the excessive importation of American goods.

That this transaction is an honest one those may believe who like. No explanation has ever been given of it. But there can be no two opinions, that it is altogether irregular and irrational; that it has seriously crippled the banks of Montreal and Quebec; and, perhaps, in the long run, will do no good to the part of the country where the money was sent to.

[14]See also Table 8.

D 13   C.E. ANDERSON TO A.N. MORIN[15]
Quebec, 17 January 1852
[*PAC, RG 19 B2b, v. 1161*]

In the absence of the Receiver-General I have the honor to report that it being desireable that all Public monies for distribution etc by Public officers should be negotiated through the Bank of Upper Canada . . . . I may add that the Receiver General for various reasons did not consider it politic to write to every public officer to change the Bank with which they kept their a/c, considering that an intimation similar to that given to Mr McDonell would have been sufficient. I may also add that the Bank of U.C. transact such business without charge while the other Banks charge a commission.

D 14   NOAH FREER,[16] ROBERT CASSELS[17] AND WILLIAM GUNN TO
E.P. TACHÉ
Quebec, 19 April 1852
[*JLA, 1852, Appendix DD*]

We would respectfully bring under the notice of yourself and the other Members of Her Majesty's Executive Council, the system at present adopted in collecting the Revenue of this Port.

The duties are paid, in almost every case, by cheques on the different Banks of this City, and these cheques are deposited by the Collector of Customs, in the Quebec Branch of the Bank of Upper Canada, in consequence of which large balances are obtained by that Institution against the other Banks, they requiring to meet these heavy demands with specie.

This operates severely against the Banks and Mercantile community, at a period of the year when increased accommodation becomes necessary and desirable.

To obviate the inconvenience and relieve the Banks and Mercantile community from the severe and injurious pressure caused by the system which now obtains, we would most respectfully suggest, that the Collector of Customs be instructed to deposit in the Banks the cheques which may be drawn on each respectively. Such deposits to be transferred to credit of the Receiver General, and drawn out when required for the Public Service.

[15]Augustin-Norbert Morin (1803–65) between 1851 and 1854 was provincial secretary, commissioner of crown lands and leader of the Lower Canadian section of the Hincks-Morin government.
[16]Noah Freer was a prominent merchant and businessman in Quebec City. He was also the long-time cashier of the Quebec Bank.
[17]Robert Cassels (1815–82) was born in Scotland and arrived in Halifax in 1837 as agent for the Bank of British North America. Over the next twenty-four years he managed branches at Chatham, New Brunswick, Quebec City and Montreal. He was a director of the Grand Trunk Railway, 1858–66, and of the Northern Railway in the 1860s. From 1861 to 1866 he was the Bank of Upper Canada's general manager.

D 15 E.P. TACHÉ TO NOAH FREER, ROBERT CASSELS AND
WILLIAM GUNN
Quebec, 21 April 1852
[JLA, 1852, Appendix DD]

I have the honour to acknowledge your joint communication of 19th instant, complaining of the manner of collecting the Revenue at this Port, by causing the same to be deposited in the Branch of the Bank of Upper Canada here, to the prejudice as you state of the other Banking Institutions.

Having communicated with some of my colleagues on the subject, I am authorized in reply to state, that during the absence of the Inspector General, the government has no intention to change the arrangements made in Toronto, in 1850, regarding the Deposit of the Provincial Revenue; but on the return of Mr. Hincks from Europe, your letter will again be brought under the consideration of the Government.

In the mean time, if I am well informed, I may be allowed to remark, that up to this period the Bank of Upper Canada has very far from invariably exacted specie in payment of the balances due by the other Banks; but on the contrary, has often taken exchange, and has almost invariably left it to the option of the Banks to pay either in specie or exchange on the usual terms.

. Having every reason to believe that the Bank of Upper Canada is not less disposed to act in the same liberal manner this season towards the other Banking Institutions as heretofore has been the case, I very much doubt if the inconveniences you anticipate will be the result under present arrangements, or that they will be so serious as you appear to apprehend.

D 16 E.P. TACHÉ TO NOAH FREER, ROBERT CASSELS
AND WILLIAM GUNN
Quebec, 24 April 1852
[JLA, 1852, Appendix DD]

. . . In answer to your concluding remark, "we are at a loss to understand what is meant by paying in exchange on the usual terms, when no such agreement exists," I have good reason to believe that the Banks in Montreal understand the "usual terms," to be a rate under that at which the Banks are drawing to the public, varying from 1/4 to 1/2 per cent, and I am informed that such has been practised in settling balances with the Bank of Upper Canada here.

D 17 H.N. WALKER[18] TO E. CORNING[19]
Detroit, 12 August 1852
[AI, Corning Papers]

. . . I am in receipt of a letter from the Secy. of the Great Western R.R.

[18]H.N. Walker was a banker and businessman operating from Detroit.

Co. requesting me as their agent to deposit monthly the money collected on Stock for that road with a man by the name of Trew of Windsor who is, I believe, an agent of the Bank of Upper Canada. I do not think it is well for our Bank to have this arrangement for the time will come when the business of the Road will be of importance and the account worth looking after. This beginning is all wrong for us. The agency of the Bank of Upper Canada in fact amounts to nothing now. They have no office worth calling such and no place in which I would ever trust £5000 for 24 hours . . . . The ground upon which Mr. Gilkinson[20] puts the change is that it is more convenient and is less expense to them neither of which it seems to me is tenable. It is certainly as convenient for them to do business with us for their disbursements here amount to much more than their receipts, and as for the expense we can do it as cheap as the Bank at Hamilton. My idea is to open some correspondence with the Bank at Hamilton and see if we cannot act together instead of one trying to get the whole and as you are doubtless acquainted with the officers of the Bank you can commence it better than anyone else . . . .

D 18   E.P. Taché to T.G. Ridout
20 October 1852
[PAC, RG 19 B2b, v. 1161]

. . . On consultation with my colleagues I conceive that it would be desirable that in this instance the Bank of Upper Canada should meet the views of the St. Lawrence & Atlantic Railway Coy. with 60 or 90 days accomodation as the £100,000 transaction referred to will no doubt receive the sanction of the Legislature. I quite however approve of your remark that the Company should be given to understand that the accomodation now granted should form no precedent for the future unless it entirely suited the operations of the Bank.

D 19   T.G. Ridout to Peter Buchanan
Toronto, 29 October 1852
[PAC, Buchanan Papers, v. 52, pp. 41716–17]

. . . In my letter of the 14th Inst I observed that we retained here 1398 shares being the balance of our stock left for sale in this Country – and I have now to inform you that it has since then been subscribed for and paid in full by various parties here. The fact of a transfer to London of the 6000 shares, having caused an immediate demand. There however remain 779 shares subscribed for some time ago on which only 10 per cent has been paid. The remainder viz. 90 per cent is now called in and

---

[19]Erastus Corning was a prominent iron merchant/manufacturer and general financier operating from Albany, New York. He was especially active in railroad matters.
[20]Jasper T. Gilkison (1814–1906) was a general businessman in the Hamilton area. He was at the time secretary for the Great Western Railway.

will be paid in a few months. When that is done, and should your sales be completed, the Capital of the Bank will then reach the extent of its charter namely £500,000 Currency.

I have already stated that £12.10 currency is the value of each share, which computed at the par of 109½ is equal to £10.5.6. Sterling within a small fraction.

It is not desirable that the 6000 shares herein set apart for the English Stock shall remain longer than two or three months in the London market for if not sold by that time – the balance whatever it may be – will be ordered to be re-transferred to this Country.

D 20   T.G. RIDOUT TO ISAAC BUCHANAN AND NOTATION
BY ISAAC BUCHANAN
1 February 1853
[*PAC, Buchanan Papers, v. 52, pp. 41735–7*]

. . . I had intended to go up to Hamilton on Thursday so as to be ready for the railroad meeting on Friday – before I recd your letter. But I am now doubly induced to take the journey – and will accordingly leave by the Boat on Monday morning.

It appears to me that the Hamilton and Toronto Railroad Company are deeply indebted to your brother for the admirable manner in which he has managed their affairs in England. I was of the same opinion from the first and his letter only confirms it. The fact is that he made hay whilst the sun shone and now there is a little cloud over the money market.

I have to thank you and the Directors of the Great Western Railroad for the very handsome preferment that they have been pleased to confer on my son Tom and hope that he will prove himself to be a good and faithful servant . . . .

It is gratifying to find that your brother Peter has selected this Bank – for the new rail road account and I trust that we shall give all concerned every satisfaction.

[Notation by Isaac Buchanan]

This letter is very [uncommittal?] seemed almost written to be shewn. And it was a great object to have him quite satisfied as thro him we can do a great deal . . . .

D 21   T.G. RIDOUT TO ISAAC BUCHANAN
Toronto, 21 February 1853
[*PAC, Buchanan Papers, v. 52, pp. 41751–52*]

. . . I beg now to acknowledge your private letter of the same date and I am puzzled to know what to say respecting the very handsome manner in which you propose to take the 40 shares in my name so as to qualify me to be a Director. I shall of course be ready to give them up at any time that they may be called for and I can undertake to do so as you may direct . . .

D 22   T.G. RIDOUT TO ISAAC BUCHANAN
Toronto, 7 May 1853
[PAC, Buchanan Papers, v. 52, pp. 41773–75]

Since I wrote to you this morning I have made further reference and find that the Bank regularly applied to you on the 7 of May for the account of the London and Sarnia Railway Company and therefore hope that all is right.

I am sure you will be pleased to learn that at the general meeting of our stock holders held yesterday for the annual election of Directors, a Resolution was passed recommending me to the new Board for an increase of salary viz from £750 to £1000 per annum from 1 January last which will be done tomorrow. This is my thirty second year of service as Cashier of this Bank having been appointed 27 January 1822 at £200 per annum.

If you want me to go up to your election on the 10th inst. I believe, please telegraph for me and I will go. If you do not I will go over to the Falls and see my wife and children who have been there for the last fortnight to get rid of the whooping cough which four of the young ones have had since September last.

D 23   GREAT WESTERN RAILROAD/BANK OF UPPER CANADA
RELATIONS
1 October 1853
[PAC, RG 30, 2]

Financial Arrangement

The Managing Director[21] reported that he had made arrangements with the Bank of Upper Canada by which this Co. would be permitted if necessary to overdraw its account to the extent of £150,000 – which was approved of.

D 24   E.P. TACHÉ TO T.G. RIDOUT
Quebec, 8 October 1853
[PAC, RG 19 B2b, v. 1161]

I have the honor to communicate to you for your guidance that between now and the end of the year I shall require to transmit to London on account of the Province for investment in English Consols say £200.000. *Two Hundred Thousands* Pounds Sterling to be paid for Ex

---

[21]Charles John Brydges (1827–89) was manager of the Great Western Railway. He eventually managed the Grand Trunk and the Intercolonial, ending up as land commissioner with the Hudson's Bay Company.

the floating funds of the Province not bearing Interest so far as it is practicable –

– As a matter of course, it will be expected that the Bank of Upper Canada will be prepared to furnish the Exchange on quite as favourable terms as any other public Institution and I would be glad to have your views on the subject as to rate of Exchange and the most favourable period for remittance.

D 25   A. SIMPSON[22] TO GLYN, MILLS (PRIVATE AND CONFIDENTIAL)
Montreal, 24 October 1853
[*PAC, Glyn, Mills Papers, A545*]

In the month of July last, you were kind enough to give me your opinion as to the responsibility of Messr. Peto, Brassey, Betts and Jackson,[23] which was very satisfactory – but as the present tightness in the Money Market in England may possibly interfere very much with their negotiating of Grand Trunk Shares and Bonds, which may inconvenience them, You will confer a particular favor on the Bank by communicating to me confidentially your opinion of their present standing and ability to meet their engagements. You will have perceived by our remittances to your firm that we have negotiated a large amount of Bills on them drawn by persons in their employ on their letters of Credit, and being at 90 dys there is now [remaining?] to maturity upwards of £160,000.

Had matters been going on prosperously as was the case a year ago, I should be under no uneasiness were the amount double of what it is, but as the times look rather squally on your side it is as well that we should look a little ahead.

D 26   E.P. TACHÉ TO T.G. RIDOUT
Quebec, 12 November 1853
[*PAC, RG 19 B2b, v. 1161*]

I have the honor to forward you herewith a statement of the Interest as it falls due upon the Sterling Bonds, shewing the periods, and where the amounts become payable. Some time since a similar statement was furnished you but alterations having been made, it is necessary that you should be again advised.

As heretofore the Interest paid by you upon the Bonds issued on account of the Railroad Companies will be refunded you upon your applying to these Companies respectively – and that paid on Government a/c you will receive in the usual manner . . . .

---

[22]Alexander Simpson was cashier of the Bank of Montreal, 1846–55.

[23]Peto, Brassey, Jackson & Betts was a prominent firm of British railway builders who became the major general contractors of much of the Grand Trunk Railway.

D 27   T.G. Ridout to Glyn, Mills
Toronto, 29 April 1854
[PAC, Glyn, Mills Papers, A542]

. . . I am now happy to inform you that the state of our account with the Great Western Rail way Company has within a few days assumed a better feature – and certain arrangements are now being made that will insure the speedy repayment of our advances to them.

In the first place, besides the £40,000 paid to you on the 13th inst. I remit to you by this mail 5000 shares of their stock for sale, equal to £102,500 Stg. This stock was delivered by the Great W.R.W.Co. to their contractors[24] on settlement of account on the 27 inst. and was transferred by them to me for sale in London out of which I have authority immediately to realize £86,000 retaining whatever balance may be left for future disposal – in making sales thereof I have at the particular desire of the Company and of the contractors to request you will be pleased to consult with their agent Mr. Peter Buchanan and with Messrs. Foster and Braithwaite[25] their brokers who are able and willing to afford you valuable assistance.

Secondly, I attended a meeting of the Great W.R.W.Co. Board of Directors on the 27 inst. when it was unanimously resolved to apply to Government for an immediate issue of £300,000 of the Provincial Guarantee to which they are by Law entitled which will enable them to pay off all their contracts and other debts, and leave them with ample funds in hand to complete their rolling stock, ballasting and other expenses, and this application has been made: and I have no doubt will be granted, as soon as Mr. Hincks arrives, if not before, as their case is of course urgent. They are entitled to receive from Government £800,000 besides the £200,000 they were paid about two years ago, but they only require the £300,000 now applied for, and say that they will not want any more.

In addition to the foregoing, it is expected that other large sums will be shortly paid into your hands by Messrs. Masterman and Co.,[26] or by their agent Mr. Peter Buchanan in the course of next month.

For your information I beg leave to enclose herewith a statement of the daily working receipts of the Great Western Railway. From the 25 of January to the 22 inst. amounting to £72,721 – cy. and these receipts are going on regularly to my knowledge as they pay into our office at Hamilton on an average £1000 per day – and this will be greatly

---

[24]This probably refers to Samuel Zimmerman (1815–57) an active and powerful railway contractor operating in Upper Canada. He was responsible for the construction of much of the Great Western Railway.

[25]Foster and Braithwaite were British financiers who invested in and acted as brokers and agents for the Great Western Railway.

[26]John Masterman & Company was a London investment banking house active in financing the Great Western Railway.

increased when they are properly supplied with Engines and Passenger Cars, as they have worked under great disadvantages during the whole winter for want of a proper stock and the completion of the ballasting. I have lately received a letter from The Hon. Col. Taché The Receiver General stating that in consequence of the unexpected fall in the Consols in which the Government had invested the £200,000 that was remitted to London for them, last autumn: he had been obliged to raise in England on the 1st instant a similar amount to meet the debentures matured on that day, and that it is now found desirable that another large sum should be placed in the hands of his agents in London by the first of July next, so as to disengage the Consols – which will then be placed to the account of the sinking fund. He therefore directs that £75,000 should be paid into your hands on the 1st of June next and a like sum of £75,000 on the first of July following for his acct. I have consequently requested this day that you would be pleased to pay the first sum of £75,000 on the 1st of June intending, in the course of next month to provide for the payment of the like amount due on the 1st of July . . . .

D 28   T.G. Ridout to R.W. Harris
Toronto, 13 June 1854
[*PAC, Buchanan Papers, v. 52, pp. 41786–90*]

I have just received a letter from Quebec from a friend apprizing me that our large advance to the Great Western Rail Way Company would shortly be brought before the Legislature with a view perhaps of depriving us of the Government account. Now this is a very serious matter and unless we can satisfactorily shew how and when that large debt will be liquidated, I fear the consequences will be most injurious to our Interests in every way.

I therefore beg to write confidentially to you to ask you how and when we are to be repaid – or what steps have been taken to reduce the Companys liabilities.

When Peter Buchanan paid in the last £40,000 about a month ago, he wrote to me that another like sum would shortly be paid to Glyn & Co. but nothing more has been done – our last letters being the 26 of May – and Glyn & Co. do not hold out any prospect of any more being likely to be paid in by him.

Last week Mr. Brydges wrote to me requesting the Bank to pay an acceptance of £10,900 that fall due on the 9th being as he said to pay for Locomotives bought in the States. At the same time he informed me that he would shortly have authority to draw a large bill on England. The Bank complied, and paid the bill, but we have heard nothing more from Mr. Brydges. I now write to him to let me know what we may expect.

There is nothing yet done I believe by the Great Western towards obtaining the Government guarantee on Quebec for £300,000 – no time should be lost – for if you let this opportunity slip you will get nothing – as the Government will say that your road is finished, and that there is no need to issue the money.

Do let me hear from you soon, – as we are very uneasy on the subject – and do not like the investigation to take place without knowing what we may have to depend upon.

D 29   T.G. RIDOUT TO R.W. HARRIS (PRIVATE, COPY)
Toronto, 15 June 1854
[*PAC, Buchanan Papers, v. 52, pp. 41800–2*]

. . . I am pleased to learn that you take a lively interest in getting the Bank account with the Great Western settled in this country by making an application to Government for £300,000 Sterling. This no doubt should have been done long ago but perhaps it is not now too late altho I apprehend some difficulty.

I think that you and Walter Dickson[27] would be the proper person to send to Quebec to effect the Loan because you are the heads of the Company independent of which your name stands higher still and you are so well known for so many years that you are identified with the Country and your negotiations will run smoothly and Walter Dickson his name and character form also a Tower of Strength and as he is on the best of terms with Sir. A.N. MacNab he will aid you much in the negotiation even then it will be no easy matter as everything looks blue. As for sending Brydges and Longsdon[28] it will never do, at least I think so for in the first place Brydges and Mr. Hincks do not agree and Sir Allan & Brydges are not on good terms and as for Mr. Longsdon he is an entire stranger and they will heed nothing that he says or does, should he insist on going down I fear the result unless you and Mr. Dickson went also.

Our letter of second June from Glyn & Co. received to day is of the most gloomy character. They have succeeded in selling 2350 out of the 5000 shares for £44383-15-0 Stg. but not a farthing has been yet paid in, the parties demur as there has been an intimation from the Great Western's Office 29 Austin Friars that the whole transaction is a sham and that the stock was transferred to Farewell & Co.[29] conditionally so making all that I have done a sham. If the GWR Co. wanted to commit suicide, they could not have hit upon a better plan for effecting their object. It is said they have thrown every difficulty in the way of making these sales even to the raising reports against their own company in this

---

[27]Walter Dickson (b. 1806) was called to the bar in 1830 and represented Niagara in the Legislative Assembly, 1844–51. He was a director of the Great Western Railway.

[28]William Longsdon was an experienced British railway manager sent over to Canada by the London investors in the Great Western Railway to assist in managing that concern.

[29]Farewell & Company was a Zimmerman-controlled railway contracting firm.

country. The consequences will therefore be disasterous unless you are able to obtain an immediate loan from Government of the £300,000 you mention.

I intend to go to Quebec on the 23rd inst and hope that by the time I arrive there you will have your affairs arranged with the Government. I hope to meet you and Mr. Dickson there and you may depend upon it all will go well if not there will be endless difficulty.

Do not send Mr. Longsdon. He will certainly fail in his object for altho he may be a man of the highest standing in England he will be looked upon as a stranger here and will have no weight with our Government but quite the contrary and as there is no cordiality between Brydges and Hincks, why send him: He will do no good. Perhaps the Grand Trunk are helping to fan the flames that is setting against your company and that is another reason why you should be very cautious in your steps this however, is all conjecture of my own.

P.S. About three weeks ago I received a letter from Mr. Peter Buchanan dated at the time that he paid in the last £40,000 Sterling in which he said that he would shortly pay in as much more, but nothing more has yet been paid – and from what Glyns say we need not expect anything from that quarter [one word?] must look to the Coy here this does not "tell a flattering tale" but we must not despair. I hope the darkest day is passed. TGR

NB   There has been a hint given at your office in London that the Books for Transfer would not be reopened on the 6th of June. Should that be the case it will be ruinous. This no doubt is the cause why buyers refused to pay in their money on the 30th and 31st of May according to the contract with the Broker. And their reason assigned, for not reopening, was that there was to be an adjourned meeting of the London Committee held after hearing from Canada. It is not a hard matter to get from bad to worse. TGR

D 30   T.G. Ridout to R.W. Harris
Toronto, 24 August 1854
[PAC, Buchanan Papers, v. 52, pp. 41804–07]

I have the pleasure to acknowledge your letter of the 23 inst. which was delivered to me by Mr. Baker[30] this morning – and who has stated the present wants of the Great Western Railway Co. and has urged the Bank to grant another advance to the extent of £20,000 to pay your most pressing debts, – it is no doubt very inconvenient for the Bank to go on this way, especially as Mr. Peter Buchanan has a veto on the sale of £300,000 sterling bonds now in London and can object to their sale at

[30]Brackstone Baker was corresponding secretary for the London board of the Great Western Railway.

the Market price, however much we may be inconvenienced for want of our money. The Bank is however disposed to assist you notwithstanding the difficulty in doing so – and I am authorized to say that if you will send me a letter addressed to Mr. Peter Buchanan in which you direct him to consent to the immediate sale of the £300,000 at such rates as Glyn and Co. and Baring and Co. may be able to obtain in the London Market this Bank will let you have bills for £10,000 on New York next week and £10,000 more on the week following, viz. in 4 bills of £5000 each, at our regular exchange rate which is 3/4% pr. – we offer this – as we do not wish to issue any more Bank notes at the present time, altho' perhaps we may find it convenient to let you have the last £10,000 in notes instead of a draft . . . .

D 31   THE SELECT COMMITTEE ON THE SUBJECT OF PUBLIC DEPOSITS,
        EVIDENCE, 27 OCTOBER 1854 (F. HINCKS, CHAIRMAN)
                   [JLA, *1854, Appendix EE*]

C.S. Ross,[31] Examined:
. . . 6. Chairman.] Do you find in conducting the business of your Bank, that the mercantile community require a large increase of accommodation at the period when the duties on spring importations become payable, and if so, will you state the extent of such increase, and the manner in which you provide for it? – I find that the customers of the Bank require increased discounts to pay Customs Duties from say 15th April to 15th June. To meet this demand, I have given orders to all the Branches to reduce discounts early in February. In 1853, from 26th February to 16th April, the discounts (aggregate) of the Bank were reduced £90,000. From 18th February, 1854, to 15th April, 1854, the reduction amounted to £70,000. From 15th April in each year, to 30th June, the discounts for duties were – say £120,000 – of which I should say one-half, or £60,000, were paid at Montreal, and the other half, equally, at Hamilton and Toronto.
. . . 8. Mr. Holton.[32]] Are you not frequently obliged to increase your aggregate of discounts to enable your customers to pay duties, very much to your own inconvenience, and are you not also obliged to deny discounts to your customers because of the destination of the proceeds? – We are obliged to increase the aggregate of local discounts,[33] say from 15th April to 15th June, to customers to pay duties, not only to extent of previous reduction in anticipation, but to a considerable amount beyond. What that amount in excess may be I

[31]C.S. Ross was cashier of the Commercial Bank.
[32]Luther Hamilton Holton (1817–80) was a businessman and politician. He was active in shipping and railway enterprises. In 1863 he became minister of finance for the reform government headed by J.S. Macdonald and A.A. Dorion.
[33]Ross defined "local discounts" as being the "class of discounts embracing what are wanted for payment of duties."

cannot state positively from memory. To give this extra discount accommodation, we have to meet balances by selling sterling exchange at the point where the rate is lowest in Canada, and this operation is always unsatisfactory. While we endeavour to meet our customers' wants for payment of duties, we are not unfrequently obliged to refuse altogether because proceeds are wanted to pay those duties. At the period named, the discount liabilities of our customers who have duties to pay are always in excess of the average.

9. Is the ability of the Banks to grant facilities to the trade restricted by the present system of confining the Public Deposits to one Bank? – We have always endeavored to make our arrangements so as to serve our customers, under the existing circumstances the Bank has thus had the ability to give its customers the required assistance, although by doing so loss has generally followed. Had the Public Deposits been partially made with the Bank in April, May and June, – this loss would have been avoided.

. . . 13. Chairman.] Have you not had from time to time a fair share of Government deposits bearing interest which you were able to make the basis of discounts, and of which there was no immediate prospect of withdrawal, and has not the Government been at all times disposed to meet your wishes regarding such deposits? – We have had a very considerable amount of Government money in deposit at interest, which naturally enabled us to assist our customers. The deposits have reached £100,000, and that amount is now with us. They have been given on stated terms and when no fixed date of withdrawal was named, notice is to be given. We have found the Government met our views, in regard to those deposits, as far as could consistently be done.

. . . 16. Hon. Mr. Cayley.] How have your weekly balances with the Bank of Upper Canada ranged for the last two years – Almost invariably in favor of the Bank of Upper Canada, the amount I could not state from memory.

Thomas G. Ridout, Examined:

17. Mr. Holton.] Will you state to the Committee what was the average weekly balance of Government Deposits in your Bank not bearing interest during the year 1853? Also the average weekly balance between the 1st April and 31st December, 1853? Also the average weekly balance between the 1st April and 24th October, 1854? – The average weekly balances during the year 1853 has been £182,381. The average weekly balances between the 1st April and 31st December, 1853, £213,072. The average weekly balances between the 1st April and 24th October, 1854, £210,056.

18. Do you include the Deposits of the Crown Lands Department? and if not can you state approximately the average amount at credit of that Department during the last two years? – They are included.

19. Will you state what amount of Government money is deposited in your Bank on interest; the length of time it has been so deposited; the

rate of interest you pay; and whether you hold it at call, or for a stipulated period? – The amount of Government deposit on interest, £100,000, not including the money belonging to Indian affairs, and it has been that, say for about three years past.

The rate of interest is three per cent.

It is held payable at call.

20. Do you make the floating balances of Government deposits as well as the amount bearing interest, the basis of discounts, or any part thereof? If not the whole, state what amount? – Taking into consideration the large and uncertain temporary advances made by the Bank on Board of Works certificates, imprest money, Post Office advances, and Pay Lists, together with the regular and current expenses of the Government, including interest on the Public Debt in London as well as the Sinking Fund, I think that the Bank freely ventures to discount to the amount of £75,000, on the public deposits; the amount of the private deposits, which generally, far exceeds that of the Government, being principally relied upon.

21. Mr. Holton.] What proportion of private deposits do you consider as forming a basis for discount? – The proportion of discount based on private deposits varies much, as it depends upon the season of the year, the demand for money, and the state of the London and New York markets – generally fifty per cent.

22. Will you state the average of private deposits in your Bank from Jany., 1853, to October, 1854? – The average is about £536,000.

. . . 24. Will you state the average monthly amount of debts due the Bank during each of the two past years? –

For the year 1853 .... £1,411,855
For the year 1854 1,903,324

. . . 26. Have you, during the past two years, made large advances to Railway Corporations, and on Railway Securities, in consequence of the Public Account being kept with your Bank? – The average amount of debts due to the Bank, within the last two years, has been much increased by the following temporary advances, viz., – To the Government, £153,348, being the average amount on account of Board of Works certificates, – Government Pay Lists, – Post Office Department and Imprest Money. To the Great Western Railway about £300,000. On the faith of, and in anticipation of, a guarantee Loan of £300,000 sterling from Government, which they had applied for, and which the Bank knew they were entitled to receive the proceeds, of which about £380,000 currency, was in due course paid into the hands of our Bankers in London. To the Ontario, Simcoe and Huron Railway Company, from £110,000 to £55,000, – based on warrants which they were entitled to receive from Government against their own moneys lodged in the hands of the Receiver General, and which we knew formed part of his deposit in the Bank, the issue of those warrants being dependent upon orders of Council after the approval of the Chief

Engineer's certificates by the Board of Works, all which has now been paid off and settled. To Railway contractors a temporary advance of £100,000, secured by 5000 Shares of Great Western Railway Stock, in my name, which was remitted to London, and was sold immediately, producing about £130,000 currency: this was considered a good and safe transaction, and remittance, although not in the form of a Bill of Exchange, but it served every purpose of such. To the Buffalo, Brantford and Goderich Railway Company, the following temporary advances were made between the 1st of July and 23rd of October this year, namely: £50,000, which was repaid by the Receiver General's cheque, about the 10th of October, out of the proceeds of Municipal Loan Fund Debentures issued for account of the Town of Brantford, and £22,000, a temporary advance made to that Company on account of £34,000 of the same Debentures purchased by the Bank, and which [Questions 26–37 missing]. . . .

. . . 38. Chairman.] Have not the balances between the Bank of Montreal and Bank of Upper Canada been generally in favour of the former Bank during the last two years? – The weekly balances at Toronto between the Bank of Montreal and the Bank of Upper Canada from the 1st of January 1853 to the 28th of Oct., 1854, have been as follows, viz:

In favor of the Bank of Montreal	£527,015
In favor of the Bank of Upper Canada	64,789
Balance in favour of the Montreal Bank	462,226

The greater part of which was paid in gold. The net balances between all the Banks at Toronto and the Bank of Upper Canada during the above period, were as follows, viz:

In favor of the Bank of Montreal	£462,226
Do Bank of British North America	271,506
Do City Bank of Montreal	217,335
Total	951,067
Deduct balances against Commercial Bank	172,037
Total balances against the Bank of Upper Canada	£779,030

Out of which the other Banks supplied themselves with specie.

The balances between the Banks in Lower Canada during the above period amount to £292,406 in favor of the Bank of Upper Canada.

39. Mr. Cauchon.[34]] What difference does it make to the trade in itself that the government deposits are made in one Bank instead of several Banks? – It is reasonable to suppose that the trade would prefer to pay their duties into their own Banks but I do not think that it makes any difference to them, as the Bank of Upper Canada generally discounts for such purposes, if required to do so.

Thomas Davidson, Examined:

[34]Joseph-Édouard Cauchon (1816–85) journalist, businessman and Conservative politician.

40. Mr. Holton.] How does the system of collecting the whole Revenue of the Country through one Bank, and keeping large sums on deposit in that Bank affect the operations of the other Banks and the convenience of the Commercial community generally? – It has the effect of creating large balances against the Banks in favour of the Bank receiving the revenue which are payable in specie. – In proof of which I may state, that in the year 1853, at Montreal alone, the Bank of Upper Canada received in settlement from the other Banks between the 15th April and the 15th July, about £145,000. The effect of this demand upon the Banks, has I believe, operated prejudicially upon the Commercial community, and has in some degree interfered with the granting of accommodation in the shape of discount.

41. Would not the collection of the revenue through several, or all of the Chartered Banks in the Province, particularly if the money were deposited with these Banks until required to be withdrawn for the public service, greatly promote the convenience of the Commercial community? – I believe it would be beneficial, more especially as in my opinion, the Funds which would be thus placed at the disposal of the several Banks could be made use of in giving facilities to the Commercial community with more general and decided advantage, than if the whole of the Revenue was entrusted to one Institution – should a Bank receiving the whole of the revenue, be tempted to employ a large portion of it in discounting commercial paper, the inconvenience which would arise when the money is called for by the Government, would be very great. No Bank can discount a large amount of paper, and insist upon the payment of it at maturity, without creating inconvenience to the trade of the Country; should the Revenue be deposited in several Banks, and a portion of it be used in granting facilities to their regular Customers, even should the money be called for by the Government, any restriction which the Banks might find it necessary to make in order to meet the demand of the Government, would be scarcely felt.

42. Would you consider it prudent for a Bank with a paid up Capital of only £500,000 to lend to a single Railway Corporation over £300,000 and a further sum at the same time to private parties on the security of the Stock of the same Corporation? – I think that no advances should be made by Banks to Public Companies, which can at all interfere with the accommodation which the Commercial community has a right to expect. If a Bank should hold a large amount of Capital for which it cannot find employment in the ordinary business of Banking, it would be justified in seeking other investments of a temporary character. I think it would not be prudent for a Bank to make use of the money it holds in deposit, except to a small extent, in making advances, upon the repayment of which, it could not with certainty calculate, within a specified period. The advance of £300,000 upon the security of its Stock to a Railway Company, would, I conceive, under any circum-

stances be highly imprudent, even if made from unemployed Capital, and not from deposits.

43. Would you consider it prudent for Government to deposit so large a sum as £600,000 in any Bank with so limited a Capital, especially after it had been known to engage in transactions of the nature and magnitude of these referred to in the preceding question? – I should not be disposed to place much confidence in the management of a Bank which entered into such transactions. No Bank can find employment in this Country for even a much less sum than £600,000 of such a nature as would enable the Bank to calculate upon having the funds thus employed at its command. Any securities which are available for investment, are not immediately convertible.

44. Would it be prudent for any Bank to employ a *large* amount of Government deposits *on call*, in discounting Commercial paper? – I think it would be highly imprudent for a Bank to employ a large amount of Government money, payable upon call, in discounting Commercial paper. I think that a Bank should not make use of more than two-thirds of its ordinary deposits in the manner referred to, but I conceive that the same proportion would be much too large in the case of a large deposit by the Government. In the one case, a Bank may safely calculate upon a certain average amount being left in its hands, but this would be very different with regard to a large deposit by the Government.

45. It appears by the public accounts of last that the Bank of Upper Canada paid only £3,000 interest on Government deposits, during that year. Do you not think the Government might make a more economical arrangement? – I have no doubt that the Government could have made a much more advantageous arrangement – looking to the large balances at the credit of the Government, the extended circulation which its payment must afford to the issues of a Bank, and the profit upon its large transactions in exchange, the account is unquestionably of very great value. In so far as I am enabled to form an opinion of the monetary operations of the Government in 1853, I have no hesitation in stating that I believe a much larger sum than £3,000 would have been gladly paid by other Banking Institutions. The Bank of British North America is now paying £3,000 per annum to the Government as interest upon £75,000 without any collateral advantage.

46. Can you state proximately what amount you have advanced to merchants of Montreal for payment of duties, during each of the past and present years? – I have ascertained that in 1853, the Bank of British North America paid Cheques of its largest Customers at Montreal, Quebec, Toronto, and Hamilton for import duties to the amount of £240,000. This sum does not include a considerable number of small amounts paid by Cheques and in Bank notes. Neither does it include the payments for Timber dues, Tolls and other sources of revenue. The whole I believe would have made up the sum to at least £300,000.

47. Chairman.] You adduce, as proof of your assertion that the

collection of the revenue through one Bank operates prejudiciously: that between 15th April and 15th July, 1853, the Bank of Upper Canada received in settlement about £145,000. Is it not the case that between 1st January, 1853, and October, 1854, the balances between the other Banks and the Bank of Upper Canada were very largely against the latter Bank? – My reply to the question can be applicable to Montreal only, and I know that the balances there during the period refered to, were very largely in favor of the Bank of Upper Canada.

48. Have your customers been unable to obtain the requisite accomodation for paying their duties? – I have never found it necessary to refuse the amount of accommodation to which I conceive the customers of the Bank were entitled, in consequence of the payment of the duties into another Bank. From the manner in which the business of the Bank is conducted, this has not been necessary.

49. Is not the real cause of the balances being in favor of the Bank of Upper Canada between April and July, that at that period the other Banks are obliged to extend their line of discounts? – I believe that any extension of discounts at the period referred to, is attributable in a large degree to the payment of duties, and in this way the balances against the Banks in favor of the Bank of Upper Canada are largely increased.

50. You state in your answer to Ques. 42 that the advance of £300,000 upon the security of its Stock, to a Railway Company, would, under any circumstance be highly improvident, are you aware that any such advance was made on the security of Railway Stock? – I know nothing of any such advance except from common rumour.

51. Would you consider it a very improvident transaction for a Bank to lend £300,000 to a Railway Company which it knew to be entitled to a larger amount of Provincial Debentures payable in London, and saleable without difficulty at a premium, and when the Agent of the Bank in London would be ready to give the full advance upon at any time? – I decidedly think so, unless the Bank held such a guarantee from the Government for the delivery of the Debentures, as would be equivalent to the actual possession of these securities, and also unless the Bank was in such a position as not to be inconvenienced by the advance of £300,000, should there have arisen any delay in the repayment of the loan, or in the delivery and sale of the Debentures.

52. Are you aware that the Bank of Upper Canada has made large advances on Commercial paper, in consequence of its having the Government Account? – I am not.

53. Why do you conceive that Government Deposits are more likely to be suddenly withdrawn than other Deposits? Is it not a most probable thing that a Bank, being fiscal agent of the Government, has the means of knowing the periods when extraordinary demands are likely to be made, and of regulating its business accordingly? – A Bank can safely calculate upon a certain average balance being left on deposit by its customers, and I have stated that two-thirds of that amount might be

safely used in discounting Commercial paper. To make use of the Funds in the same manner, of any very large Depositor, such as the Government, would not be prudent, except to a very limited extent, unless there existed a specific arrangement, that the money should remain with the Bank for a certain period . . . .

Charles E. Anderson, Examined:

. . . 60. Chairman.] Have you had, in your official position, an opportunity of forming an opinion as to the respective advantages and disadvantages to the public, of keeping the Banking account of the Province in one Bank, or indiscriminately among all, if so, will you state which system you conceive to be best? – I have been connected with the Government now nine years, and for nearly the past six years I may say, in charge of the details of the Receiver General's Department, and consequently have had ample opportunity of seeing the working of the Government deposits under both systems, viz: While the deposits were made in the various Banking institutions, and since they have been made in the Bank of Upper Canada solely, and I unhesitatingly pronounce the present, and latter system, as the best for the interest and convenience of the public service.

61. Is it not the case that the large balance apparently at the credit of the Bank of Upper Canada during the last two years, was almost constantly liable to deduction owing to large advances made by the Bank on Government account in anticipation of warrants, such advances being on account of Board of Works' certificates or imprest monies? – It is as above stated and had the old system of dividing the deposits existed, it would have been seriously to the inconvenience of the public and the government; the Bank of Upper Canada has shewn a spirit of liberality in conducting the Government account, in advancing monies in anticipation of Warrants, Board of Works certificates, &c., which forms a strong contrast with the system pursued when the account was divided. Further, the Bank of Upper Canada is constantly, I may say, in advance large sums of money for interest on the public debt due and payable in England – thus under the old system of the Deposits, for interest due in London, say on 1st January, exchange at 30 or 60 days had to be purchased and paid for here, at least one month previous, and at times it was found any thing but convenient either to get the exchange or to pay for it; for example, only certain Banks had exchange, and if cheques were drawn on one or more Banks to pay another for exchange so bought, a constant complaint and jealousy existed: whereas under the present system the Bank of Upper Canada is made aware of the amounts and periods at which the interest falls due in London, and so provides for it, being only repaid for same on production, in this country, at the Receiver General's Department of the vouchers of payment of same in England, in most cases one month after such payment has been made by that institution, without any equivalent for such advance. The amount so paid throughout the year up to 1st of

January last, on Provincial Government account was £146,666 1s. 6d. sterling, and I may further add that the £260,000 sterling, now held in Consols in England, and the £200,000 sterling, for redemption of the Bonds matured in April last was also remitted by the Bank of Upper Canada on similar terms.

62. Can you inform the Committee whether, when the Government account was kept by the Banks of Montreal and Bank of British North America the same disposition was manifested by those institutions to meet the reasonable requirements of Government that has been evinced by the Bank of Upper Canada? – The same disposition to meet the views of the Government and facilitate the public business was not manifested by the Bank of Montreal, and Bank of British North America when they held the account, as has been exhibited by the Bank of Upper Canada; what the latter institution performs readily as a duty, was looked upon by the other institutions as a favor and even then not always granted, and in most cases where the most vital interests of the Province were concerned; further the feeling shewn in carrying out the account by the Bank of Montreal and the Bank of British North America was that of a superior to an inferior and not becoming the Fiscal Agents of this Province.

63. . . . The Bank of Upper Canada in April, 1850, advanced the Government £20,000 Cy., on interest 6 per cent. being on account of £50,000 which they were pledged on accepting the account to advance the Government should it be required – no further amount was required as in the interim say in the end of May, 1850, advice was received of the completion of the sale of £500,000 Stg.: Debentures in London which made the chest easy as regarded money matters. The Bank of Upper Canada has generally held a large amount of Government Deposits . . . .

D 32   SECOND REPORT OF THE STANDING COMMITTEE ON PUBLIC ACCOUNTS, CHAIRED BY W.L. MACKENZIE, 11 DECEMBER 1854
[JLA, *1854, Appendix JJ*]

. . . 4. That the apparent balance in cash deposited with the Bank of Upper Canada by the Government is much less than it seems to be. Last 23rd of October the Bank had advanced cash on Board of Works' certificates, for which no warrants had issued, and out of which advances the Bank is on the average, kept three months, £82,907; also to "pay lists" £9,900; and to the Post Office Department, which is stated to be always in arrear to the Bank, £14,662.

D 33   E.P. TACHÉ TO W. CAYLEY
Quebec, 2 February 1855
[*PAC, RG 19 B2b, v. 1162*]

. . . You state the "daily average amount held at" call by the Bank of

U. Canada during the past year ranged somewhere near £300,000 and you assume that it was out of this average Balance that the Bank, as Agent of the Government, was directed under the terms of the understanding referred to in my letter to cash the Municipal Debentures to the amount authorised by the O in C [Order in Council] viz. £234,483.6.8.

In reply to the above I beg to state that I never at any time considered the Bank as the Agent of the Government in the matter referred to, and never authorised or considered the advances so made by the Bank to the Municipalities as a portion of the £300,000 average Balance on call in the Bank of Upper Canada, or having any reference to it, on the contrary, I should at any time have felt quite at liberty to have checked out the full amount of such average Balance had the Public Service required it, irrespective of any advance made by the Bank as herein stated; and in proof of this I may add that altho I am aware the Bank is in advance to certain Municipalities this very day to the amount of £60,300. yet the floating Balance at my credit in the Bank has been completely exhausted yesterday to meet the exigencies of the public Service.

. . . Referring again to the average amount of £300,000 held on call by the Bank of Upper Canada mentioned in your letter, I ought to remark that the average sum for the same period the previous year was no less than £339,000 whilst you should have deducted £50,000 from your calculation belonging to the Ontario & Simcoe Railroad Company, reducing by that means the amount to £250,000. It, I must say, seems to me somewhat strange that whilst in 1853 the Bank was enjoying that large capital without rendering any other services but those agreed to, the financial Departments should only have been open to the accusation of favoritism and that in 1854 when great assistance had been afforded by that Institution, independently of recognized obligations, it is apprehended that those departments will be charged with mismanagement of the Public Funds in view of favouring a particular Institution, a charge that cannot, according to me, be explained but by a feeling of political antagonism and for party purposes.

As I have had the honor to state to you verbally, I never interfered between the Municipalities and the Bank, the Parties having invariably made their financial arrangements among themselves. The payments of Interest effectuated by the Municipalities until the present time, have been made without any complaints, neither am I aware that any imputation has been made in the [Journals?] as to the course adopted by the Government.

. . . You are further desirous of being informed whether it is my opinion that the Government is pledged in the investment of the Special Funds beyond the limit fixed by the orders in Council or simply up to the specified limits; Besides the £25,000 advanced to Mr Zimmerman by my order, for which I feel I am in honor bound to make good I also think that the Government ought to take up the following sums: Ops £20,000 London £4500, Stratford £15,800 in all £40,300 – advanced by the Bank on the understanding already referred to, except that we should be able to show that the circumstances of the Country are such as would not warrant the investment of the above sums . . . .

D 34   T.G. Ridout to Isaac Buchanan
Toronto, 7 February 1855
[*PAC, Buchanan Papers, v. 52, pp. 41816–18*]

. . . With reference to the standing of the Honbe Malcolm Cameron[35] – I can only say that altho' he owns much valuable property – yet he is a good deal embarrassed at the present moment, and it will be no doubt two or three years with good luck all the time before he can extricate himself – He owes this Bank a considerable sum – it is well secured – but his payments are very small and we will have no new transactions with him – he seems to depend mostly upon his lands, and that will not do in business.

I am thankful for your hint about our credits at Hamilton and will advise Mr. Stow[36] to consult you occasionally as you kindly permit him to do so –

D 35   T.G. Ridout to T.A. Begley[37]
Toronto, 15 February 1855
[*PAC, RG 11 A1, v. 22*]

I have the honour to acknowledge the receipt of your letter of the 8 inst. with its enclosures & regret to learn that the Board of Works certificates for sums of money due to contractors have lately been refused to be paid and honoured by the agent of this Bank at Montreal; it being contrary to his instructions – and, I beg to assure you, that such an unpleasant circumstance shall not again occur. The express orders of the Bank to all its agents, being – that every facility shall be granted to all Government demands, & to pay at once, & at par, all Board of works certificates signed by the Commissioner or by the Secretary of that Department without reference to warrant or to any other authority – and to transmit them to the Bank office at Quebec – where they would be settled for in due course, at the convenience of the Government.

I have now repeated these instructions to the Bank Agent at Montreal and I trust you will be well satisfied with his future transactions regarding your Department – it being the earnest wish of the Bank to prevent all cause of complaint.

---

[35]Malcolm Cameron (1808–76) was a businessman and politician. He was active in lumber and flour mills and in shipbuilding and railway contracting. A reformer in politics, he variously represented Lanark and Huron in the Legislative Assembly.

[36]A. Stowe was the Bank of Upper Canada's agent at Hamilton.

[37]Thomas A. Begley had been secretary for the Board of Works since its formation in 1841.

D 36   T.G. RIDOUT TO T.A. BEGLEY
Toronto, 16 February 1855
[*PAC, RG 11 A1, v. 22*]

With reference to the letter I had the honour to address you yesterday, I beg to add, that besides the certificates signed by the Commissioner & Secretary to which the agents of this Bank have been directed to pay due honour: they have also been instructed to pay estimates approved & certified by the Resident Engineer of your Department – it is therefore most annoying that the Bank agent at Montreal should have taken upon himself to have deviated from this rule.

D 37   T.G. RIDOUT TO GLYN, MILLS
Toronto, 10 March 1855
[*PAC, Glyn, Mills Papers A542*]

. . . I observe the difficulty that your Brokers have in selling the remainder of the Great West Bonds. Mr. Zimmerman however authorizes me to say that he is willing to sell out at 3 or 4 per cent below the last market price, if nothing better can be done.

I still hold your £15,000 of Ontario, Simcoe and Huron Rail Way Comp. Bonds – these I am informed will be redeemed as soon as we are advised of the sale of the second lot of £100,000 Provincial Debentures hereinbefore mentioned, with interest up to date. I shall then obtain from Mr. Zimmerman his order upon you for the other £15,000 in your hands, upon which no incumbrance exists.

The Great Western Rail Way Company have succeeded in obtaining a further loan of £100,000 sterling from Government, the Debentures for which I understand are now on the way from Quebec to London, and their proceeds will be paid in due course into your hands for account of this Bank, according to the Receiver General's instructions. We hope they will be sold some time next month as the company are much in want of the money – their line of road is now yielding about £7000 per week, which they hope to increase to £10,000 as soon as they can procure a few more engineers to do the work, as there is more freight than they can carry with their present stock. I have lately been over some part of their line, it appeared to be well ballasted and better managed than it was a short time ago. Trains now pass over the Great Suspension Bridge at the Falls of Niagara.

. . . For several months past the Banks of Canada have been restricting their business as much as possible – but in general there is great prosperity throughout the country – and land is rapidly rising in value – the effect of the Reciprocity Treaty with the United States will be very beneficial to us and is already felt . . . .

D 38   T.G. RIDOUT TO GLYN, MILLS
Toronto, 31 March 1855
[*PAC, Glyn, Mills Papers, A542*]

. . . About a week ago the Receiver General forwarded to you and to Messrs. Barings a further lot of £100,000 Sterling Provincial Debentures, for sale, on account of the Great Western Railway Company accompanied as I am informed by instructions to lodge the proceeds thereof with you, to the account of this Bank, for use of said Company to whom we have made an advance thereon of £50,000 Cy. but we do not intend to pay them any more money until the sale of the Debentures is perfected. They are entitled to receive £70,000 more from Government. I do not know however when it will be granted. I think the affairs of that company are looking much better than they did last year and their weekly earnings are improving rapidly since the completion of the Great Railway Suspension bridge near the Falls of Niagara. The traffic on the line having now an uninterrupted connection with the United States rail roads.

D 39   C.S. ROSS TO ISAAC BUCHANAN
Kingston, 6 July 1855
[*PAC, Buchanan Papers, v. 53, pp. 42268–9*]

. . . Thanks also for your suggestions about Agencies. Hitherto we have found our Capital quite inadequate even to present business and then the Gov't money in deposit £100,000 has to be repaid ([just?] immediately) – This will absorb so much of new capital (for the deposit being for 3 years with us has been virtually Capital) and unless we get more paid up I don't see my way clear for extending. We have appointed an Agent at Chatham for the purpose of collecting in the first place – & possibly if found to suit it may be made a permanent Agency. Our experience is however that not one in five of these Agencies pays the Bank tho' we are obliged to continue them from other causes . . . .

D 40   T.G. RIDOUT TO GLYN, MILLS
Toronto, 28 July 1855
[*PAC, Glyn, Mills Papers, A542*]

. . . The sums that we relied upon being paid to you by Government and by the Great Western Rail way Company have not been realized so promptly as we had reason to expect, viz. the order from the Great Western for the deposit of £50,000 did not leave Hamilton until the 3rd inst whereas we supposed it had been done early in June, in the mean time we had advanced them a great part of the money – their funds in England are now however very good, and they will shortly have large sums to draw for which will keep their accounts here well supplied – as for the £38,000 due by Government to the Ontario Simcoe and Huron

Rail Way Co. alluded to by me in a former letter, there have been unforseen difficulties attending it. These are now all removed and the order of the Receiver General to yourselves and the Messrs. Barings goes by this mail to pay the amount to the account of this Bank to which it is due – having no further payments to make thereon.

The course of our business in August and in the early part of September will be such as to enable us to make you large remittances and so place our account in a very satisfactory state, as the Government imprest account and other advances made to the Board of Works will then be covered. The Receiver General having lately given notice to call in £100,000 on the 1st of September, which he has lying at interest in other banks in this province.

We may probably have occasion to draw upon you during the ensuing week something over the amount of our remittance – but that will be but temporary –

D 41   C.E. ANDERSON TO JOHN A. MACDONALD
Quebec, 10 August 1855
[PAC, RG 19 B2b, v. 1162]

. . . That in the fall of 1854 Mr Farmer[38] President of the Woodstock & Lake Erie Railway Co acting as attorney for the Treasurer of the Township of Windham received from this Department Debentures of the Consolidated Municipal Loan Fund of U.C. to the amount of £25,000 cy under an assurance that he was not to part with them *under par*; and he accordingly paid them over to the contractor of the said Railway Mr S Zimmerman *at par*, which was so far carrying out the pledge. Mr Zimmerman however not being bound by any pledge and requiring the money not the Debentures brought the later into the Market for Sale and was offering to dispose of them at 5 per Cent discount. On this coming to the knowledge of the Receiver General he sent for Mr Zimmerman and finding the above to be correct; and looking to the large amount of these securities which he had still to negotiate, he felt that by allowing such a Sale to be carried out, that it would be the means of greatly depreciating these Debentures in the Market; he consequently sent for Mr Ridout who happened to be in Quebec; & proposed to him that the Bank should take the Debentures from Mr Zimmerman *at par*, under a pledge from the Receiver General in writing that the Debentures should again be taken from the Bank on the 15 January 1855 as Investment for the Common School Fund 12 Vic CH 200, the Receiver General having in the first place learned from the

---

[38] Arthur A. Farmer was a gentleman farmer in the Woodstock area and was involved in the promotion of the Southern Railway. Through his railway activities he became heavily indebted to the Bank of Upper Canada. In August 1870 the trustees of the bank wrote his debt off, considering him to be "worthless."

Department of the Inspector General that such an arrangement might with safety be carried out –

Mr Ridout now applies that the pledge for 15 January last be now carried out and I would therefore respectfully recommend that a warrant be issued in favour of Mr Ridout Cashier Bank of Upper Canada on the Common School Fund above named for the sum of £25,000 cy. –

D 42   T.G. RIDOUT TO MATILDA
19 August 1855
[PAO, Ridout Papers]

. . . I have just received an official letter from the Great Western Railway Company dated 16 inst. accepting my offer of 3¹/₂ acres for their station and stating they had ordered their engineer to clear, grade & fence the land and to erect the necessary buildings immediately. this move I consider is worth £10,000 to me or us as I ought properly to say but we need not stand on ceremony on that score . . . .

D 43   J. BRADSHAW[39] TO C.E. ANDERSON
Quebec, 18 September 1855
[PAC, RG 1 E7, v. 42]

Referring to my communication of 24 July last to the Receiver General, relative to the Investment of £12,775 for the Great Western Railroad Co Sinking Fund, I have to request you will be pleased to draw the attention of the Hon' Mr Attorney General Macdonald, the present head of your Department in order that the Debentures held by the Bank may be reduced previous to the Government leaving Quebec . . . the Amount still held by the Bank is due now £20,000.

I am the more anxious to have the Amount as above stated taken up, as the means to do so is in the hands of the Bank already, & the Present state of the Receiver Generals Account coupled with advances on Estimates & Public Works Certificates (the later at present amounting to £40,000 & yet unpaid) renders it more desirable, that the Debentures should be taken from the Bank, & you are fully aware of the circumstances under which the Bank holds them.

D 44   C.E. ANDERSON TO JOHN A. MACDONALD
Quebec, 29 September 1855
[PAC, RG 1 E7, v. 42]

As will be seen in reference to the letter of W E Stephens Esq. Secretary Great Western Railway Co. of 12th June last herewith attached, that Company deposited on that day to credit of [this?] department the sum

---

[39]Since 1851 John Bradshaw had been cashier for the Bank of Upper Canada at Quebec City.

of £12,775 cy. to be invested by Government on account of their Sinking Fund.

It will also be seen by the letter herewith of the Manager of the Bank of Upper Canada of 14th July last, that the Bank applied to the Receiver General previous to his departure to Europe, that the amount might be invested in Debentures of the Consolidated Municipal Loan Fund of Upper Canada which the Receiver General is under pledge to take from the Bank for Investment for Special Funds, the Bank having advanced the money on same on that understanding, the amount still held by the Bank on those conditions being some £20,000 cy . . . .

Mr. Bradshaw under date 18th instant as per letter herewith again renews the application & I would therefore suggest that considering the understanding between this Department & the Bank in the matter, & the present state of the Receiver General's account with the Bank that it be recommended to Council that a warrant issue in favor of the Manager of the Bank of Upper Canada in this City, for the sum of £12750 currency to be paid him on his handing over to the Department Debentures of the Consolidated Municipal Loan Fund of Upper Canada for a similar amount.

D 45   T.G. RIDOUT TO GLYN, MILLS
Toronto, 2 April 1856
[PAC, Glyn, Mills Papers, A 542]

The publication here on the 31 ultimo of two letters written by Mr. Brassey in February last to the Hon. John Ross President of the Grand Trunk Railway Compy. stating the inability of the Contractors to continue their undertaking – without further assistance from the Provincial Government has caused a very great sensation in our Legislature now in Session as well as with the Public. I beg leave therefore to write to you on the subject & to ask you confidentially if you think that this Bank may safely continue the negotiation of the weekly drafts of Mr. Tate & Mr. Rowan, agents, on their principals in London Messrs. Peto Brassey Betts & Jackson, as we have done for the last two or three years.

The present disturbance will probably subside in a few weeks as the general impression is that the Province is in honor & interest bound to furnish means to assist the Grand Trunk Company in completing their work.

D 46   JOHN LANGTON[40] TO W. CAYLEY
Toronto, 11 April 1856
[PAC, RG 58 B2A, v. 1]

I have the honor to call your attention to the exceedingly unsatisfactory

[40]John Langton (1808–94) was the auditor general of Canada, 1855–78.

state of the Post Office Account. In the Public Accounts now being published appears a sum of £20,000 paid to the Postmaster general to meet the deficiencies of his Department for the years 1854 & 55. It appears that the amount required to cover the deficiency of 1854 was £7,000 about leaving about £12,000 only available for the deficiencies of 1855. But by the report of the Postmaster general now printed the real deficiency for that year appears to be about £30,000 leaving £18,000 unprovided for. Now the Post Office year ends on the 31st of March & therefore over & above the £20,000 for which a warrant issued, there was on the 31st of March 1855 a deficiency unprovided for of about £18,000. The same causes have been in operation this year & probably to a larger extent. The Bank of Upper Canada is now in advance to the Post Office to the extent of £57,000, which would show a deficiency on the year of £39,000. Probably this exceeds the real amount of actual deficiency as this Department is required to pay much of its expenditure before the corresponding receipts come in, but this real deficiency can certainly be not less than £30,000. There appears no reason to believe that the receipts will come any nearer this expenditure in the year which has just commenced, but rather the contrary, as I am informed that the mail contracts continue to be given at much increasing rates. If therefore no remedy is applied, by this time next year the whole deficiency will probably fall very little, if anything short, of £100,000. Unless some means of reducing the expenditure or of increasing the revenue is devised provision will have to be made in the forthcoming estimates for this sum or something near it, or else the present system must be continued of meeting the deficiency by Bank advances. It may be necessary sometimes & at other times it is no doubt convenient to resort to Bank advances, when the case which gives rise to it is unexpected & cannot otherwise be met, or when the expenditure in question is of a regular & uniform character & the only object is the convenience of issuing one warrant to the Bank instead of many to individuals, but it is a power which should be used with great caution. In the present instance the present & the future deficiency are well known & must be met sooner or later by a vote of the House, & to continue to draw upon the Bank for the sums wanted appears to me a practice the continuance of which cannot be defended. It is unjust to the Bank which is supposed to have large sums of government money in its hands but which is really heavily in advance. It prevents the government having efficient control over its expenditure, for individual Departments may thus employ money, for which the Province is responsible, without the consent or even the knowledge of the Council and it misleads the House & the public as the published accounts & the books kept in your office do not really represent the actual expenditure of the Province.

I hasten to communicate these facts to you upon their coming to my knowledge, as I believe this practice has gone on increasing to an extent which has probably never come under your notice.

D 47   FOURTH STANDING COMMITTEE ON PUBLIC ACCOUNTS,
EVIDENCE, 22 APRIL 1856
[JLA, *1856, Appendix 30*]

[C.E. Anderson, examined]
. . . 56, Can you inform the Committee, or have you any means of knowing to what extent such payments were made, on account of the Province, at any one time, without the knowledge of the Receiver General? – On the 18th of the present month of April the Bank of Upper Canada was under advances for Board of Works Certificates, Engineers' Estimates, Post Office Department, &c., and of which the Receiver General had no information and could not have, upwards of £100,000 currency . . . .

D 48   JOHN LANGTON TO WILLIAM LANGTON[41] (COPY)
Toronto, 17 April 1856
[*W.A. Langton, ed.*, Early Days in Upper Canada, Letters of John
Langton, *Toronto, 1926, pp. 242–57*]

I must give you another yarn about the public accounts, being a subject about which for want of any more agreeable one I think of all day and dream of most of the night. I expected to find a mess but the reality exceeded my expectations, especially as I have only yet got into the threshold of the dirtiest stall in the Augean stable – the Board of Works . . . .

We are a very wealthy people. We raise a large amount of revenue from a very moderate customs tariff and we hardly know how to spend it. I think we shall be relieved in this respect for the future because our railway speculations have provided a very efficient issue which will prevent us dying of plethora. It is astonishing how coolly we all bore the news that interest on debt to the amount of £300,000 a year which we had only guaranteed and never expected to pay is, by the repudiation of the Grand Trunk and other companies, to be met for the future by us. This however by the bye. Amongst the other consequences of our excess of revenue we always kept some half million idle in the banks. With an income of not much more than a million and a half in 1854 we never had less than £600,000 and sometimes upwards of £800,000 so lying. In 1855 the diminished imports and increased expenses had somewhat relieved this determination of blood to the banks, but still we generally had from 3 to 4 or £500,000 unemployed and the balances were duly reported to the Governor General every evening. Some of this was at three per cent interest, subject to two or three months' notice, in various banks, but the bulk was at call in the Bank of Upper Canada which is our financial agent, and great is the outcry against this favoured

---

[41]William Langton was John Langton's brother.

institution in consequence. I had a call from the cashier the other day who complained that whilst they were supposed to have more than £200,000 in their hands they were really put to great inconvenience in their general business by being in advance to government about £50,000 and he wanted me to speak to the Inspector General about it, who he did not believe knew how things really stood. I must say I was taken aback, but I immediately commenced investigations and I found that a practice has long existed than which nothing can be worse and which renders these balances in hand sent in to the Governor General every evening so much waste paper. At the end of every month the resident engineer gives each contractor what is called a monthly estimate showing what work he has done, how much is to be kept as drawback and what he may get payment for. He takes this to the bank who give him the money. They send it to the Board of Works who after examining and checking, etc., issue a certificate to the bank. This certificate they send to the Council office who at their leisure prepare a warrant which is sent to the Inspector General, and it is not till he signs the warrant that he knows anything about it. In the ordinary course it is at least a month after the money has been paid before it comes into the public accounts; and if a particular expenditure is of a nature which it is not desired to make known, especially whilst Parliament is in session or the public accounts are being made up for the year, there is nothing more easy than to keep it back a little in some of its numerous stages. After the warrant does come in it may be found all wrong, paid once before, unauthorized, etc., of all of which there are instances now in the office. Delay occurs in consequence and the disagreeable item does not appear in the published accounts, but the money is nevertheless really spent and irrecoverable. The bank advances to the Board of Works at this present moment are something like £100,000.

Then there is the Post Office. It is not a paying concern with us but a constant source of expense, as we have innumerable post offices scattered over the country the receipts from which do not pay a fiftieth part of the cost of conveying the mail . . . . The Postmaster General has not the smallest idea what the deficiency will be in the year just past, but the bank which has been finding the ways and means all the time has a very good idea, it is £57,000. These are goodly sums to be expended, not only without sanction of Parliament but without the consent or even knowledge of the finance minister.

The Crown Lands also have a good pull at purse, and there is another case of which I had some cognizance which illustrates the impropriety of this system. Last year we had a new Militia Bill in consequence of your taking away all our soldiers, but Parliament with the jealousy which always characterizes popular assemblies grumbled at the bill and especially the expense and put in a clause saying that the payment must depend upon an annual vote of Parliament, and the Ministry very glad to escape from an unpopular measure accepted the clause and said that as they did not intend to organize they would not ask for a vote that year. Nevertheless they did partially organize, and the pay lists came into me for audit; or rather the Deputy Inspector General asked me before payment what was to be done. I pointed out that it was not only an unprovided expense, but that the Act positively prohibited any thing being paid till a vote had been taken. So they privately instructed the bank to make an advance.

You can now understand how our apparent balances dwindle away. I have declared open war against the system and Cayley gives me a lukewarm support, but he is too timid a hand for any efficient reform. The Board of Works declare reform impossible, the Postmaster General declares it impossible, and the only warm support I get is from the bank and from the Receiver General who being the cash keeper has a commendable objection to allow any extraneous fingers to get into his purse[42] . . . . I may also mention that the bank being desirous of making a poor mouth, as the saying is, overstated the case and, if closely enquired into, I do not think they are really in advance to Government at all. The advances to contractors in strictness are and certainly ought to be pure banking transactions. I have little doubt that the bank get a discount on their advance when it would clearly not be government they were paying. It is a business which any bank would be glad to get for the security is good, and the presumptive evidence that the contractor is entitled to draw much clearer than in most cases where a bank discounts a draft; besides it is exactly the sort of business they like, for their notes are paid away to labourers and small tradesmen and are much longer in coming back upon them than if they assisted a merchant to make a large payment. Moreover £11,000 of the post office advance appears to be money not really paid but credits given to money order post offices, so that the sum is really never out of their hands though fluctuating about amongst their different branches and agencies. Then all public accountants keep their money in the bank, or ought to do . . . .

D 49   T.G. RIDOUT TO GLYN, MILLS
Toronto, 26 May 1856
[PAC, Glyn, Mills Papers, A542]

I have the pleasure to acknowledge the receipt of your private letter of the 9: inst. and note your remarks respecting the Bank account which I think will be very shortly readjusted to your satisfaction.

We are now making you considerable remittances over and above our weekly drawings.

I have been expecting to receive from government for some days past £50,000. of Exchange on London, to be drawn against £100,000.

[42]He also had assistance from John Young (1811–78), a merchant and a reform representative from Montreal who chaired the Committee on Public Accounts in 1856.

debentures lately sent to London for sale, but some political distur-bances in our Cabinet has prevented this matter being attended to. I am now however authorized to apprize you that by the ensuing mail you will receive the Receiver Generals drafts at 60 days for £100,000 and by the ensuing Packet a further remittance of his drafts at 90 days for £50,000. the latter will be drawn against another lot of £100,000 debentures now awaiting the Inspector Generals countersign.

As there is every probability that the Provincial Government will consent to convert into Grand Trunk rail way stock their loan of £3,111,000. to that Company, the government must from this time forward provide for the half yearly payments of interest due thereon in July and January of every year but I am now informed that in the course of this week this Bank will be ordered to include that interest in the government half yearly payments in London commencing 1. July next.

I must own that this is very short notice to give you, but I hope that the government bills will be considered a good remittance altho they will not mature in time for the July dividend.

We have expected that by this time a deposit will have been made with you of about £50,000 by the Great Western rail way Co. and that further large sums will be paid in during July and August for the construction of their London and Sarnia Branch – we also had reason to expect that a large sale of our stock would have been by this time effected in London through Messrs. Foster & Braithwaite but I have no certain advices yet on that subject.

Our new ministry are about being organized this day. The changes however are very few – it is said that Mr. Joseph C. Morrison[43] is to be the new Receiver General and that Col. Taché will take another Department. Sir Allan McNab and Atty. Genl. Drummond[44] will go out entirely – a good feeling is gaining ground in favor of the Grand Trunk and the changes in the government will not do them any harm.

D 50   T.G. RIDOUT TO GLYN, MILLS
Toronto, 2 June 1856
[PAC, Glyn, Mills Papers, A542]

I remit you by this mail government exchange to the amount of £90,000. Sterling. We expected it to be £100,000. but the difference £10,000. has been divided between two other parties. We shall however obtain £50,000. for next mail.

We have had letters from Mr. Hope,[45] which led us to believe that

---

[43]Joseph Curran Morrison (1816–85) was a lawyer and conservative politician and president of the Northern Railway in the 1850s. He was sometimes known as the "Honourable Member for Zimmerman" because of his close connections with that railway contractor.

[44]Lewis Thomas Drummond (1813–82) was attorney-general east.

[45]Hope may have been a London merchant banker involved in railway finance.

about £40,000. Sterling would have been deposited with you on the 5th ultimo. and about the same sum on the 29th of May being for the sale of 8000 shares of our new capital stock[46] but such does not appear to have been the case as far as we are informed up to this time.

The above was founded on a voluntary offer on the part of Mr. Hope who was out in this country last year and who on his return to England wrote to know on what terms the Bank would allow him to take up 8000 shares of our new stock & this was replied to and the matter remained in abeyance for several months, when we received another letter from Mr. Hope stating that he had made his arrangements and desired to know if the stock was still at his disposal which was answered in the affirmative and the next thing we knew was the Prospectus advertised by Foster & Braithwaite in the London times, and a letter from Mr. Hope stating that he would make the deposits with you as I have hereinbefore mentioned.

It now remains for me to say that had we supposed that the sale of the 8000 shares would be a Public affair, we should certainly have consulted you respecting its disposal, but never having had any reason to think that you would recommend our shares to be brought into the London market, we did not think it necessary to apprize you of Mr. Hope's offer to take up our stock.

In case Mr. Hope does not immediately fulfil his undertaking, the Board seem disposed to withdraw from the sale altogether – as we can sell as many shares in this country as we wish to dispose of from time to time as we require.

D 51   GRAND TRUNK RAILROAD AND BANK OF UPPER CANADA
Toronto, 10 July 1856
[PAC, RG 30, v. 1000]

The Vice President submitted his Cash Estimates to 31st August and informed the Board that he had had an interview with the Cashier of the Bank of Upper Canada and that he had negotiated a sufficient Loan to wit, £25,000 Sterling and £35,000 Currency – making a total of £65,426 – 13/ to meet current expenses to 31st August and the Vice President was authorized to issue to the Bank of Upper Canada the notes of this Company at such dates as may be judged expedient to carry out the arrangements above referred to and also for the renewal of the Notes falling due at the Commercial Bank – between this date and the 25th August next . . . .

D 52   T.G. RIDOUT TO GLYN, MILLS
Toronto, 12 July 1856
[PAC, Glyn, Mills Papers, A542]

. . . The contractors Messrs. Peto & Co. of the Grand Trunk rail way,

[46]18 Vic. c. 39.

are making great efforts to complete their line from Toronto to Montreal on or before the 1st of November next. They have consequently drawn for large sums of money on London, which this Bank has negotiated in good faith.

Besides paying the interest on the £3,111,000. Provincial Bonds in London, the government has ordered this Bank to pay over to the Grand Trunk Rail way Co. £25,000 Sterling to meet the interest due 1. July on their Portland Rail way and other stocks in Canada & the United States for which we are to receive next week bills on Messrs. Barings and yourselves guaranteed by the Receiver General, and respecting which he advises you by this mail.

Mr. Ross and Mr. Holmes the President and Vice President of the G.T. Compy. are about to proceed to England next week, at their urgent request the Bank has loaned the Company on their note, and with most satisfactory collateral security £29,000 Sterling to meet the current demands against the Co. during their absence due for wages, salaries and mechanical – and other expenses of daily occurrence – the Bank was induced to make this advance for the sake of the stockholders in England whose property was in jeopardy, from the fact of the Company here, being unable to pay its common expenses. The effect of which would be almost ruinous. The Receiver General approves of this measure altho' the government is by no means bound by it. It is the intention of the Co. to keep their cash account for Canada hereafter with this Bank commencing when the line is opened.

The foregoing are all the advances that the Bank is under to any Rail road Compy in this Country having studiously avoided all such transactions neither does the Bank hold any Rail way stock.

We certainly made at one time a very large loan to the Great Western Rail way Co. when they were in extreme distress but this was done at the special interposition of the government who undertook to see us repaid out of sale of the Public Debentures, issued for that service, all which has been long since repaid and the Company now keep their whole account with us with a balance generally of £20,000. or £30,000 in their favor, – their daily receipts being about £2000.

It does not appear to me that the act lately passed in aide of the Grand Trunk will be found beneficial further than the relief it affords for the payment of the annual interest on the loan, and the almost certainty that at the next session that loan will be converted into stock – If my opinion were asked I would recommend the Company not to make any use of the right to issue £2,000,000. of new Bonds, unless in part for the special purpose of continuing the rail way from Stratford to Sarnia Lake Huron or to Windsor opposite Detroit, if that were done, the line would rank next to Great Western in profits and all danger over – as the traffic will be very great between those points and Montreal – the line however from Toronto westward will always pay the best.

The Receiver General informs me that as soon as he learns from you and the Messrs. Barings that the 2nd lot of his £100,000 debentures has been sold, he will let this Bank have bills to the amount of £50,000. or more to cover his account.

The Provincial revenue for the present year is estimated to yield about £1,500,000 cy. it has been coming in fast for a few weeks past, but we now expect the receipts to be small for the next month.

We have a very fine season throughout Canada. The crop of wheat is of the finest quality, and most abundant.

The determined and continued claims of the United States against England – which will never cease – makes us feel uneasy. We think that our govt. ought to take example from Russia and fortify the principal points of our frontier, at any rate do something more than they have done for the last 40 years.

D 53   T.G. RIDOUT TO GLYN, MILLS
Toronto, 2 August 1856
[*PAC, Glyn, Mills Papers, A542*]

I beg to acknowledge the receipt of your note of the 11 July, and am glad to learn that notwithstanding the unsatisfactory arrangement made by the government here, with the Grand Trunk Rail way Co. during the last session, the contractors Messrs. Peto & Co. will be able to complete the line between Montreal and Toronto, in furtherance of which we are now negociating their bills on London to a very large amount.

There is no doubt I think that if the Grand Trunk Rail Way Co. will boldly demand that the Canada government loan of £3,000,000. shall be converted into stock, it will be done at the next sitting of our Legislature, for the members are generally prepared for such a course.

In my last letter I mentioned that we shortly expected a bill from the President of the Grand Trunk R.W. Co. on London for the £25,000. lately loaned to them at the request of the government, but I find now that I was mistaken, and it will not be drawn until Mr. Ross's return from England – in the meantime we hold it as an Imprest against the government under authority of Council, to be retained out of the unexpended Balance in the Receiver Generals hands belonging to the original appropriation or Loan.

The Receiver General intends to draw upon London in the course of a few days, through this Bank, for about £100,000.

The wheat harvest in Upper Canada is finished and turns out to be a very fine crop, it has been secured almost without rain.

D 54   T.G. RIDOUT TO C.E. ANDERSON
Toronto, 8 August 1856
[*PAC, RG 19 E1A, v. 3366*]

It having been communicated to me by your orders that Mr. Thomas Park the Collector at Port Colborne, has, under date of the 4 inst.

addressed a letter to the Honble: the Inspector General – complaining, that the agent of this Bank at St. Catherines has refused to receive from him the deposit of his Public Monies – the notes of the Bank of Elgin – California Gold – and the bills of the Provincial Bank of Stanstead – and as you desire an explanation of the cause of such proceedings on the part of this Bank I am directed to state for your information as follows. viz.

Bank of Elgin

The Notes of this Bank were suddenly issued – we could not send them conveniently to St. Thomas for redemption without incurring a heavy expense and loss of time – so that until we could make the necessary arrangements to have them regularly presented for payment at their place of issue – The Bank agents had orders not to take them in deposit They are now however freely received in the Public deposits and Mr. Park will not in future be annoyed under that head.

California Gold

The Fifty dollar coins of this Gold stamped at San Francisco is inferior Gold – and only passes in US. at one or two per cent discount – and will not be taken by our Banks in payment of weekly balances: besides, it is a coarse coin – and has I am told many counterfeits – we have no objection however to receive California Gold at 2 per cent discount – and our agents have instructions to that effect: Mr. Parke may therefore safely receive that description of Coin at that rate, namely two per cent discount in payment of Custom House and other duties, and pay it over to this Bank at the same rate.

The Provincial Bank of Stanstead

In May last this Bank received in deposit from the Collector of Toronto about £300. in the notes of the said Bank. These notes were forwarded to our agent at Montreal for collection. he sent them over to Stanstead – but could find no such Bank – he again sent them to the same place by a special Messenger and found that the Bank was just opened – and he was paid the amount. since which time we have taken no more of those notes. We have also lately been informed – that there are notes of that Bank in circulation – not signed by an officer of the Inspector Generals Depart.

D 55   MEMORANDUM, JOHN LANGTON
21 August 1856
[*PAC, RG 58 E1, LB*]

. . . (6) Lastly, all advances by the Bank except with due forms should be stopped, and that could certainly be done without legislative aid. Except in the case of regular monthly expenses like salaries, no money ought to be paid out of the chest except on a warrant, and then only when the correctness of the cheque is certified by the proper officer and the authority of the Receiver General is given to the Bank for the advance. In the case of advances to particular Departments as lately to the Crown Lands and to the Post Office, there can be no possible reason or convenience for the irregular practice, because an accountable warrant upon an estimate of the probable requirements can issue quarterly or oftener if necessary. In the case of the certificates of the Board of Works I also think the practice unnecessary. A warrant insures that the whole Government have knowledge of the transaction and authorize the expenditure, and this appears necessary under our form of government, where the ministry is responsible as a whole. Under the former system one Department could expend the public funds without the consent or even the knowledge of the rest. By the plan now recommended by the Board of Works an improvement would certainly be effected, because the assent of the Inspector Generals Department would also be required, and as these Departments are in fact the only ones which know anything of, or have any means of checking the expenditure, it may not practically be open to great objections. But still the Receiver General would know nothing of the money having gone out of the chest, of which he is the custodian and he would in the evening report to the Governor General a balance in hand which would be only imaginary. This certainly seems an anomaly. I cannot see any convenience in the system proposed. As long as the Commissioner or the Assistant Commissioner could on their certificate draw from the Public chest at any time without question it might no doubt have convenience to them and those with whom their business lay, although at the expense of all proper responsibility. But when no money can be raised on a certificate till it has been examined, checked, countersigned and entered in the Inspector Generals Department, such a certificate has no convenience over a warrant. The form of a warrant has to be gone through afterwards and there is no saving of trouble and very little of time. It cannot be often that a days delay is of much consequence and if it is, it has to be submitted to in all other cases except where the Board of Works is concerned. And if from the peculiar duties of that Department money is sometimes more immediately required than in others, (though I cannot see why it should be) the difficulty might be met by a sum placed at their disposal by an accountable warrant.

I desire to bring these subjects before the Board in the hope that some arrangements may be made without delaying till the reassembling of the Legislature.

D 56   T.G. RIDOUT TO GLYN, MILLS
Toronto, 23 August 1856
[*PAC, Glyn, Mills Papers, A542*]

I have the pleasure to acknowledge the receipt of your letters of the 24th ult. and 1st & 8 instant. and beg to assure you, that it has afforded the President and Directors the greatest satisfaction to learn, that you have, with so much good will, accepted the agency of this Bank as regards the transfer of its shares in London according to the act, and measures will be immediately taken to grant you the legal authority for so doing. You will also be provided with the necessary Forms, for transfers and certificates.

The conduct of Mr. McCord our City Chamberlain has surprized me, as it was no doubt your good opinion of his Bonds that led to their being taken up by other parties besides their being placed at 95, was a much higher rate than he expected to obtain when he left this country. I therefore regret the course he has taken.

The Bank of British North America paid us this morning £20,000 stg. as part of the City money raised in London, so that we suppose the remainder of those funds will come to us through the same channel. We have held that account for the last 34 years, and certainly had a right to expect that their transactions in London would have been through your House, as for that purpose the coupons for the present loan are made payable there.

I was perfectly astonished to receive in your letter yesterday protests for the non acceptance of the two bills for £20,000. each lately negociated with us by the Great Western Rail Way Company: it is well however that the proceeds remain in our hands, in a separate account, untouched, being a deposit made in conjunction with that company by Mr. Isaac Buchanan in a wild and bold scheme to control the management of the new company for constructing the Southern Rail Way line from Suspension Bridge to the Town of Amhurstburg, at the mouth of Detroit River, Lake Erie, all which you will better understand by the newspapers, one of which I now send you, containing a singular letter published by Mr. Buchanan on the subject.

The Great Western Rail Way Compy. are in a flourishing state, they ought to let well alone, and not grasp at too much; but if they persist in this undertaking they will meet with difficulties incalculable, as Mr. Buchanan holds in defiance, our government, our Legislature, and Public opinion, which latter is certainly against him: notwithstanding all this, I have no apprehension about the Bills, they must be paid, and the money will probably be ordered to be applied to the construction of the 2nd line of track on their present road, now much wanted.

In case that the Great Western should fail in their attempt to monopolize both roads, it would be well if the Grand Trunk Company had means to share in the management of the Southern Line, as it will be a very profitable concern, perhaps the very best on this continent.

Messrs. Peto & Co. are driving on their works with astonishing vigour – everything seems to prosper with them just now, and there is no doubt, that by the time the navigation closes, their line will be completed, all except the Bridge at Montreal, which ought to be a government work – rail way people should never have attempted it, and I would recommend them now to let the Province finish it – if such a thing can be done . . . .

D 57   T.G. Ridout to Glyn, Mills
Toronto, 22 November 1856
[*PAC, Glyn, Mills Papers, A542*]

This Bank has drawn upon you for large sums of money within the last few weeks owing to payments for government to the extent of £350,000 in the distribution of the balance of the clergy reserve fund amongst the municipalities of Upper Canada over and above the ordinary expenses of the country, which has entirely exhausted the Revenue in hand, and left the Receiver General nearly £100,000 in our debt. This however he has undertaken to cover, as well as to provide for the interest falling due in London on the 1. of January next by directing you, and the Messrs. Barings, to pay into our account the proceeds of the sale of the £150,000 Provincial Debentures lately sent to England, without waiting for the formality of his bills. His order for £50,000 of this money was sent by cash mail, and by this Packet the order for the remainder goes out. The Receiver General is also preparing a further lot £50,000 Stg. of Debentures for the English market, making in all £200,000. for immediate sale, after which the ordinary receipt of Customs will suffice for the current expenditure of the Province so that hereafter I trust our drawings upon you will not exceed our funds we being well aware of the rigid state of the money market throughout the world, and are preparing for it accordingly, by reducing our daily discounts.

Some new regulations made by government will tend very much to restrict the operations of the Board of Works Department and thereby relieve the Public chest, the receipts of which show a large increase this year.

At the late general election of Directors of the Grand Trunk Rail Way Company, held here on the 12th inst. I was honoured with a seat at that Board, which I have good reason to believe was conferred upon me at your suggestion, it is therefore with great pleasure that I take this opportunity to acknowledge it and to assure you that as far as my abilities will allow, I will endeavour to do my duty, in that responsible situation, being well aware that the shareholders in England, who form the great body interested, look forward with anxiety to the proceedings of the Board here, and have a right to expect all deference and attention paid to the instructions sent out by the London Board.

I am still of opinion that the company will be entirely relieved from their debt to this Province, either by the amount being converted into stock or by a free gift, the latter seems to be the most popular opinion, as there is a jealousy in having the government mixed up with so great an Institution, leading eventually to political influences.

The wheat crop in Upper Canada, this year, is larger than usual, and is of the finest quality, so much so, that it rates about 12 cents per bushel in the New York market, above the best samples of the United States, and large quantities have been exported to that country and to Lower

Canada, during this Fall. The navigation of the Lakes, and the St. Lawrence is however now about closing for the winter, so that the trade will for a few months be confined to accumulating stocks for next spring.

D 58   REPORT OF JOHN YOUNG AND R. JUSON[47] TO BOARD OF DIRECTORS, GREAT WESTERN RAILWAY, 13 FEBRUARY 1857 *[PAC, RG 30, v. 2]*

We beg leave to report that pursuant to the Finance Committee Minute No. 664 we visited Toronto yesterday to see the President & Cashier of the Bank of Upper Canada regarding the low rate of premium of Exchange allowed by the Bank on the last two lodgements of money by the London Board to the credit of the Bank with Messrs. Glyn Mills & Co. and were unable to obtain any greater concession than 3/4% additional to the rate previously allowed on the £50,000 Stg. making 8 3/4% instead of 8%. On the rate allowed for the £20,000. viz. $9^1/_2$ per cent they would make no advance but agree to allow at the rate of 10 per cent premium on any considerable lodgment which may be now made.

The Bank complains that in consequence of the non payment of the Bill for £50,000 drawn by the late Vice President[48] it suffered serious loss and inconvenience as well as from the large amount still due by the Company, which causes the Bank to have recourse to sales of Exchange in New York at low rates to meet their balances, and so long as the Company are in the hands of the Bank it is hopeless to expect to realise the highest premium that should be obtained.

We would therefore recommend that the London Board be earnestly requested to remit as early as possible such a sum as will enable the Company to repay to the Bank its present advances, and should this request not have been wholly or in part already anticipated by a further lodgement to the credit of the Bank with Messrs. Glyn & Co., that no further lodgment be made to its credit but that this Board be allowed to draw on the London Board, under such restrictions & for such sums as they may advise, such drafts being drawn payable at 60 days sight, this will enable the Company to arrange beforehand with the Bank for the highest obtainable rate of premium, in place of leaving them as at present to fix the rate after the lodgement has been made and which late experience has shown they are ready to take advantage of.

---

[47]Richard Juson (1812–73) was a hardware merchant and nail manufacturer in Hamilton. He was a longtime director of the Great Western Railway.

[48]This refers to an ill-fated attempt made by Isaac Buchanan and J.S. Radcliff, the Great Western's vice-president, to use railway funds for the promotion of the Southern Railway without first obtaining the sanction of the Great Western's shareholders.

D 59   J.C. Morrison to J.W. Dunkle[49]
16 May 1857
[*PAC, RG 19 B2A, v. 1149*]

I have the honor to request that you will be pleased to pay over to T.G. Ridout Esq[re], Cashier, Bank of Upper Canada, the Sum of £61,990 Currency and charge Same against account of this Department with Your Bank. –

You will further be pleased to ask from *Mr Ridout* Duplicate Receipts for Same Stating that the amount has been placed to credit of this Department with the Bank of Upper Canada, one of which receipts you will be pleased to transfer to me –

P.S.   *18th May 1857* – £61,990 Cy transferred to Bank of Upper Canada, in the R.G.'s Books, but I can find no Certf. of Deposit, or correspondence of any Kind. All Seems to have been arranged viva vôce

Cert. true copy   T.D. Harrington[50]
R.G.O. 31 March '62   D.R.G.

D 60   C.E. Anderson to T.L. Terrill[51]
Toronto, 23 July 1857
[*PAC, RG 19 B2b, v. 1162*]

I have the honor to request you will be pleased to process the Warrant of H.E. The Administrator of the Government in favor of Thos G. Ridout Esqre Cashier of the Bank of Upper Canada for the Sum of *Three Hundred and Seventy five Thousands, five Hundred and forty Six pounds 17/1. Cy* (being £307,265..12/2 Stg: at 10% p*m* on Exchange 4/6 Stg. per dollar) – in order to reimburse that Institution That amount paid for the Province in London on 1st Inst: on the undermentioned accounts, viz: –

For Interest due, on Govt Account	£63305..3..3 Stg.
For Redemption of 5% Debentures due	
1st Inst including the Agency of 1% –	£147.409..10..0 –
For Interest on A/C of GR. TR RR. Co.	£82,158.8/
For ditto due Ontario SHRR.	£14,392.10/.
	96..550..18..11 –
	£307..265..12..2 Stg:

As per letter from Bank of Upper Canada and the requisite vouchers from England accompanying this.

---

[49]J.W. Dunkle was cashier of the Zimmerman Bank.
[50]Thomas D. Harrington was deputy receiver general.
[51]T.L. Terrill was provincial secretary.

D 61   BANK OF UPPER CANADA'S ACCOUNT WITH THE RECEIVER GENERAL
Toronto, 30 July 1857
[PAC, RG 19 B2b, v. 1162]

Advanced O.S. & H. Railway Co.	£12,166
Advanced Grand Trunk	107,247
Advanced Ottawa & Prescott R Co.	13,000
Advanced Geo L. Read[52]	19,500
Advanced A.P. McDonald[53]	15,000
Advanced Hugh Allan[54]	29,200
Advanced Great Western Interest	28,600
Advanced Post Office Department	49,000
Advanced Education CW	25,000
Advanced Sinking Fund	73,000
Advanced Pay Lists	50,000
Interest Coupons held by Bank	30,000
	£451,713
Cash in BUC this day	55,486
due the Bank	396,227
Cash in other Banks	60,940
Deficit	335,287

signed
C.E. Anderson

D 62   GREAT WESTERN RAILROAD AND THE BANK OF UPPER CANADA, 30 JULY 1857
[PAC, RG 30, v. 6]

724   Bank of Upper Canada. Commercial Bank
The Managing Director reported that the following letter addressed to him by the Cashier of the Bank of Upper Canada dated 15th instant, had been delivered on the 18th instant, after the Bank had been afforded an opportunity of reflecting upon the consequences of the letter.

Bank of Upper Canada
Toronto 15th July 1857

My dear Sir
The Board being dissatisfied with your late reply to Mr. Stow – "that

---

[52]George Lowe Reid was the chief engineer for the Great Western Railway.

[53]A.P. Macdonald was a businessman and contractor. His debt to the Bank of Upper Canada arose from a public works contract carried out on the Chats Canal. The bank had advanced the money but the government never honoured the claim and as a result, as the bank's trustees ultimately wrote, "the account was lost."

[54]Hugh Allan (1810–82) was a shipping magnate, financier, capitalist and railway promoter. The debt referred to here related to a government subsidy for Allan's transatlantic shipping enterprise. The government did repay the bank's advance.

you had no authority to draw upon your Board in London to cover your account, and also that you could not tell when it would be paid'' – it has been determined to take legal proceedings against the Great Western Railway Company for the recovery of the debt due by them to this Bank. I therefore beg leave to give you this notice, it being the only course left to this Bank to pursue.

I remain
Yours truly,
Thos. G. Ridout
Cashier

C.J. Brydges Esq.
  Managing Director
  G.W.R.Co., Hamilton

He also reported that on the 23rd instant he had seen Mr. Ridout in Toronto who expressed his regret at the misunderstanding which had arisen & stated his expectation that, after the explanations given, the Bank Board would withdraw the above offensive letter and make satisfactory arrangements for the future. Subsequently Mr. Ridout instructed the Cashier in Hamilton to inform the Company that the Bank demanded a bond under seal payable in 3 months for the amount now overdrawn. After consultation with the Members of the Finance Committee the following communication was made to the Bank of Upper Canada.

The Company will agree to give the Bank of Upper Canada a bond under seal due in 3 months dated 1st August 1857 for the amount overdrawn on the 31st July 1857, adding interest on the amount for the 3 months and allowing 1/2% for Agency, on the following condition, "that the Company be allowed, if they want it, to overdraw their account during the six months from 1st August 1857 to the extent of £50,000 Currency, such advance being gradual, as the necessity of it arises."

This morning (30th July) the following reply by telegraph was received from Mr. Ridout . . . .

"The Board yesterday determined not to make any further advances, but will take a note at three months for your present balance as before offered."

Resolved

That the reply received from Mr. Ridout leaves this Board no alternative but to close the account with the Bank of Upper Canada.

That no cheques beyond those now out be drawn upon that Bank and no further deposits made.

That an account be opened with the Commercial Bank of Canada.

That the Managing Director be instructed to make the necessary arrangements with the Commercial Bank, on the basis that this Company is to have authority to overdraw its account to the extent of £50,000 if and when required.

That a Bond under the seal of the Company payable in 3 months from date be given to the Bank of Upper Canada on the 1st August, for the amount due on the 31st July 1857 and interest on the same for the 3 months.

That the attention of the London Board be specially called to this matter, and that this Board will have no alternative, in order to pay the Bond, demanded by the Bank of Upper Canada, but to draw for the amount (about £70,000 Currency) upon the English Board not later than 31st October 1857.

D 63   W.H. PARK[55] TO ISAAC BUCHANAN
Hamilton, 1 August 1857
[PAC, Buchanan Papers, v. 50]

. . . In 1855 the Circulation of this Bank [Commercial Bank] was £662,000; in May of the present year £300,000!! Nothing but a most rigid supervision at Head Office and a faithful discharge of duty at Branches could have enabled us to pay 4% this last half year on a considerably increased Capital and place £30,000 to credit of Surplus fund. In fact we have to look very closely into each transaction & see that it pays on the face of it and not prospectively. On circulation we don't rely beyond 20 to 30 days and my own impression not hastily formed is that the days of large Circul. in Canada are at an end. I made a calculation in '56 of the Comparative ratios of Canada Circulation and Bank Capital, to the Circul. and Capital of the principal States of the Union, the States themselves, England, Ireland & Scotland – and then the people of Canada were foolish enough and rich enough to hold B'K notes to an amount relatively only Second to Ireland the best Circulating Country in the world for the Banks, but a fact which tells against their thrift and Knowledge of the value of money.

Occasionally there may be an inflation of paper money, but it can never happen in Canada again that £12,000 will be a safe reserve against a Circul. of £230,000 as in the case of the Gore Bank in 1853. The whole tendency of the Age is to a rapid adjustment of balances, and the folly of holding Bank notes in old Chests "holes-in-the wall," and other Outlandish *natural* Banks of deposit is finding its way to be known to the rural population wherever the education of the people is advancing . . . .

D 64   J.C. MORRISON TO B. HOLMES
14 September 1857
[PAC, RG 19 B2b, v. 1162]

In reply to yours of the 11th I have to say that Mr. Macpherson having

---

[55]W.H. Park was cashier of the Commercial Bank's Hamilton branch.

called on me relative [to] the Promissary notes of Gzowski & Co.[56] mentioned in your letter and having shown me your note to that firm desiring to renew their Bills – as this department had not made the necessary Bank arrangements as would enable the Company to retire them at maturity – & Mr. Macpherson having further stated – that not only was it impossible for them to renew, but that the Com'l Bank had determined not to do so & that the Bills would go to protest – Being aware myself that these notes formed part of the Grand Trunk liabilities – to be met out of the Monies advanced by the Government – I called on Mr Ridout & instructed him to retire the notes at once – having first arranged with the Com'l Bank to transfer a little amount of their deposit to the Bank of Upper Canada to avoid inconvenience to the latter Bank – an arrangement which I assumed would meet any exigency as well as the convenience of the parties concerned –

D 65   GLYN, MILLS TO T.G. RIDOUT
London, 18 September 1857
[*PAC, Glyn, Mills Papers, A540*]

At the request of the Grand Trunk Railway we retain the bill for £25000 at present, and will take care, if paid here, that interest upon it is duly accounted for. Acting upon the Direction of the Receiver General we have withdrawn from the account of the Bank and carried to that of the Province receipts for the Province Bonds recently realised, the operation having been settled by the bills given to you by the Receiver General We congratulate you on the improved aspect of the account though we fear the return by the last Mail of the Bills of the Grand Trunk for £66720..4.. (which should not have been issued) will have deranged your calculations; we trust the drafts on us remitted by you and due on the October (issued without acceptance) may be duly honored and we learn that Every Exertion will be made by the directors to do so, but for your guidance we think it right to add that great difficulty is found, from the bad [trafic?] returns, in inducing the public to take the debentures from which source the Means of Meeting their demand is derivable We observe by your note of the 10th August that you expect a payment in [?] or Exchange on the 1st Nov. from the Great Western of Canada for £59..178 – We trust that we may now rely upon the account assuming its usual satisfactory state and that you will not depend in your operations upon such large advances from us. The recent advices from

[56]Casimir Gzowski (1813–98) was an engineer and railway contractor. He became wealthy working on contracts for the Grand Trunk. Other partners in this firm were Luther Holton, David Lewis Macpherson (1818–96) a Conservative politician, general financier and railway promoter; and Alexander Tilloch Galt (1817–93) a prominent Conservative politician and businessman who became minister of finance under John A. Macdonald in 1858.

the United States have had a detrimental Effect here upon the Market for the Sale of Bonds, and such securities – This money Market is now in some degree influenced by the increasing demand for money on the Continent, and there is no appearance of an Easier state of things here at present, though commercial credit is very sound our Harvest Abundant.

D 66   J. LANGTON TO W.H. COFFIN[57]
Toronto, 10 November 1857
[*PAC, RG 58 B2A, v. 2*]

. . . I have also received this morning an application from the Receiver General to the Provincial Secretary for a warrant to reimburse the Bank of Upper Canada the sum of £30.923.2.4 advanced to the Post Office Department – I find from your statement of cash just received that the Post Office was in arrear – £39.456. = .9 on the 30th of June, but as that amount included the remittance to England of £19.790.1.4 which was made good by the issue of a warrant for the amount a few days after the close of the quarter, the amount for which the Bank was in advance to the Post Office must have been only £19,665.19.5 – At that date the new arrangement came into force & you have received since the 1st of July warrants to the amount of £20,000, which it is presumed have prevented the necessity of any further advance – I am therefore at a loss to understand how such a large claim has arisen, & before reporting upon the application of the Receiver General I have to request that you will forward to me a statement of the present state of your account with the Bank of Upper Canada.

D 67   P.M. VANKOUGHNET[58] TO C.E. ANDERSON
Toronto, 5 December 1857
[*PAC, RG 19 B2A, v. 1149*]

Mr. Macdonald (Atty. Genl.) and myself being the only members of the Council in Town waited yesterday upon His Excellency the Governor General who authorises us to ask Mr. Ridout Cashier Bank of U.C. to loan to the Grand Trunk Railway Company £15,000, in anticipation of the weekly advance authorised by Order in Council some time since – the Co. undertaking to make this sum answer their wants for the next five weeks. In the mean time definite action will be taken by them & by us in relation to their position.

You will please endeavor to have this accommodation obtained for them.

---

[57]W.H. Coffin was deputy postmaster general.
[58]Philip VanKoughnet (1822–69) was a politician, lawyer and judge. In 1857 he was minister of agriculture.

D 68   T.G. RIDOUT TO J.C. MORRISON
Toronto, 22 December 1857
[*PAC, RG 1 E7, v. 48, 25 March 1858*]

The Bank is desirous to make a further negociation with government of
Municipal Consolidated Loan Fund Debentures payable in Canada, in
exchange for Sterling Bonds of the same Fund payable in London to the
amount of about £50,000 – in like manner as we negociated with you
some time ago £100,000 – may I therefore request you will be pleased
to sanction this arrangement which would be a great accomodation to
the Bank at this time.
Notescript: I have no objection to the application being complied with,
especially if it will relieve the Bk. in these bad times but Mr Cayley's
comment must be had. JCM

D 69   J.H. MASON[59] TO T.G. RIDOUT
22 December 1857
[*PAO, Canada Permanent Mortgage LB, 1857–58, pp. 71–2*]

I am instructed to communicate with you in reference to the account of
the Society with the Bank of Upper Canada.

The Society's account with the Bank dates from March 1850 is
entirely a deposit account, no discounts having been hitherto required
and now averages about £3000 per month, the average balance at the
credit of the society being about £1000.

From the uniform increase in the Society's business, there is little
doubt that its account with the Bank will continue to augment. The
Society is also the proprietor of 184 shares in the stock of the Bank.
Under these circumstances I beg to inquire if the Bank will allow
Interest on the balances at our credit without prejudice to us. It may be
proper for me to add that other Banks would allow interest . . .

[59]J.H. Mason was manager of the Canada Permanent Mortgage Company at
Toronto.

E. A CASUALTY OF CHANGE: 1858–66

E 1   J.L. GRANT[1] TO T. BARING (COPY)
1 February 1858
[PAC, Glyn, Mills Papers, A544, enclosed in T. Baring to G.C. Glyn, 31 March 1858]

. . . From the arrangements made the Government has now authorized us to draw on account of the general purposes of the Company a total of £300,000 of the Preferential Capital of 1858. £150,000 of which go to pay our indebtedness to the Province & the balance of our general uses. Of this sum £100,000 were drawn last week & I have now to advise you of the second £100,000 which have been drawn by this mail in favor of Mr. Ridout on Glyn Mills & Coy. at 4 months sight & I am happy to be able to inform you that arrangements have been concluded by the President & Vice President & the Bank of Upper Canada by which that institution will make such advances to us as are absolutely necessary for the carrying on of the Company in anticipation of the authority to be given by the London Board to draw exchange for the third £100,000 released by the Government & which is indispensable to enable us to continue working the Road . . . .

E 2   T.G. RIDOUT to GLYN, MILLS
Toronto, 1 February 1858
[PAC, Glyn, Mills Papers, A542]

. . . I also observe by your late letters the steady reduction of the discount rates by the Bank of England. The last arrival placing the rate at five per cent, all which will no doubt considerably relieve the Grand Trunk Rail Way Company.

You will be pleased to observe that by the present mail I remit another Grand Trunk Rail Way bill for £100,000 – but as it is at 4 months sight, it cannot be considered a regular remittance. I hope however that you will be pleased to give it your favourable consideration – their next bill, which will be drawn about the 20th inst will also be for a large sum but at 60 days as usual, out of that bill the Company propose to retire their long outstanding protested bill for £66,000 Stg. and thus redeem the £100,000. City of Toronto Debentures held by this Bank as collateral security, as the conversion of those debentures into Sterling Bonds is for the present postponed.

In consequence of the scarcity of money, the mild winter and badness of our roads, the produce of Canada in wheat and lumber has not yet begun to move – we expect however a more brisk season in the spring.

[1]J. Lewis Grant worked in the accountant's office for the Grand Trunk Railway.

Our new Legislature will meet on the 25 instant, by which time it is expected that the government will be strongly re-organized, and that no material change in the ministry will be made, or will the friendly interest now existing towards the Grand Trunk Rail Way Company be impaired.

E 3   JOHN LANGTON TO T.G. RIDOUT
Toronto, 27 March 1858
[PAC, RG 58 B2A, v. 2]

You are no doubt aware that by a late order in Council the former practice of Imprest accounts with the Bank has been abolished, & that for the future no public money is to be paid out or advanced except upon the authority of a regular warrant – As it is desirable that all the open accounts of this nature should be closed with as little delay as possible, I have the honor to request that you will furnish me with a statement of all sums, for which you hold the Government responsible, Whether they be what is usually called Imprest accounts, or advances on Board of Works certificates, or balances against any Department on their Bank account.

E 4   THE STANDING COMMITTEE ON PUBLIC ACCOUNTS, 8 JUNE 1858
[JLA, 1858, Appendix 4]

William Cayley, examined
. . . When an advance is made by the Bank, the record of it in the Receiver General's books will depend on the time it is brought to account by the Bank, & if the advance so made by the Bank is repaid before it is brought to account, it may not come into the Inspector General's books at all.

E 5   WILLIAM PROUDFOOT TO GLYN, MILLS
Toronto, 21 June 1858
[PAC, Glyn, Mills Papers, A542]

I beg leave to address you on a subject regarding myself – being desirous to borrow a sum of money for a friend, say for two years to the amount of £5000 Stg. and I would be willing to give a Bond and Mortgage in Real Estate to double the amount or more and would engage to pay at the rate of 6 or 8 per cent interest payable half yearly at your Bank in London and could procure you Mr. Thos. G. Ridouts opinion as to the entire safety of the transaction and the punctual payment of the amount & interest at maturity. In taking the liberty in making this application to you it is under the belief I am well known to you by name having been President of the Bank of Upper Canada for twenty three years and have been a director since it was first established in 1822 – induces me to apply through you for my friend and I can assure you I can offer the first class security – being myself possessed of a very large landed Estate upwards of 70,000 acres of land eligibly situated and also other large resources but the pressure of money matters here during last winter has been so great, and money still very scarce, I was unable to borrow here at any reasonable rate of interest induces me to apply through you where money is at so low a rate of interest and so abundant, and if granted the money may be paid to the credit of the Bank of Upper Canada . . . for my use *here* . . . .

Our Parliament is still in Session and has done very little business as yet, but I am now fully certain they will pass a measure to increase the rate of interest, the Banks will be allowed to charge 7 or 8 per cent, and Loans on Mortgages will probably be at the rate of 8 to 10 per cent or it may be at whatever rate the parties agree upon at long dates: this will improve the value of Bank Stock and will draw capital to this country for investment where it is greatly needed at present, and where perfect security can readily be obtained . . . .

E 6   THOMAS REIFFENSTEIN[2] TO P. VANKOUGHNET
Toronto, 31 August 1858
[*PAC, RG 19 B2b, v. 1162*]

I beg to inform you . . . that a letter has been addressed . . . [to the Receiver General] by Mr. Baby[3] the purport of which is to revoke the Power of Attorney lodged with the Dep't in favour of Mr. T.G. Ridout Cashier of the Bank of Upper Canada authorising to draw the amount of his warrants issuing from time to time.

As I am aware that the Bank of Upper Canada has made heavy advances to Mr. Baby and that he still owes that institution a large amount and that the Bank made those advances upon the faith of its interests being protected by this Dep't of the Gov't. I communicate the foregoing that instructions may be sent as to the line of conduct to be pursued by this office in the meantime.

E 7   A.T. TREMIBECKI[4] TO T. BARING
10 September 1858
[*PAC, Baring Papers, A834*]

. . . If the Bank of Upper Canada do not become anxious about the exchange for £100,000 and press for the repayment of their floating loan of £200,000 we may go on very well without drawing on London till the return of Mr. Blackwell[5] . . . . In a letter which I received yesterday the President tells me that he had some conversation with Mr. Ridout on the subject of the £100,000 exchange & that he thinks he "composed him sufficiently for the moment regarding it" . . . .

[2]Thomas Reiffenstein was deputy receiver general.
[3]Charles François Xavier Baby (1794–1864) was a general businessman and a contractor who profited immensely from government work.
[4]A.T. Tremibecki worked for the Grand Trunk.

E 8   T.G. RIDOUT TO GLYN, MILLS
Toronto, 4 October 1858
[*PAC, Glyn, Mills, Papers, A542*]

I have the pleasure to acknowledge the receipt of your private note of the 17 ultimo, the contents of which are seriously noted, and measures will of course be taken to place our account with you on a more satisfactory footing.

The unsaleable quality of the Consolidated Municipal Loan Fund Bonds in the London market owing to some unfounded opinion of their value, has led us into erroneous calculations of our remittances, as we did not anticipate that the prejudices against those Bonds would have continued so long.

Before Mr. Galt left for England I mentioned to him that we had the £150,000 still on hand, and he promised to make it one of his first investments, since then, by last mail I wrote you an official letter on the subject, and have no doubt that these Debentures will very shortly be converted into Cash, whether Mr. Galt succeeds in funding the Canada debt[6] or not, at any rate, he will afford you reliable information regarding those securities which will I am sure satisfy you, that they are first class investments.

With regard to the balance of the account after the above mentioned Bonds are realized, I shall be able by next mail to write you more particularly on that subject, as we have various resources from which we shall be able to accomplish that object, and in the meantime our valuations on you will be confined to small transactions.

After a long state of depression, the general affairs of Canada are beginning to assume a more cheering character, and I have no doubt that before the end of this year a great improvement will be visible, which already begins to show itself in the Custom House Duties.

E 9   T. BLACKWELL TO T. BARING (PRIVATE, COPY)
Montreal, 4 November 1858
[*PAC, Baring Papers, A835*]

. . . The subject [chartering a bank controlled by the Grand Trunk] is very well worthy of Consideration and there are reasons connected with present condition of public affairs in Canada which may render it in spite of the friendly feeling of its Managers to the Co. that the B.U.C. should very much curtail its accommodation to us – reasons indeed have been within the last two days pointed out why we should with all convenient speed place ourselves in a position more independent of that bank as of any other Bank relying so largely upon the Govt Acct; but I

---

[5]Thomas Blackwell was general manager of the Grand Trunk, 1858–61.

[6]This referred to a plan for recapitalizing and consolidating Canada's outstanding debt at a lower rate of interest.

have no idea that any early change can possibly take effect – Still if Mr. Cayleys Plan[7] & his Explanation are considered satisfactory the foregoing view may serve as an additional reason for giving the Plan a trial . . . .

E 10   C.S. Gzowski to [Blackwell?] (copy)
Toronto, 26 November 1858
[*PAC, Baring Papers, A835*]

In complying with your wish I will undertake to repeat in writing the remarks I made in the conversation I had the pleasure of having with you yesterday on the subject of Banking, and the field that in my opinion exists at this moment in Canada for the establishment of an additional Bank to rank with the more respectable institutions already established in the Province.

No one acquainted with the Country can doubt that there is ample room for the employment of additional banking Capital, the Bankers themselves admit this, and that there is no necessity to have recourse to any speculative or hazardous experiments to make it profitable.

Assuming that such an Institution is properly managed, the great requisites are, a respectable Capital, a good Credit and Connections in London, and a good field of operations here. By the latter, I wish it understood a steady and continuous issue of paper over a large surface so as to secure an extended circulation not liable to be suddenly or rapidly poured back upon the Bank. The connection between the Grand Trunk Co. and a new Bank, to which the conversation we had yesterday pointed, was to enable the latter to avail itself of the machinery of the former to extend its note circulation, would in my opinion effect the object admirably. You have already nearly nine hundred miles of road, with a large corps of Operatives and Labourers whose wages alone would weekly absorb a very considerable amount, while at the same time your terminal points and operations on American Ground give you the command of a field where Canada paper is preferred to that of the native Banks.

Not being a Banker, I can only give you the results of my own experience as a Contractor, having to deal with Banks and their paper as a Customer. I will not attempt to discuss the ways and means how Bank profits are made. At the same time I may observe that in this country, the issue of paper, though by no means the sole source of profit, enters more largely as an item into the account than in England where to a great extent the Bank of England supplies the circulating medium and as it may be assumed, that for every pound paid out, its equivalent is held

---

[7]Cayley and others wished to use a recently chartered but as yet inactive bank, called the Bank of Canada, as a financial arm of the Grand Trunk and, if possible, merge it with the Bank of Upper Canada. Among the promoters were Cayley, John Ross, J.C. Morrison and Frederick Cumberland. The scheme came to nothing.

by the Bank either in Bullion or Bills receivable, the paper out may be considered as bearing interest to the full extent of its average circulation, less the Cash reserve; while the paid up Capital of the Bank may be held in public Securities, readily convertible.

I may illustrate the advantage of having such means as the Grand Trunk Company would afford for putting out paper, by referring to the Molson Bank of Montreal (Chartered). This Bank commenced about four years ago. The Molsons are wealthy and of high standing, and have large mercantile & manufacturing connections. These establishments have been the means of putting out a large and constant supply of Bank notes sometimes exceeding the average of two thousand dollars a day in wages and the purchase of grain. The Capital is £250,000 and has paid regularly a dividend of eight per cent, has accumulated a handsome reserve and is eagerly sought for at a premium of eight per cent, and I may add with no sellers. A Bank established on the principles that we discussed yesterday with a larger Capital and under the auspices and management that you referred to would in a few months, command as large a premium.

Much may be said on the advantages that a Charter containing unusually liberal provisions obtained at the last Session of parliament, and which I understood from you had been placed at the Service of your friends in England as well as on the extent and certainty of profits to the Shareholders of the Bank, that must necessarily be made by its enjoying the advantages of the Grand Trunk Account; that Road with all its ramifications affording undoubtedly the best and constantly profitable circulation for a large amount of its capital . . . .

E 11   T. Blackwell to T. Baring
3 January 1859
[PAC, Baring Papers, A835]

. . . Although the Banks are not [directly?] giving us aid yet they are indirectly doing so to a large extent – which 12 months ago scarcely one of the Banks would put itself out of the way to accomodate us or our Contractors – the improved credit we have acquired have induced them to expand a very considerable credit to the Contractors who thus *collectively* have relieved us a good deal & will do so to a still larger extent . . . .

E 12   T.D. Harrington to T.G. Ridout
Toronto, 10 January 1859
[PAC, RG 19 B2b, v. 1163]

In order to reduce the Charges which Your Bank may have against the Balance appearing at the Credit of the Government at the Expiration of 1858, Either direct or indirect, I transmit you herewith two Receiver

Generals checks (one for $40.000 on the Commercial Bank, the other on Your Institution for $223.578 63/100) Amount*g* to $263.578 63/100, which will Cover all releases you have made from time to time to "The Subsidiary Lines" of Railroads by orders from this department, in anticipation of the issue of a Warrant for that purpose against the amount assigned to the Railroads in question viz.

Ottawa & Prescott Railway Co.: . . . .£45,000   Stg.
Cobourg & Peterboro' 25,000
Port Hope & Lindsay . . . . 30,000.   100000 Stg.

say one Hundred Thousand Pounds Sterling under the Grand Trunk Railway relief Act 1856 –

The above amount of *$263.578 63/100* is drawn against the Proceeds of Exchange *$281.354 16/100* deposited to [account?] of Recv. Genl. June 1858 and leaves unreleased a Bal. of that Acct of $17,775 53/100 – It comprises in addition to the *releases* on account of the Ottawa & Prescott Railway Compy the amount of the notes (matured and about to mature) given for same account by the Grand Trunk Railway Compy. and held by the Commercial Bank of Canada viz *$111.721 55/100* which You will please to retire and hand over to This Dep*t* – (one note $40.000 – is overdue and still held by Com*l* Bank). In addition to the releases out of the above *$281.354 16/100* as [follows?] viz: to the Ottawa & Prescott Road –

released	$27,478 *45*	
Grand Trunk Notes	111,721 *55*	
	$139,200	
To The Cobourg & Peterboro Road	39,557.72	
To The Port Hope & Lindsay Road	84,670 –	
(am*t* of Checks	$263,427 72	

is the amount of $150 *84* remaining unreleased (over & above the former amount of Exchange *£42,187.10 Stg.* not brought to – the Recr. Genl. Cash; 1857. – Thus the a/c of advances to the "Subsidiary Lines" will be found closed – leaving, as before stated a balance not released of *$17775 53/100* –

You will also have received a check for $49.333, Amount of Warrant to repay you for advance made in 1856 to the Northern Railroad Co. and forming a charge in "The Imprest a/c," which being the balance, closes the a/c.

I further understand that you have waived Your claim for Agency, Commission, & Postage, which enables us to Set that charge aside –

The Public Works charge *$10.798* being now in a fair way of settlement may also be taken out of the Account – now particularly as it is departmental and should not have appeared against the Receiver Generals' Balance –

The Post Office & Money Order Office a/c being partly departmental you will also please to keep separately against that Department –

The charges against the Bureau of Agriculture should also form a distinct a/c, being purely departmental and covered from time to time by Warrant.

The Compensation a/c. Should never form a charge as the Warrants Should be applied for in anticipation of the amounts required – it is also a distinct a/c –

The Crown Land Commissioners' deposits will also for the future be kept distinct from the Receiver Generals' a/c – The alterations lately adopted in the mode of deposits for a/c of the Receiver General will apply to those made for Crown Lands as they are made in credit of Receiver General for Monies due to that Department.

The late changes in the mode of deposit will also apply to the Indian monies – their a/c being also kept distinct as heretofore –

There is no necessity to Keep the Ordinance Land a/c distinct from the General Deposit a/c of this Department.

In future the only charges which should appear to the debit of the Receiver General's balance, are the advances for Salaries to departments by Customs Officers and Sums advanced by any special order from this Department Chargeable to a suspense account.

And any Officer requiring advances for Public purposes, [even?] those whose responsibility authorises it, Should be called upon by the Bank to cover any such amount, if advanced, by a Warrant before the End of the Month or Quarter as the case may require – And thus, no acct. of any officer will remain open at the close of any Quarter when in future, in addition to the usual monthly a/c, an account Current with this Department embracing all charges will be required of the Bank

E 13   A.T. GALT TO T.G. RIDOUT (PRIVATE AND CONFIDENTIAL)
Toronto, 12 January 1859
[PAC, RG 19 E1A, v. 3376]

I observe that our balance with you has been considerably reduced since the New Year. You may therefore not be displeased to learn that I have requested Mr. Sherwood to check out against our balance in the other Banks – and thus allow our fund with you to accumulate.

We expect the balance of the specie in a day or two – it is all on the North American which arrived today at Portland – With the £15000 previously received there will be in all £70,000 Sterling – which will thus go to our credit in the several Banks.

I hope you will bear in mind what I remarked on the subject of your [inspection?] it would be a great satisfaction to me as Finance Minister to know that you had been able to make such arrangements as would completely [remove?] the Bank from the [?] of its [enemies?]. I trust you will forgive my saying so much but a certain amount of responsibility rests upon me – as you are well aware – exposed as I am to attacks on all sides in any future financial policy . . . .

P.S. I shall probably go to London.

E 14   T. Blackwell to T. Baring (Private)
Montreal, 17 January 1859
[PAC, Baring Papers, A835]

. . . The reason why the Banks will not aid us *directly* is, that they have not the means and it arises only from accidental circumstances that the Bank of Upper Canada has been able to carry out its friendly disposition to us. Your suggestion about increased capital to that institution is a very valuable one, but I am afraid that a preferential capital might be injurious to its credit, – the government account has always been its main stay, but when the changes which are in prospect are completed, the increase of capital must be made, and the subject occupies serious attention at present, particularly that of the management.

With respect to drafts for our wants on the Western works, it was necessary to meet the December Certificates for £13839.4.0 Sterling but I have arranged with the B.U.C. to delay sending the draft for a week or two, so as to ensure its reaching you not before February nor maturing before May. – I also persuaded Mr. Ridout the Cashier to advance £12,000 Sterling in Detroit, as from Mr. Macpherson's representations, it was necessary that some provision should be made to meet their engagements which are all *cash*, as Mr. Gzowski will have explained to you . . . .

E 15   William Proudfoot to A. Steven (copy)
Toronto, 24 January 1859
[CIBC, Gore Bank Papers]

. . . I do not know how your bank is paid but we find an immense amount overdue & in suit – & the only chance of relief is through parties in England who are likely to invest monies on mortgages . . . .

E 16   Unsigned Memorandum Between the Government of Canada and the Bank of Upper Canada
B.U.C., 25 January 1859
[PAC, RG 19 E1A, v. 3368]

Memorandum between the Government of Canada and the Bank of Upper Canada respecting the collection of the Provincial revenue and the payment of the Public service.

The Bank undertakes to receive all money paid in at the head office or any of its branches or agencies to the credit of the Government and to account for the same on demand. The Bank further undertakes to pay all checks requisitions and pay lists duly authorized by the Government, presented at the head office or any of its branches or agencies, without charge.

In consideration of the foregoing and in lieu of any agency or other compensation for the expense attendant on the above services, the

Government undertakes to keep a cash balance in the hands of the Bank of not less than six hundred thousand dollars, such balance to be adjusted weekly in an account to be rendered by the bank every Saturday, to the Receiver General shewing the state of the deposits to the credit of the Receiver General and the several branches of the public service. It is further agreed upon between the Government and the Bank that interest at the rate of three per cent shall be paid by the Bank on all moneys exceeding the sum of seven hundred thousand dollars ascertained to be at the credit of the Government at the weekly settlement. Six months notice to be given by either party desiring to qualify or discontinue the engagement now entered into.

E 17   T.G. RIDOUT TO GLYN, MILLS
Toronto, 31 January 1859
[PAC, Glyn, Mills Papers, A542]

The Bank's account with you is still a good deal overdrawn, but we expect to receive from government Bills for £50,000 or £100,000 more next week, and Mr. Blackwell says that in the course of next month he will be able to cover our advances to the Grand Trunk Company which is a very considerable amount.

We have lately made a new arrangement with respect to the government account and on more favourable terms than heretofore, – the government engaging to keep a certain balance of $600,000 in deposit, also $100,000 more for daily payments – and for all beyond $700,000 the Bank allows interest at the rate of three per cent per annum.

For several months past the govt. account has been very low and during this month they had no balance whatever, we have therefore to receive from them bills for £100,000 Stg. before their a/c is placed according to the new agreement . . . .

E 18   T. BLACKWELL TO T. BARING (PRIVATE)
Toronto, 21 February 1859
[PAC, Baring Papers, A835]

In my last letter to you I think I enclosed copy of the letter of Mr. Davies[8] our accountant which referred to the prospect of, or at least hopes, of arranging with the Bank of Upper Canada so as to avoid drawing till the middle of March. The Bank is as it ever appears to have been ready to help us to the last degree but I feel that the present financial demands of the Country as well as our own came heavily and all at once; & I may experience some difficulty & the necessity of drawing on London somewhat earlier than expected. Of course their desire to assist us must occasion from time to time their drawing on their London agents Messrs. Glyn & Co. & therefore it would perhaps be but

[8]N. Davies worked in the chief accountant's office of the Grand Trunk.

fair that I should regard you kindly if you have the opportunity to state this to Messr. Glyn and that we are under great obligation to the B.U.C. & possibly through that channel to Messr. Glyn –

E 19   T.G. RIDOUT TO GLYN, MILLS
Toronto, 28 February 1859
[*PAC, Glyn, Mills Papers, A542*]

. . . I regret to state that we have been much disappointed to day in not being able to make you a large remittance, having expected to receive a bill of at least £50,000 from the Receiver General, but I understand that the Inspector General does not wish to draw upon the Pro. [Provincial] agents for a few days, until his new Financial Bill passes the Legislature we hope however to obtain it for next mail.

We are further disappointed in not recieving any thing from the Grand Trunk Rail Way Co. they being indebted to this Bank about £70,000 Stg. Mr. Blackwell stating that he cannot draw any more until after his return from Washington which will be about the 20th of next month. in the mean time I hold a set of the Grand Trunk rail way Exchange for £25,000 Stg. which Mr. Blackwell desired me not to remit to England until the 7th of March, as he had promised the Board in England not to draw if possible any more money this month.

As soon as the Inspector General completes his financial arrangements next month, the government will have occasion to draw largely on London to cover their account here, their expenditure being heavy at the present time, whilst their revenue receipts are light at this season.

E 20   T.G. RIDOUT TO GLYN, MILLS
Toronto, 7 March 1859
[*PAC, Glyn, Mills Papers, A542*]

. . . Your suggestion that it is expedient to increase the working capital of this Bank has received attention, that being a measure that we have long contemplated as only waiting for a favourable opportunity to bring our remaining shares into the market. These consist of 16,426 shares of £10.5.6 Sterling each, namely 14,227 in your hands, and 2199 here, and as the matter will be brought before the Board on the 10th inst. I shall be enabled by the next mail to give you official authority to reopen our London Stock Sales at par, allowing you 2 per cent thereon for your commission, to be paid for either in full at the time of subscribing, or by instalments as you may deem best, and when all sold, it will make our capital stock paid in, Four millions of Dollars.

With regard to your remarks respecting amalgamation, it occurs at this moment to me, that you allude to an amalgamation with the newly chartered Bank for which Mr. Ross, Mr. Cayley and others got a charter last year, but which has not yet been acted upon, and under this impression I have had a communication with Mr. Ross on the subject.

The result is that he seems quite willing that that Bank should be merged in this Institution with a Board of Directors in London, but never having thought before on the subject, I am not able to give any opinion, further than to say that this Bank will be willing to act in the matter in any way that you may recommend . . . .

E 21   T. BLACKWELL TO T. BARING
Toronto, 21 March 1859
[PAC, Baring Papers, A835]

. . . The *BUC* is pressing for "Exchange" in reduction of their Balance agst us now abt £70,000 (including the credit of £50,000) & I am afraid that we should be obliged to yield this [matter?] when we meet at Toronto. You may however depend on my arranging to keep the amount and dates as small & as long respectively as possible . . . .

E 22   T.G. RIDOUT TO GLYN, MILLS
Toronto, 28 March 1859
[PAC, Glyn, Mills Papers, A542]

. . . and [I] pay attention to your remarks on the Bank account, which I regret has not been for some time past in that satisfactory state which I trust it will be shortly.

The inability of the Grand Trunk Rail way Co. to keep their account covered for several months has caused us much inconvenience in consequence of their large overdrawings. The state of their several accounts this morning was as follows.

overdrawn on deposits	$192,000
Ditto on the Detroit Branch	99,500
and discounts about	75,000
besides which there will be required this week to pay interest on the Portland line – about	$45,000

On account of the above Mr. Blackwell has this day given our Montreal agent a bill on London for £25,000 Stg. and has promised the like sum next week stating that he can do no more until he receives authority from England.

I may also add that in consequence of the companys inability to pay their contractors Gzowski & Co. – their account likewise became for some time up to last week, overdrawn $77,000 dollars, part of which is now reduced by Mr. Blackwells bill on you for about £10,400 Stg. this day remitted in my official letter, and I hold a further draft for £15,000 Stg. on Messrs. Barings, which Mr. Blackwell wishes me to hold back for a fortnight to come when I may send it forward.

It may not I think be out of place here to mention that in the early part of last month the government drew from us the whole of their balance but since then the Custom House duties and other Revenue, have been coming in so fast so that their account is assuming now a prosperous aspect . . . .

E 23   T. BLACKWELL TO T. BARING (PRIVATE)
Montreal, 28 March 1859
[*PAC, Baring Papers, A835*]

. . . You may have collected from my recent letters that the BUC might soon be expressing uneasiness about its own state with respect to us & those connected with the Co. & when I reached Toronto . . . I found that there had been a full meeting of the Bank Directors and that very strong language was used towards our friend Mr. Ridout the Cashier & the President touching the large advances which they had made without authority or report – and there appears to have been great offence & recrimination which may lead to changes in the personnel for which we shall be very sorry . . . .

E 24   COMMITTEE TO ENQUIRE INTO THE WORKING OF THE BANKING AND CURRENCY SYSTEM OF THE PROVINCE, APRIL 1859
[JLA, *1859, Appendix 67*]

[T.G. Ridout:]

Ques. 1. – Do the Bank Charters of the Province generally, by the privileges they confer and the limitations and conditions they impose, appear to you to provide for the several objects which it is presumed every Legislature has in view in sanctioning the establishment of such Institutions?

Ques. 2. – Do the Charters appear too restrictive or too unguarded, in any particulars?

To Questions 1 and 2, – Many of the objects which the Legislature has had in view in granting charters to banking institutions have undoubtedly been attained, such as the supplying a circulating medium more convenient than specie, facilitating the daily transactions of the community, and economizing the use of money by means of bankers' drafts, and book credits. Some of the precautionary clauses, however, and especially in the more recent charters might in my opinion be improved.

The minimum of paid up capital might be raised, and the regulations affecting the issue of paper money made more stringent without inconvenience to, and more thoroughly securing the public.

Too great care cannot be taken to insure the integrity of the money basis on which our paper circulation and the credit system of the country rest.

Ques. 3. – What, in your opinion, is the *minimum* of Capital on which a bank should be chartered?

– Between $800,000 and $1,000,000 is little enough for a minimum limit.

Ques. 4. – Should there be a *maximum* limit?

– From five to seven millions is an ample capital for the present state of the community.

Ques. 5. – Should the present restrictions, in regard to the nature of the securities upon which Banks are authorized to grant discounts, be retained or qualified?

– Banks should be authorised to take bills of lading and railroad and warehouse receipts.[9]

Ques. 6. – What, practically, has been the effect of the late increased rate of interest which Banks are permitted to charge?

– The period during which the law has been in force is too short to afford a practical test, but I apprehend that the imposition of any limit on the procurement of money must defeat the objects for which the law was framed, that of checking over speculation and affording relief to the trading community in periods of commercial difficulty.

Ques. 7. – Would the interests of commerce, and the public advantage generally, be promoted by the removal of all restrictions as regards rates of interest?

– All restrictions should in my opinion be removed; when money is abundant the limit of seven per cent will scarcely ever be reached, except in cases where the transactions are to be extended over a lengthened period, which cannot strictly be classed under the head of banking operations. When money is tight the limit operates as an entire exclusion of a certain class of customers. Fluctuations in the rates of discounts are evidences of changes in the supply of the money market. When left free, a steady rise will give a reliable indication of coming stringent times. The imposition of a limit leaves the public without warning, until the banks taking alarm, withhold or greatly curtail their discounts, when in too many cases the refusal to discount is attributed to any but the right cause.

The complaint is frequently made that Banks give a preference to wealthy and independent customers. The limit naturally produces such a result. In England when Bankers find themselves called upon to curtail their discounts, the object is carried into effect by raising the rate, and thus by checking speculation reduce the number of customers, leaving those only as applicants whose necessities compel them to give the higher rate. But if instead of this mode of curtailing discounts, bankers are left to select which of their customers they will supply, they will naturally prefer those, whose punctuality is the most assured, whose need probably is the least, or cases from which by drawing exchange or otherwise they may expect to derive some incidental advantage, while it is evident that specula-

[9]Legislation, passed in 1859, did grant banks this privilege.

tion will not be restrained so long as there is a class of customers who can enjoy the advantage of obtaining money from the bank at six or seven per cent at a time when its value in the market is ranging possibly from nine to twelve. It is unnecessary for me to remark that many parties who have thus been excluded from Bank accommodation by the operation of the limit, have been driven to pay from one to two per cent per month for temporary loans in other quarters.

Ques. 8. – What should be the *maximum* which a Bank should be allowed to issue of its own paper, with reference to its own capital? – The present restrictions afford scope enough, perhaps too great, in the absence of any regulations with regard to the proportion of specie to be kept by the Bank.

Ques. 9. – What proportion should the specie and bullion in vault, bear to the paper circulation of a Bank? – This will in some measure depend upon the amount of funds held in London or in the United States on which the Bank can draw. One-fifth might be considered a safe limit. The amount of deposits should also be kept in view. Paper money has no intrinsic value, its credit and value are derived from the confidence the public possesses that it is convertible into specie on demand. It is not necessary that the whole of the circulation should be represented by specie to ensure this, but enough should be kept in reserve together with the power of drawing exchange to guard against exhaustion. It may be taken for granted that under no circumstances can the entire paper circulation of a country be forced back upon the Banks. But should the public become apprehensive of the stability of any particular Bank of issue, the paper of that Bank will be forced in, and its place supplied by the others.

. . . .

Ques. 18 – Have you any suggestions to offer with reference to the denominations of notes which now form the circulation; or with reference to the weekly settlement of balances between Banks? – The denominations in use appear to be adapted to the purposes of the community. In London the balances are settled daily at the clearing house and after setting off the various drafts and orders for transfer held by the banks, one against the other, the ultimate differences are settled by drafts on the Bank of England, where all the bankers kept account and where a special account is opened for the business of the clearing house; exchequer bills have also been used in settling balances. In this province, where we have neither exchequer bills nor a chief bank of issue, and where the amounts to be adjusted are held principally in the notes of the respective banks, the ultimate balances are generally settled in specie or its equivalent in exchange. Under these circumstances I am not prepared at present to suggest a change of system.

Ques. 19. – Would it be desirable, in your opinion, to make silver a legal tender to a larger amount than it is at present, and to what extent?

– Not to any considerable extent, and only in our own coin. At the present time Canada notes are more in demand in several of the neighbouring States of America than their own, and are used as a means of drawing exchange and gold from Canada. A moderate per centage, say five per cent., payable in specie would have the effect of equalizing the value of the paper circulation, and remove the inducement which now exists for picking up Canada notes.

Ques. 20. – Would a Provincial gold coinage be of advantage, and of what denominations?

– Yes, of equal fineness with American gold in four and two dollar pieces.

Ques. 21. – Is any alteration desirable in the present mode of either receiving or paying out gold by tale or weight?

– Sovereigns of full weight should be received and paid out by tale. Light sovereigns should be treated as bullion.

Ques. 22. – Referring to the commercial history of Europe and the United States, what do you find to have been the principal causes of commercial panics and depression?

– Excessive speculations, over-trading, and the abuse of credit.

Ques. 23. – Do you consider the same to have existed or to exist in Canada?

– I have no doubt of it. The large expenditure upon our Railroads and public works, and the great influx of foreign capital between 1852 and 1856 induced extravagant speculations, and excessive prices to be given for wild lands; schemes for new villages and towns were set afloat in every direction; mercantile transactions were carried to an extent far beyond the wants of the country, and bank accommodation was pressed to its utmost limit. Then came a revulsion. The large expenditures on Railroads and the foreign supplies were cut off or greatly diminished. The land speculations had absorbed the means of many a farmer and diverted them from the proper cultivation of his farm. Then followed two years of bad crops, and on the back of all, the commercial crisis in the United States which extended to Europe, and seriously aggravated the general depression under which the province was labouring.

Ques. 24. – In your opinion, can commercial depression be alleviated, or overtrading checked, by Legislative action?

– In so far only as a sound banking system, and a well regulated currency may operate as a check to rash speculations and the abuse of credit.

E 25   T.G. Ridout to T. Blackwell (copy)
Toronto, 16 April 1859
[*PAC, Glyn, Mills Papers, A542*]

Adverting to my conversation with you this morning wherein I stated the amount of the several advances made by this Bank for the Grand Trunk Railway Service exceeded $400,000 dollars and at the same time I requested that you would be pleased to cover the same by Bills on England, I regretted to learn in your reply that you were not yet authorized by your London Board to draw upon them for any such purpose; all which I have communicated to the President, and am directed by him to inform you that with every desire to meet the wishes and the convenience of the Grand Trunk Company in this matter & which the Bank has upon all occasions shewn to the utmost of its power and ability – yet there must be a limit, as the magnitude of the advances which have been made for some months past has caused much inconvenience to this Institution, and renders it necessary that you should at the very earliest moment provide funds to relieve your several accounts it being quite impossible for the Bank to continue such accommodations.

Statement of advances herein alluded to

Grand Trunk, Montreal account	$193,387
Huron & Detroit Railway account	99,517
Notes discounted	51,600
Gzowski & Co.	70,426
	$414,930 Dollars

The foregoing sums do not include Interest – also Messr. Gzowski & Co's account does not class strictly with your direct liabilities to this Bank, altho' they may be so construed indirectly.

E 26   T.G. Ridout to Glyn, Mills
Toronto, 30 April 1859
[*PAC, Glyn, Mills Papers, A542*]

. . . It may be regretted to a certain extent, that the shares of the Bank are not at the present time negociable in the London market, that being however of minor importance compared to the necessity of materially reducing as soon as possible our overdrawn account, which is the primary object that the President and Directors have in view, – and which I have no doubt will be effected in the course of the next three or four months – as large amounts of hitherto inconvertible debts will be realized. The depressed state of Trade and the failure of Harvests for the last two years, having caused an accumulation of that description of debt to an amount that was most inconvenient for the Bank to bear – altho the securities held for them are amply sufficient to cover both principal and interest, yet being chiefly in Real Estate it requires time to make sales –

The most considerable debt of the above description is that of the Zimmerman Estate, which the Bank was induced to undertake at the special request of the government, for at the time of Mr. Zimmermans death, the Receiver General had a deposit in his Bank of something over $280,000, which this Bank assumed, as well as the retirement of about $300,000 Dollars in notes, taking as security the whole of the Zimmerman Estate, valued at two millions of dollars – much of it being in land – which in course of law will be brought to Public auction in July next. We also hold on this Estate, a debt of $150,000 due by the Great Western Rail Way Company, which will shortly be paid, and also £50,000 Sterling of Port Hope Lindsay and Beaverton Rail Way Bonds, now in course of being favourably brought into the London market, the Bondholders having within a few days past obtained full possession of the Line, and are working it themselves to such advantage that there is no doubt that after paying working expenses, there will be sufficient Profit to pay the Coupons from the 1st of July next – this has been a difficult matter to accomplish – but it is now finally settled.

We should be able to relieve our account with you very much, if we could obtain Bills from the Grand Trunk Rail Way Company – whose debt to us this morning, including $110,000 due by Messr. Gzowski & Co. amounts to about $560,000. Mr. Blackwell has however promised to draw upon London as soon as he gets permission to do so. This state of their account places this Bank in a wrong position with you, which I regret exceedingly, but we trust that it will not again occur, hoping that the Grand Trunk new loan will soon be effected.

Mr. Galt the Inspector General will leave for England in the course of next month, having carried through Parliament all his Financial measures for the year, – he has engaged when in London to purchase from you, at least at par, the £150,000 Stg. of Municipal Loan Fund Debentures in your hands belonging to this Bank – and will probably make some special Deposits – as the government is morally bound to keep us covered for assuming their deposit of $280,000 in the Zimmerman Bank, until we can realize out of the Estate.

The Canada agency association (limited) of London through their agency here are investing large sums in mortgages in this Country, by which means many Debtors to this Bank are paying off their liabilities, affording us considerable relief in that way, and as the money pressure throughout Canada and the United States is becoming easier every month, and we have every appearance of a most abundant Harvest. I have no reason to doubt, that our business will again assume a flourishing shape and justify the confidence and liberality which you have always shewn towards us.

With regard to an amalgamation with the new Bank to which you are pleased to allude with friendly observations, I must own that I cannot comprehend how such a matter could be effected, however as it is of great importance I should be very glad if you would be so good as to let me know your views on the subject.

You may be assured that the President and Directors of this Bank are using their best endeavours to curtail their business here, and to increase their remittances to you by every means in their power, which they are confident they will be able to do to your satisfaction.

It has occurred to me that if I were to visit England I might be able to afford you detailed information respecting the affairs of this Bank, which cannot be well contained in letters . . . .

E 27   W. CAYLEY TO GLYN, MILLS (PRIVATE)
8 June 1859
[*PAC, Glyn, Mills Papers, A542*]

I have now the pleasure to reply to your letter of the 13th May, referring to my taking part in the management of the Bank of Upper Canada, and requesting my views as to its present position. In this latter point, the long connection which has subsisted between your House and the Bank, and the state of its account with you, entitles you to the fullest information, which I will endeavour to supply, and should there be any point on which my remarks may not be sufficiently explicit, I shall be happy to answer more particularly to any question which you may put to me. Perhaps it would be as well that I should first refer to the circumstances which led to my joining the Bank, for which I am as little prepared as the Gardener for the frost of Saturday last the 4th June which has swept every garden in the City and neighbourhood. The increasing magnitude of the transactions between the Government and the Bank and the disadvantage at which the Stock of the latter appeared to stand in comparison with the Commercial and the Bank of Montreal induced the Finance Minister to seek an interview with the Managers of the Bank, which resulted in an arrangement to increase the active Staff of the Bank, a visit from the President to myself, an adjournment to Mr. Galt for explanations and views and finally my undertaking the Office of Assistant Manager.

A very short acquaintance with the transactions of the Bank was sufficient to shew the very unsatisfactory position of its account with you, the causes of it, and the impediments to any very immediate improvement. In the beginning of the year the Government pull upon the Bank was heavy so was that of the Grand Trunk, and the latter is still much heavier than it should be, but these are by no means sufficient causes in themselves to produce our adverse position, which is attributable mainly, I may say entirely, to the fact that we have a large amount of capital locked up in securities, a large proportion in Real estate, not readily available in times like the present. The fact of the Bank being amply secured, under almost any possible contingency, by the amount of securities it holds, even tho' it should be impelled to realize at a heavy sacrifice to those who are indebted to us, cannot be considered a satisfactory explanation of the state of the account. But it is due to the Managers to state that many of those securities undertaken to cover advances made in the course of transactions originally of a strictly business character, which the depression of the times and stagnation of trade joined to the failure of two years crops and the scarcity of money, have reduced to their present shape. The Bank has also been led to make advances, arising out of its connection with the Government, and its desire to maintain the credit of the Banking Institutions of the Province, which have proved a heavy burden. As an instance I may quote the Zimmerman debt, which is our great Incubus, but which we hope speedily to shake off or at least greatly diminish. The connection with Mr. Zimmerman came in the first instance out of his position as Rail Road Contractor having large engagements and requiring the usual Bank aid, which he covered from time to time and again renewed and so on. He had also established a Bank on the Frontier and was considered wealthy. On the morning of the day on which he met with his death he made with Mr. Morrison an estimate of his property, preliminary to making his will, and their calculation of its value exceeded three millions of dollars. The government deposits in his Bank at the time of his death amounted to about £70,000. This account by an arrangement with the Receiver General was assumed by the Bank of Upper Canada, the Bank to be secured by available assets of the Zimmerman Estate. Then came in question the ability of the Z. Bank to protect its circulation about £80,000 and arrangements were made with the leading Banks of the Province to take it up, the final settlement to devolve on the Bank of Upper Canada, the latter to be again protected by the Estate. Before however the assets could be realized and the Estate turned over the general financial crisis came, purchasers disappeared, and stocks and property became unmarketable. To this day the Great Western R Road has continued to stave off the payment of $150,000 due to the Z. Estate (this sum however we now hope to obtain in a week or two).

The whole affair resulted in three-fourths of the property, valued at some $2,500,000 being handed over to the Bank to cover advances little short of $900,000. The first sales of the Estate take place next month. I have stated this case at length, as it is five times as large as any other account the Bank has, and by far the worst. We have no doubt however that the Bank claim will be ultimately paid in full. Western Canada is largely agricultural and if we could once be relieved of the strain that is now upon it by a good wheat crop, the Bank would feel the change in every sheet of its accounts.

The Farmers would settle with the Storekeepers, the Storekeepers with the Merchants etc. Another and a bad feature of the hard times is the excuse which they furnish to those even who are in a condition to pay, but who prefer to hold on or shave notes to meeting their own engagements, and it is humiliating to know that Shopkeepers have at times to beg [them?] for a percentage only of what is due to them from a wealthy customer. For some time past the Bank has been far more stringent and cautious in its transactions, confining itself to limited discounts, short business paper and quick returns, and this half year's balance sheet contrasts favorably with the last, but the progress of recovering tho' steady is slow, and will continue to be slow until a good harvest. The burden under which we are laboring owes its origin to the prosperous times of 1854–5 – had we never enjoyed the one we should never have been exposed to the pressure of the other. On the other hand the greater stringency of our regulations and the pressure we bring to bear on Defaulters are not without their disadvantages. There must be a cause, has more than once been said to me, why the Bank is so much less liberal now, and so much more exacting than formerly and the Zimmerman matter and one or two other slow accounts are pointed to, and our stock feels the depressing effect in the market. But better so in my opinion, with the prospect thereby of being earlier relieved from our cramped position than any mistaken attempt to keep up appearances. Following up this view and since I commenced this letter I urged upon the Board of Directors yesterday the prudence of reducing the Dividend from four to three per cent which I am glad to be able to say was after some little discussion adopted. Mr. Proudfoot and Mr. Ridout both concurring in the step. Yesterday being, I should have stated, the time fixed by our Charter for declaring the half yearly dividend. Within these two or three days we have had explanations with the Government. The President, the Cashier and I meeting Mr. Galt, Mr. Ross and Mr. Sherwood,[10] it was some disappointment to Mr. Galt to learn that we were not prepared to draw on England to meet the July dividends without at the same time obtaining exchange from him. The old arrangement being that the Bank should in the first instance pay the dividend and then be covered by check or drafts on London, this course however was not taken last January or with reference to the Spring Dividend. After some discussion as to the amount which the Bank would be called upon to meet on this side of the water on Government account Mr. Galt undertook to make his own arrangements for the July dividends in England. The Direction of the Bank was also discussed, the election takes place on the 26th instant, and changes were agreed to by the President, who holds a large number of proxies, which I think will prove of advantage to the Bank, and which I shall be glad to see carried out, as any poor service I may be able to render in my present position must depend upon the confidence, and frank support which I may obtain from the Board. Mr. Proudfoot suggests that I should go

[10]George Sherwood was the receiver general at this time.

into the Direction. I am not quite satisfied that this step is desirable, at least for the present. Mr. Ridout has communicated with you with respect to the Port Hope and Lindsay Debentures, these belong chiefly to the Zimmerman Estate, satisfactory arrangements for running the road which have been recently made and the guarantee of the Bank to pay the interest should, in ordinary times make them marketable. I am afraid however that that term is not applicable to the present. Mr. Galt stated yesterday that as soon as he was in funds in London he would purchase from the Bank, at par, the Municipal Loan funds debentures on which you have made advances, this proceeding will release your funds and carry a small balance to our credit, £15,000 I believe. We have just had a visit from Mr. Ross and Mr. Blackwell to make a proposition for the adjustment of the Grand Trunk account as follows: Mr. Blackwell to draw at six months for £100,000[11] Stg. which the Government will carry to the credit of the Bank on acceptance in London, Mr. Blackwell however having authority to check for the amount ags. what is now at his debit. Mr. Blackwell also proposes to give us £25,000 exchange at three months, which will go forward by Mondays mail, against which he will check in favour of Messr. Gzowski & Co. for £35,000 Stg. Mr. Ridout who appeared to see the proposition in a more favourable light than I did acquiesced in these terms.

. . . I will . . . send you an extract of the statement, shewing the result of the transactions of the Bank for the last six months, which was placed before the Bank yesterday. The Cash balance standing at the credit of the Province on Saturday the 4th June was $1,045,422 and has not materially changed since. I beg to enclose a clip from a Montreal paper of the 7th containing the annual statement of the Bank of Montreal which if you have not seen, I think you will find interesting. The report dwells strongly upon the importance of a good wheat crop, in which I entirely concur and in fact mainly rely for returning us to a healthy position.

E 28   BARING BROTHERS AND GLYN, MILLS TO A.T. GALT (COPY)
London, 1 July 1859
[PAC, Glyn, Mills Papers, A541]

. . . Your letter of 13 June also alludes to the remittance for acceptance and collection of a Bill for £100,000 of the Grand Trunk Company on Messrs. Glyn & Co. endorsed by the Bank of Upper Canada which the Receiver General has forwarded to Messrs. Glyn & Co. This bill has been received but formal objections exist to its acceptance in regular course. The usages and customs of commerce do not recognize the

---

[11]This is the beginning of a long and protracted history. This bill was bounced back and forth and the ultimate responsibility for payment was only finally assumed by the government as part of a settlement of its affairs with the Bank in 1865.

usance of a bill drawn from Canada at six months sight and the drawers naturally decline to depart so much from the customs of Bankers and although we need not say that the Directors of the Grand Trunk Rail Road Company fully feel the obligation of protecting the signature of their President and Vice President and of meeting all the engagements of the Company they cannot venture to insist on a course opposed to Banking principles, and all acceptances of Bills by the Company in England being legally prohibited the Company is unable to interfere for the honor of the signature of the drawers. We venture therefore to submit for your consideration the substitution in lieu of the present bill of one drawn by the Bank of Upper Canada on the Grand Trunk Company which would be accepted by the President and Vice President of the Company who have alone the power to accept bills for its account, and being made payable in London and endorsed to the Government would become a perfectly regular document.

E 29   T.G. RIDOUT TO GLYN, MILLS
Toronto, 4 July 1859
[*PAC, Glyn, Mills Papers, A542*]

. . . The Grand Trunk Rail Way Compy. have used up the £100,000 Stg. which they lately got indirectly from government upon their draft on you at 6 m/s and the government have run down their deposits with us to about £70,000 and which is daily diminishing as the revenue of customs is small at this time of the year under these circumstances we are led to believe, that the Receiver General will give us some Bills on England next week . . . .

The close of the half year to the 30 June has caused the Government payments to be very large so that we are under the necessity, for a few days, to draw upon you to pay our balances with other Banks, which we hope you will protect.

E 30   W. CAYLEY TO GEORGE CARR GLYN
Toronto, 11 July 1859
[*PAC, Glyn, Mills Papers, A542*]

I have just returned from visiting the agencies of Montreal & Quebec . . . . Your proposition to take security on the Zimmerman Estate for a portion of the overdrawn account will I have no doubt be viewed as very acceptable by the Directors, the proposed repayment of £25,000 every six months will very much facilitate the sale of the property. Upon these details we will consult Mr. T. Galt,[12] the Gentleman you suggest as one of the Trustees. We have to a certain extent anticipated your wishes with reference to giving security, by the Munl. L. fund bond transmitted about the date of your letter and the arrangement made with the Port

[12]Thomas Galt (1815–1901) was a Toronto lawyer and brother of Alexander T. Galt.

Hope bonds. Taking the first at par and the latter at 50 per cent will give value as a security for say £100,000 cy., if in addition to this sum we pledge the Zimmerman Estate for £150,000 making £250,000 cy. a much more managable balance will be left for us to liquidate out of Bank funds . . . .

E 31   JOHN A. MACDONALD TO G. CARTIER[13]
Toronto, 11 July 1859
[PAC, J.A. Macdonald Papers, v. 297, pp. 136235–37]

I was much surprised and chagrined at hearing from Sherwood in your prescence this morning that the Finance Minister had assumed the responsibility of giving £100,000 of Exchange to the Bank of Upper Canada without such advance being [intimated?] to & approved by His Excellency in Council.

In my view of the matter the expediency of making such an advance is not a justification for its being made without the authority of His Excellency – There was no urgency. The matter might have been discussed in Council on Saturday and the amount is very large – If the principle is once admitted the whole revenue for the year might be at any time disposed of without the knowledge or consent of the Governor General or his Council, & on the judgment of one Minister alone –

I cannot subscribe to so dangerous a principle and as I do not feel myself safe and am unwilling to incur responsibility in matters in which I have no voice. I think it advisable to relieve myself [therefrom?] by tendering to you my resignation which you will be kind enough to submit to His Excellency.

At the sametime I must beg leave to say that I am quite sure Mr Galt has acted as he thought best for the interests of the Province & that from my confidence in his judgment & ability I have every reason to believe that these interests will not be prejudiced by the Course adopted.

E 32   A.T. GALT TO T. BARING (PRIVATE)
Toronto, 14 July 1859
[PAC, Baring Papers, A834]

. . . It will be a subject of principal regret to me, if the bill for £100.000 not be accepted by Mssrs Glyn for the Grand Trunk. The Bank of U.C. as you are aware is in very straightened circumstances – and cannot continue their present large advance to The Company, which we hoped to cover by this bill – and I really do not know what they will do – I can see the difficulty you mention in regard to the date when the bill matures – but I feel sure this may be obviated by the Govt consenting to take another accepted bill at say four months in payment. Pray consider this,

[13]George-Etienne Cartier (1814–73) was a Conservative politician and for a time lawyer for the Grand Trunk.

as I do not see any way to the change you suggest – of our taking The Company's bill – endorsed by the Bank of U.C.

We were obliged by last mail to give the Bank £100.000 exchange to represent the other bill – which we hope may be accepted – but it was done with great reluctance. And I may say the same of our purchase [one word?] of the M.L. Fund Bonds. The transaction itself is a good one for the Govt – but I would rather have postponed it – until the effect of your recent sale of our Bonds had passed away. I found, however, that the Bank *had got* large advances on these Bonds payable at 4:prox° and as I know they could not other wise meet these advances, I feared a disasterous sale of the M.L.F. bonds and on the whole concluded that it was better to assume them for the Govt.

The truth is that my difficulties, financially, which have been sufficiently great arising out of the position of the Province, when I assumed office, are augmented every day by the necessity of supporting interests which it would be most disasterous to allow to succumb – I trust however, that I have now passed through the worst, And that the magnificent harvest which seems about to be vouchsafed to us – will soon restore everything. The pressure upon me, from the causes to which I allude, have obliged me to conduct our English accounts differently from what I intended, but I feel sure that both Mr. Glyn and yourself will aid me in getting through these difficulties . . . .

E 33   A.T. GALT TO BARING BROTHERS AND GLYN, MILLS (COPY)
Sherbrooke, 16 July 1859
[*PAC, Baring Papers, A834*]

. . . The Receiver General will advise you that in accordance with your suggestion the Government have consented to the substitution of the bill of the Bank of Upper Canada accepted by the Grand Trunk Company for that drawn by the latter on Messrs. Glyn & Co. – We were aware of the partial irregularity of the former bill and had declined assuming it for the Government unless accepted by Messrs. Glyn & Co. We trust the new Bill will be duly protected at maturity.

E 34   W. CAYLEY TO GEORGE CARR GLYN
18 July 1859
[*PAC, Glyn, Mills Papers, A542*]

. . . The Directors are perfectly satisfied with the terms of your proposition for a loan . . . viz. £200,000 equal to £243,333 cy. at six per cent interest, the principal payable in semi annual instalments of £25,000 or earlier if the Zimmerman Estate & securities are earlier realized. Mr. T. Galt, as I advised in my last, has consented to act as one of the two Trustees, and suggested to the Bank that I should act as the other, which has been assented to, provided it is agreeable to you. We have had a preliminary meeting and are now engaged taking steps to see that the property mortgages etc are in proper shape before they are taken over by the Trust . . . .

E 35   T.G. RIDOUT TO GLYN, MILLS
Toronto, 23 July 1859
[*PAC, Glyn, Mills Papers, A542*]

. . . With regard to the Grand Trunk Rail Way account, it now stands on our Books overdrawn about $630,000 against they will have a credit of £100,000 Stg. by a cheque from the Receiver General as soon as a bill for that amount lately drawn by me under date of the 13 June last at 6 months sight, shall be approved of by the Board in London – this bill being drawn in lieu of one for the same amount drawn by the company here upon their London Bankers, now withdrawn. The intention of our government being to aid and assist the Grand Trunk Co. by a loan of that amount for 6 or 9 months.

I have urged upon Mr. Blackwell to let us have a bill for the balance of his account, which is fast increasing against him but he says that he is not yet authorized to do so, which places this Bank in some difficulty for want of the exchange.

We have been obliged to draw very largely on you lately, owing in some measure to the removal of the government to Quebec, every demand having been paid off, many in anticipation, as the Receiver Generals office will be closed all next month, when the government Fund will so accumulate that we shall be able to make you large remittances.

Messrs. Gzowski & Co. hold a Grand Trunk bill for £35,000 Stg. which Mr. Blackwell will not allow them to negociate with us until next week altho' we have already advanced them the greater part of the money.

Our wheat Harvest commenced last week and is the finest that we have had for many years, being about double the usual yield, and of a superior quality, every other description of Produce is equally abundant and good. – This will no doubt enable the Banks to make large collections of their old debts.

E 36   A.T. GALT TO T. BARING (CONFIDENTIAL)
Sherbrooke, 8 August 1859
[*PAC, Baring Papers, A834*]

My private lines of this date will I fear not prove very encouraging to the Board, but I cannot venture to say more, and to tell the truth I do not yet see *how* the Government can aid, even if they should prove to have the disposition. We have no Legislative authority to issue Debentures for such a purpose. The amount is too large to be sent by our ordinary resources, and it will require a very good case to be made out to induce the Legislature to sanction our act when done. Ross will explain many other difficulties, which I need not notice here, but which *must* even if answered cause some delay. However the matter will in a great measure depend upon the view Mr. Cartier takes of it and whether he can make it an element in certain political changes which are imminent.

I do not see any advantage in using the Bank of Upper Canada (if anything is done) it is a source of weakness to us at present, and as the transaction, if done, must go before Parliament, it would be better to effect it openly, and directly with the Company through the financial agents . . . .

E 37   W. CAYLEY TO GLYN, MILLS
Toronto, 8 August 1859
[*PAC, Glyn, Mills Papers, A542*]

. . . The command of available means is what the Bank, for the while, is deficient in, of sums . . . in real property it has ample. The large amount of Government funds left with the Bank partly on call and at a low interest in the more [flourishing?] days of Canada induced a rather careless system of discounting. While the large and ready command of means this placed at their disposal, rendered them insensible to the gradual locking up of their capital. Two consecutive bad seasons and the crisis in the fall of 1857 – acted with two fold severity upon such a state of things. The government deposits on the one hand were gradually reduced until brought down to their minimum. On the other the Merchants and Farmers were brought to that state that they in many instances were unable to renew their paper . . .

E 38   W. CAYLEY TO GEORGE CARR GLYN
Toronto, 29 August 1859
[*PAC, Glyn, Mills Papers, A542*]

. . . I fear we have disappointed you in making remittances. I have failed to obtain exchange from Mr. Galt tho' entitled to it under the letter of our agreement. He will see how the balances stand when the offices are reopened at Quebec. We have also applied to Mr. Blackwell for £100,000. He promises £50,000 in ten days on Mr. Baring. He also leads us to expect more, when his present negotiations are completed, he speaks of them as in good train. We have not yet succeeded in bringing arbitration to a close with Mr. Bridges of the Great Western R Road. We claim $150,000.[14] This claim will be embraced in the Trust. Also $92,000 from Mr. Baby.[15] This debt is assumed by the Government but will not be paid until Parliament meets. A third item to be embraced in the Trust is our claim against the Northern Road $112,000. This amount is payable out of the Preferential bonds authorized last Session to take precedence of the Government lien . . . .

[14]The Great Western Railway owed the Zimmerman estate $150,000 on account of contracting services performed by Samuel Zimmerman.

[15]F. Baby's debts had accumulated in the early and mid-1850s when the Bank of

E 39   W. CAYLEY TO GEORGE CARR GLYN
Toronto, 1 September 1859
[PAC, Glyn, Mills Papers, A542]

. . . Our overdrawn account with you may be stated at $2,000,000. Our advances to the Grand Trunk, leaving out of sight for the moment the £100,000 draft, exceed $900,000. Had we been left perfectly free to deal with this amount, that draft which has already gone to England, and the drafts we are promised, to cover the Grand Trunk account would have reduced the overdrawn balance to $1,100,000, or say £20,000 Stg in excess of the amount proposed to be left on loan, and which the next bill of Exchange we receive from Messr. Gzowski would have covered. As it has been managed, the great pressure brought to bear, from your side of the water, upon the government here to interfere on behalf of the Company elicited from Mr. Galt a proposition, eagerly seized by Mr. Ross and Mr. Blackwell, that a six months draft should be drawn by the Company in favour of the Bank and handed to the government, and to be ultimately charged to its account. If you have by you my letters of the 9th & 13th June, you will find a reference to the transaction and my opinion adverse to it, from the Banks point of view and in regard to your account. It is true that our account with the Government was ultimately to get credit for it, but for the time it has absorbed that amount of available funds and curtailed our remittances. On the other hand the amount at the credit of the Receiver General has been gradually reducing from $1,048,000 in June to $823,000 on the 26th August and to day, according to instructions we charge that account with the £100,000 draft which reduces it in round figures to $350,000 or $250,000 below the stipulated balance to be left in our hands. With reference to the question of other sources such as sales of property, & the collection of overdue bills, from whence we may hope to realize the means of making remittances, the Province has not yet, except in anticipation, felt the effects of our good harvest. The wheat has not begun to move in any quantity. Farmers will for awhile hold out for large prices, and property is still stagnant. On the 25th July, Mr. Ridout having shewn me his letter to you of that date, I accompanied it by a short note stating my belief that he was a little to sanguine about remittances, and that we could not expect to feel the beneficial effects of the harvest for several months. I may add that we have

---

Upper Canada, often on flimsy authorization, advanced Baby money for work he claimed to have finished on various government contracts. The auditor general, John Langton, undertook a close investigation of these payments and found numerous irregularities and lack of proof of expenses claimed. At the time of the investigation, of course, Baby, courtesy of the bank, already had the money. It was the bank which had to wait for reimbursement from a reluctant government. Problems such as these fuelled Langton's crusade for tightening up government payment procedures and accounting systems.

attempted some sales of Real Estate (Zimmermans) but have met with no satisfactory offers with one exception in which the Bank desires to have Mr. Galts opinion before coming to any conclusion.

E 40   GLYN, MILLS TO R. RIDDELL[16]
London, 7 September 1859
[PAC, Glyn, Mills Papers, A543]

. . . We are perfectly aware, & it has been made the subject of a remark by us to the Bank that the management of that Institution has not kept up with the requirements of the times, & that, although it was in the hands of men of high integrity, yet that it wanted vigour & decision. To remedy this, three new directors joined the Bank at the last General Meeting. The Hon John Ross, a member of the Government, Mr Macpherson, a gentleman of whom we hear a very high character, and a third, a Commercial Man, whose name at the moment we do not recollect, & we learn from one of them, who is now in England, that effectual measures have been already taken by the Board for the improvement of the management . . . .

E 41   W. CAYLEY TO GEORGE CARR GLYN
Toronto, 11 September 1859
[PAC, Glyn, Mills Papers, A542]

. . . In consequence of your strong remonstrances respecting the over-drawn account, the Directors felt themselves compelled to intimate to Mr. Blackwell that he must confine the Grand Trunk credit to $200,000. We have received a telegraph today proposing to exceed it and with great reluctance the President has assumed the responsibility of sanctioning the increase. The inconvenience of the large checks given by the Grand Trunk is felt in the immediate return of its paper from the other Banks which are keen to pick it up, and in this way we are compelled to draw on you. Should Mr. Blackwell express his disappointment in this subject to you, the foregoing will explain the difficult position in which the Bank has found itself placed.

E 42   N. DAVIES TO T. BLACKWELL
Montreal, 19 September 1859
[PAC, Baring Papers, A835]

I regret to have to inform you, that on presenting two checks at the counter of the Bank of Upper Canada, this morning for acceptance preparatory to retiring two notes due this day at other Banks, Mr. Taylor, the Manager of the Branch here refused to accept them, having

---

[16]Robert Riddell lived in England and owned 354 shares in the Bank of Upper Canada.

received, as he states, most positive orders from the Head Office, not to allow the Company to overdraw their account, beyond the £30,000 loaned by the Bank to the Company, & which is now exhausted Under these circumstances, & as Mr. Taylor refused to depart from the instructions he has received, I see no other way of meeting the present difficulty, & which will be constantly occurring every time we have a note to meet, then by your drawing on London for say £50,000 Stg. to repay the Bank the floating balance due, with the understanding that the same accommodation will be continued to us for the future – the difficulty presses upon us, & must be met at once, for if our paper goes to protest the consequences would be most unfortunate to us. If I could see any other way of getting out of the difficulty I should be glad to suggest it, knowing how very unwilling you are to draw but I do not see any other way that we could manage, particularly as in the course of a week we shall have to remit $44,640 to Boston to meet the Interest with Atlantic Banks due on 1 October. I feel assured that with the assistance this Exchange will give us, that we shall be enabled to meet all our liabilities in this Country for some time to come; looking at the increased receipts from Traffic which we shall undoubtedly have.

E 43   T. BLACKWELL TO T. BARING
Montreal, 19 September 1859
[*PAC, Baring Papers, A835*]

. . . The Bank of Upper Canada is in straits again but this is to me unaccountable with the knowledge I have of some recent transactions and they press us most unnecessarily and vexatiously I think. Our accountant has been urging me to give them Exchange today and I feel most reluctant to do so today and if I do it will be on the understanding that Messrs. Glyn will delay the acceptance for a time. Our indebtedness to them is a little over £50,000, but they insist that while willing to give us this extent of Credit – they must have it from time to time covered by drafts . . . .

E 44   T. BLACKWELL TO T. BARING (PRIVATE AND CONFIDENTIAL)
Montreal, 23 September 1859
[*PAC, Baring Papers, A835*]

. . . Mr. Cayley as Deputy of Mr. Ridout here to endeavour to settle with me future plans of working the acct. We have not gone far yet . . .
But we must give them soon some exchange to cover further advances made on account of

Interest at Boston	$44,000
New works St. L. & Atlantic	26,000
Crossing arrangements at Sarnia	110,000
New Plant &c	

I shall of course fight off as long as possible.

E 45   W. CAYLEY TO A.T. GALT
Toronto, 20 October 1859
[*PAC, RG 19 E1A, v. 3369*]

. . . Glyn has been both patient and impatient with us. for they have borne with us at the same time that they have written us a remind nearly every week. Our account with them a few weeks ago ran over $2.000.000. by this mail it stands about $1,400.000. It would not be safe to attempt to run it up again, but we can do this. We can commence at once to remit to Baring and Glyn on your account, and run down your balance which I suppose now stands about $1,100.000 as rapidly as we can to $600000, and run it at that remitting to England the surplus as it comes in until you say stop. In the mean while if you instructed Glyn or Glyn and Baring to protect the Dividend, they would be satisfied and more content to have you in place of us, as their guarantee. Times are mending with us but getting in old arrears is always a slow process . . . .

E 46   G. SHERWOOD TO W. CAYLEY
Quebec, 10 February 1860
[*PAC, RG 19 B2b, v. 1164*]

. . . Your letter of the 7th instant seems based upon the supposition that there is an arrangement between the Government and the Bank that there shall be constantly at the credit of the Government in the Bank a balance of six hundred thousand dollars. I feel it my duty to prevent any misunderstanding to say that I Know of no such arrangements – Galt agreed with you that in the beginning of January exchange should be given to bring the balance up to that amount if after payment of the interest and sinking fund in London by the Bank it should be reduced below that sum. This arrangement was carried out and is the only one I am cognizant of –

E 47   T.G. RIDOUT TO GLYN, MILLS
Toronto, 1 March 1860
[*PAC, Glyn, Mills Papers, A542*]

. . . the Bank has just drawn upon you for a large sum over and above the remittance of this mail owing to our disappointment in not receiving our monthly bill from the Grand Trunk rail way Compy. whose indebtedness today is about $406,000 . . . .

On the 15th of this month we shall receive from the Commissary General his Bill on the Treasury for £12,750 Stg as Pensioners money quarterly due – and as the Commissariat account for Canada for the ensuing year will be transferred to us from the Bank of Montreal on the 1st of April according to general orders, we shall have a further draft on the Treasury for the military expenditure of the Province . . . .

E 48   D.L. MACPHERSON TO C.J. BRYDGES (PRIVATE)
Toronto, 2 March 1860
[PAC, A.T. Galt Papers, v. 7]

. . . the Great Western account will be one of deposit, no advance being required by the Company – all receipts to be paid into the Bank – disbursements to be made in the notes of the Bank, and in the manner best calculated to give them circulation, the Company to be at liberty to remit monthly to England, the amount at Credit of their account, in excess of $50,000, the balance standing at their Credit to be at no time less than $50,000 fifty thousand dollars.

That with regard to the Detroit and Milwaukie account the Bank shall advance that Company in course of March and April, Fifty thousand dollars, the same to be repaid during the next eight months, in instalments to be agreed upon – All the Company's receipts to be deposited with the Bank, and disbursements made; in the same way as in the Case of the Great Western Company.

Messrs. Proudfoot & Ridout fully admit the desirableness of the Great Western account kept as proposed, but as I apprehended they feel unwilling to make advances to the Detroit and Milwaukie Company, without satisfactory collateral security.

It is quite true that under the proposed arrangements, looking at the two accounts, the Bank would be under no actual advance, indeed, the transfer of the present GW Balance from the Commercial Bank to the Bank of Upper Canada, would cover the advance to be made to the D&M Company.

Still the one Company would not be liable for the debts of the other, and Messrs. P & R think circumstances might possibly arise; altho' perhaps not likely; that would prevent the prompt repayment by the D&M Company and it will be necessary for you to satisfy the Bank on this point, as no inducement would tempt the Board to take an account, involving in their opinion, that risk . . . .

E 49   D.L. MACPHERSON TO A.T. GALT (PRIVATE)
Toronto, 12 March 1860
[PAC, A.T. Galt Papers, v. 7]

. . . You will be surprised to learn that the Bank of U.C. Has taken the Great Western a/c but when you learn the terms by reading the enclosed note of mine you will admit the arrangement should be highly advantageous & profitable to the Bank. Without being under any advance – the advance to the D & M Co being covered by the Deposit of the G.W. Co – the Bank will have the benefit of a huge deposit A/C & a fine circulation. The advance to the D & M Co. is also guaranteed by Brydges & Reynolds[17] individually. so that I think the matter is placed

---

[17]Thomas Reynolds (b. 1811) was the Great Western Railway's financial director.

on a Very safe basis. & if properly managed cannot fail to be money making to the Bank . . . .

E 50   D.L. MACPHERSON TO A.T. GALT
Toronto, 23 March 1860
[PAC, A.T. Galt Papers, v. 7]

. . . When informing you touching the arrangement of the Great Western Compy. with the BUC I should have mentioned that the *inducement* was the advance of the $50,000.00 which enabled Brydges & Reynolds to pay off certain personal liabilities incurred by them in behalf of the D & M Compy. which C.S. Ross refused to advance . . . .

E 51   BANK OF UPPER CANADA, MEMORANDUM RE MR. HOPKINS[18]
Toronto, 14 April 1860
[PAC, Glyn, Mills Papers, A542]

We have just learnt that a very violent attack has been made against us by a recently dismissed officer of the Bank and that he is endeavouring by a series of charges, printed for circulation to injure the credit of the Institution . . . . In July last the Bank Inspector visited the agency of Mr. Hopkins at Lindsay and reported that amongst the paper discounted by Mr. Hopkins were several fictitious notes, renewal of other notes for a similar character . . . the notes and names were all in the handwriting of Mr. Hopkins, who had initialed one of the names as tho' acting under power of attorney. Mr. Hopkins was called upon to shew his authority or the correspondence under which he claimed to act. This he was unable or declined to do and he was then informed that his connection with the Bank must cease . . . .

E 52   D.L. MACPHERSON TO A.T. GALT (CONFIDENTIAL)
Toronto, 10 April 1860
[PAC, A.T. Galt Papers, v. 7]

. . . P.S.
. . . I wrote you that Hopkins petition had produced no effect

I was not aware that their Reserve of coin & securities was below the mark but I insisted, when the Hopkins affair occurred, they should increase their stock of specie. If there should be a run on that, or on any of the old Banks they Wd. have to stand by one another & the Govt. must support them in case of need otherwise their would be a general & total crash.

I would have looked to Your Bill[19] as the Agency [by which?] the

---

[18]J.H. Hopkins had been the agent for the Bank of Upper Canada at Lindsay.

[19]This refers to Alexander Galt's unsuccessful attempt to create a government bank of issue.

danger in the Old [system?] would be removed. There is little or no danger of a run upon them. as the rural people where the notes are held have unbounded confidence in the Institution while it remains under the long established & *the trusted* management of the President . . . .

E 53   J.H. HOPKINS TO W.L. MACKENZIE (NOT FOR PUBLICATION: CONFIDENTIAL)
Lindsay, 5 May 1860
[*PAO, Mackenzie-Lindsey Papers*]

. . . I now proceed to reply more fully. My case agt. Proudfoot is this. Last year abt May he sent to the Port Hope Agency a bill of himself & brother an agent in the Bank for abt $9000 & ordered the Agent to discount it. I saw it myself & do not doubt it is one of many other such transactions. I suppose it was to keep it out of sight of the other Directors.

It is a most improper transaction & I think should be brought before a Concl. of share-holders & not in the Public Press until then. I am certain no Bank Chairman in England could hold office one moment after such a case was proved. Do you not agree with me it is better to keep it quiet until the annual meeting in June. I cannot prove any case of undue (in time & amt) advance agt L. Robinson[20]-Ridout-Arnold,[21] C. Gamble, but undoubtedly they [one word?] & it is to enquire that I have petitioned.

More undoubtedly Glyn & Co. have made very heavy advances to the Bk of UC – it used to be abt £200,000 Stg & you may rely that in the Panic of 1857, The Provincial Debentures which were sold so low were sold to sustain the Bank by easing it with Glyn. The Govt was not in want of money at the time I must know I kept all the accounts & Cayley's pay for selling them, is his present appointment in the Bank.

It is one of a series of corrupt tricks played on poor Canada during the last few years. The Bank was also very heavily indebted to the Bank of the Interior at Albany, which is managed by a friend or relative of Mr. Streets I have heard. Nothing could have saved the Bk in 1857 but Glyn & the Bk of the I.

It is clear to me Govt are depositing large sums at Int in the Bank, formerly its Dep. at Int were from $200,000 to 300,000 now they are 2 million – no private individuals would think of depositing in it – I dont' really believe in their figures in the returns & I know other Bankers who agree with me, & as to how much of their capital is lost I dont believe anyone knows. I know a very keen judge who ought to know & who is

---

[20]James Lukin Robinson was a lawyer and director of the Bank of Upper Canada in 1851 and 1853–60. In 1857 he owned 465 shares in the bank. In 1860 he owned eighty-eight and in 1863, ten.

[21]John Arnold was a businessman and financier living in Toronto. He was a director of the Northern Railway and from 1853 to 1857 a director of the Bank of Upper Canada.

by no means an enemy of the Bank considers fully 25 per cent lost, the permanent locks up must be enormous & as you are aware convertibility is as necessary as stability to a Bank's loans, nothing could save it in the event of a European panic obliging Glyn to call in. Glyn charges them 1 per ct higher than the Bank of England rate for interest on advances. If it eventually gets thro it will be the first I ever knew of to surmount such difficulty . . . .

E 54 D.L. Macpherson to W. Cayley (copy, extract)
Toronto, 7 May 1860
[*PAC, A.T. Galt Papers, v. 7*]

You would see from my last note that I intended Mr. Ridouts duties to refer to the past rather than to the future, hence the necessity for a paid VP to attend to the current business, in conjunction with the Cashier.

I want a Cashier thoroughly posted on a good system and experienced in practical Banking, altho' I much fear, the practical Banking at the BUC for years to come, must be confined chiefly to collecting debts and other kindred transactions.

On the Cashier and VP, I would devolve the entire responsibility of management. It is useless to talk of the Board managing. A Board cannot manage a Bank or any other institution. That must be done by the Executive. All Board can do is to support the Executive, and enable the latter to conduct the business confidently and fearlessly. The first duty of our Cashier and one that would occupy him for six months or longer, would be to get a perfect understanding of every account in the Bank, a subject on which I have been able to obtain little or no information, and to place them in the best possible train for speedy liquidation.

Proudfoot has no doubt apprised you that the Banks in Montreal have resolved on daily settlements and the payment of balances in *Gold* after this day week, settlements to take place both at Montreal and Toronto. This is a blow aimed at the B.U.C. The old men see that much, but cannot tell where they will be struck, and consequently are (especially Old P) considerably frightened. I saw them on Saturday and told them what I thought they ought to do, viz.

Stop all discounts, except Short Bills on New York, payable infull at maturity, and then only when they know what is to be done with the proceeds. Renew no notes, without a payment on account 10% and upwards, the renewal to be at 30 days. Better let a note go into default and become a judgment than renew it in full. Parties with notes current, who have been in the habit of getting them renewed time out of mind, should be made aware of the change if adopted; that they may be prepared. To get in and keep always on hand, a large reserve of Gold. There must be no doubt on this point. The slightest shortcoming would be disastrous.

They should write Glyn, explaining the course taken by the other

Banks, and the one taken by themselves to meet it, that in case of need they will venture to draw a little, to place themselves in Gold, but this cannot be necessary, if they act upon my suggestions. I feel sure the balances would be in their favor regularly, I do not see how it could be otherwise.

The Govt account is increasing, the Great Western a/cs have generally $100,000 at Credit, The GT a/c is covered monthly with Exchange, The Circulation is not decreasing, nor the deposits diminishing, at least so they tell me. Why then are the balances so constantly against us. It must be in consequence of issues, improvident unwise issues, that we know nothing about at the Board. These have only to be stopped, and they must be stopped, should have been stopped long ago. It can now be done and the odium cast on the Banks in Montreal. I am sure it only requires to be done to turn the balances in our favor.

I also advised them to ask you to come up . . . .

One word more, it is of a personal character and I have done. The fact of your having been appointed under, rather *by force* of Government influence avowedly to watch and guard Government interests, gives you great authority and power. Do not hesitate to exercise them when you think the interest of the Bank requires.

It would be a poor excuse for you, and one that would not be accepted by the Government or by any person, that you have been overruled by Proudfoot. You are in a position to overrule him, placed there too, because of his notorious inefficiency and incapacity.

Great responsibility rests upon you, and when feeling this, I think I only act the part of a friend in stating my views frankly and fully, on every branch of the subject.

Some responsibility rests on myself but I can only warn, it is for you to *act*.

E 55   D.L. MACPHERSON TO A.T. GALT (PRIVATE AND
CONFIDENTIAL)
Toronto, 7 May 1860
[*PAC, A.T. Galt Papers, v. 7*]

. . . I feel much concerned about the BK. or I would not write you about it now as I am doing. when you have so much else to occupy & harrass you. But you have no more serious matter to deal with. You cannot allow it be discredited without bringing destruction upon the Gov't. & upon every Member of it for all time to come, accompanied with damaged credit abroad & wide spread ruin at home.

Notwithstanding the large amounts locked up I think with their advantages & good management the ship might be righted. but you must bring about such a change in the management as will enable you to ascertain the actual position of the Institution & this must be done in a way not to shock or disturb public confidence. Having Directors like

Ross & myself there is really of little or no use. Old Proudfoot manages the Bank & the Board Know only little of what is doing until blunders, are committed & therefore past remedy. That has been the system since the BK was established & you cannot change it without getting rid of one of the old men & putting the other in a new office.

Besides it is utterly impossible for any one who does not devote much more time to investigation than I can spare to get an understanding of their accounts much less sift them. I never had to do with anything so unpleasant, as apart from feeling that I cannot be of any great service. I am opposed & thwarted in doing what is possible by cantankerous noodles like Stayner & others. You must not ask me to serve another year . . . .

. . . If the Bank [was?] taking a Cashier from a sister Bank, he might be frightened with the first peek, resign & squack.

In spite of poor old P's incapacity one cannot help pitying them when reflecting on the terrible losses they have been led into by Govts. Zimmerman, Morton,[22] Baby, A.P. Macdonald, Cotton[23] etc making up a fearful aggregate . . . .

E 56   A.T. GALT TO T. BARING (CONFIDENTIAL)
Toronto, 7 May 1860
[PAC, Baring Papers, A834]

. . . [sorry that the Grand Trunk failed to raise new money] I can however readily see the importance to you of our extending the period for the repayment of the £500,000 beyond 1st of October – as well as of renewing the £100,000 bill – and I have every wish to meet your views on this matter – But the actions of the G.T. itself in the management of its a/c with the Bank of U.C. may possibly at the moment have put it beyond my power . . . the Coy. have drawn $650,000 from the Bank much of it during the last few weeks and have forced them into such a position that it is quite possible the bills drawn by the Bank may not meet acceptance in London – if this have unfortunately occurred, or should it occur, I must prepare not merely for the failure of this Bank, but for a [terrible?] pressure elsewhere – and it will be my duty to make every shilling available in London to meet the crisis. Until my fears are [resolved?] I can say nothing positive as to either the £500,000 or the £100,000.

. . . I felt it my duty to point out to Mr Blackwell very strongly that he ought to fulfil his engagements to the Bank and not to assume the responsibility of perhaps causing their suspension and most certainly an immediate closing of the G.T. a/c. The acceptance of his bills rests of

[22]James Morton (1808–64) was a brewer, distiller, saw miller, railway contractor and locomotive manufacturer operating from Kingston. After the economic collapse of 1857, Morton was no longer able to meet his obligations.

[23]James Cotton was a businessman and general contractor operating from Toronto.

course on your side – but in deciding on the course to be taken I must frankly warn you that the Bank is not able to stand the discredit and [restriction?] of its resources which will follow a refusal of Mr. Blackwell's bills coupled with the £100,000 bill which is also due really to the Bank . . . .

On the other hand if I could once see the Bank again in a prosperous position it would relieve the large balances (£300,000) we have in their hands and I should hope there would be no difficulty in our leaving all our unemployed balances in London – which will probably amount to the £500,000 – the £100,000 we shall, I suppose, have to renew for 90 d/s without delay . . . .

E 57   W. Cayley to George Carr Glyn
Toronto, 17 May 1860
[PAC, Glyn, Mills Papers, A542]

. . . I was sorry to find on my return here, that the Bank account with you had again run up so heavily and nothing short of Mr. Galts opinion and my own strong convictions that such a step was not only desirable but almost necessary as a measure of precaution could have induced me to urge upon the Board the propensity of increasing our reserve of specie, now almost $600000. by further drafts on you to the extent of £50.000 or £60.000 Stg. . . . The necessity also of reducing the balance against us at the Bank of the Interior assisted to absorb the funds of the Bank. Mr. Hopkins having taken special care to communicate his report & attack there. To guard against any possible apprehension in that quarter which might have been excited the Bank thought it prudent at once to balance the account, which in January stood upwards of $400,000 against us . . . .

E 58   W. Cayley to George Carr Glyn
Toronto, 19 May 1860
[PAC, Glyn, Mills Papers, A542]

. . . In the statement which I enclosed on Thursday, you may have observed the amount advanced on produce and lumber transactions, some portion of which does not fall due until late in July. It is to be regretted that these drafts, those at least for the produce of wheat were not made to mature at an earlier date. The Grand Trunk account as you will perceive is much increased . . . . The account of Messrs Gzowski & Co. stands in a different shape to what it did last year, during the period when they were constructing the Detroit & Port Huron Road they had generally a balance at their credit of $200.000 and occasionally much larger, it is just now however against them upwards of $100.000 . . . it will be necessary for the Bank to continue to hold ten per cent of its capital in Government securities until the law is altered, and with regard to which Mr. Galt had intended to bring in a bill during the

Session which has just terminated. . . . Mr. Galt has given us no intimation with reference to the July dividends. and we presume he will make his own arrangements for funds in England. His funds here are entirely inadequate . . . .

E 59   GEORGE CARR GLYN TO JOHN ROSS
London, 19 May 1860
[*PAC, Glyn, Mills Papers, A540*]

I wrote to you on the 16th inst. and have in the interval considered with my partners the position as regards the shares in the Bank of Upper Canada & have determined that, under the circumstances in which we are placed as regards that institution and the possible contingencies which may arise we are not justified in being sellers. I would rather [take?] any risk of loss upon the shares than have it said by any one that knowing the position of the Bank & what might happen (tho' I still hope everything will go on well) we had shifted upon any other person the loss which might follow – I can afford to lose money but not reputation – so you will not receive by this mail the power of attorney & authority for sale of these shares . . . [news has] again reached us from the Bank of U.C. with heavy advice of drafts without any adequate remittances. I trust there will not be a repetition of this case for we shall be compelled to refuse acceptance and I should deeply regret having to take such a course, which would create great confusion & consternation in Canada, but the time is come where some prompt and energetic measures must be taken for restoring the position of the Bank for it cannot be denied that from a variety of concurrent circumstances it is very much dis-credited: a suspension of payments would cause much mischief in Canada, & to avert it, if the directors have no other remedy, a winding up would be expedient but this could only be done with the aid of Government. The double liability of the shareholders would give security with the assets of the Bank against any possible risk of loss. You will see by these remarks that I take a very gloomy view of the position of the Bank, founded upon the entire relapse of the account to its former unjustifiable position . . . .

E 60   L.H. HOPKINS TO W.L. MACKENZIE
Lindsay, 2 June 1860
[*PAO, Mackenzie-Lindsey Papers*]

I have looked over the list of shareholders of the Bank made pursuant to order of Parliament & bearing date 27 March 1860, & I believe the following figures if not perfectly accurate may be relied on, as sufficient for all purposes of argument. The amount of stock paid up is $3,130,485, by 1050 shareholders, of these 156 holding $713,600 live in Great Britain or its dependencies, 210 Females are proprietors & 155 are described as Trustees, Executors, Public Societies &c. in all 521 or

about one half of the Proprietary, who cannot be expected to attend
Annual Meetings. The remainder (exclusive of 11 holding $45,000 &
citizens of the neighbouring republic) reside in Canada & a large
number in Toronto & its neighbourhood . . . .

E 61   GEORGE CARR GLYN TO W. CAYLEY
London, 2 June 1860
[PAC, Glyn, Mills Papers, A540]

. . . I hope the mischevious effects produced by Mr. Hopkins hostile
attacks will soon have passed away from the public mind, but it is
evident that had the BUC enjoyed the estimation & credit which
formerly attended it, they would have passed off comparatively harm-
less – I think it must have become quite clear to the Board that nothing
less than a reconstruction of the concern and a fresh organization of the
direction can effectively bring things right and I hope you and Mr. Ross
will see Mr. Galt for the purpose of devising some plan by which this
result may be effected. Matters cannot go on as they are for I feel quite
certain, if Mr. Galt had not written on the subject, we should not have
consented to increase the overdrawing by accepting these Bills if they
are drawn, Has the Bank realized any large proportion of Zimmerman's
estate? I feel the Bk direction must not expect money from this side for
G. Trunk purposes.

E 62   T.G. RIDOUT TO GLYN, MILLS
Toronto, 4 June 1860
[PAC, Glyn, Mills Papers, A542]

. . . On Mr. Cayley's return a special meeting of the Board was held
and he was armed with full power to co-operate with the President to
carry out all necessary steps to gather in the funds of the Bank. I enclose
a copy of the Resolution. It is perhaps to be regretted that these
measures were not adopted before Mr. Cayley went down to attend in
his place in Parliament. The Directors however were actuated by the
belief that temporary advances through the winter to enable the dealers
in grain and lumber to get their products to market, would hasten a
return to a more healthy and active state of things, and place the debtors
of the Bank in a better condition to meet their engagements . . . .

E 63   JOHN ROSS TO T. BARING (PRIVATE)
Toronto, 7 June 1860
[PAC, Baring Papers, A835]

Mr. Galt came to Toronto expressly to look into the state of the Bank of
Upper Canadas affairs, arriving yesterday morning & yesterday, Mr.
Blackwell received yours of the 23d ult. which he read to both Mr. Galt
& myself. – We have all considered the state of the companys affairs in

every aspect and Mr. Galt is willing to help us in every way that he can. He consents to the renewal of the £100,000 bill falling due 3d June inst. & is willing to continue the £500,000 loan arranged for last fall but this it would be out of his power to do if the Bank of UC were to collapse & this we look upon as certain unless the Company meets its engagements to that institution. I therefore have joined Mr. Galt in advising Mr. Blackwell to give the exchange necessary to cover our engagements to the Bank because if they could charge us with their failure the Company would be ruined beyond redemption, the panic would extend to the other Banks and the Govt. would be obliged to draw on every pound of its means to sustain the other Banks. The simple condition then which Mr. Galt makes on agreeing to renew the £100,000 draft & to continue the loan to the Co. guaranteed by yourselves & Mr. Glyns firm is that we keep our engagements to the Bank upon the faith of which being carried out they advanced their money to the Company. Mr. Blackwell therefore had no alternative but to draw of which he has no doubt advised you . . . .

E 64   T.G. RIDOUT TO MATILDA
10 June 1860
[*PAO, Ridout Papers*]

. . . The Bank is in much better position than it has been for several months past so that I am no longer doubtful about its affairs which I cannot help saying pressed heavily upon my mind. Since the 20 April we have remitted to Glyn £245,000 sterling & we are easy about the Government account every thing being in good train . . . .

E 65   A.T. GALT TO T. BARING (PRIVATE)
Sherbrooke, 11 June 1860
[*PAC, Baring Papers, A834*]

. . . I regret to say we do not see any relief that is within our reach on this side. As you will have gathered from my letter from Toronto the position of the Bank of U.C. is such as to make it impossible to look in that direction – nor can the Gov't. do any thing through that channel as our balance with that Institution is already in excess of $1,200,000 and I dare not take the responsibility of increasing it . . . but with the exchange given by Mr. Blackwell and the altered policy on which I have insisted my expectation is that in a few months this Institution will be out of danger and to a certain extent this relief will extend to their connection with the Grand Trunk . . . .

E 66   W. CAYLEY TO GEORGE CARR GLYN
Toronto, 2 July 1860
[*PAC, Glyn, Mills Papers, A542*]

. . . Our bank meeting went off well and has had throughout the

Province a very salutary effect. Our instructions to our local branches to contract their discounts are being responded to very generally, but they have not yet come up to what I expected or hope may be done. The cry is now wait until after harvest. We press and shall continue to press as far as it is safe. The Grand Trunk acct gives me a good deal of uneasiness. As it is now worked by the Company it is a dead weight upon us, and entirely unprofitable. The tidings which we may receive from you with regard to the bills which are now running must decide our future action
. . . .

E 67   W. CAYLEY TO GEORGE CARR GLYN
Toronto, 30 July 1860
[PAC, Glyn, Mills Papers, A542]

. . . The absence of advice leads me to infer that the aspect of Grand Trunk Affairs has not been improved and I have requested the Solicitor of the Bank to meet me in Quebec, in order that prompt steps might be taken to protect the interests of the Bank, and secure the payment of the drafts which we have transmitted to you.

E 68   GRAND TRUNK RAILWAY/BANK OF UPPER CANADA RELATIONS
Grand Trunk Office, 7 August 1860
[PAC, RG 30, v. 1000]

The President reported the arrangement made with the Bank of Upper Canada for the purpose of keeping the road running & paying the necessary expenses thereof: That all outlay on Capital Account unless when special provision for the same is made, shall cease;
    That all the revenues of the Road, arising from what source soever shall continue to be paid into the Bank of Upper Canada; that the cheques to be drawn upon, & cashed by the Bank, shall be limited strictly to what is necessary to keep the Road running & in Working order & the payment of wages for that purpose. That the [difference?] between the receipts of the Road & the Expenses thus limited should be applied to the repayment of the advance made by the Bank including the money arising from the Postal Service, after balancing the Account with the Government. The Rent of the Portland & Detroit Line be paid as part of the Working expenses of the Road.

E 69   W. CAYLEY TO GEORGE CARR GLYN
Toronto, 13 August 1860
[PAC, Glyn, Mills Papers, A542]

. . . the rumoured embarassment of the [Grand Trunk] Company is becoming the subject of comment in the papers, and our connection with it does not escape notice. This is to be regretted as our Stock has been rising steadily since the Bank meeting in June, prior to the closing of the books before dividend day the Stock stood at 80 – it is now quoted at 86 . . . .

With regard to the draft on Messrs Baring Bros. for £45500. the Directors cannot bring themselves to distrust Mr. Blackwells assurance so far as to doubt but what it will be met at maturity. In making arrangements with Mr. Blackwell prior to his leaving for England last autumn, and when he undertook to cover his bank account from time to time by drafts on England, I referred to the usual precaution, in which he acquiesced, of obtaining authority to draw each draft. This arrangement must have been advised, in fact Mr. Blackwell stated a day or two after to Mr. Macpherson that there was a difference in the amount of the credit as he had named it to Mr. Baring and the limit of the Bank.

Had Mr. Blackwell exceeded his authority in entering into such an arrangement, it should have been rectified or cancelled on his arrival in London. We have had no occasion to draw for specie since the 27th ult and the balances with the Banks continue easy. Since the 1st Inst. Mr. Cassels[24] has remitted £22000. and drawn £1300. During my recent visit to Quebec I made arrangements with Mr. Galt for the purchase of $260.000. Debentures to replace those disposed of by you, this obviates the difficulty with which we were threatened respecting our monthly statements to the Government, and enables us to have the whole amount including the batch of $48600. last transmitted, carried to our credit in account.

E 70   GRAND TRUNK RAILWAY/BANK OF UPPER CANADA RELATIONS
GTR, 19 September 1860
[PAC, RG 30, v. 1000]

RESOLVED – "That the Resolution of the Canada Board of the 7th August with reference to the Bank of Upper Canada Account and the management thereupon made with the Bank be rescinded; And that the President and Vice President of the Company be authorized to make such new arrangements as will be necessary to carry on the financial operations of the Company in a legal manner, and that they be requested accordingly to take the opinion of Counsel on the subject with due regard to the proceedings of the London Board and Canada Board and the power and restrictions of the Several Acts of the Company, and to the opinion of Mr. Wagstaff the London Solicitor referred to in the London Board Minutes, – And the President and Vice President to make such arrangements as will enable the Company to secure the use of the New Rolling Stock."

[24]Robert Scougall Cassels, brother of Robert, was the branch manager for the Bank of Upper Canada at Quebec and later at Ottawa.

E 71   T. GALT TO A.T. GALT
Quebec, 25 September 1860
[*PAC, Baring Papers, A835*]

You are aware that the claims of Messrs. Barings and the Messrs. Glyns
for cash loans to the G.T. Ry Co. long past due are in my hands for
collection. On Monday I shall obtain Judgment the whole amount is
£800,000 and I am instructed by my clients to seize and sell the Rolling
Stock and stores of The Company forthwith as other claims are being
prepared and the money loaned by my clients was advanced upon the
express understanding that in failure of payment they should have that
which under their instructions I am about to have sold. The effect of the
seizure and sale will be to stop the running of the Road for the present
and I am unwilling to create so great an amount of inconvenience and
injury to the business of the Country without first acquainting the
government and ascertaining whether any measure of relief is to be
proposed to enable the Company to pay its debts. Awaiting your reply.

E 72   JOHN ROSS TO GLYN, MILLS (PRIVATE AND CONFIDENTIAL)
Quebec, 28 September 1860
[*PAC, Glyn, Mills Papers, A545*]

. . . Cayley has shown me your last letter to the Bank & I fear that you
are inclined to press the Bank for the purpose of acting upon the
Government & I trust you will not pursue this policy because there are
some of us here who are doing our utmost to induce such action as will
secure the necessary relief & it would not in my humble opinion be wise
to bring down The Bank so long as there is a hope of our success. It may
seem unaccountable to you but if the Bank's claim in execution stood
before your own & Messrs Barings public opinion would work much
more effectively in aiding us to carry a measure of relief & when the
circumstances become known under which the Bank made its advances
to the Company that feeling will be exhibited in a much more
unmistakeable *shape*.

We ought not to have taken the money of the Bank to supply
increased rolling stock for the Company which enables it to increase its
earnings & to hand over that same stock for seizure in favour of any
other executive creditors. In this view I am quite sure both Mr. Baring
& yourself will agree & I only write you thus frankly because your letter
to Mr. Cayley has made me anxious & I am sure you do not desire to
take any action with respect to the Bank that might have the effect of
defeating our actions in favour of the *Grand Trunk*.

E 73   T. GALT TO GEORGE CARR GLYN
Toronto, 4 October 1860
[*PAC, Baring Papers, A835*]

. . . You are aware that the Company are very largely indebted to the

Bank of Upper Canada who I believe are taking steps to reduce their claim to a Judgment and will probably obtain one in the course of a few days. I think that in a political point of view and with reference to Legislative action it would be very much better that the serious responsibility of closing the Road should be taken by them rather than by Messrs. Baring and yourselves. It is my intention therefore acting in concert with Mr. Ward[25] to try and enter into an arrangement with the Bank by which they shall agree not to issue an execution on any judgment obtained by them until I hear from you and then if such a course meets with your approbation that they shall be the parties to issue the execution and stop the road, it is true that by this course they gain priority of their execution as against the Rolling stock of the Company but as I have stated in my former letters in my opinion (in which Mr. Barth[26] agrees) such a priority is I regret to say not of any great value, as I consider the holders of the Preference Bonds at all events have a prior lien and charge and I fear the Provincial lien will revive if the Company cease to work the road. The reason why I propose such a course for your consideration is that the Bank is the oldest and among the farmers of the Upper Province the best known of any of the Banking Institutions in the country and if there was a probability of their sustaining so serious a loss as the amount of their claim against the Company would occasion I am convinced that the Legislature would come to their assistance more readily than to that of other parties having equal claims in point of justice but whose loss would not press so heavily on the people of the Country. You need be under no apprehension from my submitting this suggestion for your approval that I shall in the meanwhile allow any step to be taken either by the Bank or by any other parties by which your position can be affected until I hear from you and Messr. Barings but I hope you will approve of my delaying proceedings until I am favoured with your instructions.

E 74   W. CAYLEY TO GEORGE CARR GLYN
Montreal, 26 October 1860
[PAC, Glyn, Mills Papers, A542]

I regret to have to say that the continued Newspaper attacks to which I referred in my last, and the aforesaid unprotected character of our advances to the Grand Trunk have seriously inconvenienced us, and more particularly in a quarter where we have been unable to apply a remedy. viz. in New York and with the Bank of Commerce, who have hitherto endorsed our drafts on you, whenever we have had occasion to place funds there for specie or other business purposes, and who have now declined to continue to do so.

As a temporary substitute we applied to the Government to exchange

25Samuel G. Ward was a North American representative for Baring Brothers.
26Barth was probably a London lawyer acting on behalf of the Baring Brothers.

drafts with us, to the extent of $400.000 of the particulars of which you will be advised by Mr. Galt by this mail. We have undertaken to remit commercial exchange to you to cover our drafts, I suggested however to Mr. Galt, that as we should probably be behind at first starting, not being able to purchase freely until we had replenished our reserve, that he should leave us a margin of £25000 – which we could gradually work off, and to which he assented . . . .

E 75   BANK OF MONTREAL/BANK OF UPPER CANADA RELATIONS
26 October 1860
[PAC, Bank of Montreal, Resolve Book 6, p. 192]

The position of the Bank of Upper Canada engaged the attention of the Board in connection with the reports in circulation. The Board resolved that in the event of any extraordinary demand arising for the redemption of the Notes of that Bank likely to cause Embarassment the Notes should be refused at the different establishments of the Bank but that it was desirable that the Bank of Upper Canada should be informed that this course would be adopted unless a satisfactory explanation with regard to the position of the Bank was afforded. The Cashier was instructed to put himself in communication with some of the leading Banks with the view of securing united action in the matter.

E 76   L.H. HOLTON TO GEORGE BROWN[27] (STRICTLY PRIVATE AND
CONFIDENTIAL)
Montreal, 30 October 1860
[PAC, George Brown Papers, v. 3]

You have of Course Seen the Comments of our papers on the position of the Bank of Upper Canada and the Relations of the Govt to it. The affair is assuming too alarming an aspect to admit of its being much longer ignored by public men and public journals of Canada – Of course we must all desire on public and patriotic as well as on personal grounds to See the Bank Sustain herself if it Can be done honestly and I would be the last to incur the responsibility of [serving] a partisan object at the Cost of a Commercial and financial panic but we must look the facts in the face. We Can't get rid of them by averting our own head. Nor evade a public duty by holding our tongues.

The first Question to be decided [I suppose?] is this. Is the Bank in spite of its gross Mismanagement really sound and able beyond a [peradventure?] to meet its engagements with the public? If this question can be answered affirmatively then it is clearly our duty to do every thing in our power to avert a crisis. If silence be the most effective policy let us be Silent. But what if no such answer can be given? Can

[27]George Brown (1818–80), a businessman and politician was leader of the Upper Canadian reformers at this time.

Silence and inaction *then* be justified? *I am afraid* the Bank is in any thing but a Satisfactory or even Sound Condition and that if She is Sustained at all it will be solely by the free but altogether irregular and improper use of the Public funds. Ministers have a tremendous interest in preventing an enquiry into the past management as well as the present position of the Bank and they will strain every nerve to prevent it. I believe that nearly all the Corruption that has disgraced and well nigh Ruined our Country during the last few years has been perpetrated through the agency of the Bank and that an enquiry Such as must ensue on its Suspension would drag the damning record to light. If this be So, it is easy to See that Ministers will Stick at nothing to accomplish their purpose. It is quite obvious they are preparing the way for a Grand Trunk grant which they must carry in order to Cover up the advances already made *nominally* by the London agents and the BUC but *virtually* out of Provincial funds. If either the G.T. or Bank falls – they must fall also and in *their* falling be irretrievably disgraced as public men – my belief therefore is that they intend Sustaining the Bank *at all hazards* – until Parliament meets – when they also intend *at all hazards* to Carry a Grand Trunk Bill – which will enable the Company to pay the Bank & the Bank to pay the Government, and thus make things pleasant generally. And meanwhile they are enlisting all the influence of the BKUC and to a Certain extent the Banking & Commercial interests generally – worked upon by fear of a crisis – in the Support of a Grand Trunk measure – which may thus be made the means – not of their destruction as we have Supposed – but of giving them a new lease of power. I may be all wrong in my facts & in my reasoning, but undoubtedly if there be any foundation for the one or any force in the other, Your position as Leader of a Great party impresses' upon You in my opinion a very grave responsibility, one from which I am Sure you will not shrink. At all events I felt that it was but right that I should put You in possession of my views of what we must all admit to be a very Serious matter – whether Considered in the light of public or of party interests . . . .

E 77   W. CAYLEY TO GEORGE CARR GLYN
Toronto, 5 November 1860
[PAC, Glyn, Mills Papers, A542]

Mr. Ridout starts to day for England to explain to you what has occurred here within the last fortnight and the arrangements we have made with the three principal Banks in Montreal to enable us to meet the pressure brought upon us by the combined attacks of the Montreal Press. Had this arrangement not been made, it would have been impossible for us, in the absence of a New York connection, to have raised the necessary supplies, to provide for the withdrawal of Customers deposits, and the return of our circulation. The first will to a certain extent continue, as a natural consequence of our ceasing to discount, nearly all depositors, look for occasional discounts, the demand for specie will gradually die out as the harmonious working together of the Banks becomes generally understood. The attacks of the Lower Canada Press will I think be continued if I am right in my impression that they are actuated by a feeling partly hostile to the Government, and generally to the Grand Trunk and not [more?] from jealousy of our connection with the Government and the hold we have in Western Canada. The effort to discredit our paper, alarm our depositors and force us into liquidation has been so little disguised that it can be no lack of charity to infer that our assailants have or had a definite object in view. The arrangement we have made with the Banks, and the steps we have recently taken in the States with the concurrence of Mr. Ward of Boston in re G' Trunk to obtain for us the reputation of being secured, will greatly strengthen our position, and I have now little fear of our Enemies, or perhaps I should be more correct in saying of the Enemies to Grand Trunk relief, as had we succumbed before The meeting of Parliament – we have so many connected with us in one shape or another in the two Houses of Parliament – either as stockholders, creditors, or Debtors that the Government could have expected little aid from them while smarting under the losses which such a misfortune would have entailed upon them. It will not be in our power for some short time to come, to remit exchange to any amount . . . . Until our connection in New York is re-established we should be confined to the same market for both our sales and purchases of exchange, and exposed to comments not complimentary to our financial operations. I need not say that all our arrangements with our sister Banks and our prospect of the future are predicated on the continuance of your confidence in us . . . . While hitherto you have honored all our drafts, we have not had it in our power to shew or state that we had a definite credit upon which we could calculate under all circumstances, in our relations with you. This undefined position led to the recent refusal of the Bank of Commerce to negotiate our drafts. With the Banks in the Province our settlements have been for many months past made in specie . . . .

E 78   BANK OF MONTREAL/BANK OF UPPER CANADA RELATIONS
6 November 1860
[PAC, Bank of Montreal, Resolve Book 6, pp. 194–5]

The Cashier reported that along with the General Manager of the Bank of British North America & the President of the Commercial Bank of Canada he had visited Toronto for the purpose of asking some explanation from the Bank of Upper Canada with respect to their position. That the information sought had been refused upon the ground that it was not competent for the Directors to afford it, but that assurance was given to the effect that the Bank was in a sound condition – although embarrassed for the time by the interruption of its arrangements in New York.

The Cashier informed the Board that he as well as the representatives of the other two Banks had declined to purchase the Exchange of the Bank of Upper Canada on its London Correspondents, unless accompanied with collateral security in the shape of Commercial paper & that it had been arranged that the three Banks should each in this manner become purchasers of Exchange to the extent of £25,000 stg. in Settlement of any balances which may become payable by the Bank of Upper Canada.

The Board expressed their approval of the arrangement.

The attention of the Board having been directed to an Article which appeared in the Toronto "Leader" of the 3rd. current purporting to give an account of the result of the recent interview between the Banks but containing statements completely at variance with the truth & the Board being of opinion that the Article referred to emanated from the Bank of Upper Canada instructed the Cashier in conjunction with the other Banks, to demand a contradiction of the erroneous statements, through the same channel.

E 79   L.H. Holton to George Brown (confidential)
Montreal, 6 November 1860
[*PAC, George Brown Papers, v. 3*]

I Wrote You last Week on a very important subject – but owing I presume to Your absence I am Yet without a reply. I am Sure You are satisfied by this time of the literal accuracy of what I then wrote. Just about that time the Govt. made a large additional advance to the B.U.C. to enable it to Keep its doors open – and the result of the Conference last week is not at all what was represented by the Leader. If *truly stated* it would Shut up the Bank in less than [a] Week – and yet the Govt. have made their first point and in my judgement the *Controlling one* – in the grand game I endeavored to foreshadow It is admitted that the Bank Can't Stand unless it receives its G.T. debt. It is admitted the G.T. Cannot pay without public aid – add to this the Complications arising out of the relations of Glyn & Barings to the Bank, the Railway Company, and the Govt. and then estimate the Chances of defeating them on the *second* point of their policy of voting more money to the Railway, while supporting them in the first and in many respects the Worst – viz sustaining the Bank of U.C., with the Provincial Credit, after bringing it into peril by using it for their own corrupt purposes – I look at the whole matter as a *politician*. I Know no likes or dislikes *among the Banks*. They are none of them friendly to us *as politicians*. As I Said before I should deplore a Bank Crisis from any Cause and would not promote one to secure any more partisan object – but there are greater Calamities than the Stoppage of a *political Bank*, unable to sustain itself on a legitimate Commercial basis – and these Calamities will now I fear in spite of all opposition be visited upon the Country – I hope You are getting on swimmingly with Your paper manufacture.

Pray let me hear from you on the Subject of this and my last letter. I am as you know not much given to despondency but I Confess the prospects of our party appear to me more dreary at this Moment than at any time Since the last General election –

E 80   T. GALT TO GEORGE CARR GLYN
Toronto, 8 November 1860
[*PAC, Glyn, Mills Papers, A545*]

. . . I [am] happy to learn you are satisfied with the course favored by Mr. Ward and myself. You may rely on my doing all in my power to forward your interest, but as I have already told you, the Legislature is the only authority or means on this side of the water that can afford adequate assistance . . . . My Brother . . . objected to any action at present and also stated that it was deemed *essential* that the Bank of Upper Canada should be allowed to obtain any security that could be got in the United States – Mr. Ross the next morning stated to me that such was also his opinion and the wish of Mr. Cartier. When I saw Mr. Ward which was on the 29th . . . and after consultation with him . . . he gave instructions to Mr. Bushnell[28] to withdraw the affidavits that had been taken out in his name on behalf of yourselves and Mssrs. Baring and one was issued in the name of the Bank.

It was of very great consequence that the Bank should be in a position to announce that their debt was secured as [one word?] injurious statements affecting the Bank arising out of this claim against the Company being entirely unsecured were in circulation. This I am happy to say from the correspondence and from other causes has been quieted and every thing is now calmed down. I pointed out to Mr. Ward that the whole amount of property attached would even if available go but a small way in satisfaction of your debt and that of Mssrs. Baring and therefore as The Minister of Finance and other Ministers of the Government were so desirous that the Bank should be allowed any advantage that an attachment would give them in a [one word?] that confidence might be [maintained?]. I was convinced it was for your interests and Mr. Baring that he should act as they desired, one advantage at any rate being that the Banking interests are now involved in obtaining relief for the Company. I do not wish to conceal from you that it would be a hard fight to obtain the requisite legislation but I am sanguine of success and it is of great consequence that any influence that can be brought to bear should be enlisted on our side –

---

[28]Bushnell was probably a lawyer acting on behalf of the Baring Brothers.

E 81   L.H. HOLTON TO GEORGE BROWN (PRIVATE)
Montreal, 16 November 1860
[*PAC, George Brown Papers, v. 3*]

. . . The Bank Question is I know an exceedingly delicate one on which it is difficult to decide what is best to be done. The *despondency* to which I gave expression in a former letter had not So much reference to the General and [one word?] aspects of the political field as to What I apprehended and still apprehend will be the Consequences of allowing the Govt to get over the difficulty they were in with respect to the Bank – a Subject in regard to which the General public are almost entirely uninformed and Can not therefore estimate the importance of – I Would not have urged an attack *on the Bank – but on the Gov't touching their transactions with the Bank.* Incidentally the Bank *might* have suffered but the Govt must surely in my judgement have fallen. Now my fear is that they may convert their BUC weakness into a Source of strength. I hope the result will prove that I misjudge. Of all the unscrupulous and unconstitutional things the present Govt have done – there is none So undefensible as putting their hands – without color of law into the public treasury to Sustain a tottering Bank already indebted in nearly the whole amount of its Capital to the Province . . . .

E 82   T.G. RIDOUT TO GLYN, MILLS
London, 21 November 1860
[*PAC, Glyn, Mills Papers, A542*]

The object of my visit to London on behalf of the Bank of Upper Canada is to reestablish the credit of the Bank at New York, and in Canada which has been much shaken by the large debt due to it by the Grand Trunk rail way Co. the amount of which is greatly exaggerated in the Public mind.

This object would be effectually gained by an assurance from you that you would grant an open credit of £150,000 to be negociated if need be through the Bank of Commerce at New York or through the Bank of Montreal . . . .

The debt due by the Grand Trunk Rail Way Company to the Bank of Upper Canada amounts to £181,064 Stg. including £45,500 on Messrs. Barings besides about £20,000 more due in Canada, all which no doubt will be provided for at the ensuing session of the Canadian Legislature.

E 83   A.T. GALT TO GEORGE CARR GLYN (PRIVATE)
Quebec, 30 November 1860
[*PAC, Glyn, Mills Papers, A545*]

. . . The attacks on the Bank are not yet wholly suspended – but I think the immediate danger from them is removed – and if they are enabled through your aid to secure their N. York connections – all will probably go well.

It is, however, needless to say that the Bank does not possess [considerable] capital enough, to manage so large an account as that of the Government – and that some change must soon be made for dividing it with other Banks. It is a source of great embarassment to the Government – to have not merely very large sums locked up in the Bank – but constant application for aid. At this moment, we have in the several Banks of the Province, nearly Two Millions of Dollars but I cannot venture to withdraw this large sum now indeed in the case of the B.U.C. I could not get it – and now in other cases with the state of [feeling?] in New York it would not be prudent to withdraw our Balances. It will therefore be necessary for us to remit the January Interest from resources on your side. The Balance of the Loan will not probably be great enough – but possibly some of the loans made out of it, may be called in and funds provided – I shall write officially on this point by next mail –

I am inclined to think it would be as well – if Mr. George Glyn could visit this country, and look into the Bank affairs especially in view of any modification of the Govt account with the Bank. Some changes in management ought to be made – in the *President* certainly. You will easily understand that the Govt cannot very well interfere in the personnel of the Bank – but you can do so with perfect propriety – and I could consult with your son upon the matter confidentially. Pray think this over . . . .

E 84   W. CAYLEY TO GEORGE CARR GLYN
Toronto, 10 December 1860
[*PAC, Glyn, Mills Papers, A542*]

. . . Without forebearance and some indulgence extended to us I foresee a severe struggle before us. Parliament will not meet probably till February and even then its action may not be prompt. I observe that our depositors balances since the beginning of the half year have been reduced upward of $600,000 . . . .

E 85   W. CAYLEY TO GEORGE CARR GLYN
Toronto, 27 December 1860
[*PAC, Glyn, Mills Papers, A542*]

. . . we have past the most trying period, both upon our circulation and deposits on call, the reduction on the two has been within a fraction of a million of dollars since the 1st November. Our circulation and deposits on call now stand at $2,723,869. Until we can reestablish our connection with New York we shall have to rely upon the existing arrangements with the Montreal Bank, this working much to our disadvantage both from the fact that it leaves to them to settle the rate of exchange and keeps some eighty thousand pounds sterling of our best commercial paper locked up. Were we to ask them as an alternative to rediscount that paper for us, we should transfer to them bodily our customers their accounts and deposits and close our best Agency in Quebec . . . .

E 86   W. CAYLEY TO GEORGE CARR GLYN
Toronto, 31 December 1860
[*PAC, Glyn, Mills Papers, A542*]

. . . Looking back at the several critical periods thro' which the Bank has passed in the year which closes today, I cannot but feel that we have been tried to an extent which would have staggered the strongest of our Canadian Institutions and that we stand is attributable solely to your support and the continued confidence of the Government. The attack commenced by Mr. Hopkins and continued with so much violence by the Montreal Press, the withdrawal of our New York connection, the known difficulties of the Grand Trunk and our connection with it, and the descent of the Managers of our sister Banks upon us, superadded to our Grand Trunk advances £180.000 and some £50.000 more advanced the Arthabaska[29] road at the instance of the Government, the contraction of our circulation and the removal of deposits, amounting in the aggregate to nearly half a million sterling shew the nature of the pressure to which we have been subjected and against which we have borne up. There is little doubt it was in the contemplation of the Banks when they made their formal visit, to close our doors, and assume our circulation and our depositors accounts and our transferring to them our bills receivable for collections, and leaving our foreign account to be protected by our secured debts, providing which would have rendered the collection of the latter ten fold more slow and difficult.

E 87   W. CAYLEY TO GEORGE CARR GLYN
Quebec, 10 January 1861
[*PAC, Glyn, Mills Papers, A543*]

. . . As regards the Bank of Montreal we have returned to settlement, in specie. The Commercial Bank has offered to continue the present system of settling by drafts, accompanied by the deposit of commercial paper, the drafts running at any one time not to exceed £20,000 Stg. The Bank of British North America I have little doubt would come into the same terms, and such a margin as £40,000 or £50,000 thus provided in Montreal would, with the aid of a credit of half the amount in New York, give us ample scope to work with, under all ordinary circumstances, could we be freed from the obligation of giving security, and

---

[29]The Arthabaska Railway had been guaranteed money from the Grand Trunk via the sale of a part of £2 million of second preference bonds issued under the Grand Trunk Relief Act of 1856. Pending the sale of these bonds, the government, often through the Bank of Upper Canada, advanced money to this railway. In 1863 an investigation reported that the Arthabaska line owed the government $170,000 although the bonds issued to cover it had long since been sold and the proceeds spent.

our facilities for making remittances would be increased. Mr. Ridout on his return from England to New York called upon the managers of the Bank of Commerce, and showed the letter with which you had favored him, the conversation however, it would appear, was confined to general topics and the interview terminated without result. Our Directors have had it under discussion to attempt to renew their former connection with Messr. King & Sons.

While here I have freely discussed with Mr. Galt the position of the Bank, and your suggestion of amalgamation with some other Institution. We both fear that with the present low quotations of our stock such an attempt would be attended with disappointment. No division of the government account will for the present be proceeded with, but some alteration with regard to the deposits of Customs duties may be made to meet the wishes of the mercantile community. A change in the management of the Bank has also been the subject of discussion amongst the Directors themselves, and I was requested to mention the matter to Mr. Galt, he is chary of giving his opinion, at least before he has visited Toronto, which he contemplates during next week.

E 88   A.T. GALT TO GEORGE CARR GLYN (CONFIDENTIAL)
Montreal, 4 February 1861
[*PAC, Glyn, Mills Papers, A543*]

The Directors of the Bank of U.C. about two weeks ago, decided on the immediate change in their President & Cashier – but have since reconsidered the matter, and postponed any change till their June meeting. In this I fear they have made a grave error, but the Government cannot take the responsibility of interference and we can only look to the steps required in justification of our own course as regards the public deposits. I have for some time past felt that we must look to the Resources of the country to meet all our engagements including Interest on our debt – and that we can no longer provide for this last item, by funds raised in England. And in this view it has become a most serious question how far we can venture to allow the funds required for these and other engagements to accumulate in the hands of the Bank. I cannot possibly feel the slightest confidence in obtaining at 1 July next the control of our own balances to remit to England. And yet it is extremely difficult to take any steps to remedy this which will not be fatal to the Bank. I brought the matter before my Colleagues and obtained their sanction to my placing the incoming revenue in other Banks – still paying our disbursements thro' the B.U.C. and thus securing them the circulation – and arranging for a delay in the reimbursement of the large balances they owe us. Mr. Cayley was under the impression that this arrangement would answer every purpose – but on discussing the subject confidentially with Mr. Davidson and Mr. C.S. Ross – they are both of opinion the B.U.C. is so weak that it cannot stand any change whatsoever indicating even a partial with drawal of our confidence.

It has been suggested as absolutely necessary that we should obtain a clearer insight into the assets of the Bank – as preliminary to any step. . . . . The position of the Bank towards the Government is in the last degree unsatisfactory, scarcely a week passing without an appeal for aid – and when Parliament meets I really know not how to deal with this question. The Bank is to my knowledge now carrying on its business at a frightful loss and yet, they paid a dividend last month! The question is how can this be remedied? And with the large interest your Firm have in the Bank, I feel most strongly that one of your partners should be here without delay . . . .

. . . The Government *must* make a change in their relations toward the Bank – and it cannot be delayed. If it be possible, we shall avert any crisis in their affairs, at present, but I must beg you to give your immediate and serious attention to this subject – and to advise us without delay of the course you propose to take. Without any stated credit in London, and without any agency in New York to [endorse?] their bills – and with an absolute withdrawal of confidence on the part of the other Banks here, I confess I see little prospect of their being able to maintain themselves –

E 89   W. Cayley to George Carr Glyn
Toronto, 7 February 1861
[*PAC, Glyn, Mills Papers, A543*]

. . . Mr. Proudfoot returned yesterday from New York, in my last I stated the object of his visit there was to endeavour to renew our former connection with that Firm. He was kindly received, and succeeded in effecting a temporary arrangement, the chief point however, he being authorized to draw against drafts on you remitted to them to an extent not exceeding £25,000 Stg was made to depend upon a letter of authorization from yourselves . . . .

E 90   A.T. Galt to T. G. Ridout
Quebec, 8 February 1861
[*PAC, RG 19 E1A, v. 3376*]

. . . It is essential that I should be satisfied that the public Revenues which are now paid into the Bank, are not merely ultimately safe, but are available at any moment for the public service.

The Government therefore request that you will submit this letter to your Board of Directors – with the expression of our desire to be furnished with the least possible delay with the following information –

Assets
1. Statement of Current Bills with the names of all the obligants

2. Past due Bills   ditto   ditto
3. Current deposit A/C – overdrawn
4. Special Loans
5. Real Estate – the property of the Bank
N.B. The Collateral Security held for bills to be stated – Property on Bills included in the foregoing and pledged by the Bank for loans or as Collateral Security for Bills of Exchange, to be specified.
6. Other Stocks or Securities.

Liabilities

1. Amount of Circulation – with a statement of the mode in which the same is made up. And the amount of notes [one word?] in each Branch.
2. Money at Interest.
3. Due to Depositors, or Current A/Cs – without deduction of amounts due.
4. Amount due to foreign Agents and Banks.
5. Amount due to Departments of Government.

These Returns to be furnished by the Head Office Branches & Agencies as at 31st Dec. last – with any later information that can be supplied without delay . . . .

E 91   GEORGE CARR GLYN TO W. CAYLEY
London, 13 February 1861
[*PAC, Glyn, Mills Papers, A540*]

. . . We are now anxious to call your attention and that of the directors to the overdue bills of the Grand Trunk Company which we now hold on account of the Bk of Up. Canada, as against the overdrawn account – though it is most unusual, and not in accordance with recognized rules of business to hold unpaid bills as Sufficient security for the operation of an account, Yet under the particular circumstances of the case, and looking forward to the expectations held out of relief from the Legislature to the Gr Trunk Ry. Co. in the ensuing Session, we have done so . . . we cannot consent to continue to hold the bills forever of the account, & the directors must provide against the consequence of such a deficiency – we sincerely trust such a state of things may not arise as to compel the Bank of Upper Canada to enforce its position against the Gr Trunk Co. I feel confident of the wishes of the Government in this matter & cannot doubt its powers, if exerted, to carry this out.

E 92   GEORGE CARR GLYN TO A.T. GALT
London, 20 February 1861
[*PAC, A.T. Galt Papers, v. 2*]

I beg to acknowledge the receipt of your letter of the 4th Feb and concur with you in the report expressed at the delay in carrying out the proposed changes in the executive of the Bank of Upper Canada. I shall await with much interest your further communication after the more detailed enquiry into the position of that establishment which you intended immediately to institute yourself on the spot. The other contents of your letter surprise and alarm us for the Bank of Upper Canada.

We must beg to remind you that the course of proceeding which we have adopted towards the Bank of Upper Canada and the departure from our general rules of business in its case, have entirely arisen from our knowledge of the relations of the Government towards that institution and its earnest desire to uphold it. We have acted from time to time on the representation to this effect which we have received. The firm and continued support of the Government has always been held out to us as the inducement for us to continue our support and we cannot conceive it possible for the Government to entertain the idea of withdrawing its support, and thereby at once causing the evil which we have hitherto lent our aid in averting without taking measures for carrying on the operations and concerns of the Bank of Upper Canada in some shape or under some arrangement which will prevent the evil which otherwise must occur to the Province. We shall of course after the receipt of your letter be governed in our future proceedings by the usual rules of banking.

With regard to sending out partners we are still of the same opinion as before expressed that it is not expedient. The decision upon this important matter must rest with the Government of Canada, our course must be governed by prudential considerations and the general rules of business and must be determined by what we hear from Canada and by the action of the Government. You are aware that we have frequently urged upon the Directors of the Bank of Upper Canada the necessity of winding up or if they went on of improving their position by a juncture with some other body, but whatever was to be done, must be under the sanction and with the support of the Government.

I hope the next mail will bring more reassuring accounts from you.

E 93   W. CAYLEY TO GEORGE CARR GLYN
Toronto, 4 March 1861
[PAC, Glyn, Mills Papers, A543]

. . . the Bank has no alternative between drawing upon you to meet the requirements of the Government or explicitly stating to the Minister of Finance that we are unable to meet his demands, in other words admitting our inability to continue the account. Such a course would be perfectly suicidal at this moment when we are within a fortnight of the meeting of Parliament, and the discussions of the affairs of the Grand Trunk and the claims of the Bank. In a late letter to you I stated how disappointed Mr. Galt had felt at being compelled to make his own arrangements for the redemption of $150,000 of M.L. Fund Debentures; had we declined to make provision for the more recent demand, namely an advance of $30,000 to the Arthabaska Road and $120,000 to the Grand Trunk Company to enable them to pay the wages of the men, very disastrous results might have been the consequence. In addition to the inconvenience which we experience in making these advances we experience fresh disappointments from the Grand Trunk Co. They have failed to pay one shilling on the Lease of the Cars and Engines which we bought and contracted for them at a cost of upwards of $100,000, altho this leasing system was resorted to especially to make the payments easy and convenient, nor have they retired any portion of $70,000 of their notes given to Mr. Turcotte[30] and which the Bank discounted to prevent the Company from getting into serious difficulties with the contractor of the Arthabasca Road . . . .

E 94   A.T. GALT TO GEORGE CARR GLYN (CONFIDENTIAL)
Quebec, 8 March 1861
[PAC, Glyn, Mills Papers, A543]

. . . The position of the Bank absorbs much of my attention. Mr. Cassells of whom I wrote has been engaged upon the statements and his opinion is that the Bank can go on if its G.T. debt be paid but not otherwise. I am also glad to say he will in this case, accept the management.

I am now urging this point – and hope to succeed in procuring a measure for next Session. To carry it we shall be obliged to make specific provision for the Bank debt – as well as for our own advances. The threatened failure of the Bank & Railway may carry the bill nothing else can.

If we succeed it will not, I trust be difficult for us to come to such an understanding with you, as will place the Bank once more on a satisfactory footing . . . . For our balances I am willing to be as forbearing as possible. The Bank is now in great difficulty, but I can not attempt its relief, until our G.T. policy is settled – my best arguement would be lost in this case . . . .

E 95   A.T. GALT TO GEORGE CARR GLYN (CONFIDENTIAL)
Quebec, 21 March 1861
[PAC, Glyn, Mills Paper, A543]

. . . With regard to the Bank I stated to my colleagues that whatever policy might dictate in the way of delay in re. the G.T.R. it would be fatal to the Bank – and that I desired to be able to give you a general assurance that the Government would so far as lay in their power, sustain the Bank until the Grand Trunk affair was settled. This

---

[30]Turcotte was a Grand Trunk employee.

assurance I am now happy to have it in my power to give you – though I am not yet prepared to say how it will be applied – in fact I cannot do so, until I have got the views of Mr. Cassels on what is wanted – my own idea is that we will propose to assume an amount of their debt to you, equivalent to their Grand Trunk claim – say £200.000 payable at certain dates – and conditional on your opening a new credit A/C for the Bank to a certain fixed amount – so as to enable it to reopen its New York account – without which it must stop. The new credit of course to be worked in the usual business way – and the balance of the old A/C to be covered by the Bank at such periods as you may agree with them. I do not doubt that you will consider an arrangement of this kind much more satisfactory than the present state of your A/C.

My principal confidence however in the redemption of the Bank, is in the fact that I have succeeded in getting them the services as *absolute manager* of a really able man. Mr. Robert Cassels of the Bank of B.N.A.who will take charge at once – and with whom & Mr. Cayley, I propose immediately to arrange the terms of the matters sketched out above –

The appointment of Mr. Cassels was closed yesterday and I venture to ask on behalf of his management, your support and continuance – I am sanguine, we shall soon see the affairs of the Bank in a very different position from what they have been.

I do most seriously hope, we shall not see the year close without a complete resuscitation both of the Grand Trunk and the Bank. So far as the present Government is concerned, our difficulties are now removed – which is the first step toward really effective action.

E 96   A.T. GALT TO C.S. ROSS (CONFIDENTIAL)
Quebec, 22 March 1861
[*PAC, RG 19 E1A, v. 3376*]

I am happy to be able to advise you of the completion of the new arrangements respecting the Executive of the Bank of U.C. Mr. Cassels has concluded an engagement with the Bank – to take immediate effect & which will place in his hands full power to arrange & I trust restore the affairs of the Bank . . . .

I have written Mssrs. Glyn on the subject – and have no doubt all will be well in that quarter, after the receipt of my letter – but – really matters have gone on so badly hitherto – that at this moment I am ignorant how Mssrs Glyn will act in regard to bills lately drawn on them. I do not apprehend any refusal to accept – but if such an untoward event should arise on any bills, you may have taken from the Bank, I trust you will not let it become known – as the Government will now enable the Bank to cover them . . . .

E 97 W. CAYLEY TO A.T. GALT
Quebec, 22 March 1861
[*PAC, RG 19 E1A, v. 3371*]

. . . The connections which a Bank may form in the prosecution of its business, may draw it, however insensibly at first, into a line of action from which it can scarcely afterward secede, having an important influence on its subsequent career; and there have been engagements and transactions of a financial character into which the Bank of Upper Canada has thus been brought, some dating several years back, others of a recent date, which, depending on the mode in which they are now dealt with, will have a most material bearing on the credit and ability of the Bank to maintain its position, and fulfill its engagements to the Public . . . .

The connection between the Government and the Bank laid the foundation of a business connection between the Bank and the Grand Trunk Company, through the large amounts of Provincial funds, paid to the company thro' the Bank, and more particularly under the conditions of the Relief Act.

The large unemployed balances at the credit of the Government, led to the opening of a special account at the Bank, called the suspense or impost account, to which the Departments of the Government had occasional recourse, when requiring advances for special services in anticipation of the issue of the regular official warrants. In this account several of the unsettled claims which the Bank still holds against former government contractors had their origin, & it induced an irregular system of dealing between individual Departments of the Government and the Bank, of which the transfer of the Zimmerman account was one of the fruits.

The amount of capital at the present locked up in connection with the two accounts which I have cited is large, that of the Grand Trunk may be stated at $1,200,000 and the Zimmerman Bank at $550,000. The Bank has also a large amount locked up in past due commercial paper. So long as the credit of the Bank stood unimpaired, and there was a reasonable ground of belief that the Grand Trunk Company would be true to its engagements, the Bank enjoying the use of large deposits, and a fair circulation, bore their weight of locked up capital with comparatively little inconvenience, and had every prospect of meeting the expectations of Messrs. Glyn & Co. and reducing their account tho' large to manageable dimensions within a reasonable time. But the proceedings taken by the Creditors of the Grand Trunk Company in London, and the sudden alarm which those proceedings occasioned here and the suspension which they threw upon the Bank, causing the loss of its New York connection, the withdrawal of a large amount of customer deposits and the rapid contraction of its circulation produced a very serious change in the aspect of affairs, and led to the appeal for aid which was made to the Government in October last. The promptness with which that appeal was responded to, had the immediate effect of allaying the apprehensions which had arisen in the minds of the Public, and the Bank has since been enabled to fulfill the terms on which that aid was granted. But the pressure under which the Bank continued to labor from the deprivation of the funds advanced to the Grand Trunk Company, the loss of its New York connection, its contracted business, its reduced deposits and circulation is shewn prominently in the fact that its liabilities to Messrs. Glyn & Co. on whom the Bank has been compelled to draw, have grown to a magnitude which precludes all present hope of successfully coping with, until its credit and connections in New York and Montreal are restored and the capital advanced to the Grand Trunk replaced.

The necessity of some immediate action with reference to the London account is brought home, by a recent communication received from Messrs. Glyn & Co. calling upon the Bank to make immediate provision for the overdue bills drawn by the Grand Trunk Company (£200,000 Sterling) which were cashed and remitted by the Bank as a payment on its own account to Messrs. Glyn & Co. and further calling upon the Bank to place its general account on a strictly business footing. With this demand in its present condition, the lengthened details into which I have entered will satisfy you that the Bank is utterly unable, unassisted, to comply, while on the other hand I need not point out to you the immediate and disastrous consequences which must ensue should the Bank be compelled formally to announce its inability to meet the engagements it has contracted with its London correspondents.

It is now only left me most respectfully to solicit the intervention of the Government to enable the Bank to meet its obligations to Messrs. Glyn Mills and Company to the extent of the dishonoured London bills £200,000 Stg by retiring and holding them, until arrangements can be made which shall be deemed satisfactory by the Government.

E 98   A.T. GALT TO R. CASSELS
Quebec, 3 April 1861
[*PAC, RG 19 E1A, v. 3376*]

. . . the Government are prepared to give their guarantee to Messrs. Glyn & Co. to the extent of Eighty Thousand pounds Sterling, for the purpose and on the condition of that firm assuming a new Banking credit with you to that amount to be worked on proper business principles, and to be kept wholly distinct from past transactions. The new account to date from 1 April instant.

With reference to the question of a future increase to our deposits for the purpose of enabling the Bank to complete your proposed financial arrangements, Government will be prepared to entertain favorably an application on your part to the extent of One Hundred and Twenty

Thousand pounds Sterling, or, Two Hundred Thousand with a withdrawal of the guaranteee for £80,000. Provided that the information as to the position of the Bank, to be hereafter submitted by you, is considered satisfactory & to offer proper security to the Province.

It must be clearly understood that the whole incoming revenues of the Province are at the disposal of the Government whenever required. The Balance at 1 January of say $1,200,000 will not, however, be permanently reduced, pending the result of your investigations & report, upon which a definite understanding on all these points must be come to.

E 99   T. WARD[31] TO T. BARING
Boston, 4 April 1861
[*PAC, Baring Papers, A835*]

. . . [Mr. Brooks[32] and I have been in Quebec discussing Grand Trunk Railroad affairs with A.T. Galt, Ross and T. Galt] . . . .

We [Ross and Ward] next discussed the point of any separation between the provisons for the Bank of Upper Canada and the other creditors and on this subject I found a degree of tenacity that convinced me of the importance of sticking to the point . . . .

[I visited A.T. Galt the next day] . . . but I found the same tenacity and argumentation on the subject of the position of the Bank – That I was sacrificing the substance for the shadow etc., but as I was satisfied that they could only give me personal assurances, whilst I might sacrifice positive advantages of position, I merely said, in reply to the suggestion that in our proceedings and discussions with Mr. Brooks and Mr. [?] of practical measures nothing should be advanced conflicting with the Govt't views, that unless it was understood that all the debts must be considered together I had no scheme to discuss as that was the very basis on which I [started?] . . . .

On Sunday I visited a couple of houses – Mr. Rose,[33] very satisfactorily as regards the general plans for Grand Trunk and he confirmed my views as to the importance of insisting on the Bank question . . . .

The next morning [Monday] I . . . went out of town to call on Sir Edmund Head.[34] On my return I found that Mr. [Ashvane?] had found everything particularly smooth and Mr. Galt had requested me to call at his house. This I did and had a long interview in which after some further discussion of the Bank question Mr. Galt agreed to waive all separation of the debts unconditionally and promised to write himself to you to this effect. He informed me further that the Bank was at this

[31]Thomas Ward was a North American representative for Baring Brothers.
[32]J.W. Brookes was president of the Michigan Central Railroad.
[33]John Rose (1820–88) lawyer, financier, politician and diplomat was a close confidant of the Barings and of John A. Macdonald. Until June 1861 he was chief commissioner of public works in Macdonald's cabinet.
[34]Sir Edmund Walker Head (1805–68) was governor general of Canada, 1854–61.

moment applying for aid & must be helped but that he did not look to Legislation for this purpose but to an increase of Gov't deposits. This was the first hint I had of the cause of the urgency which I had found to consent to something by which a case could be got up to give legislative aid to the Bank . . . .

On leaving him I went to see Mr. Rose – Mr. R. told me that it was quite true that the question of the Bank of Upper Canada was on the carpet and that his conversations with me had given him some anxiety on your account. I told him what the Finance Minister had promised. Mr. R. thought the matter needed watching, but he added I think we can prevent mischief. He promised to keep me advised and to telegraph me if necessary . . . .

Before leaving [for Boston] I addressed a note to Sir Edmund stating in a few words what Mr. Galt has promised in order not to leave his Excellency under a false impression and also thinking it important that he should be apprised of the understanding as he would not willingly look on at anything contravening it . . . .

E 100   A.T. GALT TO GEORGE CARR GLYN (PRIVATE)
Quebec, 9 May 1861
[*PAC, Glyn, Mills Papers, A543*]

. . . I heard yesterday from Mr. Cassels in Toronto – he writes in very good spirits about the Bank – and much to my satisfaction states its position has been very much exaggerated. He says he is *thus far* of opinion that not more than one fourth of the Capital of the Bank will be found to have been lost. He states that his views are met with the utmost alacrity by the Directors – and that he expects soon to have the whole [machine?] working harmoniously. He says the management has been *bad* almost beyond belief – which opinion I fully share – . . .

E 101   REPORT OF ROBERT CASSELS, ESQ., CASHIER TO THE SHAREHOLDERS OF THE BANK OF UPPER CANADA, AT THEIR THIRTY-EIGHTH ANNUAL GENERAL MEETING, 25TH JUNE, 1861
[*MTL, Pamphlet Collection*]

In reporting at this time on the position and prospects of the Bank, it has been considered desirable to give a full and detailed statement of its affairs, in order that the Shareholders and public generally, may be enabled to judge of its real condition . . . .

Notwithstanding the large sums which have been appropriated from time to time to meet the losses incurred in the course of business, it has been found on a close examination of the affairs of the Bank, that a much larger amount is required for this purpose than could under ordinary circumstances have been deemed necessary. It appeared to me the only sound policy was to face the difficulty, and by a full and clear

statement, place the Stockholders in a position to judge of the actual state of an institution in whose welfare they are so deeply interested
. . . .

To enable the Shareholders fully to understand the statements I have now the honor to submit, I have found it necessary to start from a date so long ago as the 30th of June, 1859, giving details of the reserve, contingent, and loss accounts, from that period up to the present time.

Hopelessly bad debts have been charged to Loss Account, and full statements prepared at the Head Office and Branches, of all past due bills and over due debts . . . .

The balance at credit of
Reserve Fund, 30th June, 1859,
was $156,393 75
Contingent Fund, 30th June, 1859,
was 400,000 00
$556,393 75

To which add –
Balance of net profits to 31st
Dec., 1859 . . . . $ 41,445 84
Balance of net profits to 30th
June, 1860 . . . . 9,812 84
Balance of net profits to 31st
Dec., 1860 . . . . 25,190 24
Profits to 31st May, 1861 . . . . 106,386 80
182,835 75[sic]
$739,229 47

From which deduct –
Bad debts written off in 1859. . . . . $961 75
    "   "   1860 . . . . . 146,140 54
76th Dividend, payable
January, 1861 . . . . 94,141 85
Bad debts written off to 30th
April, 1861 . . . . 148,941 29
Expenses, Interest, Loss on
Exchange, Tax on
Circulation, &c., to 31st
May, 1861 . . . . 180,753 55
Balance carried to credit of
loss account . . . . 168,290 99   739,229 47[sic]

Loss Account
The following sums charged to this account being irrecoverable and hopelessly bad, viz.: –
At Head Office $524,954 11
At Quebec " 99,841 35
At Montreal " 8,978 50

At Kingston "	3,561 80
At Port Hope "	10,511 65
At Brockville "	1,468 71
At Ottawa "	742 80
At Belleville "	294 43
At Barrie "	895 30
At Barrie " old account	494 52
At Lindsay "	3,701 05
At Hamilton "	28,273 77
At London "	13,645 88
At Chatham "	35,025 81
At Stratford "	1,053 14
At Goderich "	434 65
At Clifton "	637 36
At Berlin "	1,174 52
At Brantford "	15,482 47
At Windsor "	5,228 47
At Niagara "	1,026 22
At Southampton "	1,402 00

$758,808 51

To which add appropriation made for the estimated losses on past due bills and other debts –

At Head Office	$245,880 00
At Port Hope Branch	4,640 00
At Brockville "	67,000 00
At Lindsay "	2,350 00
At Kingston "	2,170 00
At Chatham "	95,900 00
At London "	60,000 00
At Sarnia "	5,550 00
At Windsor "	700 00
At Stratford "	800 00
At St. Catharines "	84,420 00
At Hamilton "	15,100 00
At Picton "	7,400 00
At Clifton "	50,500 00
At Quebec "	17,580 00

659,990 00

1,418,798 51

From which deduct

Balance from Reserve and Contingent Funds 168,290 99

Leaving to be provided for a balance of $1,250,507 52

The heavy losses incurred at Brockville, Chatham, Quebec, and St. Catharines, were made several years ago by persons not now in the service of the Bank, and are of course not attributable to the present Managers of these Branches.

Before entering on the question as to the best mode of meeting this deficiency, I shall briefly allude to several accounts of considerable magnitude, which, from time to time, have been the subject of discussion at the Annual Meetings of the Bank.

The Morton debt at the Kingston Branch has been reduced to about $200,000. The assets held as collateral security for payment of principal and interest, have been valued by Mr. Hinds, the Manager, and by Mr. Kirkpatrick, the Solicitor of the Bank, and also by other competent disinterested parties, as worth $355,000: thus leaving a sufficiently large margin for unforeseen contingencies.

The Zimmerman debt proper is $340,000, secured by lands, real estate, mortgages and other property, which at a fair and moderate valuation amount to $475,000, showing a probable surplus of $135,000.

It is right, however, to mention, that there is another sum of $256,000 due by the Zimmerman Bank not included in the above. This debt was caused by the transfer of the government deposit in that Bank, and the circumstances connected with it are, in my opinion, and in that of the Board, sufficient to constitute a strong claim for the consideration of the Provincial Government, and which will hereafter be submitted in due form.

The advances made to the Grand Trunk Railway Company, amounting to $883,000, have been secured by attachment obtained against the property of the Company in the State of Maine, worth nearly the amount of the debt . . . .

The subscribed capital of the Bank consists of 63,722 shares of $50 each, amounting to $3,186,100.

It will be at once apparent that the only course which can with propriety be adopted to meet the deficiency ascertained, is to reduce the capital of the Bank. This course was adopted with success some years ago by two Banks in Canada, both now holding deservedly high financial positions. I would therefore recommend the Stockholders to authorise the Board of Directors to apply to the Provincial Parliament at the next Session, for power to reduce the shares from $50 to $30 each, retaining the right at same time, again to raise them to their present value, when the Bank shall be in a position to do so. This reduction would place at the disposal of the Board the sum of $1,274,440, thus covering the deficiency, and leaving the sum of $23,932.48 at credit of Reserve Fund. The available capital of the Bank would then amount to nearly $2,000,000.

Application should at same time be made to Parliament for power to increase the capital again to its present limit of $4,000,000, obtaining the right to issue new shares to present stockholders first, as preference stock, in such sums and at such times, as the Board shall deem expedient; such preference stock to be first entitled to a dividend, out of the profits of the Bank, at a rate not exceeding 8 per cent, per annum, to continue at this rate until the Directors are enabled to declare a similar dividend on the whole capital of the Bank.

By this means the capital would be raised, and the Bank be again enabled to afford ample facilities to the mercantile, manufacturing, and agricultural interests of the Province.

There are two items which have not yet been alluded to, viz.: interest on over-due debts, and loss of notes in circulation.

Of the former, a large amount is still due and may ultimately be recovered. Of the latter, only £10,000 has been written off since the establishment of the Bank in 1822, and the actual gain can only be ascertained some years hence, after the old circulation shall have been withdrawn. That a considerable sum will be obtained from this source I have no doubt, considering the large and extended sphere of the Bank's operations . . . .

E 102 R. CASSELS TO GLYN, MILLS
Toronto, 27 June 1861
[*PAC, Glyn, Mills Papers, A543*]

. . . I now enclose reports & statements of the Annual General Meeting held here on 25th Inst –

It was very numerously attended, there being 3 or 400 persons present & from all parts of the Country. There was a strong feeling shown against Mr. Proudfoot, Mr. Cayley, & Mr. Ridout. The two former were not reelected Directors, & no vote was given to the latter.

The allowance to Directors was reduced one half.

I regret, from personal feeling, that Mr. Cayley was not elected, but I must admit that the Bank will now stand much higher in consequence of Mr. Proudfoot & Mr. Cayley having ceased the connection with it.

It has given universal satisfaction. Some of the Members of Government feel a little annoyed about it, but they admit at same time, that the change is rather favorable to the Bank, as far as the public are concerned . . . .

The highest number of votes polled, was for Mr. Gooderham[35] 4580 – the lowest of those elected, Col. Thomson,[36] 2821 – Mr. Cayley had 2120.

---

[35]William Gooderham (1790–1881) was a wealthy Toronto-based distiller, businessman and banker. He was a director of the Bank of Upper Canada, 1854–64. He held 357 shares in the Bank in 1857 and 129 in 1865. From 1864 to 1881 he was president of the Bank of Toronto.

[36]E.W. Thomson (1794–1865) was a militia officer and prominent promoter of improved farming techniques. He was a director of the Bank of Upper Canada, 1861–64. In 1857 he owned thirty-one shares in the Bank and in 1865 he owned sixty-eight.

Mr. Thomas Galt intends visiting England during next month; He will probably leave about the 20th or 24th and I shall probably accompany him, as his presence may be useful & necessary when arrangements are proposed regarding the Bank account.

E 103   THOMAS REIFFENSTEIN TO R.S. CASSELS
Quebec, 12 July 1861
[*PAC, RG 19 B2b, v. 1165*]

. . . I hope you did not omit mentioning to your brother when you wrote that the Public Functionaries at the various localities where your Bank is withdrawing its Agencies are experiencing a good deal of inconvenience not knowing where to deposit their Collections. I trust he will employ some Agent for such purposes as collecting the Revenue & receiving Government monies etc. in accordance with the agreement as originally made between the Gov't & the Bank of U.C. as soon as practicable if not already done in as much as those parties have to hold the Public money contrary to present rules in the interim.

E 104   R. CASSELS TO A.T. GALT (PRIVATE)
Toronto, 13 February 1862
[*PAC, A.T. Galt Papers, v. 2*]

I sent you herewith the proposed amendment to the Charter of the Bank of Upper Canada.

You will observe that we ask for a reduction of Stock from $50 to $30 or 40% –

And also power to Consolidate the Stock. The object of this is to be able at some future period to make the Shares – say *one* of $90 – instead of 3 of $30 – And also that 10% might be added to make up the Shares to $100 – if deemed expedient. Merely in fact to make the shares a More respectable Sum than $30 each.

The Next clause is asking the usual time for subscribing & paying up the Capital to an amount not exceeding $4.000.000.

The clause making it necessary for Directors to hold $2000 paid up stock is required in Consequence of the reduction of the Stock, because by the present act each Director is only required to hold 10 shares, which would be *$300* of reduced stock. Even now the qualification is much too low. In the Montreal Bank it is 20 shares of £*1.000*. The last clause is the Same as that on the same subject in the Charter of the Bank of Montreal.

We have not asked for authority to issue preference Stock – I am inclined to think it will not be necessary, and there are many objections to the plan. When we get the Grand Trunk Money there will be no difficulty in getting new Stock subscribed.

We have paid a very large amount for Government lately, nearly $400.000 reduction Since end of the Year, which has reduced our available funds quite low enough Considering the present unsettled state of matters. If you can give us funds, & be light at same time in your demands I shall be obliged to you.

Hugh Allan had a Post Office order on us for $100.000 which I had to pay by Bills on Glyn. This, together with Interest has nearly absorbed our balance.

E 105   R. CASSELS TO A.T. GALT (PRIVATE)
Toronto, 15 February 1862
[PAC, A.T. Galt Papers, v. 2]

It will give me much pleasure to meet your wishes as expressed in your Note of 12th Inst, and, I suppose it would probably be more agreeable to you to get the Money from time to time as you require it, through your brother Thomas here, whose Drafts I can Cash at any time, & he can send you a cheque for the Money – Or, if you prefer it in any other way, just say so.

If you can take Drafts on New York for part of the money, it will be a Convenience to us, as we have had pretty heavy payments to meet lately, as I mentioned in a Note to you a few days ago.

I hope the Grand Trunk Money will be forthcoming soon.

I have had a good deal of Conversation with George Brown on the subject lately & you will see he has moderated his tone considerably. He is not opposed to a fair Postal Subsidy, but had decided objections to the issue of debentures . . . .

E 106   THOMAS GALT TO GEORGE CARR GLYN (PRIVATE)
Toronto, 24 February 1862
[PAC, Glyn, Mills Papers, A545]

. . . There are several points connected with the proposed arrangement on which I should like much to hear from you – I told Mr. Watkin[37] Plainly that in any settlement he must make up his mind that the Bank of Upper Canada debt must be paid in full. I mentioned to him that I was aware Mr. Baring objected to this but I was and am satisfied it must be done. You told me in London that I had better say nothing to Mr. Baring about it then but I am convinced such a course must be consented to by Mr. Watkin, you are aware that at one time The Company agreed to appropriate an annual amount of the postal subsidy to the Bank and it certainly is no more than just that in any arrangement affecting the Postal Subsidy the claims of The Bank should be fairly treated. I do not intend writing Mr. Baring on this point at present although I think he is deeply interested in the question, from what I can learn and indeed I may say from what I know I am satisfied he is liable on the £45.000 Bill

[37]Edward William Watkin (1819–1901) was a pre-eminent railway manager-executive-promoter in Great Britain. He was president of the Grand Trunk, 1862–68.

held by you and as The Grand Trunk Company are also liable on the Bill to the Bank as endorser. If the Bank claim against the Company and are paid Mr. Baring in any demand made by The Company on him can set off an equal amount of his debt against them, whereas if The Bank are not paid in full they will call upon him for the amount. I do not really see that any difficulty need arise, it is not necessary to consult any parties but the creditors and those creditors are principally your Firm, Mssrs Baring, Mr. Peto Co & The Bank . . . .

E 107   E. WATKIN TO T. BARING (PRIVATE)
Quebec, 27 February 1862
[*PAC, Baring Papers, v. 3*]

. . . (In discussing various matters with Mr. Thomas Galt at Toronto last week he returned to the charge about the Bank of Upper Canada and stated that he thought that they ought to be paid in full. On my dissenting, and expressing wonder that he should take that view considering the parties he represented he said that he "did not act for the Bank of Upper Canada" but that he had mentioned the position of this account and the promises under which the advance was made to Mr. Glyn and also to Mr. Wheeler and that they both said they thought it was only equitable that the Bank should be paid in full.)

(I got an impression that I was being sounded on this matter for the information of other parties and I therefore said that, if so, clearly on the same showing *that half million* ought to be placed on the same footing, in which case what would the other creditors say?) . . . .

E 108   R. CASSELS TO GLYN, MILLS
Toronto, 15 March 1862
[*PAC, Glyn, Mills Papers, A543*]

. . . I am in hopes as to something definite will be done regarding payment of the Grand Trunk Bills held by you on account of the Bank, before the session of Parliament is over. The House meets on the 20th Inst, and I shall go to Quebec shortly to look after the Railway Bill.

There is no doubt the Bank claim will have to be paid in full, unless this is done, I doubt whether the postal subsidy Bill would pass.

Mr. Watkin was with me yesterday & was anxious I should write you on the subject of the debt of the Grand Trunk to the Bank. I told him *the Bank of Upper Canada* must be *paid*, and that I was under the impression that you Mr. G.T. Glyn was favorable to that Course – I am aware that Mr. Thomas Baring expressed a different opinion, which I am rather surprised at, as his house is undoubtedly liable for one of the Bills, amounting to £45.500 Stg.

The feeling amongst Members in Upper Canada in favor of the Bank of Upper Canada being paid is very strong, and this will be the chief cause of the [measure?] being carried in the house . . . .

E 109   J. ROSE TO T. BARING (PRIVATE)
Quebec, 23 May 1862
[*PAC, Baring Papers, v. 3*]

. . . I dont know whether you are aware of the fact that the Bank of Upper Canada is making extraordinary efforts to be paid *in full* by the Railway. The last phase has been that the Manager has been *Lobbying* to get the signatures of Members of both Houses on a paper urging this on the Gov't in fact that they should be paid in *full*, in *preference* to *every one* else! These combinations do much harm & promote opposition & resistance. Besides it is manifestly unjust to you. If *they* advanced their money on the faith of a promise by one of their own Directors who was President of the Coy., and also a member of the Gov't, *you* did so on the pledge of securities which a member of the Gov't represented he had power to use for that purpose . . . .

E 110   BANK OF UPPER CANADA, ANNUAL MEETING, 25 JUNE 1862
[*PAO, J.S. Cartwright Papers*]

. . . The disastrous civil war, which has been raging in the neighbouring States, and the consequent suspension of Specie payments by the Banks there, caused considerable anxiety, and rendered it necessary as a matter of precaution, to reduce and limit the Bank's operations.

The result has naturally been a decrease of circulation, and a diminution of profit. But, on the other hand, the Bank has maintained a sound and strong position.

In accordance with the Cashier's recommendation at last Annual Meeting, which received the concurrence of the Shareholders, application was made to Parliament for power to reduce the Shares of the Bank from $50 to $30 each. The Act authorizing this reduction, and the consolidation and ultimate increase of the Stock, and also other matters of minor importance, received the Royal assent, and became law on 9th instant.

By this Act, the Capital Stock has been reduced from $3,169,100 to $1,901,460, the difference of $1,267,640 having been carried to credit of "Loss Account," extinguishing it and leaving a balance of $17,132 $^{48}/_{100}$, which has been added to the Reserve Fund, thus increasing it to $638,780$^{53}/_{100}$ a sum, which, after careful investigation, is considered quite sufficient to meet the probable losses of the Bank.

The bad and doubtful debts having been provided for, the Directors do not think it desirable to allude to any special accounts, with exception of the debt due by the Grand Trunk Railway Company. The settlement of this debt is now in progress, and the Directors have much satisfaction in stating that the interests of the Bank have been protected . . . .

The net profits of the Bank for the past year, after deduction of all expenses of management, and tax paid Government on circulation,

amounted to .... $133,477.$^{44}/_{100}$
From this a Dividend of 3 per cent., or 57,043.80
has been declared, which, when paid will leave ..... $ 76,433.64
to be carried forward to the credit of Profit and Loss Account.

An issue of Notes of an improved description was commenced in 1860, the cost of which has amounted to about $22,000; of this sum, $7,000 have been deducted from profits, leaving $15,000, which will be reduced by annual payments until the whole is liquidated, or be provided for out of the anticipated gain on the old circulation.

The Old Notes were partially withdrawn from circulation in 1860, and ceased to be issued altogether in August last. On 31st ult. $329,680 still remained out, of which, no doubt, a large sum will be ultimate gain to the Shareholders. Before bringing any portion of such probable profit to account, it is thought right to allow another year to elapse, in order to arrive at a more reliable estimate.

The Bank is largely interested in Real Estate, Mortgages, and other Property, which, though at present unavailable, may, on the return of prosperity, yield a considerable profit to the Shareholders.

During the past year, the Branches at Clifton, Niagara, Picton, and Windsor, having been found unremunerative, were closed.

The Staff of the Bank has been re-organized and reduced, by which greater efficiency has been secured, combined with considerable reduction of expense. A very large saving has also been made by the introduction of a different and more economical mode of supplying Stationery to the Branches of the Bank.

Soon after the last Annual Meeting, the Cashier proceeded to England and effected a highly satisfactory arrangement with the Agents of the Bank in London, Messrs. GLYN, MILLS & CO. That eminent firm agreed to the proposals made in a liberal and friendly spirit. An Account was opened last year with the Bank of Commerce in New York, a monetary Institution of undoubted standing: the transactions of the Bank with it have been of a most satisfactory character. These Accounts have enabled the Bank to carry on its Exchange operations with facility and advantage.

The Directors recommend, that in accordance with the Amended Charter, the Capital of the Bank should be increased to $3,000,000, by the issue of 36,618 New Shares of $30 each, amounting to $1,098,540, to be called up by instalments during the next three years; such Shares to be offered in the first instance at par to present Shareholders, in proportion of one new, for every two old Shares held. The Shares not thus taken, and any others remaining, to be sold in such manner, and at such times, as the Directors may deem proper.

The Directors consider that it would be expedient to limit the Capital to 100,000 Shares of $30 each, or $3,000,000 – looking forward to the probability of being able to raise these Shares to $40 each, from the accumulated profits of the Bank, making up the Capital to the full amount of $4,000,000 – and thus returning to the Shareholders nearly the whole sum recently deducted from their Stock. The large arrears of Interest due to the Bank, the probable gain on circulation, and other contingencies, which cannot at present be valued, lead to the expectation that this desirable result may in time be accomplished . . . .

E 111   R. Cassels to W. Dickinson[38]
Toronto, 20 October 1862
[PAC, RG 19 E2A1, v. 2748]

. . . I have now the honor to state that the following Certificates issued by the Board of Works for work performed by James Cotton at Port Stanley Harbour were paid by the Bank on the undermentioned dates and that, notwithstanding repeated applications, Warrants for the same have never issued in favor of the Bank; viz. –

No. of Certificate	Issued by B. of W.	Accounts	When paid by Bank
8153	4 May 1853	£ 729.2.10	May 2/53
8168	10 May 1853	732.5/ –	Apr 6/53
8266	7 June 1853	160. –	June 4/53
8422	28 July 1853	310. –	July 26/53
8998	25 Jany 1854	1275. –	Feb. 16/54

On 17th June 1856 the Manager of this Bank in Quebec states that he had a conversation with the Hon. Mr. Cayley (then Inspector General) in Mr. Cary's[39] presence when he was given to understand "that Warrants *with Interest*, as the order in Council directs would issue for these Certificates". Now an arrangement was in force prior to the year *1854* by which Mr. Cotton was allowed by the Government Interest or Commission on the account of his outlay for work on Port Stanley Harbour at a certain fixed rate, and it was not until after Mr. Cayley took office in *1856* that this agreement or arrangement was cancelled, and this fact will probably explain the reason for the alleged promise that the Certificates would be paid, and paid with Interest. I presume the authority for the payment was an Order in Council (which in 1856 must have been an old order) but as I have no knowledge of when the Port Stanley Works were commenced, nor any copy of the Public Accounts since that period, I cannot say what is likely to be the date of that order. I therefore take the liberty of asking you to have the authority traced and of asking for a copy thereof.

E 112   R. Cassels to Glyn, Mills
Toronto, 30 January 1863
[PAC, Glyn, Mills Papers, A543]

Our Montreal Branch has had occasion to draw pretty heavily on you, in

---

[38]William Dickinson was deputy inspector general.
[39]Cary was probably deputy inspector general at that time.

consequence of the payments on Government account being extremely heavy during this month and the receipts very light. During February, the payments & receipts are nearly equal, but in March, we begin to receive large sums for duties on Imports, which will enable us to remit exchange to cover the present overdraft –

As soon as the navigation opens to Quebec, that Branch will commence to purchase Exchange on England, so that I hope in addition to remitting enough to cover all the accounts now overdrawn, I shall be able to advise a payment of £25,000 Stg on old account. I am also satisfied that the arrangement for the settlement of the Grand Trunk debt will be completed with the Company including the Bill for £100,000 Stg held by the Government, and that I shall be in a position to make a satisfactory proposal to you when this is effected . . . .

. . . when the Grand Trunk debt is arranged, I shall have no anxiety for the future.

E 113   R. Cassels to Glyn, Mills
Quebec, 5 March 1863
[*PAC, Glyn, Mills Papers, A543*]

. . . During next Summer I have no doubt we shall be able to cover our account, & effect a reduction of the old one. I have been now for some time endeavouring to hurry the passage of the Postal Arbitration Bill, which however has not yet been introduced by the Government –

I am also endeavouring to get some old matters settled with the Government which would place the Bank in an excellent & strong position –

The present party in power [40] is very new and therefore timid, and rather inclined to temporize & delay.

Our business has been progressing satisfactorily notwithstanding the deplorable events occurring in the neighbouring States.

E 114   L.H. Holton to R. Cassels
Quebec, 5 October 1863
[*PAC, RG 19 E1A, 3377*]

I am much disappointed at not having heard from you ere this.

I am most anxious to strengthen our London account & I must make a statement of our available resources in Parliament in a day or two – Pray therefore advise me immediately how soon you can furnish Exchange for the Grand Trunk Bill & how low you are prepared to let the balance of ordinary deposits be reduced.

---

[40]This refers to the reform-oriented ministry headed by John Sandfield Macdonald and Louis-Victor Sicotte.

E 115   R. Cassels to L.H. Holton (telegram)
7 October 1863
[*PAC, RG 19 E1A, v. 3371*]

Can scarcely reply to your telegram not fully understanding your allusion to payment of Grand Trunk bill as far as the ordinary account of the Government is concerned it would not be according to agreement were it reduced below one million or twelve hundred thousand dollars I leave this afternoon for Quebec.

E 116   L.H. Holton to George Brown (confidential)
Montreal, 22 October 1863
[*PAC, George Brown Papers, v. 4*]

I have come to the Conclusion that it is in all respects better that I should not go to England till after next Session. We Can go much *stronger handed* with Ample revenue measures passed – in fact we would be in a position to dictate our own terms – and besides I want the whole recess to prepare properly for the meeting of Parliament. I find I Can place *my whole loan* here on favorable terms if I can venture to deal with the public account. It would be of immense importance to me and to my Successor (*You* are to be the man the Leader Says/to have a strong institution with strong English Connections at our backs and it might be an important step towards advantageous ulterior arrangements in England. Thus comes the position of the U.C. Bank. I dont want to imperil that but if we are to have a good [one word?] balance to be gradually liquidated the Old Lady should be able to get on. It is a miserable position not only to have our money locked up but not to be able to use our account as a resource in raising money. I really think I ought to make the Change in the interest of the Country. At the same time I am bound to Consider the political effect of every step I take, as well as the immediate financial advantages – I have a great horror of going to Glyns & Baring *infirm paupers* again. nothing could have a better effect than to be able to say we have made arrangements *at home* for all we want till our new revenue laws are passed. It would strengthen us immensely *as a party*. as shewing that our home money interest is with us. Pray write me on the point *at once* at Quebec whither I go on Saturday and where I must decide at once.

E 117   George Brown to L.H. Holton (private and confidential)
Toronto, 23 October 1863
[*QUA, Alexander Mackenzie Papers*]

I have this moment received your letter of yesterday & I hasten to give you the reply you ask for.

Of course you are responsible for the financial steps to be taken at this

moment. You & you alone will bear the burden if any error is made &
you will have the credit if credit is won. It is therefore right that you
should pursue the course that seems to your own mind the best . . . .

I understand your present inclination is to borrow from the Bank of
Montreal a sufficient sum to square your account with the English
agents – & in consideration of this accommodation to transfer to the
Bank of Montreal, the Government account. I admit that some advantage is to be gained from this arrangement – but on the other hand there
are very serious dangers that may arise from it. In the first place, you
take from the Commercial circles of the Province a large portion of the
capital of the Bank of Montreal, that ought to be employed in developing the trade of the Country. In the second place you strike a blow at the
Bank of Upper Canada that *may be* disastrous to that institution & *will*
certainly be most hurtful to the Commercial interests of this section of
the Province. The Bank is not in a condition to stand a pressure – and a
pressure will certainly come if you withdraw the Govt account – in turn
they must press all their customers & where that will end who can tell? I
am led to believe that the Bank is gradually working through its
difficulties and that two years more would put it past trouble. If this is so
would it not be assuming a serious responsibility to take a step that may
bring wide-spread ruin on Upper Canada. Let me add for myself,
moreover, that I think the people of Upper Canada would have a good
cause to dread the accumulation of this great additional power in the
hands of the directors of the Bank of Montreal. It is a Montreal
institution soul & body, & most hostile to Upper Canada interests. Its
true spirit was displayed in the panic of 1857. I am persuaded that the
removal of the Government account to the Bank of Montreal at this
moment – while the Bank of U.C. is bravely & successfully struggling
through its difficulties, would not only be an act of great injustice, but
highly impolitic as regards the general interests of the country. It will
certainly be viewed as coming from you, as a Montreal blow Aimed at
Upper Canada. I know well that no such feeling animates you, but
assuredly this will be believed here – and it will very much surprise me
if a strong & excited feeling in Upper Canada does not flow from it.

Frankly, the step would be a very grave one in my opinion, politically
financially & every other way. I would not like to have the responsibility for it on my shoulders. Nothing but absolute necessity could
justify a step involving risks so serious – and I confess I do not see the
necessity. You are not responsible for the debt. No one will blame you
for borrowing to square accounts & start anew under better auspices.
You can easily borrow in England – I have no doubt you can make what
arrangements you like with Barings & Glyns – but failing them, you can
get whatever you want in London for any length of time you wish by
hypothicating debentures on moderate terms. All the Bank of Montreal
proposes is to do with the money of the Canadian Merchants what you
can do with the money of English capitalists.

From an Upper Canada view, I could fancy few acts on the part of the present Government more suicidal.

I have written you my full mind in this matter – but of course with only partial knowledge of the subject. I am persuaded however, that I have expressed what will be the strong feeling of nine tenths of the people of Upper Canada until the contrary is known –

E 118   L.H. HOLTON TO GEORGE BROWN (CONFIDENTIAL)
Montreal, 1 November 1863
[*PAC, George Brown Papers, v. 4*]

. . . I deeply regret that in the matter referred to my conclusions do not Coincide with yours. I am persuaded that if we could *talk* the matter over for an hour or two we should agree. As a simple financial question, the aspect in which I must as Minister of Finance primarily regard it I am sure we *could not* differ. The advantage of avoiding further loans in England till our revenue measures are accomplished, the greater [one word?] of managing our finances at all times, through a strong than a weak (or worse) fiscal agent – the importance of rendering available the disposal of the public account as a financial resource, the desirableness per se of terminating a connection with an institution So ill qualified in all essential respects to perform the higher functions of a Govt Bank as the Bank of Upper Canada notoriously is; are points that hardly admit of dispute and which being conceded, dispose of the whole question considered merely as one of *financial administration*. There remains the political side of the question and in regard to that I confess there is much more difficulty but I am convinced the [one word?] proper [one word?] of argument is in favor of the Course I am disposed to adopt. The Bank of U.C. has been [involved?] in all the worst transactions of the Coalition Since 1854, and I believe the severance of the Connection between the Govt and this instrument of manifold Corruption would be the most striking endeavor that Could be given that we have entered upon a New era. The Bank of U.C. is indissolubly bound up with the Grand Trunk and with Glyns. The Grand Trunk is waging war [two words?] with our administration. The Bank can not if it would and I think we have almost reason to Say would not if it Could render us any assistance. and You at least will admit that it is most desirable we should get into a position of independence of Glyn at the earliest possible moment. Now I hold that my plan would be a staggering blow to the Grand Trunk influence both in this Country and in England, would give us the assistance we so much need and that in the most effective way, and would be a most important step towards Such ulterior arrangements as we may desire to effect in England either by modifying or, altogether suspending our existing arrangements with Barings & Glyns.

A Sectional cry may be raised – *will* no doubt be raised but much can not be made of it. Nothing with sensible men – I would gladly deal with an U.C. institution if there was one that Could undertake to do for us what the Montreal Bank Can do. If I have *any* bias and were disposed to Yield to it in my public Conduct it is in favor of the Commercial with which I have done my own business for twenty Years and of which I was for many years a director. I did in fact ask the President last summer if they Could do any thing for us and he replied frankly they Could not. The truth is Montreal is as much the Commercial and monetary Capital of Canada as New York of the U.S. or London of Great Britain, and when people want to borrow large Sums of money they generally go where it is to be found – in fact they must go to the great money Centers.

We have no idea of pushing the Bank of U.C. to the wall – I propose treating her with the utmost consideration with respect to the large balance she owes. If She Cant get on with her own resources and the use of $1.300.000 of public money, that very fact Constitutes the Strongest possible reason for a Change. In truth the Change we propose ought not to Cripple her at all. You Say and truly that I am not responsible for the present Condition of things, but I can not escape the responsibility of permitting it to Continue, and of Seeing my way as I Clearly do to an advantageous Change – any disaster now to flow from a want of Courage to adopt it, the blame *would* rest upon me and most righteously too. It is quite clear that the Bank of U.C. So far from being able to assist the Govt must be assisted by the Govt. This I maintain is just reversing the natural order of things. How is She a perfectly *Safe Custodian* of the public funds? I ask you as a Keen eyed man of business to take up any one of her recently published monthly statements. and Say after scrutinizing it closely that She is in a position to stand the shock of a Commercial panic resulting from Short Crops or any other potent Cause? And if this question should be answered negatively, does it not follow that this is the very time to make the Change – When money is easy – and everything prosperous?

The Loan that I propose getting taken up – is not as You Seem to have inferred the whole Amount of our floating debt, but the Million and a half authorised by the last Supply Bill. This Could be done in the present state of our money market and with the great resources of the Bank of Montreal using if need be her English Connection without interfering in the Slightest degree with her means of doing general business here – Depend upon it the moral effect of our being able to Announce that we had made Such an arrangement would be tremendous in this Country and greatly to our advantage in England. You Say I Could borrow money on a pledge of Bonds in England. no doubt of it, but we have too much borrowed in that way already. I am utterly averse to increasing the Amount and want to diminish it as Soon as possible
. . . .

E 119   L.H. HOLTON TO GLYN, MILLS AND BARING BROTHERS
Montreal, 11 November 1863
[*PAC, RG 19 E1A, v. 3376*]

. . . It is proposed to issue Currency Debentures having three years to run, and bearing five per cent interest to the amount of $1,500,000. which amounts will suffice for the redemption of about $800,000 currency debentures due next month, and with the revenue receipts, to meet all the public liabilities, that require to be provided for, until permanent arrangements founded on the Legislation of the next session of Parliament, can be concluded. The Bank of Montreal, the leading monetary Institution of the Province, has agreed to purchase the whole of this proposed issue, on favorable terms, and to become the fiscal agents of the Government in this country . . . .

I ought perhaps to mention, that in transferring the Government account from the Bank of Upper Canada, to the Bank of Montreal, the former institution will be treated with the utmost consideration, so that no shock may be given to its credit. The sole object of the change is to secure to the government the services of an institution possessing resources so ample that it can without restricting its ordinary operations, greatly facilitate the financial operations of the Government . . . .

E 120   L.H. HOLTON TO GEORGE BROWN (CONFIDENTIAL)
Quebec, 21 November 1863
[*PAC, George Brown Papers, v. 4*]

. . . Cassels did not behave well in his interviews with me – He tried bullying, Coaxing and whining alternately. When all failed and I had told him frankly what I prepared doing with the Bank of Montreal and the terms I was to get the loan upon, he said (and Subsequently put a letter in my hands repeating it/*he* could do for me all that the Bank of Montreal proposed to do. This was no doubt thought a very clever dodge – but to me it appeared exceedingly weak and rather shabby. My answer was in effect – "Your offer is ridiculous! You are in no position to undertake a Loan on Your own account of a million and a half. You *must* take the Bonds to England which I could do myself but *that* is the very thing I *want to avoid*. Besides You must remember that if You are in a position to pay me what You owe me I should have no occasion to borrow at all!" I fear that the Story of my sending him to England emanated from himself – Altogether his conduct has not elevated him in my eyes. There Can be no doubt that all through the Session he was anxiously hoping for our downfall. I shall not shew any feeling towards him however – and of course will not visit his Sins on the Bank which So far as it depends on me – Will be treated with the Greatest possible Consideration.

I wish I could shew you my recent correspondence with the London

Agents – *They* are always polite sometimes *almost* flattering but the hoof will occasionally shew itself through the diplomatic drapery [one word?] to conceal it – of my replies I will not speak beyond saying that I have striven to be [gracious?] courteous and diplomatic but to let them understand at the sametime that *they* are understood – I suppose the Correspondence will see the light when Parliament meets unless indeed which I consider not improbable they take another tack – I have been studiously careful to avoid writing a word at which they could fairly take umbrage – . . .

E 121   L.H. HOLTON TO B.U.C. COMMITTEE (COPY)
Montreal, 26 November 1863
[*PAC, RG 19 E1A, v. 3376*]

I have the honor to acknowledge the receipt of your letter, of yesterday's date, applying on behalf of the Bank of Upper Canada, to be allowed, in consequence of the loss, and inconvenience, that would arise, from so hasty a realization of its assets, as would be necessary to enable it to meet an immediate or early demand for the whole amount, in which it is indebted to the Government, to spread the payment thereof over a series of years. In consideration of this application being complied with, and of the low rates of interest mentioned by you, being accepted for the first five years, you propose, that the Bank shall waive the claim it has heretofore advanced in respect of the Bill of the Grand Trunk Company, for £100,000 Sterling, and of the liability assumed by the Bank, in passing to the credit of the Government, the balance of Public deposits held by the Zimmerman Bank. Although, as the Receiver General, and I, have repeatedly stated to you, the Government cannot admit the validity of either of these claims, they yet felt that the circumstances surrounding the origin of the transactions themselves, might fairly be urged, in support, of an application for some consideration, in adjusting so much of the balance, as is represented by the amounts of those transactions. The main, if not the only ground however, in which we could consider the application of the Bank for so large a measure of forbearance and favour as was sought by you, had reference to the position of the Bank, and its inability, without seriously crippling its operations, to pay the amount due the Government, unless terms as favorable as those indicated by you were accorded, and you will remember, that throughout our conferences, you have uniformly, and explicitly, urged this view on our attention. On no other basis, could we in point of fact, justify ourselves, for consenting to leave a large amount of public money, in the hands of a private corporation, subject to a rate of interest, below that paid by the government, for its own borrowings. Considering the important public interests that are involved in the maintenance of the stability, and the credit of an old and valuable monetary institution, like the Bank of Upper Canada, the

Receiver General and I are disposed to recommend your application to the favourable consideration of the Government, on being informed by you, that I have correctly stated the grounds, on which it was urged, in our several personal interviews with you.

E 122   L.H. Holton to R. Cassels
Quebec, 11 December 1863
[*PAC, RG 19 E1A, v. 3376*]

I have the honor to transmit, herewith, a copy of a minute of Council on the application of the Bank of Upper Canada to be allowed to liquidate by instalments spread over a series of years its indebtedness to the Government, the total amount of which indebtedness, it was proposed should be reduced by the first of January next to $1,486,666.00 including the Grand Trunk Bill for £100,000 Sterling.

You will observe there is a discrepancy of $20,000 between the amount of the Balance (irrespective of the special deposit of $220,000) as stated in the letter of application of the 26th November and in the minute of Council; being stated at $1,286,666.00 in the former, and at $1,266,666.00 The latter is of course the correct amount. It was proposed that the Balance in the hands of the Bank exclusive of the Grand Trunk Bill should be $1,000,000
add Grand Trunk Bill
£100,000 Sterling   486,666.00
                                                                                      1,486,666
special Deposit repayable in 1864   220,000
Balance as stated in minute of Council, $1,266,666.00
after providing for payment of
special Deposit

E 123   George Brown to L.H. Holton
Toronto, 19 January 1864
[*QUA, Alexander Mackenzie Papers*]

I dare say you begin to think that you are never to hear from me again – & perhaps you think I am out of sorts about the Bank matter. But you worry me if such is your notion. I thought you wrong in the Bank matter – I think so still – but it was your own affair & had I been in your place I would have carried out my own ideas. But I totally decline to discuss the matter after it is a *fait accompli*. I dont look at it from your point of view – I dont think your arguments satisfactory – but what would it avail for us now to argue it out? The thing is done – let it rest there . . . .

E 124   Bank of Upper Canada, Annual Meeting, June 1864
[*Toronto* Globe, *27 June 1864*]

. . . After providing for the dividend paid in January last, for that payable on Second July next, for the balance of expenses of new issue of notes, for Government tax on circulation, and for the Zimmerman Bank debt, (according to agreement made with the Provincial Government) a balance of $26,127 still remains at the credit of Profit and Loss

Since the last annual meeting, many old, bad, and doubtful debts have been arranged, paid or written off. The balance now at credit of Reserve Account, to meet doubtful debts still unsettled, is $221,238.17, which, with other items not yet credited to account, are considered amply sufficient for that purpose.

The Shareholders will be happy to learn, that the claim against the Grand Trunk Railway Company of Canada has been finally arranged and secured; the Bill for £100,000 sterling, about which so much has been said, having been included in the Bank's claim against that Company. The settlement of this claim, and the arrangement made with the Government, has finally disposed of all matters in dispute, or which were previously not clearly understood, and in a doubtful position.

The old issue of notes having been withdrawn from circulation since August, 1861, the Board considered it advisable to authorise the writing off a portion of the amount, still leaving nearly $90,000 at credit of the account, on which it is not improbably there may yet be a gain to the bank.

It was considered desirable to close the Branches at Belleville and at Lindsay, and the Agency at Three Rivers, and thus concentrate the operations of the bank at points where already a profitable business was transacted.

The removal on the 1st January last of the Government account from this Bank was unexpected and uncalled for. The intimate connection subsisting between the Government and the bank for many years, and the various and extended ramifications of the business operations, were suddenly brought to a close by Hon. Mr. Holton, then Finance Minister, after a short notice of a few weeks. The cashier did not fail during repeated interviews with that gentleman, to urge upon him the inexpediency and injustice of so summary a proceeding, but without avail. It was only on the 7th November last that Mr. Cassels ascertained from Mr. Holton what the requirements of the Government then were, all allusions to the subject at previous interviews having been vague and undefined. He immediately addressed a letter to the Finance Minister, offering terms which Mr. Holton declined to accept, though more favourable than those which he subsequently obtained from the Bank of Montreal.

When it was found that the Government had determined upon removing the account, a committee was appointed by the board, consisting of the Hon. Mr. Speaker Wallbridge,[41] T.C. Street, Esq.,

[41] Lewis Wallbridge (1816–87), a lawyer and politician from Belleville, was a director of the Bank of Upper Canada from 1862–65.

M.P.P., and the cashier, to confer with the Hon. Mr. Holton, then Minister of Finance, and the Hon. Mr. Howland,[42] then Receiver General, as to the final settlement of the Government balance, and others matters in dispute. These gentlemen effected what, under the circumstances, may be considered a satisfactory arrangement.

The course which the late Government thought fit to pursue towards the bank is much to be regretted. Under the policy of their predecessors, the bank was rapidly recovering its position, and would soon have been able to dispense with the Government account without inconvenience. Now, however, it will be necessary to restrict the operations of the bank which must necessarily affect, to some extent, the profits, and at the same time, be injurious to the whole community.

A painful result arising from this change was the necessity for dispensing with nearly thirty officers, many of whom, it is satisfactory to know, have found employment elsewhere, while others who have spent the best part of their lives in the service of the bank, are left without provision in their old age. The board would name the following gentlemen: – Messrs. E. Goldsmith, T. McCormick, R.G. Anderson, C.S. Murray, and M. Scollard – as those requiring your notice and liberal consideration.

E 125   W. McMaster[43] to T. Dakin[44] (copy)
Toronto, 30 December 1864
[*UWO, Thomas Swinyard Papers, LB1*]

. . . Amongst other things, the Banking arrangements of the Company [Great Western Railway], which were exceedingly faulty has occupied our attention for Some time past, and the result can hardly be otherwise than Satisfactory. Besides being relieved from Various Commissions formerly paid, The aggregate of which was Considerable, the Company under the new arrangement will get 4^1/2% Interest on all balances whether in New York or Canada, which must amt. to a larger Sum annually, but what I regard as being of still greater importance, is the fact that the funds of the Company, which the peculiar Circumstances of the Bank of Upper Canada, and the reckless business now being done by the Banks in New York – rendered very unsafe, will in future be in the Keeping of – and Secured by the Bank of Montreal an Institution which is as Sound in every respect as the Bank of England . . . .

---

[42]William Pearce Howland (1811–1907) was a Toronto businessman and at this time a reform politician.

[43]William McMaster (1811–87) was a businessman, politician and banker. He commenced the Canadian Bank of Commerce in 1867. He was or soon became chairman of the Great Western Railway's Canadian board of directors.

[44]Thomas Dakin was the British-based president of the Great Western Railway, 1862–74.

E 126   A.T. GALT TO C.J. BRYDGES (COPY)
13 February 1865
[*PAC, RG 19 E1a, v. 3376*]

In accordance with your desire I willingly put in writing the opinion I have already strongly expressed to you in regard to the [Grand Trunk] Railway a/c with the Bank of Upper Canada. That it is expressly undesireable in the present state of money matters in the Province to remove the account, or, to refuse to place any additional advances you may require in the shape of Exchange. After all the difficulties entailed upon the Bank by its past connection with the Railway Company it would appear to be a most ungenerous course to deprive them of the account at a moment when the general state of business is far from satisfactory . . . .

E 127   J. ROSE TO T. BARING (PRIVATE)
Montreal, 26 October 1865
[*PAC, Baring Papers, v. 4*]

I hinted in my last as to the probability of an arrangement between the Bank of Montreal & the Grand Trunk.

It is now completed. We *buy* £100,000 of the Equipment Mortg. Bonds at 9% & *advance* £90,000 Stg more on the security of another £100,000. The Comy. is to be at liberty to redeem this Loan in which case we give them an open credit of £50,000 Stg. The details of working the a/c have been arranged on fair terms satisfactory to both. I hope this arrangement coupled with the increase in the returns may do something for the credit of the Comy. The exchange will be sent to the Messrs Glyn through whom the transaction will be completed. I hope their interest in the Bank of U.C. may not be seriously affected . . . .

E 128   BANK OF UPPER CANADA, PUBLIC NOTICE,
19 SEPTEMBER 1866
[*PAC, Glyn, Mills Papers, A543*]

The Directors of the Bank of Upper Canada, while awaiting the returns from the several Branches to enable them to complete a balance-sheet of its affairs up to yesterday, would announce to the Public that such statement will be prepared and published at the very earliest moment, and that a special general meeting of the shareholders will be called as soon as possible.

In the meantime the Directors entreat all those who are interested to retain their securities and not to make any sacrifice, as the result, which will be exhibited in a few days, will establish the safety of all note-holders and depositors.

Bank of Upper Canada, Toronto, 19th Sept. 1866
George W. Allan,
President[45]

Robert Cassels, Cashier	Peter Paterson,	Directors
	Vice-President[46]	present
	George Alexander[47]	
	Joseph D. Ridout[48]	
	Thomas C. Street	

E 129   LYDIA PAYNE[49] TO J. BROWNE[50]
circa September 1866
[*PAC, RG 19 C1, v. 1181, file 9*]

. . . Is there any probability of the poor Shareholders getting any thing eventually from the assets of the late U.C Bank? The failure is of serious consequence to me, as I depended on my stock invested in it, for support in my old Age – . . . .

I wrote to Mr. Cassells before the Bank suspended payment to dispose of my shares, but I was not favored with an answer –

I am much obliged to you for writing –, & I hope you will kindly pardon the questions I have asked –

Pray do what you think is best for me.

E 130   J. ROSE TO T. Baring
Montreal, 20 September 1866
[*PAC, Baring Brothers Papers, v. 4*]

. . . You will not be surprised to hear of the closing of the Bank of Upper Canada. I dont apprehend any immediate disasterous result from the Event – beyond loss to the shareholders & the distrust which it will not unnaturally reflect on other Institutions. We have several weak ones here, who but for Galt's facilitating disposition, should never have had an existance. It would not surprise me if they went to the Wall, & if they

[45]George W. Allan (1822–1901), lawyer and son of William Allan, was a director of the Bank of Upper Canada in 1860 and from 1861–65 was its president. In 1857 he owned twenty-eight shares and in 1865 he owned seventy shares of the bank.

[46]Peter Paterson (1807–83) was a hardware merchant and agricultural implement manufacturer operating in Toronto. He was a director of the Bank of Upper Canada, 1861–64. He owned 104 shares in 1857 and 315 in 1865.

[47]George Alexander was a Conservative politician and a director of the Bank of Upper Canada, 1861–65. Between 1857 and 1865 his stockholdings in that bank increased from forty-four to 234.

[48]Joseph Davis Ridout (1809–84) was a wholesale hardware merchant operating in Toronto. He was a director of the Bank of Upper Canada, 1843–65. His shares increased from forty in 1857 to sixty-eight in 1865.

[49]Lydia Payne was a resident of England and owned 215 shares in the Bank of Upper Canada.

[50]J. Browne was land agent for the Bank of Upper Canada.

did, we should have a healthier condition of affairs. I enclose you a slip
from the mornings paper which will put you *au fait* on the B.U.C.
matters. I hope your friends Messrs Glyn have got out. I warned them
personally more than [18 days?] ago that Mr. Cassels was too sanguine
& that they ought to stand from under . . . .

E 131   AMELIUS IRVING[51] TO SYDNEY BELLINGHAM[52]
Hamilton, 21 September 1866
[PAO, Amelius Irving Private Letterbook]

In answer to your note of the 19: inst: I think there can be no doubt that
the rumour that Mr. Street had transferred his shares in the Bank of U.C.
to men of Straw, to avoid future liability is incorrect.

I will ask him, when first I have an opportunity of so doing: The
rumour here is, that about 10 days ago he bought in a large amount at
[one word?] per cent –

I am as you assume, heavily interested, in the first place, personally,
and secondly on behalf of several near relatives.

In answer to your queries – I say as follows:

I believe the Stock is worth something – that there is sufficient to pay
the creditors, and divide something over, but this in my opinion, will
greatly depend upon the judgement and integrity with which the
Property is sold, and the old debts realized –

If however, the Assets do not meet the debts of the Bank – the
shareholders will be mulcted to the extent of $20 per share – being the
value of their shares as reduced by Act of Parliament –

– (the responsibility is not on the Old Value of $50).

If any knowing ones have transferred their stock, as you suggest, and
which I think not the fact, and such transfer was to a man of Straw – that
would be looked on as a Sham, and not release the Knowing one from
his responsibility.

But I think the double Liability as it is called is rather a remote
security – as I think the Creditors must first exhaust the Securities of the
Bank before they can call on the Shareholders – and the process of
exhaustion would take some time –

And I further think – that if a Call is to be made on the shareholders, it
would be rateable on the whole – say 1/5 or 1/2 or 3/4ths, and that each
shareholder would be called upon for his proportion, quite irrespective
of whether other shareholders were able to make up their own Calls.

These are my impressions only, but this would satisfactorily answer
your question – that individuals could not be picked out and plucked –

[51]Amelius Irving (1823–1913) was a Toronto lawyer and businessman.
[52]Sydney Robert Bellingham (1807–1900) was a businessman and politician from
Lower Canada.

I do not know whether Mr. Cassels has deceived, or been deceived, or deceived himself.

By an article in the Globe of today, I observe that, the idea of assignees being appointed is noted. This agrees with my own view – if good assignees can be obtained they should be free from any Connection with the old management in my opinion – for reasons which I think will present themselves readily to every one.

And I also understand that a Shareholders meeting will be called at an early day – I think Shareholders should be prepared to act together on the occasion and would therefore Suggest that the Gentlemen of Montreal should send up some one to represent them – indeed, the more who come the better, and I should like a preliminary meeting, to agree on the adoption of a course.

I have not a late list of Shareholders – but I have reason to believe that the following persons have a considerable [stake?] namely

Alfred Nelson[53]
Rev. Ph. Wolff[54]
Dr. G. W. Campbell[55]

perhaps this may be of some service to you, in organizing a movement among the shareholders, of a protective nature. Our interests are –
1. to Know the worst
2. to see that the assets are fairly realized – . . . .

E 132   Report of the Directors of the Bank of Upper Canada, Presented to the Shareholders at a Special General Meeting, 13 November, 1866
[QUA, Magill Papers]

Your Directors regret that it has been necessary to call a Special General Meeting of the Shareholders, to consider the position of the Bank, in consequence of its having been compelled to suspend Specie payments, on the 18th September last.

The pressure which led to this unfortunate event, arose from various causes.

The business of the country, during the early part of the summer, was greatly depressed and disturbed, and at a later period, the new financial measures of the Government caused much anxiety to the Banking establishments of the Province – added to which, the harvest was unusually late.

These circumstances combined, produced a stringency in the money market of a more serious character than has occurred for many years, reducing the circulation and deposits of the Banks, and being peculiarly

[53]Nelson does not appear on any Bank of Upper Canada shareholder lists.
[54]Rev. Ph. Wolff owned 103 Bank of Upper Canada shares.
[55]Dr. G.W. Campbell owned 133 Bank of Upper Canada shares.

embarrassing to this Bank, in consequence of the large amount locked up in inconvertible assets. Assistance to a moderate extent was obtained from the Government, and on the 18th September, the Commercial Bank, the Bank of Toronto, Ontario Bank, and Royal Canadian Bank, were prepared to advance an amount which most probably would have been sufficient to meet the emergency, but on that day, the Bank of Montreal refused to receive Bank of Upper Canada Notes, thus rendering a suspension of Specie payments unavoidable.

Your Directors have earnestly endeavoured to meet the difficulties in which they have been placed, and have done everything in their power to protect the Shareholders from loss.

Early in October a Deputation was sent to England by the Board for the purpose of settling with the English creditors of the Bank, and these gentlemen have recently returned, after having made satisfactory arrangements.

The liabilities of the Bank on 9th November instant, the latest period to which a statement could be prepared, were as follows: –

Circulation	$ 722,086 00
Due to Depositors	369,601 59
Due to Banks in Canada	22,562 61
Due to Agents in England, £61,500 stg., at 9½ per cent	299,300 00
Due to Provincial Government	1,149,430 75
Dividends unclaimed	9,026 56
	$2,572,007 51

To meet this the Assets are: –

Gold and Silver coin	$ 39,808 42
Notes of other Banks	2,134 82
Due by other Banks	5,450 61
Government Debentures	17,519 99
Municipal and Other Debentures	35, 282 52
Real Estate	1,657,573 37
Bank Furniture	16,050 00
Notes and Bills Discounted	2,224,488 80
Current Accounts overdrawn	980 50
Mortgages	62 580 85
	$4,061,869 88

This shows a surplus of $1,488,862 37[sic], which must, however, be greatly diminished when allowance is made for bad and doubtful debts, and probable loss on realizing Real Estate.

Your Directors are of opinion that under careful and judicious management, a considerable surplus will ultimately remain for division amongst the Shareholders, after the whole liabilities of the Bank have been paid.

Under the peculiar circumstances in which the Bank is placed, Your

Directors think it due to the Cashier to contrast the present position of the Bank with that in which it stood on 13th April, 1861, when he undertook the management, viz:

Circulation	$2,047,749
Due to Depositors	1,336,674
Due to Government, including G.T. Ry. £100,000 St. Bill subsequently assumed by the Bank	2,360,730
Due to other Banks and Bankers	2,674,074
Dividends unclaimed	12,371
	$8,431,598

You will observe from these statements, that during the past five years, the liabilities of the Bank have been reduced from $8,431,598 to $2,572,007, shewing the enormous reduction of $5,859,591. There cannot be a doubt that had the Bank stopped payment in 1861, which it was in imminent danger of doing, it would not only have been a great public calamity, but would have entailed far more serious loss on the Shareholders.

After mature consideration, and acting by the advice and with the consent of the Government, your Directors have executed under seal of the Bank, a deed of assignment, appointing the following gentlemen to wind-up the affairs of the Bank, viz.: – Thomas C. Street, Peter Paterson, Robert Cassels, Hugh C. Barwick,[56] and Peleg Howland,[57] Esquires.

The details of this deed have received the fullest and most careful consideration of the Directors, have been prepared under the supervision of the Bank Solicitor, and the Standing Counsel, and have received the entire sanction of the Government.

The Directors believe that its provisions are such, that under them, the assignees will be enabled to wind up the affairs of the Bank in the most advantageous manner, both for the Creditors and the Shareholders.

> Approved by the Board,
> ROBERT CASSELS,
> Cashier.

E 133   BANK OF UPPER CANADA, TRUSTEES MEETING, 5 JUNE 1868
[PAC, RG 19 C1, v. 1210]

BUC vs. Cassels: Mr. Gamble submitted an offer of settlement of the claims of the Trust against Robert Cassels Esq. the late Cashier, as follows,   .

---

[56]Hugh C. Barwick was a businessman and politician from the Woodstock area.
[57]Peleg Howland was probably a local Toronto businessman related to William Pearce Howland, a merchant and later mayor of Toronto.

The Stock purchased by him as he says for B.U.C. in connection with T. C. Street	$8,000
Interest	600
Difference between what was paid for £15,000 of Port Hope and Lindsay Debentures and what they were taken at by Covert & Fowler[58]	12,000
Interest	2,160
Commissions received as Trustee at Lynn Kingston & Chippawa from the time the Trusts were created till the failure of the B.U.C.	8,167
Amount lost in conversion of Amern. funds with the National Bank of New York through James Cassels[59] at Montreal	4,416
Interest	420
	$35,763

Mr. Cassels claimed from the Trustees the amount that would accrue under his Bond from B.U.C. *$23,333*, but would not admit any liability on his part on any one of the said items.

The Trustees declined admitting any claim under the Bond but after considerable discussion in order to bring the matter to a close it was agreed that the Trustees would accept in full of all claims against Mr. Cassels the sum of $20,000 in B.U.C. Funds paid as follows.

> $5,000 down
> 5,000 in one year
> 5,000 in two years
> 5,000 in three years

or if he prefers it pay these instalments in current funds taking B.U.C. funds at 80 cts. in the $, and to pledge as security for these payments $5,000 paid up Capital in B.A.A. Coy. and $5,000 in Canada L. Credit until the whole amount is paid. All recourse on the Bank at New York for loss on conversion of American funds at Montreal reserved for the benefit of the Trust.

Mutual releases to be executed . . . .

E 134   JOHN A. MACDONALD TO GEORGE ALEXANDER (PRIVATE AND
CONFIDENTIAL)
23 November 1869
[PAC, J.A. Macdonald Letterbook, 516]

I have yours of the 20th. You are right in supposing that I had a good deal to do in [effecting?] the settlement of the Bank of Upper Canada debt by the Government; & it is on account of this same settlement that I desire very much that there should be no investigation into the affairs of

---

[58]Covert and Fowler were railroad contractors operating in Upper Canada.
[59]James Cassels was a brother of Robert Cassels.

the Bank just now. Whether the settlement after an investigation [will be found?] either good or bad, it would equally afford food for those opposed to the Government. The fact is that you must manage to lay over the whole matter not only until the prorogation of the Local House, but until after the rising of the Parliament of the Dominion. I am afraid of a strong pressure being brought to bear in the latter body upon the Government to press the *double security* clause, & if there is an authoritative statement of assets & liabilities, it will give the basis of action.

Now I greatly sympathize with the shareholders of the Bank & think that in all justness & fairness the Country should be satisfied with taking the property that has been handed over & let the shareholders alone. So long as the state of the assets & liabilities is unknown we can manage to avoid a direct attack upon these poor people.

I have not yet had an opportunity of discussing the question with the Finance Minister but hope to do so in a few days. Meanwhile we must leave the postponement to your management. I need not say that this matter is entirely confidential.

E 135   JOHN LANGTON'S MEMORANDUM ON MR. COURTNEY'S[60]
REPORT
circa January 1870
[*PAC, RG 58 B2b, v. 2*]

. . . The Bank of Upper Canada: There has for many years been an unexplained difference between the Receiver General & the Bank. Under the former systems of making deposits the Bank was constantly receiving money of which the Receiver General had no notice; this arose principally in the Crown Lands Department. There was also great confusion from the practice of the Bank making payments on Board of Works certificates which at that time were given to the individual & not sent in, as now, for a warrant to issue. From these two causes most of the differences arose. The system in both cases was altered 10 or 12 years ago but many of the old differences remained unexplained. Upon our closing our transactions with the Bank the balance of the differences was on the whole in favour of Government, the Bank having as much as $48,000 at the credit of the Indian Fund, which had in the meantime been transferred to the Province, of which the Books of the Indian Department knew nothing. This was for sometime kept in a suspense account & no interest was allowed on it, but on Confederation it was added to the general fund & went to the credit of the general management account, there being no record of what particular tribe it belonged to. There remained a difference against Government in the [one word?] account with the Bank. But the main portion of the difference Mr.

[60]Courtney worked in the Department of Finance for the Dominion government.

Courtney speaks of consists of one item arising out of the closing of the Zimmerman Bank, which we have charged against the Bank of Upper Canada, but which the Trustees repudiate . . . .

E 136   FRANCIS HINCKS, MINISTER OF FINANCE MEMO
Ottawa, 31 January 1870
[PAC, RG 19 C1, v. 1183]

. . . it seems very desirable to adopt more efficacious measures than have hitherto been taken to wind up the affairs of the Bank of Upper Canada, the present Trust being needlessly expensive.

The Creditors may be divided into three classes, 1st The unsecured creditors holding Either certificates of deposit or notes and which are bearing interest. 2nd The secured creditors Messrs Glyn Mills Currie & Coy of London, and 3rdly the Government.

There is no reason to anticipate that the lands mortgaged to Messrs Glyn Mills & Co will sell for more than sufficient to pay their debt – At present they are managed by the Trustees practically at the expense of the other creditors.

It would be better to allow Messrs Glyn & Co. to dispose of their Lands through their own agents – The claims of the general creditors do not Exceed $300.000 with some interest, and if these creditors were paid off, the remainder of the assets would become the property of the Government, & ought to be managed in the same way as other lands, by Government Officers; and without Expense. The undersigned has had the opportunity of consulting with the Trustees, and with other gentlemen having a general knowledge of the facts, and they concur in recommending the course which seems to him best, which is to sell without delay the most available assets, taking the payment Either in cash or the Trustees' certificates. The effect of the recommendation would be to give the holders of certificates a preference over the Government, but not a greater one than has been obtained by all those who have paid in the notes of the Bank at par.

It may require authority from Parliament to carry the suggestion into Effect, but the undersigned strongly recommends that such authority be applied, so that the Government may be in a position to state, that the trust will be brought to a close with as little delay as possible.

E 137   R. MORTON[61] TO FRANCIS HINCKS
Toronto, 31 August 1870
[PAC, RG 19 C1, v. 1183]

. . . I send herewith Lists of the Claims still unsettled, accounting in the aggregate to $117,987.73 and Interest; and with these I beg to send a

[61]R. Morton was employed by the bank's trustees to help wind up the sale of the bank's land holdings.

memo shewing that in my opinion something like $88,000 would cover
the whole (including Interest) which are ever likely to be presented
. . . .

. . . I may say however that I have very little doubt almost all would
compromise at 90 cents including Interest (which was the rate the
Trustees paid) or that they would take Real Estate at a fair valuation for
their respective claims. Probably $80,000 in Cash would quench *all*
outside claims except Glyn's if holders were approached cautiously
. . . .

. . . The charges for losses on lands are alarmingly large, but of
course unavoidable, and I may add that during this year they have been
exceptionally heavy from the fact that they include some fearfully
overvalued properties, as for instance

Lots in Collingwood held at $10,000 sold for	$1175
Largess lands held at $9000 sold for	$4000
Wharf property in Kingston held at $8000 sold for	$3000
Chippawa Distillery held at $40,000 sold for	$9500
Niagara Dock property held at $40,000 sold for	$9018

As regards the Duke St. premises the Dominion gave the Bank credit
for $10,000; our Trustees paid Galt & Cayley $10,000 in cash; and Galt
& Cayley made a Deed to the Crown. There cannot be a doubt it belongs
to the Dominion . . . .

E 138   C. GAMBLE TO FRANCIS HINCKS
Toronto, 12 November 1870
[*PAC, RG 19 C1, v. 1183*]

You omitted to enclose Hicksons[62] letter so I cant report therein – the
only way he can be mixed up with or interested in any BUC matter must
be in respect to the Grand Trunk mortgage to BUC for £221.000 Stg @
4% on some small property not worth, I was going to say as many cents.
The principal not payable until Grand Trunk *may be in funds* – This was
assigned (together with Postal Subsidy Bonds and other like Securities)
absolutely to Glyn and BUC received credit therefore at the sum of
£178.000 Stg. *It was taken absolutely,* and we have had nothing to do
with principal or interest since – The latter if paid at all has been paid
thru'. Hickson – I have no doubt Glyn would be delighted to put the
same security off upon the Dominion – with others if they could – but
the arrangt then made was one most favourable to BUC and should not be
disturbed or interfered with in any way. The lands of the Glyn Trust –
have been sold as Glyn Lands by Smith as Agent of the Glyn Trustees.
Nothing has been done to mix up the two estates. They have always
been Kept distinct and the Trustees of BUC under my advice studiously

---

[62]Sir Joseph Hickson (1830–97), after working for the Grand Trunk from the early
1860s, became general manager in 1874, a position he held until 1890.

avoid anything and everything that Could by any possibility alter the position of BUC Estate.

I have received Mr. Langtons dispatch enclosing a Copy of the Order in Council – I wish I had seen it before it passed – I could have altered it for the better in many respects but I must work along as well as I can for the present – but my powers will have to be considerably enlarged upon [one word?] to wind up the estate in any reasonable time. *Now with regard to the Books* – The lease of the Office expires on the 14 day of March 1872. Rent $450. Taxes – Care Taker. So long as Morton & Smith remain in our employment they have the right to use half of the Office. This right expires with the Current six months 1st Febry next. They offer to take the Office off our hands at once and assume all responsibilities therefor – to find room for such Books as we shall require to Keep with right of preference at all times – if we will give them the Office furniture valued at $200 by me and *the old Books not required* to be Kept – giving a Covenant to see personally to the destruction of them. The Current years taxes have been paid – Morton & Smith have offered to take the Office furniture from us at $180 – there must be at least ten tons of Books worth $20 per Ton – that is the Paper maker would take it at that – unless destroyed by damp – a large quantity has been under water this spring – and looking at it with the view of winding up the matter and getting it well in hand at the earliest moment, I would advise that Morton & Smiths Offer be accepted.

E 139   C. GAMBLE TO FRANCIS HINCKS
Toronto, 17 November 1870
[*PAC, RG 19 C1, v. 1183*]

Glyn Mortgages

I see Mr. Hickson refers to Mortgages arising out of Sales made by Galt and Cayley only – I beg to report that the arrangt made by the Bank with the Trustees of Glyn was, that when Sales were made of the Land credit should at once be given to the Bank for the full amount of the purchase money – Glyns Trustee arranging with the purchasers for the terms of sale. These Terms were 1/4 Cash – rest due in 3 years Int at 7% – The Mortgages were taken in the name of Glyn or his Trustees and the latter have always collected the Interest and Instalments which I am informed have been regularly paid. The Mortgages ought therefore to be first class. The property so far as I can learn, has been sold to [one word?] parties – a considerable sum has been paid on each purchase and every year the Security is proving better – no doubt among so many there may be a few speculators, but I am informed that they are few and that their payments have been made promptly.

I was led astray from Mr. Hicksons connection with the Grand Trunk – and the fear that our friends the Glyns – might try and make the reassuming of the GT mortgage by the Dominion one of the Conditions of our arrangement.

I have such a horror of the GT [interconnections?] with the Bank UC that the very idea of opening up any thing connected with their A/C almost makes me shudder.

I return you Mr. Hicksons letter.

E 140   C. GAMBLE TO FRANCIS HINCKS
Toronto, 18 November 1870
[*PAC, RG 19 C1, v. 1183*]

. . . The old Books where they can be worked over again are worth $20 per Ton delivered at the Office of the paper manufacturer. It will have to be sorted where it is however – that part [fit?] for the Factory – Cut up and sent [away?] and the refuse destroyed. It will take months to do this and I have stipulated that Smith himself shall superintend it. Then Morton & Smith are to give Office room for all the Books we Keep with free access to them by those authorised to use them at all times. I have considered the matter in all its bearing and have made up my mind that it would be well to arrange with them upon this basis and I trust upon my explanation you will not consider that I have made a bad bargain.

E 141   T. GALT TO C. GAMBLE
17 September 1872
[*PAC, RG 19 C1, v. 1183*]

I have received authority from Messrs Glyn to accept the sum of Thirty Thousand dollars in discharge of the Balance due to them by the late Bank of Upper Canada. The balance appearing to be due for Principal was on the first July last the sum of $35172^{80}/100 to this amount has to be added a sum of $5300 for interest since July 1, 1870 – I have gone into this with you & I believe you are satisfied that it is correct. You will please understand that I am to receive the $30,000 free from any charges & that the expenses of the conveyances are to be borne by the Government.

I now beg to offer for the consideration of the Hon. the Finance Minister the following proposition: I will accept the sum of Thirty Thousand dollars in full of the balance due & will convey to the Government the residue of Lands & securities held by me. The Government to be at the expense of the necessary conveyance.

E 142   C. GAMBLE TO FRANCIS HINCKS
Toronto, 27 September 1872
[*PAC, RG 19 C1, v. 1183*]

Among the assets of the Bank of Upper Canada at the time of its failure was a mortgage of the late James Morton of Kingston for $300,000 upon properties in all parts of the Country, among others the Kingston Distillery and dwelling house of the deceased. At that time the distillery was being worked under a lease to Messrs. Cassel and Kirkpatrick for the benefit of the Bank, when the lease expired Mrs. Morton bought from the Trustees the Distillery and residence at $50,000 and paid a first instalment of $4000 since when now three years ago no part of principal or interest has been paid and the property has been suffered to go so much to decay particularly the Distillery – frequent applications have been made to the Govt by her and her friends for delay and I have been requested to delay proceedings from time to time by persons in authority. The only source from which means were to come to pay for the purchase was a claim the Estate of Morton had or fancied they had on the Southern Railway Charter.

This was recognized to a certain extent and some arrangement made for its payment thro James O'Reilly Esq. Q.C.[63] but I am given to understand that no portion of it has yet been paid and the exact amount I do not know. There are other lands contained in the mortgage besides the Distillery and residence, of considerable value the rents of which Mrs. Morton has hitherto received. Mrs. Morton and her family always maintained that no such amt as $300,000 was due at the time the mortgage was given and that such sum was inserted to cover everything that might be due and I never could get at the real figures Mr. Thomas Kirkpatrick now dead was the only man who could explain anything about the transaction and for some reason or other why, I could never discover he counselled delay and lenient measures toward Mrs. Morton which in fact he himself carried out almost to the day of his death. He sold some of the land contained in the mortgage under the [one word?] of sale and accounted to BUC and the Trustees for the proceeds and I have received the balances on some of them and accounted for them in my accounts to your department. Mrs. Morton died suddenly last week in possession of the Distillery and Residence and has devised her whole interest in her husbands estate to C. Price Esq. Barrister at Kingston her last words to her children being "to fight the matter of BUC to the last". I have received a letter from Mr. Price offering on behalf of the Estate to accept $4,000 the instalment paid and give a release and perfect the title in anything in the Govnt. and also a communication from Mr. George A. Kirkpatrick Esq. M.P. of Kingston[64] strongly recommending that such arrangement be carried out. My own opinion is that it would be advisable to do so and close this long and most unsatisfactory matter. I have no doubt the heirs and Trustee could give us a great deal of trouble and postpone the settlement of BUC affairs for years almost besides keeping us before the public by a suit in Chancery, altho in the end we should recover something, but *that carrying on the business at Kingston*

[63]James O'Reilly (1823–75) was a Kingston lawyer and from 1872–74 represented South Renfrew as a Conservative in the Dominion Parliament.

[64]George Airey Kirkpatrick (1841–99) was the son of Thomas Kirkpatrick and a Conservative politician.

by the Cashier of the Bank, the Kingston agent and Solicitor was a very bad affair. Mr. Price offers to take the $4,000.00 or property to the value of $4,000. The better plan would be to authorise me out of the moneys of BUC estate in my hands to make the best arrangement at anything below the $4,000 or to the extent of $4,000 that I can effect. I fear if we go to the valuation of land we shall never come to an arrangement.

No one will understand the difficulties that surround us in this matter better than the Hon the Minister of Justice, to whom I desire that my letter may be submitted.

E 143   C. GAMBLE TO J.M. COURTNEY
Toronto, 20 September 1876
[PAC, RG 19 C1, v. 1183]

In reply to your letter of the 23rd Inst. No. 546, I beg to state for the Information of the Hon the Minister of Finance, that I do not think it possible, to make out such a statement of the affairs of the Bank of Upper Canada, at the time Mr. Cassels took charge say in 1861 as you mention. You are aware that in consequence of the flooding of the premises, in which the Books of the Bank were kept it was found necessary to have them put away, and that they were sold to the paper manufactory, and worked up again into new paper. All that were saved were those only in use by the Trustees at the time, which you have seen in my present office and from them it would be simply impossible to compile the schedule required. 2nd I have never seen the Minute Books referred to and having enquired of the party into whose Care the Books came, after the failure of the Bank, he informs me that they never came under his notice, that to his Knowledge no reference was ever required to be made to them, and that they must have been among those destroyed by the flooding of the premises already referred to.

I was never present at the meetings of the Directors, except when some particular matter was referred to me, some special business, upon which the Board required Counsel and advice, and had no opportunity of learning the nature and extent of the statements usually laid before the Directors at their Board meetings. I do not recollect ever seeing one and certainly was never consulted upon the subject.

I know of but one man, who could give satisfactory information upon the subject matter of your communication, and that man is the last Cashier, Robert Cassels Esq of Quebec.

APPENDIXES

APPENDIX 1A

Alphabetical List of Directors of the Bank of Upper Canada

Name	Dates	Place of Birth[a]	Religion[b]	Principal Occupation	BUC Share Ownership[c]	Years as Director BUC
ALEXANDER, George	1822–1901	UC	CoE	lawyer	1857: 44; 1860: 90; 1863: 234; 1865: 234	1861–5
ALLAN, George W., Hon.	1822–1901				1857: 28; 1860: 45; 1863: 70; 1865: 70	1860–5 Pres. 1861–3, 1865
ALLAN, William, Hon.	1770–1853	S	P	merchant	1830: 105	1822–34 Pres. 1822–4, 1826–34
ANDERSON, Robert G.		S		merchant	1857: 32; 1860: 56; 1863: 100; 1865: 100	1824–7
ARNOLD, John		E	CoE	financier	1857: 90	1853–7
BABY, James, Hon.	1762–1833	US	RC	fur	1830: 20	1822–32
BALDWIN, Augustus Warren	1776–1866	I	CoE	navy financier	1830: 40; 1838; 1857: 273; 1860: 273; 1863: 284; 1865: 284	1832, 1834–7, 1839, 1841, 1843–4, 1847–56
BALDWIN, John S.	1787–1843	I	CoE	merchant	1830: 40	1823–4, 1826, 1828–33, 1837–42
BALDWIN, William W., Dr.	1775–1844	I	CoE	lawyer; doctor	1830: 20, 1857: 5	1823–4
BARWICK, John				miller	1857: 3; 1863: 70; 1865: 70	1838–9, 1864–5
BERCZY, Charles Albert	1794–1858	UC		general businessman	1838	1840–3
BETHUNE, Angus	1783–1858	I		general businessman	1857: 103; 1860: 63; 1863: 63; 1865: 63	1843–54

Name	Dates	Place of Birth[a]	Religion[b]	Principal Occupation	BUC Share Ownership[c]	Years as Director BUC
BILLINGS, F.T.	d. 1875				1857: 4	1827, 1831
BOULTON, D'Arcy	1759–1834	E	CoE	lawyer	1857: 4	1827, 1831
BOULTON, D'Arcy, Jr.	1785–1846	E	CoE	lawyer	1830:104; 1838	1824–6, 1828, 1831–3
BOULTON, Henry John	1790–1870	E	CoE	lawyer	1838, 1857: 320; 1860: 242	1822–8
BOYD, Francis	d. 1865				1838, 1857: 100; 1860: 100	1842–59
CAMERON, Duncan, Hon.	1765–1838	S	CoE	merchant		1822
CATLET, William						1837
CAWTHRA, Joseph	1759–1842	E		merchant	1830: 34, 1838	1835–39
CAWTHRA, William	1801–1880	E		merchant	1838: 1857: 45	1848–50, 1852–3, 1855–6, 1858
CAYLEY, Francis M.				financier	1838: 1857: 121; 1860: 161; 1863: 161; 1865: 161	1841, 1843–7
CAYLEY, William	1807–1890	R	CoE	lawyer	1838: 1857: 80; 1860: 15; 1863: 71; 1865: 7	1839–43, 1845–7
CHEWETT, James Grant	1793–1862	E	CoE	surveyor; financier	1830: 20; 1838; 1857: 217	1828, 1839, 1842–4, 1846–56, V. Pres: 1849–56
CROOKS, James, Capt.	1778–1860	S		miller	1830: 20	1822
CROOKSHANK, George, Hon.	1773–1859	US	CoE	financier	1830: 20; 1857: 400; 1860: 10; 1863: 10; 1865: 10	1822–6, Pres: 1825
DALY, J. Porter, Dr.				doctor		1826

Name	Dates	Place of Birth[a]	Religion[b]	Principal Occupation	BUC Share Ownership[c]	Years as Director BUC
DRAPER, William Henry	1801–1877	E	CoE	lawyer	1838	1833–4, 1838–9
DUNN, John Henry, Hon.	1794–1854	F	CoE	financier	1830: 601; 1838	1822–3, 1826–36, 1841, 1843–5
ELMSLEY, John	1801–1863	UC	CoE-RC	navy; financier	1830: 264	1828–30, 1832, 1834
FITZGIBBON, James, Col.	1780–1863	I		army	1838	1825, 1827
FITZPATRICK, F.						1850
GAMBLE, William	1805–1881	UC	CoE	merchant; miller	1830: 20; 1838	1829–1830, 1832–9, 1841–7
GILLESPIE, Robert, Jr.	1785–1863	S		general businessman	1863: 10	1833–4
GOODERHAM, William	1790–1881	E	CoE	general businessman	1857: 357; 1860: 257; 1863: 129; 1865: 129	1854–64
GOODHUE, George Jervis, Hon.	1799–1870	US	CoE	merchant	1857: 202	1848–54
GWYNNE, William Charles, Dr.	1806–1875	I		doctor	1838	1836
HARRIS, John					1830: 10; 1838; 1865: 38	1846
HAWKE, A.B.		E			1857: 24; 1860: 24	1850–8
HELLIWELL, Thomas	1795–1862	E		merchant	1830: 25; 1838; 1857: 52; 1860: 52; 1863: 52	1829–30, 1834–5, 1837–8, 1840–3, 1846–7, 1849–52, 1854–8
HENDERSON, Jas. A.		E	CoE	lawyer	1857: 8; 1860: 64; 1863: 80; 1865: 80; 1857: 27	1861–5
HOLDSWORTH, Frederick						1848
IRVING, Jacob Aemilius, Hon.	1797–1856	US				1848

Name	Dates	Place of Birth[a]	Religion[b]	Principal Occupation	BUC Share Ownership[c]	Years as Director BUC
JARVIS, Samuel Peters	1792–1857	UC		lawyer	1830: 20; 1838	1825–44, 1846–7
JONES, Thomas Mercer	1795–1868	E		general businessman		1832
KETCHUM, Jesse	1782–1867	US	P	tanner	1830: 20; 1838; 1857: 53; 1860: 53	1840–4
KIRKPATRICK, Thomas	1805–1870	I		lawyer	1838; 1857: 209; 1860: 153; 1863: 153; 1865: 153	1846, 1848–9, 1851–3
LAWRASON, Lawrence	1803–1882	UC	CoE	merchant	1857: 205; 1860: 205; 1863: 205; 1865: 205	1855–6
LORING, Robert Roberts, Lt. Col.	1790–1848			army		1845–7
MACAULAY, John	1792–1857	UC	CoE	businessman	1830; 1838; 1857: 160	1837–9
MACAULAY, John Simcoe	1791–1855	CoE		businessman		1836–42
MACPHERSON, Sir David Lewis, Hon.	1818–1896	S		general businessman	1860: 40; 1863: 90; 1865: 156	1859–60
MAGRATH, Thomas				general businessman		1841–2
MARKLAND, George Herchmer	1790–1862	UC	CoE			1833
MCDONNELL, Alexander, Hon.	1762–1842	S	RC			1835
MCGILL, John, Hon.	1752–1834	S		financier	1830: 25; 1838	1822–3, 1825
MONRO, George	1801–1878	S	CoE	merchant	1830: 60; 1838; 1857: 90; 1860: 100; 1863: 91; 1865: 91	1822–4, 1829–31
MONRO, John	1788–1830	S		merchant	1830: 20	1825–8

Name	Dates	Place of Birth[a]	Religion[b]	Principal Occupation	BUC Share Ownership[c]	Years as Director BUC
MURRAY, Alexander	1806–1838		P	merchant	1838	1836–7
NEWBIGGING, James	1787–1874	I	P	merchant		1835
O'HARA, Walter, Col.	1807–1883	S		army; lawyer		1835–6, 1838, 1842
PATERSON, Peter	1802–1866	S	CoE	merchant	1838	1861–4
PROUDFOOT, William		UC	P	merchant; financier	1857: 104; 1863: 194; 1865: 315	1822, 1826, 1828–61, Pres: 1835–61
RIDOUT, George	1791–1871	E	CoE	lawyer	1830: 20; 1838; 1857: 305; 1860: 11	1822, 1824
RIDOUT, Joseph Davis	1809–1884	E		general businessman	1830: 20	1843–65
RIDOUT, Samuel Smith	1778–1855			merchant	1857: 40; 1860: 40; 1863: 70; 1865: 68	1824, 1827, 1829, 1834, 1838
RIDOUT, Thomas	1754–1829			public official	1830: 24	1822–23
ROBINSON, Sir James Lukin		LC	CoE	lawyer	1838	1851, 1853–60, V. Pres: 1857
ROBINSON, Sir John Beverley, Hon.	1791–1863	NB		merchant	1857: 465; 1860: 88; 1863: 10	1824–6
ROBINSON, Peter	1785–1838	I		lawyer	1838	1823, 1825, 1827–8, 1835
ROSS, John, Hon.	1818–1871	I		lawyer	1830: 80; 1838	1859–60
RUTHERFORD, E.H.	1821–		CoE	merchant	1860: 102; 1863: 50; 1865: 50	1859–65, V. Pres: 1861
SMALL, Charles Coxwell	1800–1864	UC		public official	1857: 120; 1860: 40; 1863: 80; 1865: 80	1826–28
SMITH, Larratt	1782–1860	E		army		1840, 1843

Name	Dates	Place of Birth[a]	Religion[b]	Principal Occupation	BUC Share Ownership[c]	Years as Director BUC
SMITH, Larratt, W.	1820–1905	E	CoE	lawyer	1857: 40; 1863: 24: 1865: 50	1864–5
SMYTHE, Thomas S.					1830: 20	1831
STAYNER, Thomas Allen	1788–1868	NS		public official	1838; **1857:485;** 1860: 963; 1863: 33; 1865: 33	1854–60, V. Pres: 1860
STEGMAN, David	1797–1834			army merchant		1833
STRACHAN, Dr. John, Hon.	1778–1867	S	CoE	minister	1830: 282; 1838	1822
STREET, Samuel	1775–1844			general businessman	1830: 400	1840, 1844
STREET, Thomas Clark	1814–1872	UC	CoE	lawyer, general businessman	1857: 800; 1860: 800; 1863: 875; 1865, 1175	1845, 1847–51, 1853–63, 1865
SULLIVAN, Robert Baldwin	1802–1853	I		lawyer	1830: 16; 1838	1836–40
TANNABILL, John					1830: 22	1825
THOMPSON, Edward William, Col.	1794–1865	UC	P	army; financier	1857: 31; 1860: 31; 1863: 68; 1865: 68	1861–4
THORNE, Benjamin				miller	1838	1824, 1831, 1833–5
TURNER, C. Barker, Col.	d. 1853			army		1848–52
WALLBRIDGE, Lewis	1816–1887	UC	CoE	lawyer	1863: 72; 1865: 72	1862–5
WELLS, Joseph, Hon.	1757–1853			army	1830: 285; 1838	1822–6, 1828–38
WIDMER, Christopher	1780–1858	E		doctor	1830: 35; 1838; 1857: 80	1822–4, 1827–56, V. Pres: 1843–8
WINNIETT, James, Maj.				army	1830: 119	1829–32

Name	Dates	Place of Birth[a]	Religion[b]	Principal Occupation	BUC Share Ownership[c]	Years as Director BUC
WOOD, Alexander	1772–1844	S		merchant	1830: 24; 1838	1829–41
WOODRUFF, Richard	d. 1863			general businessman	1830; 1838; 1857: 240; 1860: 432; 1863: 648; 1865: 648	1849–50

a. The following symbols are used: E – England; F –France; G – Germany; I – Ireland; LC – Lower Canada; NB – New Brunswick; NS – Nova Scotia; R – Russia; S – Scotland; UC – Upper Canada; US – United States.
b. The following symbols are used: CoE – Church of England; P – Presbyterian; RC – Roman Catholic.
c. The earliest available date and number of shares in the BUC owned by the director.

APPENDIX 1B

Bank of Upper Canada Directorates, 1823–65

1822
William Allan (P)
James Baby
Henry John Boulton
Duncan Cameron
James Crooks
George Crookshank
John Henry Dunn
John McGill
George Monro
George Ridout
Thomas Ridout
John Strachan
Joseph Wells
Christopher Widmer

1823
William Allan (P)
James Baby (G)
John S. Baldwin
William Warren Baldwin
D'Arcy Boulton
Henry John Boulton (G)
George Crookshank
John Henry Dunn (G)
John McGill
George Monro
Thomas Ridout
Peter Robinson
William B. Robinson (G)
Joseph Wells
Christopher Widmer

1824
William Allan (P)
Robert G. Anderson
James Baby (G)
John S. Baldwin
William Warren Baldwin
D'Arcy Boulton Jr. (G)
Henry John Boulton (G)
George Crookshank
George Monro
George Ridout
Samuel Ridout
John Beverly Robinson (G)
Benjamin Thorne
Joseph Wells
Christopher Widmer

1825
George Crookshank (P)
William Allan
Robert G. Anderson
James Baby (G)
D'Arcy Boulton Jr.
Henry John Boulton
James Fitzgibbon
Samuel P. Jarvis
John McGill (G)
John Monro
John Beverly Robinson
Peter Robinson (G)
John Tannabill
Joseph Wells (G)

1826
William Allan (P)
Robert G. Anderson
James Baby (G)
John Baldwin
D'Arcy Boulton Jr.
Henry John Boulton (G)
George Crookshank (G)
J.J. Daly
John Henry Dunn
Samuel P. Jarvis
John Monro
William Proudfoot
John Beverly Robinson
Charles C. Small
Joseph Wells (G)

1827
William Allan (P)
Robert G. Anderson
James Baby (G)
F.T. Billings
D'Arcy Boulton Jr. (G)
Henry John Boulton
John Henry Dunn
James Fitzgibbon
Samuel P. Jarvis
John Monro
Samuel Ridout
Peter Robinson (G)
Charles Coxwell Small (G)
Christopher Widmer

1828
William Allan (P)
James Baby (G)
John S. Baldwin
D'Arcy Boulton Jr.
Henry John Boulton
James Chewitt
John Henry Dunn (G)
John Elmsley (G)
Samuel P. Jarvis
James Monro
William Proudfoot
Peter Robinson
Charles Coxwell Small
Joseph Wells (G)
Christopher Widmer

1829
William Allan (P)
James Baby (G)
John S. Baldwin
John Henry Dunn (G)
John Elmsley
William Gamble
Thomas Helliwell
Samuel P. Jarvis
George Monro
William Proudfoot
Samuel Ridout
Joseph Wells (G)
Christopher Widmer
James Winniett (G)
Alexander Wood

1830
William Allan (P)
James Baby (G)
John S. Baldwin
John Henry Dunn (G)
John Elmsley
William Gamble
Thomas Helliwell
Samuel P. Jarvis
George Monro
William Proudfoot
Joseph Wells (G)
Christopher Widmer
James Winniett (G)
Alexander Wood

1831
William Allan (P)
James Baby (G)
John S. Baldwin
Francis T. Billings
D'Arcy Boulton Jr.

John Henry Dunn (G)
Samuel P. Jarvis
George Monro
William Proudfoot
Thomas S. Smythe
Benjamin Thorne
Joseph Wells (G)
Christopher Widmer (G)
James Winniett
Alexander Wood

1832
William Allan (P)
James Baby (G)
Augustus Baldwin (G)
John S. Baldwin
D'Arcy Boulton Jr.
John Henry Dunn (G)
John Elmsley
William Gamble
Samuel P. Jarvis
Thomas Mercer Jones
William Proudfoot
Joseph Wells (G)
Christopher Widmer
James Winniett
Alexander Wood

1833
William Allan (P)
John S. Baldwin
D'Arcy Boulton Jr.
John Henry Dunn (G)
William H. Draper
William Gamble
Robert Gillespie Jr.
Samuel P. Jarvis
George H. Markland (G)
William Proudfoot
David Stegman
Benjamin Thorne
Joseph Wells (G)
Christopher Widmer (G)

1834
William Allan (P)
Augustus Baldwin (G)
William Henry Draper
John Henry Dunn (G)
John Elmsley
William Gamble
Robert Gillespie Jr.
Thomas Helliwell
Samuel P. Jarvis
William Proudfoot
Samuel Ridout

Benjamin Thorne
Joseph Wells (G)
Christopher Widmer (G)
Alexander Wood

1835
William Proudfoot (P)
Augustus Baldwin (G)
Joseph Cawthra
John Henry Dunn (G)
William Gamble
Thomas Helliwell
Samuel P. Jarvis
Alexander McDonnell
James Newbigging
Walter O'Hara (G)
Peter Robinson
Benjamin Thorne
Joseph Wells (G)
Christopher Widmer
Alexander Wood

1836
William Proudfoot (P)
Augustus Baldwin (G)
Joseph Cawthra
John Henry Dunn (G)
William Gamble
William C. Gwynne
Samuel P. Jarvis
John S. Macaulay
Alexander Murray
Walter O'Hara
Robert Baldwin Sullivan (G)
Joseph Wells (G)
Christopher Widmer
Alexander Wood

1837
William Proudfoot (P)
Augustus Baldwin (G)
John S. Baldwin
William Catlet
Joseph Cawthra
William Gamble
Thomas Helliwell
Samuel P. Jarvis
John Macaulay (G)
John S. Macaulay
Alexander Murray
Robert Baldwin Sullivan (G)
Joseph Wells (G)
Christopher Widmer
Alexander Wood

1838
William Proudfoot (P)

John S. Baldwin
John Barwick
William Henry Draper (G)
William Gamble
Thomas Helliwell
Samuel P. Jarvis
John Macaulay (G)
John S. Macaulay
Walter O'Hara
Samuel Ridout
Robert Baldwin Sullivan (G)
Joseph Wells (G)
Christopher Widmer
Alexander Wood

1839
William Proudfoot (P)
Augustus Baldwin (G)
John S. Baldwin
John Barwick
William Cawthra
William Cayley
James G. Chewett
William Henry Draper (G)
William Gamble
Samuel P. Jarvis
John Macaulay (G)
John S. Macaulay
Robert Baldwin Sullivan (G)
Christopher Widmer
Alexander Wood

1840
William Proudfoot (P)
John S. Baldwin
Charles Berczy
William Cayley
Thomas Helliwell
Samuel P. Jarvis
Jesse Ketchum
John S. Macaulay
Larratt Smith
Samuel Street
Robert Baldwin Sullivan
Christopher Widmer
Alexander Wood

1841
William Proudfoot (P)
Augustus Baldwin
John S. Baldwin
Charles Berczy
Francis M. Cayley
William Cayley
John Henry Dunn
William Gamble

Thomas Helliwell
Samuel P. Jarvis
Jesse Ketchum
John S. Macaulay
Thomas Magrath
Christopher Widmer
Alexander Wood

1842
William Proudfoot (P)
John S. Baldwin
Charles Berczy
Francis Boyd
William Cayley
James G. Chewett
William Gamble
Thomas Helliwell
Samuel P. Jarvis
Jesse Ketchum
John S. Macaulay
Thomas Magrath
Walter O'Hara
Christopher Widmer

1843
William Proudfoot (P)
Christopher Widmer (VP)
Charles Berczy
Angus Bethune
Francis Boyd
Francis M. Cayley
William Cayley
James G. Chewett
John Henry Dunn
William Gamble
Thomas Helliwell
Samuel P. Jarvis
Jesse Ketchum
Joseph D. Ridout
Larratt Smith

1844
William Proudfoot (P)
Christopher Widmer (VP)
Augustus Baldwin
Angus Bethune
Francis Boyd
Francis M. Cayley
James G. Chewett
John Henry Dunn
William Gamble
Samuel P. Jarvis
Jesse Ketchum
Joseph D. Ridout

1845
William Proudfoot (P)

Christopher Widmer (VP)
Augustus Baldwin
Angus Bethune
Francis Boyd
Francis M. Cayley
William Cayley
John Henry Dunn
William Gamble
Robert Roberts Loring
Joseph D. Ridout
Thomas C. Street

1846
William Proudfoot (P)
Christopher Widmer (VP)
Angus Bethune
Francis Boyd
Francis M. Cayley
William Cayley
James G. Chewett
William Gamble
John Harris
Thomas Helliwell
Samuel P. Jarvis
Thomas Kirkpatrick
Robert Roberts Loring
Joseph D. Ridout

1847
William Proudfoot (P)
Christopher Widmer (VP)
Augustus Baldwin
Angus Bethune
Francis Boyd
Francis M. Cayley
William Cayley
James G. Chewett
William Gamble
Thomas Helliwell
Samuel P. Jarvis
Robert Roberts Loring
Joseph D. Ridout

1848
William Proudfoot (P)
Christopher Widmer (VP)
Augustus Baldwin
Angus Bethune
Francis Boyd
William Cawthra
James G. Chewett
George Jervis Goodhue
Frederick Holdsworth
Jacob Aemilius Irving
Thomas Kirkpatrick
Joseph D. Ridout

Thomas C. Street
C. Barker Turner

1849
William Proudfoot (P)
James G. Chewett (VP)
Augustus Baldwin
Angus Bethune
Francis Boyd
William Cawthra
George Jervis Goodhue
Thomas Helliwell
Thomas Kirkpatrick
Joseph D. Ridout
Thomas C. Street
C. Barker Turner

1850
William Proudfoot (P)
James G. Chewett (VP)
Augustus Baldwin
Angus Bethune
Francis Boyd
William Cawthra
F. Fitzpatrick
George Jervis Goodhue
Anthony B. Hawke
Thomas Helliwell
Joseph D. Ridout
Thomas C. Street
C. Barker Turner
Christopher Widmer
Joseph Woodruff

1851
William Proudfoot (P)
James G. Chewett (VP)
Augustus Baldwin
Angus Bethune
Francis Boyd
George Jervis Goodhue
Anthony B. Hawke
Thomas Helliwell
Thomas Kirkpatrick
Joseph D. Ridout
James Lukin Robinson
Thomas C. Street
C. Barker Turner

1852
William Proudfoot (P)
James G. Chewett (VP)
Augustus Baldwin
Angus Bethune
Francis Boyd
William Cawthra

George Jervis Goodhue
Anthony B. Hawke
Thomas Helliwell
Thomas Kirkpatrick
Joseph D. Ridout
James Lukin Robinson
Thomas C. Street
C. Barker Turner
Christopher Widmer

1853
William Proudfoot (P)
James G. Chewett (VP)
John Arnold
Augustus Baldwin
Angus Bethune
Francis Boyd
William Cawthra
George Jervis Goodhue
Anthony B. Hawke
Thomas Kirkpatrick
Joseph D. Ridout
James Lukin Robinson
Thomas C. Street
Christopher Widmer

1854
William Proudfoot (P)
John Arnold
Augustus Baldwin
Angus Bethune
Francis Boyd
James G. Chewett
William Gooderham
George Jervis Goodhue
Anthony B. Hawke
Thomas Helliwell
Joseph D. Ridout
James Lukin Robinson
Thomas A. Stayner
Thomas C. Street
Christopher Widmer

1855
William Proudfoot (P)
James G. Chewett (VP)
John Arnold
Augustus Baldwin
Francis Boyd
William Cawthra
William Gooderham
Anthony B. Hawke
Thomas Helliwell
Lawrence Lawrason
Joseph D. Ridout
James Lukin Robinson

Thomas A. Stayner
Thomas C. Street
Christopher Widmer

1856
William Proudfoot (P)
James G. Chewett (VP)
John Arnold
Augustus Baldwin
Francis Boyd
William Cawthra
William Gooderham
Anthony B. Hawke
Thomas Helliwell
Lawrence Lawrason
Joseph D. Ridout
James Lukin Robinson
Thomas A. Stayner
Thomas C. Street
Christopher Widmer

1857
William Proudfoot (P)
James Lukin Robinson (VP)
John Arnold
Francis Boyd
William Gooderham
Anthony B. Hawke
Thomas Helliwell
Joseph D. Ridout
Thomas A. Stayner
Thomas C. Street

1858
William Proudfoot (P)
Francis Boyd
William Cawthra
William Gooderham
Anthony B. Hawke
Thomas Helliwell
Joseph D. Ridout
James Lukin Robinson
Thomas A. Stayner
Thomas C. Street

1859
William Proudfoot (P)
Francis Boyd
William Gooderham
David Lewis Macpherson
Joseph D. Ridout
James Lukin Robinson
John Ross
E.H. Rutherford
Thomas A. Stayner
Thomas C. Street

1860
William Proudfoot (P)
Thomas A. Stayner (VP)
George W. Allan
William Gooderham
David Lewis Macpherson
Joseph D. Ridout
James Lukin Robinson
John Ross
E.H. Rutherford
Thomas C. Street

1861
George W. Allan (P)
E.H. Rutherford (VP)
George Alexander
William Gooderham
James A. Henderson
Peter Paterson
Joseph D. Ridout
Thomas C. Street
Edward William Thomson

1862
George W. Allan (P)
George Alexander
William Gooderham
James Alexander Henderson
Peter Paterson
Joseph D. Ridout
E.H. Rutherford
Thomas C. Street
Edward William Thomson
Lewis Wallbridge

1863
George W. Allan (P)
George Alexander
William Gooderham
James Alexander Henderson
Peter Paterson
Joseph D. Ridout
E.H. Rutherford
Thomas C. Street
Edward William Thomson
Lewis Wallbridge

1864
George W. Allan (P)
John Barwick
William Gooderham (resigned during year,
  replaced by George Alexander)
James A. Henderson
Peter Paterson
Joseph D. Ridout
E.H. Rutherford

Edward William Thomson (died,
   replaced by Larratt W. Smith)
Lewis Wallbridge

1865
George W. Allan (P)
E.H. Rutherford (VP)

George Alexander
John Barwick
James A. Henderson
Joseph D. Ridout
Larratt W. Smith
Thomas C. Street
Lewis Wallbridge

Key: P President; VP Vice President; G Government appointee

Source: QUA, Magill Papers

APPENDIX 2

Bank of Upper Canada: Selected Statutes, 1821–62

An Act to incorporate sundry persons under the style and title of the president, directors and company of the Bank of Upper Canada [Revised Statutes of Upper Canada, 59 Geo III, c. 24]

Whereas the establishment of a bank in the province of Upper Canada will conduce to the prosperity and advantage of commerce and agriculture in the said province; and whereas William Allan, Robert Charles Horne, John Scarlett, Francis Jackson, William Warren Baldwin, Alexander Legge, Thomas Ridout, Samuel Ridout, D'Arcy Boulton, junior, William B. Robinson, James Macaulay, Duncan Cameron, Guy C. Wood, Robert Anderson, John Baldwin, and others, by their petitions presented to the legislature, have prayed for the privilege of being incorporated; be it enacted by the King's most excellent Majesty, by and with the advice and consent of the legislative council and assembly of the province of Upper Canada, constituted and assembled by virtue of and under the authority of an act passed in the parliament of Great Britain, entitled, ''An act to repeal certain parts of an act passed in the fourteenth year of his Majesty's reign, entitled, 'An act for making more effectual provision for the government of the province of Quebec, in North America, and to make further provision for the government of the said province,' '' and by the authority of the same, That [the above named] and all such persons as hereafter shall become stockholders of the said bank, shall be, and hereby are, ordained, constituted, and declared to be, from time to time, and until the first day of June, which will be in the year of our Lord one thousand eight hundred and forty-eight, a body corporate and politic, in fact and in name, of the president, directors and company of the bank of Upper Canada, ...

II. And be it further enacted by the authority aforesaid, That a share in the stock of the said bank shall be twelve pounds ten shillings, or the equivalent thereof in specie, and the number of shares shall not exceed sixteen thousand, and that books of subscription shall be opened at the same time in the towns of Kingston, Niagara, York, Brockville, Amherstburgh, Ancaster, Vittoria, Hamilton, in the district of Newcastle, and Cornwall, in the Eastern district, within two months after the passing of this act, by such person or persons, and under such regulations, as the majority of the said petitioners shall direct.

III. And be it further enacted by the authority aforesaid, That it shall and may be lawful for the governor, lieutenant governor, or person administering the government of this province, for the time being, to subscribe and hold in the capital stock of the said bank, for and on behalf of this province, any number of shares therein, not exceeding two thousand, the amount whereof the said governor, lieutenant governor, or person administering the government of this province for the time being, is hereby authorized, by a warrant or warrants under his hand and seal, directed to the receiver general of this province for the time being, to take out of the unappropriated monies which now remain or hereafter may remain in the hands of the said receiver general, for the future disposition of the parliament of this province.

IV. And be it further enacted by the authority aforesaid, That it shall be lawful for any person, his Majesty's subjects or foreigners, to subscribe for such and so many shares as he, she, or they may think fit, not however exceeding in the first instance, eighty; and that the shares respectively subscribed shall be payable in gold or silver, that is to say; ten per centum to be ready as a deposit at the time of subscribing, to be called for by the directors hereafter appointed by virtue of this act, as soon as they may deem expedient, and the remainder shall be payable in such instalments as a majority of the stockholders, at a meeting to be expressly convened for that purpose, shall agree upon; Provided no instalment shall exceed ten per centum upon the capital stock, or be called for or become payable in less than sixty days after public notice shall have been given in the Upper Canada Gazette and Kingston Chronicle, to that effect; Provided always, That if any stockholder or stockholders, as aforesaid, shall refuse or neglect to pay to the said directors the instalment due upon any share or shares held by him, her or them, at the time required by law so to do, such stockholder or stockholders, as aforesaid, shall forfeit such shares, as aforesaid, with the amount previously paid thereon, and the said share or shares may be sold by the said directors, and the sum arising therefrom, together with the amount previously paid thereon, shall be accounted for and divided in like manner as other monies of the bank.

v. Provided also, and it is further enacted by the authority aforesaid, That if the whole number of shares shall not be subscribed within two months after the said books of subscription shall be opened, then and in such case it shall be lawful for any former subscriber or subscribers to increase his, her, or their subscriptions, and, Provided further, That if the total amount of subscriptions within the period aforesaid shall exceed the capital stock limited by this act, then and in such case the shares of each subscriber or subscribers above ten shares, shall, as nearly as may be, be proportionably reduced until that the total number of shares be brought down to the limits above said, and, Provided nevertheless, That the said limitation in respect to persons subscribing to the said capital stock, shall not extend, or be construed to extend, to prevent the acquisition of a greater number of shares by purchase after the said bank shall have commenced its operations.

vi. And be it further enacted by the authority aforesaid, That the whole amount of the stock estate and property which the said corporation shall be authorized to hold, including the capital stock or shares before mentioned, shall never exceed in value two hundred thousand pounds.

vii. And be it further enacted by the authority aforesaid, That as soon as the sum of fifty thousand pounds shall have been subscribed, it shall and may be lawful for such subscribers, or the majority of them to call a meeting at some place to be named at the seat of the government of this province, for the purpose of proceeding to the election of the number of directors hereinafter mentioned, and such election shall then and there be made by a majority of shares, voted in manner hereinafter prescribed, in respect of the annual elections of directors, and the persons then and there chosen shall be the first directors, and be capable of serving until the expiration of the first Monday in June in the year of our Lord one thousand eight hundred and twenty-one; and the directors so chosen shall, as soon as the deposit amounting to twenty thousand pounds subscribed, as aforesaid, shall be paid to the said directors, commence the business and operations of the said Bank: Provided always, That no such meeting of the said subscribers shall take place until a notice is published in all the public newspapers of this province, at the distance of not less than thirty days from the time of such notification.

viii. And be it further enacted by the authority aforesaid, That the stock, property, affairs, and concerns of the said corporation, shall be managed and conducted by fifteen directors, one of whom to be the president, who, excepting as is hereinbefore provided for, shall hold their offices for one year; which directors shall be stockholders, and shall be subjects of his Majesty, residing in this province, and be elected on the first Monday in June in every year, at such time of the day, and at such place at the seat of government, as a majority of the directors for the time being shall appoint, and public notice shall be given by the said directors in the different newspapers printed within the province, of such time and place, not more than sixty nor less than thirty days previous to the time of holding the said election, and the said election shall be held and made by such of the said stockholders of the said bank, as shall attend for that purpose in their own proper persons, or by proxy; and all elections for directors shall be by ballot, and the fifteen persons who shall have the greatest number of votes at any election shall be the directors, except as is hereinafter directed; and if it should happen at any election

that two or more persons have an equal number of votes, in such manner that a greater
number of persons than fifteen shall by plurality of votes appear to be chosen as
directors, then the said stockholders hereinbefore authorized to hold such election, shall
proceed to ballot a second time, and by plurality of votes determine which of the said
persons so having an equal number of votes shall be the director or directors, so as to
complete the whole number of fifteen; and the said directors, so soon as may be after the
said election, shall proceed in like manner to elect by ballot one of their number to be
their president and four of the directors which shall be chosen at any year, excepting the
president, shall be ineligible to the office of director for one year after the expiration of
the time for which they shall be chosen directors; and in case a greater number than ten
of the directors, exclusive of the president who served for the last year, shall appear to
be elected, then the election of such person or persons above the said number, and who
shall have the fewest votes, shall be considered void, and such other of the stockholders
as shall be eligible, and shall have the next greatest number of votes, shall be considered
as elected in the room of such last described person or persons, and who are hereby
declared ineligible as aforesaid; and the president for the time being shall always be
eligible to the office of director; but stockholders, not residing within the province, shall
be ineligible, and if any director shall move out of the said province, his office shall be
considered as vacant; and if any vacancy or vacancies should at any time happen among
the directors, by death, resignation, or removal from the said province, such vacancy or
vacancies shall be filled for the remainder of the year in which they may happen, by a
special election for that purpose, to be held in the same manner as is hereinbefore
directed respecting annual elections, at such time and place at the seat of government as
the remainder of the directors, or the major part of them, shall appoint; Provided
always, That no person shall be eligible to be a director who shall not be a stockholder to
the amount of at least twenty shares. . . . .

x. And be it further enacted by the authority aforesaid, That each stockholder shall
be entitled to a number of votes, proportioned to the number of shares which he or she
shall have held in his or her own name, at least three months prior to the time of voting,
according to the following ratios, that is to say, at the rate of one vote for each share not
exceeding four, five votes for six shares, six votes for eight shares, seven votes for ten
shares, and one vote for every five shares above ten; stockholders actually resident
within the province of Upper Canada, and none others, may vote in election by proxy:
Provided always, That no person, co-partnership, or body politic, shall be entitled to
more than fifteen votes at any such election.

xi. And be it further enacted by the authority aforesaid, That it shall be the duty of
the directors to make half yearly dividends of so much of the profits of the said bank, as
to them, or the majority of them, shall appear advisable, and that once in every three
years, and oftener, if thereunto required by a majority of the votes of the stockholders,
to be given agreeable to the ratios hereinbefore established, at a general meeting to be
called for that purpose, an exact and particular statement of the debts which shall have
remained unpaid, after the expiration of the original credit, for a period of treble the
term of that credit, and of the surplus of profits, if any, after deducting losses and
dividends.

xii. And be it further enacted by the authority aforesaid, That the directors for the
time being, or a major part of them, shall have power to make and subscribe such rules
and regulations, as to them shall appear needful and proper, touching the management
and disposition of the stock, property, estate, and effects, of the said corporation, and
touching the duties and conduct of the officers, clerks, and servants employed therein,
and all such as many officers, clerks, and servants, for carrying on the said business,
and with such salaries and allowances as to them shall seem meet, provided that such
rules and regulations be not repugnant to the laws of this province.

xiii. And be it further enacted by the authority aforesaid, That the total amount of the
debts which the said corporation shall at any time owe, whether by bond, bill, note or
other contract, over and above the monies then actually deposited in the bank, shall not
exceed three times the sum of the capital stock subscribed, and actually paid into the

bank, and in case of such excess, the directors, under whose administration it shall happen, shall be liable for the same, in their natural and private capacities; but this shall not be construed to exempt the said corporation, or any estate, real or personal, which they may hold as a body corporate, from being also liable for and chargeable with the said excess; but such of the said directors who may have been absent when the said excess was contracted, or who may have dissented from the said resolution or act whereby the same was so contracted, may respectively exonerate themselves from being so liable, by giving immediate notice of the fact, and of their absence or dissent, to the stockholders, at a general meeting which they shall have power to call for that purpose.

xiv. And be it further enacted by the authority aforesaid, That it shall not be lawful for the said corporation to issue any note or bill under the value of five shillings, of lawful money of the province of Upper Canada.

xv. And be it further enacted by the authority aforesaid, That the lands, tenements, and hereditaments, which it shall be lawful for the said corporation to hold, shall be only such as shall be requisite for its immediate accommodation, in relation to the convenient transactions of its business, or such as shall have been bona fide mortgaged to it, by way of security, or conveyed to it in satisfaction of debts previously contracted in the course of its dealings, or purchased at sales upon judgements, which shall have been obtained for such debts, and further the said corporation shall not directly or indirectly deal or trade in buying or selling any goods, wares, or merchandize, or commodities whatsoever: Provided, That nothing herein contained shall any wise be construed to hinder the said corporation from dealing in bonds, bills of exchange, or promissory notes, or in buying or selling bullion, gold, or silver.

xvi. And be it further enacted by the authority aforesaid, That the shares of the said capital stock shall be transferable, and may be from time to time transferred by the respective persons so subscribing the same: Provided always, That such transfer be entered or registered in a book or books to be kept for that purpose by the directors.

xvii. And be it further enacted by the authority aforesaid, That the bills obligatory and of credit, under the seal of said corporation, which shall be made to any person or persons, shall be assignable by indorsement thereupon, under the hand or hands of such person or persons, and of his, her or their assignee or assignees, and so as absolutely to transfer and vest the property thereof in each and every assignee or assignees successively, and to enable such assignee or assignees to bring and maintain an action thereupon in his, her, or their own name or names; and bills or notes which may be issued by order of the said corporation, signed by the president, and countersigned by the principal cashier or treasurer, promising the payment of money to any person or persons, his, her, or their order, or to bearer, though not under the seal of the said corporation, shall be binding and obligatory upon the same in like manner, and with the like force and effect, as upon any private person or persons, if issued by him, her, or their, in his, her, or their private or natural capacity or capacites, and shall be assignable or negotiable in like manner as if they were so issued by such private person or persons.

xviii. And be it further enacted by the authority aforesaid, That every cashier and clerk, before he enters into the duties of his office, shall give bond, with two or more sureties, in such sum as may be satisfactory to the directors, with condition for the faithful discharge of his duty.

xix. And be it further enacted by the authority aforesaid, That the said corporation shall not demand any greater interest on any loan or discount than at the rate of six per centum per annum.

xx. And be it further enacted by the authority aforesaid, That the directors, excepting the president, shall not be entitled to any emolument for their services, and that seven directors shall constitute a board for the transaction of business, of whom the president shall be one, except in the case of sickness or absence, in which case, the directors present may choose a chairman for the said meeting.

xxi. And be it further enacted by the authority aforesaid, That the said bank shall be established, and the buildings necessary for the accommodation thereof erected, purchased, or leased, and the business thereof at all times hereafter transacted, at such place at the seat of the government of this province as the directors, or the majority of them may appoint: Provided always, as soon as it may be deemed expedient, branches of the said bank, and offices of deposit and discount may be authorized by the said directors, or the majority of them, in any other part of the said province, under such rules and regulations as the said directors, or the major part of them, may think proper, not repugnant to the general rules of the said corporation.

xxii. And be it further enacted by the authority aforesaid, That if at any time after the passing of this act, the said president, directors and company should refuse, on demand being made at their banking house, or any branch or branches hereafter to be established, during the regular hours of doing business, to redeem in specie, or other lawful money of this province, their said bills, notes, or other evidences of debt, issued by the said company, the said president, directors and company shall, on pain of forfeiture of their charter, wholly discontinue and close their said banking operations, either by way of discount or otherwise, until such time as the president, directors and company shall resume the redemption of their bills, notes or other evidences of debt, in specie or other lawful money of this province.

xxiii. And be it further enacted by the authority aforesaid, That it shall and may be the duty of the president and cashier of the said bank for the time being, to make a return under oath to the provincial parliament, once in each year, if required either by the legislative council or house of assembly, which return shall contain a full and true account of the funds and property of the said bank, the amount of its capital stock subscribed and paid, the amount of debts due to and from the said bank in circulation, and the amount of specie in the said bank, at the time of making such return.

xxiv. And be it further enacted by the authority aforesaid, That this act be, and is hereby declared to be, a public act, and that the same may be construed as such in his Majesty's courts in this province.

xxv. And be it further enacted by the authority aforesaid, That this present act of incorporation shall in no wise be forfeited by any non-user, at any time before the first day of January one thousand eight hundred and twenty-two.

An Act to extend the Charter of the Bank of Upper Canada and to increase the Capital Stock thereof [6 Victoria, c. 27, October 12, 1842]

Whereas the President and Directors of the Bank of Upper Canada, have by their petition prayed that the duration and powers of the said Bank of Upper Canada, as a Corporation, be extended, and that the Capital Stock thereof be increased from Two hundred thousand pounds, to Five hundred thousand pounds, current money of this Province, and that the Act of the Parliament of the Province of Upper Canada, incorporating the said Company may be amended: and whereas it is expedient to grant the prayer of their petition; Be it therefore enacted . . . that William Proudfoot, Thomas Helliwell, James G. Chewett, William Gamble, Samuel P. Jarvis, Jesse Ketchum, Christopher Widmer, The Honorable John Simcoe Macaulay, Francis Boyd, Angus Bethune, John S. Baldwin, William Cayley, Walter O'Hara, Thomas W. Magrath and Charles Berczy all of the City of Toronto, in the Province, and such other persons as now are Shareholders of the Capital Stock of the Corporation, created and constituted by the Act of Incorporation of the said Bank, and their respective Heirs, Executors, Administrators and Assigns, shall continue to be and shall be a Body Corporate and Politic, in fact and in name, by and under the name, style and title of "The Bank of Upper Canada," and as such, shall during the continuance of this Act have all, each, and every the rights, powers and authorities in and by the said Act of the Legislature of the Province of Upper Canada, incorporating the same, conferred upon or vested in the said Corporation, and subject to the provisions, enactments, limitations and restrictions in the said Act of Incorporation contained: Provided always that so much of the said Act of Incorporation and the several Acts of the Parliament of Upper Canada amending the same, as may be inconsistent with or repugnant to the provisions of this Act, shall be and is hereby repealed and made wholly void; and the said Corporation shall, during the continuance of this Act, have succession and a common seal, with power to break, renew, change and alter the same at pleasure; and shall be capable of sueing and being sued, and of pleading and being impleaded, in all Courts of Law and Equity, and other places, in all manner of actions, causes and matters whatsoever; and for the convenient management of their business, but for no other purpose, shall and may purchase, acquire and hold real or immovable estates and property, not exceeding the yearly value of two thousand pounds, current money of this Province, and may sell, alienate and dispose of the same, and purchase, acquire and hold others in their stead, not exceeding in the whole the yearly value aforesaid.

II. And be it enacted, that it shall be lawful for the Stockholders of the said Bank of Upper Canada, to raise and contribute among themselves, or by the admission of new subscribers, a further sum of Three hundred thousand pounds, in addition to the present Capital Stock of the said Bank of Upper Canada, which said additional sum of Three hundred thousand pounds, currency, shall be divided into Twenty four thousand shares of twelve pounds ten shillings each, and every person subscribing for or taking any share or shares, in the said additional Capital Stock of Three hundred thousand pounds, shall have the same rights and be subject to the same rules and liabilities, as the original subscribers and shareholders of the said Bank of Upper Canada.

III. And be it enacted, that the Books of subscription for the Capital Stock, authorized to be added to the Capital Stock of the said Corporation, shall be opened . . . . Provided always, that no share or shares shall be held to be lawfully subscribed for unless a sum equal to ten pounds per centum, on the amount subscribed for, be actually paid at the time of subscribing: Provided also that all the said Capital Stock shall be paid in full within five years from and after the passing of this Act.

IV. And be it enacted, that if any Shareholder or Shareholders, shall refuse or neglect to pay any or either of the instalments upon his, her or their shares of the said Capital Stock, at the time or times required by public notice as aforesaid, such Shareholder or Shareholders, shall incur a forfeiture to the use of the said Corporation, of a sum of money equal to ten pounds per centum on the amount of such shares; and moreover it shall be lawful for the Directors of the said Corporation, (without any previous formality other than thirty days of public notice of their intention) to sell at public auction, the said shares or so many of the said shares as shall after deducting the reasonable expenses of the same, yield a sum of money sufficient to pay the unpaid instalments due on the remainder of the said shares and the amount of forfeitures incurred upon the whole; and the President or Vice-President or Cashier of the said Corporation, shall execute the transfer to the purchaser of the shares of stock so sold, and such transfer being accepted, shall be as valid and effectual in Law, as if the same had been executed by the original holder or holders of the shares of Stock thereby transferred: Provided always, that nothing in this section contained shall be held to debar the Directors or Shareholders, at a general meeting, from remitting either in whole or in part, and conditionally or unconditionally, any forfeiture incurred by the non-payment of instalments as aforesaid.

V. And be it enacted, that the chief place or seat of business of the said Corporation, shall be in the City of Toronto aforesaid, but it shall and may be lawful for the Directors of the Corporation, to open and establish in other Cities, Towns, and Places in this Province, branches or offices of discount and deposit of the said Corporation, ...

VI. And be it enacted, that for the management of the affairs of the said Corporation, there shall be Fifteen Directors who shall be annually elected by the Shareholders of the Capital Stock of the Corporation, at a general meeting of them to be held annually on the first Monday in June, beginning on the first Monday in June, in the year one thousand eight hundred and forty-three; at which meeting the Shareholders shall vote according to the rule or scale of votes hereinafter established; and the Directors elected by a majority of votes given in conformity to such rule or scale, shall be capable of serving as Directors for the ensuing twelve months; and at their first meeting after such election shall choose out of their number a President and a Vice President, who shall hold their offices respectively during the same period; and in case of a vacancy occurring in the said number of fifteen Directors, the remaining Directors shall fill the same by election from among the Shareholders, and the Director so elected shall be capable of serving as a Director, until the next annual general meeting of the Shareholders; and if the vacancy occurring in the said number of fifteen Directors shall also cause the vacancy of the office of President or of Vice President, the Directors at their first meeting after their number shall have been completed as aforesaid, shall fill the vacant office by choice or election from among themselves, and the Director shall fill the office to which he shall be so chosen or elected, until the next general annual meeting of the Shareholders: Provided always, that each of the Directors shall be the holder and proprietor in his own name of not less than twenty shares of the Capital Stock of the said Corporation, wholly paid up, and shall be a natural born or naturalized subject of Her Majesty, and provided also, that eight of the Directors in office at the period of each annual election, shall be re-elected for the next ensuing twelve months. . . . .

viii. And be it enacted that the Books, Correspondence and Accounts of the Corporation, shall at all times be subject to the inspection of the Directors, but no Shareholder not being a Director, shall inspect, or be allowed to inspect the account or accounts of any person or persons dealing with the Corporation.

ix. And be it enacted, that at all meetings of the Directors of the said Corporation, not less than five of them shall constitute a board or quorum for the transaction of business; and at the said meetings the President, or in his absence the Vice-President, or in their absence one of the Directors present, to be chosen *pro tempore*, shall preside; and the President, Vice-President or President *pro tempore*, so presiding, shall have a casting vote. . . .

xi. And be it enacted, that it shall and may be lawful for the Directors of the said Corporation from time to time, to make and enact Bye-laws, Rules and Regulations, (the same not being repugnant to this Act or to the Laws of this Province) for the proper management of the affairs of the said Corporation, and from time to time, to alter or repeal the same, and others to make and enact in their stead: Provided always, that the present Bye-Laws of the Corporation, in so far as they are not repugnant to this Act or to Law, shall continue to be the Bye-Laws of the Corporation, until repealed or amended in the manner provided by this Act.

xii. And be it enacted, that no Director of the said Corporation shall during the period of his service act as a private Banker, nor shall any Director other than the President, be entitled to any salary or emolument for his services as a Director, but the President may be compensated for his services as President, either by an annual vote of a sum of money by the Shareholders, at their annual general meetings, or by a fixed salary; and in the latter case, for the purpose of securing to the Corporation the undivided attention and services of the President, it shall be lawful for the Directors if they see fit, to choose and appoint annually from among themselves, a person duly qualified, who shall be the President of the Corporation, and to award to him such remuneration for his services as they in their judgement shall see fit; and nothing hereinbefore contained to the contrary notwithstanding. . . .

xiv. And be it enacted, that it shall be the duty of the Directors to make half yearly dividends of so much of the profits of the Corporation as to them shall appear advisable, and such dividends shall be payable at such place or places as the Directors shall appoint, and of which they shall give public notice thirty days previously: Provided always, that such dividends shall not in any manner lessen or impair the Capital Stock of the Corporation.

xv. And be it enacted, that a general meeting of the Shareholders of the Corporation shall be held in the City of Toronto, on the first Monday of the month of June, in every year during the continuance of this Act, for the purpose of electing Directors in the manner hereinbefore provided, and for all other general purposes touching the affairs and the management of the affairs of the Corporation; and at each of the said annual general meetings, the Directors shall submit a full and clear statement of the affairs of the Corporation, containing on the one part the amount of Capital Stock paid in, the amount of notes of the Bank in circulation, the net profits in hand, the balances due to other Banks and Institutions, and the Cash deposited in the Bank, distinguishing deposits bearing interest from those not bearing interest; and on the other part, the amount of current coins and gold, and silver bullion in the vaults of the Bank, the value of buildings and other real estate belonging to the Bank, the balances due to the Bank from other Banks and Institutions, and the amount of debts owing to the Bank, including and particularising the amounts so owing on Bills of Exchange, discounted notes, mortgages and *hypothèques*, and other securities; thus exhibiting on the one hand the liabilities of or debts due by the Bank, and on the other hand, the assets and resources thereof, and the said statement shall also exhibit the rate and amount of the then last dividend declared by the Directors, the amount of profits reserved at the time of declaring such dividend, and the amount of debts to the Bank overdue and not paid, with an estimate of the loss which may probably be incurred from the non payment of such debts.

xvi. And be it enacted, that the number of votes which the Shareholders of the said Corporation shall respectively be entitled to give at their meetings, shall be according to the following scale, that is to say, for one share and not more than two, one vote; for every two shares, above two and not exceeding ten, one vote, making five votes for ten shares; for every four shares above ten and not exceeding thirty, one vote, making ten votes for thirty shares; for every six shares above thirty and not exceeding sixty, one vote, making fifteen votes for sixty shares; and for every eight shares above sixty and not exceeding one hundred, one vote, making twenty votes for one hundred shares; and no Shareholder shall be entitled to give a greater number of votes than twenty; and it shall be lawful for absent Shareholders to give their votes by proxy, such proxy being also a Shareholder and not being either a Cashier or other Officer in the said Bank, and being provided with a written authority from his constituent or constituents, in such form as shall be established by a Bye-Law, and which authority shall be lodged in the Bank: Provided always, that a share or shares of the Capital Stock of the said Corporation, that shall have been held for a less period than three Calendar months immediately prior to any meeting of the Shareholders, shall not entitle the holder or holders to vote at such meeting, either in person or by proxy: provided also that where two or more persons are joint holders of shares, it shall be lawful that one only of such joint holders, or a majority of them, to represent the said shares and vote accordingly: and provided also and it is hereby enacted, that no Shareholder who shall not be a natural born or naturalized subject of Her Majesty, or who shall be a subject of any Foreign Prince or State, shall either in person or by proxy, vote at any meeting whatever of the Shareholders of the said Corporation, or shall assist in calling any meeting of the Shareholders, any thing in this Act to the contrary notwithstanding.

xvii. And be it enacted, that any number not less than twenty of the Shareholders of the said Corporation, who together shall be proprietors of at least two hundred and fifty shares of the paid up Capital Stock of the Corporation by themselves or proxies, or the Directors of the Corporation, or any seven of them, shall respectively have power at any time to call a Special General Meeting of the Shareholders of the Corporation, to be held at their usual place of meeting in the City of Toronto, upon giving six weeks previous public notice thereof, and specifying in such notice the object or objects of such meeting, ...

xviii. And be it enacted, that the shares of the Capital Stock of the said Corporation, shall be held and adjudged to be personal estate, and be transmissible accordingly, and shall be assignable and transferable at the Bank, according to the form of Schedule A, annexed to this Act, but no assignment or transfer shall be valid and effectual unless it be made and registered in a Book or Books to be kept by the Directors for that purpose; nor until the person or persons making the same shall previously discharge all debts actually due by him, her or them to the Corporation, which may exceed in amount the remaining Stock, (if any) belonging to such person or persons, ...

xix. And be it enacted, that the said Corporation hereby constituted shall not either directly or indirectly hold any lands or tenements, (save and except such as by the first section of this Act they are specially authorized to acquire and hold) or any ships or other vessels, or any share or shares of the Capital Stock of the Corporation, or of any Bank in this Province; nor shall the said Corporation either directly or indirectly, lend money or make advances upon the security, mortgage or hypothecation of any lands or tenements, or of any ships or other vessels, nor upon the security or pledge of any goods, wares or merchandize; nor shall the said Corporation either directly or indirectly, raise loans of money or deal in the buying, selling or bartering of goods, wares, or merchandize, or engage or be engaged in any trade whatever, except as dealers in gold and silver, bullion, bills of exchange, discounting of promissory notes and negotiable security, and in such Trade generally as appertains to the business of Banking: Provided always that the said Corporation, may take and hold mortgages and *hypothèques* on real estates and property in this Province, by way of additional security, for debts contracted to the Corporation in the course of their dealings.

xx. And be it enacted, that the aggregate amount of discounts and advances made by the said Corporation upon commercial paper or securities bearing the name of any Director or Officer, or the copartnership name or firm of any Director of the said Corporation, shall not at any one time, exceed one third of the total amount of discounts or advances made by the Corporation at the same time.

xxi. And be it enacted, that it shall and may be lawful for the said Corporation, to allow and pay interest (but not exceeding the legal rate of interest in this Province) upon moneys deposited in the Bank; and also it shall and may be lawful for the Corporation in discounting promissory notes or other negotiable securities, to receive or retain the discount thereon at the time of the discounting or negotiating the same; any law, or usage to the contrary notwithstanding. . . . .

xxiii. And be it enacted, that the notes or Bills of the said Corporation made payable to order or to bearer, and intended for general circulation, whether the same shall issue from the chief place or seat of business of the Corporation, in the City of Toronto, or from any of the Branches of the Corporation under the management of a local Board of Directors in other places in the Province, shall bear date at the place of issue and not elsewhere, and shall be payable on demand in specie at the same place of issue; and that each and every office of discount and deposit established or hereafter to be established under the management or direction of a local Board of Directors shall be considered and held to be a Branch Bank, and subject to the restriction as to the issuing and redemption of notes provided in this Act.

xxiv. And be it enacted, that a suspension by the said Corporation, (either at the chief place or seat of business in the said City of Toronto, or at any of their branches or offices of discount and deposit at other places in this Province,) of payment on demand in specie of the notes or bills of the said Corporation payable on demand, shall if the time of suspension extend to sixty days consecutively, or at intervals within any twelve consecutive months, operate as and be a forfeiture of the privileges conferred by this Act or by the Act of Incorporation aforesaid, and of all and every the privileges hereby or thereby granted.

xxv. And be it enacted, that the total amount of the notes or bills of the said Corporation, being for a less sum than one pound current money of Canada each, that shall be or may have been issued and put in circulation, shall not exceed at any one time one fifth of the amount of the Capital Stock of the Corporation then paid in: Provided always that no notes under the nominal value of five shillings, shall at any time be issued or put into circulation by the Corporation; nor shall any further limitation by the Legislature of the total amount of notes to be issued be held to be any infringement of the privileges hereby granted.

xxvi. And be it enacted, that the total amount of the debts which the said Corporation shall at any time owe, whether by bond, bill, note or otherwise shall not exceed three times the aggregate amount of the Capital Stock paid in and the deposits made in the Bank in specie, and Government securities for money; and at no one period after the passing of this Act, shall the notes or bills payable on demand and to bearer exceed the amount of the paid up Capital of the said Corporation, and in case of excess, the said

Corporation shall forfeit this Act of Incorporation, and all the privileges hereby granted, and the Directors under whose administration the excess shall happen, shall be liable jointly and severally for the same in their private capacities, as well to the Shareholders as to the holders of the bonds, bills and notes of the Corporation, and an action or actions in this behalf may be brought against them or any of them, and the heirs, executors, administrators, or curators of them or any of them, and be prosecuted to judgment and execution according to law, but such action or actions, shall not exempt the Corporation or their lands, tenements, goods or chattels, from being also liable for such excess: Provided always, that if any Director present at the time of contracting any such excess of debt, do forthwith, or if any Director absent at the time of the contracting any such excess of debt, do within twenty-four hours after he shall have obtained a knowledge thereof, enter on the minutes or register of proceedings of the Corporation, his protest against the same, and do within eight days thereafter publish such protest in at least two Newspapers published in the City of Toronto, such Director may thereby, and not otherwise, exonerate and discharge himself, his heirs, executors, and administrators or curators, from the liability aforesaid, any thing herein contained or any law to the contrary notwithstanding: and provided always, that such publication shall not exonerate any Director from his liability as a shareholder.

xxvii. And be it enacted, that besides the detailed statement of the affairs of the said Corporation hereinbefore required to be laid before the Shareholders thereof, at their annual general meetings, the Directors shall make up and publish on the first days of March and September, in every year, statements of the Assets and Liabilities of the Corporation, in the form of the Schedule B., hereunto annexed shewing under the heads specified in the said form the average of the amount of the notes of the Corporation in circulation, and other liabilities, at the termination of each Month, during the period to which the statement shall refer, and the average amount of specie and other Assets, that at the same times were available to meet the same: and it shall also be the duty of the Directors to submit to the Governor, Lieutenant Governor or person administering the Government of this Province a copy of such half-yearly statements, and if by him required to verify all or any part of the said statements, the said Directors shall verify the same by the production of the monthly or weekly balance sheets from which the said statements shall have been compiled: and furthermore the said Directors shall from time to time when required, furnish to the said Governor, Lieutenant Governor, or person administering the Government of this Province, such further information respecting the state and proceedings of the Corporation, and of the several branches and offices of discount and deposit thereof as such Governor, Lieutenant Governor, or person administering the Government of this Province may reasonably see fit to call for: Provided always, that the weekly or monthly balance sheets, and the further information that shall be so produced and given, shall be held by the said Governor, Lieutenant Governor, or person administering the Government of this Province, as being produced and given in strict confidence that he shall not divulge any part of the contents of the said weekly or monthly balance sheets, or of the information that shall be so given; and provided also, that the Directors shall not, nor shall any thing herein contained be construed to authorize them or any of them, to make known the private account or accounts of any person or persons whatever having dealings with the Corporation.

xxviii. And be it enacted, that in the event of the property and assets of the said Corporation becoming insufficient to liquidate the liabilities and engagements or debts thereof, the Shareholders of the Corporation, in their private or natural capacities, shall be liable and responsible for the deficiency, but to no greater extent than to double the amount of the paid up Capital Stock, that is to say, that the liability and responsibility of each Shareholder shall be limited to the amount of his or her share or shares of the said paid up Capital Stock, and a sum of money equal in amounts thereto: Provided always, that nothing in this section contained shall be construed to alter or diminish the additional liabilities of the Directors of the Corporation hereinbefore mentioned and declared.

xxix. And be it enacted, that it shall not be lawful for the said Corporation, at any time whatever, directly or indirectly, to advance or lend to or for the use of or on account of any Foreign Prince, Power or State, any sum or sums of money or any securities for money: and if such unlawful advance or loan be made, then and from thenceforth, the said Corporation shall be dissolved, and all the powers, authorities, rights, privileges and advantages, hereby granted, shall cease and determine, any thing in this Act to the contrary notwithstanding. . . .

xxxviii. And be it enacted, that this Act shall be and remain in force until the first day of June, which will be in the Year of Our Lord, one thousand eight hundred and sixty-two, and from that time until the end of the then next Session of the Parliament of this Province, and no longer.

An Act to Amend and Consolidate the Acts Forming the Charter of the Bank of Upper Canada [19–20 Victoria, c. 121]

Whereas the Corporation called and known as "The Bank of Upper Canada," was created and constituted by and under the Act of the Legislature of Upper Canada passed in the fifty-ninth year of the Reign of King George the Third, and intituled, *An Act to incorporate sundry persons under the style and title of The President, Directors and Company of the Bank of Upper Canada* [59 G. 3, c. 24.], which said Act was amended by the Act of the said Legislature passed in the second year of the Reign of King George the Fourth, and chaptered seven [2 G. 4, c. 7.], and by the Act thereof passed in the second year of the Reign of His late Majesty King William the Fourth, and chaptered ten [2 W. 4, c. 10.]; And whereas the said Acts were again amended by the Act of the Legislature of this Province passed in the session thereof held in the fourth and fifth years of Her Majesty's Reign, and chaptered ninety-five (4 & 5 V. c. 95], and the charter and privileges of the said Corporation were confirmed and extended by the Act of the said Legislature passed in the sixth year of Her Majesty's Reign, and intituled, *An Act to extend the charter of the Bank of Upper Canada, and to increase the Capital Stock thereof* [6 V. c. 27.], which said Act hath since been amended and the privileges of the said Corporation have been further extended by the Act of the said Legislature passed in the ninth year of Her Majesty's Reign, and chaptered eighty-six [9 V. c. 86.], and by that of the said Legislature passed in the session held in the thirteenth and fourteenth years of Her Majesty's Reign, chaptered one hundred and thirty-seven [13 & 14 V. c. 137.], and the said Acts were further amended and an increase of the Capital Stock of the said Corporation was authorized by the Act of the said Legislature passed in the eighteenth year of Her Majesty's Reign, chaptered thirty-nine [18 V. c. 39.]. And whereas the said Corporation hath by its Petition prayed that the provisions of the said several Acts may be consolidated with certain amendments and extensions of the powers and privileges thereby conferred, and it is expedient to grant the prayer of the said Petition: Therefore, Her Majesty, by and with the advice and consent of the Legislative Council and Assembly of Canada, enacts as follows:

i. So much of the Acts hereinbefore cited, or any of them, as may be inconsistent with or repugnant to the provisions of this Act, or as makes any provision in any matter provided for by this Act, other than such as is hereby made, shall be and is hereby repealed.

ii. The said corporation of the Bank of Upper Canada shall, during the time this Act shall remain in force, continue to have all each and every of the rights, powers and authority in and by the Acts hereinbefore cited, or any of them, conferred upon or vested in it, subject always to the provisions of this Act; and shall continue to have perpetual succession and a common seal, with power to break, renew, change and alter the same at pleasure; and shall be capable of suing and being sued, pleading and being impleaded in all Courts of law and equity, and other places, in all manner of actions, causes and matters whatsoever; and for the convenient management of its business, but for no other purpose, shall and may purchase, acquire and hold real or immoveable estates and property, not exceeding the yearly value of five thousand pounds currency, and may sell, alienate and dispose of the same, and purchase, acquire and hold others in their stead, not exceeding in the whole the yearly value aforesaid.

III. The Capital Stock of the said Bank, (the words "the said Bank" meaning throughout this Act the Corporation aforesaid), shall be one million of pounds currency, divided into shares of twelve pounds ten shillings currency, or fifty dollars each; and so many of the said shares as may be unsubscribed for when this Act shall come into force, may be subscribed for either within or out of this Province, in such proportions or numbers and at such times and places, and under such regulations, and at such rate of premium, to be paid by the subscribers over and above the amount of the shares, as the Directors of the said Bank shall from time to time establish; and the shares so subscribed for shall be paid in such instalments, and at such times and places as the said Directors shall from time to time appoint, and executors, administrators and curators paying instalments upon shares of deceased shareholders, shall be and are hereby respectively indemnified for paying and are required to pay the same: Provided always, that no share shall be held to be lawfully subscribed for, unless the premium (if any) which shall have been fixed by the Directors, and at least ten per centum on the amount of such share be paid at the time of subscribing: And provided also, that no part of the Capital Stock unsubscribed for at the time when this Act shall come into force, shall be subscribed for after the end of six years from that time; and the whole of the stock subscribed for shall be called in before the thirty-first day of December, one thousand eight hundred and sixty-one: And provided further, that it shall not be obligatory upon the said Bank to raise the full amount of the Capital Stock hereby allowed, but the number of shares to be thereafter subscribed for, may at any time be limited by a By-law of the said Bank, in such manner as the shareholders shall deem most advantageous for the interests of the Bank.

IV. If any person or party, subscribing for shares of the Capital Stock of the said Bank, shall also be willing to pay up at the time of subscribing the full amount of the shares subscribed for, together with such premium thereon as aforesaid, it shall and may be lawful for the Directors of the Bank, and at any time within the period hereinbefore limited for subscribing for such Stock, to admit and receive such subscriptions and full payment, or payment of any number of instalments, together with such premium; and in every case, the premium so received on any Stock subscribed for, shall be carried to the account of the ordinary profits of the said Bank.

V. If any Shareholder or Shareholders shall refuse or neglect to pay any instalment upon his, her or their shares of the said Capital Stock, at the time or times required by the Directors as aforesaid, such Shareholder or Shareholders shall incur a forfeiture to the use of the said Bank, of a sum of money equal to ten pounds per centum on the amount of such shares; and moreover, it shall be lawful for the Directors of the said Bank (without any previous formality other than thirty days' public notice of their intention) to sell at public auction the said shares, or so many of the said shares as shall, after deducting the reasonable expenses of the sale, yield a sum of money sufficient to pay the unpaid instalments due on the remainder of the said shares and the amount of forfeitures incurred upon the whole; and the President, with the Vice-President or the Cashier of the said Bank, shall execute the transfer to the purchaser of the shares of Stock so sold, and such transfer being accepted, shall be as valid and effectual in law as if the same had been executed by the original holder or holders of the shares of Stock thereby transferred: Provided always, that nothing in this section contained shall be held to debar the Directors or shareholders, at a general meeting, from remitting either in whole or in part, and conditionally or unconditionally, any forfeiture incurred by the non-payment of any instalment as aforesaid.

VI. The chief place or seat of business of the said Bank, shall be in the City of Toronto, but it shall and may be lawful for the Directors of the Bank, to open and establish in other Cities, Towns and Places in this Province, Branches or Agencies or offices of discount and deposit of the said Bank, under such rules and regulations for the good and faithful management of the same, as to the said Directors shall from time to time seem meet, not being repugnant to any law of this Province, to this Act, or to the By-laws of the said Bank.

VII. For the management of the affairs of the said Bank, there shall continue to be Ten Directors annually elected by the Shareholders of the Capital Stock thereof, at a general meeting of them to be held annually on the twenty-fifth day of June in each year, (except when that day shall be a Sunday or legal holiday, and then on the next day which shall not be a Sunday or legal holiday,) beginning in the month of June, in the year of our Lord one thousand eight hundred and fifty-seven; at which meeting the Shareholders shall vote according to the rule or scale of votes hereinafter established; and the Directors elected by a majority of votes given in conformity to such rule or scale, shall be capable of serving as Directors for the ensuing twelve months; and at their first meeting after such election the Directors shall choose out of their number a President and a Vice-President, who shall hold their offices respectively during the same period: and in case of a vacancy occurring in the said number of ten Directors, the remaining Directors shall fill the same by election from among the Shareholders, and each Director so elected shall be capable of serving as a Director, until the next annual general meeting of the Shareholders; and if the vacancy occurring in the said number of ten Directors shall also cause the vacancy of the office of President or of Vice-President, the Directors at their first meeting after their number shall have been completed as aforesaid, shall fill the vacant office by choice or election from among themselves, and the Director so chosen or elected to be President or Vice-President shall fill the office to which he shall be so chosen or elected, until the next general annual meeting of the Shareholders: Provided always, that each of the Directors shall be the holder and proprietor in his own name of not less than ten shares of Capital Stock of the said Bank, wholly paid up, and shall be a natural born or naturalized subject of Her Majesty: And provided also, that it shall be lawful for the Stockholders at any annual general meeting, to pass a By-law directing that five of the Directors in office at the period of each annual election, shall be re-elected for the next ensuing twelve months.

VIII. If at any time it shall happen that an election of Directors shall not be made or take effect on the day fixed by this Act, the said Corporation shall not be deemed or taken to be thereby dissolved, but it shall be lawful at any subsequent time to make such election, at a general meeting of the Shareholders to be called for that purpose, and the Directors in office, when such failure of election shall take place, shall remain in office until such election shall be made.

IX. The Books, Correspondence and Funds of the said Bank, shall at all times be subject to the inspection of the Directors, but no Shareholder not being a Director, shall inspect, or be allowed to inspect, the account or accounts of any person or persons dealing with the said Bank.

X. At all meetings of the Directors of the said Bank, not less than five of them shall constitute a board or quorum for the transaction of business; and at the said meetings the President or in his absence the Vice-President, or in their absence one of the Directors present, to be chosen *pro tempore*, shall preside; and the President, Vice-President or President *pro tempore*, so presiding, shall vote as a Director, and if there be an equal division on any question, shall also have a casting vote.

XI. The Shareholders of the said Bank, who at the time this Act shall come into force shall be Directors thereof, shall be and continue to be Directors thereof until the first election of Directors under this Act, and shall then go out of office; and the said Directors shall, until the first election under this Act, have in all respects the rights, duties and powers assigned to the Directors of the said Bank by this Act, and be governed by its provisions as if elected under it.

XII. It shall and may be lawful for the Directors of the said Bank from time to time to make and enact By-laws, Rules and Regulations, (the same not being repugnant to this Act or to the Laws of this Province) for the proper management of the affairs of the said Corporation, and, from time to time, to alter or repeal the same, and others to make and enact in their stead; Provided always, that no By-law, Rule or Regulation so made by the Directors, shall have force or effect until the same shall, after six weeks' public notice, have been confirmed by the Shareholders at an annual general meeting or at a special general meeting called for that purpose; And provided also, that the By-laws of the said Bank in force at the time when this Act shall come into force, in so far as they are not repugnant to this Act, or to Law, shall continue to be the By-laws thereof until others shall have been made and enacted and confirmed as provided for by this section.

xiii. The Shareholders may by a By-law appropriate a sum of money for the remuneration of the services of the President and Directors as such, and the President and Directors may annually apportion the same among themselves as they may think fit: No Director shall act as a Private Banker.

xiv. The Directors of the said Bank, shall have power to appoint a Cashier, Assistant Cashier and Secretary, and Clerks and Servants under them, and such other Officers as shall be necessary for conducting the business of the Bank, and to allow reasonable compensation for their services respectively, and shall also be capable of exercising such powers and authority, for the well governing and ordering of the affairs of the Corporation, as shall be prescribed by the By-laws thereof; Provided always, that before permitting any Cashier, Assistant Cashier, Officer, Clerk or Servant of the Bank, to enter upon the duties of his office, the Directors shall require him to give bond, with sureties, to the satisfaction of the Directors, that is to say, every Cashier in a sum not less than five thousand pounds currency, and every other Officer, Clerk or Servant, in such sum of money as the Directors shall consider adequate to the trust to be reposed in him, with condition for good and faithful behaviour.

xv. It shall be the duty of the Directors to make half yearly dividends of so much of the profits of the said Bank as to them shall appear advisable, and such dividends shall be payable at such place or places as the Directors shall appoint, and of which they shall give public notice thirty days previously: Provided always, that such dividends shall not in any manner lessen or impair the Capital Stock of the said Bank.

xvi. The general meetings of the Shareholders of the said Bank to be held annually as aforesaid in the City of Toronto, for the purpose of electing Directors in the manner hereinbefore provided, shall be general meetings also for all other general purposes touching the affairs and the management of the affairs of the said Bank; and at each of the said annual general meetings, the Directors shall exhibit a full and clear statement of the affairs of said Bank.

xvii. The number of votes which the Shareholders of the said Bank shall respectively be entitled to give at their meetings, shall be according to the following scale, that is to say: for one share and not more than two, one vote, making five votes for ten shares; for every four shares above ten and not exceeding thirty, one vote, making ten votes for every thirty shares; for every six shares above thirty and not exceeding sixty, one vote, making fifteen votes for sixty shares; and for every eight shares above sixty and not exceeding one hundred, one vote, making twenty votes for one hundred shares; and no Shareholder shall be entitled to give a greater number of votes than twenty; and it shall be lawful for absent Shareholders to give their votes by proxy, such proxy being also a Shareholder, and being provided with a written authority from his constituent or constituents, in such form as shall be established by a By-law, and which authority shall be lodged in the Bank: Provided always, that a share or shares of the Capital Stock of the said Bank which shall have been held for a less period than three calendar months immediately prior to any meeting of the Shareholders, shall not entitle the holder or holders to vote at such meeting, either in person or by proxy: Provided also, that where two or more persons are joint holders of shares, it shall be lawful that one only of such joint holders be empowered by Letter of Attorney from the other joint holder or holders, or a majority of them, to represent the said shares and vote accordingly: And provided also that no Shareholder who shall not be a natural-born or naturalized subject of Her Majesty, or who shall be a subject or citizen of any Foreign Prince or State, shall either in person or by proxy, vote at any meeting whatever of the Shareholders of the said Bank, or shall assist in calling any meeting of the Shareholders; any thing in this Act to the contrary notwithstanding.

xvIII. No Cashier, Assistant Cashier, Bank Clerk or other Officer of the Bank, shall vote either in person or by proxy at any meeting for the election of Directors, or hold a proxy for that purpose.

xIx. Any number not less than twenty of the Shareholders of the said Bank, who together shall be proprietors of at least one thousand shares of the paid up Capital Stock of the said Bank, by themselves or their proxies, or the Directors of the said Bank or any seven of them, shall respectively have power at any time to call a Special General Meeting of the Shareholders of the said Bank, to be held at their usual place of meeting in the City of Toronto, upon giving six weeks' previous public notice thereof, and specifying in such notice the object or objects of such meeting; and if the object of any such Special General Meeting be to consider of the proposed removal of the President or Vice-President, or of a Director or Directors of the Corporation, for mal-administration, or other specified and apparently just cause, then and in any such case the person or persons whom it shall be so proposed to remove, shall from the day on which the notice shall be first published, be suspended from the duties of his or their office or offices; and if it be the President or Vice-President whose removal shall be proposed as aforesaid, his office shall be filled up by the remaining Directors (in the manner hereinbefore provided in the case of a vacancy occurring in the office of President or Vice-President,) who shall choose or elect a Director to serve as such President or Vice-President, during the time such suspension shall continue or be undecided upon.

xx. The shares of the Capital Stock of the said Bank, shall be held and adjudged to be personal estate, and shall be transmissible accordingly, and shall be assignable and transferable at the chief place of business of the said Bank, or at any of its Branches which the Directors shall appoint for that purpose, and according to such form as the Directors shall from time to time prescribe; but no assignment or transfer shall be valid and effectual unless it be made and registered in a Book or Books to be kept by the Directors for that purpose, nor until the person or persons making the same shall previously discharge all debts actually due by him, her or them to the Bank, which may exceed in amount the remaining Stock, (if any) belonging to such person or persons; and no fractional part or parts of a share, or other than a whole share, shall be assignable or transferable; and when any share or shares of the said Capital Stock shall have been sold under a writ of execution, the Sheriff by whom the writ shall have been executed, shall within thirty days after the sale, leave with the Cashier of the Bank, an attested copy of the writ with the certificate of such Sheriff indorsed thereon, certifying to whom the sale has been made, and thereupon (but not until after all debts due by the original holder or holders of the said shares to the Bank, shall have been discharged as aforesaid) the President, or Vice-President, or Cashier of the Corporation, shall execute the transfer of the share or shares so sold to the purchaser, and such transfer being duly accepted, shall be to all intents and purposes as valid and effectual in Law as if it had been executed by the original holder or holders of the said share or shares; any law or usage to the contrary notwithstanding.

xxI. Shares in the Capital Stock of the said Bank may be made transferable, and the dividends accruing thereon may be made payable in the United Kingdom, in like manner as such shares and dividends are respectively transferable and payable at the Chief office of the said Bank in the City of Toronto; and to that end, the Directors may, from time to time, make such rules and regulations, and prescribe such forms, and appoint such agent or agents, as they may deem necessary; Provided always, that at no time shall more than one half of the whole Capital Stock be registered in the book to be kept for that purpose in the United Kingdom.

xxII. If the interest in any share in the said Bank become transmitted in consequence of the death, or bankruptcy, or insolvency of any Shareholder, or in consequence of the marriage of a Female Shareholder, or by any other lawful means than by a transfer according to the provisions of this Act, such transmission shall be authenticated by a declaration in writing as hereinafter mentioned, or in such other manner as the Directors of the Bank shall require; and every such declaration shall distinctly state the manner in which and the party to whom such share shall have been so transmitted, and shall be, by such party made and signed; and every such declaration shall be, by the party making and signing the same, acknowledged before a Judge or Justice of a Court of Record, or before the Mayor, Provost, or Chief Magistrate of a City, Town, Borough, or other place, or before a Public Notary, where the same shall be made and signed; and every such declaration, so signed and acknowledged, shall be left with the Cashier, or other officer or agent of the Bank, who shall thereupon enter the name of the party entitled under such transmission, in the Register of Shareholders; and until such transmission shall have been so authenticated, no party or person claiming by virtue of any such transmission shall be entitled to receive any share of the profits of the bank, nor to vote in respect of any such share, as the holder thereof; Provided always, that every such declaration and instrument as by this and the following section of this Act is required to perfect the transmission of a share of the Bank, which shall be made in any other Country than in this or some other of the British Colonies in North America, or in the United Kingdom of Great Britain and Ireland, shall be further authenticated by the British Consul or Vice-Consul, or other the accredited representative of the British Government in the Country where the declaration shall be made, or shall be made directly before such British Consul or Vice-Consul, or other accredited representative: And provided also, that nothing in this Act contained shall be held to debar the Directors, Cashier, or other officer or agent of the Bank from requiring corroborative evidence of any fact or facts alleged in such declaration.

xxiii. If the transmission of any Share of the Bank be by virtue of the marriage of a Female Shareholder, the declaration shall contain a copy of the Register of such marriage, or other particulars of the celebration thereof, and shall declare the identity of the wife with the holder of such share; and if the transmission have taken place by virtue of any testamentary instrument or by intestacy, the Probate of the Will, or the Letters of Administration, or Act of Curatorship, or an official extract therefrom, shall, together with such declaration, be produced and left with the Cashier, or other Officer or Agent of the Bank, who shall thereupon enter the name of the party entitled under such transmission, in the Register of Shareholders.

xxiv. If the transmission of any share or shares in the Capital Stock of the said Bank be by decease of any Shareholder, the production to the Directors, and deposit with them, of any probate of the will of the deceased Shareholder, or of letters of administration in his estate, granted by any Court in this Province having power to grant such probate or letters of administration, or by prerogative, diocesan or peculiar Court or authority in England, Wales, Ireland, India or any other British Colony, – or of any testament-testamentary or testament-dative expede in Scotland, – or if the deceased Shareholder shall have died out of Her Majesty's dominions, the production to and deposit with the Directors of any probate of his will or letters of administration of his property or other document of like import, granted by any Court or authority having the requisite power in such matters, – shall be sufficient justification and authority to the Directors for paying any dividend or transferring or authorizing the transfer of any share in pursuance of and in conformity to such probate, letters of administration or other such document as aforesaid.

xxv. The said Bank shall not be bound to see the execution of any trust, whether express, implied or constructive, to which any of the shares of its Stock may be subject; and the receipt of the party in whose name any such share shall stand in the Books of the Bank, or if it stand in the name of more parties than one, the receipt of one of the parties shall, from time to time, be a sufficient discharge to the Bank for any dividend or other sum of money, payable in respect of such share, notwithstanding any trust to which such share may then be subject, and whether or not the Bank have had notice of such trust and the Bank shall not be bound to see to the application of the money paid upon such receipt; any law or usage to the contrary notwithstanding.

xxvi. It shall be the duty of the Directors of the said Bank to invest, as speedily as the debentures hereinafter mentioned can be procured from the Receiver General, and to keep invested at all times, in the debentures of this Province payable within the same, or secured upon the Consolidated Municipal Loan Fund, one-tenth part of the whole paid up Capital of the said Bank, and to make a Return of the numbers and amount of such debentures, verified by the oaths and signatures of the President and Chief Cashier or Manager of the said Bank, to the Inspector General, in the month of January in each year, under the penalty of the forfeiture of the Charter of the said Bank in default of such investment and return: Provided always, that said Bank shall not be bound to invest any portion of its Capital in debentures under the provisions of this section unless it shall have availed itself of the power to increase its Capital Stock to an amount exceeding five hundred thousand pounds, under this Act or the said Act passed in the Eighteenth year of Her Majesty's Reign, and chaptered thirty-nine.

xxvii. The said Bank shall not either directly or indirectly hold any lands or tenements, (save and except such as by the third [sic-second] section of this Act it is specially authorized to acquire and hold) or any ships or other vessels, or any share or shares of the Capital Stock of the said Bank, or of any other Bank in this province; nor shall the said Bank either directly or indirectly, lend money or make advances upon the security, mortgage or hypothecation (hypothèque) of any lands or tenements, or of any ships or other vessels, nor upon the security or pledge of any share or shares of the Capital Stock of the said Bank, or of any goods, wares or merchandize; nor shall the said Bank either directly or indirectly, raise loans of money or deal in the buying, selling or bartering of goods, wares or merchandize, or engage or be engaged in any trade whatever, except as a dealer in gold and silver bullion, bills of exchange, discounting of promissory notes and negotiable securities, and in such trade generally as legitimately appertains to the business of Banking; Provided always, that the said Bank may take and hold mortgages and hypothèques on real estate, ships, vessels and other personal property in this Province, by way of additional security for debts contracted to the Bank in the course of its dealings, and may also for such purpose purchase and take any outstanding mortgages, judgments or other shares upon the real or personal property of any debtor of the said Bank.

xxviii. The aggregate amount of discounts and advances made by the said Bank upon commercial paper or securities bearing the name of any Director of the said Bank, or the name of any copartnership or firm in which any Director of the said Bank shall be a partner, shall not at any one time, exceed one-twentieth of the total amount of discounts or advances made by the Bank at the same time.

xxix. The Bank may allow and pay interest not exceeding the legal rate in this Province, upon moneys deposited in the Bank, and in discounting promissory notes, bills, or other negotiable securities or paper, may receive or retain the discount thereon at the time of discounting or negotiating the same; and when notes, bills, or other negotiable securities or paper, are bonâ fide payable at a place within the Province different from that at which they are discounted, the Bank may also in addition to the discount receive or retain an amount not exceeding one half per centum on the amount of every such note, bill or other negotiable security or paper, to defray the expenses of agency and exchange attending the collection of every such note, bill, or other negotiable security or paper; And the Bank may charge any note or bill held by and payable at the Bank, against the deposit account of the maker of such note or acceptor of such bill, at the maturity thereof; any law, statute or usage to the contrary notwithstanding.

xxx. The bonds, obligations and bills obligatory or of credit of the said Bank, under its common seal and signed by the President or Vice-President, and countersigned by a Cashier (or Assistant Cashier) thereof, which shall be made payable to any person or persons, shall be assignable by indorsement thereon under the hand or hands of such person or persons, and of his, her or their assignee or assignees, and so as absolutely to transfer and vest the property thereof in the several assignments successively, and to enable such assignee or assignees to bring and maintain an action or actions thereon in his, her or their own name or names; and signification of any assignment by indorsement shall not be necessary, any law or usage to the contrary notwithstanding; and bills or notes of the said Bank, signed by the President, Vice-President, Cashier or other officer appointed by the Directors of the said Bank to sign the same, promising the payment of money to any person or persons, his or their order or to the bearer, though not under the corporate seal of the said Bank, shall be binding and obligatory upon it, in the like manner and with the like force and effort as they would be upon any private person if issued by him in his private or natural capacity, and shall be assignable in like manner as if they were so issued by a private person in his natural capacity; Provided always that nothing in this Act shall be held to debar the Directors of the said Bank from authorizing or deputing from time to time, any Cashier, Assistant Cashier or Officer of the Bank, or any Director other than the President or Vice-President, or any Cashier, Manager or local Director of any branch or office of discount and deposit of the said Bank, to sign the bills or notes of the Corporation intended for general circulation and payable to order or to bearer on demand.

xxxi. And whereas it may be deemed expedient, that the name or names of the person or persons intrusted and authorized by the Bank to sign bank-notes and bills on behalf of the Bank, should be impressed by machinery, in such form as may from time to time be adopted by the Bank, instead of being subscribed in the hand-writing of such person or persons respectively: And whereas doubts might arise respecting the validity of such notes: Be it therefore further declared and enacted, That all bank-notes and bills of the Bank of Upper Canada, whereon the name or names of any person or persons intrusted or authorized to sign such notes or bills on behalf of the Bank, shall or may become impressed by machinery provided for that purpose by or with the authority of the Bank, shall be and be taken to be good and valid, to all intents and purposes as if such notes and bills had been subscribed in the proper handwriting of the person or persons intrusted and authorized by the Bank to sign the same respectively, and shall be deemed and taken to be bank-notes or bills within the meaning of all laws and statutes whatever; and shall and may be described as bank-notes or bills, in all indictments and other criminal proceedings whatsoever; any law, statute or usage to the contrary notwithstanding.

xxxii. The notes or bills of the said Bank made payable to order or to bearer and intended for general circulation, whether the same shall issue from the chief seat or place of business of the said Bank in the City of Toronto, or from any of its branches, shall be payable on demand in specie at the place where they bear date.

xxxiii. A suspension by the said Bank, either at its chief place or seat of business in the said City of Toronto, or at any of its branches or offices of discount and deposit at any other place in this Province, of payment on demand in specie of the notes or bills of the said Bank payable there on demand, shall, if the time of suspension extend to sixty days, consecutively or at intervals within any twelve consecutive months, operate as and be a forfeiture of its charter, and of all and every privileges granted to it by this or any other Act.

xxxiv. The total amount of the bank-notes and bills of the Bank, of all values, in circulation at any one time, shall never exceed the aggregate amount of the paid up capital stock of the Bank, and the gold and silver coin and bullion, and debentures or other securities, reckoned at par, issued or guaranteed by the Government under the authority of the Legislature of this Province, on hand; and of the bank-notes and bills in circulation at any one time, not more than one-fifth of the said aggregate amount shall be in bank-notes or bills under the nominal value of one pound currency each; but no bank-note or bill of the Bank, under the nominal value of five shillings, shall be issued or put in circulation.

xxxv. The total amount of the debts which the said Bank shall at one time owe, whether by bond, bill, note or otherwise, shall not exceed three times the aggregate amount of its Capital Stock paid in, and the deposits made in the Bank in specie and Government securities for money; and in case of excess or in case the total amount of the bills or notes of the said Bank payable to order or to bearer on demand and intended for general circulation shall at any time exceed the amount hereinbefore limited, the said Bank shall forfeit its charter and all the privileges granted to it by this or any other

Act and the Directors under whose administration the excess shall happen, shall be liable jointly and severally for the same in their private capacity, as well to the Shareholders as to the holders of the bonds, bills and notes of the said Bank, and an action or actions in this behalf may be brought against them or any of them, and the heirs, executors, administrators, or curators of them or any of them, and be prosecuted to judgment and execution according to law, but such action or actions shall not exempt the said Bank or its lands, tenements, goods or chattels, from being also liable for such excess: Provided always, that if any Director present at the time of contracting any such excess of debt, do forthwith, or if any Director absent at the time of contracting any such excess of debt, do within twenty-four hours after he shall have obtained a knowledge thereof, enter on the minutes or register of the Bank, his protest against the same, and do within eight days thereafter publish such protest in at least two Newspapers published in the City of Toronto such Director may thereby, and not otherwise, exonerate and discharge himself, his heirs, executors, and administrators or curators, from the liability aforesaid, any thing herein contained or any law to the contrary notwithstanding: Provided always that such publication shall not exonerate any Director from his liability as a shareholder.

xxxvi. In the event of the property and assets of the said Bank becoming insufficient to liquidate the liabilities and engagements or debts thereof, the Shareholders of its stock, in their private or natural capacities, shall be liable and responsible for the deficiency, but to no greater extent than to double the amount of their respective shares, that is to say, the liability and responsibility of each Shareholder to the creditors of the said Bank, shall be limited to a sum of money equal in amount to his stock therein, over and above any instalment or instalments which may be unpaid on such stock, for which he shall also remain liable and shall pay up: Provided always that nothing in this section contained shall be construed to alter or diminish the additional liabilities of the Directors of the said Bank hereinbefore mentioned and declared.

xxxvii. Besides the detailed statement of the affairs of the said Bank hereinbefore required to be laid before the Shareholders thereof, at their annual general meeting, the Directors shall make up and publish on the first Monday in each and every month, statements of the Assets and Liabilities of the said Bank, in the form of the Schedule A, hereunto annexed, showing under the heads specified in the said form, the average amount of the notes of the said Bank in circulation, and other liabilities, at the termination of the month to which the statement shall refer, and the average amount of specie and other Assets, that at the same times were available to meet the same: and it shall be the duty of the Directors to submit to the Governor of this Province, if required, a copy of such monthly statements, and, if by him required to verify all or any part of the said statements, the said Directors shall verify the same by the production of the weekly or monthly balance-sheets from which the said statements shall have been compiled: and furthermore, the said Directors shall from time to time when required, furnish to the said Governor of this Province, such further reasonable information respecting the state and proceedings of the said Bank, and of the several branches and offices of discount and deposit thereof, as such Governor of this Province, may reasonably see fit to call for: Provided always that the weekly or monthly balance-sheets, and the further information that shall be so produced and given, shall be held by the said Governor of this Province, as being produced and given in strict confidence that he shall not divulge any part of the contents of the said weekly or monthly balance-sheets, or of the information that shall be so given; And provided also, that the Directors shall not, nor shall any thing herein contained be construed to authorize them or any of them, to make known the private account or accounts of any person or persons whatever having dealings with the said Bank.

xxxviii. It shall not be lawful for the said Bank, at any time whatever, directly or indirectly, to advance or lend to or for the use of or on account of any Foreign Prince, Power or State, any sum or sums of money or any securities for money: and if such unlawful advance or loan be made, then and from thenceforth, the said Corporation shall be dissolved, and all the powers, authorities, rights, privileges and advantages granted to it by this or any other Act, shall cease and determine.

xxxix. The several public notices of this Act required to be given, shall be given by advertisement, in one or more of the Newspapers published in the City of Toronto, and in the *Canada Gazette*, or such other Gazette as shall be generally known and accredited as the Official Gazette for the publication of official documents and notices emanating from the Civil Government of this Province, if any such Gazette be then published.

xl. If any Cashier, Assistant Cashier, Manager, Clerk or Servant of the said Bank, shall secrete, embezzle or abscond with, any Bond, Obligation, Bill Obligatory or of Credit, or other Bill or Note, or any Security for money, or any moneys or effects, intrusted to him as such Cashier, Assistant Cashier, Manager, Clerk or Servant, whether the same belong to the said Bank, or belonging to any other person or persons, body or bodies politic or corporate, or institution or institutions, be lodged and deposited with the said Bank, the Cashier, Assistant Cashier, Manager, Clerk or Servant, so offending, and being thereof convicted in due form of Law, shall be deemed guilty of felony.

xli. Every person convicted of felony under this Act shall be punished by imprisonment at hard labor, in the Provincial Penitentiary, for any term not less than two years, or by imprisonment in any other Gaol or place of confinement for any less term than two years, in the discretion of the Court before which he shall be convicted.

xlii. It shall and may be lawful to and for any Justice of the Peace, on complaint made before him, upon the oath of one credible person, that there is just cause to suspect that any one or more person or persons is or are or hath, or have been concerned in making or counterfeiting any false bills of exchange, promissory notes, undertakings or orders of the said Bank, or hath in his possession any plates, presses or other instruments, tools or materials for making or counterfeiting the same or any part thereof, by warrant under the hand of such Justice, to cause the dwelling house, room, workshop, or outhouse or other building, yard, garden or other place, belonging to such suspected person or persons, or where any such person or persons shall be suspected of carrying on any such making or counterfeiting, to be searched; and if any such false bills of exchange, promissory notes, undertakings or orders, or any plates, presses or other tools, instruments or materials, shall be found in the custody or possession of any person or persons whomsoever, not having the same by some lawful authority, it shall and may be lawful to and for any person or persons whomsoever discovering the same to seize such false or counterfeit bills of exchange, promissory notes, undertakings or orders, and such plates, presses, or other tools, instruments or materials, and to carry the same forthwith before a Justice of the Peace of the County or District, (or if more convenient, of the adjoining County or District) in which the same shall be seized, who shall cause the same to be secured and produced in evidence against any person or persons who shall or may be prosecuted for any of the offences aforesaid, in some Court of Justice proper for the determination thereof, and the same, after being so produced in evidence, shall by order of the Court be defaced or destroyed, or otherwise disposed of as such Court shall direct.

xliii. Nothing in this Act contained shall in any manner derogate from, or affect, or be construed to derogate from or affect the rights of Her Majesty, Her Heirs and Successors, or of any person or persons, or of any body or bodies politic or corporate, except in so far as the same may be specially derogated from or affected by the provisions of this Act.

xliv. This Act shall be held, and taken to be a Public Act, and shall be judicially taken notice of and have the effect of a Public Act, without being specially pleaded, and shall be known as the *Charter of the Bank of Upper Canada,* and the Interpretation Act shall apply thereto.

xlv. This Act, and so much of the Acts mentioned in the preamble as is not repealed by this Act, shall be and remain in force until the first day of January, which will be in the year of Our Lord one thousand eight hundred and seventy, and from that time until the end of the then next Session of the Parliament of this Province, and no longer.

xLvi. The foregoing sections of this Act shall have force and effect upon, from and after the first day of January in the year of Our Lord, one thousand eight hundred and fifty-seven, and not before, and the said sections only shall be understood as intended, by the words "this Act," whenever in any of them the time when this Act shall be in force is mentioned.

SCHEDULE A

Referred to in the Thirty-seventh Section of the foregoing Act.

Return of the Average Amount of Liabilities and Assets of the Bank of Upper Canada, during the period from first   to   one thousand eight hundred and

Liabilities

Promissory Notes in circulation not bearing interest	£
Bills of Exchange in circulation not bearing interest	£
Bills and notes in circulation bearing interest	£
Balances due to other Banks	£
Cash deposits, not bearing interest	£
Cash deposits, bearing interest	£
Total average Liabilities	£

Assets

Coin and Bullion	£
Landed or other property of the Bank	£
Government Securities	£
Promissory Notes or Bills of other Banks	£
Balances due from other Banks	£
Notes and Bills discounted	£
Other Debts due to the Bank, not included under the foregoing heads	£
Total average Assets	£

An Act further to amend the Charter of the Bank of Upper Canada, June 9, 1862 [25 Victoria, c. 63]

1. For and notwithstanding any thing contained in the Act passed in the Session held in the nineteenth and twentieth years of Her Majesty's Reign, and intituled: *An Act to amend and consolidate the Acts forming the Charter of the Bank of Upper Canada*, each and every share in the Capital Stock of the said Bank shall, from and after the passing of this Act, be held to represent and be equal to the sum of seven pounds ten shillings currency, or thirty dollars, and not twelve pounds ten shillings currency, or fifty dollars, as heretofore, and the total amount of the Capital Stock of the said Bank now paid up, shall also be reduced in proportion; Provided always, that the Directors of the said Bank may, if they shall deem it advantageous for the interests of the said Bank, at any time hereafter, consolidate the said reduced shares of thirty dollars each, to shares not exceeding one hundred dollars each; And provided also, that the Directors of the said Bank may, at any time and from time to time, with the consent of the Shareholders, if the said reduced shares be not so consolidated, add any portions of the profits of the said Bank, not exceeding in the whole twenty dollars per share, to the Capital Stock thereof; or if the said reduced shares be consolidated in any sum not exceeding sixty dollars each, then the Directors of the said Bank may, at any time, with the consent of the Shareholders, add such portions of the profits of the said Bank as shall raise the said shares to an amount not exceeding one hundred dollars each.

2. The terms in and by the third section of the said Act hereinbefore recited, limited for subscribing for, and wholly paying up such shares of the said Capital Stock as should be unsubscribed for when the said Act came into force, and which by the said Act were thereby authorized to be raised, shall be and the same are hereby authorized to be extended as follows, that is to say: for subscribing for the said additional shares, until two years after the passing of this Act, and for wholly paying up the said shares, until five years after the same.

3. Notwithstanding any thing in the said Act hereinbefore recited contained, no Shareholder shall be capable of serving as a Director of the said Bank, unless he shall be the holder and proprietor, in his own name, of not less than two thousand dollars of the shares of the Capital Stock of the said Bank wholly paid up.

4. Notwithstanding any thing in the said Act thereinbefore recited contained, no transfer of the Capital Stock of the said Bank shall be valid or effectual in law until the transferring actually due by him to the said Bank, but all his liabilities to the said Bank which may exceed in amount the value of his remaining shares, if any, unless with the consent of the Directors . . . .

Appendix 3

Bank of Upper Canada: Branches and Agencies

1825   York (Head Office)

Agencies
Kingston
Niagara

1833   York (Head Office)

Branches	*Agencies*
Hamilton	Amherstburg
Niagara	Sandwich
Cobourg	London
Kingston	Perth
Brockville	Cornwall

1846   Toronto (Head Office)

Branches	*Agencies*
Kingston	Chatham
Niagara	Chippawa
London	Port Hope
St. Catharines	Bytown
Montreal	Cornwall
	Goderich
	Barrie

1859   Toronto (Head Office)

Branches	*Agencies*
Brockville	Barrie
Hamilton	Belleville
Chatham	Clifton
Kingston	Goderich
London	Lindsay
St. Catharines	Niagara
Montreal	Ottawa
Quebec	Port Hope
	Sarnia
	Stratford
	Windsor
	Picton
	Three Rivers (CE)

Sources: PAC, CO 42, vol. 417, p. 188, W.L. Mackenzie to Lord Goderich, 19 March 1833; PAC, RG 19B 2A, 1146, T.G. Ridout to William Morris, 12 June 1846; PAO, Mackenzie/Lindsey Papers, *Journal of Banking, Commerce and Finance*, 1859. For the distinction between agencies and branches see P. Baskerville, "The Entrepreneur and the Metropolitan Impulse: James Grey Bethune and Cobourg, 1825–1836," in J. Petryshyn et al., eds., *Victorian Cobourg: A Nineteenth Century Profile* (Belleville 1976), 61.

TABLES

Table 1 Operating Ratios of Selected Chartered Banks, 1823–41

Bank	8 Dec. 1823	22 Feb. 1825	13 Dec. 1826	19 Feb. 1828	17 Mar. 1829	15 Feb. 1830	25 Jan. 1831	30 Jan. 1833	18 Dec. 1833
Bank of Upper Canada									
Capital stock as a percent of bank notes	45.5	51.8	62.1	58.8	51.5	49.5	53.5	57.5	91.7
Specie as a percent of bank notes[1a]	39.4	27.9	21.8	17.2	16.5	21.2	22.8	32.9	22.5

Bank									16 Dec. 1833
Commercial Bank									
Capital stock as a percent of bank notes									111.1
Specie as a percent of bank notes[1a]									28.1

Bank	8 Jan. 1824	6 Feb. 1825	31 Jan. 1826	1 Dec. 1828	18 Feb. 1830	1 Feb. 1831	18 Jan. 1834
Bank of Montreal							
Capital stock as a percent of bank notes	204.1	137.0	140.8	140.8	133.3	112.4	109.9
Specie as a percent of bank notes[1a]	109.9	47.4	74.6	49.3	44.8	44.1	32.6

Table 1 Operating Ratios of Selected Chartered Banks, 1823–41 (continued)

Bank	21 Jan. 1835	3 Feb. 1836	16 Nov. 1836	17 Jun. 1837	1 Jan. 1838	5 Mar. 1839	5 Dec. 1839	30 Jul. 1841
Bank of Upper Canada								
Capital stock as a percent of bank notes	81.9	90.9	88.5	135.0	250.0	62.1	125.0	140.8
	22 Jan. 1835	1 Feb. 1836	7 Nov. 1836	16 Jun. 1837	11 Sep. 1837	11 Mar. 1839		1 Jul. 1841
Specie as a percent of bank notes[1a]	41.3	46.7	28.2	22.1	172.4	29.9	64.5	38.6
Commercial Bank								
Capital stock as a percent of bank notes	85.5	69.0	106.4	158.7	250.0	71.4		97.1
Specie as a percent of bank notes[1a]	25.1	24.0	26.8	18.6	16.6	20.9		40.3
Bank of Montreal				1 Jun. 1837				
Capital stock as a percent of bank notes				137.0				
Specie as a percent of bank notes[1a]				38.0				

Table 1   Operating Ratios of Selected Chartered Banks, 1823–41 (continued)

	28 Nov. 1836	16 Jun. 1837	8 Jan. 1838	11 Mar. 1839	30 Jun. 1841
Gore Bank					
Capital stock as a percent of bank notes	217.4	232.5	500.0	111.1	129.9
Specie as a percent of bank notes[a]	74.6	52.4	122.0	28.0	34.2

Sources: Financial statements for dates shown in *JUC*, 1823–41

[a]Specie as a percent of bank notes is referred to as the reserve ratio in the text and in Table 2. It differs from current usage in that it does not include deposits.

Table 2 Reserve Ratio, 1841–66[a]

	BUC	Average All Banks
1841 (July)	38.5	40.0
(9 banks)		
1846 (Feb-Mar)	25.0	26.3
(8 banks)		
1847 (May-Jun)	15.2	25.0
(8 banks)		
1849 (Jan)	18.2	34.5
(8 banks)		
1850 (Jun-Jul)	25.6	27.0
(8 banks)		
1851–2 (Apr 51-Mar 52)	18.5	27.7
(average 8 banks)		
1852–3 (Apr 52-Mar 53)	24.4	27.0
(average 8 banks)		
1853–4 (Apr 53-Mar 54)	21.3	23.3
(average 8 banks)		
1854–5 (Apr 54-Mar 55)	11.1	20.4
(average 8 banks)		
1855–6 (Apr 55-Mar 56)	10.2	21.7
(average 8 banks)		
1857 (Oct)	9.6	22.7
(13 banks)		
1858 (Mar)	17.5	27.0
(13 banks)		
1859 (Jul)	20.0	30.3
(14 banks)		
1860 (Apr)	20.8	34.5
(14 banks)		
1862 (Sep)	52.6	58.8
(16 banks)		
1864 (Aug)	38.5	55.6
(16 banks)		
1866 (Feb)	35.7	47.6
(17 banks)		

Sources: Computed from data in Table 12B and financial information in *JLA*, various years.
    a. Specie as a percent of bank notes, see Table 1, note a.

Table 3   Profit and Loss Statement: Selected Chartered Banks, 1818–58

Year	Bank of Upper Canada				Bank of Montreal Net Profit as a % of Paid in Capital	Commercial Bank Net Profit as a % of Paid in Capital
	Dividend	Change in Rest	Estimated Net Profit	Net Profit as a % of Paid in Capital		
1817–18					3.0	
1818–19					8.6	
1819–20					7.0	
1820–1					5.8	
1821–2					7.5	
1823	£ 493 cy.	− 15	478	3.6	6.8	
1824	1624	285	1909	6.7	7.0	
1825	2953	− 115	2838	7.7	6.0	
1826	3863	1610	5473	10.1	0.5	
1827	8606	683	9289	14.7	5.5	
1828	5790	3073	8863	12.2	7.2	
1829	6036	2505	8541	11.1	0.2	
1830	13574	− 2929	10655	10.6	− .7	
1831	8000	4552	12552	12.5	9.6	
1832	26000	− 9554	16554	16.5	12.6	
1833	12264	6736	19000	10.4	15.4	
1834	15695	1477	17172	8.6	14.0	8.9
1835	24000	− 2510	21490	10.7	13.3	10.1
1836	16000	6896	24896	12.4	14.8	7.9
1837	16000	2657	18657	9.3	16.9	9.5
1838	16000	2039	18039	9.0	6.3	9.1
1839	16000	− 4224	11776	5.8	9.2	8.2
1840	16000	10936	26936	13.5	6.3	10.5
1841	16000	3200	19200	9.6	9.3	10.1
1842	16000	− 758	15242	7.6	9.3	
1843	32617	21687	10930	4.9	6.2	
1844	15171	4176	19347	7.9	7.3	
1845	18041	2912	20953	7.7	9.3	
1846	20154	958	21112	6.9	9.1	
1847	23851	− 1036	22815	6.1	6.5	
1848	15199	− 6268	8931	2.3	− 1.0	
1849	17135	2923	14212	3.7	6.5	
1850	20949	1929	22878	6.0	7.5	
1851	22870	7932	30802	8.1	9.2	
1852	24041	12505	36546	8.7	10.0	
1853	31546	27463	59009	11.9	9.9	
1854	97421	− 2466	94955	19.0	13.6	
1855	47688	20490	68178	11.2	11.6	
1856	54146	− 6438	47708	6.6	5.0	
1857	53654	10000	63654	8.2	8.7	
1858	62302	− 9157	53145	6.8	7.0	

Notes: Estimated Net Profit is Dividend ± Change in Rest. Figures derived from data in *JLA*, 1859, Appendix 67, *Report of Banking Committee*, and randomly checked against statements in *Journals* for various years.

Calculations for Bank of Montreal and Commercial Bank not shown. Year-end dates are for Bank of Upper Canada. Year-end for Bank of Montreal and Commercial Bank not necessarily the same as indicated for Bank of Upper Canada. Commercial Bank data not comparable for other than dates shown.

Calculations for the years 1823 to 1858, inclusive, as of 31 December.

Table 4   Bank of Upper Canada: Sale of Exchange on London, Profit and Loss, 1824–41[a]

Year	Amount Sold	Profit from Sale of Exchange on London	As a % of Total Exchange Sales	As a % Total of Net Bank Profit[b]
1824	12135	183	1.5	9.5
1825	22228	− 164	− 0.74	
1826	31011	863	2.8	15.7
1827	31302	1554	4.9	16.7
1828	68477	594	0.9	6.7
1829	86065	455	0.5	5.3
1830	75695	12	0.01	0.1
1831	59389	1259	2.1	10.0
1832	120188	1020	0.84	6.2
1833	120358	− 1212	− 1.0	
1834	254431	− 971	− 0.38	
1835	305203	3551	1.16	16.5
1836	190065	3717	1.9	14.9
1837	165074	16715	10.1	89.5
1838	461643	9868	2.13	54.7
1839	623017	− 12702	− 2.0	
1840	289903	3825	1.3	14.2
1841	128694[c]	1195[c]	0.9 [c]	6.2[c]

a. *JLA*, Appendix O, Section G.
b. See Table 3, Net Profit figure.
c. 1/2 year only to 30 June 1841.

Table 5 The Bank of Upper Canada as a Holder of Government Debentures, 1822–41

Year	A Government Debentures Purchased[a]	B Government Debentures Sold[a]	C Net Debentures on Hand[a]	D Total Debt Due Bank[b]	E C/D × 100[c]
1822	11666		11666		
1823			11666	31525	37
1824		2222	9444		
1825			9444	80453	12
1826	25000	19222	15222	107598	14
1827	35000	11255	38967		
1828	500	16188	23279	171869	14
1829	17388	25333	15334	180854	8
1830	47555	40655	22234	214045	10
1831	27016	12800	36450	260577	14
1832	6683	31033	12100		
1833	21185	13391	19894	309659	6
1834	63626	70300	13220		
1835	41016	43466	10770	376634	3
1836	21930	19346	13354	479321	3
1837	69900	25356	57898	444958	13
1838	42592	26772	73718	261689	28
1839	4387	14946	63159	363867	17
1840	4754	7882	60031		
1841	700	9800	50931	406927	13

a. Adapted from *JLA*, 1841, Appendix O, Section G.
b. Taken from statements for years indicated as listed in Appendix 12A and 12B
c. These percentages are only rough indications as the statement dates of debentures on hand and total debt due bank are not the same.

Table 6 Financial Data: Bank of Upper Canada, 1837–39

Date	Specie	Notes in Circulation	Cash Deposited	Balance Due from Other Banks and Foreign Agencies on Exchange Transactions	Debts Due Bank of Upper Canada
1837					
May 03	49,700	204,990			
15	49,700	212,356			473,905
16	39,742	201,406	134,324		
June 15	37,850	168,906			
17	32,366	146,852	155,725	36,458	444,958
24	30,184	135,106	149,751	42,600	431,712
28	48,641	127,000			
Jul 19	40,182	108,650	187,208	49,286	396,506
Aug 15	71,303[a]				
Sep 16	73,000	97,000			
Nov 21	138,000				
1838					
Jan 01	139,225	80,079	75,516	−48,943	261,689
29		85,000			
Feb 01	74,000[a]				
Mar 05	63,013	154,000		200,000	
Dec 15	130,369[a]				
Dec 18				330,000	
1839					
Mar 05	96,376	321,853	253,751	300,277	363,867
Apr 14			150,000	300,000	
Apr 15	93,034[a]				
Jun 01		330,041			
Dec 05	103,718	160,472	113,854	23,537	311,232

Source: PAC, RG 5 A1, Ridout to Joseph, 27 June 1837, cited in PAC, A. Shortt Papers, 3; Report on Monetary System, 1837, Statement A & A59; *JUC*, second session, 1837, 9; PAO, Macaulay Papers, Macaulay to Kirby, 16 Sept., 21 Nov. 1837; Report of Committee on Finance, 1837–8, 95; PAC, Colborne Papers, 16, Ridout to Macaulay, 18 August 1838; PAO, Ridout Papers, T.G. Ridout to Matilda, 2 November, 18 December 1838; PAC, Ellice Papers, C4637, S. Gerrard to E. Ellice, 14 April 1839; *JLA*, 1841, Appendix O, D2; and financial statements, Table 12B.

Note: All figures are in pounds currency.

a. *JLA*, 1841, Appendix 0, B3

Table 7 Summer Note Issue as a Percent of Yearly Issue[a]

1 Nov-31 Oct.	Bank of Upper Canada	Commercial Bank	Gore Bank	Bank of Montreal
1841–2	23.7	18.7	21.5	23.7
1842–3	.			
1843–4	26.6	23.8	23.7	24.4
1844–5	24.4	22.4	22.8	25.6
1845–6	22.2	20.8	20.3	22.8
1846–7	25.6	23.8	25.6	25.0
1847–8	22.2	22.1	22.5	22.8

a. June, July, and August. Computed from data in *JLA*, 1849, Appendix Z.

Table 8   Government Money at Deposit: Bank of Upper Canada, 1851–56

Date	Not Bearing Interest	Percent of Total Government Deposits in Domestic Banks Not Bearing Interest	Bearing 3 Percent Interest	Percent of Total Government Deposits in Domestic Banks Bearing Interest	Percent of Total Government Deposits in Domestic Banks
1 June 1851	199,643 £	92	123,333	46	67
1 Aug 1852	84,452	73	165,633	34	42
1 Apr 1853	37,466	84	100,000	28	34
1 Oct 1854	202,008	71	100,000	30	49
5 Jun 1855	not known	not known	100,000	26	not known
31 Mar 1856	165,441	88	100,000	0	49

Sources: Montreal *Transcript*, 31 Dec. 1851; *JLA*, 1852; Appendix DD; 1853, Appendix FFFF; 1854, Appendix NN; 1856, Appendix 30; PAC, RG 19 B2b, 1162, Taché to Merritt, 5 June, 1855

Table 9 Province of Canada: Railway and Municipal Loan Fund Debentures Issued, 1851–55 (£ stg)

	1851	1852	1853	1854	1855	Total
St. Lawrence & Atlantic Rwy[a]	28 Oct.: 300,000	14 Jul.: 100,000 14 Dec.: 60,000	24 Jan.: 7,500			467,500
Quebec & Richmond Rwy[a]			5 Oct.: 100,000	17 Aug.: 150,000		250,000
Grand Trunk Rwy				2 Mar.: 100,000 22 May: 100,000 31 Jul.: 110,000 50,000 8 Nov.: 174,000 17 Nov.: 26,000	26 Jan.: 498,768 2 Jun.: 900,000 23 Jul.: 122,511 N.D.: 312,720	2,393,999
Ontario, Simcoe & Huron Rwy (later named Northern)		8 Nov.: 100,000	9 Apr.: 175,000	28 Nov.: 200,000		475,000
Great Western Rwy		1 Oct.: 200,000		3 Jul.: 300,000 17 Nov.: 100,000	15 Jan.: 100,000 1 Jun.: 70,000	770,000
Total Rwy Debt	300,000	460,000	282,500	1,310,000	2,003,999	4,356,499
Municipal Loan Fund			406,474	560,879	253,402	1,220,755
Total	300,000	460,000	688,974	1,870,879	2,257,401	5,577,254

Sources: *Public Accounts, 1860, JLA,* 1861, Sessional Paper No. 3; RG 19 B2b 1162, Memorandum of Provincial Guarantee to various Railway Companies, 25 July 1855.

a. Became part of Grand Trunk Railway subsidy during period under review.

Table 10   The Great Western Railway's Bank of Upper Canada Debt, 1852–55 (£ cy)

21 February 1852	55,845
1 October 1853	150,000 line of credit opened
31 May 1854	218,000
28 August 1854	298,897
4 September 1854	308,414
21 September 1854	317,108
3 October 1854	36,142
28 November 1854	84,650
8 December 1854	98,906
2 January 1855	121,140

Sources: PAC, RG 30, 5; AI, Corning Papers, W. Longsdon to E. Corning, 31 July 1854

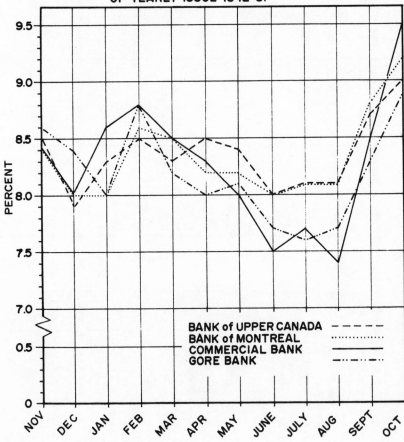

FIGURE I: AVERAGE MONTHLY NOTE ISSUE AS A PERCENT OF YEARLY ISSUE 1842-8.

BANK of UPPER CANADA — — — —
BANK of MONTREAL ....
COMMERCIAL BANK ————
GORE BANK —··—··—··

Table 11 Bank of Upper Canada: Financial Standing within the Canadian Banking Sector, 1841–66 (£ cy)[a]

		1841 (July) (9 banks)	1846 (Feb-Mar) (8 banks)	1847 (May-Jun) (8 banks)	1849 (Jan) (8 banks)	1850 (Jun-Jul) (8 banks)	1852 (Aug) (8 banks)	1854 (Aug 30-Oct 4) (8 banks)	1856 (mainly Oct) (12 banks)
Capital	Total	1,435,881	2,005,066	2,870,610	2,967,729c	2,879,870	2,934,580(est)	3,414,983	4,660,907
	BUC	200,000	281,667	333,101	379,166	380,877	381,248	498,952	687,638
	%	14	14	12	13	13	13	15	15
Circulation	Total	909,198	1,703,675	1,664,184	1,101,188	1,309,931	1,897,415	3,849,574	3,206,823
	BUC	142,849	182,338	208,651	149,610	194,216	363,422	746,315	658,684
	%	16	11	13	14	15	19	19	21
Deposits	Total	717,127	1,169,692	1,212,817	712,112	1,547,117	1,784,796	3,013,161	2,996,755
	BUC	144,093	184,702	136,694	88,010	429,992	539,215	839,407	648,837
	%	20	16	11	12	28	30	28	22
Specie	Total	355,933	454,020	420,310	379,489	356,681	528,061	722,293	819,552
	BUC	55,125	45,085	31,832	27,355	49,706	106,265	119,315	95,187
	%	16	10	8	7	14	20	17	12
Discounts[b]	Total	2,952,118	5,123,628	5,081,164	3,961,046	4,426,947	5,862,299	9,645,724	10,237,959
	BUC	406,927	595,943	579,282	564,459	692,290	1,101,569	1,867,822	1,771,685
	%	14	12	11	14	16	19	19	17
Sources		JLA, 1841, App. O, Section F; App. C	JLA, 1846, App. 4	JLA, 1847, App. P	JLA, 1849, App. P	JLA, 1850, App. H	JLA, 1852, App. R	JLA, 1854, App. EE	PAO, Mackenzie/ Lindsey Papers, 1856 Clippings, 721D; PAO, D. Thorburn Papers, 5 July 1856; JLA, 1856, App. 5

a. All calculations are my own.

b. Discount figures up to 1851 include government securities and other debts. Gradually after 1850 and especially after 1856 government securities and other debts were separated from discount figure. Since holdings of government securities in the 1840s were relatively small, no corrections have been made in the figures listed above.

c. Capital stock estimated for 4 banks.

d. Returns for Gore Bank and the Bank of British North America are estimated.

e. Returns for Gore Bank are estimated.

Table 11 Bank of Upper Canada: Financial Standing, 1841–66 (continued)

		1857 (Oct)^d (13 banks)	1858 (Mar) (13 banks)	1859 (Jul) (14 banks)	1860 (Apr)^e (14 banks)	1862 (Sep) (16 banks)	1864 (Aug) (16 banks)	1866 (Feb) (17 banks)
Capital	Total	5,349,589	5,472,277	5,657,288	5,772,928	—	6,927,364	6,771,726
	BUC	776,137	777,568	781,755	782,621	—	483,025	484,821
	%	15	14	14	14	—	7	7
Circulation	Total	3,100,000	2,435,327	2,282,113	2,630,474	2,621,741	2,131,368	3,076,340
	BUC	719,807	537,673	528,955	588,329	411,689	295,774	238,556
	%	23	22	23	22	16	14	8
Deposits	Total	2,460,563	2,184,183	3,319,465	3,539,943	—	6,121,740	7,282,027
	BUC	600,451	538,750	1,212,243	1,125,171	—	2,343,178	607,906
	%	24	25	37	32	—	38	8
Specie	Total	708,814	649,846	692,447	911,607	1,563,768	1,159,848	1,455,763
	BUC	69,004	94,450	106,796	121,512	211,743	111,707	86,309
	%	10	15	15	13	14	10	6
Discounts	Total	10,340,371	9,614,113	10,196,973	10,675,261	10,354,422	11,577,349	11,106,424
	BUC	1,885,602	1,845,825	2,166,169	2,389,288	1,583,460	1,098,046	914,376
	%	18	19	21	22	15	9	8
Sources		PAO, Mackenzie/Lindsey Papers, Clippings, 721 E	JLA, 1858, App. No. 8; PAO, Mackenzie/Lindsey Papers, clippings, 721E	PAO, Mackenzie/Lindsey Papers, clippings, 721 D	PAO, Mackenzie/Lindsey Papers, Clippings, 721 D	Globe, 22 Oct. 1862	Globe, 21 Sept. 1864	Globe, 21 Mar. 1866

Table 12A   Bank of Upper Canada Financial Statements, 1823–31[a] (in £ cy)

	8 Dec 1823	22 Feb 1825	13 Dec 1826	19 Feb 1828	17 Mar 1829	15 Feb 1830	25 Jan 1831
Funds & property	8056 132	13,126	38,391	37,765	47,271	26,412 6,571	15,618 6,715
Capital stock paid in	12,155	31,600	54,039	72,067	72,410	77,462	100,000
Debts due to the bank	31,525	80,453	107,598	171,869	180,854	214,045	260,577
Debts due by the bank	11,466	17,468	19,484	32,376	35,102	38,303	33,621
Bank notes in circulation	26,699	61,298	87,339	122,858	140,488	156,296	187,039
Specie in vault	10,523	17,145	19,066	21,177	23,190	33,134	42,664
Source	JUC, 1823, *Report of Archives*, 1914, 543	PAC, Upper Canada Sundries, 1825, cited in PAC, A. Shortt Papers, 1	*JUC*, 1825–6, 13	*JUC*, 1828, 61	*JUC*, 1829, 67	*JUC*, 1830, 56	*JUC*, 1831, 31

a. The government required a different and more detailed public statement following 1832; see Table 12B.

Table 12B Bank of Upper Canada Financial Statements, 1833–66 (in £ cy)

	30 Jan. 1833	18 Dec. 1833	21 Jan. 1835	3 Feb. 1836	16 Nov. 1836	17 June 1837	1 Jan. 1838	5 Mar. 1839
Capital stock paid in	109,361	182,847	200,000	200,000	200,000	200,000	200,000	200,000
Amount of notes in circulation, not bearing interest:[1]								
$5 upwards	135,256	156,227	198,510	170,481	180,826	101,778	52,355	249,150
under $5	54,452	42,181	45,329	49,542	45,828	45,073	27,724	72,703
Total	189,708	198,408	243,839	220,023	226,654	146,852	80,079	321,853
Balances due to other banks	11,748	7,860	14,993	29,768	4,362	59,506	52,164[7]	7,695
Dividends unpaid								
Net profit on hand							23,512[8]	
Cash deposited, including all sums due from the bank, not bearing interest (its bills in circulation & balances due other banks excepted)	107,097	117,780	180,735	157,755	154,604	155,725	75,516	253,751
Balances due at this date to the officers & agencies of the bank	799	1,993	1,799		788	1,129		
Cash deposited bearing interest[2]		919		8,763	3,016	2,822	2,669	2,702
Total amount due from bank	418,985	509,809	641,368	616,285	589,426	566,035	433,941	786,003
Resources or Assets								
Specie: gold, silver, & other coined metals in the bank & its offices	62,437	44,653	100,746[4]	102,859[5]	63,796	32,366	139,225	96,376
Bank property								
Bank furniture								
Bank real estate								
Total	9,109	9,186	8,698	8,858	8,880	8,659	8,676	8,701
Bills of other banks	5,808	8,929	10,936	16,092	18,045	43,594	21,127	16,780

Table 12B (continued)

	30 Jan. 1833	18 Dec. 1833	21 Jan. 1835	3 Feb. 1836	16 Nov. 1836	17 June 1837	1 Jan. 1838	5 Mar. 1839
Balances due from other banks & foreign agencies on exchange transactions	25,165	67,177[3]	140,502[3]	7,408[6]	84,728	36,458	3,221[6]	300,277
Balances due at this office from offices & agencies of the bank, being money in transit	6,804		3,849	1,745				
Amount of all debts due, excepting the balance due from other banks:								
Notes & bills discounted								
Mortgages								
Government debentures								
Municipal debentures								
Other								
Total	309,659	379,862	376,634	479,321	413,976	444,958	261,689	363,867
Total amount of resources of bank	418,985	509,809	641,368	616,285	589,426	566,035	433,941	786,003
Miscellaneous								
Amount of overdue debts due to the bank not considered doubtful or bad	9,572	22,503	31,452	37,214	50,905	43,904		61,350
Amount of overdue debts considered bad or doubtful	0	572	2,160	3,955	5,450	6,000		3,000
Source for statement	JUC, 1832–3, p. 118	JUC, 1833–4, p. 65	JUC, 1835, p. 57	JUC, 1836, p. 118	JUC, 1837, p. 73	JUC, 1837, 2nd Session, p. 9	JUC, 1838, p. 104	JUC, 1839, p. 40, i, k

Table 12B (continued)

	5 Dec. 1839	30 July 1841	20 Sept. 1842	17 Oct. 1843	14 Jan. 1845	8 Apr. 1846	21 June 1847	13 Mar. 1848
Capital stock paid in	200,000	200,000	200,000	217,210	246,076	281,667	333,101	379,166
Amount of notes in circulation, not bearing interest[1]								
$5 upwards	107,281	94,493	98,006	82,008	142,582	107,994	125,794	113,479
under $5	53,191	48,355	37,329	21,921	30,717	74,344	82,857	76,365
Total	160,472	142,849	135,336	103,929	176,299	182,338	208,651	189,844
Balances due to other banks	5,059	27,573[9]	21,281[9]	49,477	35,019	43,194	5,669	26,603
Dividends unpaid								
Reserve fund								
Net profit on hand								
Cash deposited, including all sums due from the bank, not bearing interest (its bills in circulation & balances due other banks excepted)	113,854	140,111	116,155	105,830	134,545	115,931	90,114	87,432
Balances due at this date to the officers & agencies of the bank								
Cash deposited bearing interest	3,776	3,982	6,358	10,707	30,988	68,771	46,580	24,667
Total amount due from bank	483,162	514,516	479,131	487,154	619,929	691,903	684,118	707,713
Resources or Assets								
Specie: gold, silver, & other coined metals in the bank & its offices	103,718	55,125	24,894	32,170	52,265	45,085	31,832	34,680
Bank property								
Bank furniture								
Bank real estate	9,549	13,209	13,443	20,067	18,217	19,236	22,083	21,548
Total								
Bills of other banks	35,123	15,218	20,807	6,863	20,358	13,452	12,251	13,329

Table 12B (continued)

	5 Dec. 1839	30 July 1841	20 Sept. 1842	17 Oct. 1843	14 Jan. 1845	8 Apr. 1846	21 June 1847	13 Mar. 1848
Balances due from other banks & foreign agencies on exchange transactions	23,537	24,035[10]	34,570[10]	53,164	12,291	18,184	38,667	24,013
Balances due at this office from offices & agencies of the bank, being money in transit								
Amount of all debts due, excepting the balance due from other banks:								
Notes & bills discounted								
Mortgages								
Government debentures								
Municipal debentures								
Other								
Total	311,232	406,927	385,416	374,888	516,796	595,943	579,282	614,141
Total amount of resources of bank	483,162	514,516	479,131	487,154	619,929	691,903	684,118	707,713
Miscellaneous								
Amount of overdue debts due to the bank not considered doubtful or bad	67,169	44,878	50,835					
Amount of overdue debts considered bad or doubtful	4,000	7,000	7,500	4,000	7,500	8,000	10,000	10,000
Source for statement	JUC, 1839, App. 2, p. 761	JLA, 1841, App. C	JLA, 1842, App. R	JLA, 1843, App. Y	JLA, 1844–5, App. Q	JLA, 1846, App. U	JLA, 1847, App. U	JLA, 1848, App. T

Table 12B (continued)

	30 Jan. 1849	29 July 1850	9 June 1851	4 June 1852	6 June 1853	2 Oct. 1854	29 May 1856	13 Mar. 1858[14]
Capital stock paid in	380,787	380,877	381,192	381,248	440,033	498,952	633,631	777,568
Amount of notes in circulation, not bearing interest:[1]								
$5 upwards	88,600	123,206	151,568			508,030		375,085
under $5	61,010	71,010	99,466			238,285		162,588
Total	149,610	194,216	251,035	304,561	418,777	746,315	698,864	537,673
Balances due to other banks	34,375[7]	6,119	11,397[7]	12,302	10,130	42,021[13]	65,681	344,313[7]
Dividends unpaid				4,764	1,541		4,305	
Reserve fund								
Net profit on hand				33,770	45,815		76,079	
Cash deposited, including all sums due from the bank, not bearing interest (its bills in circulation & balances due other banks excepted)	76,942	268,722	396,956	427,267	521,442	714,184	455,390	501,986
Balances due at this date to the officers & agencies of the bank								
Cash deposited bearing interest[2]	11,068	161,270	149,227	181,535	468,483	125,223	79,756	36,764
Total amount due from bank	652,784	1,011,206	1,189,808	1,345,450	1,906,224	2,126,696	2,013,710	2,198,306
Resources or assets								
Specie: gold, silver, & other coined metals in the bank & its offices	27,355	49,703	51,206	71,255	115,777	119,315	81,759	94,450
Bank property								
Bank furniture								
Bank real estate								
Total	31,935	31,204	35,914	35,838	32,817	30,695	24,683	46,654
Bills of other banks	13,082	20,216	33,773	32,584	44,099	56,198	68,182	52,164

Table 12B (continued)

	25 June 1859	16 June 1860	31 May 1861	31 May 1862	23 May 1863	25 May 1864	25 May 1865	28 Feb. 1866
Balances due from other banks & foreign agencies on exchange transactions	15,952	217,787	53,580	41,697	391,393	52,666	69,656	159,211
Balances due at this office from offices & agencies of the bank being money in transit								
Amount of all debts due, excepting the balance due from other banks:								
Notes & bills discounted				955,536	1,313,524[12]	1,867,822	1,556,912[12]	1,845,825
Mortgages				144,011			186,063	
Government debentures								
Municipal debentures							26,453	
Other				64,556[11]	8,611[11]			
Total	564,459	692,290	1,015,333	1,164,103	1,322,135	1,867,822	1,769,428	1,845,825
Total amount of resources of bank	652,784	1,011,206	1,189,808	1,345,450	1,906,224	2,126,696	2,013,710	2,198,306
Miscellaneous								
Amount of overdue debts due to the bank not considered doubtful or bad	8,500	10,000	7,000					
Amount of overdue debts considered bad or doubtful								
Source for statement	*JLA*, 1849, App. P	*JLA*, 1850, App. H	*JLA*, 1851, App. I	PAC, Glyn, Mills Papers, A542	PAC, Glyn, Mills Papers, A542	*JLA*, 1854, App. JJ	PAO, Misc. Collection, BUC, 1856	*JLA*, 1858, App. # 8

Table 12B (continued)

	25 June 1859	16 June 1860	31 May 1861	31 May 1862	23 May 1863	25 May 1864	25 May 1865	28 Feb. 1866
Capital stock paid in	781,567	782,621	790,517	792,275	478,302	482,597	484,382	484,822
Amount of notes in circulation, not bearing interest:[1]								
£5 upwards								
under £5								
Total	522,764	546,600	475,483	409,645	388,985	299,236	260,160	238,556
Balances due to other banks	348,599	56,895	6,381	47,700	66,640	219,348	189,318	35,748
Dividends unpaid	4,082	3,616	2,308	714	2,146	2,708	2,803	
Reserve fund				155,412	101,132[23]	55,322[23]	54,479[23]	
Net profit on hand	155,715	194,026		33,369	29,307[24]	20,990[27]	6,946	
Cash deposited, including all sums due from the bank, not bearing interest (its bills in circulation & balances due other banks excepted)	703,002	614,901	678,093	715,262	640,937	521,610	185,153	210,692
Balances due at this date to the officers & agencies of the bank								
Cash deposited bearing interest[2]	284,266	652,467[15]	818,423	687,163	669,492	408,698	552,976	470,011
Total amount due from bank	2,799,998	2,851,130	2,771,208	2,796,544	2,376,944	2,010,513	1,736,219	1,439,829
Resources or assets								
Specie: gold, silver, & other coined metals in the bank & its offices	134,779	228,331	141,144	272,062	130,766	114,380	130,928	86,310
Bank property			49,066[16]	35,394[21]	43,866	45,250[21]	42,500	
Bank furniture					3,950		4,275	
Bank real estate			124,475[17]	131,213	160,368	275,958	322,289	
Total	59,837	95,070	173,541	166,607	208,184	321,208	369,064	378,769
Bills of other banks	37,765	48,022	51,207	36,180	33,785	31,495	22,892	17,296
Balances due from other banks & foreign agencies on exchange transactions	158,120	163,479	150,566	123,998	73,077	43,857	12,028	8,174

Table 12B (continued)

	25 June 1859	16 June 1860	31 May 1861	31 May 1862	23 May 1863	25 May 1864	25 May 1865	28 Feb. 1866
Balances due at this office from offices & agencies of the bank, being money in transit			312,626[18]	312,626[18]				
Amount of all debts due, excepting the balance due from other banks:								
Notes & bills discounted	2,161,774[12]	2,224,161[12]	1,379,503	1,602,852	1,697,565	1,183,070	873,661	679,355
Mortgages	234,458	79,351	78,585	78,690	58,214	41,357	26,399	
Government debentures	13,262	12,714		79,416	77,278[25]	50,916	49,316	49,174
Municipal debentures			72,377[19]	23,032[19]				
Other			411,654[20]	101,075[22]	98,072[20]	224,225[28]	251,927[29]	2325,096[30]
Total	2,409,494	2,316,226	1,942,119	1,885,065	1,931,129	1,499,568	1,201,303	963,625
Total amount of resources of bank	2,799,998	2,851,130	2,771,208	2,796,544	2,376,944	2,010,513	1,736,219	1,454,174[31]
Miscellaneous								
Amount of overdue debts due to the bank not considered doubtful or bad								
Amount of overdue debts considered bad or doubtful								
Source for statement	QUA, Magill Papers	PAO, Mackenzie Lindsey Papers	MTL, Rpt. of R. Cassels to Shareholders of BUC, 27 June 1861	PAO, J.S. Cartwright Papers	QUA, Magill Papers	Toronto *Globe*, 27 June 1864	PAC, Glyn, Mills Papers, A543	Toronto *Globe*, 21 Mar. 1866

NOTES TO TABLE 12B

[1] An entry often appeared for "Bills & Notes in circulation bearing Interest," but was always entered as "none" so the entry has not been included here.

[2] Up to 1842 this money was generally listed as deposited in the Home District Savings Bank at an annual interest of 5 per cent. In 1842 and after this money appears as deposited in the Bank of Upper Canada.

[3] The foreign agencies were listed as London and New York.

[4] At Toronto, £76,049; at agencies, £24,697.

[5] At Toronto, £98,730; at agencies, £4,129.

[6] The entry refers to "Balances due from other Banks." It does not mention foreign agencies.

[7] This includes due to "foreign agents."

[8] It is entered as "Contingent Fund."

[9] Entry reads "Balances due to other Banks & Bankers."

[10] Entry reads "Balances due from other Banks & Bankers."

[11] Includes Government and Municipal Debentures.

[12] Includes Bills and Notes Discounted and Mortgages.

[13] Entry includes "and agents."

[14] From 1857 all accounts were rendered in dollars. These have been converted to pounds currency for the purpose of comparison (£1 = $4).

[15] £161,998 of this was described as "Special Account."

[16] Bank Premises at Toronto and Branches.

[17] Mortgages and Real Estate.

[18] Loss Account.

[19] Municipal and Other Debentures.

[20] Other Debts: Cash Credits & Due by Depositors at Head
Office & Branches – 40848
Estate of Late S. Zimmerman – 85383
Debts secured by Mortgages on Real
Estate & other Securities – 285347

[21] Bank Premises.

[22] Cash Credits & due by Depositors – 22890
Other Debts secured by Mortgages on
Real Estate & other Securities – 74435
Balance of Expenses on New Issue – 3750

[23] "Reserve Fund to meet Bad & Doubtful Debts."

[24] £14339 of this was slated for the 79th Dividend payable 6 July 1863.

[25] Includes Government, Municipal & other Debentures.

[26] Cash Credits, Overdrawn Accounts & other
debts due to the Bank – 94322
Balance of Expense on New Issue – 3750

[27] £14459 of this was slated for the 81st Dividend payable 2 July 1864.

[28] Postal Subsidy, Municipal & other Debentures – 204208
Cash Credits & other debts due to the Bank – 20017

[29] Postal Subsidy, Municipal & Other Debentures – 198363
Cash Credits & other Debts due to the Bank – 53564

[30] Other debts not specified.

[31] Note that this statement does not balance. For statement in Nov. 1866 see F132.

Table 12C   Bank of Upper Canada: Additional Financial Information, 1823–65

Yearly Periods	Capital Stock Paid Up	Dividends rate	Dividends amount	Bonuses rate	Bonuses amount	Bank Rests
30 June, 1823	£ 10,640 cy	5	523			161
31 Dec., 1823	13,415	8	493			146
31 Dec., 1824	28,181	8	1,624			431
31 Dec., 1825	37,950	8	2,953			316
31 Dec., 1826	54,037	8	3,863			1,926
31 Dec., 1827	63,230	8	4,813	6	3,793	2,609
31 Dec., 1828	72,410	8	5,790			5,682
31 Dec., 1829	76,993	8	6,036			8,187
31 Dec., 1830	100,000	8	7,574	6	6,000	5,258
31 Dec., 1831	100,000	8	8,000			9,810
31 Dec., 1832	100,000	8	8,000	18	18,000	256
31 Dec., 1833	183,241	8	12,264			6,992
31 Dec., 1834	200,000	8	15,695			8,469
31 Dec., 1835	200,000	8	16,000	4	8,000	5,959
31 Dec., 1836	200,000	8	16,000			12,855
31 Dec., 1837	200,000	8	16,000			15,512
31 Dec., 1838	200,000	8	16,000			17,551
31 Dec., 1839	200,000	8	16,000			13,227
31 Dec., 1840	200,000	8	16,000			24,163
31 Dec., 1841	200,000	8	16,000			27,363
31 Dec., 1842	200,000	8	16,000			26,605
31 Dec., 1843	223,270	6	12,617	10	20,000	4,918
31 Dec., 1844	244,951	6$^{1}/_{2}$	15,171			9,094
31 Dec., 1845	270,660	7	18,041			12,006
31 Dec., 1846	307,388	7	20,154			12,964
31 Dec., 1847	375,303	7	23,851			11,928
31 Dec., 1848	380,763	4	15,199			5,660
31 Dec., 1849	380,810	4$^{1}/_{2}$	17,135			8,583
31 Dec., 1850	380,922	5$^{1}/_{2}$	20,949			10,514
31 Dec., 1851	381,226	6	22,870			18,446
31 Dec., 1852	420,128	6	24,041			30,951
31 Dec., 1853	497,393	7	31,546			58,414
31 Dec., 1854	499,162	7	34,921	12$^{1}/_{2}$	62,500	55,948
31 Dec., 1855	607,612	8	47,688			76,438
31 Dec., 1856	721,870	8	54,146			70,000
31 Dec., 1857	777,017	7	53,654			80,000
31 Dec., 1858	780,170	8	62,302			70,843
31 June, 1859	781,567	7	54,605			39,098[a]
31 June, 1860	782,621	6	46,916			39,098[b]
31 May, 1861	790,517	3	23,535			(312,626)[c]
31 July, 1862	475,365	3	14,260			159,695[d]
31 July, 1863	478,302	6	28,616			101,216[e]
31 July, 1864	482,597	6	28,881			
31 June, 1865	484,382	3	14,498			54,479[e]
Total			£891,224			

Sources: JLA, 1859, Appendix 67, *Report of Banking Committee*. For period following 1858 see appropriate sources listed in Table 12B.

    a. £100,000 also in a separate contingency fund for bad debts.

    b. £39,314 also in a separate contingency fund for bad debts.

    c. See Report of Directors, 1861, reprinted above p. 277 for explanation of loss.

    d. See Report of Directors, 1862, reprinted above p. 285 for explanation of profit.

    e. Includes contingency fund for bad debts.

BIBLIOGRAPHY

GOVERNMENT RECORDS

Public Archives of Canada, Ottawa (PAC)
Auditor General, Canada, Papers, 1856–1870 (RG 58)
Canadian National Railway Papers, 1850–1866 (RG 30), vols. 1–10, 1000–1002, Deposit 55
Colonial Office 42 Series, 1817–1837 (CO 42), vols. 359–438, microfilm of originals in Public Record Office, London
Department of Finance, Bank of Upper Canada, 1839–1888 (RG 19 C1), vols. 1181–1212
Department of Finance, Departmental Correspondence, 1856–1866 (RG 19E1A), vols. 3366–77
Department of Finance, Receiver General of Upper Canada Correspondence Received, 1821–1857 (RG 19 B2A), vols. 1130–49
Department of Finance, Receiver General of Upper Canada Letter Books, 1820–1866 (RG 19 B2b), vols. 1160–75
Department of Public Works, Records, 1845–1855 (RG 11), vols. 6, 119, 636, A1–22
Governor General's Office, Despatches from the Colonial Office, 1837 (RG 7 G1), vol. 35
Governor General's Office, 1844–1847 (RG 7 G14), vols. 46–48
Executive Council, Canada, Minute Books, Upper Canada, 1821, 1827 (RG 1 E1), vol. C-98
Executive Council, Canada, Submission to Council, 1850–1866 (RG 1 E7), vols. 35–67
Executive Council, Canada, State Records, 1850–1864 (RG 1 E8), vols. 34–82
Treasury Board, Canada, Records, 1870–1872 (RG 55 A1 and A3)
Upper Canada Sundries, 1819–1840 (RG 5 A1), vols. 48–221

MANUSCRIPTS

Albany Institute of History and Art, Albany, New York (AI)
E. Corning Papers
Archives, Canadian Imperial Bank of Commerce, Toronto (CIBC)
Gore Bank Papers
Archives, Midland Bank, London, England
Midland Bank Papers

Archives Nationales du Québec, Québec (ANQ)
Quesnel Papers
Archives of Ontario, Toronto (PAO)
Canada Company Papers
Canada Permanent Mortgage Letter Book
J.S. Cartwright Papers
Crookshank-Lambert Papers
F. Cumberland Papers
Amelius Irving Collection
S.P. Jarvis Papers
Jarvis-Powell Papers
Macaulay Papers
Mackenzie-Lindsey Papers, Mackenzie Correspondence and Clippings
W.H. Merritt Papers
T.G. Ridout Diaries
Ridout Papers
Samuel Street Papers
Hamilton Public Library, Hamilton (HPL)
John Young Papers
Metropolitan Toronto Library, Baldwin Room, Toronto (MTL)
William Allan Papers
Robert Baldwin Papers
S.P. Jarvis Papers
Thomas Shenston Papers
Larratt Smith Papers
Public Archives of Canada, Ottawa
Bank of Montreal Papers (MG 28 II2)
Baring Papers (MG 24 D21)
George Brown Papers (MG 24 B40)
Buchanan Papers (MG 24 D16)
Colborne Papers (MG 24 A40)
Edward Ellice Papers (MG 24 A2)
A. T. Galt Papers (MG 27 D8)
Alexander Hamilton Papers (MG 24 I26)
Glyn, Mills Papers (MG 24 D36)
J.A. Macdonald Papers (MG 26a)
W.H. Merritt Papers (MG 24 E1)
Ridout Papers (MG 24 D65)
A. Shortt Papers (MG 30 D101)
John Young Papers (MG 24 D79)
Queen's University Archives, Kingston (QUA)
J.S. Cartwright Papers
J. Macaulay Papers
Alexander Mackenzie Papers
Magill Papers

Toronto City Archives, Toronto (TCA)
Toronto City Council Papers
University of Toronto, Fisher Library, Toronto (UTL–TF)
J. Elmsley Papers
A.N. MacNab Papers
University of Western Ontario Library, Regional History Collection, London (UWO)
H.C. Becher Papers
Hamilton and Warren Papers
John Harris Papers
Thomas Swinyard Papers
Talbot Papers

PRINTED PRIMARY SOURCES

GOVERNMENT PUBLICATIONS

Appendix to the Journal of the Legislative Assembly of the Province of Canada, 1841–1866
Appendix to the Journal of the Legislative Assembly of Upper Canada, 1821–1840
Appendix to the Journal of the Legislative Council of the Province of Canada, 1856
Canada, Financial and Departmental Commission, First Report and Evidence, May 1863
Journals of the Legislative Assembly of Upper Canada, 1817–1824, Report of the Bureau of Archives for the Province of Ontario, 1911–1914
Province of Canada, Statutes, 1841–1866
Upper Canada Court of Queen's Bench, Reports, 1830–66
Upper Canada, Statutes, 1821–1840

NEWSPAPERS

Chronicle (Kingston)
Colonial Advocate (Toronto)
Courier (Upper Canada)
Gazette (Kingston)
Gazette (Montreal)
Gazette (Upper Canada)
Globe (Toronto)
Patriot (Toronto)

PAMPHLETS

James Morris to the Stockholders of the Commercial Bank, Brockville, 1850

Report of Robert Cassels, Bank of Upper Canada, Thirty-Eighth General Meeting, June 25, 1861, Toronto

Rules and Regulations for Conducting the Business of the Chartered Bank of Upper Canada, York, 1822

CONTEMPORARY MATERIAL OF LATER PRINTING

CRUICKSHANK, E.A., ed. *The Correspondence of Lieutenant-Governor John Graves Simcoe.* Vol. 1, Toronto, 1923.

FIRTH, EDITH, G., ed. *The Town of York, 1815–1834.* Toronto, 1966.

INNIS, H.A., and A.R.M. LOWER, eds. *Select Documents in Canadian Economic History, 1783–1885.* Toronto, 1937.

KNAPLUND, P., ed. *Letters from Lord Sydenham to Lord John Russell.* London, 1931.

LANGTON, W.A., ed. *Early Days in Upper Canada, Letters of John Langton.* Toronto, 1926.

NISH, E. *Debates of the Legislative Assembly of Canada, 1841.* Montreal, 1970.

PRESTON, RICHARD, ed. *Kingston Before the War of 1812.* Toronto, 1959.

SMITH, M.L., ed. *Young Mr. Smith in Upper Canada.* Toronto, 1980.

SECONDARY SOURCES

BOOKS, THESES

AITKEN, H.G.J. *The Welland Canal Company: A Study in Canadian Enterprise.* Cambridge, Mass., 1954.

ANDERSON, B.L. and P.L. COTTRELL. *Money and Banking in England, 1694–1914.* London, 1974.

BASTER, A.S.J. *The Imperial Banks.* New York, 1929.

BRECKENRIDGE, R.M. *The History of Banking in Canada.* Washington, 1910.

BROWN, LUCY F. *The Board of Trade and the Free Trade Movement, 1830–1842.* Oxford, 1958.

CARELESS, J.M.S. *The Union of the Canadas.* Toronto, 1967.

CRAIG, G.M. *Upper Canada: The Formative Years, 1784–1841.* Toronto, 1963.

CURRIE, A.W. *The Grand Trunk Railway of Canada.* Toronto, 1957.

DENISON, MERRILL. *Canada's First Bank: A History of the Bank of Montreal.* 2 vols. Toronto, 1966–67.

FRASER, R.L. " 'Like Eden in Her Summer Dress': Gentry, Economy and Society, 1812–40.'' Ph.D. thesis, University of Toronto, 1979.

FULFORD, R. *Glyn's: 1753–1953*. London, 1953.

HALPENNY, FRANCESS, G., gen. ed. *Dictionary of Canadian Biography*. X: *1871–1880*. Toronto, 1972.

————. *Dictionary of Canadian Biography*, XI: *1881–1890*. Toronto, 1982.

HIDY, R.W. *The House of Baring in American Trade and Finance, 1763–1861*. Cambridge, Mass., 1949.

HILTON, BOYD. *Corn, Cash and Commerce: The Economic Policies of the Tory Governments, 1815–1830*. Oxford, 1977.

JONES, R.L. *History of Agriculture in Ontario, 1613–1880*. Toronto, 1946.

KNAPLUND, PAUL. *James Stephen and the British Colonial System, 1813–47*. Madison, 1953.

MCCALLA, DOUGLAS. *The Upper Canada Trade, 1834–1872: A Study of the Buchanans' Business*. Toronto, 1979.

MCCALLUM, J. *Unequal Beginnings: Agriculture and Economic Development in Quebec and Ontario Until 1870*. Toronto, 1980.

MCCULLOUGH, A.B. *Money and Exchange in Canada to 1900*. Toronto, 1984.

MCCULLOUGH, J.R. *A Dictionary of Commerce and Commercial Navigation*. London, 1869.

MCCUSKER, JOHN. *Money and Exchange in Europe and America, 1600–1775: A Handbook*. Chapel Hill, 1978.

MCIVOR, R.C. *Canadian Monetary, Banking and Fiscal Development*. Toronto, 1958.

MARR, W.L. and D.G. PATERSON. *Canada: An Economic History*. Toronto, 1980.

MINTS, LLOYD, W. *A History of Banking Theory in Great Britain and the United States*. Chicago, 1945.

PENTLAND, H.C. *Labour and Capital in Canada, 1650–1860*. Toronto, 1981.

PRESNELL, L.S. *Country Banking in the Industrial Revolution*. Oxford, 1956.

RAUDZENS, G. *The British Ordnance Department and Canada's Canals, 1815–55*. Waterloo, 1979.

REDLICH, F. *The Moulding of American Banking*. Vol. 1. New York, 1968.

ROSS, V. *The History of the Canadian Bank of Commerce*. Toronto, 1920.

SCHUMPETER, JOSEPH. *Business Cycles*. Toronto, 1964.

SCROPE, G. POULETT. *Life of Lord Sydenham*. London, 1843.

SWINFEN, D.B. *Imperial Control of Colonial Legislation, 1813–1865*. Oxford, 1970.

TEMIN, PETER. *The Jacksonian Economy*. New York, 1969.

WILSON, BRUCE. *The Enterprises of Robert Hamilton: A Study of Wealth and Influence in Early Upper Canada: 1776–1812.* Toronto, 1983.

ARTICLES

ACHESON, T.W. "The Nature and Structure of York Commerce in the 1820s." In *Historical Essays on Upper Canada.* Ed. J.K. Johnson (Toronto, 1975), 171–93.

AITKEN, H.G.J. "A Note on the Capital Resources of Upper Canada." *Canadian Journal of Economics and Political Science* xviii, (1952) 525–33.

Anon. "The Canadian Financial Agency." *Three Banks Review* (Mar. 1961), 29–40

————. "Glyns and the Bank of Upper Canada." *Three Banks Review* (Sept. 1962), 40–52

————. "Glyns and the Grand Trunk Railway." *Three Banks Review* (Dec. 1961), 28–40

BAEHRE, RAINER. "Pauper Emigration to Upper Canada in the 1830s." *Histoire sociale/Social History* xiv (1981), 339–68.

BALLS, HERBERT. "John Langton and the Canadian Audit Office." *Canadian Historical Review* xxi (1940), 150–176.

BASKERVILLE, P. "Americans in Britain's Backyard: The Railway Era in Upper Canada, 1850–1880." *Business History Review* LV (1981), 315–24.

————. "Donald Bethune's Steamboat Business: A Study of Upper Canadian Commercial and Financial Practice." *Ontario History* LXVII (1975), 135–49.

————. "The Entrepreneur and the Metropolitan Impulse: James Grey Bethune and Cobourg, 1825–1836." In *Victorian Cobourg: A Nineteenth Century Profile.* Ed. Jerry Petryshyn, Belleville, 1976, 56–70.

————. "Entrepreneurship and the Family Compact: York-Toronto, 1822–55." *Urban History Review* ix (1981), 15–34.

————. "The Pet Bank, the Local State and the Imperial Centre, 1850–1864." *Journal of Canadian Studies* xx (1985), 22–46.

BRECKENRIDGE, R.M. "The Canadian Banking System, 1817–90." *Journal of the Canadian Bankers' Association* ii (1894–95).

BURNS, R. "God's Chosen People: The Origins of Toronto Society, 1793–1818." *Historical Papers* (1973), 213–28.

CUNEO, C.J. "Surplus Labour in Staple Commodities: Merchant and Early Industrial Capitalism." *Studies in Political Economy* vii (1982), 61–88.

DEN OTTER, A.A. "Alexander Galt, the 1859 Tariff and Canadian Economic Nationalism." *Canadian Historical review* LXIII (1982), 151–78.

FAUCHER, ALBERT. "Some Aspects of the Financial Difficulties of the Province of Canada." *Canadian Journal of Economics and Political Science* XXVI (1960), 617–24.

FENSTERMAKER, JOSEPH VAN. "Bank Profitability in the 1820s." In *Papers of the Fifteenth Annual Meeting of the Business History Conference.* Ed. Fred Bateman and J.D. Forest, Indiana, 1968, 72–85.

GOODWIN, C.D.W. "John Rae: Undiscovered Exponent of Canadian Banking." *The Canadian Banker* LXVI (1959), 111–15.

GWYN, J. "The Impact of British Military Spending on the Colonial American Money Markets, 1760–1783." *Historical Papers* (1980), 77–99.

HAEGER, J.D. "Eastern Financiers and Institutional Change: The Origins of the New York Life Insurance and Trust Company and the Ohio Life Insurance and Trust Company." *Journal of Economic History* XXXIX (1979), 259–73.

KNAPLUND, P. "James Stephen on Canadian Banking Laws, 1821–1846." *Canadian Historical Review* XXXI (1950), 177–87.

LONGLEY, R.S. "Francis Hincks and Canadian Public Finance." Canadian Historical Association, *Annual Report* (1934), 30–39.

MCCALLA, DOUGLAS, "The 'Loyalist' Economy of Upper Canada." *Histoire sociale/Social History* XVI (1983), 279–304.

———. "The Wheat Staple and Upper Canadian Development." *Historical Papers* (1978), 34–46.

MAGILL, M.L. "John H. Dunn and the Bankers." *Ontario History* LXII (1970), 83–100.

———. "William Allan: A Pioneer Business Executive." In *Aspects of Nineteenth Century Ontario.* Ed. F.H. Armstrong *et al.,* Toronto, 1974, 101–13.

NAYLOR, T. "The Rise and Fall of the Commercial Empire of the St. Lawrence." In *Capitalism and the National Question in Canada.* Ed. Gary Teeple, Toronto, 1972, 1–42.

NORTH, D.C. "The United States Balance of Payments, 1790–1860." In *Trends in the American Economy in the Nineteenth Century.* Ed. National Bureau of Economic Research 24, Princeton, 1960.

OWRAM, D. "Management by Enthusiasm: The First Board of Works of the Province of Canada, 1841–1846." *Ontario History* LXX (1978), 171–88.

PARKER, BRUCE, A. "The Niagara Harbour and Dock Company." *Ontario History* LXXII (1980), 93–121.

PENTLAND, H.C. "Further Observations on Canadian Development." *Canadian Journal of Economics and Political Science* XIX (1953), 403–10.

———. "The Role of Capital in Canadian Economic Development Before 1875." *Canadian Journal of Economics and Political Science* XVI (1950), 457–74.

Piva, M.J. "The Canadian Public Debt, 1848–1856." Paper presented to the Canadian Historical Association, Montreal, 1980.

_____. "Continuity and Crisis: Francis Hincks and Canadian Economic Policy." *Canadian Historical Review* LXVI (1985), 185–210.

Redish, A. "The Economic Crisis of 1837–1839: Case Study of a Temporary Suspension of Specie Payments." *Explorations in Economic History* XX (1983), 402–17.

_____. "Why was Specie Scarce in Colonial Economies? An Analysis of the Canadian Currency, 1796–1830." *Journal of Economic History* XLIV (1984), 713–28.

Redlich, F. "American Banking and Growth in the Nineteenth Century: Epistemological Reflections." *Explorations in Economic History* X (1972–73), 305–18.

Shortt, A. "Crisis and Resumption." *Journal of the Canadian Bankers' Association* IX (1901–2), 101–21.

_____. "The Crisis of 1857–58." *Journal of the Canadian Bankers' Association* XI (1903–4), 199–218.

_____. "Criticism, Prosperity and Expansion." *Journal of the Canadian Bankers' Association* VIII (1900–1), 145–64.

_____. "Currency and Exchange as Influenced by the Union." *Journal of the Canadian Bankers' Association* X (1902–3), 25–40.

_____. "The Early History of Canadian Banking, 1791–1812." *Journal of the Canadian Bankers' Association* IV (1897), 235–52.

_____. "Early Metallic Currency and its Regulation." *Journal of the Canadian Bankers' Association* VII (1899–1900), 209–26.

_____. "Experiment and Inflation." *Journal of the Canadian Bankers' Association* VIII (1900–1), 305–26.

_____. "The First Banks in Lower Canada." *Journal of the Canadian Bankers' Association* IV (1897), 341–60.

_____. "The First Banks in Upper Canada." *Journal of the Canadian Bankers' Association* V (1897), 1–21.

_____. "Free Banking and Currency Amendments." *Journal of the Canadian Bankers' Association* X (1902–3), 12–29.

_____. "Lord Sydenham's Measures." *Journal of the Canadian Bankers' Association* X (1902–3), 21–40.

_____. "One Currency for the Empire." *Journal of the Canadian Bankers' Association* VII (1899–1900), 311–32.

_____. "Origin of the Canadian Banking System." *Journal of the Canadian Bankers' Association* IV (1896), 1–19.

_____. "The Passing of the Upper Canadian and Commercial Banks." *Journal of the Canadian Bankers' Association* XII (1904–5), 193–216.

_____. "Prosperity and Expansion in Upper Canada." *Journal of the Canadian Bankers' Association* VIII (1900–1), 227–43.

_____. "Reconstruction and New Schemes." *Journal of the Canadian Bankers' Association* VIII (1900–1), 227–43.

STELTER, G. "Urban Planning and Development in Upper Canada." In *Urbanization in the Americas: The Background in Comparative Perspective*. Ed. G. Stelter *et al.*, Ottawa, 1980.

SWEENY, ROBERT. "Colony and Crisis: Montreal and the First Capitalist Crisis." In *Protesting History: Four Papers*. Robert Sweeny, Montreal, 1984, 8–52.

SYLLA, RICHARD. "American Banking and Growth in the Nineteenth Century: A Partial View of the Terrain." *Explorations in Economic History* IX (1971/72), 197–227.

TOUSIGNANT, PIERRE. "Problematique pour une nouvelle approche de la constitution de 1791." *Revue d'histoire de l'Amérique française* XXVII (1973), 181–234.

VAUGHAN, C.L. "The Bank of Upper Canada in Politics, 1817–40." *Ontario History* LX (1968), 185–204.

WILSON, BRUCE. "The Struggle for Wealth and Power at Fort Niagara, 1775–1783." *Ontario History* LXVIII (1976), 137–54.

WINKS, R.W. "On Decolonization and Informal Empire." *American Historical Review* LXXXI (1976), 540–56.

INDEX

Honourary Treasurer:
  John K. Armour, Toronto, Ontario
Executive Secretary-Treasurer:
  Anne Lato
Committee on Publications:
  Prof. P.D.W. McCalla, Dr. Sylvia Van Kirk, Prof. S.F. Wise, Dr. Morris
  Zaslow and Miss Edith Firth

PUBLICATIONS OF THE CHAMPLAIN SOCIETY

Ontario Series